R. I. Gilbert is Emeritus Professor of Structural Engineering at the University of New South Wales, Sydney, Australia, and former Head of the School of Civil and Environmental Engineering at UNSW. His research interests over a 35-year academic career are in structural engineering, where he has published 8 books and over 450 technical papers. He also has had a lifelong interest in test cricket and has spent much of the last two decades researching and cataloguing the statistics of the game.

To my family

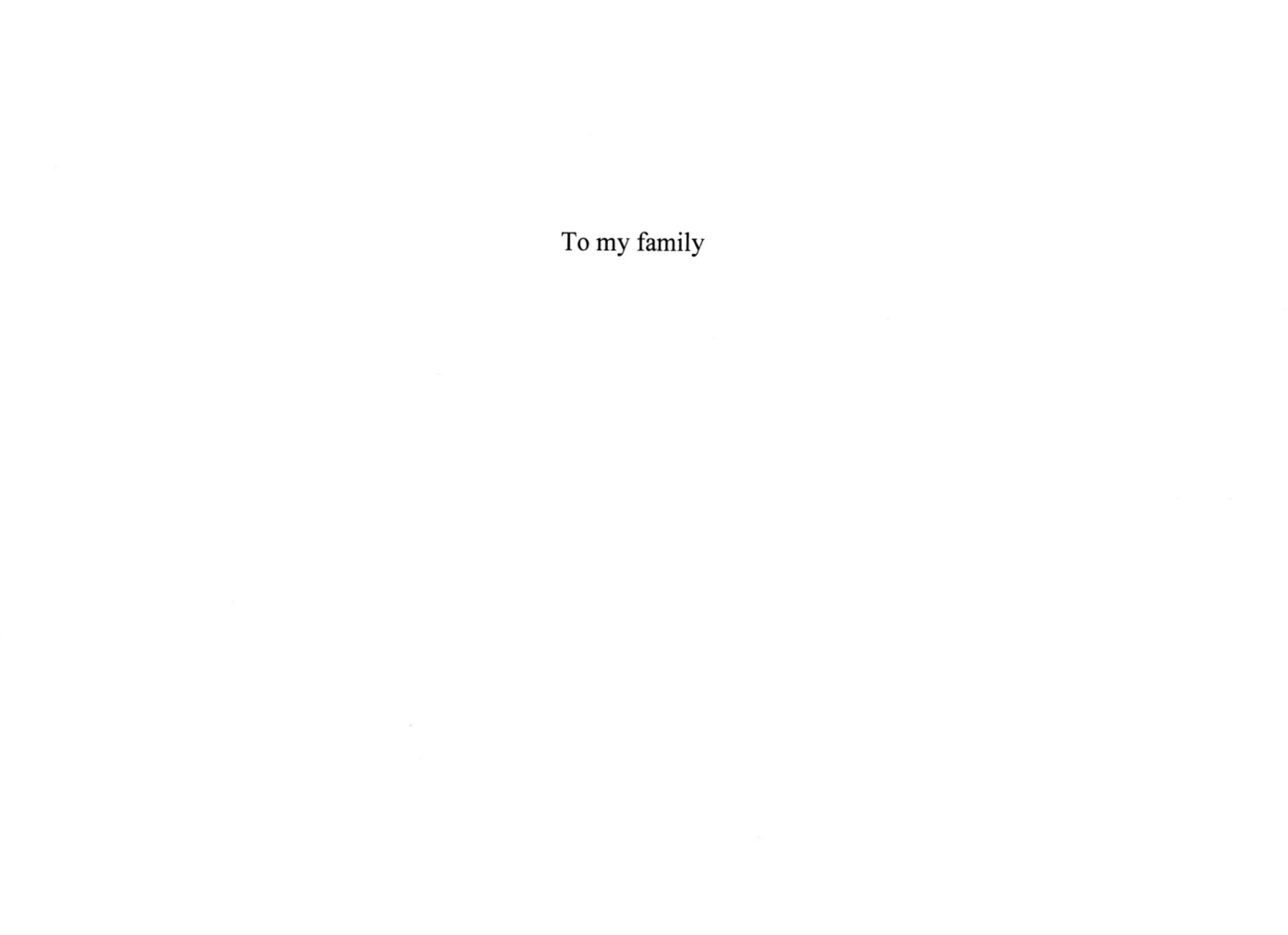

R. I. Gilbert

GREATEST TEAMS AND GREATEST PLAYERS – A HISTORY OF TEST CRICKET

AUSTIN MACAULEY PUBLISHERS
LONDON * CAMBRIDGE * NEW YORK * SHARJAH

Copyright © R. I. Gilbert 2025

The right of R. I. Gilbert to be identified as author of this work has been asserted by the author in accordance with sections 77 and 78 of the Copyright, Designs and Patents Act 1988.

All rights reserved. No part of this publication may be reproduced, stored in a retrieval system, or transmitted in any form or by any means, electronic, mechanical, photocopying, recording, or otherwise, without the prior permission of the publishers.

Any person who commits any unauthorised act in relation to this publication may be liable to criminal prosecution and civil claims for damages.

The story, experiences, and words are the author's alone.

A CIP catalogue record for this title is available from the British Library.

ISBN 9781035877669 (Paperback)
ISBN 9781035877676 (ePub e-book)

www.austinmacauley.com

First Published 2025
Austin Macauley Publishers Ltd®
1 Canada Square
Canary Wharf
London
E14 5AA

Table of Contents

Preface	9
Notation List	10
Chapter 1: Background and Motivation	12
Chapter 2: Rating the Players	25
Chapter 3: The Best World Team before World-War 1 1877 to 1914	53
Chapter 4: The Best World Team — 1920 to 1949	61
Chapter 5: The Best World Team — 1950 to 1959	72
Chapter 6: The Best World Team – 1960 to 1969	81
Chapter 7: The Best World Team — 1970 to 1979	90
Chapter 8: The Best World Team — 1980 to 1989	99
Chapter 9: The Best World Team — 1990 to 1999	109
Chapter 10: The Best World Team — 2000 to 2009	122
Chapter 11: The Best World Team — 2010 to 2019	136
Chapter 12: The Best World Team — 2020 to 2024	150
Chapter 13: The Best World and National Teams of All Time — 1877 to 2024	156
Appendix A: The Highest Rating Test Batsmen and Bowlers	206
Appendix B: Modes of Dismissing a Batsman and Test Venues	218
Appendix C: The Distribution of Batting Averages – Top-Order Batsmen	222
Appendix D: Best National Teams Before World War 1 — 1877-1914	223
Appendix E: Best National Teams — 1920 To 1949	226
Appendix F: Best National Teams — 1950 To 1959	230
Appendix G: Best National Teams — 1960 To 1969	236
Appendix H: Best National Teams — 1970 To 1979	243
Appendix I: Best National Teams — 1980 To 1989	249
Appendix J: Best National Teams — 1990 To 1999	256
Appendix K: Best National Teams — 2000 To 2009	265
Appendix L: Best National Teams — 2010 To 2019	275
Appendix M: Highest Rating National Players - 2020 To 2024	284
Indexes	289

Preface

In this player-based history of test cricket, the best world and national test cricket teams have been selected for each era of the game, including the *golden age* of test cricket before World War 1, the 30-year period from 1920 to 1949, and each subsequent decade until the present. Finally, the best world and national teams of all time are selected. Selections are based only on the batting and bowling statistics of every player who has played 20 or more test matches. Simple and consistent approaches have been used to determine a batting rating for each batsman during a particular time period and a bowling rating for each bowler based only on their on-field performances. The achievements and background of each of the key players are discussed and the performances of the various national teams in each era are compared. For each team, the top-rating players are selected and include two specialist opening batsmen, four other top-order batsmen, a wicketkeeper and four specialist bowlers.

In Chapter 1, the motivation and background for the book are outlined. A brief description of the basics of test cricket is presented, including the countries that have participated in test cricket and the eras in which they played. Also included in Chapter 1 are explanations of some of the commonly used terms and expressions that are peculiar to test cricket.

The methods used to calculate the batting and bowling ratings of each player are explained and justified in Chapter 2. Typical example calculations are provided and the ratings of the top 100 batsmen and the top 100 bowlers in test history are presented. Also rated and compared are the top performing all-rounders and wicketkeepers.

The highest rating players and the top-rating world teams in each of the 10 eras of test cricket are selected and discussed in Chapters 3 to 12. In Chapter 13, the best world and national teams are selected over the entire 147-year history of test cricket from 1877 until the end of 2024. In each chapter, the exploits and achievements of the greatest cricketers of all time are discussed and compared.

Thirteen appendices are also included. The highest rating batsmen and bowlers in test history are listed in Appendix A. The modes of dismissing batsmen and the venues at which test cricket is played are listed in Appendix B and a statistical analysis of the batting averages of all top-order batsmen who have played more than 20 test matches is presented in Appendix C. Appendices D to M contain the batting and bowling statistics of the players in the top performing national teams for each era considered.

The idea for the book first came to me twenty years ago during the Boxing Day test in 2004 played between Australia and Pakistan at the Melbourne Cricket Ground. I was watching the match on television with my ten-year-old grandson who was just discovering cricket. As we watched the Pakistan 1st innings, he asked a steady stream of questions. Is Shane Warne the best spin bowler? Is Yousuf Youhana a better batsman than Younis Khan? Is Shoaib Akhtar a better fast bowler than Glenn McGrath? Who is the best batsman you ever saw? To most of his questions, I gave a confident answer — my opinion. I started to look at the players' statistics and have been doing so ever since. Some of the comparisons have confirmed my opinion, but some have changed it. I hope that the lovers of test cricket will enjoy the outcome of my research and that the book will prove to be an enjoyable and informative read.

Ian Gilbert
January 2025

Notation List

Symbol	Meaning
DNB	Did not bowl
LAF	Bowling style – left arm fast
LAFM	Bowling style – left arm fast medium
LAM	Bowling style – left arm medium
LAMF	Bowling style – left arm medium fast
LAO	Bowling style – left arm orthodox
LAWS	Bowling style – left arm wrist spin (Chinaman)
HS	A batsman's highest score in a specified time period
n_0	Number of scores of 0
n_5	Number of 5 or more wickets in an innings
n_{10}	Number of 10 or more wickets in a match
n_{50}	Number of half centuries scored (scores in the range 50 to 99)
n_{100}	Number of centuries scored (scores in excess of 100)
n_{balls}	Number of balls bowled
n_{overs}	Number of overs bowled
$n_{innings}$	Number of innings played
$n_{maidens}$	Number of maiden overs bowled
n_{runs}	Number of runs scored
$n_{wickets}$	Number of wickets taken
RAF	Bowling style – right arm fast
RAFM	Bowling style – right arm fast medium
RAL	Bowling style – right arm leg break
RAM	Bowling style – right arm medium
RAMF	Bowling style – right arm medium fast
RAO	Bowling style – right arm off break
w_{avge}	Batting average or bowling average
w_{econ}	Bowling economy rate
w_{sr}	Batting strike rate or bowling strike rate
WS1	Weighted batting score based on batting average
WS2	Weighted batting score based on total number of runs scored
WS3	Weighted batting score based on batting strike rate
WS4	Weighted batting score based on centuries, half centuries and ducks

WS5	Weighted batting score based on the highest score
WS6	Weighted batting score based on number of innings
WS7	Weighted bowling score based on bowling average
WS8	Weighted bowling score based on number of wickets taken
WS9	Weighted bowling score based on bowling strike rate
WS10	Weighted bowling score based on bowling economy rate
WS11	Weighted bowling score based on 5 and 10 wicket hauls
WS12	Weighted bowling score based on number of balls bowled
WS13	Weighted bowling score based on number of maiden overs
< 100	Less than 100 overs

Chapter 1
Background and Motivation

Introduction

Test cricket pits country against country in a five-day struggle for cricket supremacy. It is the ultimate cricketing challenge for those players who are skilful enough and dedicated enough to represent their country at the highest level. But test cricket is much more than that, it is a source of national pride and a mechanism that brings together vastly different cultures and communities, encouraging mutual respect, as well as a shared admiration for the heroes of the game.

It has been said by the cricket establishment that "cricket is a gentleman's game played by gentlemen". On the village greens of England long ago, perhaps this was so, and "gentlemanly" was an appropriate word to describe the game, but on the test cricket grounds of the world, in the heat of battle, it is often not the case. When something was underhanded or not achieved with honour, anywhere in the British Empire, it was *"simply not cricket"*. Since Douglas Jardine implemented *bodyline*, and probably long before, test cricket has been *"simply not cricket"*. It is true that the great majority of test cricketers are indeed *gentlemen*, on the field as well as off it, but the game itself is uncompromising, demanding and ruthless, requiring outstanding hand-eye coordination, the sharpest of reflexes, stamina, concentration and strength of body and mind under pressure. Of the millions who have played cricket, only 3,215 men have been good enough to play test cricket for their countries and, of these, 847 were successful enough to play more than 20 test matches. This book is about those few — the best of the best.

Both men and women play test cricket and there have been some outstanding performances in the women's game. However, up until the end 2024, only 149 test matches have been played by women, compared to 2,573 played by men, and very few women have played more than 20 test matches. As a consequence, reliable statistical comparisons between individuals are difficult. This book is therefore concerned only with the men's game.

Ever since the first test match in March 1877 between England and Australia at the Melbourne Cricket Ground, lovers of cricket have argued over who was the best, the best team, the best batsman, the best spin bowler, the best fast bowler, the best wicketkeeper, the best captain, the best slips fielder and so on. Some old men argue that the players of today are not nearly as good as the players of yesteryear. Are they right or has the passing of the years made the feats of past players seem grander and more impressive than they actually were?

How do today's players compare against the greats of the past? Is it possible to make such a comparison, given that the game has changed so much? Pitches are better prepared today, and they are now protected from rain both before and during the game. This was not always the case. Equipment has also gradually improved over the years, bats are heavier, balls are better made, and the protective gear is far superior to that of years gone by. These factors suggest that the batsmen of the modern era have a distinct advantage. On the other hand, the advent of limited overs cricket has encouraged a more reckless approach to batting and has reduced the opportunities for young batsmen to learn to build an innings and bat for long periods. In addition, the training techniques and fitness of the bowlers have improved significantly, perhaps putting the batsman of today at a disadvantage and levelling out the playing field a little.

Based only on statistics, and we have the statistics for every player who ever played test cricket, it is possible to make a reasonable comparison between players of the same era, provided of course that they played enough matches to ensure that the statistics provide a reliable representation of their abilities. It is even possible to make less reliable, but still sensible, comparisons between players of different eras.

In the following chapters, based solely on the players' statistics, the best test team for each era has been selected from every test cricketer who played more than 20 test matches in that particular time period. The best national teams in each era for each participating country have also been selected, as have the best national teams and best world team of all time. The methods for determining the batting and bowling ratings of each player are described in Chapter 2. The statistics considered for each player, the comparisons made between the players and the facts presented herein are based on data from every test match played before the end of 2024.

When selecting the best team for each era, the best two opening batsmen, the best four middle-order batsmen, the best four bowlers and the best wicketkeeper have been determined. An attempt has been made to include two specialist opening batsman in each side and, in doing so, some middle-order batsmen with higher batting ratings may have been unlucky not to have been selected. In addition, an attempt has been made to include at least two seamers (fast or fast-medium bowlers) to open the bowling attack and, as a consequence, some spin bowlers may also have been unlucky. In these cases, the unlucky players have been identified and included in the discussion.

It is hoped that the national and world teams selected herein, and the comparisons between players, provide for enjoyable reading, both settling old arguments and creating new ones.

National Teams and Eras

Twelve national teams have played test cricket, and all are still competing. An ICC World team also played a single test against Australia in 2005. The teams, their test debuts, the total number of tests played before the end of 2024 and the outcomes are provided in Table 1.1. The teams are listed in the table in chronological order based on the dates of their test debuts. Both Ireland and Afghanistan joined the ranks of test playing nations in 2018 and have played insufficient test matches for further consideration here.

The English team actually represents England and Wales (and, until 1992, Scotland as well). The West Indies team represents several individual nations and dependencies from the Caribbean region (including Antigua and Barbuda, Barbados, Dominica, Grenada, Guyana, Jamaica, Saint Lucia, Saint Vincent and Grenadines, Trinidad and Tobago, Saint Kitts and Nevis, Anguilla, Montserrat, British Virgin Islands, Saint Maarten and US Virgin Islands).

When selecting the best world and national teams, ten eras have been considered here:

(i) before World War 1;   (ii) 1920 to 1949;   (iii) 1950s;   (iv) 1960s;
(v) 1970s;   (vi) 1980s;   (vii) 1990s; (viii) 2000s;
ix) 2010s; and   (x) 2020 to 2024.

The number of tests played in each decade is illustrated In Figure 1.1.

For the purposes of team selections, the period before 1950 has been divided into two eras rather than decades, before and after World War 1. This is simply because there were too few players who played in 20 or more test matches in each decade to make sensible selections. Indeed, in the early years of test cricket, some national teams played fewer than twenty test matches in some decades.

Table 1.1 Participating nations, tests played and overall results (up to the end of 2024).

Team	Date of debut test	Total tests	Won	Lost	Tied	Drawn	% wins
England	15-03-1877	1,083	400	328	0	355	36.9
Australia	15-03-1877	870	416	233	2	219	47.8
South Africa	12-03-1889	471	184	161	0	126	39.1
West Indies	23-06-1928	582	184	215	1	182	31.6
New Zealand	10-01-1930	478	119	189	0	170	24.9
India	25-06-1932	588	181	183	1	223	30.8
Pakistan	16-10-1952	462	150	146	0	166	32.5
Sri Lanka	17-02-1982	323	106	125	0	92	32.8
Zimbabwe	18-10-1992	119	14	76	0	29	11.8
Bangladesh	10-11-2000	150	22	110	0	18	14.7
Ireland	11-05-2018	9	2	7	0	0	22.2
Afghanistan	14-06-2018	10	3	7	0	0	30.0
ICC World XI	14-10-2005	1	0	1	0	0	0

Total tests	2,573	Total tests Won/lost	1,781	Total tests tied	2	Total tests drawn	790

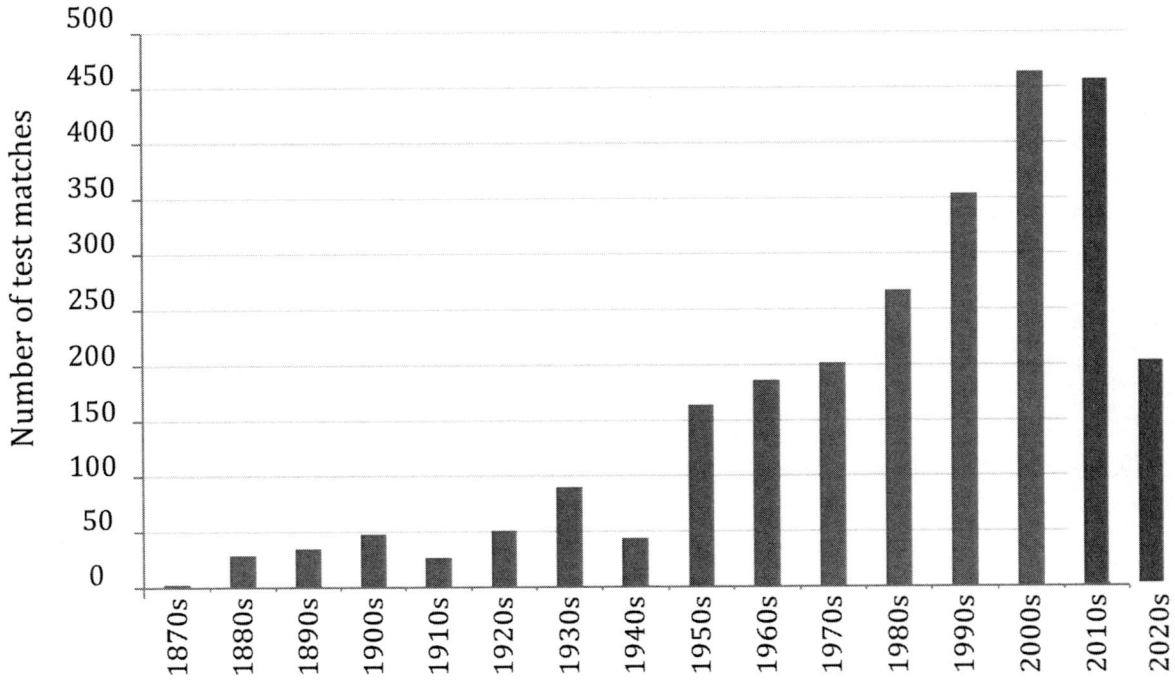

Figure 1.1 Number of tests played in each decade.

Eras Considered

(i) 1877-1914 (before World War 1):

In what has been called the golden age of cricket, before World War 1, 134 test matches were played, with only England, Australia and South Africa participating. England played in 123 test matches, Australia in 105 and South Africa in 40.

(ii) 1920-1949:

In this 30-year period, 185 test matches were played, with West Indies, India and New Zealand joining the ranks of test cricketing countries. England played 152 tests, Australia 85, South Africa 62, West Indies 31, New Zealand 20 and India 20.

(iii) 1950-1959:

In the decade of the 1950s, 164 test matches were played (almost as many as in the previous 30 years), with Pakistan making its test cricket debut. England played 83 tests, Australia 57, South Africa 35, West Indies 48, New Zealand 32, India 44 and Pakistan 29.

(iv) 1960-1969:

In the 1960s, 186 test matches were played. England played 100 of them, Australia 67, South Africa 31, West Indies 49, New Zealand 43, India 52 and Pakistan 30.

(v) 1970-1979:

In the decade of the 1970s, 198 test matches were played. England played 95 tests, Australia 83, South Africa 4 (having been banned from test cricket in 1970), West Indies 63, New Zealand 41, India 64 and Pakistan 46.

(vi) 1980-1989:

The 1980s saw the introduction of Sri Lanka into test cricket and the continuation of the ban on South Africa. 266 test matches were played in the decade, with England playing 104 tests, Australia 97, West Indies 82, New Zealand 59, India 81, Pakistan 80 and Sri Lanka 29.

(vii) 1990-1999:

In the 1990s, Zimbabwe commenced playing test cricket and South Africa were reinstated. 347 test matches were played, with England playing 107 tests, Australia 108, West Indies and New Zealand 81 each, India 69, Pakistan 76, Sri Lanka 67, South Africa 66 and Zimbabwe 39.

(viii) 2000-2009:

Bangladesh played its first test match in November 2000. In the decade, a total of 464 test matches were played (far more than in any previous decade), with England playing 129 tests, Australia 115, West Indies and South Africa 108 each, New Zealand 80, India 103, Pakistan 83, Sri Lanka 96, Zimbabwe 44 and Bangladesh 61.

(ix) 2010-2019:

In the 2010s, a total of 433 test matches were played, with England playing 126 tests, Australia 112, South Africa 90, West Indies 83, New Zealand 83, India 107, Pakistan 83, Sri Lanka 95, Zimbabwe 24, Bangladesh 56, Afghanistan 4 and Ireland 3.

(x) 2020-2024:

In the 2020s (up to the end of 2024), a total of 196 test matches were played, with England playing 64 tests, Australia 41, South Africa 35, West Indies 37, New Zealand 39, India 48, Pakistan 35, Sri Lanka 36, Zimbabwe 12, Bangladesh 33, Afghanistan 6 and Ireland 6.

In a couple of the teams, particularly those from the 2020s and the early years of test cricket when relatively few test matches were played, players were considered who had played as few as 18 test matches, but only when insufficient qualified players (i.e., players with more than 20 test matches) were available to fill all the specialist positions in the team.

In addition to selecting the best teams from each era, the best performances by batsman and bowlers across all eras are compared. The best all-rounders and the best wicketkeepers have also been identified.

The Basics of the Game

It is assumed that the reader is familiar with the rules of cricket and is a follower of the game. However, for the uninitiated, a very brief outline of the basics is provided here.

A test match is played over a maximum period of 5 days (generally) between two national teams and forms part of a test series between the two nations. Each series consists of between 1 and 6 test matches all played on the test venues of the host nation. Each national team comprises 11 players selected for each test match by a national selection committee often consisting of past test players. Also selected is a 12th man, who can field, if one of the playing 11 is incapacitated, but who is not permitted to bat or bowl. In 2019, the International Cricket Council (ICC) introduced the 'concussion substitution', whereby a batsman who is concussed while batting may be replaced by another player from outside the playing 11.

The make-up of the test team can vary from country to country depending on the strengths of the individuals considered for selection, but generally a team consists of six specialist batsmen, a wicketkeeper and four specialist bowlers. Often, a specialist batsman is a strong enough bowler to contribute to the bowling attack and a specialist bowler may be a good enough batsman to score a substantial number of runs. Specialist batsmen who are also front-line bowlers are known as batting all-rounders. Specialist bowlers who regularly contribute with the bat are known as bowling all-rounders. Wicketkeepers are generally selected because of their skills behind the stumps, but a wicketkeeper who is also a successful batsman is often favoured by selectors, particularly in the modern era.

A day of test cricket consists of three 2-hour sessions of play. A 40-minute lunch break separates the first and second sessions of play and a 20-minute tea break separates the final two sessions of the day. The starting and ending times can vary, but are traditionally around 11.00 am and 6.00 pm, respectively. In recent years, in an attempt to curb slow play, a requirement has been introduced to ensure that a minimum number of 90 six-ball overs is bowled in each day, and this has often seen play extend beyond the scheduled close of play. In 2015, the first day/night test match took place, and, by the end of 2024, 23 day/night test matches have been played. Australia has played in thirteen of these matches and won twelve of them.

Figure 1.2 below shows a plan view of a cricket field. The field may be circular or oval with the dimensions varying depending on the location and size of the ground. The pitch is the rectangular stretch of turf near to the centre of the field that is carefully prepared by mowing and rolling to form a flat surface that is suitable for both bowling and batting. The pitch is always 22 yards (20.12 m) long between the wickets and 10 feet (3.05 m) across.

A wicket is set at each end of the pitch. Each wicket consists of three stumps with two bails on top. The wicket stands 28 inches (71.1 cm) high and 9 inches (22.86 cm) wide. The popping crease is a marked line drawn across the pitch and set 48 inches (1.22 m) in front of the stumps.

Test matches are played over four innings, with each team batting twice and each team bowling twice. In an innings, after each 6-ball over is bowled from one end of the pitch, a different bowler bowls the next over from the opposite end, and so the game progresses as the batsmen score runs and the bowlers take wickets. A batsman scores a single run, if he hits the ball and the two batsmen can run the length of the pitch and touch their bats down over the popping crease before the fielding side can break the wickets, i.e., remove the bails with the ball or with a hand holding the ball. Two runs are scored, if after the ball is hit, the two batsmen can each run the length of the pitch twice touching their bats beyond the popping crease at each end of the pitch before the fielding side can break the wickets. Similarly, three runs involve each batsman safety running the length of the pitch three times after the ball is hit usually into the outfield. Four runs are score if the batsman hits the ball along the ground (or with at least one bounce) to the boundary of the field. Six runs are scored if the batsman can hit the ball over the boundary fence (or rope) on the full.

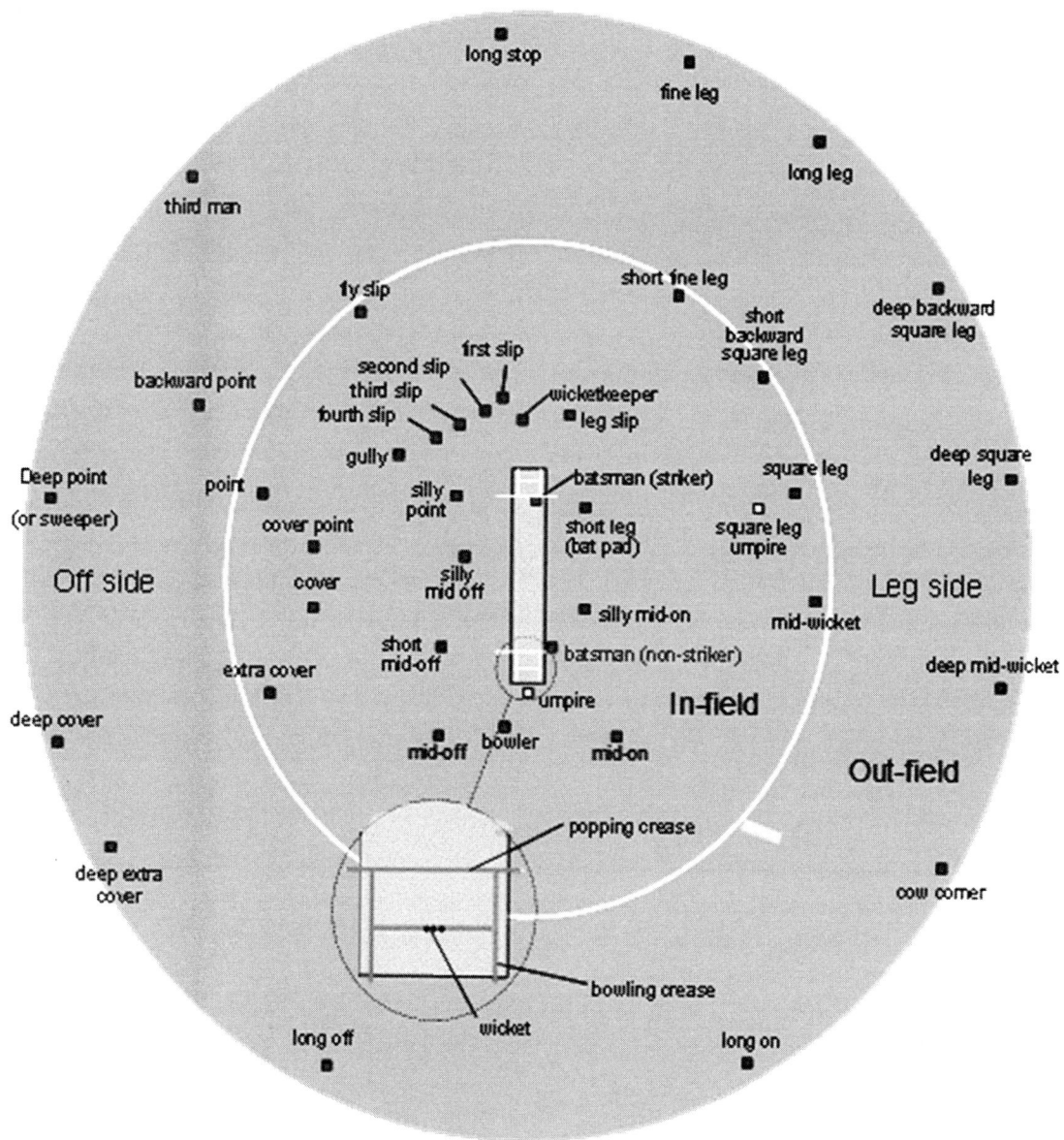

Figure 1.2 Layout of a cricket field and fielding positions.

At the beginning of an innings, the two specialist opening batsmen go out to face the opposition bowling attack. The opening bowlers are usually fast bowlers who make the most of the bounce and swing provided by the hard, new ball. The opening batsmen are required to see off the new ball and score as many runs as they can before being dismissed.

As each batsman is dismissed, a new batsman comes out to bat, so that two batsmen are at the wicket at all times. As the innings progresses and the number of overs increases, the ball becomes softer and roughened, and the pitch may become worn. Spin bowlers often make use of the older ball and the cracked or roughened pitch to turn the ball and deceive the batsmen. Some fast bowlers are able to swing the old ball and are also successful later in the innings.

An innings is completed, when ten of the eleven batsmen are dismissed. An innings may be terminated earlier if the batting captain decides that enough runs have been scored, and the innings is declared closed. The final innings (or fourth innings) of the match comes to an end either when the batting side has scored more total runs than the opposition (in which case the batting side wins) or when all ten batsmen are dismissed, and the batting side has not scored more total runs than the opposition (in which case the batting side loses). To win the match, a team must bowl the other team out twice and score more total runs. If the maximum number of scheduled days is completed and no result has been reached (i.e., the fourth innings has not been completed), the match is drawn. If both sides are dismissed twice for the same total number of runs, the result is a tie. In the history of test cricket, there have been only two ties, Australia versus the West Indies in Brisbane in December 1961 and Australia versus India in Chennai in September 1986.

The most common ways for a batsman to get out (be dismissed) are bowled, caught, leg before wicket (LBW), stumped and run out. Other, rarer modes of dismissal are hit-wicket, hit the ball twice, obstructing the field and timed out. The bowler is credited with having taken the wicket if the batsman is either bowled, LBW, caught, stumped, or hit-wicket. A description of each mode of dismissal is provided in Appendix B (Section B.1).

One umpire stands at the bowler's end of the pitch to adjudicate on dismissals and no-balls (i.e., when the bowler oversteps the popping crease with his front foot in the process of delivering the ball). A second umpire stands square of the batting crease at square leg (see Figure 1.2). The umpire at the bowling end makes decisions when the fielding side appeals for a dismissal of either bowled, caught, LBW, hit-wicket or run out at the bowler's end. The square leg umpire decides on stumping dismissals or on appeals for run outs at the batting end and may be asked to assist in decisions involving hit-wicket, catches or hitting the ball twice.

The different fielding positions that may be taken up by members of the bowling team when bowling to a right-hand batsman are also shown in Figure 1.2. For a left-hand batsman taking strike, the fielding positions are a mirror-image of those shown in Figure 1.2 (taken about a line running parallel to the pitch through the middle stumps). The "*leg*" side of the field is the side closest to the legs of the batsman at strike (the striker) and, in Figure 1.2, it is the right side (from *fine leg* to *long on*). The other side of the field closest to the batsman's head when in his normal batting stance is the "*off*" side and, in Figure 1.2, it is the left side of the field (from long stop to long off).

Test cricket has been played in venues in each of the test playing nations, as well as in the United Arab Emirates (where Pakistan has played many of its recent "home" test matches) and 1 test has been played in Ireland. A full list of the test playing venues in each country, including the number of tests played at each venue, is provided in Appendix B. Lords Cricket Ground in London is often called "the home of cricket".

Some Cricket Jargon

There are many words and expressions relating to cricket that are a mystery to the uninitiated. The origins of much of the jargon are often a mystery even to devotees of the game. The names of some of the fielding positions shown in Figure 1.2, such as first slip, gully, point, cover, cow corner, third man and so on, are known and accepted by cricketers and cricket followers throughout the world, but relatively few could explain their origins. Some of the cricketing terms that are used in this book are explained here.

All-rounder:	A player who is both a good batsman and a good bowler. In test cricket, most all-rounders are selected as either specialist bowlers who are competent batsmen (bowling all-rounders) or specialist batsmen who are competent bowlers (batting all-rounders). The term all-rounder is also used to describe a wicketkeeper who is also a good batsman.
Appeal:	The fielding team asking the umpire whether the batsman is out. Often this involves the bowler and fielders shouting "howzat" ("how-is-that") at the umpire.
Arm Ball:	A type of delivery where the bowler imparts back-spin on the ball by rolling his fingers down the back of the ball on release. The ball does not turn appreciably off the pitch.
Around the wicket:	Describes the side of the wicket from which the ball is delivered. A right arm bowler delivers the ball around the wicket when he runs in and bowls on the right side of the stumps. A left-arm bowler delivers the ball around the wicket when he runs in and bowls on the left side of the stumps.
Ashes, the:	The prize for the victors when England plays Australia in a test series. The story goes that the bails used at the Oval in 1882, when Australia first won in England, were burned and the ashes are housed in a small wooden urn that has come to be called the Ashes.
Bat-pad:	A fielding position close to the wicket (usually on the leg side), so called because the chances are good of a catch to that position coming off the edge of the bat and popping up off the batsman's pad.
Bouncer (or bumper):	A short-pitched delivery from a fast or medium pace bowler that reaches the batsman at or above shoulder height.
Bowling Crease:	The line drawn across the pitch through the centres of the three stumps at each end of the pitch. It is 8 feet 8 inches (2.64 m) long, with the stumps in the centre (see inset in Figure 1.2).
Bump ball:	A ball that after being struck by the batsman bounces close to the batsman's foot and may appear to have come from the bat without contacting the ground. To the crowd a bump ball may appear to have been caught by a close-to-the-wicket fielder — a so-called crowd catch.
Bye:	An extra scored when both the batsman and the wicketkeeper miss a legal delivery, and the batsmen are able to take a run (or runs).
Cap:	Awarded for each appearance at test level. Usually, a national cap is presented to each test player on debut.
Carrum Ball:	A delivery usually by an off-spin bowler whereby at release the ball is flicked between the thumb and a bent middle finger in order to impart spin.
Carried his bat:	An opening batsman "carries his bat" when he opens the innings and remains not out when all 10 other batsmen have been dismissed.
Cherry:	The name given to the new (red) cricket ball at the start of an innings.
Chinaman:	A left-arm wrist spin bowler is known as a Chinaman, named after Ellis Achong, who played 6 test matches for the West Indies between 1930 and 1935 and was the first person of Chinese descent to play test cricket.
Cover drive:	A drive through the covers between cover point and extra cover.
Cut:	A shot played on the off-side to a short-pitched delivery outside the off stump and includes square cuts, back cuts and late cuts. The ball may travel between cover point and third man.
Delivery:	Each ball bowled is referred to as a delivery.
Dolly:	A simple catch that should be easy to take.

Doosra:	A ball delivered by an off-spin bowler that turns from leg to off (i.e., in the opposite direction to a standard off break). The development of the doosra is credited to Pakistan's Saqlain Mushtaq and was used to greatest effect by Sri Lanka's Muttiah Muralitharan.
Dot ball:	A ball from which no runs are scored and indicated in the scorebook by a single dot.
Drive:	The act of firmly hitting a full pitched ball usually with a straight bat in the arc between cover point on the off side of the field and mid-wicket on the leg side and include cover drives, off drives, straight drives and on drives.
Duck:	When a batsman is out without scoring, he has made a duck. A golden duck is when the batsman is dismissed for zero from the first ball faced. A diamond duck is when a batsman is run out for zero without facing a delivery. Needless to say, a batsman would prefer not to be out without troubling the scorers.
Edge (or snick or nick or feather or tickle):	A slight deviation of the ball off the edge of the bat (usually unintentional).
Extra (or sundry):	A run awarded to the batting side that is not attributed to a batsman. Extras include byes, leg byes, wides and no-balls. Wides and no-balls are attributed to the bowler and are added to the number of runs conceded in the over off the bat. Byes and leg byes are deemed fielding extras and are not attributed to the bowler.
Fast bowling (or pace bowling):	The ball is delivered at high speeds (often in excess of 140 km/hour), often utilizing swing.
First-class cricket:	The senior form of the game and includes county cricket, state or provincial cricket and test cricket. All first-class matches consist of four innings (two per side) and played over three or more days.
Flipper:	A leg-spin delivery with back-spin that causes the ball to stay low and scoot off the pitch. The flipper was first developed by Australia's Clarrie Grimmett and, in more recent years, has been used to great effect by Australia's Shane Warne.
Follow-on:	If the team batting second falls short of the oppositions first innings total by more than 200 runs, the opposing captain may enforce the follow-on and ask them to bat again (the 3rd innings of the game).
Full-length:	A ball that pitches closer to the batsman than does a good length ball.
Full-toss:	A delivery that reaches the batsman on the full, i.e., does not bounce off the pitch.
Good length:	A good length ball pitches between 3 and 5 m from the batsman (depending on the bowler) making it difficult for the batsman to decide whether to come forward and play a front-foot shot or go back and play a back-foot shot.
Googly (or wrong 'un):	A ball bowled by a leg-spin bowler with an over-the-wrist leg spin action that turns from off to leg (i.e., in the opposite direction to a standard leg break). The googly was first developed by Bernard Bosanquet who played 7 test matches for England from 1903 to 1905 and, as a consequence, is also known as a bosie.
Half-volley:	A delivery that bounces just short of the batsman and is relatively easy to drive or steer through the off side or glance down the leg side.
Hat-trick:	A bowler takes a wicket off three consecutive deliveries.
Hook:	A shot played on the leg-side between fine leg and mid-wicket and struck by the batsman often when the ball is at or above the batsman's shoulder.
ICC:	International Cricket Council

In-cutter (or off-cutter):	A ball that deviates towards the batsman after it hits the pitch.
In-swinger:	A ball that swings into the batsman from off to leg.
Infield:	That part of the field inside the 30-yard circle (see Figure 1.2).
Innings:	A player's or a team's turn to bat (or bowl).
Jaffa:	An unplayable delivery.
Late cut:	A cut shot played late when the ball is almost past the batsman and the ball runs down through the slips towards third man.
Leading edge:	A ball hitting the front edge of the bat when hitting across the line of the ball.
Left arm orthodox:	A left-arm finger-spin bowler whose stock ball turns away from a right-hand batsman (from leg to off).
Leg break:	A leg spin delivery that turns from the leg to the off side (away from a right-and batsman).
Leg Bye:	A run taken after a delivery hits and deflects off any part of the batsman's body (other than the bat or gloved hand holding the bat) provided the batsman has played at the ball with the bat.
Leg-cutter:	A ball usually delivered at pace that deviates away from the batsman after it hits the pitch.
Leg glance:	A shot played between fine leg and backward square leg off the face of a straight bat with a glancing action.
Leg spin (or wrist spin):	Bowling where spin is imparted by turning the wrist as the ball is delivered out of the back of the hand. A leg-spinner's stock delivery is the leg break, but he may deceive the batsman with the googly, the top spinner or the flipper.
Legitimate Delivery:	A delivery that is not a no-ball.
Length:	The place on the pitch where the ball bounces (see full-toss, full-length, half-volley, good length, short-pitched, long-hop).
Line and length bowling:	Bowling on a good length just on or outside the off stump.
Long hop:	A delivery that is pitched short but without the venom of a bouncer. Usually considered to be a bad delivery and easy to score off.
Lower-order or tail-ender:	A batsman who bats from No. 8 to No. 11 in the batting order. Usually includes the specialist bowlers who are not expected to contribute much with the bat.
Maiden over:	An over in which the batsman does not score, and no wides and no-balls are bowled.
Mankading:	The act of a bowler running out the batsman at the bowler's end by removing the bails before the ball has been bowled when the batsman is out of his crease. The practice of 'mankading' is named after Indian all-rounder Vinoo Mankad who first affected such a dismissal in 1947.
MCC:	Marylebone Cricket Club, the owner of Lords Cricket Ground in London, the governing body of cricket in England and Wales until 1997 and widely recognised as the authority on the laws of cricket.
Medium pace:	Bowling that is slower than pace bowling but faster than spin bowling, relying on good line and length and movement off the seam or swing in the air.
Middle-order:	Batsmen who bat from No. 5 to No. 8 in the batting order. Often includes all-rounders and wicketkeeper batsmen.
Non-striker:	The batsman at the bowler's end.

Nightwatchman:	Usually, a lower-order batsman who is sent in to bat to protect higher order batsmen when the end of the day's play is approaching or when the light is poor.
No-ball:	An illegal delivery (bowl), because part of the bowler's front foot is not behind the popping crease when he releases the ball or when the bowlers back foot in the delivery stride touches or falls outside the return crease. A no-ball is also called if the ball is a full-toss that passes the batsman above waist height. A no-ball results in a single run (an extra) for the batting side and must be re-bowled.
ODI:	One-day International (50 overs per side).
Off break:	An off-spin delivery that turns from the off to the leg side (in towards a right-hand batsman).
Off-cutter:	A ball usually delivered at pace that deviates towards the batsman after it hits the pitch.
Off drive:	A drive through the off-side towards mid-off.
Off-spin (or finger-spin):	Bowling where spin is imparted with the fingers. An off-spinner's stock delivery is the off break, but he may also bowl an arm ball or a doosra.
On drive:	A drive through the on side towards mid-on.
Outfield:	That part of the field outside the 30-yard circle (shown in Figure 1.2).
Out-dipper:	A ball that curves away from the batsman before pitching,
Out-swinger (or away-swinger):	A ball that swings away from the batsman from leg to off.
Over:	Six consecutive legitimate balls bowled at one end of the pitch. Before 1978, the number of balls in an over varied from country to country and ranged between 4 and 8.
Overpitched:	A full-length ball that is short of Yorker length. It is relatively easy to drive an overpitched ball in front of the wicket.
Over rate:	The number of overs bowled per hour.
Over the wicket:	Describes the side of the wicket from which the ball is delivered. A right arm bowler delivers the ball over the wicket when he runs in and bowls at the left of the stumps. A left-arm bowler delivers the ball over the wicket when he runs in and bowls at the right of the stumps.
Partnership:	The number of runs scored between two batsmen while both are at the crease and before one of them gets out. It may also refer to the period when two players bowl consecutive overs from either end unchanged.
Peach:	Similar to a Jaffa.
Pitch:	The 22-yard-long rectangular stretch of turf near the centre of the field that is carefully prepared by mowing and rolling to form a flat surface that is suitable for both bowling and batting.
Popping Crease:	The line drawn across the pitch 4 feet (1.22m) in front of the stumps at each end of the pitch. The popping crease is parallel to the bowling crease (see inset in Figure 1.2).
Pull:	A shot played on the leg side between backward square leg and mid-wicket to a short-pitched ball that reaches the batsman between knee and shoulder height.
Rabbit:	A lower-order batsman, usually a specialist bowler, with a poor batting record.
Return Crease:	The return creases are lines perpendicular to the popping crease and the bowling crease, 4 feet 4 inches (1.32 m) either side of the middle stumps at each end of the pitch. Each return crease line starts at the popping crease and is used to determine whether the bowler has bowled a no-ball (see inset in Figure 1.2).

Reverse sweep:	A right-hand batsman turning around and sweeping the ball like a left-hand batsman, and vice-versa.
Seam:	The stitching running around the cricket ball.
Seam bowling	Usually, medium pace to fast bowling that relies on the raised seam hitting the pitch to cause deviation and bounce.
Seamer:	A seam bowler
Session	The period of play between the start of the day's play and lunch or between lunch and tea or between tea and stumps. A session is usually of 2 hours duration.
Short-pitched:	A delivery that bounces short of a good length (see bouncer and long-hop). It is relatively easy to cut, pull or hook a short-pitched ball.
Shot:	A shot is played by a batsman when he hits the ball. Different shots include forward or backward defensive shots, cover drives, off drives, on drives, square cuts, back cuts and late cuts, hooks, pulls, sweeps, lap sweeps, glances, slogs, steers and more.
Sitter:	An easy catch.
Slip:	A close-to-the-wicket fielder behind the stumps on the off-side adjacent to the wicketkeeper. There may be four slips for a fast bowler (see Figure 1.2).
Slog:	An attempt to hit the ball for six, usually with a lot of power but little technique.
Slog sweep:	An aggressive sweep in the air to the leg side usually off a spin bowler.
Slower ball:	A bowl delivered with essentially the same action that is significantly slower than usual. It is designed to deceive the batsman into playing too early.
Spin Bowling:	Generally slow bowling where spin is imparted to the ball either by fingers (see off-spin or finger-spin) or by wrist (see leg spin or wrist spin).
Spinner:	A spin bowler
Square cut:	A cut shot square of the wicket through point or gully.
Stance:	The posture taken by a batsman as he prepares to play a ball.
Straight drive:	A drive back along the pitch.
Striker:	The batsman facing the delivery (see Figure 1.2).
Sweep:	A shot in which the batsman gets down on one knee and sweeps a good length ball with a horizontal bat towards the leg-side fence. The shot is usually played against a spin bowler.
Swing bowling:	Usually employed by fast or medium pace bowlers. The fielding team polishes the ball on one side of the seam. If the seam is held upright, the air travels faster over one side of the ball than the other causing the ball to swing in the air. Conventional swing is when the ball curves in the air away from the shiny side (usually when the ball is relatively new). Reverse swing is when the ball curves the other way (usually as the ball becomes older and more worn).
Through the gate:	When a batsman is bowled by a ball passing between his bat and pad.
Ton:	When a batsman scores a century, i.e., 100 or more runs in a single innings.
Top-order:	Batsmen who bat from No. 1 to No. 4 in the batting order, including the two opening batsmen.
Top spin:	When a bowler imparts forward rotation spin on a ball causing it bounce unexpectedly.
T20 or Twenty20:	Twenty overs per side limited overs cricket.

Walk: When a batsman walks off the pitch because he knows he is out and does not wait for the umpire's decision. It is generally considered to be a sporting gesture, but some consider it rather foolish.

Wide: A delivery that falls outside the return crease and wide of the wickets. When the umpire calls a delivery a wide, the batting side is awarded one run (an extra) and the delivery must be re-bowled.

Yorker: A fast bowl that pitches right under the bat or on the batsman's toes. A good yorker is difficult to keep out, but a bad attempt at a Yorker may result in a full-toss or a half-volley and easy runs.

Chapter 2
Rating the Players

The comparisons between players (and teams) in the following chapters are based on a batting and a bowling rating calculated for each cricketer who played more than 20 test matches in any of the time periods under consideration. Some of the great players, played more than 20 test matches in more than one decade (or in more than one era) and so their performances in each period are assessed separately. For example, Rohan Kanhai, Sir Garfield Sobers, Clive Lloyd, Shivnarine Chanderpaul and Courtney Walsh (West Indies), Geoffrey Boycott (England), Javed Miandad (Pakistan), Kapil Dev, Sachin Tendulkar and Rahul Dravid (India), Stephen Waugh and Ricky Ponting (Australia), Mahela Jayawardene (Sri Lanka), and Jacques Kallis (South Africa) all played more than 20 tests in three different decades and all performed well enough in each decade to be selected here in their respective highest rating national teams.

A batting rating has been determined for each player in each decade or era considering the following statistics:

(a) the batting average (the total number of runs scored divided by the number of times dismissed);
(b) the total number of runs scored;
(c) the strike rate (the average number of runs scored off every 100 balls faced);
(d) the numbers of centuries (scores of 100 or more in an innings), half-centuries (scores of 50 or more but less than 100 in an innings) and ducks (scores of zero);
(e) the highest score in the period under consideration; and
(f) the total number of innings played in the period.

A bowling rating has been determined for each player who bowled more than 100 overs during the period under consideration. The bowling rating takes into consideration:

(g) the bowling average (the average number of runs scored off the bowler per wicket taken);
(h) the number of wickets taken;
(i) the strike rate (number of balls bowled divided by number of wickets taken);
(j) the economy rate (average number of runs scored off every six balls bowled);
(k) the number and frequency of times the bowler took 5 or more wickets in an innings and 10 or more wickets in a match;
(l) the total number of balls bowled; and
(m) the ratio of maiden overs to total overs bowled.

The numerical rating assigned to each factor is explained in this chapter and the formulas and relationships from which the batting and bowling ratings have been calculated are presented. An attempt has been made to place an appropriate weighting on the various factors so that each player's performance is represented fairly, and that reasonable comparisons can be made between players.

The Batting Rating

For each period under consideration, the batting rating for each player is taken as the sum of the weighted scores WS1 to WS6. The score WS1 depends on the batting average, WS2 depends on the total number of runs scored, WS3 depends on the batting strike rate, WS4 depends on the number of 100s, 50s and 0s, WS5 depends on the highest score and WS6 depends on the number of innings played.

Batting Rating = WS1 + WS2 + WS3 + WS4 + WS5 + WS6   (2.1)

WS1 — Batting average:

A player's batting average in any period (w_{avge}) is the total number of runs scored divided by the number of times the batsman was dismissed. It is the usual way and the safest way to compare the batting performances of players. Consequently, WS1 is assigned a relatively large proportion of the batting rating. For most batsmen, the value of WS1 (calculated using Equation 2.2) is between 40% and 45% of the batting rating.

The relationship used here to determine the weighted score for batting average (WS1) is:

$$WS1 = 0.02\, (w_{avge})^2 \qquad (2.2)$$

And the relationship is graphed in Figure 2.1. The variation of WS1 with batting average is also shown in Table 2.1.

Table 2.1 Values of WS1

w_{avge}	0	10	20	30	40	50	60	70	80	90	100
WS1	0	2.0	8.0	18.0	32.0	50.0	72.0	98.0	128	162	200

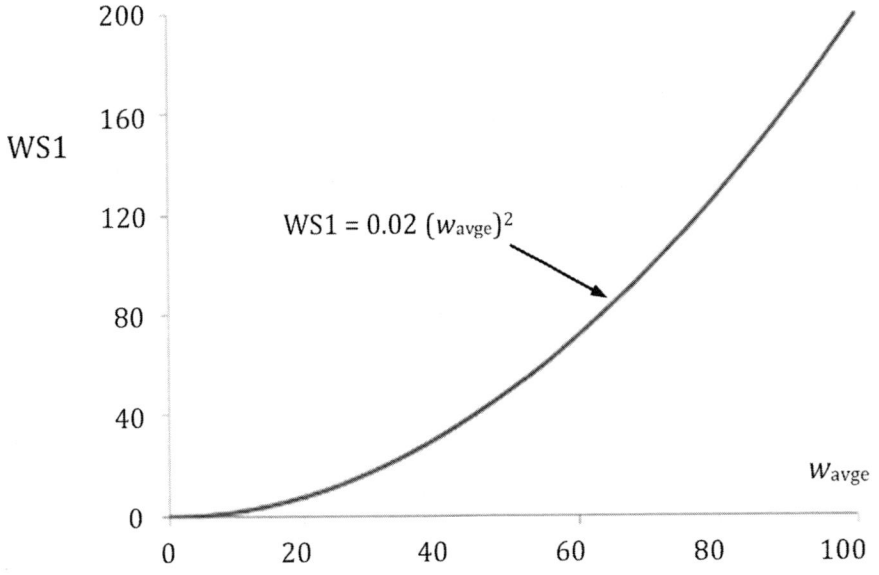

Figure 2.1 Variation of WS1 with batting average, w_{avge}.

In test cricket, a batting average of below 30 is acceptable for a bowler who bats in the lower-order but is generally considered unacceptable for a top-order batsman. An average of 30 to 40 is satisfactory for a top-order batsman but is unlikely to be considered acceptable over a long period by the national selectors of the test team. An average in the low 40s is considered good for an established test batsman and an average of 50 is outstanding. Up to the end of 2024, of those players who have played 20 or more test matches, only 39 of them have averaged over 50 in their test careers (see Table 2.2).

The distribution of batting averages for all eligible top-order players is shown in Appendix C (Figure C.1). For the statistically minded, the mean batting average of all the top-order batsmen with more than 20 test matches is 38.00 and the standard deviation is 8.84. Only five batsmen have averaged over 60 per innings, Adam Voges (Australia) 61.88, Graeme Pollock (South Africa) 60.97, George Headley (West Indies) 60.83, Herbert Sutcliffe (England) 60.73, and Sir Donald Bradman (Australia) 99.94, with only Bradman, and Sutcliffe playing more than 25 tests. Bradman's average is so much higher than his peers, it is statistically so improbable as to be almost impossible. If the batting averages of the top-order batsmen are assumed to be *normally distributed* (with a mean of 38.00 and a standard deviation of 8.84), the probability of an average of 99.94 is one in about 100,000,000,000. In no other sport has any individual been statistically so much better than everyone else who ever played.

Table 2.2 Batsmen with a career batting average over 50
(20 or more tests before the end of 2024).

Batsman	Country	Career	Tests	w_{avge}	WS1	Batsman	Country	Career	Tests	w_{avge}	WS1
1. Bradman, DG	Australia	1928-48	52	99.94	199.8	21. Tendulkar, SR	India	1989-13	200	53.79	57.9
2. Voges, AC	Australia	2015-16	20	61.88	76.6	22. Lara, BC	W Indies	1990-06	131	52.89	55.9
3. Pollock, RG	Sth Africa	1963-70	23	60.97	74.4	23. Javed Miandad	Pakistan	1976-93	124	52.57	55.3
4. Headley, GA	W Indies	1930-54	22	60.83	74.0	24. Dravid, R	India	1996-12	164	52.31	54.7
5. Sutcliffe, H	England	1924-35	54	60.73	73.8	25. Mohd. Yousuf	Pakistan	1998-10	90	52.29	54.7
6. Paynter, E	England	1931-39	20	59.23	70.2	26. Younis Khan	Pakistan	2000-17	118	52.06	54.2
7. Barrington, KF	England	1955-68	82	58.67	68.8	27. Ponting, RT	Australia	1995-12	168	51.85	53.8
8. Weekes, EDC	W Indies	1948-58	48	58.62	68.7	28. Ryder, J	Australia	1920-29	20	51.63	53.3
9. Brook, HC [1]	England	2022-24	24	58.49	68.4	29. Flower, A	Zimbabwe	1992-02	63	51.55	53.1
10. Hammond, WR	England	1927-47	85	58.46	68.4	30. Hussey, MEK	Australia	2005-13	79	51.53	53.1
11. Sobers, GStA	W Indies	1954-74	93	57.78	66.8	31. Chanderpaul, S	W Indies	1994-15	164	51.37	52.8
12. Sangakkara, KC	Sri Lanka	2000-15	134	57.41	65.9	32. Gavaskar, SM	India	1971-87	125	51.12	52.3
13. Hobbs, JB	England	1908-30	61	56.95	64.9	33. Waugh, SR	Australia	1985-04	168	51.06	52.1
14. Walcott, CL	W Indies	1948-60	44	56.69	64.3	34. Root, JE [1]	England	2012-24	152	50.87	51.8
15. Hutton, L	England	1937-55	79	56.67	64.2	35. Hayden, ML	Australia	1994-09	103	50.74	51.5
16. Smith, SPD [1]	Australia	2010-24	113	56.28	63.3	36. de Villiers, AB	Sth Africa	2004-18	114	50.66	51.3
17. Kallis, JH	Sth Africa	1995-13	166	55.37	61.3	37. Border, AR	Australia	1978-94	156	50.56	51.1
18. Williamson, KS [1]	N Zealand	2010-24	105	54.89	60.3	38. Richards, IVA	W Indies	1974-91	121	50.24	50.5
19. Chappell, GS	Australia	1970-84	87	53.86	58.0	39. Compton, DCS	England	1937-57	78	50.06	50.1
20. Nourse, AD	Sth Africa	1935-51	34	53.82	57.9						

[1] Still playing in 2024

WS2 — Number of Runs Scored:

The total number of runs scored (n_{runs}) is also an indicator of a batsman's value to his team. Comparing two players with the same batting average, the batsman who plays the most innings and scores the most runs is clearly more valuable. There are now far more tests played each year than in the early years of test cricket, so batsmen in the modern era have the opportunity to play more tests and score more runs than in years gone by. This complicates matters when attempting to compare players from different eras. The WS2 score assigned to each batsman is determined using:

$$\text{WS2} = 0.003\, n_{runs} \qquad (2.3)$$

Fourteen batsmen have scored more than 10,000 runs in test cricket, with India's Sachin Tendulkar heading the list with 15,921 runs. After Tendulkar comes Australia's Ricky Ponting (13,378 runs), South Africa's Jacques Kallis

(13,289 runs), India's Rahul Dravid (13,288 runs), England's Joe Root (12,972 runs) and Alastair Cook (12,472 runs), Sri Lanka's Kumar Sangakkara (12,400 runs), West Indians Brian Lara (11,953 runs) and Shiv Chanderpaul (11,867 runs), Sri Lanka' Mahela Jayawardene (11,814 runs), Australians Allan Border (11,174 runs) and Steve Waugh (10,927 runs), India's Sunil Gavaskar (10,122 runs) and Pakistan's Younis Khan (10,099 runs). Of these fourteen batsmen, only Joe Root is still playing in 2024 and is likely to increase his aggregate of runs in the future.

WS3 — Batting Strike Rate:

A player's batting strike rate w_{sr} is the number of runs scored off every 100 balls faced, averaged over the time period in question. A strike rate in the 30s (or less) indicates a rather defensive batsman who scored slowly. A strike rate between 40 and 50 is typical of most top-order batsmen. A strike rate of between 50 and 65 is typical of an attacking stroke player. Few batsmen have career strike rates in test cricket exceeding 65. Only 11 top-order batsmen who have played more than 20 matches have recorded strike rates above 70: Harry Brook (England) 88.38, Shahid Afridi (Pakistan) 86.97, Ben Duckett (England) 85.89, Virender Sehwag (India) 82.21, Adam Gilchrist (Australia) 81.96, Colin de Grandhomme (New Zealand) 80.45, Rishabh Pant (India) 73.51, Kusal Perera (Sri Lanka) 72.25, Quinton de Kock (South Africa) 70.94, David Warner (Australia) 70.19, and Sarfaraz Ahmed (Pakistan) 70.16.

It is only since the late 1970s that the strike rates for batsmen have been recorded regularly, so the strike rates for the greats of yesteryear are often unknown. However, Don Bradman (Australia) scored 309 runs in a day in the test match against England at Leeds in 1930 (the highest number of runs ever scored in a day by an individual). He also scored 271 in a day at the same ground in 1934 and 244 runs in a day at the Oval in 1934. Walter Hammond (England) scored 295 runs in a day against New Zealand in 1933 at Auckland. He also scored 223 runs in a day in the same series at Christchurch and he scored 217 runs in a day against India at the Oval in 1936. So, the strike rates of these great players must have been reasonably high.

In the list of the top 16 highest number of runs scored in a day by an individual, 8 were scored before 1960 when strike rates were not routinely recorded. Bradman features 4 times in that list, Hammond twice, and Denis Compton (England) and Frank Worrell (West Indies) once each. The batsmen on the list whose strike rates were recorded all played after 1990 and include Virender Sehwag (India) 3 times, David Warner (Australia), Karun Nair (India), Brian Lara (West Indies), Herschelle Gibbs (South Africa) and Michael Clarke (Australia) once each.

Although a high strike rate is generally more valuable to a team in limited overs cricket than in test cricket, strike rate is nevertheless a significant part of the batting rating. However, to be meaningful, the weighted score for strike rate in test cricket must be tied to the batting average. A high batting strike rate is of little value if the batsman's average is low. A high strike rate linked with a high average is valuable, since the batsman has scored his runs quickly, giving the bowlers more time to get the opposition out. The relationship adopted to determine the weighted score WS3 is:

$$WS3 = 0.002 \, w_{avge} \, (w_{sr})^{1.25} \qquad (2.4)$$

And is illustrated in Figure 2.2. The values of WS3 are tabulated in Table 2.3 for the realistic range of strike rates for batsmen with batting averages of $w_{avge} = 60.0$ (i.e. with WS1 = 72), $w_{avge} = 50.0$ (with WS1 = 50.0) and $w_{avge} = 40.0$ (with WS1 = 32.0).

When determining the batting rating of a batsman who played in an era when strike rates were not recorded, a strike rate of 50 has been assumed in each of the years for which the actual strike rate is unavailable.

Table 2.3 Values of WS3.

Strike rate, w_{sr}	30	40	50	60	70	80	90	100
WS2 for Batsmen with $w_{avge} = 60$	8.4	12.1	16.0	20.0	24.3	28.7	33.3	37.9
WS2 for Batsmen with $w_{avge} = 50$	7.0	10.1	13.3	16.7	20.2	23.9	27.7	31.6
WS2 for Batsmen with $w_{avge} = 40$	5.6	8.0	10.6	13.4	16.2	19.1	22.2	25.3

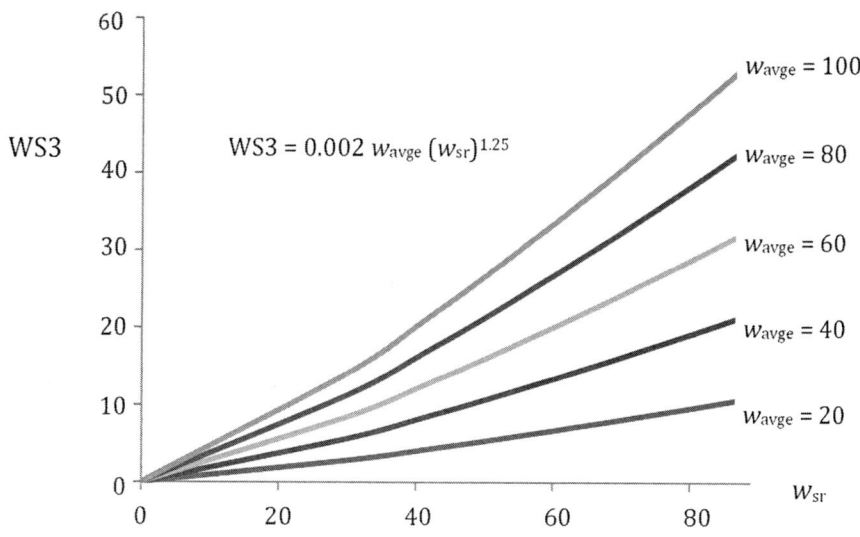

Figure 2.2 Relationship between WS3 and batting strike rate w_{sr}.

Table 2.4 contains the list of all batsmen who played in 20 or more tests, scored over 1,000 runs and had a career batting strike rates greater than 60. Also included in the table for each player are their batting averages, their strike rates and their calculated WS3 scores. The player with the 4th highest strike rate, Tim Southee of New Zealand, is a specialist opening bowler with a modest batting average. Consequently, his WS3 score is significantly lower than, for example, that of the 5th player on the list Virender Sehwag (India) who was an opening batsman with a batting average of almost 50. Of the players listed in Table 2.4, only Harry Brook (England), Brian Lara (West Indies), Viv Richards (West Indies) and Matthew Hayden (Australia) have a career batting average greater than 50.0.

Table 2.4 Batsmen with career strike rates over 60
(with 20 or more tests before the end of 2024).

Batsman	Country	Runs	w_{avge}	w_{sr}	WS3	Batsman	Country	Runs	w_{avge}	w_{sr}	WS3
1. Brook, HC [1]	England	2,281	58.49	88.38	31.7	23. Mohd. Rafique	Bangladesh	1,059	18.58	64.93	6.8
2. Shahid Afridi	Pakistan	1,716	36.51	86.97	19.4	24. Harbhajan Singh	India	2,225	18.24	64.83	6.7
3. Duckett, BM [1]	England	2,270	39.82	85.89	19.1	25. Symonds, A	Australia	1462	40.61	64.8	14.9
4. Southee, TG [1]	N Zealand	2,245	15.48	82.69	7.7	26. McCullum, BB	N Zealand	6,453	38.64	64.6	14.2
5. Sehwag, V	India	8,586	49.34	82.21	24.4	27. Pope, OJD [1]	England	3,130	34.02	63.68	12.2
6. Gilchrist, AC	Australia	5,570	47.61	81.96	23.5	28. Smith, IDS	N. Zealand	1,815	25.56	63.17	9.1
7. de Grandhomme, C	N Zealand	1,432	38.70	80.45	18.6	29. Kamran Akmal	Pakistan	2,648	30.79	63.12	11.0
8. Swann, GP	England	1,370	22.10	76.49	10.0	30. Flintoff, A	England	3,845	31.78	62.05	11.1
9. Pant, RR [1]	India	2,847	41.87	73.51	18.0	31. Lehmann, DS	Australia	1,798	44.95	61.81	15.6
10. Perera, MDKJ	Sri Lanka	1,177	30.97	72.25	13.0	32. Pietersen, KP	England	8,181	47.29	61.72	16.4
11. de Kock, Q	Sth Africa	3,300	38.82	70.94	16.0	33. Shakib Al Hasan [1]	Bangladesh	4,609	37.78	61.68	13.1
12. Muralitharan, M	Sri Lanka	1,261	11.68	70.29	4.8	34. Richards, IVA	W Indies	8,540	50.24	60.82	17.1
13. Warner, DA	Australia	8,786	44.60	70.19	18.1	35. Prior, MJ	England	4,099	40.19	61.67	13.9
14. Sarfaraz Ahmed	Pakistan	3,031	37.42	70.16	15.2	36. Botham, I T	England	5,200	33.55	60.71	11.4
15. Sammy, DJG	W Indies	1,323	21.69	67.88	8.5	37. Carey, AT [1]	Australia	1,534	31.96	60.61	10.8
16. Head, TM [1]	Australia	3,583	43.17	67.02	16.6	38. Lara, BC	W Indies	11,953	52.89	60.52	17.9
17. Dhawan, S	India	2,315	40.61	66.95	15.6	39. Shubman Gill [1]	India	1,860	35.77	60.39	12.0
18. Dickwella, N	Sri Lanka	2,757	30.98	66.47	11.8	40. Kaluwitharana, RS	Sri Lanka	1,933	26.12	60.35	8.8
19. Crawley, Z [1]	England	2,899	30.52	65.72	11.4	41. Habibul Bashar	Bangladesh	3,026	30.88	60.28	10.4
20. Dilshan, TM	Sri Lanka	5,492	40.99	65.55	15.3	42. Gayle, CH	W Indies	7,214	42.19	60.27	14.2
21. Broad, SCJ	England	3,662	18.04	65.31	6.7	43. Starc, MA [1]	Australia	2,189	20.27	60.19	6.8
22. Jayasuriya, ST	Sri Lanka	6,973	40.07	65.13	14.8	44. Hayden, ML	Australia	8,625	50.74	60.11	17.0

[1] Still playing in 2024
[2] Players who played before the late 1970s when strike rates were not always recorded are not included.

WS4 — Number of 100s, 50s and 0s:

Players are often rated depending on the number of centuries (n_{100}) and half centuries (n_{50}) they scored and the frequency with which they scored them. These figures reflect their ability, their powers of concentration, their temperament and so on. If a player scored one or more centuries or half centuries, then WS3 is calculated from:

$$\text{WS4} = \frac{100\, n_{100} + 50\, n_{50} - 20\, n_0}{n_{\text{innings}}} \geq 0 \qquad (2.5)$$

Where n_0 is the number of ducks (i.e., the number of times the batsman was dismissed without scoring) and n_{innings} is the number of innings played in the period under consideration. If a player did not score any centuries or half centuries, WS4 = 0, even though he may not have troubled the scorers on one or more occasions.

In Equation 2.5, the number and frequency of centuries and half-centuries are rewarded, and the number and frequency of ducks are penalised. For example, the WS4 score for a player with 150 innings who scored 12 centuries, 20 half centuries and 6 ducks is:

$$\text{WS4} = (100 \times 12 + 50 \times 20 - 20 \times 6) / 150 = 13.9$$

The list of the great batsmen who scored 25 or more centuries during their test careers is shown in Table 2.5. Sachin Tendulkar (India) heads the list with 51 centuries. However, Don Bradman scored a century every 2.76 innings he played, much more frequently than all the rest, and this is reflected in the WS4 scores shown in the right-hand column of Table 2.5. Interestingly, 22 of the 25 batsmen listed in Table 2.5 played at least some of their matches in the 21st century, reflecting the greater number of test matches played each year in the modern era and the general trend in the modern era for the bat to dominate the ball.

Only eight players in the history of test cricket have scored more than 30 ducks, with Courtney Walsh (West Indies, 43) heading the list, followed by Stuart Broad (England, 39), Chris Martin (New Zealand, 36), Glenn McGrath (Australia, 35), Shane Warne (Australia, 34), Ishant Sharma (India, 34), James Anderson (England, 34) and Muttiah Muralitharan (Sri Lanka, 33). All played some of their matches in the 21st century. Walsh, McGrath, Broad, Warne, Muralitharan and Anderson all played over 120 tests and all were magnificent bowlers. Merwyn Dillon (West Indies) played 38 tests and scored a duck every 2.62 innings, the highest frequency of any player with more than 20 test matches.

Table 2.5 Batsmen with 25 or more career hundreds (up to the end of 2024) and their WS4 score.

Batsman	Country	Career	n_{innings}	Runs	n_0	n_{50}	n_{100}	n_{200}	n_{300}	W_{avge}	WS4
Tendulkar, SR	India	1989-13	329	15,921	14	68	51	6	0	53.79	25.0
Kallis, JH	Sth Africa	1995-13	280	13,289	16	58	45	2	0	55.37	25.3
Ponting, RT	Australia	1995-12	287	13,378	17	62	41	6	0	51.85	23.9
Sangakkara, KC	Sri Lanka	2000-15	233	12,400	11	52	38	11	1	57.41	26.5
Dravid, R	India	1996-12	286	13,288	8	63	36	5	0	52.31	23.0
Root, JE [1]	England	2012-24	278	12,972	13	65	36	6	0	50.87	23.7
Gavaskar, SM	India	1971-87	214	10,122	12	45	34	4	0	51.12	25.3
Lara, BC	W Indies	1990-06	232	11,953	17	48	34	9	2	52.89	23.5
Jayawardene, DPMdS	Sri Lanka	1997-14	252	11,814	15	50	34	7	1	49.85	22.2
Younis Khan	Pakistan	2000-17	213	10,099	19	33	34	6	1	52.06	21.9
Smith, SPD [1]	Australia	2010-24	202	9,962	11	41	34	4	0	56.28	25.9
Cook, AN	England	2006-18	291	12,472	9	57	33	5	0	45.35	20.5
Williamson, KS [1]	N Zealand	2010-24	186	9,276	11	37	33	6	0	54.89	26.5
Waugh, SR	Australia	1985-04	260	10,927	22	50	32	1	0	51.06	20.2

Batsman	Country	Career	$n_{innings}$	Runs	n_0	n_{50}	n_{100}	n_{200}	n_{300}	w_{avge}	WS4
Hayden, ML	Australia	1994-09	184	8,625	14	29	30	2	1	50.74	22.7
Chanderpaul, S	W Indies	1994-15	280	11,867	15	66	30	2	0	51.37	21.4
Kohli, V [1]	India	2011-24	207	9,202	15	31	30	7	0	47.43	20.5
Bradman, DG	Australia	1928-48	80	6,996	7	13	29	12	2	99.94	42.6
Clarke, MJ	Australia	2004-15	198	8,643	9	27	28	4	1	49.11	20.1
Amla, H M	Sth Africa	2004-19	215	9,282	13	41	28	4	1	46.64	21.3
Smith, GC	Sth Africa	2002-14	205	9,265	11	38	27	5	0	48.26	21.4
Border, AR	Australia	1978-94	265	11,174	11	63	27	2	0	50.56	21.2
Sobers, GSA	W Indies	1954-74	160	8,032	12	30	26	2	1	57.78	24.1
Warner, DA	Australia	2011-24	205	8,886	13	37	26	3	1	44.59	20.4
Inzamam-ul-Haq	Pakistan	1992-07	200	8,830	15	46	25	2	1	49.61	22.5

[1] Still playing in 2024

WS5 – Highest Scores:

A relatively small part of a batman's rating is dependent on his highest score (HS) in the period under consideration. Many players did not score double or triple centuries, simply because they could not maintain their powers of concentration for long enough periods. Only one player has ever scored a quadruple century in test cricket. Brian Lara scored exactly 400 for the West Indies against England at Antigua in April 2004 and for this he receives WS5 = 15. The following linear relationship has been adopted between WS5 and HS:

$$WS5 = (HS - 100)/20 \geq 0 \qquad (2.6)$$

A batsman with a highest score of less than 100 receives WS5 = 0. Numerical values of WS5 are given in Table 2.6.

Individual scores of 300 or more have been made only 32 times in test cricket, with only Don Bradman (Australia), Brian Lara (West Indies), Chris Gayle (West Indies) and Virender Sehwag (India) scoring triple centuries on more than one occasion. Double centuries are more common, but still rare. Don Bradman scored a double century on 12 occasions (out of a total of 80 innings), the most times in history. He is followed by Kumar Sangakkara (Sri Lanka) on 11 occasions (from 233 innings) and Brian Lara on 9 occasions (from 232 innings). Double centuries were scored on 7 occasions by Wally Hammond (England – 140 innings), Virat Kohli (India – 207 innings) and Mahela Jayawardene (Sri Lanka – 252 innings) and, on 6 occasions, by Sachin Tendulkar (India – 329 innings), Ricky Ponting (Australia – 287 innings), Younis Khan (Pakistan – 213 innings), Javed Miandad (Pakistan – 189 innings), Virender Sehwag (India – 180 innings), Kane Williamson (New Zealand – 186 innings), Marvan Atapattu (Sri Lanka – 156 innings) and Joe Root (England – 278 innings).

WS6 – Number of Innings:

A batsman's rating and value in a particular decade (or era) also depends on the number of innings played ($n_{innings}$) and this is reflected in the value assigned to WS6. A batsman who played 100 innings for his country was of more value than a player with the same batting average and strike rate who played 50 innings. The relationship between WS6 and the number of innings played for a batsman with a batting average over 20 is given in by:

$$WS6 = (n_{innings} - 30)/10 \geq 0 \qquad (2.7)$$

Numerical values of WS6 are given in Table 2.6. For players with less than 30 innings in the time period under consideration WS6 = 0. For specialist bowlers with a batting average below 20.0, WS6 is taken as zero (as Equation 2.7 may unreasonably enhance their batting rating, particularly for bowlers who played many test matches).

Table 2.6 Values of WS4 and WS5.

Highest score, HS	0 to 100	150	200	250	300	350	400
WS5 (Eq. 2.6)	0	2.5	5	7.5	10	12.5	15

Number of innings, $n_{innings}$	≤ 30	50	100	150	200	250	300
WS6 (Eq. 2.7)	0	2	7	12	17	22	27

Example Batting Ratings:

To illustrate the calculation of the batting rating, we will consider three top-order batsmen for the decade 2000 to 2009:

(1) Virender Sehwag opened the batting for India in 72 test matches from 2001 to 2009.

Input data:

w_{avge}	w_{sr}	$n_{innings}$	n_{runs}	HS	n_{100}	n_{50}	n_0
52.50	80.41	123	6,248	319	17	19	10

From Eq. 2.2:   WS1 = $0.02 \times (52.50)^2$ = 55.1
From Eq. 2.3:   WS2 = $0.003 \times 6{,}248$ = 18.7
From Eq. 2.4:   WS3 = $0.002 \times 52.5 \times (80.41)^{1.25}$ = 25.3
From Eq. 2.5:   WS4 = $(100 \times 17 + 50 \times 19 - 20 \times 10)/123$ = 19.9
From Eq. 2.6:   WS5 = $(319 - 100)/20$ = 11.0
From Eq. 2.7:   WS6 = $(123 - 30)/10$ = 9.3
From Eq. 2.1:   Batting Rating = WS1 + WS2 + WS3 + WS4 + WS5 + WS6 = 139.3

(2) Marvan Atapattu opened the batting for Sri Lanka 61 tests from 2000 to 2007.

Input data:

w_{avge}	w_{sr}	$n_{innings}$	n_{runs}	HS	n_{100}	n_{50}	n_0
42.68	44.86	105	4,055	249	13	14	12

WS1	WS2	WS3	WS4	WS5	WS6	Batting Rating
36.4	12.2	9.9	16.8	7.5	7.5	90.2

(3) Justin Langer opened the batting for Australia in 76 tests from 2000 to 2007.

Input data:

w_{avge}	w_{sr}	$n_{innings}$	n_{runs}	HS	n_{100}	n_{50}	n_0
48.73	58.98	134	5,994	250	18	21	7

WS1	WS2	WS3	WS4	WS5	WS6	Batting Rating
47.5	18.0	15.9	20.2	7.5	10.4	119.5

Ratings Of the Top 100 Batsmen of All Time:

The career batting details for the 100 highest rating batsmen in the history of test cricket (up to the end of 2024) are provided in Table 2.7. A more comprehensive list of all batsmen with a batting rating of over 50 is provided in Appendix A (Table A.1). Only batsmen who played 20 or more test matches have been considered and, where records of strike rates are not available in a particular year, a strike rate of 50 has been adopted for that year.

Of the top 100 players listed in Table 2.7, there are 22 Australians, 22 Englishmen, 14 West Indians, 11 Indians, 9 Pakistanis, 8 South Africans, 8 Sri Lankans, 5 New Zealanders and 1 Zimbabwean. There are 31 left-hand batsmen and 69 right handers. Only 1 of the top 100 batsmen made his test debut before the First World War, 13 between 1920 and 1949, 7 in the 1950s, 7 in the 1960s, 10 in the 1970s, 9 in the 1980s, 21 in the 1990s, 19 in the 2000s and 13 in the 2010s. Ten of the batsmen on the list are still playing at the end of 2024 and so their positions on the table will almost certainly change as their careers progress. The affected players are Joe Root of England (at No. 7), Steven Smith of Australia (at No. 9), Kane Williamson of New Zealand (at No.12), Harry Brook of England (No. 15), Virat Kohli of India (at No. 40), Angelo Mathews of Sri Lanka (No. 58), Manus Labuschagne of Australia (at No. 79), Dimuth Karunaratne of Sri Lanka (at No. 86), Dinesh Chandimal of Sri Lanka (at No. 90) and Usman Khawaja of Australia (at No. 95).

All the players in Table 2.7 were or are brilliant batsmen, but Bradman, with a rating almost 70% higher than the next best, was unique. Based on his statistics, he was much more successful than anyone before or since, despite playing just 52 test matches. No one has ever scored more runs per innings, more centuries per innings, more double centuries and more triple centuries per innings. Although his strike rate is unavailable for some of his career, he scored more runs in a single day than anyone else has ever scored. In the list of the batsmen with the most runs scored in a single day of test cricket, Bradman features 3 times in the top 7, so his strike rate was probably well in excess of the value of 54.95 assigned to him here for the calculation of his career batting rating.

After Bradman, the next five highest rating batsmen on the list are India's Sachin Tendulkar (2nd), Sri Lanka's Kumar Sangakkara (3rd), South Africa's Jacques Kallis (4th), West Indian Brian Lara (5th) and Australia's Ricky Ponting (6th). All played in excess of 130 test matches. Tendulkar had a test career longer than anyone else on the list (24 years, 1 day), the 5th longest career in test history. He played more tests and scored more test runs than anyone else. However, Sangakkara had a higher batting average and a higher strike rate than Tendulkar and he scored almost twice as many double centuries. For a significant part of his career, Sangakkara also kept wickets for Sri Lanka. Rounding out the top 12 test batsmen in Table 2.7 are England's Joe Root (7th), India's Rahul Dravid (8th), Australia's Steven Smith (9th), Sri Lanka's Mahela Jayawardene (10th), West Indian Sir Garfield Sobers (11th) and New Zealand's Kane Williamson (12th).

The two greatest ever batting all-rounders feature in the top twelve batsmen in Table 2.7, Jacques Kallis and Sir Garfield Sobers. With Kallis having a slightly higher bowling rating than Sobers, it would appear from a statistical point of view that he was the greatest batting all-rounder in history. However, those who saw Sobers bat will probably disagree.

Table 2.7 The top 100 career test batting ratings (20 or more matches before the end of 2024).

Batsman	Country	Career	Tests	$n_{innings}$	Runs	w_{avge}	w_{sr}	HS	n_{100}	n_{50}	n_0	Rating
1. Bradman, DG	Australia	1928-48	52	80	6996	99.94	55.95	334	29	13	7	310.0
2. Tendulkar, SR	India	1989-13	200	329	15921	53.79	54.12	248	51	68	14	183.7
3. Sangakkara, KC	Sri Lanka	2000-15	134	233	12400	57.41	54.19	319	38	52	11	177.8
4. Kallis, JH	Sth Africa	1995-13	166	280	13289	55.37	45.98	224	45	58	16	170.9
5. Lara, BC	W Indies	1990-06	131	232	11953	52.89	60.52	400	34	48	17	168.4
6. Ponting, RT	Australia	1995-12	168	287	13378	51.85	58.72	257	41	62	17	168.2
7. Root, JE [1]	England	2012-24	152	278	12972	50.87	57.48	270	36	65	13	163.4
8. Dravid, R	India	1996-12	164	286	13288	52.31	42.51	239	36	63	8	163.1
9. Smith, SPD [1]	Australia	2010-24	113	202	9962	56.28	53.54	374	34	41	11	159.6

Batsman	Country	Career	Tests	$n_{innings}$	Runs	w_{avge}	w_{sr}	HS	n_{100}	n_{50}	n_0	Rating
10. Jayawardene, DPMD	Sri Lanka	1997-14	149	252	11814	49.85	51.47	365	34	50	15	157.0
11. Sobers, GStA	W Indies	1954-74	93	160	8032	57.78	49.62	254	26	30	12	156.5
12. Williamson, KS [1]	N Zealand	2010-24	105	186	9276	54.89	51.78	336	33	37	11	153.0
13. Hammond, WR	England	1927-47	85	140	7249	58.46	49.53	203	22	24	4	152.0
14. Chanderpaul, S	W Indies	1994-15	164	280	11867	51.37	43.32	256	30	66	15	151.4
15. Brook, HC [1]	England	2022-24	24	40	2281	58.49	88.38	313	8	10	2	150.3
16. Barrington, KF	England	1955-68	82	131	6806	58.67	48.86	256	20	35	5	150.2
17. Younis Khan	Pakistan	2000-17	118	213	10099	52.06	52.12	313	34	33	19	150.0
18. Hutton, L	England	1937-55	79	138	6971	56.67	50.00	364	19	33	5	149.2
19. Hayden, ML	Australia	1994-09	103	184	8625	50.74	60.11	380	30	29	14	146.4
20. Waugh, SR	Australia	1985-04	168	260	10927	51.06	48.65	200	32	50	22	146.3
21. Gavaskar, SM	India	1971-87	125	214	10122	51.12	48.03	236	34	45	12	146.0
22. Cook, AN	England	2006-18	161	291	12472	45.35	46.96	294	33	57	9	146.0
23. Border, AR	Australia	1978-94	156	265	11174	50.56	40.98	205	27	63	11	145.1
24. Sehwag, V	India	2001-13	104	180	8586	49.34	82.21	319	23	32	16	144.7
25. Sutcliffe, H	England	1924-35	54	84	4555	60.73	46.77	194	16	23	2	144.7
26. Javed Miandad	Pakistan	1976-93	124	189	8832	52.57	48.36	280	23	43	6	143.0
27. Richards, IVA	W Indies	1974-91	121	182	8540	50.24	60.82	291	24	45	10	142.4
28. Inzamam-ul-Haq	Pakistan	1992-07	120	200	8830	49.61	54.02	329	25	46	15	141.2
29. De Villiers, AB	Sth Africa	2004-18	114	191	8765	50.66	54.53	278	22	46	8	140.4
30. Chappell, GS	Australia	1970-84	87	151	7110	53.86	51.52	247	24	31	12	138.2
31. Smith, GC	Sth Africa	2002-14	117	205	9265	48.26	59.69	277	27	38	11	138.1
32. Clarke, MJ	Australia	2004-15	115	198	8643	49.11	55.92	329	28	27	9	137.5
33. Pollock, RG	Sth Africa	1963-70	23	41	2256	60.97	50.83	274	7	11	1	137.5
34. Weekes, E	W Indies	1948-58	48	81	4455	58.62	50.00	207	15	19	6	136.9
35. Hobbs, JB	England	1908-30	61	102	5410	56.95	49.69	211	15	28	4	136.5
36. Headley, GA	W Indies	1930-54	22	40	2190	60.83	50.00	270	10	5	2	136.5
37. Mohammad Yousuf	Pakistan	1998-10	90	156	7530	52.29	52.4	223	24	33	11	135.3
38. Amla, HM	Sth Africa	2004-19	124	215	9282	46.64	49.97	311	28	41	13	134.1
39. Warner, DA	Australia	2011-24	112	205	8786	44.60	70.19	335	26	37	13	134.0
40. Kohli, V [1]	India	2011-24	122	208	9207	47.22	55.71	254	30	31	15	132.5
41. Walcott, CL	W Indies	1948-60	44	74	3798	56.69	50.00	220	15	14	1	130.6
42. Voges, AC	Australia	2015-16	20	31	1485	61.88	55.68	269	5	4	2	129.7
43. Pietersen, KP	England	2005-14	104	181	8181	47.29	61.72	227	23	35	10	128.4
44. Laxman, VVS	India	1996-12	134	225	8781	45.97	49.37	281	17	56	14	127.9
45. Boycott, G	England	1964-82	108	193	8114	47.73	38.17	246	22	42	10	123.8
46. Hussey, MEK	Australia	2005-13	79	137	6235	51.53	50.13	195	19	29	12	123.7
47. Gooch, GA	England	1975-95	118	215	8900	42.58	49.24	333	20	46	13	123.0
48. Lloyd, CH	W Indies	1966-84	110	175	7515	46.68	51.22	242	19	39	4	122.1
49. Compton, DCS	England	1937-57	78	131	5807	50.06	50.12	278	17	28	10	122.0
50. Gilchrist, AC	Australia	1999-08	96	137	5570	47.61	81.96	204	17	26	14	121.3
51. Taylor, LRPL	N Zealand	2007-22	112	196	7683	44.67	59.28	290	19	35	14	120.9
52. Paynter, E	England	1931-39	20	31	1540	59.23	50.00	243	4	7	3	120.0
53. Langer, JL	Australia	1993-07	105	182	7696	45.27	54.23	250	23	30	11	119.8
54. Taylor, MA	Australia	1989-99	104	186	7525	43.5	41.48	334	19	40	5	117.3
55. Harvey, RN	Australia	1948-63	79	137	6149	48.42	50.00	205	21	24	7	117.2
56. Walters, KD	Australia	1965-81	74	125	5357	48.26	49.56	250	15	33	4	116.9
57. Gower, DI	England	1978-92	117	204	8231	44.25	50.6	215	18	39	7	116.6
58. Mathews, AD [1]	Sri Lanka	2009-24	116	206	8042	44.93	48.43	200	16	44	6	116.4
59. Kirsten, G	Sth Africa	1993-04	101	176	7289	45.27	43.43	275	21	34	13	116.4
60. Flower, A	Zimbabwe	1992-02	63	112	4794	51.55	45.07	232	12	27	5	116.2
61. Nourse, AD	Sth Africa	1935-51	34	62	2960	53.82	50.00	231	9	14	3	115.7
62. Bell, IR	England	2004-15	118	205	7727	42.69	49.46	235	22	46	14	115.7
63. Kanhai, RB	W Indies	1957-74	79	137	6227	47.53	49.93	256	15	28	7	115.1
64. Gayle, CH	W Indies	2000-14	103	182	7214	42.19	60.27	333	15	37	15	115.0
65. Greenidge, CG	W Indies	1974-91	108	185	7558	44.72	50.09	226	19	34	11	114.7

Batsman	Country	Career	Tests	$n_{innings}$	Runs	w_{avge}	w_{sr}	HS	n_{100}	n_{50}	n_0	Rating
66. Cowdrey, MC	England	1954-75	114	188	7624	44.07	47.51	182	22	38	9	113.5
67. Samaraweera, TT	Sri Lanka	2001-13	81	132	5462	48.77	46.92	231	14	30	11	113.0
68. Azharuddin, M	India	1984-00	99	147	6215	45.04	54.64	199	22	21	5	110.7
69. Waugh, ME	Australia	1991-02	128	209	8029	41.82	52.27	153	20	47	19	110.4
70. Jayasuriya, ST	Sri Lanka	1991-07	110	188	6973	40.07	65.13	340	14	31	15	109.8
71. Azhar Ali	Pakistan	2010-22	97	180	7142	42.26	41.93	302	19	35	19	109.4
72. Thorpe, GP	England	1993-05	100	179	6744	44.66	45.90	200	16	39	12	109.2
73. Simpson, RB	Australia	1957-78	62	111	4869	46.82	49.23	311	10	27	8	109.0
74. Pujara, CA	India	2010-23	103	176	7195	43.61	44.37	206	19	35	12	108.9
75. Boon, DC	Australia	1984-96	107	190	7422	43.66	40.97	200	21	32	16	108.2
76. Ganguly, SC	India	1996-08	113	188	7212	42.18	51.26	239	16	35	13	108.0
77. Worrell, FMM	W Indies	1948-63	51	87	3860	49.49	49.72	261	9	22	11	107.8
78. May, PBH	England	1951-61	66	106	4537	46.77	50.00	285	13	22	8	107.8
79. Labuschagne, M [1]	Australia	2018-24	54	97	4338	48.20	52.01	215	11	23	4	107.8
80. De Silva, PA	Sri Lanka	1984-02	93	159	6361	42.98	50.94	267	20	22	7	107.6
81. Lawry, WM	Australia	1961-71	67	123	5234	47.15	47.11	210	13	27	6	107.2
82. Haynes, DL	W Indies	1978-94	116	202	7487	42.30	45.22	184	18	39	10	107.1
83. Stewart, AJ	England	1990-03	133	235	8463	39.55	48.67	190	15	45	14	106.6
84. Crowe, MD	N Zealand	1982-95	77	131	5444	45.37	44.66	299	17	18	9	106.5
85. Dexter, ER	England	1958-68	62	102	4502	47.89	49.71	205	9	27	6	105.4
86. Karunaratne, FDM [1]	Sri Lanka	2012-24	98	187	7165	39.81	51.56	244	16	39	12	104.8
87. Trescothick, ME	England	2000-06	76	143	5825	43.8	54.52	219	14	29	12	104.3
88. Misbah-ul-Haq	Pakistan	2001-17	75	132	5222	46.63	44.53	161	10	39	9	104.1
89. Saleem Malik	Pakistan	1982-99	103	154	5768	43.70	50.28	237	15	29	12	104.0
90. Chandimal, LD [1]	Sri Lanka	2011-24	86	154	6019	43.3	50.18	206	16	30	8	103.9
91. Richardson, RB	W Indies	1983-95	86	146	5949	44.40	47.78	194	16	27	8	103.8
92. Mitchell, B	Sth Africa	1929-49	42	80	3471	48.89	50.00	189	8	21	3	103.0
93. Fleming, SP	N Zealand	1994-08	111	189	7172	40.07	45.83	274	9	46	16	103.0
94. Vengsarkar, DB	India	1976-92	116	185	6868	42.13	47.76	166	17	35	15	102.5
95. Khawaja, UT [1]	Australia	2011-24	77	139	5592	44.38	48.17	195	15	27	8	102.4
96. Zaheer Abbas	Pakistan	1969-85	78	124	5062	44.80	52.66	274	12	20	10	102.3
97. McCullum, BB	N Zealand	2004-16	101	176	6453	38.64	64.6	302	12	31	14	102.1
98. Saeed Anwar	Pakistan	1990-01	55	91	4052	45.53	55.77	188	11	25	8	102.1
99. Viswanath, GR	India	1969-83	91	155	6080	41.93	48.33	222	14	35	10	101.7
100. Strauss, AJ	England	2004-12	100	178	7037	40.91	48.92	177	21	27	15	101.5

[1] Still playing at the end of 2024

The Bowling Rating:

A bowling rating has been determined for each player who bowled more than 600 balls (i.e., the equivalent of 100 six-ball overs) during the period under consideration. Any player who played 20 or more test matches in a particular period and who is under consideration as a front-line bowler (or genuine all-rounder) will usually have bowled more than 3000 balls in that period (i.e., the equivalent of 500 six-ball overs. Their bowling rating is determined as the sum of seven scores WS7 to WS13 as indicated in Equation 2.8a. Many batsmen were part-time bowlers who may have bowled more than 600 but less than 3000 balls in their 20 or more matches. The bowling ratings of these part-time bowlers have been determined using Equation 2.8b.

When $n_{balls} \geq 3{,}000$:

$$\text{Bowling Rating} = WS7 + WS8 + WS9 + WS10 + WS11 + WS12 + WS13 \tag{2.8a}$$

When $n_{balls} < 3{,}000$:

$$\text{Bowling Rating} = (WS7 + WS8 + WS9 + WS10 + WS11 + WS12 + WS13)\sqrt{(n_{balls}/3000)} \tag{2.8b}$$

Where n_{balls} is the number of balls bowled in the period under consideration.

The score WS7 depends on the bowling average; WS8 depends on the number of wickets taken; WS9 depends on the bowling strike rate; WS10 depends on the bowler's economy rate; W11 depends on the number of times the bowler took 5 or more wickets in an innings and the number of times he took 10 or more wickets in a match; WS12 depends on the total number of balls bowled; and WS13 depends on the proportion of maiden overs bowled.

WS7 — Bowling average:

A player's bowling average w_{avge} over a particular period is the total number of runs scored off his bowling divided by the number of wickets taken. The bowling average has traditionally been one of the key measures used to determine the relative merits of bowlers; generally, the lower the figure, the better the bowler is regarded.

In test cricket, a value of w_{avge} between 30 and 35 over the career of a front-line bowler is very respectable. Many of the long-serving test bowlers have career averages in the low 30s. An average in the range 25 to 30 is very good, and less than 25 is outstanding.

The relationship used to determine WS7 is:

$$WS7 = 3 \times \left(e^{(4-0.05 w_{avge})} - 1\right)_{\geq 0} \tag{2.9}$$

And is illustrated in Figure 2.4. Numerical values of WS7 for the practical range of bowling averages are also provided in Figure 2.4. Most front-line bowlers have a bowling average of between 20 and 40 and so their WS7 score is between 57 and 19.

In the history of test cricket, only five bowlers who played more than 20 matches, and bowled more than 3,000 balls, have a career bowling average of less than 20 and four of these were Englishmen who played before World War 1: William Barnes (1880-90) - w_{avge} = 15.55; Sydney Barnes (1901-14) - w_{avge} = 16.43; Robert Peel (1884-96) - w_{avge} = 16.98; and John Briggs (1884-99) - w_{avge} = 17.75. The only bowler of the modern era to have a bowling average of less than 20 is India's current opening bowler Jasprit Bumrah (2019-2024) - w_{avge} = 19.43.

A special mention must be made of another outstanding English bowler from the period before World War 1, George Lohmann (1886-96), who played just 18 test matches. Lohmann bowled over 3,830 balls taking 112 wickets at an average of just 10.75. The Australian Fred Spofforth (1877-87) averaged 18.41 but also played only 18 matches.

$$WS7 = 3 \times \left(e^{(4-0.05 w_{avge})} - 1\right) \geq 0$$

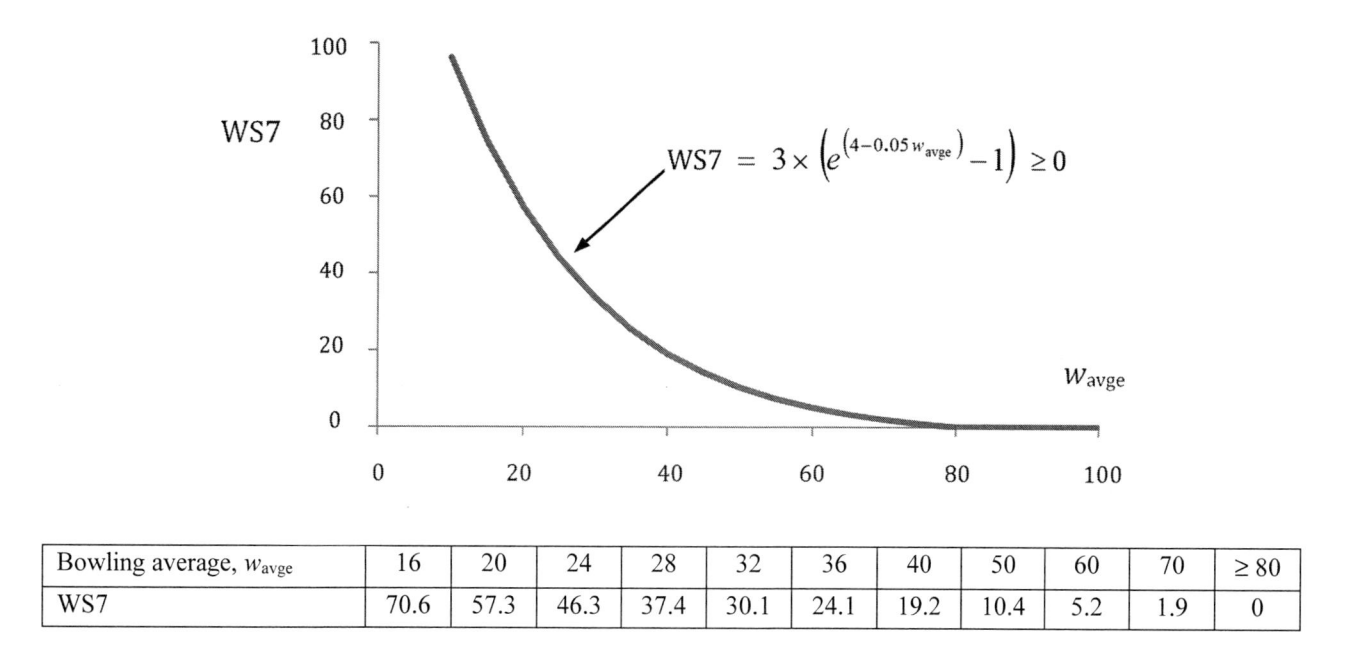

Bowling average, w_{avge}	16	20	24	28	32	36	40	50	60	70	≥ 80
WS7	70.6	57.3	46.3	37.4	30.1	24.1	19.2	10.4	5.2	1.9	0

Figure 2.4 Relationship between WS7 and the bowling average.

From 1920 until the present, of the bowlers who played 20 or more test matches and bowled more than 3000 balls, only the 22 bowlers shown in Table 2.8 had a career bowling average less than 23.0.

Table 2.8 Bowlers since World War 1 with a bowling average less than 23.

Player	Country	Career	w_{avge}	Player	Country	Career	w_{avge}
1. Bumrah, JJ [1]	India	2018-24	19.43	12. Donald, AA	Sth Africa	1992–02	22.25
2. Wardle, JH	England	1948-57	20.39	13. Hadlee, RJ	N Zealand	1973–90	22.30
3. Davidson, AK	Australia	1953–63	20.53	14. Philander, VD	Sth Africa	2011–20	22.32
4. Marshall, MD	W Indies	1978-91	20.95	15. Cummins, PJ [1]	Australia	2011–24	22.55
5. Garner, J	W Indies	1977-87	20.98	16. O'Reilly, WJ	Australia	1932–46	22.60
6. Ambrose, CEL	W Indies	1988-00	20.99	17. Muralitharan, M	Sri Lanka	1992–10	22.73
7. Adcock, NAT	Sth Africa	1953–62	21.11	18. Mohammed Abbas [1]	Pakistan	2017–24	22.73
8. Laker, JC	England	1948-59	21.25	19. Imran Khan	Pakistan	1971–92	22.81
9. Trueman, FS	England	1952-65	21.58	20. Robinson, OE [1]	England	2021–24	22.92
10. McGrath, GD	Australia	1993–07	21.64	21. Steyn, DW	Sth Africa	2004–19	22.95
11. Rabada, K [1]	Sth Africa	2015–24	21.89	22. Miller, KR	Australia	1946–56	22.98

[1] Still playing in 2024

WS8 — Wickets taken

The number of wickets taken during any time period ($n_{wickets}$) also affects the bowling rating as follows:

$$WS8 = n_{wickets}/20 \qquad (2.10)$$

The 50 bowlers with the most test wickets are shown in Table 2.9. Three of the top four wicket takers, Sri Lanka's Muttiah Muralitharan (800 wickets), Australia's Shane Warne (708) and India's Anil Kumble (619) are spin bowlers. Of the top 50 wicket takers: 14 are spin bowlers and 36 are fast or fast-medium pace bowlers; there are 11 Australians, 8 Indians, 6 Englishmen, 7 South Africans, 6 West Indians, 5 New Zealanders, 4 Pakistanis and 3 Sri Lankans; 2 made their test debuts in the 1950s, 2 in the 1960s, 8 in the 1970s, 5 in the 1980s, 14 in the 1990s, 10 in the 2000s and 9 in the 2010s.

Table 2.9 Top fifty wicket takers in test cricket history (up to the end of 2024).

Bowler	Country	Career	Tests	n_wickets	Bowler	Country	Career	Tests	n_wickets
1. Muralitharan, M	Sri Lanka	1992–10	133	800	26. Lillee, DK	Australia	1971–84	70	355
2. Warne, SK	Australia	1992–07	145	708	27. Vaas, WPUJC	Sri Lanka	1994–09	111	355
3. Anderson, JM [1]	England	2003–24	188	704	28. Donald, AA	Sth Africa	1992–02	72	330
4. Kumble, A	India	1990–08	132	619	29. Willis, RGB	England	1971–84	90	325
5. Broad, SCJ [1]	England	2007–23	167	604	30. Jadeja, RA [1]	India	2012–24	79	323
6. McGrath, GD	Australia	1993–07	124	563	31. Rabada, K [1]	Sth Africa	2015–24	69	321
7. Lyon, NM [1]	Australia	2011–24	133	538	32. Boult, TA	N Zealand	2011–22	78	317
8. Ashwin, R [1]	India	2011–23	95	490	33. Johnson, MG	Australia	2007–15	73	313
9. Walsh, CA	W Indies	1984–01	132	519	34. Sharma, I	India	2007–21	105	311
10. Steyn, DW	Sth Africa	2004–19	93	439	35. Zaheer Khan	India	2000–14	92	311
11. Kapil Dev	India	1978–94	131	434	36. Lee, B	Australia	1999–08	76	310
12. Herath, HMRKB	Sri Lanka	1999–18	93	433	37. Gibbs, LR	W Indies	1958–76	79	309
13. Hadlee, RJ	N Zealand	1973–90	86	431	38. Morkel, M	Sth Africa	2006–18	86	309
14. Pollock, SM	Sth Africa	1995–06	108	421	39. Trueman, FS	England	1952–65	67	307
15. Harbhajan Singh	India	1998–15	103	417	40. Underwood, DL	England	1966–82	86	297
16. Wasim Akram	Pakistan	1985–02	104	414	41. Kallis, JH	Sth Africa	1995–13	166	292
17. Ambrose, CEL	W Indies	1988–00	98	405	42. McDermott, CJ	Australia	1984–96	71	291
18. Southee, TG [1]	N Zealand	2008–24	107	391	43. Cummins, PJ [1]	Australia	2012–24	66	289
19. Ntini, M	Sth Africa	1998–09	101	390	44. Roach, KAJ [1]	W Indies	2009-23	79	275
20. Botham, IT	England	1977–92	102	383	45. Hazlewood, JR [1]	Australia	2014–24	72	279
21. Marshall, MD	W Indies	1978–91	81	376	46. Bedi, BS	India	1967–79	67	266
22. Waqar Younis	Pakistan	1989–03	87	373	47. Kaneria, D	Pakistan	2000–10	61	261
23. Starc, MA [1]	Australia	2011–24	93	373	48. Wagner, N	N Zealand	2012–24	64	260
24. Imran Khan	Pakistan	1971–92	88	362	49. Garner, J	W Indies	1977–87	58	259
25. Vettori, DL	N Zealand	1997–14	113	362	50. Gillespie, JN	Australia	1996–06	71	259

[1] Still playing in 2024

WS9 — Bowling strike rate

The bowling strike rate w_{sr} is the average number of balls bowled for each wicket taken. Again, the lower the strike rate, the more potent is the bowler. The bowling strike rate is an important measure in test cricket, more so than in limited overs cricket, since in test cricket the primary aim of a bowler is to take wickets, whereas in limited overs cricket, restricting the run rate per over is arguably more important.

The value of WS9 awarded for the bowling strike rate is determined from:

$$\text{WS9} = 2 \times \left(e^{(5-0.05 w_{sr})} - 1\right) \geq 0 \qquad (2.11)$$

And the relationship is shown in Figure 2.5. Numerical values of WS9 are also given in Figure 2.5. Most frontline bowlers have a strike rate between 45 and 70 and so their WS9 score is between 29.3 and 7.0.

George Lohmann of England (1886-96) had a strike rate of just 34.20 in his 18 tests. At the end of 2024, the current South African pace bowler, Kagiso Rabada, with a strike rate of 39.43, has the lowest strike rate of any bowler who played more than 20 test matches. England's Sydney Barnes (1901-14) with a strike rate of 41.66 is second on the list. Of the bowlers who have taken more than 150 test wickets, the 20 with the lowest career strike rates at the end of 2024 are shown in Table 2.10, and interestingly, all but one are fast bowlers. India's Ravi Ashwin is the spin bowler with the lowest strike (50.68) and of all the other spin bowlers with more than 150 test wickets Australia's Stuart MacGill has the next lowest strike rate of 54.02.

Figure 2.5 Relationship between WS9 and bowling strike rate.

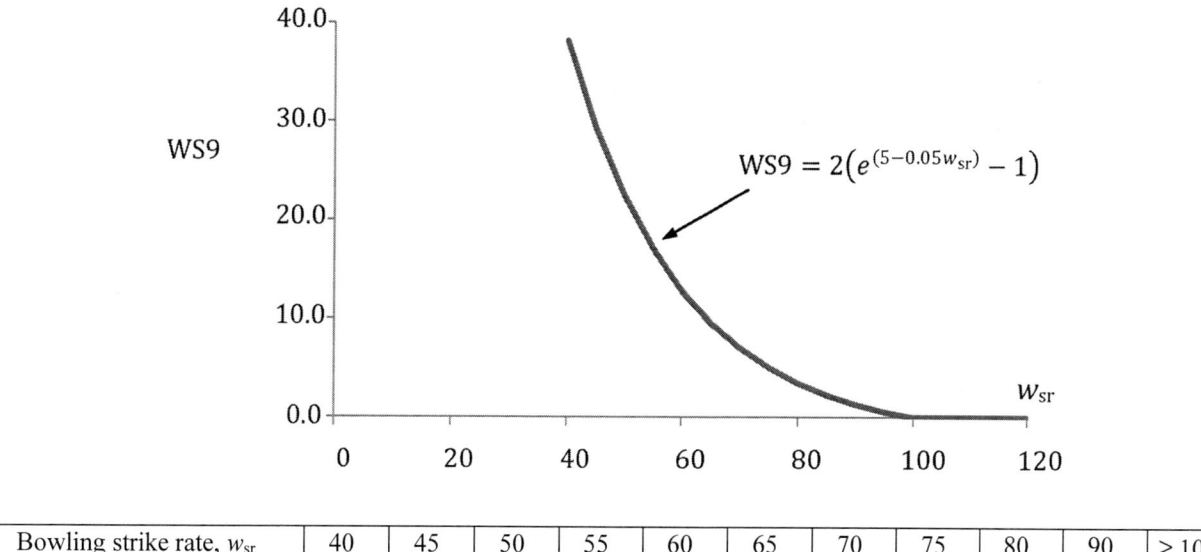

$$WS9 = 2\left(e^{(5-0.05 w_{sr})} - 1\right)$$

Bowling strike rate, w_{sr}	40	45	50	55	60	65	70	75	80	90	≥ 100
WS9	38.2	29.3	22.4	17.0	12.8	9.5	7.0	5.0	3.4	1.3	0

Table 2.10 Bowlers with strike rates less than 52.0 (150 wickets or more).

Player	Country	w_{sr}
1. Rabada, K [1]	S Africa	39.40
2. Barnes, SF	England	41.66
3. Bumrah, JJ [1]	India	42.22
4. Steyn, DW	S Africa	42.39
5. Waqar Younis	Pakistan	43.50
6. Shoaib Akhtar	Pakistan	45.75
7. Cummins, PJ [1]	Australia	46.48

Player	Country	w_{sr}
8. Marshall, MD	W Indies	46.77
9. Donald, AA	S Africa	47.03
10. Starc, MA [1]	Australia	48.81
11. Trueman, FS	England	49.44
12. Mohd. Shami	India	50.28
13. Ashwin, R [1]	India	50.68
14. Hadlee, RJ	N Zealand	50.85

Player	Country	w_{sr}
15. Garner, J	W Indies	50.85
16. Philander, VD	S Africa	50.85
17. Holding, MA	W Indies	50.92
18. Johnson, MG	Australia	51.12
19. Gough, D	England	51.62
20. McGrath, GD	Australia	51.95
21. Lillee, DK	Australia	52.00

[1] Still playing in 2024

WS10 — Bowling Economy Rate:

The bowling economy rate, w_{econ}, adopted in this book is the average number of runs conceded off every 6 balls bowled. Generally, the lower the figure, the more difficulty the opposition batsman had in scoring.

The value of WS10 awarded for the bowling economy rate is determined from:

$$WS10 = 20 \times \left(e^{(1-(w_{econ}/6))} - 1\right) \geq 0 \qquad (2.12)$$

and the relationship is illustrated in Figure 2.6 together with numerical values of WS10.

The career economy rates for test bowlers are usually in the range from 2.0 to 4.0, rarely below 2.0. The lower end of the range represents the most frugal of bowlers, who kept the oppositions scoring rate in check. Often these bowlers were defensive rather than attacking, with relatively high strike rates. Such bowlers often played an important role when bowling in partnership with a more attacking bowler (i.e., a bowler with a lower strike rate). Of the test bowlers who played more than 20 matches and bowled more than 3,000 balls after World War 1, the five with the lowest economy rates are South Africa's Trevor Goddard (w_{econ} =1.65), India's Bapu Nadkarni (w_{econ} =1.68), Australia's Ken Mackay (w_{econ} =1.78), West Indian Gerry Gomez (w_{econ} =1.82) and India's Polly Umrigar (w_{econ} =1.87). However, with strike rates of 95.4, 104.2, 115.8, 90.3 and 135.0, respectively, none of these players could be considered to be attacking bowlers.

The economy rates of the 20 attacking bowlers listed in Table 2.10, all with strike rates less than 52, are given in Table 2.11.

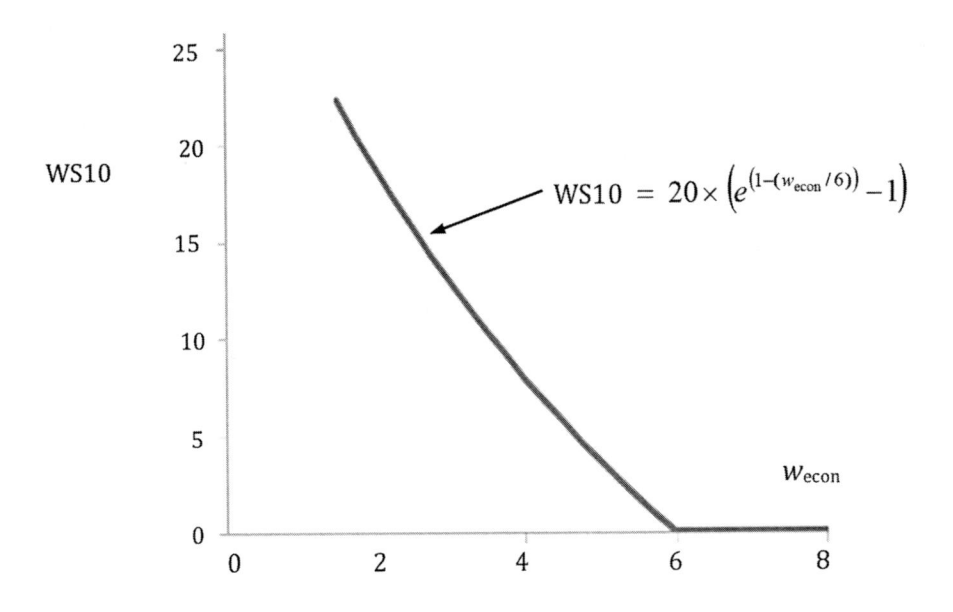

$$WS10 = 20 \times \left(e^{(1-(w_{econ}/6))} - 1\right)$$

Bowling economy rate, w_{econ}	1.5	2.0	2.5	3.0	3.5	4.0	4.5	5.0	5.5	≥ 6.0
WS10	22.3	19.0	15.8	13.0	10.3	7.9	5.7	3.6	1.7	0

Figure 2.6 Relationship between WS10 and bowling economy rate.

Table 2.11 Economy rates of attacking bowlers listed in Table 2.10.

Player	Country	w_{econ}
1. Rabada, K [1]	Sth Africa	3.33
2. Barnes, SF	England	2.37
3. Bumrah, JJ [1]	India	2.76
4. Steyn, DW	Sth Africa	3.25
5. Waqar Younis	Pakistan	3.25
6. Shoaib Akhtar	Pakistan	3.37
7. Cummins, PJ [1]	Australia	2.91

Player	Country	w_{econ}
8. Marshall, MD	W Indies	2.69
9. Donald, AA	Sth Africa	2.84
10. Starc, MA [1]	Australia	3.42
11. Trueman, FS	England	2.62
12. Mohd. Shami	India	3.31
13. Ashwin, R [1]	India	2.83
14. Hadlee, RJ	N Zealand	2.63

Player	Country	w_{econ}
15. Garner, J	W Indies	2.48
16. Philander, VD	Sth Africa	2.63
17. Holding, MA	W Indies	2.79
18. Johnson, MG	Australia	3.33
19. Gough, D	England	3.30
20. McGrath, GD	Australia	2.50
21. Lillee, DK	Australia	2.76

[1] Still playing in 2024

WS11 — 5 And 10 Wicket Hauls:

The number of times that a bowler takes 5 or more wickets in an innings (n_5) and 10 or more wickets in a match (n_{10}) are also measures of the bowler's value to the team. The number of 5 wicket hauls for a bowler is often held in the same regard as the number of centuries scored by a batsman. The frequency at which a player achieves these milestones is also a consideration. The rating score WS11 is given by:

$$WS11 = \frac{5 \times (n_5 + 3n_{10})}{\sqrt{n_{matches}}} \qquad (2.13)$$

where $n_{matches}$ is the number of matches played in the time period in question.

The 37 bowlers with WS11 scores above 15.0 (at the end of 2024) are listed in Table 2.12, together with their numbers of 5 and 10 wicket hauls.

Table 2.12 Top 37 bowlers in test cricket history in terms of 5 and 10 wicket hauls.

Bowler	Country	Career	Matches	n_5	n_{10}	Bowling type	WS11
1. Muralitharan, M	Sri Lanka	1992–2010	133	67	22	right arm off break	57.7
2. Barnes, SF	England	1901-1914	27	24	7	right arm medium fast	43.3
3. Grimmett, CV	Australia	1925–1936	37	21	7	right arm leg break	34.5
4. Hadlee, RJ	N Zealand	1973–1990	86	36	9	right arm fast	34.0
5. Herath, HMRKB	Sri Lanka	1999–2018	93	34	9	left arm orthodox	31.6
6. Ashwin, R [1]	India	2011-2024	106	37	8	right arm off break	29.6
7. Warne, SK	Australia	1992–2007	145	37	10	right arm leg break	27.8
8. Lillee, DK	Australia	1971–1984	70	23	7	right arm fast	26.3
9. Kumble, A	India	1990-2008	132	35	8	right arm leg break	25.7
10. Imran Khan	Pakistan	1971–1992	88	23	6	right arm fast	21.9
11. Fazal Mahmood	Pakistan	1952–1962	34	13	4	right arm fast medium	21.4
12. Steyn, DW	Sth Africa	2004–2019	93	26	5	right arm fast	21.3
13. Bedser, AV	England	1946-1955	51	15	5	right arm medium fast	21.0
14. Waqar Younis	Pakistan	1989–2003	87	22	5	right arm fast	19.8
15. Singh, H	India	1998-2015	103	25	5	right arm off break	19.7
16. Wasim Akram	Pakistan	1985–2002	104	25	5	left arm fast	19.6
17. Botham, IT	England	1977-1992	102	27	4	right arm fast medium	19.3
18. O'Reilly, WJ	Australia	1932–1946	27	11	3	right arm leg break	19.2
19. Marshall, MD	W Indies	1978-1991	81	22	4	right arm fast	18.9
20. Underwood, DL	England	1966-1982	86	17	6	left arm orthodox	18.9
21. Saeed Ajmal	Pakistan	2009–2014	35	10	4	right arm off break	18.6
22. Abdul Qadir	Pakistan	1977–1990	67	15	5	right arm leg break	18.3
23. Briggs, J	England	1884-1899	33	9	4	left arm orthodox	18.3
24. Yasir Shah	Pakistan	2014–2022	48	16	3	right arm leg break	18.0
25. Donald, AA	Sth Africa	1992–2002	72	20	3	right arm fast	17.1
26. McGrath, GD	Australia	1993–2007	124	29	3	right arm fast medium	17.1
27. Lyon, NM [1]	Australia	2011–2024	133	24	5	right arm off break	16.9
28. Rabada, K [1]	Sth Africa	2015–2024	69	16	4	right arm fast	16.9
29. Swann, GP	England	2008-2013	60	17	3	right arm off break	16.8
30. Tayfield, HJ	Sth Africa	1949–1960	37	14	2	right arm off break	16.4
31. McKenzie, GD	Australia	1961–1971	60	16	3	right arm fast	16.1
32. Trumble, H	Australia	1890–1904	32	9	3	right arm off break	15.9
33. Trueman, FS	England	1952-1965	67	17	3	right arm fast	15.9
34. Saqlain Mushtaq	Pakistan	1995–2004	49	13	3	right arm off break	15.7
35. Ambrose, CEL	W Indies	1988-2000	98	22	3	right arm fast	15.7
36. Davidson, AK	Australia	1953–1963	44	14	2	left arm fast medium	15.1
37. Anderson, JM [1]	England	2003-2023	188	32	3	right arm fast medium	15.0

[1] Still playing in 2024

At a first glance of the numbers of 5 and 10 wicket hauls, the performance of Sri Lanka's Muttiah Muralitharan looks *Bradmanesque*, and indeed his success rate was magnificent. With $n_5 = 67$ and $n_{10} = 22$, he took 5 wickets in an innings 30 times more than anyone else and he took 10 wickets in a match more than twice as many times as anyone else. The next highest values of n_5 and n_{10} both belong to Shane Warne of Australia.

Two bowlers listed in Table 2.12 took five wicket hauls more frequently than Muralitharan. Sydney Barnes (England) took a 5 wicket in an innings every 1.13 matches and Clarrie Grimmett (Australia) every 1.76 matches, whereas Murali took a 5 wicket haul every 1.99 matches. The frequency of their 5 and 10 wicket tallies has resulted in Barnes and Grimmett achieving the second and third highest positions in Table 2.12. After Barnes, the highest ranked fast bowler in the table is Sir Richard Hadlee at No. 4, with the third highest n_5 score in history. Hadlee took 5 wickets in an innings every 2.39 matches. Interestingly, about half of the bowlers in Table 2.12 are spin bowlers, including five of the top seven. Table 2.12 includes some of the greatest bowling all-rounders in the history of the game, including Sir Richard Hadlee (New Zealand), Imran Khan (Pakistan), Wasim Akram (Pakistan), Sir Ian Botham (England), whose careers all overlapped in the 1980s, and current spin bowler Ravi Ashwin (India).

WS12 — Balls Bowled:

A bowler's rating and value to his team also depend on the number of balls bowled (n_{balls}) in a particular time span and are reflected in the value assigned to WS12 using:

$$WS12 = 0.005\, n_{balls}/6 \qquad (2.14)$$

Numerical values of WS12 are given in Table 2.13.

Table 2.13 Values of WS12.

Number of balls, n_{balls}	0	3,000	6,000	12,000	18,000	24,000	30,000	36,000	42,000
WS12	0	2.5	5.0	10.0	15.0	20.0	25.0	30.0	35.0

The WS12 score for a particular time period is taken as 0.005 times the equivalent number of 6 ball overs. Statistics for bowlers are generally recorded in terms of the number of overs bowled rather than the number of balls bowled in a match. However, in comparisons between bowlers from different eras and different countries, it is important to consider the number of balls bowled rather than the number of overs. Since 1979, the number of legitimate balls bowled in each over of every test match has been 6, irrespective of the host country. However, for the first century of test cricket, the number of balls per over has been either 4, 5, 6 or 8 depending on the country in which the test was being played and the year it was played. For example, the number of balls in each over in test matches played in England from 1880 to 1888 was 4, from 1889 to 1899 was 5 and from 1900 to the present was 6. In Australia, the number of balls per over in test cricket from 1876 to 1888 was 4, from 1891 to 1921 was 6, from 1924 to 1925 was 8, from 1928 to 1933 was 6, from 1936 to 1979 was 8 and from 1979 to the present was 6.

At the end of 2024, only 34 bowlers have bowled more than 18,000 balls in test cricket (the equivalent of 3000 six-ball overs) and their records are listed in Table 2.15. Of these 34, 13 were spin bowlers and 21 were pace bowlers. Not only did Muttiah Muralitharan bowl more overs than anyone else on the list, but he bowled more overs per match than anyone else. The value of WS12 for each of these players over their entire careers is also given in the table.

The first 10 bowlers in Table 2.15 all played at least some test cricket in the 21st century. This reflects the increased frequency of tests in the modern era. In the time periods considered for the team selections in this book, rarely did any bowler, bowl more than 18,000 balls, and so the scores for WS12 were generally less than 15.0.

WS13 — Number of Maidens:

A *maiden over* is an over in which no runs are conceded. A relatively small part of a bowler's rating (WS13) is dependent on the ratio of the number of maiden overs ($n_{maidens}$) to the total number of overs bowled (n_{overs}), with the WS13 score taken as

$$WS13 = \frac{40 \times n_{maidens}}{n_{overs}} \qquad (2.15)$$

Numerical values are given in Table 2.14.

Table 2.14 Numerical values of WS13.

$n_{maidens}/n_{overs}$	0	0.1	0.2	0.3	0.4	0.5
WS13	0	4.0	8.0	12.0	16.0	20.0

The values of WS13 for the 34 bowlers who bowled more than 18,000 balls are shown in the right-hand column of Table 2.15. Only eleven of these bowlers had their ratio of maiden overs to total overs greater than 0.25:

Derick Underwood (0.358)   Bishen Bedi (0.318)   Lance Gibbs (0.312)   Glenn McGrath (0.302)
Shaun Pollock (0.298)   Richie Benaud (0.295)   Sir Garfield Sobers (0.284)   Curtly Ambrose (0.272)
Shane Warne (0.260)   James Anderson (0.258)   Jacques Kallis (0.251)

Only Derick Underwood bowled a maiden more frequently than 1 in 3.

Table 2.15 Bowlers who had bowled more than 18,000 balls up to the end of 2024 and career values of WS12 and WS13.

Bowler	Country	Career	Mat.	n_{balls}	n_{overs}	$n_{maidens}$	Bowling type	WS12	WS13
1. Muralitharan, M	Sri Lanka	1992–10	133	43,984	7,339.5	1792	right arm off break	36.7	9.8
2. Kumble, A	India	1990–08	132	40,789	6,808.2	1575	right arm leg break	34.0	9.3
3. Warne, SK	Australia	1992–07	145	40,743	6,784.1	1762	right arm leg break	34.0	10.4
4. Anderson, JM [1]	England	2003–23	188	40.058	6,672.5	1721	right arm fast-med	33.4	10.3
5. Broad, SCJ	England	2007–23	167	33,662	5,616.2	1304	right arm fast-med	28.1	9.3
6. Lyon, NM [1]	Australia	2011–24	133	33,512	5,576.5	1061	right arm off break	27.9	7.6
7. Walsh, CA	W Indies	1984-01	132	29,962	5,003.1	1144	right arm fast	25.0	9.1
8. McGrath, GD	Australia	1993–07	124	29,246	4,874.4	1470	right arm fast-med	24.4	12.1
9. Vettori, DL	N Zealand	1997–14	113	28,821	4,802.2	1197	left arm orthodox	24.0	10.0
10. Singh, H	India	1998-15	103	28,599	4,763.2	869	right arm off break	23.8	7.3
11. Kapil Dev	India	1978-94	131	27,771	4,623.2	1060	right arm fast-med	23.1	9.2
12. Ashwin, R [1]	India	2011-23	106	27,220	4,536.0	907	right arm off break	22.7	8.0
13. Gibbs, LR	W Indies	1958-76	79	27,103	4,207.5	1313	right arm off break	22.6	12.5
14. Herath, HMRKB	Sri Lanka	1999–18	93	25,958	4,332.1	816	left arm orthodox	21.6	7.5
15. Pollock, SM	Sth Africa	1995–08	108	24,333	4,058.5	1211	right arm fast-med	20.3	11.9
16. Southee, TG [1]	N Zealand	2008–23	81	23,507	3,915.0	893	right arm fast-med	19.6	9.1
17. Vaas, WPUJC	Sri Lanka	1994–09	111	23,422	3,906.2	895	left arm fast-med	19.5	9.2
18. Wasim Akram	Pakistan	1985–02	104	22,654	3,771.1	871	left arm fast	18.9	9.2
19. Ambrose, CEL	W Indies	1988-00	98	22,083	3,683.5	1001	right arm fast	18.4	10.9
20. Hadlee, RJ	N Zealand	1973–90	86	21,926	3,461.4	809	right arm fast	18.3	9.3
21. Botham, IT	England	1977-92	102	21,829	3,550.3	788	right arm fast-med	18.2	8.9
22. Underwood, DL	England	1966-82	86	21,822	3,464.0	1239	left arm orthodox	18.2	14.3
23. Sobers, GSA	W Indies	1954-74	93	21,619	3,432.5	974	left arm med-fast	18.0	11.4
24. Bedi, BS	India	1966-79	67	21,412	3,441.4	1096	left arm orthodox	17.8	12.7
25. Ntini, M	Sth Africa	1998–09	101	20,819	3,472.2	759	right arm fast	17.3	8.7

Bowler	Country	Career	Mat.	n_{balls}	n_{overs}	$n_{maidens}$	Bowling type	WS12	WS13
26. Kallis, JH	Sth Africa	1995–13	166	20,216	3,372.0	848	right arm fast-med	16.8	10.1
27. Imran Khan	Pakistan	1971–92	88	19,431	3,107.2	727	right arm fast	16.2	9.4
28. Sharma, I	India	2007–21	105	19,135	3,193.2	640	right arm fast-med	15.9	8.0
29. Benaud, R	Australia	1952–64	63	19,064	2,729.0	805	right arm leg break	15.9	11.8
30. Zaheer Khan	India	2000–14	92	18,802	3,130.5	624	left arm med-fast	15.7	8.0
31. Steyn, DW	Sth Africa	2004–19	93	18,604	3,101.2	660	right arm fast	15.5	8.5
32. Lillee, DK	Australia	1971–84	70	18,463	2,836.1	652	right arm fast	15.4	9.2
33. Jadeja, RA	India	2012–24	79	18,425	3,067.5	728	left arm orthodox	15.4	9.5
34. Starc, MA	Australia	2011–24	93	18,181	3,034.1	579	left arm fast	15.2	7.6

[1] Still playing in 2024

Example Ratings:

To illustrate the rating of bowlers, we will consider two front line bowlers for the decade 2000 to 2009 and one part-time bowler:

(1) Shoaib Akhtar – right arm fast bowler for Pakistan (33 tests from 2000-2007).

w_{avge}	w_{sr}	w_{econ}	$n_{matches}$	n_{balls}	n_{overs}	$n_{maidens}$	$n_{wickets}$	n_5	n_{10}
22.22	39.68	3.36	33	5,714	951	175	144	11	2

From Equation 2.9:	WS7	$= 3 \times (e^{(4-0.05 \times 22.22)} - 1)$	$= 50.9$
From Equation 2.10:	WS8		$= 7.2$
From Equation 2.11:	WS9	$= 2 \times (e^{(5-0.05 \times 39.68)} - 1)$	$= 38.8$
From Equation 2.12:	WS10	$= 20 \times (e^{(1-3.36/6)} - 1)$	$= 11.0$
From Equation 2.13:	WS11	$= (5 \times (11 + 3 \times 2))/\sqrt{33}$	$= 14.8$
From Equation 2.14:	WS12	$= 0.005 \times 5,714/6$	$= 4.8$
From Equation 2.15:	WS13	$= 40 \times 175/951$	$= 7.4$
From Equation 2.8a:	Bowling Rating		$= 134.9$

(2) Daniel Vettori – left arm orthodox spinner for New Zealand (69 tests from 2000-2009).

w_{avge}	w_{sr}	w_{econ}	$n_{matches}$	n_{balls}	n_{overs}	$n_{maidens}$	$n_{wickets}$	n_5	n_{10}
33.15	74.56	2.67	69	16,552	2,758	650	222	15	3

WS7	WS8	WS9	WS10	WS11	WS12	WS13	Bowling rating (Eq. 2.8a)
28.2	11.1	5.1	14.9	14.5	13.8	9.4	97.0

(3) Michael Clarke - batted at No.4 for Australia, but occasionally bowled left arm orthodox (56 tests from 2004 to 2009 inclusive).

w_{avge}	w_{sr}	w_{econ}	$n_{matches}$	n_{balls}	n_{overs}	$n_{maidens}$	$n_{wickets}$	n_5	n_{10}
39.74	81.04	2.94	56	1,540	257	42	19	1	0

WS7	WS8	WS9	WS10	WS11	WS12	WS13	Bowling rating (Eq. 2.8b)
19.5	0.9	3.2	13.3	0.7	1.3	6.5	32.5

Ratings Of the Top 100 Bowlers of All Time:

The career bowling details for the 100 highest rating bowlers in the history of test cricket (up until the end of 2024) are provided in Table 2.16.

Table 2.16 The top 100 career test bowling ratings (20 or more matches before the end of 2024).

Bowlers	Country	Career	Style[3]	n_{match}	n_{balls}	n_{overs}	n_{maids}	Runs	Wkts	n_5	n_{10}	w_{avge}	w_{sr}	w_{ecom}	Rating
1. Muralitharan, M	S.L.	1992–10	RAO	133	43,984	7,339.5	1792	18,180	800	67	22	22.73	55.05	2.48	226.5
2. Barnes, SF	Eng	1901-14	RAMF	27	7,863	1,312.1	356	3,106	189	24	7	16.43	41.66	2.37	190.8
3. Warne, SK	Austa	1992–07	RAL	145	40,743	6,784.1	1762	17,995	708	37	10	25.42	57.49	2.65	180.2
4. Hadlee, RJ	N.Z.	1973–90	RAF	86	21,926	3,461.4	809	9,611	431	36	9	22.30	50.85	2.63	170.3
5. McGrath, GD	Aust	1993–07	RAFM	124	29,246	4,874.4	1470	12,186	563	29	3	21.64	51.95	2.50	170.1
6. Ashwin, R[1]	India	2011-24	RAO	106	27,220	4,536.0	907	12,839	537	37	8	23.91	50.68	2.83	169.2
7. Anderson, JM[1]	Eng	2003-24	RAFM	188	40,058	6,672.5	1721	18,627	704	32	3	26.46	56.87	2.79	163.9
8. Steyn, DW	S.A.	2004–19	RAF	93	18,604	3,101.2	660	10,077	439	26	5	22.95	42.39	3.25	161.5
9. Kumble, A	India	1990-08	RAL	132	40,789	6,808.2	1575	18,355	619	35	8	29.65	65.99	2.70	157.7
10. Marshall, MD	W.I.	1978-91	RAF	81	17,567	2,930.4	613	7,876	376	22	4	20.95	46.77	2.69	156.5
11. Ambrose, CEL	W.I.	1988-00	RAF	98	22,083	3,683.5	1001	8,502	405	22	3	20.99	54.58	2.31	153.9
12. Rabada, K[1]	S.A	2015-24	RAF	69	12,659	2,109.3	422	7,026	321	16	4	21.89	39.43	3.33	153.8
13. Briggs, J	Eng	1884-99	LAO	33	5,324	1,051.5	385	2,094	118	9	4	17.75	45.19	2.36	153.4
14. Waqar Younis	Pak	1989-03	RAF	87	16,224	2,704.0	516	8,788	373	22	5	23.56	43.50	3.25	150.4
15. Lillee, DK	Aust	1971-84	RAF	70	18,463	2,836.1	652	8,493	355	23	7	23.92	52.00	2.76	149.5
16. Walsh, CA	W.I.	1984-01	RAF	132	29,962	5,003.1	1144	12,684	519	22	3	24.44	57.84	2.54	148.9
17. Imran Khan	Pak	1971-92	RAF	88	19,431	3,107.2	727	8,258	362	23	6	22.81	53.75	2.55	148.6
18. Wasim Akram	Pak	1985-02	LAF	104	22,654	3,771.1	871	9,779	414	25	5	23.62	54.65	2.59	148.3
19. Donald, AA	S.A.	1992-02	RAF	72	15,515	2,586.3	661	7,344	330	20	3	22.25	47.03	2.84	147.7
20. Herath, HMRKB	S.L.	1999-18	LAO	93	25,958	4,332.1	816	12,157	433	34	9	28.08	60.03	2.81	146.5
21. Broad, SCJ[1]	Eng	2007-23	RAMF	167	33,662	5,616.2	1304	16,719	604	20	3	27.68	55.79	2.98	146.1
22. Bumrah, JJ[1]	India	2018-24	RAF	44	8574	1428.2	344	3,944	203	13	0	19.43	42.22	2.76	144.0
23. Trueman, FS	Eng	1952-65	RAF	67	15,172	2,448.2	522	6,625	307	17	3	21.58	49.44	2.62	143.3
24. Pollock, SM	S.A.	1995-08	RAFM	108	24,333	4,058.5	1211	9,733	421	16	1	23.12	57.85	2.40	141.9
25. Grimmett, CV	Aust	1925-36	RAL	37	14,531	2,408.5	736	5,231	216	21	7	24.22	67.19	2.16	141.7
26. Peel, R	Eng	1884-96	LAO	20	5,223	1,072.5	444	1,715	101	5	1	16.98	51.64	1.97	141.6
27. Lyon, NM[1]	Aust	2011-24	RAO	133	33,512	5,576.5	1061	16,365	538	24	5	30.42	62.20	2.93	136.7
28. Cummins, PJ[1]	Aust	2011-24	RAF	66	13,435	2,239.0	489	6516	289	13	2	22.55	46.48	2.91	136.6
29. Underwood, DL	Eng	1966-82	LAO	86	21,822	3,464.0	1239	7,674	297	17	6	25.84	73.61	2.11	131.9
30. Jadeja, RA[1]	India	2012-24	LAO	79	18,425	3,067.5	728	7,769	323	15	3	24.05	56.99	2.53	131.5
31. Garner, J	W.I.	1977-87	RAF	58	13,144	2,194.5	575	5,433	259	7	0	20.98	50.85	2.48	130.7
32. Laker, JC	Eng	1948-59	RAO	46	12,003	1,913.5	674	4,101	193	9	3	21.25	62.32	2.05	130.4
33. Botham, IT	Eng	1977-92	RAMF	102	21,829	3,550.3	788	10,878	383	27	4	28.40	56.96	2.99	130.4
34. Philander, VD	S.A.	2011-20	RAFM	64	11,407	1,898.3	507	5,000	224	13	2	22.32	50.85	2.63	130.3
35. Davidson, AK	Aust	1953-63	LAFM	44	11573	1,665.1	431	3,819	186	14	2	20.53	62.30	1.98	130.3
36. Barnes, W	Eng	1880-90	RAM	21	2,288	568.1	271	793	51	3	0	15.55	44.88	2.08	128.4
37. Holding, MA	W.I.	1975-87	RAF	60	12,684	2,067.0	459	5,898	249	13	2	23.69	50.92	2.79	126.7
38. Ntini, M	S.A.	1998-09	RAF	101	20,819	3,472.2	759	11,242	390	18	4	28.83	53.42	3.24	126.5
39. Trumble, H	Aust	1890-04	RAO	32	8,084	1,431.2	452	3,072	141	9	3	21.79	57.44	2.28	126.4
40. O'Reilly, WJ	Aust	1932-46	RAL	27	10,012	1,588.2	585	3,254	144	11	3	22.60	69.61	1.95	125.9
41. Bedser, AV	Eng	1946-55	RAMF	51	15,953	2,425.4	574	5,876	236	15	5	24.90	67.45	2.21	125.5
42. Kapil Dev	India	1978-94	RAFM	131	27,771	4,623.2	1060	12,867	434	23	2	29.65	63.92	2.78	125.2
43. Starc, MA[1]	Aust	2011-24	LAF	93	18181	3034.1	579	10,363	373	15	2	27.78	48.81	3.42	124.8

Bowlers	Country	Career	Style [3]	n_{match}	n_{balls}	n_{overs}	n_{maids}	Runs	Wkts	n_5	n_{10}	w_{avge}	w_{sr}	w_{ecom}	Rating
44. Willis, RGB	Eng	1971-84	RAF	90	17,364	2,700.1	554	8,190	325	16	0	25.20	53.41	2.83	123.3
45. Singh, H	India	1998-15	RAO	103	28,599	4,763.2	869	13,537	417	25	5	32.46	68.54	2.84	122.5
46. Hazlewood, JR	Aust	2014–24	RAFM	72	14,799	2,469.3	635	6,857	279	12	0	24.58	53.11	2.78	121.6
47. Gibbs, LR	W. I.	1958-76	RAO	79	27,103	4,207.5	1313	8,989	309	18	2	29.09	87.75	1.99	120.0
48. Fazal Mahmood	Pak	1952–62	RAFM	34	9,811	1,639.0	563	3,434	139	13	4	24.71	70.75	2.10	119.9
49. Wardle, JH	Eng	1948-57	LAO/WS	28	6,603	1,030.1	403	2,080	102	5	1	20.39	64.68	1.89	119.3
50. Johnson, MG	Aust	2007–15	LAF	73	16,020	2,666.5	514	8,891	313	12	3	28.41	51.12	3.33	117.8
51. Lindwall, RR	Aust	1946–60	RAF	61	13,639	1,971.2	419	5,251	228	12	0	23.03	59.87	2.31	117.6
52. Shoaib Akhtar	Pak	1997–07	RAF	46	8,144	1,357.1	238	4,574	178	12	2	25.70	45.75	3.37	117.4
53. Southee, TG[1]	N. Z.	2008–24	RAMF	107	23,507	3,915.0	893	11,832	391	15	1	30.26	60.08	3.02	115.6
54. Boult, TA	N. Z.	2011–22	LAFM	78	17,434	2,902.5	656	8,717	317	10	1	27.50	54.94	3.00	115.2
55. Statham, JB	Eng	1951-65	RAF	70	16,054	2,495.2	595	6,261	252	9	1	24.85	63.71	2.34	114.1
56. Benaud, R	Aust	1952-64	RAL	63	19,064	2,729.0	805	6,704	248	16	1	27.03	77.05	2.11	114.0
57. Lock, GAR	Eng	1952-68	LAO	49	13,156	2,140.5	819	4,451	174	9	3	25.58	75.56	2.03	114.0
58. Roberts, AME	W. I.	1974-83	RAF	47	11,127	1,778.5	382	5,174	202	11	2	25.61	55.12	2.79	113.9
59. Tayfield, HJ	S. A.	1949–60	RAO	37	13,554	1,852.4	602	4,405	170	14	2	25.91	79.81	1.95	113.8
60. Roach, KAJ[1]	W. I.	2009–24	RAFM	84	14913	2483.4	539	7,705	282	11	1	27.32	52.84	3.10	113.2
61. Vaas, WPUJC	S. L.	1994–09	LAFM	111	23,422	3,906.2	895	10,501	355	12	2	29.58	66.02	2.69	113.0
62. McDermott, CJ	Aust	1984–96	RAFM	71	16,609	2,764.2	583	8,332	291	14	2	28.63	57.00	3.01	112.9
63. Gillespie, JN	Aust	1996–06	RAF	71	14,253	2,372.2	630	6,770	259	8	0	26.14	54.96	2.85	112.3
64. Bedi, BS	India	1966-79	LAO	67	21,412	3,441.4	1096	7,637	266	14	1	28.71	80.32	2.14	111.7
65. Mohd. Abbas[1]	Pak	2017–24	RAF	26	5,378	896.1	271	2,205	97	5	1	22.73	55.43	2.46	111.5
66. Morkel, M	S. A.	2006–18	RAF	86	16,495	2,749.4	605	8,550	309	8	0	27.67	53.39	3.11	111.3
67. Mohammad Asif	Pak	2005–10	RAFM	23	5,184	862.4	196	2,592	106	7	1	24.45	48.83	3.00	111.2
68. Miller, KR	Aust	1946-56	RAF	55	10,463	1,497.1	337	3,906	170	7	1	22.98	61.54	2.24	111.0
69. Vettori, DL	N. Z.	1997-14	LAO	113	28,821	4,802.2	1197	12,441	362	20	3	34.37	79.60	2.59	111.0
70. Pollock, PM	S. A.	1961-70	RAF	28	6,526	1,034.2	270	2,806	116	9	1	24.19	56.22	2.58	110.1
71. Swann, GP	Eng	2008-13	RAO	60	15,335	2,558.1	493	7,642	255	17	3	29.97	60.19	2.99	109.3
72. Adcock, NAT	S. A.	1953-62	RAF	26	6,393	917.5	218	2,195	104	5	0	21.11	61.45	2.06	109.2
73. Harris, RJ	Aust	2010–15	RAFM	27	5,737	956.0	258	2,658	113	5	0	23.52	50.76	2.78	109.2
74. Ulyett, G	Eng	1877-90	RAF	25	2,627	653.4	299	1,020	50	1	0	20.40	52.54	2.33	108.9
75. Verity, H	Eng	1931-39	LAO	40	11,202	1,693.3	604	3,510	144	5	2	24.38	77.59	1.88	108.8
76. Noble, MA	Aust	1898-09	RAO	42	7,118	1,213.0	361	3,025	121	9	2	25.00	58.75	2.55	108.7
77. Wagner, N	N. Z.	2012-24	LAMF	64	13,742	2,287.3	473	7,169	260	9	0	27.57	52.79	3.13	108.1
78. Croft, CEH	W. I.	1977-82	RAF	27	6,154	1,027.3	211	2,913	125	3	0	23.30	49.32	2.84	107.6
79. McKenzie, GD	Aust	1961–71	RAF	60	17,658	2,630.5	547	7,328	246	16	3	29.79	71.87	2.49	107.5
80. Bishop, IR	W. I.	1989-98	RAF	43	8,471	1,411.1	288	3,911	161	6	0	24.29	52.59	2.77	107.1
81. Reid, BA	Aust	1985–92	LAFM	27	6,233	1,040.4	244	2,784	113	5	2	24.64	55.26	2.68	107.1
82. Saeed Ajmal	Pak	2009–14	RAO	35	11,590	1,932.4	386	5,003	178	10	4	28.11	65.15	2.59	107.0
83. Alderman, TM	Aust	1981–91	RAFM	41	10,182	1,696.5	432	4,616	170	14	1	27.15	59.89	2.72	107.0
84. Fraser, ARC	Eng	1989-98	RAFM	46	10,867	1,812.4	439	4,836	177	13	2	27.32	61.45	2.67	107.0
85. Chandrasekhar, BS	India	1964-79	RAL	58	15,939	2,549.5	584	7,199	242	16	2	29.75	65.96	2.71	106.6
86 Hall, WW	W. I.	1958-69	RAF	48	10,410	1,658.5	312	5,066	192	9	1	26.39	54.28	2.92	106.3
87. Robinson, OE[1]	Eng	2021-24	RAMF	20	3,801	632.4	159	1,742	76	3	0	22.92	49.95	2.75	106.3
88. MacGill, SCG	Aust	1998-08	RAL	44	11,249	1,872.5	365	6,037	208	12	2	29.02	54.02	3.22	106.2
89. Yasir Shah	Pak	2014–22	RAL	48	14,268	2,375.5	359	7,657	244	16	3	31.38	58.42	3.22	105.1

Bowlers	Country	Career	Style [3]	n_{match}	n_{balls}	n_{overs}	n_{maids}	Runs	Wkts	n_5	n_{10}	w_{avge}	w_{sr}	w_{ecom}	Rating
90. Johnston, WA	Aust	1947–55	LAFM	40	11,037	1,517.0	372	3,826	160	7	0	23.91	69.05	2.08	104.9
91. Snow, JA	Eng	1965–76	RAF	49	12,016	1,928.5	415	5,387	202	8	1	26.67	59.51	2.69	104.6
92. Lee, B	Aust	1999–08	RAF	76	16,522	2,755.1	547	9,555	310	10	0	30.82	53.33	3.47	104.1
93. Saqlain Mushtaq	Pak	1995–04	RAO	49	14,051	2,345.0	541	6,206	208	13	3	29.84	67.64	2.65	103.9
94. Mohd. Shami	India	2013–23	RAF	64	11,503	1,919.1	364	6,346	229	6	0	27.71	50.28	3.31	103.7
95. Cairns, CL	N. Z.	1989–04	RAFM	62	11,690	1,949.4	414	6,410	218	13	1	29.40	53.66	3.29	103.7
96. Gough, D	Eng	1994–03	RAF	58	11,824	1,970.1	368	6,503	229	9	0	28.40	51.62	3.30	103.1
97. Caddick, AR	Eng	1993–03	RAFM	62	13,546	2,259.4	500	6,999	234	13	1	29.91	57.94	3.10	102.5
98. Abdul Qadir	Pak	1977–90	RAL	67	17,141	2,810.4	608	7,742	236	15	5	32.81	72.57	2.71	102.3
99. Tate, MW	Eng	1924–35	RAMF/O	39	12,541	1,982.5	581	4,055	155	7	1	26.16	80.79	1.94	101.8
100. Hughes, MG	Aust	1985–94	RAF	53	12,280	2,047.3	499	6,017	212	7	1	28.38	57.95	2.94	101.8
Lohmann GA [2]	Eng	1886–96	RAM	18	3,825	800.1	364	1,205	112	9	5	10.76	34.12	1.89	219.5
Spofforth FR [2]	Aust	1877–87	RAMF	18	4,188	1,045.3	416	1,731	94	7	4	18.41	44.52	2.48	154.7

[1] Still playing in 2024

[2] Only 18 matches played

[3] RAO — Right arm off break   RAL — Right arm leg break   RAM — Right arm medium
RAF — Right arm fast   RAFM — Right arm fast medium   RAMF — Right arm medium fast
LAO — Left arm orthodox   LAF — Left arm fast   LAFM — Left arm fast medium
LAMF — Left arm medium fast   LAM — Left arm medium

At the top of the list is Sri Lanka's Muttiah Muralitharan. His career bowling rating of 226.5 is 18.7% higher than the next best (England's Sydney Barnes) and 25.7% higher than the next best bowler since World War 1 (Australia's Shane Warne). Muralitharan's performances with the ball were truly remarkable. He took wickets all around the world, on all types of pitches, over a career that spanned 19 years. He took more test wickets than anyone else. He bowled more overs and more maidens than anyone else. He took more five-wicket hauls than anyone else and he took 10 wickets in a match more than twice as many times as the next highest.

Of the top 100 in Table 2.16, there are 26 Australians, 24 Englishmen, 11 Pakistanis, 11 West Indians, 10 South Africans, 9 Indians, 6 New Zealanders and 3 Sri Lankans. Seventeen of the top 100 were left-arm bowlers, with 7 left-arm pace bowlers (fast, fast medium or medium) and 10 left-arm orthodox spinners. Of the 83 right arm bowlers, 61 were pace bowlers (fast, fast medium, medium fast or medium), 9 were leg-spin bowlers and 13 bowled off-spin. Only 7 of the top 100 made their test debuts before the First World War, 11 between 1920 and 1949, 9 in the 1950s, 6 in the 1960s, 12 in the 1970s, 11 in the 1980s, 18 in the 1990s, 10 in the 2000s and 16 in the 2010s. 14 of the top 100 were still playing at the end of 2024 and so their positions on the table may vary in the years ahead.

At the foot of Table 2.16, the performances of George Lohmann of England and Fred Spofforth of Australia are also recorded. Both played in the 19th Century and had outstanding records, but they were not included in the main table because they each played only 18 test matches. They are included here because of their fine records and because they have each been included in their national teams before 1914, due to the relatively small number of tests played in that era and the relatively small pool of eligible players with more than 20 test caps.

Lohman's record is staggering. He has a lower bowling average, a lower strike rate and a lower economy rate than any of the bowlers in Table 2.16. Had he played 20 test matches with these figures, he would have featured in Table 2.16 in the row one below Muralitharan. Spofforth was also a wonderful bowler and, had he played 20 matches, he would have featured in Table 2.16 at No. 11, in the row immediately after Malcolm Marshall and before Curtly Ambrose.

Rating the All-Rounders:

In Chapter 1, an all-rounder is described as a player who is both a good batsman and a good bowler. In test cricket, most all-rounders are selected as either specialist bowlers who are competent batsmen (bowling all-rounders) or specialist batsmen who are competent bowlers (batting all-rounders). In this book, for a player to be considered for classification as a genuine batting all-rounder, his career batting rating must be greater than 60 and his career bowling rating must exceed 40. For a player to be considered for classification as a genuine bowling all-rounder, his career bowling rating must be greater than 60 and his career batting rating must be greater than 40.

In the history of test cricket, just 80 cricketers who played 20 or more matches meet these requirements and they are ranked in Table 2.17. The rankings are based on the sum of the career batting and bowling ratings of each player minus one half the difference between the two ratings. There are 40 batting all-rounders and 40 bowling all-rounders in Table 2.17. There are 19 Australians, 15 Englishmen, 10 Pakistanis, 9 New Zealanders, 9 Indians, 8 South Africans, 7 West Indians, 2 Sri Lankan and 1 from Bangladesh.

Sixteen of the batting all-rounders are among the top 100 rating batsmen of all time (Table 2.7) and fourteen of the bowling all-rounders feature in the top 100 bowlers (Table 2.16), but no players feature in both Tables 2.7 and 2.16. However, some of the all-rounders in Table 2.17 were good enough to have made their national test teams as a specialist batsman and also good enough to have made the team as a specialist bowler. Of the all-rounders, there are only 26 who had both batting and bowling ratings greater than 65 (up to the end of 2024). This select group of outstanding all-rounders and their positions in Table 2.17 are as follows:

England:	Ian Botham (3), Ben Stokes (6), Tong Greig (13), Andrew Flintoff (30), Frank Woolley (33).
Australia:	Doug Walters (10), Charlie Macartney (16), Keith Miller (17), Bob Cowper (26), Warwick Armstrong (34), Shane Watson (35).
New Zealand:	Daniel Vettori (23), Chris Cairns (24), John Reid (40).
Pakistan:	Imran Khan (4), Mushtaq Mohammad (18), Asif Iqbal (22).
South Africa:	Jacques Kallis (1), George Faulkner (20), Hansie Cronje (32).
India:	Kapil Dev (7), Ravi Jadeja (8), Ravi Shastri (37).
West Indies:	Sir Garfield Sobers (2).
Sri Lanka:	Sanath Jayasuriya (21).
Bangladesh:	Shakib Al Hasan (5).

Rating the Wicketkeepers:

The term wicketkeeping all-rounder is used to describe a wicketkeeper who is also a good batsman. When comparing or ranking two wicketkeepers with equivalent performances behind the stumps, the one with the highest batting rating is of more value. The wicketkeeping rating is therefore affected by the batting rating and is calculated as the sum of three weighted scores WS14, WS15 and WS16:

$$\text{Wicketkeeper Rating} = WS14 + WS15 + WS16 \qquad (2.16)$$

The weighted score WS14 depends on the total number of dismissals n_{dis}, where n_{dis} is the sum of the number of catches taken by the wicketkeeper and the number of stumpings. The weighted score WS15 depends on the frequency of the dismissals, i.e., the number of dismissals per innings behind the stumps ($n_{dis}/n_{innings}$) and WS16 depends on the wicketkeeper's batting rating. When determining the career ratings of each wicketkeeper, the following has been adopted:

$$WS14 = 0.15\, n_{dis}; \qquad (2.17)$$
$$WS15 = 30\, n_{dis}/n_{innings}; \qquad (2.18)$$
$$WS16 = 0.40 \times \text{Batting Rating} \qquad (2.19)$$

The performances, weighted scores and rating of every wicketkeeper who has taken more than 70 wickets in test cricket up to the end of 2024 is given in Table 2.18 (ranked from the highest to the lowest wicketkeeper rating).

A wicketkeeper's performance depends on the number of catches at the wicket and the number of stumping opportunities available to him and, therefore, to some extent, the wicketkeeper's rating depends on the quality of the bowlers in his team. However, the catches still need to be taken and the stumpings still need to be made. Perhaps a better estimate of a wicketkeeper's value would be based on how few errors he makes. A valuable wicketkeeper is one who does not drop too many catches, does not miss many stumping or run out opportunities, does not permit too many byes and is generally tidy behind the stumps. However, these attributes are far more difficult to quantify than the number of dismissals.

The two most successful wicketkeepers of all time are Adam Gilchrist of Australia and Mark Boucher of South Africa. Boucher was the South African wicketkeeper in 281 test innings from 1997 to 2012, making 555 dismissals at 1.98 dismissals per innings. Boucher played more test matches as wicketkeeper and made more wicketkeeping dismissals than any other player. Gilchrist kept wickets for Australia in 191 test innings from 1999 to 2008, making 416 dismissals at 2.18 dismissals per innings. Boucher and Gilchrist are the only two wicketkeepers to have made more than 400 dismissals. Gilchrist rates higher than Boucher in Table 2.18 because of his superior batting performance. Boucher was a fine batsman, as well as a magnificent wicketkeeper, with a batting rating of 71.1. However, Gilchrist's career batting rating of 121.3, places him at No. 50 in the list of the highest rating batsman of all time (see Table 2.7).

In addition to Boucher and Gilchrist, only 12 other wicketkeepers have made more than 220 career dismissals behind the stumps, Ian Healy (Australia, 395), Rod Marsh (Australia, 355), MS Dhoni (India, 294), Brad Haddin (Australia, 270), Jeff Dujon (West Indies, 270), Alan Knott (England, 269), BJ Watling (New Zealand, 265), Matt Prior (England, 256), Alec Stewart (England, 241), Quinton de Kock (South Africa, 232), Wasim Bari (Pakistan, 228) and Jonny Bairstow (England, 223).

Besides Gilchrist, five other wicketkeepers also feature in the list of the 100 highest rating batsmen of all time in Table 2.7, Sri Lanka's Kumar Sangakkara (No. 3), South Africa's A.B. de Villiers (No. 29), Zimbabwe's Andrew Flower (No. 60), England's Alec Stewart (No. 83) and New Zealand's Brendon McCullum (No. 97). Despite featuring in the top 4 rating wicketkeepers in Table 2.18, both Sangakkara and de Villiers were not full-time wicketkeepers, playing most of their test cricket as specialist batsmen. Sangakkara is the 3rd highest rating batsman of all time, but he played just 48 of his 134 test matches as wicketkeeper, making 151 dismissals at 1.68 dismissals per innings. AB de Villiers ranks 28th in Table 2.7 and played just 24 of his 114 tests as wicketkeeper. He made 106 wicketkeeping dismissals at 2.36 dismissals per innings. Only South Africa's Quinton de Koch has a higher number of dismissals per innings.

Table 2.17 The genuine all-rounders and their ratings (20 or more matches before the end of 2024).

	All-Rounder	Country	Career	No. of tests	Runs	w_{avge}	n_{100}	Rating	Wickets	w_{avge}	w_{sr}	Rating	All-rounder rating	Batting or bowling
1	Kallis, JH	S. A.	1995-13	166	13,289	55.37	45	170.9	292	32.65	69.29	93.7	226.0	batting
2	Sobers, GSA	W. I.	1954-74	93	8,032	57.78	26	156.5	235	34.04	91.91	89.6	212.7	batting
3	Botham, IT	Eng	1977-92	102	5,200	33.55	14	81.8	383	28.4	56.96	130.4	187.9	bowling
4	Imran Khan	Pak	1971-91	88	3,807	37.69	6	71.7	362	22.81	53.75	148.6	181.9	bowling
5	Shakib Al Hasan [1]	Bang	2007-24	71	4,609	37.78	5	86.1	246	31.72	63.72	101.4	179.9	bowling
6	Stokes, BA [1]	Eng	2013-24	110	6,719	35.55	13	95.8	210	32.37	58.34	84.4	174.5	batting
7	Kapil Dev	India	1978-94	131	5,248	31.05	8	72.8	434	29.65	63.92	125.2	171.8	bowling
8	Jadeja, RA [1]	India	2012-24	79	3,331	35.06	4	69.8	323	24.05	56.99	131.5	170.5	bowling
9	Hammond, WR	Eng	1927-47	85	7,249	58.46	22	152.0	83	37.81	95.99	60.1	166.2	batting
10	Walters, K D	Aust	1965-81	74	5,357	48.26	15	117.1	49	29.08	67.24	71.7	166.1	batting

All-Rounder	Country	Career	No. of tests	Batting Runs	w_{avge}	n_{100}	Rating	Bowling Wickets	w_{avge}	w_{sr}	Rating	All-rounder rating	Batting or bowling
11 Waugh, SR	Aust	1985-04	168	10,927	51.06	32	146.3	92	37.45	84.84	61.9	166.0	batting
12 Ashwin, R [1]	India	2011-24	106	3,503	25.76	6	52.1	537	23.91	50.68	169.2	162.8	bowling
13 Greig, AW	Eng	1972-77	58	3,599	40.44	8	80.3	141	32.21	69.52	82.9	161.9	bowling
14 Hadlee, RJ	N. Z.	1973-90	86	3,124	27.17	2	50.7	431	22.3	50.85	170.3	161.2	bowling
15 Pollock, SM	S. A.	1995-08	108	3,781	32.32	2	59.8	421	23.12	57.85	141.9	160.7	bowling
16 Macartney, CG	Aust	1907-26	35	2,131	41.78	7	79.5	45	27.56	79.00	81.7	160.1	bowling
17 Miller, KR	Aust	1946-56	55	2,958	36.98	7	68.5	170	22.98	61.54	111.0	158.3	bowling
18 Mushtaq Mohd.	Pak	1959-79	57	3,643	39.17	10	81.8	79	29.23	66.58	77.9	157.8	batting
19 Border, AR	Aust	1978-94	156	11,174	50.56	27	145.1	39	39.10	102.79	56.8	157.8	batting
20 Faulkner, GA	S. A.	1906-14	25	1,754	40.79	4	73.0	82	26.59	51.55	92.0	155.6	bowling
21 Jayasuriya, ST	S. L.	1991-07	110	6,973	40.07	14	109.8	98	34.35	83.55	67.1	155.5	batting
22 Asif Iqbal	Pak	1964-79	58	3,575	38.86	11	77.1	53	28.34	72.91	78.3	154.8	bowling
23 Vettori, DL	N. Z.	1997-14	113	4,531	30.01	6	65.4	362	34.37	79.60	111.0	153.6	bowling
24 Cairns, CL	N. Z.	1989-04	62	3,320	33.54	5	67.3	218	29.40	53.66	103.7	152.8	bowling
25 Chappell, GS	Aust	1970-84	87	7,110	53.86	24	138.2	47	40.70	113.34	54.3	150.6	batting
26 Cowper, RM	Aust	1964-68	27	2,061	46.84	5	94.9	36	31.64	83.47	66.8	147.7	batting
27 Root, JE [1]	Eng	2012-24	152	12,972	50.87	36	163.4	71	45.37	82.41	43.5	146.95	batting
28 Wasim Akram	Pak	1985-02	104	2,898	22.64	3	46.9	414	23.62	54.65	148.3	144.5	bowling
29 Dexter, ER	Eng	1958-68	62	4,502	47.89	9	105.3	66	34.94	80.56	60.5	143.5	batting
30 Flintoff, A	Eng	1998-09	79	3,845	31.78	5	67.4	226	32.79	66.15	84.4	143.3	bowling
31 Worrell, FMM	W. I.	1948-63	51	3,860	49.49	9	107.8	69	38.72	103.49	58.6	141.9	batting
32 Cronje, WJ	S. A.	1992-00	68	3,714	36.41	6	69.7	43	29.95	88.37	74.6	141.9	bowling
33 Woolley, FE	Eng	1909-30	64	3,283	36.08	5	69.3	83	33.92	78.25	69.7	138.8	bowling
34 Armstrong, WW	Aust	1902-21	50	2,863	38.69	6	68.0	87	33.60	92.21	71.5	137.8	bowling
35 Watson, SR	Aust	2005-15	59	3,731	35.20	4	71.2	75	33.68	73.27	68.0	137.6	batting
36 Barlow, EJ	S. A.	1961-70	30	2,516	45.75	6	91.3	40	34.05	75.53	61.1	137.3	batting
37. Shastri, RJ	India	1981-92	80	3,830	35.79	11	71.8	151	40.97	104.31	66.6	135.8	batting
38 Goddard, TL	S. A.	1955-70	41	2,516	34.47	1	57.5	123	26.23	95.41	98.7	135.6	bowling
39 Clarke, MJ	Aust	2004-15	115	8,643	49.11	28	137.5	31	38.19	78.55	44.3	135.2	batting
40 Reid, JR	N. Z.	1949-65	58	3,428	33.28	6	65.9	85	33.35	90.88	72.4	135.1	bowling
41 Simpson, RB	Aust	1957-78	62	4,869	46.82	10	109.0	71	42.27	96.92	52.8	133.7	batting
42 Gayle, CH	W. I.	2000-14	103	7,214	42.19	15	115.0	73	42.74	97.38	49.9	132.4	batting
43 Umrigar, PR	India	1948-62	59	3,631	42.22	12	89.5	35	42.09	135.00	57.1	130.4	batting
44 Waugh, ME	Aust	1991-02	128	8,029	41.82	20	110.4	59	41.17	82.25	49.6	129.6	batting
45 Holder, JO [1]	W. I.	2014-24	69	3,073	29.83	3	56.7	1162	30.38	69.76	89.6	129.5	bowling
46 de Grandhomme, C	N. Z.	2016-22	29	1,432	38.70	2	66.2	49	32.96	82.73	64.2	129.4	batting
47 Noble, MA	Aust	1898-09	42	1,997	30.26	1	49.5	121	25.00	58.75	108.7	128.6	bowling
48 McMillan, BM	S. A.	1992-98	38	1,968	39.36	3	63.7	75	33.83	80.72	65.1	128.1	bowling
49 Mankad, MH	India	1946-59	44	2,109	31.48	5	54.4	162	32.32	90.65	92.7	127.9	bowling
50 Mohd. Hafeez	Pak	2003-18	55	3,652	37.65	10	78.3	53	34.11	76.74	59.0	127.6	batting
51 Hooper, CL	W. I.	1987-02	102	5,762	36.47	13	88.4	114	49.43	121.00	55.4	127.3	batting
52 D'Oliveira, BL	Eng	1966-72	44	2,484	40.06	5	72.8	47	39.55	121.40	60.0	126.4	batting
53 Astle, NJ	N. Z.	1996-06	81	4,702	37.02	11	83.2	51	42.02	111.53	55.5	124.9	batting
54 Mudassar Nazar	Pak	1976-89	76	4,114	38.09	10	80.3	66	38.36	90.41	55.5	123.4	batting
55 Gooch, GA	Eng	1978-95	118	8,900	42.58	20	123.0	23	46.48	115.4	41.1	123.2	batting
56 Rhodes, W	Eng	1899-30	58	2,325	30.19	2	50.3	127	26.97	64.81	94.6	122.7	bowling
57 Gregory, JM	Aust	1920-28	24	1,146	36.97	2	56.7	85	31.15	65.67	73.8	122.0	bowling
58 Vaas, WPUJC	S. L.	1994-09	111	3,089	24.32	1	42.9	355	29.58	66.02	113.0	120.9	bowling
59 Oram, JDP	N. Z.	2002-09	33	1,780	36.33	5	58.2	60	32.92	82.63	66.6	120.7	bowling
60 Shahid Afridi	Pak	1998-10	27	1,716	36.51	5	72.1	48	35.60	66.54	56.3	120.5	batting

All-Rounder	Country	Career	No. of tests	Runs	w_{avge}	n_{100}	Rating	Wickets	w_{avge}	w_{sr}	Rating	All-rounder rating	Batting or bowling
61 Congdon, BE	N.Z.	1965-78	61	3,448	32.22	7	63.6	59	36.51	95.25	58.8	120.1	batting
62 Coney, J	N.Z.	1974-87	52	2,668	37.58	3	65.9	27	35.78	105.00	57.3	118.9	batting
63 Kelleway, CE	Aust	1910-28	26	1,422	37.42	3	57.6	52	32.37	83.90	64.9	118.9	bowling
64 Wasim Raja	Pak	1973-85	57	2,821	36.17	4	64.2	51	35.80	80.04	56.8	117.4	batting
65 McCabe, SJ	Aust	1930-38	39	2,748	48.21	6	97.6	36	42.86	104.1	45.5	117.1	batting
66 Ali, MM	Eng	2014-23	68	3,094	28.13	5	52.5	204	37.31	61.81	74.7	116.1	bowling
67 Jackson, FS	Eng	1893-05	20	1,415	48.79	5	89.8	24	33.29	66.13	46.5	114.6	batting
68 Klusener, L	S.A.	1996-04	49	1,906	32.86	4	56.3	80	37.91	86.09	60.2	114.5	bowling
69 Bailey, TE	Eng	1949-59	61	2,290	29.74	1	45.2	132	29.21	73.58	87.0	111.2	bowling
70 Matthews, GRJ	Aust	1983-93	33	1,849	41.09	4	70.6	61	48.23	102.80	48.2	107.6	batting
71 Smith, OG	W.I.	1955-59	26	1,331	31.69	4	50.0	48	33.85	92.31	65.2	107.6	bowling
72 Mackay, KD	Aust	1956-63	37	1,507	33.49	0	48.3	50	34.42	115.84	68.1	106.5	bowling
73 Edrich, WJ	Eng	1938-54	39	2,440	40.00	6	77.6	41	41.29	78.88	44.4	105.4	batting
74 Saeed Ahmed	Pak	1958-72	41	2,991	40.42	5	76.7	22	36.45	90.00	44.1	104.5	batting
75 Atkinson, DStE	W.I.	1948-58	22	922	31.79	1	45.6	47	35.04	110.66	69.3	103.1	bowling
76 Phadkar, DG	India	1947-58	31	1,229	32.34	2	47.8	62	36.85	96.68	62.5	103.0	bowling
77 Borde, CG	India	1958-65	55	3,061	35.59	5	66.3	52	46.48	109.52	46.5	102.9	batting
78 Symonds, A	Aust	2004-08	26	1,462	40.61	2	71.6	24	37.33	87.25	43.3	100.8	batting
79 Prabhakar, MM	India	1985-95	39	1,600	32.65	1	44.7	96	37.3	77.86	62.4	98.3	bowling
80 Abdul Razzaq	Pak	1999-06	46	1,946	28.62	3	42.0	100	36.94	70.08	60.9	93.5	bowling

[1] Still playing in 2024

Table 2.18 The wicketkeepers with 70 dismissals up to the end of 2024 and their ratings.

Wicketkeeper	Country	Career	No. of Inns	Catches	Stumpings	Total	Dismissals /Inns	WS14	WS15	WS16	Batting Rating	Wicket-keeper Rating
1 Gilchrist, AC	Aust	1999-08	191	379	37	416	2.18	62.4	65.3	48.5	121.3	176.3
2 Boucher, MV	S.A.	1997-12	281	532	23	555	1.98	83.3	59.3	28.4	71.1	170.9
3 Sangakkara, KC	S.L.	2000-15	90	131	20	151	1.68	22.7	50.3	71.1	177.8	144.1
4 de Villiers, AB	S.A.	2004-18	45	101	5	106	2.36	15.9	70.7	56.2	140.4	142.7
5 de Kock, Q	S.A.	2014-21	98	221	11	232	2.37	34.8	71.0	32.5	81.3	138.3
6 Healy, IA	Aust	1988-99	224	366	29	395	1.76	59.3	52.9	23.9	59.8	136.1
7 Bairstow, JM	Eng	2012-23	104	209	14	223	2.14	33.5	64.3	34.9	86.8	132.5
8 Dhoni, MS	India	2005-14	166	256	38	294	1.77	44.1	53.1	35.2	88.0	132.4
9 Watling, BJ	N.Z.	2009-21	127	257	8	265	2.09	39.8	62.6	30.0	74.9	132.3
10 Marsh, RW	Aust	1970-84	182	343	12	355	1.95	53.3	58.5	20.2	50.4	131.9
11 Stewart, AJ	Eng	1990-03	141	227	14	241	1.71	36.2	51.3	42.6	106.6	130.1
12 Haddin, BJ	Aust	2008-15	128	262	8	270	2.11	40.5	63.3	25.6	64.1	129.4
13 Prior, MJ	Eng	2007-14	146	243	13	256	1.75	38.4	52.6	33.7	84.3	124.7
14 McCullum, BB	N.Z.	2004-16	95	168	11	179	1.88	26.9	56.5	40.8	102.1	124.2
15 Dujon, PJL	W.I.	1981-91	150	265	5	270	1.80	40.5	54.0	23.4	58.5	117.9
16 Pant, RR [1]	India	2018-24	83	147	15	162	1.95	24.3	58.6	34.6	86.6	117.5
17 Flower, A	Zimb	1992-02	96	142	9	151	1.57	22.7	47.2	46.5	116.2	116.3
18 Kamran Akmal	Pak	2002-10	99	184	22	206	2.08	30.9	62.4	22.8	57.0	116.1
19 Knott, APE	Eng	1967-81	174	250	19	269	1.55	40.4	46.4	27.5	68.8	114.2
20 Paine, TD	Aust	2010-21	68	150	7	157	2.31	23.6	69.3	17.2	42.9	110.0
21 Sarfaraz Ahmed	Pak	2010-23	104	160	23	183	1.75	27.3	52.5	29.6	74.1	109.4
22 Carey, AT [1]	Aus	2021-24	68	137	14	151	2.22	22.7	66.6	19.2	47.9	108.4
23 Jacobs, RD	W.I.	1998-04	122	207	12	219	1.80	32.9	53.9	18.7	46.8	105.4
24 Ramdin, D	W.I.	2005-16	131	205	12	217	1.66	32.6	49.7	19.8	49.4	102.0
25 Buttler, JC	Eng	2014-22	70	130	1	131	1.87	19.7	56.1	22.9	57.3	98.7
26 Parore, AC	N.Z.	1990-02	121	194	7	201	1.66	30.2	49.8	17.6	43.9	97.5
27 Dickwella, DPDN	S.L.	2014-23	96	133	27	160	1.67	24.0	50.0	22.6	56.5	96.6
28 Blundell, TA [1]	N.Z.	2017-24	65	100	16	116	1.78	17.4	53.5	23.8	59.4	94.7
29 Chandimal, LD	S.L.	2011-23	50	63	10	73	1.46	11.0	43.8	39.8	99.6	94.6
30 Richardson, DJ	S.A.	1992-98	77	150	2	152	1.97	22.8	59.2	12.3	30.7	94.3
31 Litton Das [1]	Bang	2015-24	62	94	14	108	1.74	16.2	52.3	25.8	64.4	94.2
32 Jones, GO	Eng	2004-06	66	128	5	133	2.02	20.0	60.5	12.4	31.1	92.8
33 Mohammad Rizwan [1]	Pak	2016-24	60	92	7	99	1.65	14.9	49.5	28.0	70.1	92.4

Wicketkeeper	Country	Career	No. of Inns	Catches	Stumpings	Total	Dismissals/Inns	WS14	WS15	WS16	Batting Rating	Wicketkeeper Rating
34 Rashid Latif	Pak	1992-03	69	119	11	130	1.88	19.5	56.5	15.8	39.5	91.8
35 Da Silva, J [1]	W.I.	2020-24	45	121	6	127	2.05	19.1	61.5	11.3	28.3	91.8
36 Smith, IDS	N.Z.	1980-92	109	168	8	176	1.61	26.4	48.4	16.5	41.2	91.3
37 Russell, RC	Eng	1988-98	96	153	12	165	1.72	24.8	51.6	14.4	36.1	90.8
38 Grout, ATW	Aust	1957-66	98	163	24	187	1.91	28.1	57.2	4.5	11.2	89.8
39 Murray, DL	W.I.	1963-80	119	181	8	189	1.59	28.4	47.6	13.3	33.3	89.3
40 Waite, JHB	S.A.	1951-65	92	124	17	141	1.53	21.2	46.0	21.2	53.0	88.3
41 Jayawardene, HAPW	S.L.	2000-15	102	124	32	156	1.53	23.4	45.9	18.0	45.0	87.3
42 Kirmani, SMH	India	1976-86	151	160	38	198	1.31	29.7	39.3	17.8	44.5	86.8
43 Alexander, FCM	W.I.	1957-61	47	85	5	90	1.91	13.5	57.4	15.7	39.3	86.7
44 Mushfiqur Rahim	Bang	2005-23	99	98	15	113	1.14	17.0	34.2	35.2	87.9	86.4
45 Wasim Bari	Pak	1967-84	146	201	27	228	1.56	34.2	46.8	5.1	12.8	86.2
46 Verreynne, K [1]	S.A.	2021-24	38	67	6	73	1.92	11.0	57.6	17.2	43.0	85.8
47 Evans, TG	Eng	1946-59	175	173	46	219	1.25	32.9	37.5	13.4	33.6	83.8
48 Browne, CO	W.I.	1995-05	36	79	2	81	2.25	12.2	67.5	3.8	9.6	83.5
49 Saleem Yousuf	Pak	1982-90	58	91	13	104	1.79	15.6	53.8	12.5	31.2	81.9
50 Wade, MS	Aust	2012-21	42	63	11	74	1.76	11.1	52.9	17.7	44.2	81.6
51 Moin Khan	Pak	1990-04	118	127	20	147	1.25	22.1	37.4	20.7	51.7	80.1
52 Taylor, RW	Eng	1971-84	106	167	7	174	1.64	26.1	49.2	4.3	10.8	79.7
53 Parks, JM	Eng	1954-68	80	101	11	112	1.40	16.8	42.0	19.2	47.9	78.0
54 Ames, LEG	Eng	1929-39	81	72	23	95	1.17	14.3	35.2	28.5	71.3	78.0
55 Dowrich, SO	W.I.	2015-20	57	85	5	90	1.58	13.5	47.4	17.1	42.7	77.9
56 Murray, JR	W.I.	1993-02	57	98	3	101	1.77	15.2	53.2	9.0	22.6	77.3
57 Adnan Akmal	Pak	2010-14	41	66	11	77	1.88	11.6	56.3	9.3	23.3	77.2
58 Kaluwitharana, RS	S.L.	1992-04	85	93	26	119	1.40	17.9	42.0	17.2	43.0	77.1
59 Langley, GRA	Aust	1951-56	51	83	15	98	1.92	14.7	57.6	3.8	9.6	76.2
60 Imtiaz Ahmed	Pak	1952-62	64	74	16	90	1.41	13.5	42.2	20.0	50.1	75.7
61 More, KS	India	1986-93	90	110	20	130	1.44	19.5	43.3	11.5	28.8	74.4
62 Wadsworth, KJ	N.Z.	1969-76	59	92	4	96	1.63	14.4	48.8	9.1	22.7	72.3
63 Saha, WP	India	2010-21	76	92	12	104	1.37	15.6	41.1	15.5	38.8	72.2
64 Patel, PA	India	2002-18	47	62	10	72	1.53	10.8	46.0	14.7	36.7	71.4
65 Mongia, NR	India	1994-01	77	99	8	107	1.39	16.1	41.7	12.4	31.0	70.1
66 Oldfield, WAS	Aust	1920-37	101	78	52	130	1.29	19.5	38.6	9.9	24.7	68.0
67 Engineer, FM	India	1961-75	83	66	16	82	0.99	12.3	29.6	20.9	52.2	62.8
68 Lilley, AFA	Eng	1896-09	67	70	22	92	1.37	13.8	41.2	7.5	18.8	62.5
69 Khaled Mashud	Bang	2000-07	61	78	9	87	1.43	13.1	42.8	6.0	15.1	61.9
70 Downton, PR	Eng	1981-88	51	70	5	75	1.47	11.3	44.1	6.1	15.2	61.4
71 Strudwick, H	Eng	1910-26	48	61	12	73	1.52	11.0	45.6	1.6	4.0	58.2

[1] Still playing in 2024

Chapter 3
The Best World Team before World-War 1
1877 to 1914

The first ever test match was played in March 1877 between England and Australia at the Melbourne Cricket Ground. Australia won by 45 runs in a low scoring match, with Charles Bannerman scoring 165 not out in Australia's first innings (more than a quarter of the total match runs). England's Alfred Shaw and Australia's Tom Kendall each took 8 wickets in the match. The era of test cricket had begun.

Before World War 1, the only test playing nations were England, Australia and South Africa. In what is often called the Golden Age of cricket, a total of 134 test matches were played; England featured in 123 of them, Australia in 105 and South Africa in 40. England's win/loss/draw record against Australia was 40/35/19 and against South Africa was 19/7/3. In tests between Australia and South Africa, Australia won 8, lost 1 and drew 2. In the 37 years before World War 1, 379 individuals played test cricket, with 180, 105 and 94 players representing England, Australia and South Africa, respectively. Of these, only 42 played more than 20 test matches. Based on the batting and bowling ratings of these eligible players, the most highly rating team of the Golden Age is as follows:

The Team:

Batting Order:	Country	No. of tests	Playing career	Batting rating	Bowling rating
1. Hobbs, JB	England	28	1908-14	120.1	-
2. Bardsley, W	Australia	20	1909-12	85.8	-
3. Hill, C	Australia	49	1896-12	79.4	-
4. Trumper, VT	Australia	48	1899-12	77.9	-
5. Jackson, FS	England	20	1893-05	89.8	46.5
6. Faulkner, GA	South Africa	24	1906-12	75.6	96.3
7. Rhodes, W	England	47	1899-14	51.6	101.3
8. Lilley, AFA	England	35	1896-09	18.8	-
9. Briggs, J	England	33	1884-99	14.9	153.4
10. Lohmann, GA	England	18	1886-96	4.6	219.5
11. Barnes, SF	England	27	1901-14	4.2	190.8
			Total	622.7	807.8

Note: Batting and bowling statistics are given in Tables 3.1 and 3.2, respectively.

It was an era when the ball dominated the bat. This team has the highest bowling rating of any of the world teams selected in this book, and the lowest batting rating. The top three bowlers in the team Johnny Briggs, George Lohmann and Sydney Barnes, together with William Barnes and Robert Peel who both missed out on selection in the first 11, were the only bowlers in the history of test cricket to have a bowling average of less than 18, and they were all English. Although the figures suggest that this bowling attack was the finest in history, the statistics here must be viewed with some caution. This was an era in which the preparation of pitches was far inferior to today, the outfields were not as well manicured as they are today, the pitches remained uncovered throughout the match, and the development of bats and protective equipment for batsmen was in its infancy. It is not surprising therefore that, in general, the bowlers outshone the batsmen. Despite the advantages that these bowlers enjoyed, there is no question that they would have been a formidable attacking unit.

Nine of the players who played before 1914 have been inducted into the International Cricket Council's (ICC) Cricket Hall of Fame that was established in 2009: W.G. Grace, Jack Hobbs, Wilfred Rhodes, Frank Woolley, George Lohmann and Sydney Barnes (England), Victor Trumper, Fred Spofforth and Monty Noble (Australia) and Aubrey Faulkner (South Africa).

The batting and bowling performances of the best World team for the era are shown in Tables 3.1 and 3.2 and the performances of the top all-rounders and the highest rating wicket keepers are compared in Table 3.3 and 3.4, respectively. The statistics for the best English and Australian teams before World War 1 are provided in Appendix D (Tables D.1 and D.2, respectively). The batting and bowling records of the 5 eligible South Africans are shown in Table D.3. Batting strike rates in this era were often not recorded and so, in the determination of the batting rating for each player, a strike rate of 50 has been assumed in each year where strike rates were not available.

The Top 11 Players:

No. 1: The English opening batsmen Jack Hobbs is the highest rating batsman of the time. He was born in Cambridge in December 1882 and, after spending two years qualifying to play for Surrey, he commenced his first-class career in 1905. He played for Surrey for the next 29 years. He was a right-hand opening batsman, occasional right arm medium pace bowler and an agile cover point fieldsman. He made his test debut in 1908 and by the start of World War 1 was widely regarded as the best batsman in the world. His test career continued for the next 22 years. His batting rating before the war of 120.1 and his batting average of 57.33 are the highest of any player in any national team before World War 1 and are consistent with his batting rating of 136.5 and batting average of 56.95 over his long test career. Hobbs is considered by many as perhaps the greatest opening batsman of all-time and he ranks 35th in the list of the highest career test batting ratings (see Table 2.7).

No. 2: Opening the batting with Hobbs in the top world team before World War 1 is Australia's Warren Bardsley. He was born in Warren, New South Wales in December 1882 (the same month as Jack Hobbs). His test career spanned from 1909 to 1926, with a total of 41 tests, 20 of them before the war. He made his test debut against England at Edgbaston in 1909 but failed to impress with scores of 2 and 6. However in the final test of that series at the Oval, he scored 136 in the first innings and 130 in the second to become the first cricketer to score a century in each innings of a test match. In the test series against South Africa in the 2010-11 Australian summer, he scored 573 runs at an average of 63.67, including 132 at the Sydney Cricket ground at a strike rate of 88.0. In the triangular series between England, South Africa and Australia in 1912, he was the leading run scorer with 392 runs at 65.33. A classical stroke maker, he played over 200 first-class games for New South Wales from 1903 to 1926. He was named one of Wisden's Cricketers of the Year in 1910. His career batting rating places him 200th in the list of the highest rating test batsmen of all time (see Table A.1 in Appendix A).

No. 3: At No. 3 is the Australian, Clement "Clem" Hill, the first of the great left-handed test batsmen. He was born in Adelaide on the rest day of the first ever test match in March 1877 and made his test debut as a 19-year-old in 1896. He played first-class cricket for South Australia for 31 years, from 1892 until 1923 and played 49 test matches before the end of his test career in 1912. He captained Australia in its last ten test matches before World War 1, in the Australian summers of 1910-11 and 1911-12. Hill was a prolific run-scorer. In the 1900-01 domestic season, he scored 365 for South Australia against New South Wales, a first-class record in Australia that stood for the next 27 years. In 1902, he became the first batsman to score 1000 test runs in a calendar year, a feat that was not repeated for the next 45 years. At the beginning of World War 1, Hill had played more test matches than any other player and had scored more test runs than any other player. He is rated 194th in Table A.1.

No. 4: Although he usually opened the batting for Australia, Victor Trumper is selected here at No.4. He played 48 test matches from his test debut against England at Trent Bridge in 1899 until his final test against England at the Sydney Cricket Ground in 1912. Born in November 1877 in Sydney, he was widely regarded as the most stylish and versatile batsman of his era. In England in 1902, in one of the wettest summers on record, Trumper scored 2,570 runs in 53 innings. He scored runs on wet wickets that his peers found unplayable. Describing Trumper, Plum Warner wrote: "No one ever played so naturally. Batting seemed just part of himself, and he was as modest as he was magnificent." In arguably his greatest innings that summer, he scored 103 before lunch against England at Old Trafford and became the first player to make a century on the first morning of a test match. He is the 201st highest rating test batsman in Table A.1. Best known for his cricketing skills, Trumper was also a keen rugby player and was a key figure in the establishment of rugby league in Australia in 1907 and 1908. In 1914, his health deteriorated rapidly, and he died at the age of 37 in June 1915. Australia mourned. In what was the largest funeral procession ever seen in Australia, 250,000 mourners lined the route through the streets of Sydney.

No. 5: England's Stanley Jackson is selected at No. 5. With a test batting average of 48.79, five test centuries in 33 innings and a batting rating of 89.8, he is the second-best performing batsman in the side (behind Jack Hobbs) and the 139th highest rating test batsman (Table A.1). He has been described as a very correct batsman, strong infront of the wicket and a good player of fast bowling. He was also a respectable right arm medium pace bowler. He is the 67th highest rating all-rounder in Table 2.17. Born in 1870 in Leeds, he went to Harrow School and later Cambridge University. As a senior student at Harrow in the late 1880s, his fag was the young Winston Churchill. He played county cricket for Yorkshire from 1890 to 1907 and test cricket for England on and off from 1893 to 1905. His test career was interrupted by his military career, serving in the Second Boer War in 1900 as a captain in the King's Own Royal Lancaster Regiment. All 20 of his tests were played at home because he insisted that he did not have the time to tour abroad. He took over as captain of England for his final five tests in 1905 against Australia, winning the series 2-0 and retaining the Ashes. In that series, he topped the batting and bowling averages for both sides, with 492 runs at 70.28 and 13 wickets at 15.46.

Jackson had a distinguished career after cricket as a soldier, politician and diplomat. By 1914, he had risen to Lieutenant Colonel in the West Yorkshire regiment, and he was elected to parliament in February 1915. He served as Financial Secretary to the War Office 1922-23 and Chairman of the Conservative Party from 1923 to 1926. He was knighted in 1927 and that same year he was appointed as Governor of Bengal, a position he held until 1932.

No. 6: The highest rating of the three genuine all-rounders in the side and batting at No. 6 is George Aubrey Faulkner, the only South African in the team. Born in December 1881 in Port Elizabeth, Faulkner made his test debut against England at Johannesburg in January 1906. He was one of the first effective leg spin bowlers, an elegant right-hand batsman and an outstanding fielder, both in the outfield and close to the wicket. On the South African tour of England in 1907, he took 6/17 in eleven overs in the test match at Headingley.

Faulkner was considered by Wisden to be the best all-rounder in the world following his performances when England toured South Africa in 1909-10. He was the leading run scorer from either team, scoring 545 runs at 60.55 and the second highest wicket taker with 29 at 21.89. In his next series, in Australia in 1910/11, he scored 732 runs at 73.20, including a highest score of 204 in the second Test at Melbourne. He is ranked at No. 20 in the list of the greatest all-rounders in test cricket history (Table 2.17) and he was the highest rating South African test bowler and the highest rating South African test batsman at the start of World War 1.

No. 7: The English all-rounder Wilfred Rhodes is at No. 7. He was born in Kirkheaton, West Yorkshire in 1877 and played for Yorkshire from 1898 until 1930. He played regularly for England between 1899 and 1921, but he was recalled for one test in 1926 and 4 tests in 1930. In his final test he was 52 years and 165 days old — the oldest person ever to play test cricket.

Early in his test career, Rhodes gained the reputation as the finest slow bowler in England, but by 1912 he had established himself as one of England's best batsmen, often opening the batting for England with Jack Hobbs. The pair put on an opening stand of 323 at the MCG in 1912. Rhodes' cricket longevity is amazing. He played more first-class matches than any other cricketer in the history of the game and, with 4,207 first-class wickets, he is the most successful first-class bowler of all time. Indeed, only four bowlers have taken more than 3,000 first class wickets, with Rhodes the only bowler to pass 3,800. He is the 56th highest rating all-rounder in test history (see Table 2.17) and the 123rd highest rating test bowler (see Table A.2).

No. 8: The wicketkeeper is Dick Lilley selected at No. 8 in the batting line-up. In 35 tests, he took 70 catches and made 22 stumpings to average 1.37 dismissals per innings. His wicketkeeper rating calculated using Equation 2.16 is 62.5 and he ranks 68th in Table 2.18. Born in Birmingham in 1866, he played county cricket for Warwickshire from 1888 to 1911 and kept wickets for 23 years. He was considered to be the best wicketkeeper in England for much of his career. He averaged 20.52 with the bat in test cricket and was a forceful, hard-hitting batsman.

No. 9: Johnny Briggs was an outstanding left-arm orthodox spin bowler. He played for Lancashire between 1879 and 1900 and remains second on the list of players with most wickets for that county. Born in 1862, he played his first test in 1885 and continued playing test cricket until 1899 when injury and illness ended his career. His rating of 153.4 places him 13th on the list of the highest bowling ratings in test cricket (Table 2.16). Briggs had some amazing performances. In the second test against South Africa in March 1889 at Newlands, he took 7 for 17 runs in the first innings and 8 for 11 in the second innings, clean bowling 14 of the 17 South Africans. He took 12 wickets against Australia at the Adelaide Oval in the 3rd test of the 1892 series and 10 Australian wickets at the Oval in 1893. He was the first bowler ever to take 100 wickets in test cricket. His first-class career was even more impressive than his test career, taking 2,221 wickets in 535 matches at an average of 15.95. Briggs was agile in the field and a competent, usually aggressive batsman, often overly aggressive. Briggs scored a test century against Australia at the Melbourne Cricket Ground in 1885 in only his second test match.

No. 10: George Lohmann, who only played 18 test matches between 1886 and 1896, could not be left out of this side. As mentioned in Chapter 1, Lohmann has a lower bowling average, a lower strike rate and a lower economy rate than any other test bowler and he has a bowling rating of 219.5, second only to Sri Lanka's Muttiah Muralitharan who played a century later. Born in Middlesex in 1865, he played county cricket for Surrey from 1884 to 1896. His cricket career was cut tragically short by tuberculosis, and he died at age 36 in 1901.

Lohmann was a medium pace bowler, but on the pitches of his day he could spin the ball deceptively and vary his pace and flight to confuse the finest of batsmen. He was regarded as the best slip fielder of his time and, in his early years of county cricket, a hard-hitting batsman. His feats with the ball were staggering. In the test series against South Africa in 1896, he took 35 wickets in the 3 tests at just 5.80 runs per wicket, with 15/45 in the first test, including a hat-trick at the end of the second innings to win the match.

No. 11: Sydney Barnes is generally regarded as one of the greatest bowlers of all time and his bowling rating of 190.8 places him 2nd in the list of the highest 100 rated test bowlers shown in Table 2.16. He bowled medium to fast-medium pace with the ability to swing the ball and cut the ball both ways off the wicket. Born in 1873 in Staffordshire, Barnes commenced his cricketing career in 1888 and played in the Lancashire League from 1894. He had a long cricketing career as a top-class player, still playing into his 60s, but he spent little more than two seasons in first-class cricket. He preferred league and minor counties cricket for mostly financial reasons. Barnes played 27 test matches for England and took 189 wickets at 16.43 runs per wicket, the lowest test bowling average of any player who bowled more than 1000 overs and played more than 20 matches. He took 34 wickets in the test series against Australia in 1911-12 and, in the 1913-14 series against South Africa, the last test series before World War 1 and Barnes' final series, he took 49 wickets — still the most wickets ever in a series.

Next Best Batsmen:

The next four highest rating batsmen who missed out on selection were Australia's Warwick Armstrong and Vernon Ransford and England's Tom Hayward and Archie MacLaren.

[1] Warwick Armstrong was born in rural Victoria in May 1879 and made his test debut in 1902 as an all-rounder. He ranks 34th in list of the most highly rated all-rounders in history (Table 2.17), the 255th highest rating test batsman (see Table A.1) and the 236th highest rating test bowler (see Table A.2). He was regarded as an effective, if not stylish, batsman, with a sound defence and a good temperament. At 1.9 m tall and weighing 133 kg, he was perhaps the largest ever test cricketer, but he bowled rather gentle leg spin, relying on accuracy and flight to get his wickets. He played first-class cricket for Victoria from 1898 until 1922,

scoring 16,158 first class runs at 46.83 and taking 832 wickets at 19.71. Armstrong went on to captain Australia in the first 10 tests after the war, winning the ashes in Australia (1920-21) and retaining them in England (1921) with a record as captain of 8 wins, 2 draws and zero losses.

[2] Tom Hayward was born Cambridge in March 1871 and played first-class cricket for Surrey from 1894 to 2014. He played 35 test matches from 1896 to 1909 and scored 1,999 runs at an average of 34.47. He is the 328th highest rating test batsman (see Table A.1). Selected primarily as a right-hand opening batsman in test cricket, Hayward was an outstanding all-rounder for Surrey, scoring over 43,551 runs in 712 first-class matches at an average of 41.79 (including 104 centuries) and taking 481 wickets at 22.95 with accurate medium pace bowling.

[3] Archie MacLaren captained England in 22 of his 35 test matches between 1898 and 1909. Born in 1871 in Manchester, he was a stylish right-hand batsman who played county cricket for Lancashire from 1890 until 1914. His score of 428 for Lancashire against Somerset in 1895 remained the highest first-class score by a batsman in England for the next 80 years. His test performances, however, were relatively modest. He is the 329th highest rating test batsman (see Table A.1).

[4] Vernon Ransford was an elegant left-hand batsman who played 20 tests from 1907 to 1912. He topped the Australian batting averages on the 1909 tour of England, scoring a century at Lords. He is the 331st highest rating test batsman (see Table A.1). Born in Melbourne, he played first-class cricket for Victoria from 1903 to 1928, scoring 8,268 first-class runs at an average of 42.40, including 25 centuries. Ransford was one of the so-called Big Six test cricketers who refused to tour England in 1912 after a dispute with the Australian Board of Control (the others were Victor Trumper, Clem Hill, Sammy Carter, Tibby Cotter and Warwick Armstrong). This, and the onset of World War 1, ended Ransford's test career.

Next Best Bowlers:

The next four highest rating bowlers who missed out on selection were Englishmen Robert Peel and Billy Barnes and Australians Fred Spofforth and Hugh Trumble.

[1] Robert Peel would have been one of the first bowlers picked in any other era and is therefore unlucky to have missed selection. With a bowling rating of 141.6, he was one of the best left arm orthodox spinners to play test cricket, but he played in an era of great English bowlers and, although coming 26th in the list of the highest test cricket bowling ratings (Table 2.16), he could not force his way into this bowling attack. He played county cricket for Yorkshire from 1883 to 1897 and played for England at the same time as Johnny Briggs. The two competed with each other as left-arm orthodox spinners. Never, before or since, has a national team had two such outstanding spinners vying for test selection.

[2] The bowling all-rounder William "Billy" Barnes was one of the great English bowlers of his era. His bowling rating of 128.4 is significantly higher than Rhodes', but Rhodes was selected ahead of Barnes to strengthen the team's batting rating. With a bowling average of 15.55 in his 21-match test career and a strike rate of 44.88, Barnes was an outstanding medium pace bowler and despite being the 36th highest rating test bowler (see Table 2.16), he could not make the best team for England before World War 1. Born at Sutton-in-Ashfield in 1852, he played for Nottinghamshire from 1875 until 1894. His first-class career was as impressive as his test career, taking 902 wickets at an average of 17.12. Barnes was also a competent batsman averaging 23.39 with the bat in tests and scoring 15,425 runs in 459 first-class matches.

[3] Known as the "Demon", Fred Spofforth is arguably the best test fast bowler of the 19th century. He played just 18 tests for Australia, all against England, from the first ever test in 1877 to the match at the Sydney Cricket Ground in February 1887. He was the first bowler ever to take 50 wickets in test cricket. He ended his test career with a bowling average of 18.41, a strike rate of 44.52 and a bowling rating of 154.7, placing him among the great bowlers of all time.

[4] Hugh Trumble played 32 tests between 1890 and 1904. He was a quicker than average off-spin bowler who took 141 test wickets (a world record at the time of his retirement) at an average of 21.78 runs per wicket. He is one of only four bowlers to twice take a hat-trick in test cricket. He ranks 39th in the list of the highest rating test bowlers (see Table 2.16). With four half-centuries and a batting average of almost 20, he was also a fair lower-order batsman.

The Top All-Rounders:

The statistics of the top-rated all-rounders of the era are provided in Table 3.3. George Faulkner and Wilfred Rhodes have already been mentioned. Unlucky to miss selection in the first 11 was Australia's Monty Noble. Wilfred Rhodes at No. 7 was preferred ahead of Noble for his batting in a relatively weak batting team. However, Noble was a fine batsman with numerous first-class batting records for New South Wales over his long career from 1893 to 1919. He was also a deceptive medium paced off-spin bowler who played 42 test matches between 1898 and 1909, taking 121 wickets at a bowling average of 25.0. He is the 47th highest rating all-rounder in test history (Table 2.17) and the 76th highest rating test bowler (Table 2.16). The MA Noble Stand is located at the northern end of the Sydney Cricket Ground.

The all-rounder of the era who must be mentioned is William Gilbert (W.G.) Grace. Although his statistics in test cricket are not impressive, he was undoubtedly the greatest all-rounder of the 19th century. He played first-class cricket from 1865 to 1908 (predominantly for Gloucestershire) and test cricket for England between 1880 and 1899. He played a major role in the development of cricket in the 19th Century and is widely regarded as the father of the modern game. He is the only first-class cricketer to score more than 50,000 runs (including 124 centuries) and take more than 2,500 wickets.

The Top Wicketkeepers:

The performances of the highest-ranking wicketkeepers who played 20 or more matches are provided in Table 3.4. After Dick Lilley are Australian's Sammy Carter and Jack Blackham. Sammy Carter played first-class cricket for New South Wales (1897-1925) and Australia (1907-1921). Born in Yorkshire in 1878, his family emigrated to Australia, and he grew up in Sydney. In total, he kept wickets in 28 tests taking 44 catches and making 21 stumpings. Jack Blackham was the Australian wicketkeeper in the first ever test match in March 1877 and he was wicketkeeper in 35 of Australia's first 40 tests. Born in Melbourne in 1854 and known in his day as the "prince of wicketkeepers", he played first-class cricket for Victoria (1874-95) and Australia (1877-94).

Plate 3.1 The English team at Trent Bridge for the 1st test against Australia in June 1899. (public domain)

Back row: Dick Barlow (umpire), Tom Hayward, George Hirst, Billy Gunn, John Hearne, Bill Storer (wicketkeeper), Bill Brockwell (12th man), V.A. Titchmarsh (umpire). Middle row: Charles Fry, Kumar Ranjitsinhji, W.G. Grace (captain), Stanley Jackson. Front row: Wilfred Rhodes, Johnny Tyldesley.

Table 3.1 Best World Team before World War 1 (1877 to 1914, inclusive) — Batting Performances.

The team

Players	Country	Batting style	Matches	Innings	Not outs	100s/50s/0s	Highest score	Runs scored	Batting average	Strike rate	Batting rating
1. Hobbs, JB	England	right	28	49	6	5/16/3	187	2,465	57.33	50.49	120.1
2. Bardsley, W	Australia	left	20	33	0	5/7/4	164	1,490	45.15	55.60	85.8
3. Hill, C	Australia	left	49	89	2	7/19/9	191	3,412	39.22	53.67	79.4
4. Trumper, VT	Australia	right	48	89	8	8/13/7	214	3,163	39.05	54.55	77.9
5. Jackson, FS	England	right	20	33	4	5/6/3	144	1,415	48.79	50	89.8
6. Faulkner, GA	S. Africa	right	24	45	4	4/8/2	204	1,717	41.88	52.20	75.6
7. Rhodes, W	England	right	47	77	16	2/10/5	179	1,965	32.21	49.87	51.6
8. Lilley, AFA	England	right	35	52	8	0/4/10	84	903	20.52	50	18.8
9. Briggs, J	England	right	33	50	5	1/2/10	121	815	18.11	50	14.9
10. Lohmann, GA	England	right	18	26	2	0/1/7	62	213	8.88	50	4.6
11. Barnes, SF	England	right	27	39	9	0/0/8	38	242	8.07	49.59	4.2
										Total	622.7

Next Batters

Armstrong, WW	Australia	right	40	71	8	3/7/4	159	2,247	35.67	50.76	56.9
Hayward, T	England	right	35	60	2	3/12/7	137	1,999	34.47	50	56.4
MacLaren, AC	England	right	35	61	4	5/8/4	140	1,931	33.88	50	56.3
Ransford, VS	Australia	left	20	38	6	1/7/2	143	1,211	37.84	50.67	56.2

Table 3.2 Best World Team before World War 1 (1877 to 1914, inclusive)—Bowling Performances.

The team

Players	Country	Overs	Balls	Maids.	Runs against	Bowl style	Wickets	5w/10w	Best	Bowl average	Strike rate	Econ rate	Bowling rating
1. Hobbs, JB	England	\multicolumn{11}{c}{Less than 100 overs}	-
2. Bardsley, W	Australia	\multicolumn{11}{c}{Did not bowl}	-
3. Hill, C	Australia	\multicolumn{11}{c}{Did not bowl}	-
4. Trumper, VT	Australia	\multicolumn{11}{c}{Less than 100 overs}	-
4. Jackson, FS	England	291	1,587	77	799	RAM	24	1/0	5/52	33.29	66.13	3.02	46.5
5. Faulkner, GA	S. Africa	687	4,125	124	2,093	RAL	82	4/0	7/84	25.52	50.31	3.04	96.3
6. Rhodes, W	England	996	5,830	231	2,615	LAO	105	6/1	8/68	24.90	55.55	2.69	101.3
8. Lilley, AFA	England	\multicolumn{5}{c}{Wicketkeeper}	\multicolumn{6}{c}{Less than 100 overs}	-
9. Briggs, J	England	1,052	5,324	385	2,094	LAO	118	9/4	8/11	17.75	45.19	2.36	153.4
10. Lohmann, GA	England	801	3,825	364	1,205	RAM	112	9/5	9/28	10.76	34.12	1.89	219.5
11. Barnes, SF	England	1,312	7,863	356	3,106	RAMF	189	24/7	9/103	16.43	41.66	2.37	190.8
												Total	807.8

Next Bowlers

Player	Country	Overs	Balls	Maids	Runs against	Bowl style	Wickets	5w/10w	Best	Bowl average	Strike rate	Econ rate	Bowling rating
Spofforth F.R.	Australia	1,046	4,188	416	1,731	RAFM	94	7/4	7/44	18.41	44.52	2.48	154.7
Peel, R.	England	1,073	5,223	444	1,715	LAO	101	5/1	7/31	16.98	51.64	1.97	141.6
Barnes, W	England	569	2,288	271	793	RAM	51	3/0	6/28	15.55	44.88	2.08	128.4
Trumble, H.	Australia	1,431	8,084	452	3,072	RAO	141	9/3	8/65	21.79	57.44	2.28	126.4

Table 3.3 Performances of the best all-rounders (1877 to 1914, inclusive).

Player	Country	No. of tests	Years played	Batting style	Runs scored	Batting average	Batting rating	Bowl style	Wickets taken	Bowl average	Bowl rating	All-rounder Rating
Faulkner, GA	S Africa	24	1906-14	right	1,717	41.88	75.6	RAL	82	25.52	96.3	161.6
Noble, MA	Australia	42	1898-09	right	1,997	30.26	49.5	RAO	121	25.00	108.7	128.6
Rhodes, W	England	47	1899-14	right	1,965	32.21	51.6	LAO	105	24.90	101.3	128.1

Table 3.4 Wicketkeeping performances (1877 to 1914, inclusive).

Player	Country	No. of tests	Years played	Batting style	Runs scored	Batting average	Batting rating	Catches	Stumpings	Total dismissals	Wicket keeper rating
Lilley, AFA	England	35	1896-09	right	903	20.52	18.8	70	22	92	62.5
Carter, H	Australia	20	1907-12	right	655	21.83	22.3	28	10	38	45.4
Blackham, JM	Australia	35	1877-94	right	800	15.69	12.7	35	24	57	43.5

Chapter 4
The Best World Team — 1920 to 1949

No tests were played during World War 1 and the first test after the war commenced in December 1920. From 1920 to 1949 inclusive, 185 test matches were played. England played in 152 of them, Australia in 85, South Africa in 62, West Indies in 31, New Zealand in 20 and India in 20. The highest rating team for this 30-year period is shown below. Of the 11 players selected, 6 are English, 4 are Australian and 1 is West Indian. The team is the strongest batting side of any era in the history of test cricket.

The highest rating team — 1920 to 1949

Batting Order:	Country	No. of tests	Period	Batting Rating	Bowling Rating
1. Sutcliffe, H.	England	54	1924-35	144.7	-
2. Hutton, L	England	41	1937-49	134.0	-
3. Bradman, DG	Australia	52	1928-48	310.0	-
4. Hammond, WR	England	85	1927-47	152.0	60.1
5. Headley, GA	West Indies	21	1930-49	146.4	-
6. Compton, DCS	England	36	1937-49	137.5	28.8
7. Tate, MW	England	39	1924-35	30.4	101.8
8. Oldfield, WAS	Australia	54	1920-37	24.9	-
9. Voce, W	England	27	1930-47	8.1	89.9
10. Grimmett, CV	Australia	37	1925-36	8.3	141.7
11. O'Reilly, WJ	Australia	27	1932-46	7.6	125.9
			Total	1,103.9	548.2

Note: Batting and bowling statistics are given in Tables 4.1 and 4.2.

The win/loss/draw results for each of the participating countries are shown below. Of the 185 tests played, 110 were won and lost and 75 (40.5%) were drawn. Australia was the most successful national team, winning 50, losing 16 and drawing 19. All except one of Australia's losses were against England, but so too were 29 of its victories.

Country	\multicolumn{7}{c}{Win/Loss/Draw results versus}
	England	Australia	South Africa	West Indies	New Zealand	India	All matches
England	-	15/29/15	15/5/25	8/5/8	3/0/14	6/0/4	47/39/66
Australia	29/15/15	-	12/0/3	4/1/0	1/0/0	4/0/1	50/16/19
South Africa	5/15/25	0/12/3	-	Did not play	2/0/0	Did not play	7/27/28
West Indies	5/8/8	1/4/0	Did not play	-	Did not play	1/0/4	7/12/12
New Zealand	0/3/14	0/1/0	0/2/0	Did not play	-	Did not play	0/6/14
India	0/6/4	0/4/1	Did not play	0/1/4	Did not play	-	0/11/9

Plate 4.1 Don Bradman – Simply the best. (public domain)

Based on these figures, one would expect that Australia would be the team to be most represented in the best 11 of the era. This is not the case. Only one of Australia's top-order batsmen rated highly enough to earn selection in the world team, the phenomenal Don Bradman. Four of the 5 top-order batsmen are English, and one is West Indian. It is the highest rating batting side of any team from any era. The six top-order batsman all feature in the top 50 rated batsman in the history of the game, three of them are in the top 18 (see Table 2.7). Australia had some other fine batsmen in Bill Ponsford, Stan McCabe, Bill Brown, Jack Ryder and Lindsay Hassett, but all ranked well below the top 6 and below the next four batsmen who missed out on selection, England's Jack Hobbs and Eddie Paynter and South Africa's Dudley Nourse and Bruce Mitchell.

The bowling strength of the world team for the era does not match the batting strength. No world team in any other era of 10 years or more has a lower bowling rating. Two English specialist pace bowlers, Maurice Tate and Bill Voce, earned selection in the World team, while the two spinners are Australians, Clarrie Grimmett and Bill O'Reilly. Very unlucky not to be included in the first 11 is the 3rd ranked bowler, Hedley Verity. He had a higher bowling rating than both Tate and Voce, but with two spinners already in the side, the pace pair were preferred in the interest of a balanced attack.

They say bowlers win test matches, but it is clear from the records that Bradman was Australia's match winner, together with a fine group of bowlers, including the most successful two spinners of the years before World War 2 (Grimmett and O'Reilly) and an outstanding pair of fast bowlers in the years immediately after the war, Ray Lindwall and Keith Miller. Lindwall's bowling rating in the era is second only to Grimmett, but he played just 17 tests before 1950 and is therefore ineligible. Bert Oldfield of Australia has been preferred as wicketkeeper ahead of England's Les Ames, despite Ames' higher batting rating. Oldfield had a higher number of dismissals per innings than Ames and he was a superb keeper to spin bowlers. He made 52 dismissals by stumping, more than any other test wicketkeeper. George Headley was the only West Indian to play more than 20 test matches and he is selected to bat at No.5 in the World team. No Indians or New Zealanders played more than 20 test matches before the end of 1949.

The batting and bowling performances of the best World team are presented in Tables 4.1 and 4.2. Only 3 eligible players qualified as all-rounders in the era and their performances are provided in Table 4.3. The statistics of the top 4 wicketkeepers are shown in 4.4. The performances of the most highly rated national teams and eligible players for the era are presented in Appendix E (Tables E.1 to E.4). From this era, 19 players were subsequently inducted into the ICC's Cricket Hall of Fame. They are:

England:	Sir Jack Hobbs, Frank Woolley, Wilfred Rhodes, Herbert Sutcliffe, Harold Larwood, Wally Hammond, Sir Len Hutton, Denis Compton and Sir Alec Bedser.
Australia:	Clarrie Grimmett, Sir Don Bradman, Bill O'Reilly, Stan McCabe, Arthur Morris, Ray Lindwall and Keith Miller.
West Indies:	George Headley and Learie Constantine.
India:	Vinoo Mankad.

The Top 11 Players:

Nos. 1 and 2: The opening batsmen in the top team are England's Sir Leonard Hutton and Herbert Sutcliffe. Very unlucky to miss out is Sir Jack Hobbs. Hobbs and Sutcliffe formed an outstanding opening combination for England for six years from 1924, when Sutcliffe debuted, until Hobbs' retirement in 1930. In 38 innings their partnerships yielded 3249 runs at an average of 87.81, the highest average for an opening partnership in test cricket history. The pair scored 268 at Lords against South Africa in 1924 in only Sutcliffe's second test and 283 against Australia at the MCG six months later in 1925. However, Hutton who played after both Hobbs and Sutcliffe had a slightly better batting rating than Hobbs in this period (the last ten years of Hobb's career) and has therefore relegated him to the position of next best batsman.

Jack Hobbs is the only player to have made the best English teams before and after World War 1. He ended his 22-year test career in 1930 just short of his 48th birthday and he retired from first class cricket in 1934 at the age of 52. He scored 199 first-class centuries and over 60,000 first-class runs — more centuries and more runs than any other player in the history of cricket. He was knighted in 1953, the first professional cricketer to be so honoured. For much of his career, Hobbs was considered by critics as the best batsman in the world. He was Wisden's Cricketer of the year in 1909 and 1926, and in 2000 he was named as one of Wisden's five cricketers of the 20th century. In 2009, he was selected by cricket writers and historians in England's best team of all-time and in the best ever team from all cricketing countries. In his 49 tests from 1910 until the end of 1929, Hobbs' batting average was 63.18. Only Sir Donald Bradman has a higher test batting average.

In has been argued by some that Herbert Sutcliffe was an even better opening batsman than Hobbs and there is no question that he deserves his place at the top of the batting order. Born in Yorkshire in 1894, he played county cricket for Yorkshire from 1919 to 1945 and test cricket for England from 1924 to 1935. He finished his test career with an average of 60.73, higher than any other Englishman and the 5th highest in test cricket history (see Table 2.2). He is the only player whose test batting average never dropped below 60 throughout his entire career. In fact, only one other player with more than 20 tests has had a batting average above 50 throughout his career.

In his first 41 tests, Sutcliffe's batting average was 68.84 and, had he retired at this time (the end of 1932), his batting rating would have been 169.5 moving him from 25th to 5th on the list of the best batting ratings in Table 2.7. Sutcliffe had an even temperament, never appearing rattled or intimidated, and was at his best on big occasions. He had a sound defence, as well as a strong off-side drive, and he was regarded as the best hooker and puller of his time. He was noted for his courage when facing fast bowling. Sutcliffe has been described as "cool, beyond disturbance, the master of survival". At the end of the bodyline series, England's captain Douglas Jardine commented that "Sutcliffe rather enjoys appearing to be in difficulties: he so rarely fails to surmount them".

Sir Leonard Hutton was another outstanding opening batsman for England during this era, starting his test career two years after Sutcliffe retired. He was born in Leeds in 1916 and played for Yorkshire from 1934 to 1955 and for England from 1937 to 1955. His talents were recognised at an early age. Initially regarded as a defensive or even a dower batsman, Hutton became one of England's most prodigious scorers. At the Oval in 1938, he set a new world record, scoring 364 against Australia in England's massive first innings total of 903 for 7. This still remains the highest test score by an English batsman and the longest test innings. In accumulating his 364, he faced 847 balls — still the most balls ever faced by a batsman in a single innings.

His career was interrupted by the Second World War but by the start of the war he was a national hero. During the war, he injured his arm in a training exercise, and this forced him to alter his batting style, but it did not affect his scoring ability. He was the mainstay of England's batting in the decade after the war. Hutton was knighted for services to cricket in 1956. That he displaced Hobbs at the top of the batting order in this team is testimony to his outstanding performances. Hutton sits 18th in the list of the highest rating batsmen of all time (see Table 2.7).

No. 3: Sir Donald Bradman was without peer as a batsman. In the history of sport, all sports, no individual has been statistically so much better than every other player. His career test batting average of 99.94 is 60% higher than the next best player. Bradman scored a century every 2.76 innings he played — more than twice as frequently as the next most successful batsman in history. He passed 200 in an innings more than any other player in history and 3 times more frequently than the next best player. He scored more runs in a day than any other player has ever done. He was magnificent against both pace and spin bowling and absolutely without peer in the history of the game. Throughout the cricket world, he is known simply as "The Don".

Born in Cootamundra, New South Wales in 2008, Bradman grew up in the Southern Highlands of New South Wales in the town of Bowral. He played first class cricket for New South Wales from 1927 to 1934 when he moved to South Australia, where he lived for the rest of his life. He represented South Australia in first-class cricket until his retirement in 1949. He played 52 tests between 1928 and 1948, captaining Australia 24 times. In 37 tests before the Second World War from 1928 to 1938, he scored 5093 runs at an average of 97.94. He played no test cricket from age 30 to 38, due to World War 2, the best years for most batsmen. After the war, from 1946 to 1948, he played 15 more tests scoring 1903 runs at an average of 105.7. His first-class statistics are just as astonishing as his test statistics. He played 234 first class matches, with a batting average of 95.14 (the highest in history), scoring 117 centuries — on average a century every second match.

Bradman has a unique place in the Australian psyche. He became a national hero during the Great Depression and has remained a national hero ever since. Just after his retirement, he was knighted for services to cricket— the only Australian to be so honoured. He was named the greatest living Australian in 2001 (over 50 years after his retirement from cricket), his image has appeared on Australian coins and postage stamps and his batting average of 99.94 is known by cricket lovers everywhere and most Australians (even those misguided Australians who are not fans of test cricket).

No. 4: Wally Hammond selects himself at No. 4. He features at No. 13 in the table of career-best batting ratings (Table 2.7) and the greatest English batsman of his era. Born in 1903, he played cricket for Gloucestershire from 1920 to 1951 and test cricket from 1927 to 1947, captaining his country on 20 occasions. His test career ran parallel with Bradman and the two were great rivals.

Hammond was a prodigious middle-order batsman, a more than useful fast-medium bowler and an outstanding slips fieldsman. He is the 4th highest rating batting all-rounder in test history and ranks 9th overall in Table 2.17. His total number of runs in test cricket (7,249) remained the highest test individual aggregate until overtaken by Colin Cowdery in 1970 and his total of 22 test centuries was the highest by an Englishman until passed by Alastair Cook in 2012. He scored 167 first-class centuries. Only Jack Hobbs and Patsy Hendren have scored more. In 1933, he scored a then world record score of 336 not out against New Zealand, breaking Bradman's record score of 334 set three years earlier. He scored more test runs between the two World Wars than any other player.

No. 5: George Headley has been selected at No.5 and, in this team of outstanding batsmen, only Bradman and Hammond have a higher batting rating in this period. He scored a test century every 4th time he batted, second only to Bradman. Headley was the first of the great West Indian batsmen. He played 22 test matches between 1930 and 1954, 19 of them before World War II. He also represented Jamaica and played professional club cricket in England. The West Indies played relatively few test matches during Headley's career, so his opportunities were limited. In his 19 test matches before the war, he averaged 66.7 with the bat and was the mainstay of the West Indian batting, usually coming in at No. 3.

In first-class cricket, for batsman who played more than 50 innings, his batting average of 69.86 remains the 3rd highest in history (behind Bradman and India's Vijay Merchant). He sits 36th in the list of the highest rating test batsmen of all time (Table 2.7). Headley was born in Panama in 1909 and grew up in Jamaica. He is generally regarded as the yardstick by which all West Indian batsmen are measured. His son Ron and his grandson Dean each played test cricket, Ron for the West Indies and Dean for England.

No. 6: The dashing Denis Compton is at No.6. Born in 1918 in north London, he was an outstanding all-round sportsman, excelling at both cricket and football. He played county cricket for Middlesex from 1936 to 1958 and football for Arsenal from 1936 to 1950. He was a member of Arsenal's FA cup winning side in 1950. However, it is his cricketing performances that are most remembered. Like his countrymen Hobbs, Sutcliffe, Hutton and Hammond, Compton features in the top 12 on the list of players with over 100 first class centuries. He was a dashing batsman and a slow left-arm *Chinaman* bowler, who first played test cricket in 1937, just 83 days past his 19th birthday. He made a promising start in test cricket, with centuries against Australia in 1938 and West Indies in 1939, but like so many others, the Second World War robbed him of six of his best cricketing years.

After the war, the summer of 1947 established Compton as a household name in England and the hero of the war-weary and heavily rationed English public. He scored 4 test centuries against the touring South Africans and thrilled crowds with his good looks and dashing batting style. In that summer, he scored 3,816 first class runs (still a world record) and 18 first class centuries (also still a world record). In the test series against the Australians in 1948 (Bradman's *Invincibles*), he scored 562 runs at an average of 62.44 and was England's best performer with the bat, albeit in a losing side. For all his batting brilliance, he was well known as a poor judge of a run and frequently ran out either himself or his partner. Trevor Bailey famously said of him: "a call for a run from Compton should be treated as no more than a basis for negotiation". He is the 49th highest rating test batsman (Table 2.7).

No. 7: Maurice Tate was England's opening bowler for much of the 1920s and the greatest all-rounder of his day. Born in 1895 in Brighton, he played county cricket for Sussex from 1912 to 1937. He made his test debut in 1924 aged 29, taking a wicket with his very first ball. He first came to notice as a batsman in 1919 when he scored a thousand first-class runs in the season, a feat he was to repeat for the next 10 consecutive seasons. Enjoying only modest success as an off-spin spin bowler, he changed his style to pace bowling with immediate results. He was the first of the great post-war seam bowlers and the 99th highest bowler in test cricket (Table 2.16).

In the mid-1920s, Tate carried a heavy bowling load for Sussex, as well as opening the batting. He seemed tireless, with an easy, seemingly effortless approach to the wicket. In the 1924-25 tour of Australia, he bowled over 2500 balls in the 5 test matches and took 38 wickets at 23.18, still a record number of wickets by an Englishman in a series on Australian pitches. In the 1926-27 season in India and Sri Lanka, he took 116 first-class wickets at 13.78, still a record for the most wickets in a season by an Englishman outside England. In that same season, he scored almost 1200 runs. Tate is one of only five all-rounders to achieve the career double of 20,000 runs and 2,500 wickets in first-class cricket.

No. 8: The wicketkeeper is Australia's Bert Oldfield. Born in Sydney in 1894, Oldfield served in World War 1 and was shot in the leg in 1917. After the war, he played 28 first-class matches in Britain, South Africa and Australia for the Australian Imperial Forces team. Oldfield made his test debut against England in Sydney in 1920. From the Ashes series against England in the 1924-25 season until his retirement from test cricket in 1937, he missed only one other test, the fourth Test of the infamous 1932-33 *Bodyline series* against England. In the 3rd test at the Adelaide Oval, Oldfield was hit in the head off a top edge while facing Harold Larwood. He was carried from the ground unconscious but recovered in time for the fifth Test of the series.

In his 54 Tests for Australia, Oldfield scored 1,427 runs at an average of 22.65. He took 78 catches behind the stumps and made 52 stumpings, the highest number of stumping by any wicketkeeper in test cricket. He played 245 matches in first-class cricket, scoring 6,135 runs at an average of 23.77, taking 399 catches and affecting 263 stumpings.

Oldfield's selection ahead of England's Les Ames is arguable. Ames was an outstanding wicketkeeper/ batsman who played for England from 1929 until 1939 and for Kent from 1926 until 1951. Ames played 47 tests, scoring 2,434 runs at an average of 40.56, with 74 catches behind the stumps and 23 stumpings. He was England's wicketkeeper in the *Bodyline series* against Australia in 1932-33. At 54th in Table 2.18, he rates higher than Oldfield because of his superior batting, but in the greatest batting team of any era, Oldfield's superior record behind the stumps has seen him selected ahead of Ames.

No. 9: Bill Voce was a left-arm fast bowler who played for England in 27 test matches between 1930 and 1947. Born in Nottingham in 1909 to a working-class family, he made his debut for Nottinghamshire as a left-arm spinner. He changed his style to left-arm fast bowling in 1928 but continued to bowl spin when the pitch suited. He had success bowling fast on the hard pitches in the West Indies in 1930 and continued fast bowling from then on.

Voce will forever be remembered, along with Harold Larwood, for his role in what has become known as *bodyline*. After a meeting with the English captain Douglas Jardine in 1930, a plan was hatched to restrict Bradman and so defeat the Australians in the upcoming 1932-33 tour of Australia. Jardine encouraged his fast bowlers to concentrate on bowling at a batsman's body to intimidate and restrict scoring. Voce and Larwood, who both opened the bowling for Nottinghamshire, practiced *leg side theory* (bodyline) over the next two years. Voce took 123 wickets at 19.29 runs per wicket in 1931 and 136 wickets at 16.87 in 1932. Not as fast as Larwood, but taller, he could achieve steep bounce from left arm over the wicket.

Jardine's plan worked. England won the bodyline series 4-1 and Bradman only averaged 56.7, with just 1 century in his 8 innings (well below his usual standards). Voce and Larwood bowled relentlessly at the Australians causing great ill-feeing, many bruises and several more serious injuries. Jardine's side included 4 of the 6 Englishmen selected here in the best team of the era (Sutcliffe, Hammond, Tate and Voce), the next two best eligible bowlers (Hedley Verity and Harold Larwood), one of the three next highest rating batsmen (Eddie Paynter) and the next best wicketkeeper (Les Ames). The Australians selected here in the best 11 of the era (Bradman, Oldfield, Grimmett and O'Reilly) were all on the receiving end of bodyline. *Leg side theory* is clearly seen in the photograph on the next page. The Australian captain Bill Woodfull is seen ducking a short-pitched ball from Larwood in the 4th test in Brisbane in 1933, with six close-in catchers on the leg side waiting for a ball fended off the body.

Jardine's tactics were deplored in Australia, including by some members of his own team, and embarrassed the English establishment. Of the four fast bowlers in the side, Gubby Allen refused to bowl at the body. The rules of the game were changed the following year. The MCC deemed *direct attack* bowling to be unfair and that it was the responsibility of the umpires to identify and stop it. Larwood was the scape goat and, after refusing to sign an apology to the MCC for obeying his captain's directions, never played for England again. The fallout and repercussions after the series also affected Voce's subsequent performances, but he remained an effective bowler and hard-hitting batsman until well after World War 2. Voce is the 139th highest rating test bowler (Table A.2).

Plate 4.2 The Australian captain Bill Woodfull ducks a short-pitched ball from Larwood in the bodyline test in Brisbane 1933. (public domain)

No. 10: Clarrie Grimmett was born in New Zealand and commenced his first-class career in Wellington in 1909. He moved to Australia at the age of 23, but by the time he first played test cricket for Australia in 1925, Grimmett was 33 years old. He played 37 Tests between 1925 and 1936, taking 216 wickets at a bowling average of 24.21. He was the first bowler to take 200 test wickets, and he did it in his 36th test — a record that would stand for 82 years until December 2018 when Pakistan's Yasir Shah took his 200th test wicket in just 33 tests. Grimmett's total of 216 wickets remained a world record until surpassed by Alec Bedser in 1953.

Grimmett was a wonderful leg-spin bowler — the 25th highest rating test bowler (Table 2.16) and the 3rd highest rating leg-spinner. He was the first to develop the *flipper*, a ball with back spin that stays low and skids through often surprising even the best of batsmen. Grimmett took two 5-wicket hauls on his test debut (against England in Sydney in 1925) and another two in his final test (against South Africa in Durban in 1936) at the age of 44. In his last test series, against South Africa in the 1935-36 season, he took 44 wickets at 14.59 runs per wicket. During the 3rd test at Newlands in January 1936, he broke Sydney Barnes' record as the leading wicket taker in test cricket. His test career ended at the end of that series, after taking ten or more wickets in each of his last three tests. Despite continuing success at first-class level, Grimmett never played for Australia again.

No. 11: Grimmett's spinning partner for Australia, Bill ("Tiger") O'Reilly, also selects himself in the top 11. Bill O'Reilly has been retrospectively ranked by the International Cricket Council (ICC) as the best bowler in the world for much of his career (1934-46) and he ranks 40th in Table 2.16. He gripped the ball with two fingers and delivered the ball at close to medium pace, bowling leg breaks, top spinners and googlies with no obvious change of action. With his career interrupted by the war, he played just 27 test matches, taking 144 test wickets at an average of 22.59. His first-class bowling average was 16.60.

O'Reilly was known for his competitiveness, with a hostility that is usually reserved for pace bowlers and that earned him the handle "Tiger". After his retirement as a player, he became a well-respected cricket writer and broadcaster. When he died in 1992, Sir Donald Bradman said that Bill O'Reilly was the greatest bowler he had ever faced or watched.

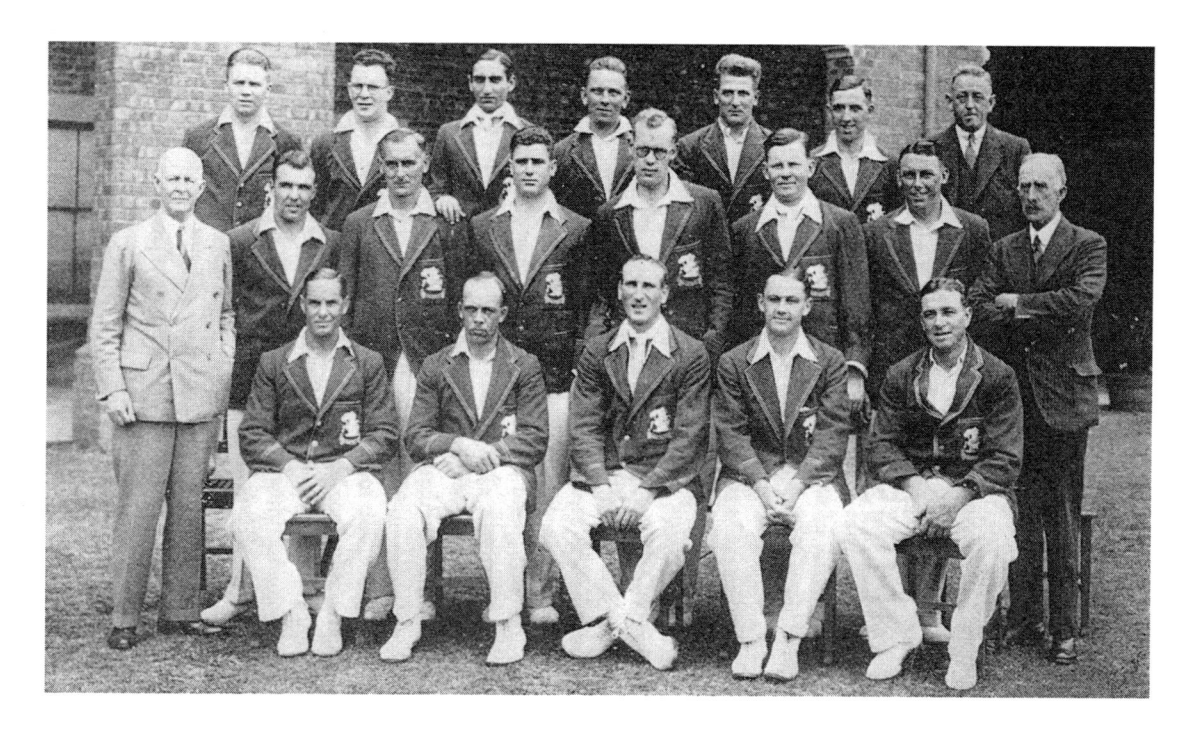

Plate 4.3 The English touring team to Australia in 1932–33 — the Bodyline team. (public domain)

Back row: George Duckworth, Tommy Mitchell, Nawab of Pataudi, Maurice Leyland, Harold Larwood, Eddie Paynter, W. Ferguson (scorer). Middle row: Pelham Warner (co-manager), Les Ames, Hedley Verity, Bill Voce, Bill Bowes, Freddie Brown, Maurice Tate, R. C. N. Pet (co-manager). Front row: Herbert Sutcliffe, Bob Wyatt, Douglas Jardine, Gubby Allen, Walter Hammond.

Next Best Batsmen:

The three most highly rated batsmen who just missed selection were Jack Hobbs, South Africa's Dudley Nourse and England's Eddie Paynter.

[1] Arthur Dudley Nourse played 26 tests before 1950 averaging an impressive 58.79 with the bat. He was the son of a successful South African test cricketer, Arthur William "Dave" Nourse, who played 45 consecutive tests between 1902 and 1924. Dudley played first-class cricket for Natal from 1931-52 and test cricket from 1934 to 1951, captaining his country in 15 test matches. He was an aggressive back-foot batsman, stocky in build and a strong hooker and cutter of the ball. He scored his maiden test century against Australia in Johannesburg in 1935, an impressive 231, and in the famous 10-day "timeless" test at Durban in 1939 he took 6 hours to score a century. He ranks 61st in Table 2.7

[2] Eddie Paynter was a gritty left-hand batsman who only played 20 tests in the 1930s. Born in 1901 in Lancashire, he played first-class cricket for that county from 1926 to 1945. He was a relatively late starter

who performed better in tests towards the end of his career in his late 30s. His test career batting average is 59.23, higher than any other Englishman, with the exception of Herbert Sutcliffe. In his seven tests against Australia, he averaged an impressive 84.43. He averaged 61.33 in his five innings in the bodyline series. In his final 11 tests played in 1938 and 1939, he averaged 75.67. In the series against Australia in 1938, he averaged 101.75 scoring 216 not out at Trent Bridge, a then record score in Ashes tests in England. The Second World War brought an abrupt end to Paynter's test career. He ranks 52nd in Table 2.7.

Next Best Bowlers:

The next three most highly rated bowlers are England's Hedley Verity, Gubby Allen and Harold Larwood.

[1] Hedley Verity was the third ranked bowler in the era, but being a left-arm orthodox bowler, there was no place for a 3rd spinner in the top 11. Verity played for Yorkshire and England in the 1930s. Starting as a left-arm medium pace bowler in the Lancashire League in the late 1920s, he changed his style to spin bowling early in 1929. By the beginning of World War 2, he had taken almost 2000 first-class wickets at an average of just 14.90. He took 5 wickets in an innings 164 times. In 1932 against Nottinghamshire, he took all 10 wickets in an innings for just 10 runs. His bowling helped Yorkshire win the county championship seven times in the 1930s. In his test career, he played 40 matches took 144 wickets at an average of 23.37. Verity is the 75th highest rating test bowler (Table 2.16). He was successful in the bodyline series, taking 8 wickets in the 5th test in Sydney. At Lords in the 2nd test against Australia in 1934, he took 15 wickets for 104 runs, including the prized wicket of Bradman in both innings. Verity dismissed Bradman 8 times in test cricket, more than any other bowler. During World War 2, Verity saw active service in the British Army in India, the Middle East, Egypt and Italy. He was killed in the invasion of Sicily in 1943.

[2] George "Gubby" Allen was a fast bowler and effective lower-order batsman who played for Middlesex (1921- 51), Cambridge University (1922-23) and England (1930-48). Born in Sydney, Australia in 1902, he grew up in England. He played first-class cricket rather irregularly through the 1920s due to work commitments but was eventually selected to play for England in 1930. He met with little success in his first few tests but had a successful tour of Australia in the bodyline series of 1932-33. He took 21 wickets at 28.24 but refused to follow Jardine's instructions to intimidate the opposition and he left *bodyline* bowling to Larwood and Voce. Allen was appointed England captain for the 1936-37 tour of Australia, winning the first two tests but losing the series 3-2. After World War 2, he led England in a final test series in the West Indies in 1947-48 at the age of 45. After cricket, he became an influential and successful cricket administrator. He was chairman of selectors for England from 1955 to 1961 and became MCC President in 1963. He was knighted for his services to cricket in 1986. Allen ranks 156th in Table A.2.

[3] Harold Larwood was a faster and more intimidating bowler than either Allen or Voce, and he was Jardine's most devastating attacking weapon in the bodyline series. He played first-class cricket for Nottinghamshire from 1924 to 1938 and test cricket for England from 1926 to 1933. He took 1427 first-class wickets at a bowling average of 17.51. His test career was cut short at the end of the bodyline tour after just 21 matches when he refused to apologise for following Jardine's instructions. Larwood's treatment by the cricketing establishment when he returned to England after the tour is now widely regarded as disgraceful.

Denis Compton considered Larwood and Voce to be the most accurate fast-bowling combination he ever faced, and that Larwood was the fastest. Jack Hobbs is said to have considered Larwood not just the fastest but also the most accurate bowler he had seen. Larwood emigrated to Australia in 1950 and lived there for the next 45 years. At the age of 88 in 1993, two years before his death, he was awarded an MBE for services to cricket. The UK newspaper *Today* recalling his treatment in 1933 commented: "At last the ruling classes honour the man who carried the can for their savage arrogance".

Highest Rating All-Rounders:

Wally Hammond is the most highly rated all-rounder of the era followed by Australia's Jack Gregory and England's Frank Woolley. Gregory played first-class cricket for New South Wales and Australia from 1920 until 1928, when a knee injury ended his career. He spearheaded the Australian bowling attack for most of the 1920s and was an accurate and often hostile fast bowler. He was also an aggressive left-hand batsman, who scored a test century against South Africa in 1921 off just 67 balls. This remained the fastest test century until 1985 when West Indian Viv Richard scored a ton off just 56 balls. Gregory is the 57th highest rating test all-rounder (Table 2.17).

Frank Woolley played test cricket both before and after World War 1 and his performances were discussed in Chapter 3. Although he scored more than 3,000 test runs and took more than 80 wickets, his performances in test cricket pale compared to his performances in first-class cricket. In a first-class career for Kent and England from 1906 to 1938, he scored 58,959 runs at an average of 40.77, including 145 centuries, and he took 2,066 wickets at a bowling average of 19.8. No other player has scored over 55,000 first-class runs and taken over 2,000 first-class wickets. He is the 33rd highest rating test all-rounder (Table 2.17).

Highest rating wicketkeepers:

Besides Bert Oldfield, the 3 other eligible wicketkeepers are England's Les Ames, Godfrey Evans and George Duckworth.

Evans' test career started in 1946, and he went on to be the most highly rated wicketkeeper in the 1950s. His performances are discussed in more detail in Chapter 5.

Les Ames was a superb wicketkeeper batsman for England between his test debut in 1929 and his final test in 1939. He played first-class cricket for Kent from 1926 to 1951. He scored 2,434 test runs at 40.57, including 8 test centuries. He is the only wicketkeeper batsman to score 100 first-class centuries, and he still holds the record for the most runs (120) in a single session before lunch in a test match. In this extremely strong batting side, Oldfield's performances behind the stumps keeping to Grimmett and O'Reilly have earned him the wicketkeeping duties, but Ames can be considered unlucky to miss selection.

George Duckworth was wicketkeeper for England in 24 tests between 1924 and 1936 and the wicketkeeper for Lancashire between 1923 and 1938. He still holds the record for the most wicketkeeping dismissals (925) for Lancashire. His career overlapped with that of Les Ames, who was a much better batsman, so his test opportunities were limited.

Plate 4.4 The Australian squad for the 1930 tour of England (public domain)

Back row: Kelly WL (Manager), Jackson A, Wall TW, a'Beckett EL, Hornibrook PM, Hurwood A, Grimmett CV, Howard T, (Treasurer). Middle row: Fairfax A, Ponsford WH, Richardson VY, Woodfull WM (captain), Kippax AF, Bradman DG, Walker CV. Front row: McCabe SJ, Oldfield WAS.

Table 4.1 Best World team 1920-1949 (inclusive) — Batting Performances.

Players	Country	Batting style	Matches	Innings	Not outs	100s/ 50s/0s	Highest score	Runs scored	Batting average	Strike rate	Batting rating
1. Sutcliffe, H	England	right	54	84	9	16/23/2	194	4555	60.73	56.77	144.7
2. Hutton, L	England	right	41	72	5	11/17/3	364	3788	56.54	50	134.0
3. Bradman, DG	Australia	right	52	80	10	29/13/7	334	6996	99.94	54.95	310.0
4. Hammond, WR	England	right	85	140	16	22/24/4	336	7249	58.46	49.53	152.0
5. Headley, GA	W Indies	right	21	38	4	10/5/2	270	2173	63.91	50	146.4
6. Compton, DCS	England	right	36	60	8	13/12/2	208	3132	60.23	50.22	137.5
7. Tate, MW	England	right	39	52	5	1/5/5	100	1198	25.49	50	30.4
8. Oldfield, WAS	Australia	right	54	80	17	0/4/9	65	1427	22.65	43.79	24.9
9. Voce, W	England	right	27	38	15	0/1/6	66	308	13.39	50	8.1
10. Grimmett, CV	Australia	right	37	50	10	0/1/7	50	557	13.93	39.90	8.3
11. O'Reilly, WJ	Australia	left	27	39	7	0/1/6	56	410	12.81	46.43	7.6
										Total	1,103.9

Next Batters:

Nourse, AD	S Africa	right	26	49	7	8/12/3	120	2469	58.79	50	128.0
Hobbs, JB	England	right	33	53	1	10/12/1	211	2945	56.63	49.03	125.3
Paynter, E	England	right	20	31	5	4/7/3	243	1540	59.23	50	120.0

Table 4.2 Best World team 1920-1949 (inclusive) — Bowling Performances.

The team

Players	Country	Overs	Balls	Maids.	Runs against	Bowl style	Wickets	5w/10w	Best	Bowl average	Strike rate	Econ rate	Bowling rating
1. Sutcliffe, H	England	\multicolumn{11}{c}{Did not bowl}	-
2. Hutton, L	England	\multicolumn{11}{c}{Less than 100 overs}	-
3. Bradman, DG	Australia	\multicolumn{11}{c}{Less than 100 overs}	-
4. Hammond, WR	England	1,278	7,978	300	3,138	RAMF	83	2/0	5/36	37.81	95.99	2.36	60.1
5. Headley, GA	W Indies												-
6. Compton, DCS	England	314	2,132	60	1,031	LAWS	20	1/0	5/70	51.55	106.6	2.90	28.8
7. Tate, MW	England	1,982	12,541	581	4,055	RAMF	155	7/1	6/42	26.16	80.79	1.94	101.8
8. Oldfield, WAS	Australia	Wicketkeeper					Less than 100 overs						-
9. Voce, W	England	991	6,356	211	2,733	LAF	98	3/2	7/70	27.89	64.90	2.58	89.9
10. Grimmett, CV	Australia	2,408	14,531	736	5,231	RAL	216	21/7	7/40	24.22	67.19	2.16	141.7
11. O'Reilly, WJ	Australia	1,588	10,012	585	3,254	RAL	144	11/3	7/54	27.60	69.61	1.95	125.9
												Total	548.2

Next Bowlers:

Verity, H	England	1,692	11,202	604	3,510	LAO	144	5/2	8/42	24.38	77.59	1.88	108.8
Allen, GOB	England	688	4,392	116	2,379	RAF	81	5/1	7/80	29.37	54.15	3.25	86.6
Larwood, H	England	828	4,971	167	2,212	RAF	78	4/1	6/32	28.36	63.71	2.67	85.5

Table 4.3 Performances of the best all-rounders 1920 to 1949, inclusive.

Player	Country	No. of tests	Years played	Batting style	Runs scored	Batting average	Batting rating	Bowling style	Wickets taken	Bowl avge	Bowl rating	All-rounder Rating
Hammond, WB	Eng	85	1927-47	right	7,249	58.46	152.0	RAMF	83	37.81	60.1	162.2
Gregory, JM	Aust	24	1920-28	right	1,146	36.97	56.7	RAF	85	31.15	73.8	122.0
Woolley, FE	Eng	42	1920-34	right	2,346	37.84	66.6	LAO	44	43.00	48.6	106.2

Table 4.4 Wicketkeeping performances 1920 to 1949, inclusive.

Player	Country	No. of tests	Years played	Batting style	Runs scored	Batting average	Batting rating	Catches	Stumpings	Total dismissals	Wicket-keeper rating
Ames, LEG	Eng	47	1929-39	right	2,434	40.57	71.3	72	23	95	78.0
Oldfield, WAS	Aust	54	1920-37	right	1,427	22.65	24.9	78	52	130	68.1
Evans, TG	Eng	27	1946-49	right	746	22.61	21.0	48	18	66	59.6
Duckworth, G	Eng	24	1924-36	right	234	14.63	8.9	45	15	60	54.4

Note: The ratings are determined from the number of tests played as wicketkeeper

Chapter 5
The Best World Team — 1950 to 1959

In the decade of the 1950s (1950 to 1959, inclusive), 164 test matches were played (almost as many as in the previous 30 years). England played in 83 of them, Australia in 57, South Africa in 35, West Indies in 48, New Zealand in 32, India in 44 and Pakistan in 29. The most highly rated team for this decade is shown below. Of the first 11 players selected, 5 are English, 3 are West Indian, two are Pakistani and one is Australian. The batting is not nearly as strong as for the team selected before 1950 in Chapter 4, but the bowling attack is stronger.

The highest rating team of the 1950s

Batting Order:	Country	No. of tests	Period	Batting Rating	Bowling Rating
1. Hutton, L	England	38	1950-55	121.8	-
2. Hanif Mohammad	Pakistan	27	1952-59	86.9	-
3. Harvey, RN	Australia	59	1950-59	113.5	-
4. Weekes, EDC	West Indies	39	1950-58	116.7	-
5. Walcott, CL	West Indies	33	1950-58	141.8	39.1
6. Sobers, GStA	West Indies	27	1954-59	121.2	48.8
7. Evans, TG	England	64	1950-59	20.4	WK
8. Fazal Mahmood	Pakistan	26	1952-59	11.4	130.6
9. Laker, J.C	England	38	1950-59	7.8	139.7
10. Lock, GAR	England	31	1952-59	6.3	127.9
11. Bedser, AV	England	28	1950-55	5.3	136.8
			Total	753.1	622.9

Notes: 1. Batting and bowling statistics are given in Tables 5.1 and 5.2, respectively.
2. Of the 10 eras considered in this book, the team of the 1950s has the 9th highest batting rating and the 7th highest bowling rating.

The win/loss/draw results for each of the participating countries during the 1950s are shown below:

Country	Win/Loss/Draw results versus							
	England	Australia	South Africa	West Indies	New	India	Pakistan	All matches
England	-	7/10/8	8/5/2	6/5/3	8/0/3	9/1/4	1/1/2	39/22/22
Australia	10/7/8	-	7/2/4	7/1/2	Did not play	3/1/1	2/1/1	29/12/16
South Africa	5/8/2	2/7/4	-	Did not play	5/0/2	Did not play	Did not play	12/15/8
West Indies	5/6/3	1/7/2	Did not play	-	4/1/1	4/0/6	4/3/1	18/17/13
New Zealand	0/8/3	Did not play	0/5/2	1/4/1	-	0/2/3	0/2/1	1/21/10
India	1/9/4	1/3/1	Did not play	0/4/6	2/0/3	-	2/1/7	6/17/21
Pakistan	1/1/2	1/2/1	Did not play	3/4/1	2/0/1	1/2/7	-	8/9/12

Australia was the most successful national team, winning 51% of its matches, losing 21% and drawing 28%. The next most successful teams were England, winning 47%, losing 26.5% and drawing 26.5% and the West Indies, winning 38%, losing 35% and drawing 27%. With 69% of all matches being won and lost and only 31% drawn, the cricket was more attractive than in previous years (40.5% of matches were drawn in the period 1920-1949). Despite the Australian team's success in the 1950s, only one Australian rated highly enough for selection in the World 11. Also surprising is England's high representation in the side.

Len Hutton was the highest rating opening batsman in the decade and is the only player to earn selection in the two world teams before and after 1950. The other specialist opener is Hanif Mohammad of Pakistan. The next four batsmen are Australia's Neil Harvey, and the West Indian trio of Everton Weekes, Clyde Walcott and Garfield (Garry) Sobers. Unlucky to miss selection are England's Peter May and West Indian Frank Worrell, who both rated more highly than Hanif Mohammad but were not specialist openers. Godfrey Evans of England is the wicketkeeper, Pakistan's Fazal Mahmood and England's Alec Bedser were the standout quicks of the decade, and the spinners are England's Jim Laker and Tony Lock. The next best bowlers are South African Hugh Tayfield, Englishmen John Wardle and Fred Trueman, and the Australian pair of Alan Davidson and Richie Benaud.

The batting and bowling performances of the world team of the 1950s are presented in Tables 5.1 and 5.2, respectively, and the statistics of the top all-rounders and the three best wicketkeepers in the decade are provided in Table 5.3 and 5.4, respectively. The statistics for the best national teams and eligible players are presented in Appendix F (Tables F.1 to F.7). By comparison with the ratings of the world teams in other eras, the team of the 1950s is not a particularly strong one. Its batting rating is the second lowest, with only the team before World War 1 having a lower rating, and its bowling rating is the fourth lowest of any era.

Of the players who played 20 or more test matches in the 1950s, 22 have been subsequently inducted into the ICC's Cricket Hall of Fame. They are:

England: Len Hutton, Denis Compton, Alec Bedser, Jim Laker, Tom Graveney, Peter May, Brian Statham, Fred Trueman and Colin Cowdrey.
Australia: Ray Lindwall, Keith Miller, Arthur Morris, Neil Harvey, Richie Benaud and Alan Davidson.
West Indies: Clyde Walcott, Everton Weekes, Frank Worrell, Rohan Kanhai and Garfield Sobers.
Pakistan: Hanif Mohammad.
India: Vinoo Mankad

The Top 11 Players:

No. 1: Len Hutton's test career began in 1937 and ended in 1955. His performances towards the end of his career in the 1950s were as good as they had ever been, maintaining a batting average of 56.84 in his mid to late 30s. However, his batting in the 1950s was more defensive and more cautious than it had been before the war, perhaps due to changes he was forced to make to compensate for a serious arm injury, but more likely due to the responsibility of opening the batting in what were relatively weak Yorkshire and England teams in the years after the war. He was essentially a back-foot player with a rock-solid defense. Hutton was the first professional cricketer to be appointed as captain of England. He captained England in 23 tests from 1952 to 1955, winning 11 of them. In the early 1950s, Hutton was widely regarded as the finest batsman in the world. He ranks 18th in the list of the most highly rated test batsmen of all time (Table 2.7). In the All-time World Team selected by ESPNcricinfo in 2010 by a jury of former test cricket captains and cricket historians, Hutton was selected to open the innings with Jack Hobbs.

No. 2: Hutton's opening partner is Hanif Mohammad, the outstanding Pakistani batsman of his day. Hanif was born in Junagadh in 1936 and played 55 tests for Pakistan between 1952 and 1969. He was a member of an amazingly successful Pakistani cricketing family. His elder brother Wazir played 20 tests, his younger brothers Mushtaq and Sadiq played 57 and 41 tests, respectively, and his son Shoaib played 45 tests for Pakistan. Another brother (Raees), four nephews and a grandson have all had first-class cricket careers in Pakistan. At his death in 2016, Hanif was described as the original *Little Master*. He was the first Pakistani batsman to score a triple century in a test match, in a marathon innings of over 800 minutes against the West Indies in Bridgetown in 1958. It is still the longest innings in test cricket history. He once scored 20 runs off 233 balls, in what is considered to be the slowest 20 of all time. He could also score more quickly, and in 1958-59, he passed Don Bradman's record first-class score of 452 by making 499 for Karachi against Bahawalpur. He was unfortunately run out attempting to get to 500. This remained the world record until passed by Brian Lara in 1994. In 2009, Hanif was one of 3 Pakistani players in the first group to be inducted into the ICC's Hall of Fame, the other two being Imran Khan and Javed Miandad. Hanif is the 106th highest rating test batsman (Table A.1).

No. 3: Neil Harvey was a stylish, left-handed Australian batsman, admired for his superb timing and his controlled aggression. He was also an outstanding cover fieldsman. In total, he played 79 tests for Australia between 1948 and 1963, scoring 6,149 test runs at an averaging 48.42 runs per innings. After making 153 against India in his second test, to become the youngest Australian ever to make a test century, he was selected in Bradman's Australian side (dubbed "The Invincibles") that toured England undefeated in 1948. He was Australia's best batsman throughout the 1950s and vice-captain under Richie Benaud from 1957 until his retirement in 1963.

Harvey grew up in Melbourne in a cricketing family. Three of his five brothers played for Victoria and his eldest brother Merv also played test cricket for Australia. Harvey played first-class cricket for Victoria from 1946 to 1957 and for New South Wales from 1958 until 1963, scoring 21,699 first-class runs at an average of 50.93. At his retirement, he had scored more runs and made more centuries in test cricket than any other Australian, except for Don Bradman. He is ranked 55th in the list of most highly rated test batsmen (see Table 2.7).

Nos. 4, 5 and 6: The remaining three top-order batsmen are the West Indian trio, Everton Weekes, Clyde Walcott and Garfield Sobers. All three have been knighted for their services to cricket. Together with Frank Worrell, who just missed selection in the top team of the 1950s and who was one of the four leading all-rounders in the decade, Weekes and Walcott form a trio of outstanding batsmen from Barbados known as the "Three Ws". The three were all born within 18 months of each other (from August 1924 to January 1926), all within a mile of Kensington Oval in Barbados, and they all made their test debuts against England in 1948.

Weekes debuted at his beloved Kensington Oval, where today a stand is named in honour of the "Three Ws". In 1948, in his first year of test cricket Everton Weekes set a still current world record by scoring 5 test centuries in consecutive innings and, in his next two innings (in 1949), he scored 90 and 56, making him the only player in the 20th century to pass 50 in 7 consecutive innings. By the end of the West Indies tour of the subcontinent in 1949, Weekes had a batting average of 82.46 and had scored 1,000 test runs in his first 12innings. No other player has reached this milestone in fewer innings, although Herbert Sutcliffe of England also reached the target in his 12th innings.

In the West Indies' next test series, against England in England, Weekes scored 338 test runs at an average of 56.33 and, in all first-class matches on that tour, he scored 2,310 runs at an average of 79.65, including the only ever triple century by a West Indian on tour of England. Weekes was a hard-hitting, stylish batsman, masterful on both sides of the wicket, and an excellent fieldsman, both in the covers and in the slips. In his 48 tests, he scored 4,455 runs at an average of 58.62 (the 8th highest average in test cricket history). He ranks 34rd in the list of the most highly rated batsmen of all time (Table 2.7).

Clyde Walcott played 44 test matches for the West Indies between 1948 and 1960 scoring 3,798 runs at a batting average of 56.69, the 14th highest average of all time (see Table 2.2). He first came to notice at the age of 20 when he scored 314 not out for Barbados against Trinidad as part of an unbroken stand of 574 for the fourth wicket with his school friend Frank Worrell (255 not out) — a world record partnership in first-class cricket that remains a record in the West Indies. Although Walcott was a big man weighing over 15 stone and standing over 6 feet tall, he was agile, and for his first 15 tests, he kept wickets. He retained his place in the side as a specialist batsman when a back injury forced him to give up the gloves. He was a fine stroke-player, mainly off the back foot. In 1950, he scored 168 not out at Lords to help the Windies win its first test against England and then its first series against England. In 1954, he made 698 runs in the series against England in the Caribbean, and in 1955, he made 827 runs against an Australian bowling attack that included Lindwall, Miller and Benaud. In that series, he became the first batsman to score 5 centuries in a test series, scoring a century in both innings in both the 2nd and 5th tests. He ranks 41st in the list of the most highly rated batsmen of all time (Table 2.7).

Walcott retired from playing Test cricket in 1960. He was President of the Guyana Cricket Board of Control from 1968 to 1970, and then vice-president of the Barbados Cricket Association. He was chairman of the West Indies selectors from 1973 to 1988 and managed the West Indies teams that won the Cricket World Cup in 1975 and 1979. He was president of the West Indies Cricket Board from 1988 to 1993. He became chairman of the International Cricket Council in 1993, the first non-English person and the first black man to hold the position. In 1997, he was in charge of the ICC Code of Conduct, and oversaw the investigations into allegations of match fixing.

Sir Garfield Sobers, also known as Gary Sobers, is regarded by many as the game's greatest ever batting all-rounder and is selected at No.6 — the only left-handed batsman in the team. Like the "Three Ws", Weekes, Worrell and Walcott, Sobers was born in Barbados. He played 93 test matches for the West Indies between 1954 and 1974, making his test debut at the age of 17. He scored 8,032 test runs with a batting average of 57.78. In the history of test cricket, 36 great batsmen have scored more than 8,000 runs. Sobers has a higher batting average than all of them. Of the batsmen with over 5,000 runs, only Don Bradman, Wally Hammond and Ken Barrington have higher batting averages. He is the 11th highest rating test batsman (Table 2.7). Sobers did not score a century in his first 16 test matches but made up for his relatively slow start with 365 not out in his 17th test (against Pakistan at Sabina Park, Jamaica in 1958), breaking Len Hutton's world record individual score. Sobers' score remained the world record until 1994 when fellow countryman Brian Lara scored 375.

In addition to his batting, Sobers could bowl — left arm medium pace, left arm orthodox and left arm Chinaman. In his test career, he took 235 wickets at an average of 34.04 runs per wicket. Originally selected in test cricket as a bowler (batting at No. 9 in his first test), his batting improved remarkably through the 1950s (averaging 56.74 by the end of the decade), but his bowling declined ending the decade with a bowling average of 46.78 (compared to 32.30 in the 1960s and 31.50 in the 1970s). He sits 2nd on the list of the highest rating all-rounders in test history (Table 2.17).

No. 7: England's Godfrey Evans was one of three excellent contenders for the wicketkeeping role in the 1950s. Although rating 3rd in Table 5.3, he was selected ahead of Australia's Gil Langley and South Africa's John Waite, because the bowling attack in the team was predominantly English and he took more wickets and played more matches in the 1950s than any other wicketkeeper. Evans played for Kent between 1939 and 1966 and for England from 1946 to 1959. After one season with Kent in 1939, his career was interrupted by World War 2 and he lost the opportunity to play test cricket until 1946. He played 91 test matches between 1946 and 1959, taking 173 catches and affecting 46 stumpings in 175 innings as wicketkeeper. Evans' 46 dismissals by stumping is the second highest number in history, behind Bert Oldfield. With the bat, he scored 2,439 runs at 20.50. He was the first wicketkeeper to make 200 test dismissals, and he is the 47th highest rating test wicketkeeper of all time (see Table 2.18).

No. 8: Fazal Mahmood was a right-arm fast-medium bowler who played a significant role in the new nation of Pakistan obtaining test cricket status and was the spearhead of Pakistan's attack in that country's first ever test series — against India in 1952. He was born in Lahore in 1927 and played in 34 tests between 1952 and 1962 taking 139 wickets at a bowling average of 24.71. He began his first-class career at the age of 17 in 1944 playing for Northern India and he was selected for India's first tour of Australia in 1947. However, Pakistan was granted independence before the tour began, and being a devout Muslim, Fazal decided to withdraw and concentrate on playing for his new country.

Fazal Mahmood holds a unique place in the history of Pakistani test cricket. In Pakistan's second ever test, and its first ever test victory, Fazal took 12 wickets for 94 runs against India. In 1954, in Pakistan's first ever test victory over England, Fazal took 12 wickets for 99 runs and, in 1956, in Pakistan's first ever test against Australia, Fazel rattled the Australians taking 13 wickets for 114 runs and bowling Pakistan to victory. In Australia's first innings, only the two opening bowlers were used, Fazal and Khan Mohammad, who both bowled unchanged. Fazal took 6 for 34 in 27 straight overs. In 1959 against the West Indies in Dhaka, he took 12 wickets for 100 runs making him the first player ever to take 12 or more wickets in a match against four different countries. He ranks 48th in the list of the most highly rated bowlers in test history (Table 2.16).

No. 9: English off-spin bowler Jim Laker is at No. 9. After serving in North Africa during World War 2, Laker played 46 test matches between 1948 and 1959, taking 193 wickets with a bowling average of 21.25. In first-class cricket, playing most of his career for Surrey, he took 1,944 wickets at 18.41. He was an integral part of the Surrey side that won seven successive County Championships from 1952 to 1958. Laker has the best bowling figures for a single test match in the history of the game. Against the Australians at Old Trafford in the 4th test of the 1956 Ashes series (known forevermore as *Laker's test*), he took 9 for 37 of 16.4 overs in the Australian first innings and then followed with 10 for 53 off 51.2 overs in the second innings to win the match. No other player has taken 19 wickets in a test match (or 18 wickets in a match for that matter). He was the first bowler to take 10 wickets in a test innings (only ever repeated twice — once by Anil Kumble of India against Pakistan in 1999 and once by New Zealand's Ajaz Patel against India in 2021). Laker's 10/53 remains the best-ever bowling figures in a test innings. In that same series against Australia in 1956, Laker took 46 wickets — the most wickets by any bowler in an Ashes series. He ranks 32nd in the list of the most highly rated test bowlers (Table 2.16). After his retirement, he had a successful career as a cricket commentator for both ITV and BBC television from the 1960s until his death in 1986 at the age of 64.

No. 10: Left-arm orthodox spinner Tony Lock had a very successful bowling partnership for England with Jim Laker and earned his place as the second spinner in the best world team for the 1950s. Lock made his test debut against India in 1952 and played his final test in 1968 against the West Indies. In total, he took 174 test wickets at a bowling average of 25.58. The most notable was probably his dismissal of the Australian opener Jim Burke caught by Colin Cowdrey at Old Trafford in 1956 in *Laker's test* when Jim Laker took the other 19 Australian wickets. In a long first-class career for Surrey, Western Australia and Leicestershire, he took 2,844 wickets at 19.23 runs per wicket and holds the dubious honour of being the only player in history to score 10,000 first-class runs without ever making a century. He was an outstanding short-leg fieldsman, taking 831 catches in first-class cricket — the third highest by a fielder in history behind Frank Woolley and W.G. Grace. In the 5-test series against New Zealand in 1958 in England, Lock took 35 wickets at an average of just 7.26 and followed this up against the same opponents in the 2-test series in 1959 with 13 wickets at 8.69. He ranks 57th in the list of the highest rating bowlers of all time (Table 2.16).

No. 11: Sir Alec Bedser was an outstanding right-arm medium-fast bowler who opened the bowling for England in the decade after World War 2. He played 51 test matches between 1946 and 1955 taking 236 wickets at 24.90 runs per wicket. He was at the peak of his career in the 1950s when he took 147 wickets at 19.84. He became test cricket's highest wicket taker when he passed Clarrie Grimmett's record in 1953. Bedser held the record for the next decade until 1963 when fellow countryman Brian Statham took his 237th wicket. Both Alec and his twin brother Eric played first-class cricket for Surrey from 1939 until 1960.

Bedser was a remarkably accurate in-swing bowler who could bowl a lethal in-swinging leg break at pace. He took 11 wickets in each of his first two test matches (against India in 1946). He bowled Don Bradman for a duck in the Adelaide test match in 1946 with an in-swinger that pitched on the leg stump and cut sharply off the pitch taking the middle and off stumps. Bradman described that ball as the finest to ever take his wicket. Despite England's 4-1 loss in the 1950-1951 Ashes Series in Australia, Bedser had a successful series taking 30 wickets at an average of 16.06. In the 5th tests in Melbourne, he bowled England to victory taking 10 for 105 in the match and ending Australia's run of 26 tests without loss. In the return series against the Australians in England in 1953, he helped England regain the ashes taking 39 wickets in the series at 17.48 runs per wicket. His career statistics place him 41st on the list of the most highly rated bowlers of all time (Table 2.16).

After retiring from cricket as a player, Bedser served as a national selector for England from 1962 until 1985 and was the chairman of selectors from 1968 until 1981. He was knighted for his services to cricket in 1997.

Next Best Batsmen:

The next four most highly rated batsmen in the decade were England's Peter May, Australian Lindsay Hassett, West Indian Frank Worrell and South African Jackie McGlew.

[1] Sir Peter May was the most consistent and highest scoring English batsman in the 1950s in both first-class and test cricket. He played domestic cricket for Surrey, the County Champions for seven years in a row in the 1950s, the last two under May's leadership. He scored a century in his test debut in 1951 against South Africa at Headingley. In 1955, May took over the English captaincy from Len Hutton after England's successful defence of the Ashes in Australia in 1954-55 and he went on to captain his country in 41 test matches, with a win/loss/draw ratio as captain of 20/10/12. His test batting average as captain was 54.03, significantly higher than his career average of 46.77. May's batting technique was straight out of the textbook. He played with the straightest of bats and had a complete range of strokes. In 1957 at Edgbaston, he made 285 not out, putting on a 3rd wicket partnership of 411 with Colin Cowdrey (154) to save the game — still an English record partnership for any wicket. He sits 78th in the list of the highest rating batsmen of all time (Table 2.7). Peter May was inducted posthumously into the ICC Cricket Hall of Fame in 2009.

[2] Sir Frank Worrell was a stylish right-handed batsman, and a left-arm seam bowler. He is the 77th highest rating batsman (Table 2.7) and the 31st highest rating test all-rounder (Table 2.17). He was the 3rd highest rating all-rounder in the 1950s (Table 5.3). He was born in Barbados on 1st August 1924, 6 months before Everton Weekes and 18 months before Clyde Walcott. He was the first black man to captain the West Indies in a full test series, thereby ending the colour barrier that had existed until then in West Indian cricket. Worrell was a successful captain and a fine batsman (averaging 49.49 runs per innings in 51 tests). He twice participated in first-class cricket partnerships of over 500 runs. Against England at Trent Bridge in 1950, he made his highest test score of 261. In 1967, just three years after his last test, Frank Worrell died of leukaemia aged 42. The Frank Worrell Trophy is awarded to the winning side in every West Indies-Australia test series since the 1960–61 series in Australia, where Worrell was praised for his attacking cricket and his sportsmanship.

[3] Lindsay Hassett began his test career in 1938 and played his final test in 1953 at the age of 40. In total, he played 43 tests scoring 3,073 runs at an average of 46.56. He is the 121st highest rating test batsman (Table A.1). Like many others, his career was interrupted by World War 2. Hassett enlisted in the Second Australian Imperial Force and served in North Africa and New Guinea. He was vice-captain under Don Bradman for three series after the war (including the "Invincibles" tour of England in 1948) and took over the captaincy of Australia in 1949 until his retirement. He captained his country in 24 tests, winning 14 and losing only 4. A small man, Hassett was admired for his stylish stroke play, quick footwork and determination. After retirement, Hassett became a well- respected cricket commentator for the Australian Broadcasting Commission on radio and was popular for his dry sense of humour and his insightful comments on the game.

[4] Derrick John 'Jackie' McGlew was mainstay of South African batting in the 1950s. As a schoolboy, he was outstanding at both cricket and rugby but went on to excel at cricket. He played first-class cricket for Natal and, in 34 tests for South Africa between 1951 and 1962, he scored 2,440 runs at 42.07. He is the 174th highest rating test batsman (Table A.1). He was a gritty and stubborn right-hand batsman who was difficult to dislodge. He made his test debut against England in 1951 and was made vice-captain for the series in Australia in 1952-53. He scored an unbeaten 255 against New Zealand at the Basin Reserve in 1953, which was at that time the highest ever score by a South African batsman. Despite gaining a reputation for slow scoring, he was named a Wisden Cricketer of the Year in 1956. Wisden noted that his dour batting was a contrast to his lively fielding in the covers. McGlew captained South Africa in 14 tests between 1955 and 1962, winning 4 and losing 6, with 4 draws.

Next Best Bowlers:

The bowlers who just missed selection, were England's John Wardle and Fred Trueman, South African Hugh Tayfield and Australians Alan Davidson and Richie Benaud.

[1] Hugh Tayfield was born in Durban in 1929 and played domestic first-class cricket for Natal, debuting as a 17-year-old in 1946. He was an off-spin bowler who played 37 test matches for South Africa between 1949 and 1960 taking 170 wickets at 25.91 runs per wicket. He took 7 for 23 at Durban against Australia in 1950 and bowled South Africa to victory against England at Johannesburg in 1957. In that match, he took 9 for 113 in England's second innings, bowling unchanged on the last day. In that same series against England at Durban, he bowled 137 consecutive deliveries without conceding a run, a test and first-class cricket record that still stands today. He ranks 59th in the list of most highly rated test bowlers (see Table 2.16).

[2] Johnny Wardle was a left-arm orthodox spinner for Yorkshire and England. Between 1948 and 1957, he played 28 test matches taking 102 wickets at an average of 20.39, including 12 wickets against South Africa at Newlands in 1957. He was England's 3rd highest rating spin bowler for the decade but, playing for England at the same time as Lock (also a left-arm orthodox bowler) and Laker, his opportunities were limited. An outstanding bowler, his career test bowling average is the lowest of any spin bowler since World War 1 and he is the 49th highest rating test bowler (Table 2.16).

[3] Fred Trueman was a right-arm fast bowler who played for Yorkshire from 1949 to 1968 and for England between 1952 and 1965. He bowled outswingers at genuine pace and his strength and freedom from injury were responsible for his longevity. In total, he played 67 test matches taking 307 wickets at 21.58 runs per wicket. In first-class cricket, he took 2,304 wickets in 603 matches at an average of 18.29. Known as "Fiery Fred", his total of 307 test wickets was a world record until overtaken by Lance Gibbs of the West Indies in 1976. He ranks 23rd in Table 2.16.

[4] Alan Davidson of Australia was a consistently accurate left-arm fast-medium bowler with a bustling approach to the wicket and a classical bowling action. He was known for his deceptive late in-swingers. He was also a hard-hitting lower-order batsman. He played first-class cricket for New South Wales from 1949 to 1963 and 44 test matches for Australia between 1953 and 1963 taking 186 wickets at 20.53. Of the bowlers who have taken more than 120 test wickets in their career, Davidson's bowling average is second only to England's Sydney Barnes (1901-1914). He has the lowest bowling average of any bowler who played more than 40 test matches, and he also has a remarkably low economy rate for a fast bowler. At 1.98 runs per over in his test career, he was harder to score off than any other fast bowler since World War 2. He was also an excellent close-to-the-wicket fielder. He ranks 35th in Table 2.16.

[5] Richie Benaud was a leg break bowler who played first-class cricket for New South Wales and from 1948 to 1964 and test cricket for Australia from 1952 to 1964. In 63 tests, he took 248 wickets at 27.03 and scored 2,201 runs at 24.46. At the time of his retirement, he had taken more test wickets than any other Australian. He is the 56th ranked bowler in Table 2.16. On 6th December 1963, against South Africa at the Brisbane Cricket ground, he became the first test cricketer to reach the milestone of 2,000 runs and 200 wickets. Benaud was an outstanding leader, captaining Australia from 1958 to 1964 in 28 tests, winning 12 and losing 4. After retirement from the game, Benaud became a popular and influential cricket journalist, writer and commentator, both in Australia and overseas. Known to television viewers in the UK and in Australia as the *voice of cricket*, Benaud was influential in the development of the game, including the establishment of World Series Cricket in the late 1970s.

The Top-Rating All-Rounders:

In the 1960s, Sobers emerged as the leading all-rounder in the game. However, Australia's Keith Miller, at the time of his retirement in 1956, was the highest rating all-rounder. Miller was a charismatic, crowd favourite wherever he went, an outstanding fast bowler and a swash buckling batsman. He is 68th highest rating test bowlers (Table 2.16) and the 11th highest rating bowling all-rounder (Table 2.17). The four highest rating test all-rounders in the 1950s are given in Table 5.3 and, in addition to Miller and Sobers, include India's Vinoo Mankad and West Indian Frank Worrell.

Vinoo Mankad was the third highest rating all-rounder of the decade and the 49th highest rating all-rounder in test history (Table 2.17). He was a right-hand opening batsman and left arm orthodox spin bowler who played 44 tests for India between 1946 and 1959, scoring 2,109 runs at 31.48 and taking 162 wickets at 32.32. In 1956 in Chennai against New Zealand, Mankad scored 236 in a world record opening partnership of 413 with Pankaj Roy. This record stood for the next 52 years and remains the second highest opening partnerships in test history. In December 1947, Mankad controversially ran out the Australian opening batsman Bill Brown in a test match in Sydney, when Brown prematurely left his crease, and Mankad removed the bails at the bowler's end without delivering the ball. Since that day, this method of dismissal is known as *mankading*.

The Top-Rating Wicketkeepers:

The leading wicketkeepers of the 1950s are listed in Table 5.4. The Australian wicketkeeper Gil Langley had a better record behind the stumps than Godfrey Evans, but Evans had a better batting record. Langley kept wickets for Australia in 26 test matches taking 83 catches and making 15 stumpings. He affected 1.92 dismissals per innings as wicketkeeper compared to Evans' 1.25. Langley is the 59th highest rating wicketkeeper in Table 2.18. An outstanding all-round sportsman, Langley played Australian Rules football as well as cricket for South Australia, starting his test cricket career after he retired from football. After retirement from cricket, he entered politics and served as an elected member of South Australian House of Assembly from 1962 to 1982.

John Waite was born in Johannesburg in 1930. He was a wicketkeeper batsman in 50 test matches for South Africa from his debut against England at Trent Bridge in 1951 to his final test in 1965, also against England at St George's Park in Port Elizabeth. He took 124 career catches and made 17 stumpings, averaging 1.53 dismissals per innings. He also scored 2,405 runs at 30.44. Waite was the first South African to play 50 test matches and he held the South African record for most test dismissals by a wicketkeeper until overtaken by Dave Richardson during the boxing day test against Australia at the Melbourne Cricket Ground in 1997. John Waite is the 40th highest rating wicketkeeper in Table 2.18.

Table 5.1 Best World team of the 1950s (1950 to 1959, inclusive) — Batting Performances.

The Team:

Players	Country	Batting style	Matches	Innings	Not outs	100s/50s/0s	Highest score	Runs scored	Batting average	Strike rate	Batting rating
1. Hutton, L	England	right	38	66	10	8/16/2	205	3,183	56.84	50	121.8
2. Hanif Mohammad	Pakistan	right	27	48	3	5/9/2	337	1,937	43.04	50	86.9
3. Harvey, RN	Australia	left	56	99	8	15/19/5	205	4,573	50.25	49.99	113.5
4. Weekes, EDC	W Indies	right	39	68	5	10/17/6	207	3,383	53.70	50	116.7
5. Walcott, CL	W Indies	right	33	57	6	13/11/1	220	3,129	61.35	50	141.8
6. Sobers, GStA	W Indies	left	27	46	7	6/7/1	365	2,213	56.74	50	121.2
7. Evans, TG	England	right	64	93	7	2/6/15	104	1,693	19.69	50	20.4
8. Fazal Mahmood	Pakistan	right	26	39	6	0/1/8	60	541	16.39	50	11.4
9. Laker, JC	England	right	38	49	13	0/0/4	48	453	12.58	49.08	7.8
10. Lock, GAR	England	right	31	39	6	0/0/5	25	375	11.36	44.53	6.3
11. Bedser, AV	England	right	28	36	9	0/0/6	30	263	9.74	50	5.3
										Total	753.1

Next Batters:

May, PBH	England	right	59	93	8	13/20/6	285	4,182	49.20	50	113.0
Worrell, FMM	W. Indies	right	29	53	3	7/10/4	261	2,397	47.94	50	97.4
Hassett, AL	Australia	right	22	39	1	6/7/0	167	1,712	45.05	50	86.3
McGlew, DJ	S Africa	right	24	45	3	5/9/3	255	1,825	43.45	50	83.8

Table 5.2 Best World team of the 1950s (1950 to 1959, inclusive) — Bowling Performances.

Players	Country	Overs	Balls	Maids	Runs against	Bowl style	Wickets	5w/10w	Best	Bowl average	Strike rate	Econ rate	Bowling rating
1. Hutton, L	England	\multicolumn{7}{c}{Less than 100 overs}					-
2. Hanif Mohammad	Pakistan	\multicolumn{7}{c}{Less than 100 overs}					-
3. Harvey, RN	Australia	\multicolumn{7}{c}{Less than 100 overs}					-
4. Weekes, EDC	W Indies	\multicolumn{7}{c}{Less than 100 overs}					-
5. Walcott, CL	W Indies	176	1,057	68	326	RAFM	10	0/0	3/50	32.60	105.6	1.85	39.1
6. Sobers, GStA [1]	W Indies	661	3,967	218	1,444	LAMF	31	0/0	4/26	46.58	128.0	2.18	48.8
7. Evans, TG	England	Wicketkeeper					Did not bowl						-
8. Fazal Mahmood	Pakistan	1,302	7,808	452	2,765	RAFM	125	12/4	7/42	22.12	62.52	2.12	130.6
9. Laker, JC	England	1,539	9,790	578	2,992	RAO	162	8/3	10/53	18.47	60.39	1.84	139.7
10. Lock, GAR	England	1,302	8,116	524	2,554	LAO	123	8/3	7/35	20.76	65.99	1.89	127.9
11. Bedser, AV	England	1,318	8,377	343	2,917	RAMF	147	13/3	7/44	19.84	56.94	2.09	136.8
												Total	622.9

Wardle, JH [2]	England	1,026	4,791	403	2,071	LAO[2]	102	5/1	7/36	20.30	64.50	1.89	119.8
Trueman, FS	England	1,003	4 4,316	232	2,685	RAF	128	5/0	8/31	20.98	48.44	2.60	119.3
Tayfield, HJ	S. Africa	1,594	11,885	526	3,686	RAO	153	14/2	9/113	24.09	77.61	1.86	119.1
Benaud, R	Australia	1,633	11,197	476	3,952	RAL	165	11/1	7/72	23.95	68.19	2.12	112.7
Davidson, AK	Australia	894	6,264	249	1,886	LAFM	92	5/1	7/93	20.50	68.19	1.80	112.5

Notes: 1. In addition to left arm medium fast, Sobers also bowled left arm orthodox and left arm chinaman.
2. In addition to left arm orthodox, Wardle also bowled left arm chinaman.

Table 5.3 Performances of the best all-rounders (1950 to 1959, inclusive).

Player	Country	No. of tests	Years played	Batting style	Runs scored	Batting average	Batting rating	Bowling style	Wickets taken	Bowl avge	Bowl rating	All-rounder Rating
Miller, KR	Australia	37	1950-56	right	2,080	34.67	58.9	RAF	122	23.59	104.0	140.4
Worrell, MM	W Indies	29	1950-57	right	2,397	47.94	97.4	LAO	47	36.19	58.2	136.0
Mankad, MH	India	31	1951-59	right	1,536	35.72	58.2	LAO	122	29.26	97.1	135.9
Sobers, GStA	W Indies	27	1954-59	left	2,213	56.74	121.2	LAMF	31	46.58	48.8	133.8

Table 5.4 Wicketkeeping performances (1950 to 1959, inclusive).

Player	Country	No. of tests	Years played	Batting style	Runs scored	Batting average	Batting rating	Catches	Stumpings	Total dismissals	Wicket-keeper rating
Langley, GRA	Australia	26	1951-56	right	374	14.96	9.6	83	15	98	76.2
Waite, JHB	S Africa	31	1951-58	right	1,518	29.19	43.6	74	13	87	74.7
Evans, TG	England	64	1950-59	right	1,693	19.69	20.4	125	28	153	69.4
Walcott, CL [2]	W Indies	15	1950-58	right	888	40.36	69.6	27	11	38	72.9

Notes: 1. The ratings are determined from the number of tests played as wicketkeeper.
2. Walcott played only 15 matches as wicketkeeper.

Chapter 6
The Best World Team – 1960 to 1969

In the decade of the 1960s (1960 to 1969, inclusive), 186 test matches were played. England played in 100 of them, Australia in 67, South Africa in 31, West Indies in 49, New Zealand in 43, India in 52 and Pakistan in 30. The highest rating team for this decade is shown below. Of the 11 players selected, 3 are English, 4 are Australian, 2 are South African and 2 are West Indian. Both the batting and bowling ratings for the team are stronger than for the best team of the 1950s.

The highest rating team of the 1960s

Batting Order:	Country	No. of tests	Period	Batting Rating	Bowling Rating
1. Simpson, RB	Australia	46	1960-68	115.7	56.6
2. Lawry, WM	Australia	58	1960-69	112.0	-
3. Pollock, RG	South Africa	19	1963-67	122.5	-
4. Barrington, KF	England	75	1960-68	151.6	34.3
5. Walters, KD	Australia	21	1965-69	152.9	25.6
6. Sobers, GStA	West Indies	49	1960-69	140.4	82.6
7. Parks, JM	England	45	1960-68	48.3	WK
8. Pollock, PM	South Africa	24	1961-67	19.5	104.3
9. McKenzie, GD	Australia	54	1961-69	9.4	112.4
10. Trueman, FS	England	36	1960-65	8.3	130.7
11. Gibbs, LR	West Indies	42	1961-69	2.7	107.5
			Total	883.3	654.0

Notes: 1. Batting and bowling statistics are given in Tables 6.1 and 6.2, respectively.
2. Of the 10 eras considered in this book, the team of the 1960s has the 6th highest batting rating and the 5th highest bowling rating.

The win/loss/draw results for each of the participating countries during the 1960s are shown below:

Country	Win/Loss/Draw results versus							
	England	Australia	South Africa	West Indies	New Zealand	India	Pakistan	All matches
England	-	4/6/15	4/1/8	6/6/11	8/0/4	3/2/8	7/0/7	32/15/53
Australia	6/4/15	-	2/4/4	6/4/5	Did not play	9/2/4	0/0/2	23/14/29
South Africa	1/4/8	4/2/4	-	Did not play	2/2/4	Did not play	Did not play	7/8/16
West Indies	6/6/11	4/6/5	Did not play	-	1/1/1	7/0/1	Did not play	18/13/17
New Zealand	0/8/4	Did not play	2/2/4	1/1/1	-	2/5/4	1/2/6	6/18/19
India	2/3/8	2/9/4	Did not play	0/7/1	5/2/4	-	0/0/5	9/21/22
Pakistan	0/7/7	0/0/2	Did not play	Did not play	2/1/6	0/0/5	-	2/8/20

Australia, England and the West Indies won more matches than they lost, but with 47.3% of the test matches drawn, test cricket in the decade is best characterised as dour. Only the West Indies drew less than 40% of its matches. The tragedy of the apartheid policy of the South African government that was to see South Africa banned from test cricket for the next two decades is evident from the above table. South Africa did not play against the West Indies, India or Pakistan.

The two highest rating opening batsmen in the decade are Bob Simpson and Bill Lawry. They opened the batting for Australia 62 times between 1961 and 1967 averaging 59.93 runs per innings. Of all the opening batting combinations to have scored more than 3500 runs in opening partnerships, Simpson and Lawry have the highest average runs per innings. The four other top-order batsmen are South Africa's Graeme Pollock, England's Ken Barrington, Australia's Doug Walters and West Indian Garfield Sobers, who is also the No.6 batsman in the 1950s world team and holds his place here. The next most highly rated batsmen are the English trio, Ted Dexter, Colin Cowdrey and Tom Graveney, and West Indian Rohan Kanhai.

Jim Parks of England has been selected as wicketkeeper ahead of a rather unlucky Wally Grout of Australia. Parks was a wicketkeeping all-rounder with a batting average of 32.45 and a batting rating of 48.3, whereas Grout was a specialist wicketkeeper with a batting average of just 11.96 in the 1960s. However, in the 1960s Grout had the superior wicketkeeping performances making 132 dismissals in 37 matches compared to Parks' 113 dismissals in 45 matches. The four top ranked bowlers of the decade are the three right-arm fast bowlers, Fred Trueman (England), Graham McKenzie (Australia) and Peter Pollock (South Africa) and the West Indian off-spinner Lance Gibbs. The next most highly rated bowlers are India's Erapally Prasanna and Bapu Nadkarni and South Africa's Trevor Goddard.

The batting and bowling statistics of the World team of the 1960s are presented in Tables 6.1 and 6.2 and the performances of the most highly rated all-rounders and wicketkeepers in the decade are shown in Tables 6.3 and 6.4, respectively. The players in the best national teams, and their batting and bowling statistics, are presented in Appendix G (Tables G.1 to G.7). Of the players who played 20 or more test matches in the 1960s, 17 have been inducted subsequently into the ICC's Cricket Hall of Fame. They are:

England:	Tom Graveney, Brian Statham, Fred Trueman, Colin Cowdrey, Ken Barrington, Geoffrey Boycott and Ted Dexter.
Australia:	Richie Benaud, Alan Davidson, Bob Simpson and Ian Chappell.
West Indies:	Garfield Sobers, Rohan Kanhai, Lance Gibbs and Wes Hall.
South Africa:	Graeme Pollock.
Pakistan:	Hanif Mohammad.

The Top 11 Players:

No. 1: Bob Simpson was a right-hand opening batsman and useful right-arm leg-spinner who played 52 test matches for Australia between 1957 and 1968. He then came back a decade later to captain Australia in 10 additional test matches in 1977 and 1978 when the majority of the then current Australian test team decided to play in Kerry Packer's World Series Cricket. In the 1960s, Simpson played 46 tests scoring 3,995 runs at an average of 51.22 and he took 60 wickets at an average of 39.2. In domestic cricket, he played for New South Wales (1953-56, 1961-68, 1977-78) and Western Australia (1956-1961). In addition to being a fine batsman, he was widely regarded as the best slips fielder in the game. He took 110 catches at an average of 0.94 catches per innings. No other non-wicketkeeping fieldsman with more than 60 catches has taken a higher number of catches per innings in the history of test cricket.

After failing to score a century in his first 29 tests, he scored 311 in his 30th test - against England at Old Trafford in 1964. His 13-hour marathon innings was instrumental in Australia retaining the Ashes, but he was heavily criticised in England at the time for slow, unattractive test cricket. He took over from Richie Benaud as captain of the Australian team at the beginning of 1964 and captained his country in 28 test matches, scoring 8 test centuries before he retired (for the first time) in 1968. He scored two more test centuries at the age of 41 against India in the 1977-78 Australian summer. After cricket, Simpson went on to become perhaps the most successful Australian test cricket coach of all time. He is ranked 73rd in the list of the most highly rated batsmen in test cricket (Table 2.7) and sits 41st in the list of most highly rated test all-rounders (Table 2.17).

No. 2: Victorian and Australian left-hander Bill Lawry was Simpson's opening partner for Australia for much of the 1960s. A patient batsman with an outstanding defence, Lawry could bat for long periods and was regularly the backbone of the Australian innings. He played 67 tests between 1961 and 1971. In the 1960s, he scored 4,717 runs in tests at an average of 49.65, with 13 centuries. Lawry's slow defensive batting caused him to be described by an English journalist as "the corpse with pads". In Australia, he was called more affectionately the Phantom ("the Ghost who walks"). Lawry and Simpson put on 382 runs against the West Indies in 1965 in what remains an Australian record opening partnership, with both players scoring double centuries. Lawry scored another double century against the West Indies in the Boxing Day test at his beloved Melbourne Cricket Ground in 1968. He took over the Australian captaincy from Bob Simpson in 1968 and captained Australia in 25 tests until he was unceremoniously sacked in 1971. He ranks at No. 81 in Table 2.7. After cricket, Lawry began a long career as a popular commentator on free-to-air television in Australia.

No. 3: South Africa's Graeme Pollock is the younger of the two Pollock brothers in the side. Graeme was an outstanding left-hand batsman whose test career was cut short by the sporting boycott imposed on South Africa in the early 1970s. In a career of just 23 test matches from 1963 until 1970, he scored 2,256 runs at an average of 60.97. Only Don Bradman and Adam Voges of Australia have higher test batting averages (see Table 2.2). He is widely regarded as South Africa's best ever batsman and despite his relatively few tests, he is 33rd on the list of the highest rating batsmen of all time (Table 2.7).

It is unfortunate that test cricket was denied Graeme Pollock in his prime. Born in Durban in 1944, Pollock was a prodigious talent as a schoolboy, and he remains the youngest South African to score a test century when he scored 122 against Australia in Sydney in January 1964. Two weeks later in the next test in Adelaide, he scored 175. In his final test series, he scored 274 against Australia in Durban in 1970. Pollock played first-class cricket in South Africa for Eastern Provence from 1960 until 1978 and then for Transvaal until 1987. In his long first-class cricket career, he played 262 matches, scoring 20,940 runs at an average of 54.67 runs per innings.

No. 4: England's Ken Barrington earned selection at No.4. He was a right-handed middle-order batsman known for his determination, concentration and ability to bat for long periods in test cricket. He played 81 test matches scoring 6,806 test runs at an average of 58.67 — the highest batting average of any Englishman since World War 2.

Barrington is 16th on the list of the highest rating batsmen of all time (Table 2.7). He was remarkable in that his batting improved with the quality of the opposition bowling. His average in English county cricket was just 39.87, lower than his first-class average of 45.63 and lower than his test average 58.67. Against Australia, his average was still higher at 63.96. Barrington established many records. He made centuries in four consecutive test matches on two different occasions. His 256 at Old Trafford in 1964 is the highest score by an Englishman against Australia since World War 2 and he was the first English batsman to make a century on each of England's six traditional test venues, Lords, the Oval, Trent Bridge, Old Trafford, Headingley and Edgbaston.

In 1968, during a double wicket championship in Australia, Barrington had a heart attack, and he never played test cricket again. He did recover, however, and from 1975 to 1981 was an English selector. He was the English tour manager in the West Indies in 1981 when he collapsed and died from a second heart attack aged 50.

No. 5: Australia's Doug Walters was a middle-order batsman from New South Wales who played 74 test matches between 1965 and 1981, scoring 5,357 runs at an average of 48.26, with 15 centuries. However, at the end of the 1960s, after just 21 test matches, he had scored almost 2,000 runs at an average of 66.40 runs per innings, with a batting rating for the decade of 152.1. Affectionately known in Australia as "Dashing Doug", he was an attacking right-hand batsman, a useful right-arm medium pace bowler, an excellent fieldsman and a much-loved Australian larrikin. With a career bowling rating of 71.7, Walters qualifies as a genuine batting all-rounder, sitting 5th in the list of the top batting all-rounders in test history (Table 2.17).

Walters made his test debut in the 1965-1966 Ashes Series. He scored 155 in his first test innings and followed that with a century in his second test. He was conscripted into the Army in 1967 and essentially lost two years of test cricket in his batting prime. In four tests matches against the West Indies in the Australian summer of 1968-69, Walters scored 699 runs at an average of 116.5. In the final test of the series at the Sydney Cricket Ground, he became the first player to score a double century and a single century in the same match. He is ranked 56th in Table 2.7.

Walters generally performed much better in Australia than overseas. In the 1960s, he had one tour of England and one tour of India. In England, he played 5 tests, scoring 343 runs at an average of 38.11, and in India, he played 5 tests, scoring 286 runs at an average of 40.86. By comparison in Australia, he played 11 tests, scoring 1363 runs at an average of 97.36.

No.6: As in the team of the previous decade, the No. 6 batsman is Sir Garfield Sobers - the swashbuckling batting all-rounder from Barbados and the West Indies. Sobers reached cricketing heights in the 1960s that stamped him as the best all-rounder the world had seen. His performances with both bat and ball in the1960s were even better than his outstanding performances in the 1950s. In 49 test matches in the 1960s, his batting average was 60.04 (compared to 56.74 in the 1950s) and his bowling average was 32.30 (compared to 46.58 in the 1950s). He is the 11th highest rating batsman (Table 2.7) and the 2nd highest rating all-rounder (Table 2.17). He was a remarkably versatile left-arm bowler who could open the bowling with deceptively late swing at pace, and bowl accurate left-arm finger-spinners or wrist spinners if required. He was also a magnificent fielder in all positions. His accomplishments in cricket are many. In 1968 playing for Nottinghamshire against Glamorgan, he became the first batsman to hit six sixes in a single over in first-class cricket when he belted the hapless Malcolm Nash out of the attack and out of the park.

In 2000, a 100-member panel of experts was charged with selecting the five Wisden Cricketers of the Century. Each member nominated 5 cricketers. The five individuals to receive the most votes, and who were consequently named as the five cricketers of the century, were Don Bradman (100 votes), Garfield Sobers (90 votes), Jack Hobbs (30 votes), Shane Warne (27 votes) and Viv Richards (25 votes). In 2004, the International Cricket Council inaugurated an award to be given annually to the ICC Player of the Year. The award was named the Sir Garfield Sobers Trophy and it has become what the ICC have called "cricket's ultimate individual award".

No. 7: Jim Parks kept wickets for England in the 1960s. Parks made his first-class debut for Sussex in 1949 as an attacking batsman and spin bowler. He was picked as a specialist batsman for his first test (against Pakistan at Old Trafford in 1954), but after being bowled by Fazal Mahmood for 15 in his only bat, he was dropped and waited 6 years before restarting his test career in 1960. He took up wicketkeeping for Sussex in 1958 and was selected as the English wicketkeeper in the final test of the series against the West Indies in Trinidad in 1960, impressing with one catch, two stumpings and an unbeaten century in the 2nd innings to help England salvage a draw. Between 1960 and 1968, he played 45 tests scoring 1,947 runs at an average of 32.45, taking 101 catches and making 11 stumpings in 80 innings as wicketkeeper. He ranks 53rd in the list of highest rating wicketkeepers (Table 2.18). Parks was not considered as gifted a keeper as Godfrey Evans, who kept wicket for England in the 1950s, but he was a better batsman. In his first-class career, he played 739 matches, scored 36,673 runs at an average of 34.76, including 51 centuries, and he made 1,087 catches and 92 stumpings. He also took 51 wickets with the ball.

Jim Parks is part of a successful cricketing family — his father Jim Parks senior played over 400 first class matches for Sussex between 1924 and 1939 and a single test match in 1937. His son Bobby Parks kept wickets for Hampshire and Kent between 1980 and 1993 in over 250 first-class matches. Bobby also kept wickets in a Test match for a single day against New Zealand at Lords in 1986, as a substitute fieldsman.

No. 8: The first of the three fast bowlers in the side is South Africa's Peter Pollock. He was born in Pietermaritzburg in 1941and he played domestic cricket for Eastern Province (1958-72). He played 28 test matches between 1961 and 1970, taking 116 wickets at 24.19 runs per wicket. In his first test match, he took 6 wickets in New Zealand's second innings at Durban. He was South Africa's leading bowler throughout his career. After his first series against New Zealand, he played in every South African test until the Apartheid ban in 1970 ended his test career. At Trent Bridge in 1965 against England, Pollock had match figures of 10 wickets for 87 runs, helping

South Africa win the match and the series. The test was a family affair, with brother Graeme making scores of 125 and 59. Peter Pollock is the 70th highest rating test bowler (Table 2.16).

The two Pollock brothers were part of the famous walk-off at Newlands, Cape Town, in April 1971 in protest of the South African Government's apartheid policy that was about to end their test careers. The Currie Cup champions Transvaal were playing a Rest of South Africa team and both teams walked off in protest after the first ball was bowled. Among the talented group of players whose test careers were ended at that time and who also participated in the walk-off with the Pollocks were Barry Richards, Mike Procter, Clive Rice and Denis Lindsay.

Twenty years later when South Africa was re-admitted into test cricket, Peter Pollock became convener of selectors for South Africa. He is credited with encouraging the discipline within the team of the early 1990s that led to South Africa's rapid rise in the test rankings based largely on accurate and hostile fast bowling, a trend that continues to this day.

No. 9: Graham McKenzie was the spearhead of the Australian attack for most of the 1960s. Between 1961 and 1971, McKenzie played 60 test matches and took 246 wickets at 29.79 runs per wicket. He played first-class cricket for Western Australia from 1960 to 1974, Leicestershire from 1969 to 1975 and Transvaal from 1979 to 1980. He was selected as a 19-year-old for the 1961 Ashes tour of England where he made his test debut in the 2nd Test at Lords taking 5 for 37 in the 2nd innings to help Australia to a 5-wicket victory. He was successful on wickets around the world and gained a reputation for taking wickets on good batting pitches. In 1964, he took 71 wickets in 14 test matches on pitches in Australia, England, India and Pakistan to become the highest wicket taker in a 12-month period.

In 1968, McKenzie became a full-time professional cricketer. He played test cricket until 1971, when Dennis Lillee took over his mantle as Australia's leading fast bowler. McKenzie continued to play county cricket in England, taking over 400 wickets for Leicestershire and helping that county win four one-day cricket trophies and its first county championship. An aggressive fast bowler, he often forced batsman to take evasive action. For what it is worth, McKenzie dismissed more batsmen hit-wicket in test cricket than anyone else (4 in total). He is the 79th highest rating bowler in test history (Table 2.16).

No. 10: England's Fred Trueman has the highest bowling rating of any player in the 1960s. He was introduced in Chapter 5 for his bowling performances in the 1950s. This right-arm fast bowler from Yorkshire played 36 tests in the 1960s, taking 176 wickets at 22.01. The 1960 home season was the most successful of Trueman's career. He played 36 first-class matches in that year and took 175 wickets at just 13.98, with 10 or more wickets in a match on four occasions and 5 or more wickets in an innings on 12 occasions.

On the 1962-63 tour of Australia and New Zealand, Trueman passed Brian Statham's world record for the most wickets taken by a bowler. He took the record to 250 test wickets with his 7 for 75 in the second Test against New Zealand. He would subsequently take the record to 307 wickets before he had finished with test cricket. In 1963, Trueman took 57 test wickets at an average of 17.53 and was ICC's No. 1 ranked bowler. He also spearheaded Yorkshire to win another County Championship. His career statistics place him 23rd on the list of the most highly rated test bowlers (Table 2.16). After his retirement, Trueman became a popular media personality and commentator for the BBC on radio and television.

No. 11: West Indian Lance Gibbs was the best spin bowler of the 1960s. Gibbs had a test career spanning 18 years. He was a remarkably accurate and economical off-spin bowler, with a career economy rate of less than 2.0. At the time of his retirement in 1976, he had taken more wickets (309) in test cricket than anyone else and he had bowled more overs in test matches (4,206) than anyone else. Born in Guyana in 1934, Gibbs ranks 47th in the list of the most highly rated test bowlers (Table 2.16). In the 1960s, he took 184 test wickets at an average of 27.85 and an economy rate of 2.16. He played test cricket from 1958 to 1976, domestic cricket for Guyana from 1953-1975, County cricket for Warwickshire, and a season for South Australia in the Australian domestic Sheffield Shield in 1969-70. It was during the West Indies eventful tour down under in the 1960-61 Australian summer that Gibbs first showed his great potential. After missing the first two tests, including the first ever tied test in Brisbane, he took 19 wickets in the last three tests, including a hat-trick in the famous drawn 4th Test in Adelaide.

In what has been described as the greatest spell of bowling in test cricket history, Gibbs bowled the West Indies to victory against India at Bridgetown in 1962. In India's second innings, Gibbs commenced his spell when India was 149 for 2. In the next 15.3 overs, he took all 8 remaining Indian wickets for just 6 runs. India was all out for 187 and Gibbs' final figures of 8/38 were the best of his career. The following year in England, he took 26 test wickets at 21.30 runs per wicket. Gibbs was ranked by the ICC retrospectively as the top bowler in test cricket each year from 1964 to 1968, inclusive, and from January 1976 until December 1981, he held the record for most wickets in test cricket. His deeds with the ball were unfortunately not matched with the bat; he never once made 50 in first-class cricket.

Towards the end of his career, Gibbs played several test matches with his cousin Clive Lloyd, who captained the great West Indian side of the late 1970s and early 1980s.

Next Best Batsman:

In the 1960s', the English side shown in Table G.1 had the highest batting rating of any national side, thanks to its specialist batsmen in the middle-order. These include three of the four next most highly rated batsmen (after the top six discussed above), Ted Dexter, Colin Cowdrey and Tom Graveney.

[1] Ted Dexter was an attacking batsman and a fine right arm medium pace bowler. Between 1958 and 1965, he played 60 tests for England, scoring 4,405 runs at an average of 48.94. He also took 66 wickets with a bowling average of 34.52. His cricket career was almost ended by a car accident in 1965. He made a rather unsuccessful comeback to test cricket in 1968, playing 2 additional tests against Australia. He is the 85th highest rating test batsman (Table 2.7) and is ranked the 13th highest rating batting all-rounder (Table 2.17). In 1987, Dexter had the idea of a ranking system for test cricket, which has since been developed into the Deloitte's Ratings. This was adopted by the ICC for its official Player Rankings in 2003.

[2] Colin Cowdrey had a long and distinguished cricket career. He played for England 114 times between 1954 and 1976 and for Kent from 1950 to 1975. He was a stylish and effective batsman who made 22 test centuries for England, equalling Walter Hammond's record. He was the first cricketer to play 100 tests. He reached that milestone against Australia at Edgbaston in 1968, fittingly scoring a century in the first innings. He was the first cricketer to make test centuries against all 6 test playing countries in his era, both at home and away. At his prime in the 1960s, he played 65 tests scoring 4,788 runs at an average of 48.86. His batting career places him 66th in Table 2.7. He was a fine close to the wicket fielder taking 120 catches in test cricket. He was knighted in 1992 and became a life peer in 1997 — Baron Cowdrey of Tonbridge.

[3] Like Cowdrey, Tom Graveney had a long and successful career as a middle-order batsman, playing for England from 1951 to 1969, scoring 4,882 runs at an average of 44.38. He played country cricket for Gloucestershire and Worcestershire and his first-class career spanned from 1948 to 1972. He is the only player ever to have scored more than 10,000 runs for two different counties. Although he played most of his 79 tests matches in the 1950s, he was at his best in the 1960s, playing 31 tests and averaging 52.09 runs per innings. He was a graceful attacking batsman who like a good wine got better with age. After several years out of test cricket, he was called back into the English side in 1966 after England had lost the first test against the West Indies. His comeback test started on his 39th birthday. In that series, he scored 459 runs at an average of 76.50, including 165 in the 5th test.

[4] The next most highly rated test batsman in the 1960s was the West Indian Rohan Kanhai. Born in British Guiana in 1935, Kanhai was a stylish right-hand batsman who played 79 tests between 1957 and 1974 scoring 6,227 runs at 47.53. His average in the 1960s was 49.85. He ranks 63rd in Table 2.7. He played first-class cricket for a variety of teams in the West Indies, England, Australia and South Africa. He went on to captain the test side in the early 1970s and was appointed to coach the West Indies twenty years later. The great Indian opening batsman Sunil Gavaskar wrote that Kanhai was one of the finest batsmen and finest sportsman he had seen.

Next Best Bowlers:

The next three most highly rated bowlers in the 1960s are Indian spinners E.R.S. Prasanna and R.G. Nadkarni and South African medium pacer Trevor Goddard.

[1] Erapally Prasanna was a right-arm off-break bowler who played 49 tests for India between 1962 and 1978. After a disappointing start to his test career in 1962, he left the sport to complete his engineering degree and returned to play for India in 1967. In the 1960s, he played just 22 matches taking 113 wickets at 27.05. He was an attacking bowler who could deceive batsmen with flight, unexpected bounce and unerring accuracy of line and length. He held the record for the fastest 100 wickets in tests by an Indian bowler (set in 20 matches), until in 2013 Ravi Ashwin reached that milestone in 18 matches. Prasanna is the 117th highest rating test bowler (see Table A.2).

[2] Bapu Nadkarni was a bowling all-rounder who played 41 tests for India between 1955 and 1968. He scored 1,414 runs at a batting average of just over 25 and took 88 wickets with slow left arm orthodox bowling at 29.08 runs per wicket. Nadkarni was an accurate bowler, with a persistent line and length. It is said that he practiced with a coin on the pitch, hitting the coin with every delivery. Batsmen found it difficult to score off his bowling. In the 1960s, his economy rate was 1.57. Of all the bowlers who played more than 20 test matches, Nadkarni's career economy rate of 1.68 is the 2nd lowest in the history of test cricket. He is the 136th highest rating test bowler (see Table A.2).

[3] Trevor Goddard of South Africa had the next highest bowling rating for the 1960s. He was an all-rounder who played 41 tests between 1955 and 1970 and took 123 wickets at 26.23 with medium pace left-arm bowling. He was a good looking and classically correct left-handed opening batsman who scored 2,516 test runs at 34.47. He opened the batting for South Africa in 74 of his 78 test innings. In the mid-1960s, he captained South Africa in 13 tests. As a bowler, he was accurate and difficult to get away. Of all the cricketers who have played 20 test matches, Goddard has the lowest career economy rate (1.65). Goddard was perhaps the best bowling all-rounder of his day. He ranks 38th in Table 2.17.

Highest Rating All-Rounders:

The highest rating all-rounders in the 1960s are listed in Table 6.3. Sobers, Simpson and Goddard have already been mentioned.

Bob Cowper was born in Melbourne and played first-class cricket for Victoria from 1960 to 1970 and test cricket for Australia for just four years from 1964 to 1968. He made the first triple century in test matches in Australia scoring 307 against England at the Melbourne Cricket Ground in 1966. He averaged 46.84 with the bat in test cricket and took 36 wickets at a bowling average of 31.64. He is the 26th highest rating test all-rounder (Table 2.17).

New Zealand's John Reid was born in Auckland in 1928 and played 58 test matches for New Zealand from 1949 to 1965, captaining his country in 34 tests from 1956 until his retirement in 1965. He scored 3,428 runs at an average of 33.28 and he took 85 test wickets at 33.35. Reid was a right-hand top-order batsman and an aggressive medium fast bowler, turning to off-cutters and off-spin later in his career. Both his batting rating and his bowling rating improved in the last five years of his career (in the 1960s). He is the 40th highest rating test all-rounder (Table 2.17).

Highest Rating Wicketkeepers:

The leading wicketkeepers of the 1960s are listed in Table 6.4.

Wally Grout of Australia was the most successful specialist wicketkeeper, but his batting performances were modest compared to the others in Table 6.4, Jim Parks and John Waite. Grout played 51 tests between 1957 and 1966, taking 163 catches, making 24 stumpings and averaging 1.91 dismissals per innings. He is the 38th highest rating test wicketkeeper (Table 2.18). He was born in Mackay in 1927 and debuted for Queensland in first-class cricket in 1949, but in the early 1950s, he played second fiddle to the incumbent Queensland and Australian wicketkeeper Don Tallon. Against Western Australia in a first-class match in 1960, Grout set a world record by taking 8 catches in an innings. He died suddenly of a heart attack in 1968 at the age of just 41, less than 3 years after his final test match.

John Waite was introduced in Chapter 5 for his wicketkeeping performances for South Africa in the 1950s. He played just 19 test matches in the 1960s, with 50 catches and 4 stumpings (1.50 dismissals per innings). Waite is the 40th highest rating test wicketkeeper (Table 2.18).

Table 6.1 Best World team of the 1960s (1960 to 1969, inclusive) — Batting Performances.

The Team:

Players	Country	Batting style	Matches	Innings	Not outs	100s/50s/0s	Highest score	Runs scored	Batting average	Strike rate	Batting rating
1. Simpson, RB	Australia	right	46	84	6	8/23/6	311	3,995	51.22	49.66	115.7
2. Lawry, WM	Australia	left	58	105	10	13/23/5	210	4,717	49.65	50	112.0
3. Pollock, RG	S Africa	left	19	34	4	6/8/1	209	1,739	57.97	50	122.5
4. Barrington, KF	England	right	75	122	15	20/31/4	256	6,397	59.79	48.79	151.6
5. Walters, KD	Australia	right	21	34	4	7/11/3	242	1,992	66.40	46.79	152.9
6. Sobers, GStA	W Indies	left	49	86	10	15/19/7	226	4,563	60.04	49.62	140.4
7. Parks, JM	England	right	45	67	7	2/9/3	108	1,947	32.45	49.59	48.3
8. Pollock, PM	S Africa	right	24	34	10	0/2/2	75	533	22.21	50	19.5
9. McKenzie, GD	Australia	right	54	78	9	0/2/14	76	886	12.84	50	9.4
10. Trueman, FS	England	right	36	51	5	0/0/5	38	580	12.61	50	8.3
11. Gibbs, LR	W Indies	right	42	62	22	0/0/11	18	226	5.65	47.78	2.7
										Total	883.3

Next Batters:

Dexter, ER	England	right	55	92	8	8/26/4	205	4,232	50.38	49.69	110.2
Cowdrey, MC	England	right	65	110	12	16/21/6	182	4,788	48.86	49.67	110.1
Kanhai, RB	W Indies	right	43	76	1	10/18/2	153	3,739	49.85	50.06	105.9
Graveney, TW	England	right	31	47	3	7/9/1	165	2,292	52.09	47.15	103.0

Table 6.2 Best World team of the 1960s (1960 to 1969, inclusive) — Bowling Performances.

Players	Country	Overs	Balls	Maids	Runs against	Bowl style	Wickets	5w/10w	Best	Bowl average	Strike rate	Econ rate	Bowling rating
1. Simpson, RB	Australia	846	5,754	226	2,352	RAL	60	2/0	5/57	39.20	95.95	2.45	56.6
2. Lawry, WM	Australia	Less than 100 overs											-
3. Pollock, RG	S Africa	Less than 100 overs											-
4. Barrington, KF	England	390	2,434	95	1,165	RAL	24	0/0	3/4	48.54	101.4	2.87	34.3
5. Walters, KD	Australia	133	1,011	21	432	RAM	11	0/0	4/53	39.27	91.82	2.57	25.6
6. Sobers, GStA [1]	W Indies	2,066	13,395	514	5,232	LAMF	162	6/0	6/73	32.30	82.71	2.34	82.6
7. Parks, JM	England	Wicketkeeper					Did not bowl						-
8. Pollock, PM	S Africa	919	5,829	231	2,548	RAF	101	8/1	6/38	25.23	57.74	2.62	104.3
9. McKenzie, GD	Australia	2,408	16,127	512	6,644	RAF	238	16/3	8/71	27.92	67.78	2.47	112.4
10. Trueman, FS	England	1,442	8,974	290	3,940	RAF	179	12/3	7/44	22.01	50.16	2.63	130.7
11. Gibbs, LR	W Indies	2,375	15,480	733	5,124	RAO	184	12/2	8/38	27.85	84.15	1.99	107.5
												Total	654.0

Prasanna, EAS	India	1,194	7,553	344	3,057	RAO	113	8/1	6/74	27.05	66.87	2.43	99.3
Nadkarni, RG	India	1,255	7,677	587	1,975	LAO	76	4/1	6/43	25.99	101.0	1.54	98.7
Goddard, TL	S Africa	921	5,841	350	1,708	LAM	67	3/0	6/53	25.49	87.27	1.75	91.7

Note: In addition to left arm medium fast, Sobers also bowled left arm orthodox and left arm chinaman.

Table 6.3 Performances of the best all-rounders (1960 to 1969, inclusive).

Player	Country	No. of tests	Years played	Batting style	Runs scored	Batting average	Batting rating	Bowling style	Wickets taken	Bowl avge	Bowl rating	All-rounder Rating
Sobers, GStA	W Indies	49	1960-69	left	4,563	60.04	140.4	LAMF	162	32.30	82.6	194.1
Cowper, RM	Australia	27	1964-68	left	2,061	46.84	94.9	RAO	36	31.64	66.8	147.7
Goddard, TL	S Africa	23	1960-67	left	1,606	40.15	64.7	LAM	67	25.49	91.7	142.9
Simpson, RB	Australia	46	1960-68	right	3,995	51.22	115.7	RAL	60	39.2	56.6	142.8
Reid, JR	N. Zealand	24	1961-65	right	1,768	40.18	70.7	RAMF	38	30.84	73.4	142.8

Table 6.4 Wicketkeeping performances (1960 to 1969, inclusive).

Player	Country	No. of tests	Years played	Batting style	Runs scored	Batting average	Batting rating	Catches	Stumpings	Total dismissals	Wicket-keeper rating
Parks, JM	England	45	1960-68	right	1,947	32.45	48.3	101	11	112	78.1
Grout, ATW	Australia	37	1960-66	right	538	11.96	7.6	118	14	132	79.4
Waite, JHB	S Africa	19	1960-65	right	887	32,85	48.9	50	4	54	73.9

Note: The ratings are determined from the number of tests played as wicketkeeper.

Chapter 7
The Best World Team — 1970 to 1979

A total of 198 test matches were played in the decade 1970 to 1979, inclusive. England played 95 of them, Australia 83, South Africa 4, West Indies 63, New Zealand 41, India 64 and Pakistan 46. The best team for this decade is shown below. Of the 11 players selected, 3 are English, 3 are Australian, 3 are West Indian and one each are from India and Pakistan. The sum of the batting ratings for the decade is a little greater than the corresponding total for the team of the 1960s, but the sum of the bowling ratings is less.

The highest rating team of the 1970s

Batting Order:	Country	No. of tests	Period	Batting Rating	Bowling Rating
1. Gavaskar, SM	India	60	1971-79	138.4	-
2. Boycott, G	England	44	1970-79	121.5	-
3. Richards, IVA	West Indies	30	1974-79	130.0	12.0
4. Javed Miandad	Pakistan	25	1976-79	137.3	37.6
5. Chappell, GS	Australia	54	1970-79	122.6	50.2
6. Kallicharran, AI	West Indies	53	1972-79	106.2	-
7. Botham, IT	England	22	1977-79	59.7	142.5
8. Marsh, RW	Australia	55	1970-79	50.6	-
9. Lillee, DK	Australia	35	1971-79	10.3	127.8
10. Underwood, DL	England	59	1970-79	6.5	110.9
11. Roberts, AME	West Indies	29	1974-79	4.8	112.1
			Total	887.9	593.1

Notes: 1. Batting and bowling statistics are given in Tables 7.1 and 7.2, respectively.
2. Of the 10 eras considered in this book, the team of the 1970s has the 5th highest batting rating and the 8th highest bowling rating.

The win/loss/draw results for each of the participating countries during are shown below:

Country	Win/Loss/Draw results versus							
	England	Australia	South Africa	West Indies	New Zealand	India	Pakistan	All matches
England	-	13/10/11	0/0/0	1/6/6	8/1/4	8/4/8	3/0/12	33/21/41
Australia	10/13/11	-	0/4/0	8/5/5	4/1/3	3/4/4	5/2/1	30/29/24
South Africa	0/0/0	4/0/0	-	0/0/0	0/0/0	0/0/0	0/0/0	4/0/0
West Indies	6/1/6	5/8/5	0/0/0	-	0/0/5	5/5/10	2/1/4	18/15/30
New Zealand	1/8/4	1/4/3	0/0/0	0/0/5	-	1/3/2	0/4/5	3/19/19
India	4/8/8	4/3/4	0/0/0	5/5/10	3/1/2	-	1/2/4	17/19/28
Pakistan	0/3/12	2/5/1	0/0/0	1/2/4	4/0/5	2/1/4	-	9/11/26

South Africa played just 4 matches in 1970, winning them all, before the apartheid policies of the South African Government saw its team banned from international cricket. The ban ended the test careers of many outstanding cricketers, including Graeme Pollock, Peter Pollock, Barry Richards, Mike Procter, Denis Lindsay, Eddie Barlow and more.

England, Australia and the West Indies won more matches than they lost in the 1970s. The percentage of matches drawn was down from 47.3% in the 1960s to 42.4 in the 70s, but still significantly higher than in the modern era. Australia drew 28.9% of its games, England 43.2%, India 43.8%, New Zealand 46.3%, West Indies 47.6% and Pakistan 56.5%.

The two highest rating opening batsmen in the decade were Sunil Gavaskar of India (138.4) and Geoffrey Boycott of England (121.5). The four other top- order batsmen are West Indians Viv Richards (130.0) at No. 3, Pakistan's Javed Miandad (137.3) at No. 4 and Australia's Greg Chappell (122.6) at No.5 and Alvin Kallicharran (106.2) at No.6. The next three most highly rated opening batsmen in the decade are England's Dennis Amiss (101.5), Australia's Ian Redpath (99.8), and New and Zealand's Glenn Turner (92.2). The next most highly rated middle-order batsmen are India's Gundappa Viswanath (101.3) and West Indian Clive Lloyd (96.1).

At No.7 is the all-rounder Ian Botham of England, the top-rated bowler of the decade and an aggressive, attacking batsman. Rod Marsh of Australia is the wicketkeeper, selected ahead of Alan Knott of England, despite Knott's better batting rating. In the 1970s, Marsh made 209 dismissals in 55 tests at 3.80 dismissals per match, significantly higher than Knott's 192 dismissals in 71 tests at 2.70 dismissals per match. The three ranked bowlers of the decade behind Botham are the fast bowlers, Dennis Lillee (Australia) and Andy Roberts (West Indies) and England's left arm orthodox spinner Derek Underwood. After the top four, the next most highly rated bowlers of the 1970s are right arm pace bowlers Bob Willis (England) and Jeff Thomson (Australia) and India's two spinners Bhagwath Chandrasekhar and Bishen Bedi.

The batting and bowling statistics of the World team of the decade are presented in Tables 7.1 and 7.2 and the performances of the most highly rated all-rounders and wicketkeepers are shown in Tables 7.3 and 7.4, respectively. The statistics of the eligible players in the best national teams are contained in Appendix H (Tables H.1 to H.6). Of the cricketers who played 20 or more test matches in the 1970s, 21 have been inducted subsequently into the ICC's Cricket Hall of Fame. They are:

England:	Geoffrey Boycott, Derek Underwood, Alan Knott, Bob Willis and Ian Botham.
Australia:	Ian Chappell, Greg Chappell, Rod Marsh and Dennis Lillee.
West Indies:	Lance Gibbs, Clive Lloyd, Gordon Greenidge, Viv Richards and Andy Roberts.
Indian:	Bishen Bedi, Sunil Gavaskar and Kapil Dev.
Pakistan:	Imran Khan, Zaheer Abbas and Javed Miandad
New Zealand:	Richard Hadlee.

The Top 11 Players:

No. 1: The top-rating batsman in the 1970s is India's Sunil Gavaskar. He was a right-handed opening batsman with a great defence and the ability to keep the score ticking over, often without appearing to attack the bowling. He played 125 test matches between 1971 and 1987, scoring 10,122 runs at 51.12, placing him 21st on the list of highest rating test batsmen in Table 2.7. In the 1970s, for the first half of his long career, he averaged 55.91 and made over 1,000 runs more than any other player in test cricket.

He played domestic cricket for Bombay from 1967 to 1987, and he captained India in 13 tests in the 1970s. His technique was admired by all who saw him bat, particularly against fast bowling. Against the West Indies in the second half of the 1970s, with one of the fiercest fast-bowling attacks in the history of the game, Gavaskar averaged 71.5 runs per innings. He was remarkably consistent throughout his career breaking numerous records. In the 1970s, he scored two centuries in a single test on three separate occasions, the first player to do so. He would finish his career as the leading scorer of runs and the leading century-maker in test cricket. In addition to opening the batting in the best team of the 1970s, he was good enough to hold his place in the best team of the 1980s.

No. 2: The second opening batsman is Geoffrey Boycott of England and Yorkshire. Boycott rated highly enough throughout his long career to earn the opening batting position in England's best national side in each of three decades, the 60s, 70s and 80s, as well as in the best World team in the 70s. Between 1964 and 1982, he played 108 test matches and scored 8,114 runs at 47.73 runs per innings. Despite missing three years of test cricket through a self-imposed exile between 1974 and 1977, his test average in the 1970s was 55.97, significantly higher than his career average, and he scored 12 of his 22 test centuries in that decade.

Boycott was a defensive batsman who could occupy the crease for long periods. Although he had a reputation as a loner and was sometimes critical of the cricket establishment, he was renowned for his concentration and self-belief. With 151 first-class centuries, Boycott scored more first-class 100s than any other player since World War 2 and, at his retirement, he had scored more test runs than any other player. He is the 45th highest rating test batsman in Table 2.7.

No. 3: Flamboyant West Indian Sir Vivian Richards, affectionately known as the "Master Blaster", is at No. 3. Richards played 121 tests between 1974 and 1991 scoring 8,540 runs at 50.24, with 24 test centuries. He also played 14 "Supertests" in Kerry Packer's World Series Cricket from 1977 to 1979, scoring 1281 runs at 55.69, with 4 centuries. He played county cricket for Somerset for much of his career and represented the Leeward Islands in domestic cricket from 1971-1991. In the 1970s, at the beginning of his test career, his batting average was 58.21 and he made his highest test score of 291 against England at the Oval in 1976. In that calendar year, he played 11 test matches and scored 1,710 runs at an average of 90.00. Sir Vivian Richards was voted one of the five Wisden Cricketers of the 20th Century.

At the wicket, Richards always appeared to be confident and relaxed, with an air of arrogance that often intimidated bowlers. He looked like he owned the ground. As well as being a destructive batsman, who could take charge of a game in a few overs, he was an outstanding fielder, with a deadly accurate throw and a great pair of hands. He was also a better than average off-spin bowler. A wonderful test batsman, Richards was an even better One Day International (ODI) batsman. In the ICC rankings of the best-ever test batsmen, Richards is 9th, but in the ICC rankings of the best-ever ODI batsman, he is at the top of the list. He ranks 27th in Table 2.7.

No. 4: Batting at No.4 is Pakistan's Javed Miandad, the second highest rating batsman of the decade. Javed was born in Karachi in 1957 and played 124 test matches between 1976 and 1993, scoring 8,832 runs at an average of 52.57. He is one of only two batsmen in history to have averaged over 50 throughout his career (the other being England's Herbert Sutcliffe before World War 2). He rated highly enough to win selection in the best Pakistani team in the 1970s, 80s and 90s. He had an outstanding start to his test career, playing 25 tests in the late 1970s and scoring over 2,000 runs at an average of 64.34, significantly higher than his career average. At this time, he also played for Sussex in county cricket and for Habib Bank Limited in first-class domestic cricked in Pakistan.

Javed scored 163 in his maiden test innings to become the youngest player to score a century on debut (at the age of 19 years and 119 days). Three weeks later he became the youngest player to ever score a double century when he scored 206 against a New Zealand attack that included Richard Hadlee. He was to become the captain of Pakistan at the age of 22. In the 3-test series against India in 1978 on home soil, he guided Pakistan to a 2-0 series victory scoring 357 runs at an average of 178.5. He scored centuries away against both Australia and New Zealand in 1979. He is the 26th highest rating test batsmen in Table 2.7.

No. 5: The stylish Australian Greg Chappell is selected at No. 5. Chappell played his first-class cricket with South Australia (1966-1973) and Queensland (1973-84). He played 87 test matches between 1970 and 1984, scoring 7,110 runs at 53.86, with 24 centuries. He also played 14 "Supertests" in World Series Cricket scoring 1,415 runs at 56.60, with 5 centuries and a top score of 246. Chappell scored a century in his first test inning (108 against England at the WACA ground in Perth) and a century in his last test innings (182 against Pakistan at the Sydney Cricket Ground). He took over the captaincy of the Australian test team from his brother Ian Chappell for the series against the West Indies in Australia in 1975. He captained his country in the next 48 tests, winning 21, losing 13 and drawing 14.

Chappell was an elegant stroke-maker, with a very correct technique and the ability to concentrate for long periods. He was also a useful medium pace bowler and an excellent slip fielder, taking 122 catches in test cricket (a world record at the time of his retirement). He is the 30th highest rating test batsman and, with a career bowling rating of 54.3, he is 25th in the list of genuine all-rounders in Table 2.17 and the 10th highest rating batting all-rounder.

No. 6: The diminutive West Indian left-handed batsman Alvin Kallicharran makes up the top 6. Born in Georgetown Guyana, Kallicharran played 66 tests for the West Indies from 1972 to 1981, scoring 4,399 runs at 44.43. He is the 123rd highest rating batsman in test cricket (see Table A.1). He was a steady and patient batsman who accumulated runs and often held the batting together for the West Indies, usually at No.4. He took over as captain of the West Indies in 1978 for the third test against a depleted Australian team, when Clive Lloyd and many in the West Indian team joined Kerry Packer's World Series Cricket. He captained the team for 9 tests until Clive Lloyd and the others returned to test cricket. Kallicharran played domestic cricket for Guyana from 1967 to 1981 and county cricket for Warwickshire from 1971 to 1990. He also had stints in Australia with Queensland and in South Africa with Transvaal and Orange Free State.

No. 7: England's all-rounder Ian Botham is selected at No. 7 and, despite only playing 22 tests in the 1970s, he qualifies for the team as the most highly rated bowler of the decade. Like Miandad, Botham had an outstanding start to his test career in the late 1970s. In 22 test matches from 1976 to 1979, he took 118 wickets at an average of just 19.27, with an excellent economy rate for a pace bowler. He also made 1,068 runs at 36.83, including 4 centuries. He was a right-arm medium-fast swing bowler, an aggressive right-handed batsman and a brilliant close-to-the-wicket fieldsman — a true all-rounder. He is the highest rating bowling all-rounder in test history and the 3rd highest rating all-rounder overall behind Jacques Kallis and Sir Garfield Sobers (see Table 2.17).

A natural sportsman, Botham excelled at many sports, including football and golf. He played professional football for Scunthorpe United before concentrating on cricket. He played county cricket for Somerset from 1974 to 1986, with stints at Worcestershire and Durham between 1987 and his retirement in 1993. He played for Queensland in the Australian summer of 1987/88. In first-class cricket, he scored 19,399 runs and took 1,172 wickets. This included making 38 centuries, taking 5 wickets in an innings 59 times and taking 354 catches. He had a relatively unsuccessful period as captain of England, leading the side in 12 tests, losing 4 and drawing 8.

Over his career, Botham played 102 test matches between 1976 and 1992. He took 383 wickets at 28.40 runs per wicket, with an economy rate of 2.99, and he scored 5,200 runs at an average of 33.55 and a strike rate of 60.71. For a two-year period from 1986 to 1988, he held the world record for the greatest number of test wickets. In 1980 against India in Mumbai, Botham became only the second player in history to take 10 wickets and make 100 runs in the same match. The first player to achieve this feat was Australia's Alan Davidson in 1960. This double has only twice been repeated, by Pakistan's Imran Khan in 1983 and Bangladesh's Shakib Al Hasan in 2014. Botham scored a century and took a 5-wicket haul in the same test match on five separate occasions between 1978 and 1984, more times than any other player. In fact, no other player has achieved this double more than twice. Ian Botham is the 33rd highest rated bowler of all time (Table 2.16).

After cricket, Botham became a successful commentator and was actively involved in fund-raising for several prominent charities, including *"Bloodwise"*, a leading blood cancer charity in the UK. He was knighted in 2007 for his services to charity and to cricket.

No 8: Rod Marsh of Australia is selected as wicketkeeper. Between 1970 and 1984, Marsh played 96 test matches, taking 343 catches and making 12 stumpings in 182 innings as wicketkeeper. He also scored 3,633 runs at an average of 26.52. He was also the first Australian wicketkeeper to score a test century. At the time of his retirement, he held the world record for the most dismissals by a wicketkeeper. Marsh is the 10th highest rating wicketkeeper of all time (Table 2.18).

Marsh is one half of the most successful wicketkeeper-bowler combination in test history. A total of 95 batsman were caught Marsh bowled Lillee. No other combination has made more than 90 dismissals. They both played domestic cricket for Western Australia from 1969 to 1984. They both made their test debuts in the 1970/71 Ashes Series against England, and they played their final test together, the 5th test against Pakistan at the Sydney Cricket Ground in 1984. Marsh made exactly 355 test dismissals and, remarkably, Lillee took exactly 355 test wickets.

Fittingly, Marsh's 355th dismissal in his final test was that of Pakistani batsman Abdul Qadir — caught Marsh bowled Lillee.

Apart from his skill and athleticism keeping to Dennis Lillee and Jeff Thomson, perhaps the fastest bowler of them all, Marsh was the heart and soul of the Australian team for much of his career. He was disciplined and competitive, fiercely so, and he instilled this aggression into the rest of the team.

No. 9: Australian fast bowler Dennis Lillee is widely regarded as Australia' greatest ever pace bowler. Like Marsh, Lillee was a competitive and aggressive West Australian. His fiery temperament made him popular with cricket fans, particularly Australian fans, and unpopular with opposing batsmen. He made an immediate and lasting impression in test cricket. In his first test, against England in 1971 at the Adelaide Oval, he took 5 for 84 in the first innings and, in the second innings, John Hampshire became the first of many batsmen to be caught Marsh bowled Lillee. In December 1971, he took 8 for 29 in an "unofficial" test match against a Rest-of-the-World team with a batting line-up that included, Sunil Gavaskar, Farokh Engineer, Zaheer Abbas, Rohan Kanhai, Garfield Sobers, Clive Lloyd and Tony Grieg.

At the beginning of his career, he was very fast and hostile, but stress fractures to his back in February 1973 almost ended his career. After almost two years of rehabilitation, he returned to test cricket for the Ashes series in 1974-75 forming a formidable opening combination with Jeff Thomson. In that series, he took 25 wickets at 23.84. Despite losing some pace, his bowling speed was measured in 1975 at 154.8 km/hour.

Lillee lost more time to test cricket when he joined World Series Cricket in 1977, and he became one of the marketing faces of the break-away group. Although his pace slowed as he neared the end of his career, his accuracy and aggression never waived, and he remained an effective bowler throughout.

Between 1971 and 1984, Lillee played 70 tests, taking 355 wickets at an average of 23.92, a strike rate of 52.02 and an economy rate of 2.76. He also took 67 wickets in 14 "Supertests" in World Series Cricket and he participated in several unofficial tests against combined world teams. At the end of his test career, he held the world record for the highest number of test wickets. He held that record until 1986 when Ian Botham took his 356th wicket. Dennis Lillee is the 15th highest rating test bowler in Table 2.16.

No. 10: The most highly rated spin bowler of the decade is England's Derek Underwood selected at No. 10. He played 86 test matches between 1966 and 1982, taking 297 wickets at an average of 25.84 and an economy rate of 2.11. He bowled left-arm orthodox spin, almost at medium pace, with a consistent accuracy that earned him the nickname 'Deadly Derek'. He took more test wickets in the 1970s than any other player.

Underwood played county cricket for Kent from 1963 to 1987, making his debut at age 17. By 1971, at the age of 25, he had already taken 100 test wickets and 1000 first-class wickets, the youngest player to achieve that feat since George Lohmann and Wilfred Rhodes before World War 1. Underwood was retrospectively ranked by the ICC as the No.1 bowler in the world from September 1969 to August 1973. Underwood was one of five English players to join Kerry Packer's World Series Cricket in 1977. He is the 29th highest rating test bowler in Table 2.16.

No. 11: West Indian fast bowler Andy Roberts was the first cricketer from Antigua to play test cricket for the West Indies. Between 1974 and 1983, Roberts played 47 test matches, taking 202 wickets at 25.61 and an economy rate of 2.79. In 13 World Series Cricket "Supertests" between 1977 and 1979, he took 50 wickets at an average of 24.14. In domestic cricket, he played for the Leeward Islands between 1970 and 1984, and in county cricket, he played for Hampshire from 1973 to 1978 and Leicestershire from 1981 to 1984. He also played a season for New South Wales in the Australian Sheffield Shield competition. Roberts was the leader of the West Indian quartet of fast bowlers that saw the West Indies dominate test cricket in the mid-1970s to early 1980s. The other three fast bowlers of that time were Michael Holding, Joel Garner and Colin Croft.

Roberts' performances away from home were better than his performances in the West Indies. In 18 tests in the West Indies, he took 72 wickets at 28.75 but, in 27 tests away from home, he took 130 wickets at 23.88. In 5 tests against India during his first overseas tour to the subcontinent in 1974-1975, he took 32 wickets at 18.28. In the 5-test series in England in 1976, he took 28 English wickets at 19.18. One of the most feared bowlers of his time, Andy Roberts is the 58th highest rating test bowler (Table 2.16). In 2014, he was knighted by the Antiguan Barbudan government for services to West Indian cricket.

Next Best Batsmen:

After the top 6 batsmen, the next 5 most highly rated batsmen are Dennis Amiss (England), Gundappa Viswanath (India), Ian Redpath (Australia), Glenn Turner (New Zealand) and Clive Lloyd (West Indies).

[1] Dennis Amiss played 50 test matches for England between 1966 and 1977, opening the batting in 69 of his 88 test innings. He scored 3,612 runs at 46.31, with 11 centuries and a top score of 262 not out against the West Indies at Sabina Park in 1974. He is the 126th highest rating test batsman (Table A.1). Amiss was one of the 5 English players to participate in World Series Cricket, playing 15 WSC one-day internationals and 1 "Supertest". He was one of the first batsmen to regularly wear a protective helmet.

[2] Gundappa Viswanath was born in Bhadravathi in 1949 and played first-class cricket for Karnataka throughout his career and test cricket from 1969 to 1983. He played 91 tests for India scoring 6,080 runs at 41.93 and making 14 test centuries. His average in the 1970s was 46.11. In 1979, he scored 1,388 runs at an average of 58.55, including 5 centuries (2 against the West Indies, 2 against Australia and 1 against England). He was a stylish and wristy player, who relied on timing and elegant stroke-play rather than power. At his best in difficult situations, Viswanath was a match winner for India. In India's victory against the West Indies in Madras in 1975, his innings of 97 not out in an Indian total of 190, on a difficult pitch, has been rated by Wisden as one of best of all time. He top-scored with 112 in India's world record successful run chase of 406 against the West Indies at Port of Spain in 1976. His brother-in law, Sunil Gavaskar, made it a family affair scoring 102 in the same run chase. He is the 99th highest rating test batsman (Table 2.7).

[3] Ian Redpath played 66 tests for Australia between 1964 and 1976, opening the batting in 59 of his 120 innings and scoring 4,737 runs at 43.46. In his 33 test matches in the 1970s, he averaged 50.19. He came out of retirement to play 2 "Supertests" and 5 one-day internationals in World Series Cricket. He scored 3 centuries in his final test series against the West Indies in 1975-1976, against an attack that included Andy Roberts, Michael Holding and Lance Gibbs. Redpath is the 130th highest rating test batsman (Table A.1).

[4] Glenn Turner played 41 tests for New Zealand between 1969 and 1983 opening the batting in 67 of his 73 innings and scoring 2,991 runs at 44.64. In the 1970s, he averaged 49.38. In the 5-test series against the West Indies in 1972, he scored 672 runs at an average of 96.00, including two double centuries. At the time of his retirement, he had the highest test batting average of any New Zealand player. His batting rating is 135th in Table A.1.

[5] Clive Lloyd played 110 tests for the West Indies between 1966 and 1984 scoring 7,515 runs at 46.68. He sits 48th on the list of highest rating test batsmen (Table 2.7). Between 1974 and 1984, he captained the West Indies in 74 tests, winning 36 of them and losing only 12. He led the West Indies as it developed into the best cricket team in the world. Lloyd was a powerful, middle-order batsman who could bludgeon any attack and who had a rock-solid defence. Lloyd's bat always looked wider than everyone else's.

Next Best Bowlers:

After the top 4 bowlers, the next 4 most highly rated bowlers are Bob Willis (England), Jeff Thomson (Australia), Bhagwath Chandrasekhar (India) and Bishen Bedi (India).

[1] Bob Willis played 90 test matches for England between 1971 and 1984 taking 325 wickets at a bowling average of 25.20 and captaining England in 18 tests in the early 1980s. A great team man with a never-give-in attitude, he spearheaded the English attack for over a decade. In England's 3-0 win over Australia in the 1977 Ashes Series, Willis took 27 wickets at 19.78, including three 5-wicket hauls and his then career-best figures of 7/78 in the first test at Lords. In 1981, he demolished Australia with a career-best 8/43, bowling England to victory in its famous *come from behind* win in the 3rd test at Headingley. He is the 44th

highest rated test bowler (Table 2.16). After cricket, Willis became a successful television commentator and writer.

[2] Jeff Thomson played 51 test matches for Australia between 1972 and 1985 taking 200 wickets at a bowling average of 28.01. He is the 104th highest rating test bowler (Table A.2). He is widely regarded as the fastest bowler of all time. His bowling speed was timed at over 160 km/hr in 1975 and many of the great batsmen of his day, including Viv Richards, Sunil Gavaskar and Clive Lloyd, consider Thomson the fastest they ever saw. In the mid-1970s, Thomson and Dennis Lillee formed the fastest and most feared opening combination in the game. During the 1974-1975 Ashes Series, in which Thomson took 33 wickets at 17.94, a photograph in the cricket pages of a Sydney newspaper included the caption "Ashes to Ashes, dust to dust, if Thomo don't get ya, Lillee must." The English comedian Eric Morecombe told his straight man Ernie Wise that the fastest bowler in the world was a woman. "Who?" asked Ernie. "Lillian Thomson".

[3] Bhagwath Chandrasekhar played 58 test matches for India between 1964 and 1979, taking 242 wickets at 29.75. He was an accurate leg-spin bowler, one of several outstanding spin bowlers who represented India in the 1960s and 1970s. Born in Mysore, he grew up and played his early cricket in Bangalore. He bowled India to victory over England at The Oval in 1971 with 6/38, in what Wisden described in 2002 as the "Indian bowling performance of the century". In the third test of the 1977-78 series against Australia at the Melbourne Cricket Ground, Chandrasekhar had figures of 6/52 in both innings. He is the 85th highest rating test bowler in Table 2.16. His success with the ball was not matched with the bat. He scored 167 career runs in tests; fewer runs off his bat than wickets taken (a dubious distinction held only by one other player — Chris Martin of New Zealand).

[4] Bishen Bedi was born in Amritsar in north-western India in 1946 and played first-class cricket for Northern Punjab (1961-67), Delhi (1968-81) and Northamptonshire (1972-77). He was a left-arm orthodox spin bowler who played 67 tests between 1966 and 1979, taking 266 wickets at 28.71. He captained India in 22 tests between 1976 and 1978. He was a stylish bowler, with a relaxed and economical action. Using flight, spin and deceptive bounce to confuse the batsman, he was renowned for his accuracy and guile. He could bowl long spells and maintain his rhythm and accuracy throughout. His most productive series was against Australia in 1977-78 when he took 31 wickets at 23.87. He is the 64th highest rated bowler in the history of the game (Table 2.16). After a somewhat controversial period as captain of India, Bedi has remained a passionate supporter of the game and sometimes an outspoken critic. He was appointed coach of India from 1990 until 1991.

Highest Rating All-Rounders:

The most highly rated all-rounders in the decade are shown in Table 7.3. With an all-rounder rating of 161.9, England's Tony Greig is the highest rating all-rounder, followed closely by Ian Botham (160.8) and Pakistan's Mushtaq Mohammad (157.3).

With batting and bowling ratings both over 80, Tong Greig was a genuine all-rounder, rating 13th in Table 2.17. He played 58 tests for England from 1972 to 1977, captaining England in 14 tests from 1975 to 1977. He scored 3,599 test runs at 40.44 and took 141 wickets at 32.21. Greig was a tall right-hand batsman who bowled medium pace and off-spin (the 190th highest rating test batsman in Table A.1 and the 180th highest rating test bowler in Table A.2). He lost the captaincy of England when he helped to sign up players from England, the West Indies and Pakistan for 'World Series Cricket' in 1977. Following his retirement as a player after World Series Cricket, Greig became an outspoken TV Commentator later emigrating to Australia.

Mushtaq Mohammad was a right-hand batsman and right arm leg break bowler. Like Tony Greig, both his batting and bowling ratings were over 75. He is the 18th highest rating all-rounder (Table 2.17). The younger brother of Hanif Mohammad and one of four brothers who all played test cricket for Pakistan, Mushtaq played 57 tests between 1959 and 1979 scoring 3,643 runs at 39.17 and taking 79 wickets at 29.23. He is the only Pakistan player to have scored a century and taken a 5-wicket haul in the same match twice. Against New Zealand in 1973 at

Dunedin, he scored 201 in Pakistan's 1st innings and took 5/49 in New Zealand's 2nd innings to win the match for Pakistan. At Queen's Park Oval against the West Indies in 1977, he scored 121 and took 5/28 and 3/69 to again bowl Pakistan to victory. He captained Pakistan in 19 tests from 1976 to 1979, winning 8 and losing 4. Since retirement, Mushtaq has been a successful coach of the Pakistan National team and commentator for Pakistani television.

Highest Rating Wicketkeepers:

The ratings of the wicketkeepers in the 1970s are provided in Table 7.4.

After Rod Marsh, the two leading wicketkeepers are England's Alan Knott and New Zealand's Ken Wadsworth. Knott had a better batting rating than Marsh, but Marsh made on average 3.8 dismissals per match, while Knott averaged 2.7. Knott played first-class cricket for Kent from 1964 to 1985. He kept wickets for England in 95 test matches from 1967 to 1981 making 269 dismissals (250 catches and 19 stumpings). He made 4,389 test runs at 32.75. In 2004, Knott was voted by Wisden as the wicketkeeper in 'England's Greatest Post-War XI'.

Ken Wadsworth was the wicketkeeper for New Zealand in 33 tests between 1969 and 1976, making 96 dismissals (92 catches and 4 stumpings) and scoring 1,010 runs at 21.49. His 2.9 dismissals per match is higher than Knott's 2.7 but less than Marsh's 3.8. Wadsworth's career was tragically cut short when he died in 1976 from an aggressive melanoma at the age of 29 just 6 months after his final test match.

Table 7.1 Best World team of the 1970s (1970 to 1979, inclusive) — Batting Performances.

The Team:

Players	Country	Batting style	Matches	Innings	Not outs	100s/ 50s/0s	Highest score	Runs scored	Batting average	Strike rate	Batting rating
1. Gavaskar, SM	India	right	60	108	7	22/25/6	221	5,647	55.91	48.36	138.4
2. Boycott, G	England	right	44	77	9	12/21/2	191	3,806	55.97	34.97	121.5
3. Richards, IVA	W Indies	right	30	49	2	9/9/2	291	2,736	58.21	50.96	130.0
4. Javed Miandad	Pakistan	right	25	43	11	6/10/2	206	2,059	64.34	50	137.3
5. Chappell, GS	Australia	right	54	96	13	15/21/6	247	4,398	52.99	49.76	122.6
6. Kallicharran, AI	W Indies	left	53	89	9	11/20/7	187	3,956	49.45	50	106.2
7. Botham, IT	England	right	22	30	1	4/3/2	137	1,068	36.83	52.80	59.7
8. Marsh, RW	Australia	left	55	88	9	3/12/6	132	2,471	31.28	45.17	50.6
9. Lillee, DK	Australia	right	35	45	14	0/1/6	73	497	16.03	44.81	10.3
10. Underwood, DL	England	right	59	83	23	0/0/13	43	661	11.02	37.71	6.5
11. Roberts, AME	W Indies	right	29	38	5	0/1/5	54	290	8.79	51.06	4.8
										Total	887.9

Next Batters:

Amiss, DL	England	right	45	80	9	11/11/8	262	3,487	49.11	43.72	101.5
Viswanath, GR	India	right	62	108	8	10/28/5	179	4,611	46.11	48.97	101.3
Redpath, IR	Australia	right	33	64	7	7/18/3	171	2,861	50.19	39.09	99.8
Turner, GM	N Zealand	right	30	52	4	6/11/0	259	2,370	49.38	43.63	99.2
Lloyd, CH	W Indies	left	48	81	5	8/17/3	242	3,475	45.72	49.76	96.1

Table 7.2 Best World team of the 1970s (1970 to 1979, inclusive) — Bowling Performances.

The Team:

Players	Country	Overs	Balls	Maids	Runs against	Bowl style	Wickets	5w/10w	Best	Bowl average	Strike rate	Econ rate	Bowling rating
1. Gavaskar, SM	India	\multicolumn{11}{c}{Less than 100 overs}	-
2. Boycott, G	England					Less than 100 overs							-
3. Richards, IVA	W Indies	102	644	27	235	RAO	4	0/0	2/34	58.75	160.9	2.19	12.0
4. Javed Miandad	Pakistan	165	1,255	29	556	RAL	17	0/0	3/74	32.71	73.80	2.66	37.6
5. Chappell, GS	Australia	558	3,958	139	1,438	RAM	34	1/0	5/61	42.29	116.4	2.18	50.2
6. Kallicharran, AI	W Indies					Less than 100 overs							-
7. Botham, IT	England	811	5,386	191	2,274	RAMF	118	12/2	8/34	19.27	45.64	2.53	142.5
8. Marsh, RW	Australia		Wicketkeeper				Did not bowl						-
9. Lillee, DK	Australia	1,343	9,515	296	4,376	RAF	184	12/4	6/26	23.78	51.77	2.76	127.8
10. Underwood, DL	England	2383	15,374	787	5,587	LAO	202	10/4	8/51	27.66	76.11	2.18	110.9
11. Roberts, AME	W Indies	1,145	7,331	234	3,521	RAF	140	9/2	7/54	25.15	52.36	2.88	112.1
												Total	593.1

Willis, RGD	England	1,460	9,917	280	4,511	RAF	182	11/0	7/78	24.79	54.49	2.73	109.1
Thomson, JR	Australia	1,086	7,513	210	3,892	RAF	152	6/0	6/46	25.61	49.43	3.11	104.7
Chandrasekhar, BS	India	1,773	11,211	362	5,257	RAO	180	14/1	8/79	29.21	62.28	2.81	99.9
Bedi, BS	India	2,544	15,812	755	5,839	LAO	196	10/1	6/71	29.79	80.68	2.22	99.0

Table 7.3 Performances of the best all-rounders (1970 to 1979, inclusive).

Player	Country	No. of tests	Years played	Batting style	Runs scored	Batting average	Batting rating	Bowling style	Wickets taken	Bowl avge	Bowl rating	All-rounder Rating
Greig, AW	England	58	1972-77	right	3,599	40.44	80.3	RAMF	141	32.21	82.9	161.9
Botham, IT	England	22	1977-79	right	1,068	36.83	59.7	RAMF	118	19.27	142.5	160.8
Mushtaq Mohd.	Pakistan	35	1971-79	right	2,449	42.22	83.2	RAL	65	29.12	77.1	157.3

Table 7.4 Wicketkeeping performances (1970 to 1979, inclusive).

Player	Country	No. of tests	Years played	Batting style	Runs scored	Batting average	Batting rating	Catches	Stumpings	Total dismissals	Wicket-keeper rating
Marsh, RW	Australia	55	1970-79	left	2,471	31.28	50.6	201	8	209	112.5
Knott, APE	England	71	1970-77	right	3,509	34.40	66.6	181	11	192	98.1
Wadsworth, KJ	N Zealand	24	1971-76	right	886	27.69	26.7	70	2	72	69.5

Note: The ratings are determined from the number of tests played as wicketkeeper.

Chapter 8
The Best World Team — 1980 to 1989

The 1980s saw the introduction of Sri Lanka into test cricket and the continuation of the ban on South Africa. In the decade (1980 to 1989, inclusive), 266 test matches were played. England played 104 tests, Australia 97, West Indies 82, New Zealand 59, India 81, Pakistan 80 and Sri Lanka 29. The best team for the decade is shown below. Of the first 11 players selected, England was not represented, the West Indies had 5 representatives, Australia and Pakistan had 2 each, and New Zealand and India had 1 each.

The highest rating team of the 1980s

Batting Order:	Country	No. of tests	Period	Batting Rating	Bowling Rating
1. Gavaskar, SM	India	65	1980-87	101.5	-
2. Greenidge, CG	West Indies	75	1980-89	103.6	-
3. Richards, IVA	West Indies	78	1980-89	120.7	38.4
4. Javed Miandad	Pakistan	76	1980-89	134.0	-
5. Chappell, GS	Australia	33	1980-84	118.4	37.6
6. Border, AR	Australia	97	1980-89	137.3	46.8
7. Imran Khan	Pakistan	54	1980-89	80.1	157.4
8. Dujon, PJL	West Indies	64	1981-89	63.9	-
9. Hadlee, RJ	New Zealand	53	1980-89	49.7	171.4
10. Marshall, MD	West Indies	63	1980-89	20.3	160.3
11. Garner, J	West Indies	49	1980-87	6.7	127.6
			Total	936.2	739.5

Notes: 1. Batting and bowling statistics are given in Tables 8.1 and 8.2, respectively.
2. Of the 10 eras considered in this book, the team of the 1980s has the 4th highest batting rating and the 4th highest bowling rating.

The win/loss/draw results for each of the participating countries during are shown below:

Country	Win/Loss/Draw results versus							
	England	Australia	West Indies	New Zealand	India	Pakistan	Sri Lanka	All matches
England	-	9/11/12	0/17/7	3/3/7	4/4/10	2/4/8	2/0/1	20/39/45
Australia	11/9/12	-	3/11/5	5/4/7	1/1/6	4/6/7	3/0/1	27/31/38
West Indies	17/0/7	11/3/5	-	3/2/5	9/1/9	3/2/5	Did not play	43/8/31
New Zealand	3/3/7	4/5/7	2/3/5	-	2/2/2	2/2/4	4/0/2	17/15/27
India	4/4/10	1/1/7	1/9/9	2/2/2	-	1/4/17	2/1/4	11/21/48
Pakistan	4/2/8	6/4/7	2/3/5	2/2/4	4/1/17	-	5/1/3	23/13/44
Sri Lanka	0/2/1	0/3/1	Did not play	0/4/2	1/2/4	1/5/3	-	2/16/11

Note: Australia and India tied a single test match in India in September 1986.

The West Indian team of the 1980s dominated test cricket, with arguably the greatest fast-bowling attack in the history of the game, it lost just one series out of 20 played. In fact, the 80s was a decade of great fast bowlers. So much so, that all of the top six ranked bowlers in the decade were right-arm fast bowlers. It was also a decade where the fortunes of teams changed. For the first time England lost more games than it won, as did Australia for the first time since World War 1. Both Pakistan and New Zealand won more games than they lost for the first time in their history. However, the cricket was generally still defensive with the percentage of matches drawn at 45.9%. England drew 43.3% of its matches, Australia 39.2%, India 59.3%, New Zealand 45.8%, West Indies 37.8%, Pakistan 55.0% and Sri Lanka 37.9%.

Four of the top 6 batsmen who featured in the best team of the 1970s retained their places in the 1980s team, albeit with lower batting ratings. Sunil Gavaskar retains his place at the top of the order with a batting rating of 101.5 (down from 138.4 in the 1970s). Viv Richards is at 3 with a rating of 120.7 (compared to 130.0 in the 1970s), Javed Miandad is at 4 with a rating of 134.0 (compared to 137.3 in the 1970s) and Greg Chappell is at 5 with a rating of 118.4 (compared to 122.6 in the 1970s). The other opening batsman is West Indian Gordon Greenidge with a rating of 103.6. At No.6, and the highest rating batsman of the decade, is Allan Border of Australia (137.3). The next three most highly rated batsman each rated more highly than at least one of the two specialist openers, but they were middle-order players with little opening experience — West Indies captain Clive Lloyd (111.6), Australia's Dean Jones (101.7) and England's David Gower (101.6). The next two most highly rated batsmen were India's Dillip Vengsarkar (100.0) and West Indian Richie Richardson (98.2).

At No.7 is the all-rounder Imran Khan of Pakistan, at the top of his powers with bat (80.1) and ball (157.4). The standout wicketkeeper batsman is Jeffrey Dujon of the West Indies. The decade's top ranked bowler is New Zealand's Richard Hadlee (171.4) at No. 9, followed by the West Indian pair of quicks Malcolm Marshall (160.3) at No. 10 and Joel Garner (127.6) at No. 11. The four specialist bowlers all feature in the top 31 in history (Table 2.16) and all were devastating right arm fast bowlers.

Comparing the performances of the three top ranked bowlers Richard Hadlee, Imran Khan and Malcolm Marshall, all had similar bowling averages, strike rates and economy rates. The significant difference between Hadlee's rating and those of Imran and Marshall lies in Hadlee's higher number of 5 and 10 wicket hauls. Malcolm Marshall played alongside a number of wonderful West Indian bowlers, including Joel Garner, Michael Holding, Andy Roberts, Courtney Walsh and Curtly Ambrose — all feature in the top 58 in Table 2.16. Imran Khan also played alongside a number of outstanding Pakistani bowlers, including Wasim Akram, Abdul Qadir and Iqbal Qasim (all feature in the top 102 test bowlers Table A.2). By contrast, Richard Hadlee was the only world-class bowler playing at that time for New Zealand. For Imran Khan and Malcolm Marshall there were fewer opportunities to take 5 and 10 wicket hauls in matches despite playing more matches than Hadlee. Nevertheless, Hadlee's performances justify his position at the top of the bowler ratings for the 1980s.

After the top four, the next most highly rated bowlers are Australian Dennis Lillee (122.5), West Indians Michael Holding (118.6) and Courtney Walsh (104.5), India's Kapil Dev (108.2) and Pakistan's two spin bowlers Iqbal Qasim (104.8) and Abdul Qadir (102.1). In addition to the three great bowling all-rounders already mentioned, Imran Khan, Richard Hadlee and Kapil Dev, England's top-rating bowling all-rounder Ian Botham (ranked 3rd in Table 2.17) also played in the 1980s.

The batting and bowling statistics of the World team of the 1980s are presented in Tables 8.1 and 8.2, respectively, and the performances of the highly rated all-rounders and wicketkeepers who played in the 1980s are compared in Tables 8.3 and 8.4, respectively. The statistics of the eligible players in the best national teams are presented in Appendix I (Tables I.1 to I.7). Of those who played 20 or more test matches in the 1980s, 25 have been inducted subsequently into the ICC's Cricket Hall of Fame. They are:

England:	Geoffrey Boycott, Ian Botham, Graeme Gooch, David Gower and Bob Willis.
Australia:	Greg Chappell, Rod Marsh, Dennis Lillee, Allan Border and Steve Waugh.
West Indies:	Clive Lloyd, Gordon Greenidge, Desmond Haynes, Viv Richards, Courtney Walsh, Joel Garner, Michael Holding and Malcolm Marshall.
Indian:	Sunil Gavaskar and Kapil Dev.
Pakistan:	Imran Khan, Zaheer Abbas, Javed Miandad and Wasim Akram.
New Zealand:	Richard Hadlee and Martin Crowe.

The Top 11 Players:

No. 1: Opening the batting of the top world team for the second consecutive decade is India's Sunil Gavaskar. In the 1980s, during the second half of his career, he was widely regarded as India's best ever batsman. In this decade, he became the first test batsman to pass the 10,000-run mark and the first player to score 30 test centuries, bringing up his 30th century with 236 not out against the West Indies in 1983. He finished his career with more test runs and more test centuries than any other player. Gavaskar's record of 34 test centuries remained the record until beaten by fellow countryman Sachin Tendulkar in 2005. In Table 2.7, he ranks 21st on the list of the highest career test batting ratings.

No. 2: West Indian Gordon Greenidge is Gavaskar's opening partner. He was an aggressive and powerful opening batsman who played 108 test matches between 1974 and 1991 scoring 7,558 runs at an average of 44.72 with 19 test centuries. He had a stout defence when needed, but was a stylish stroke-player, who could, and often did, take apart the opposition attack. Throughout the 1980s, Greenidge was the senior partner in a wonderful West Indian opening batting combination with Desmond Haynes. In 148 partnerships between 1978 and 1991, Greenidge and Haynes scored 6,482 runs at an average of 46.63 runs per partnership, the most prolific opening batting combination in test cricket history.

Born in Barbados in 1951, Greenidge moved from Barbados to England at the age of 14 and began his first-class career with Hampshire. Eligible to play for England, he chose to play for his native West Indies. He played for Hampshire from 1970 to 1987 (forming another great opening partnership with South African Barry Richards) and for Barbados from 1973 to 1991. In the series against England in 1984, famously won 5-0 by the West Indies (and rather unfortunately dubbed the "blackwash" by the English press), Greenidge scored 214 not out on the 5th day of the 2nd Test at Lords as the West Indies successfully chased down 342 to win by 9 wickets. The target was reached in just 66.1 overs, and all who saw Greenidge bat that day will never forget his power and controlled aggression. In the same series, he scored 233 in the 4th test at Old Trafford. Earlier the same year, he had scored two centuries in Australia. Less than two weeks before his 40th birthday in 1991, Greenidge scored 226 against Australia at Kensington Oval to set up a West Indies win. He is the 65th highest rating test batsmen (Table 2.7). After retirement, he coached Bangladesh in the late 1990s assisting that nation to ICC full membership status and to enter test cricket in 2000.

No. 3: Sir Vivian Richards is the No.3 batsman, retaining the same position he held in the top team of the 1970s. He played 78 tests in the 1980s, scoring 5,113 runs at 49.16, with 15 centuries and an impressive strike rate of 66.77. Throughout his career, Richards never appeared to be intimidated by any bowler, it was he who did the intimidating. He was one of the most destructive batsmen of all time. His power and exquisite stroke-play have caused him to be rated by many experts as the greatest of post-war batsmen. However, style and presence at the crease are not always reflected in the statistics and his ranking at No. 27 in Table 2.7 will be disputed by many who saw the "master blaster" in action.

In 1986 against England in Antigua, Richards scored 110 not out at a strike rate of 189.66 to set up the West Indies win in the final test. It was the fastest test century in history taking just 56 balls. He is one of only four non-English players to have scored more than 100 first-class centuries. He holds numerous records in one-day cricket as well as test cricket. He was the first player to score a fifty and take 5 wickets in the same ODI and the first player to score a century and take 5 wickets in the same ODI. Richards captained the West Indies in 50 tests in the 1980s and early 1990s, winning 27, losing 8 and drawing 15. He was the only West Indian captain never to lose a test series.

No. 4: For the second decade in a row, Javed Miandad fills the No. 4 position in the batting line-up. In the 1980s, he scored 5,642 test runs at an average of 54.78 with 16 test centuries. Rating higher than Viv Richards and Greg Chappell in both the 1970s and 1980s, Javed Miandad was a truly outstanding batsman. In the seven tests against India in the calendar year 1983, he scored 763 runs at a batting average of 127.2. In the 2nd test against New Zealand in 1984, he scored centuries in both innings finishing that series with 337 runs at an average of 84.25. Javed scored 5 double centuries in the 1980s, more than any other player. He is the 26th highest rating test batsman (Table 2.7). In addition to his long and distinguished test career for Pakistan, Javed also excelled as a one-day batsman. The ICC currently rank Javed at 7th in the list of the best ever ODI batsmen. After retirement, Javed served three terms as coach of Pakistan and has continued his involvement in the game.

No. 5: Greg Chappell at No.5 is the fourth of the batsman to retain his place in the best side of the decade. At the later end of his career, Chappell played 33 test matches from 1980 to 1984, scoring 2,712 runs at 55.35, with 10 test centuries. In each of these 5 years, his top scores were over 150, with double centuries in 1980 and 1981. In Chappell's last test series, against Pakistan in the Australian summer of 1983-84, he scored 364 runs at a batting average of 72.80, including two scores in excess of 150, against an attack that included Imran Khan, Sarfraz Nawaz and Abdul Qadir. Chappell's retirement after the Pakistan series coincided with the retirements of Dennis Lillee and Rodney Marsh and signalled a downturn for the next half decade in the fortunes of the Australian test team. After retirement, Chappell coached South Australia at first-class level for 5 years and served a term as the national coach of India. As a coach, he was not nearly as successful as he was as a player. His name is forever linked as the villain in the infamous underarm bowling incident in an ODI match against New Zealand in 1981.

No. 6: Allan Border of Australia fills the No. 6 slot and is the highest rating batsman of the 1980s. A gritty and defiant left-handed batsman and a handy left arm orthodox bowler, he played 156 test matches between 1978 and 1994, scoring 11,174 runs at 50.56. He is the 23rd highest rating test batsman (Table 2.7) and he is the 8th highest rating batting all-rounder in test history (Table 2.17). He played domestic cricket for New South Wales (1976-80) and Queensland (1980-96), and county cricket for Gloucestershire (1977) and Essex (1986-88).

Border left an indelible mark on Australian cricket. When he retired, he had played more test matches than any other player, he had scored more test runs than any other player and he had scored more one-day international runs than any other Australian. From his 4th test against Pakistan in March 1979 until his final test against South Africa in March 1994, Border played in every Australian test match, 153 consecutive appearances — a world record for the next 24 years. In the 1980s, he scored over 1,100 test runs more than any other player.

Border's mark on Australian cricket goes well beyond his feats with the bat or his longevity as a player. Following the retirements of Greg Chappell, Rod Marsh and Dennis Lillee in February 1984, Border took over the captaincy of a young and inexperienced Australian team. In partnership with new coach Bob Simpson, Border rebuilt the Australian test team over the next decade, instilling a determination and work ethic that has characterised Australian cricket ever since.

For the remainder of the 1980s, Border was the backbone of the Australian batting line-up. In the 1985 Ashes Series in England, which Australia lost 1-3, Border scored 597 runs at a batting average of 66.33. In the loss to England (1-2) in the next Ashes Series, he scored 473 runs at 52.56. By the next Ashes Series in England in 1989, the Australian team under Border's leadership had developed sufficiently to win 4-0, with Border scoring 442 runs at 73.67. Border would go on to captain the team that retained the Ashes at home in 1990-91 and in England in 1993. In total, he captained Australia in 93 tests (the most by any Australian), winning 32, losing 22 and drawing 39.

After his retirement, Border has become a popular cricket commentator and has been honoured in many ways. In every series between India and Australia since 1996-97, the teams have played for the Border-Gavaskar Trophy. The Allan Border Medal is awarded at a gala dinner each year and is the highest individual award in Australian cricket. First-class cricket is often played on the Allan Border field in Brisbane.

No. 7: The first bowling all-rounder in the side is Imran Khan, the "Tiger of Pakistan". Born in Lahore in 1952, Imran was a swash buckling, aggressive striker of the ball and a devastating right-arm fast bowler. Imran played 88 test matches between 1971 and 1992, scoring 3,807 runs at a batting average of 37.69 and taking 362 wickets at a bowling average of 22.81. He sits at No. 17 on the list of the highest rating bowlers of all time (Table 2.16) and he is the 2nd highest rating bowling all-rounder in test history (Table 2.17). He is one of the few all-rounders to have achieved the 'double', 3500 test runs and 350 test wickets.

At his peak in the first half of the 1980s, he played 27 test matches between January 1981 and December 1986 taking 154 wickets at an average of just 14.85, passing 5 wickets in an innings 11 times and 10 wickets in a match 3 times. In the calendar year 1982, Imran played 9 test matches, 1 against Sri Lanka, 3 against England, 3 against Australia and 2 against India. He took 62 wickets at an average of 13.19, with best figures of 8/58 against Sri Lanka and 8/60 against India. His match figures of 14 for 116 against Sri Lanka are the best ever by a Pakistani bowler. Of all the players who have taken 50 wickets in a calendar year, Imran's bowling average in 1982 is the lowest in test history. In the 6-test series against India in 1982-83, Imran's performances are arguably the best by a bowling all-rounder in a single test series in history. He scored 247 runs at a batting average 61.75 and took 40 wickets at a bowling average of 13.95, spearheading Pakistan to a 3-0 series win.

Imran captained Pakistan in 48 tests and retired from cricket after he led Pakistan to victory in the 1992 One-Day Cricket World Cup. Since his retirement, Imran has rarely left the public eye. He has been a writer, a generous philanthropist and an outspoken, and often controversial, politician in Pakistan. He also served as the Chancellor of the University of Bradford from 2005 to 2014. In 2018, Imran was elected as the 22nd Prime Minister of Pakistan.

No. 8: The wicketkeeper is West Indian Jeffrey Dujon. He played domestic cricket for Jamaica from 1974 to 1993 and test cricket for the West Indies between 1981 and 1991. Dujon scored 3,322 runs in 81 tests at a batting average 31.94. As a wicketkeeper, he took 265 catches and made 5 stumpings in 150 innings behind the stumps — only 5 other wicketkeepers in test history have made more dismissals. He is the 15th highest rating wicketkeeper in Table 2.18.

Throughout his test career, Dujon kept wickets to the greatest fast bowling attack of all time. Originally selected as a batsman in his first two tests, he took over the gloves for his third test. He was an athletic and energetic keeper, agile and quick with a safe pair of hands. He had little opportunity to demonstrate his keeping skills up to the stumps for spin bowlers. In a decade of test cricket, Dujon played in 19 series, never losing a single series. He was a key player in one of the most consistently successful test teams of all time.

No. 9: Sir Richard Hadlee of New Zealand is the highest rating bowler of the 1980s. It was a decade of great bowling all-rounders; Hadlee's career coincided with the careers of Imran Khan, Kapil Dev and Ian Botham. While Hadlee's batting statistics are not as good as the other three, his bowling statistics in the 1980s were better than the rest. In fact, in a decade that included 5 or 6 of the greatest fast bowlers in history at the height of their careers, he rated highest. He was the top ranked ICC test bowler each year from 1984 to 1988.

Hadlee is regarded by many good judges as the best new ball bowler of all time and his ranking at No.4 in Table 2.16, and his position as the 8th highest rating bowling all-rounder in Table 2.17, support this assessment. In the 1980s, he took 289 wickets in 53 tests at a bowling average of 19.29. Over his test career, between 1973 and 1990, he played 86 test matches taking 431 wickets at a bowling average of 22.30 and scoring 3,124 runs at 27.17. At the time of his retirement, he had taken more test wickets than any other bowler.

Hadlee started the decade by taking 11 wickets in a home test against the West Indies in February 1980 at Dunedin and, in the next test a couple of weeks later, he scored his maiden test century. In the away series against England in 1983, Hadlee topped both the batting and bowling averages for New Zealand. In the second test of the return series against England in 1984 at Christchurch, New Zealand won by an innings in less than 3 days, dismissing England in both innings for less than 100. Hadlee was player of the match taking 8 wickets for 44 runs and top scoring for New Zealand in their only innings with 99 runs off just 81 balls. In 1985, Hadlee spearheaded New Zealand to its first ever series win in Australia. He was named player of the match in the first test in Brisbane, where he demolished Australia taking 9 for 52 in the first innings and 6 for 71 in the second. He also scored 54 runs off just 45 balls in New Zealand's only innings. In the 3-test series, he took 33 wickets at 12.15 runs per wicket. In February 1990, Hadlee became the first bowler in history to take 400 test wickets.

Richard Hadlee comes from a prominent New Zealand cricketing family. His father, Walter Hadlee, played 11 tests for New Zealand between 1937 and 1951, captaining New Zealand for the 1949 tour of England. His brothers, Dayle and Barry also played cricket for New Zealand, with Dayle playing 26 tests between 1969 and 1978. Richard's wife Karen also played cricket for New Zealand. Hadlee was knighted for services to cricket in 1990 and a bronze bust of him stands outside the Arts Centre in his hometown of Christchurch.

No. 10: The West Indian fast bowler Malcolm Marshall was another of the great cricketers from Barbados. In total, he played 81 test matches between 1978 and 1991 taking 376 wickets at an average of 20.95 runs per wicket. His performances in the 1980s were even better, taking 323 wickets at just 19.92 runs per wicket. Of all the bowlers who have taken more than 300 test wickets, Marshall's bowling average is the lowest and only Dale Steyn of South Africa and Waqar Younis of Pakistan have a lower strike rate. He is widely regarded as the best of the many great West Indian fast bowlers.

Marshall was relatively short in stature, but he was both fast and accurate. He could swing the ball both ways and he had a great leg-cutter and a fearsome bouncer. He was also a useful lower-order batsman, scoring over 1,800 test runs, including ten fifties, at a batting average of 18.85. He ranks 10th on the list of the highest rating test bowlers (see Table 2.16). Born in Bridgetown in 1958, he made his first-class debut for Barbados against Jamaica at the age of 19, taking 6-77 in Jamaica's first innings. Based on this single first-class performance, he was selected to tour India with the West Indies in 1978-79, when many of the established West Indies players were unavailable due to World Series Cricket commitments.

The West Indies lost that series against India. However, Marshall would go on to play a further 20 test series between 1980 and 1991 and the West Indies did not lose any of them. He was a key member of the most successful national team in test cricket history. He took more wickets in the 1980s than any other player. Of his many dominant bowling performances in the 1980s, his best was arguably during the 5-test series in England in 1988. He took 35 wickets at 12.66 runs per wicket to spearhead the West Indians to a 4-0 series win.

No. 11: West Indian speedster Joel Garner, affectionately known as "Big Bird", was one of the group of devastating fast bowlers that led the West Indian attack in their most successful period. He stood 6 feet 8 inches tall (2.03 m) and delivered the ball from an unprecedented height, thereby extracting prodigious bounce even from the most docile of pitches. As well as a dangerous bouncer, he could deliver a deadly accurate yorker. Garner played first-class cricket for Barbados from 1975 to 1987, for Somerset from 1977 to 1986 and for South Australia from 1982 to 1983.

In a 10-year career from 1977 to 1987, he played 58 tests, taking 259 wickets at an average of 20.98 runs per wicket. Of all the bowlers who have taken more than 200 test wickets, only Malcolm Marshall has a lower bowling average. Joel Garner is ranked 31st in Table 2.16.

Next Best Batsmen:

After the top 6 batsmen, the next 5 most highly rated batsmen in the 1980s are Clive Lloyd (West Indies), Dean Jones (Australia), David Gower (England), Dillip Vengsarkar (India), and Richie Richardson (West Indies).

[1] Clive Lloyd also just missed out on selection for the top 11 in the 1970s. Lloyd captained the West Indies team for the first 5 years of the 1980s, in what was the first five years of a 15-year period in which the West Indies did not lose a test series. His was the most successful national team in history. He is most remembered for his leadership, but he was an exceptional batsman. His batting average in the 1980s was higher than any other West Indian, including Viv Richards and Gordon Greenidge. After his retirement, he remained active in cricket, serving periods coaching and managing the West Indies, serving as an ICC match referee (from 2001-06) and a highly respected commentator.

[2] Dean Jones was a top-order batsman who played 52 test matches for Australia between 1984 and 1992 averaging 46.55. He played domestic cricket for Victoria (1981-98) and he had stints in county cricket for Durham and Derbyshire. His most memorable test innings was in the famous tied test against India in Chennai in 1986, where Jones scored 210 in Australia's first innings in the most trying of conditions. This remains the highest test score by an Australian in India. In addition to his fine record in test cricket, Jones was an outstanding ODI batsman, rating as the top ODI batsman in the ICC rankings for each year from 1989 to 1992. He was an outstanding fielder, quick between the wickets and noted for his footwork against both spin and pace bowling. He is the 119th highest rating test batsman (see Table A.1).

[3] David Gower was a stylish left-handed top-order batsman who played 117 test matches for England between 1978 and 1992, scoring 8,231 runs at an average of 44.25. He played county cricket for Leicestershire (1975-1989) and Hampshire (1990-93), scoring more than 26,000 first-class runs. His relaxed style and seemingly effortless stroke-play were often interpreted as lazy or aloof, but few who saw him bat could doubt his effectiveness. He captained England in 32 tests in the 1980s, with 5 wins, 18 losses and 9 draws. He is the 57th highest rating test batsman (Table 2.7).

[4] Dillip Vengsarkar was a top-order Indian batsman who played 116 test matches between 1976 and 1992, scoring 6,868 runs at an average of 42.13. Born in Rajapur, he played domestic cricket for Bombay (1975-1992) and county cricket for Staffordshire (1985). An elegant right-handed stroke-maker, strong in front of the wicket, he was one of the mainstays of the Indian batting throughout the decade, scoring 4,501 runs at an average of 46.89. He scored 6 test centuries against the strong West Indian bowling attack between 1979 and 1986 and he holds the unique distinction of being the only overseas batsman to score 3 test centuries at Lords, and he did it in three consecutive India versus England tests in 1979, 1882 and 1986. Vengsarkar captained India in 10 test matches from 1987 to 1989, but his period as captain was relatively unsuccessful, with just 2 test victories. He is the 94th highest rating test batsman (Table 2.7).

[5] Richie Richardson played 86 tests for the West Indies between 1983 and 1995, scoring 5,949 runs at an average of 44.40, generally batting at No.3. He played domestic cricket for the Leeward Islands (1981-96) and the Windward Islands (1997-98). He also played first-class cricket for Yorkshire (1993-94) and Northern Transvaal (1996-97). He was an elegant batsman, particularly effective against pace bowling and instantly recognisable at the crease by his wide-brimmed hat. In 1991, he took over the captaincy of the highly successful West Indian team from Viv Richards and led the national side until his retirement in 1995. He is the 91st highest rating test batsman (Table 2.7).

Next Best Bowlers:

After the top 4 bowlers, the next 6 most highly rated bowlers are Dennis Lillee (Australia), Michael Holding (West Indies), Kapil Dev (India), Iqbal Qasim (Pakistan), Courtney Walsh (West Indies) and Abdul Qadir (Pakistan).

[1] Dennis Lillee of Australia was the opening bowler in the top team of the 1970s and he was the next most highly rated bowler in the team of the 1980s. Approaching the end of his career in the 1980s, Lillee had lost some of his pace but none of his skill and accuracy. From 1980 to his retirement in 1984, Lillee took 171 wickets in 35 test matches at an average of 24.08. His bowling rating of 122.5 in the 1980s is only a little down on his rating in the 1970s (127.8) and he was by far the most consistent of the highly rated bowlers over both decades. He became more consistently accurate in the 1980s, using guile rather than extreme pace to bother batsmen. At the time of his retirement, Lillee had taken more test wickets than anyone else (355). He is the 15th highest rating test bowler in Table 2.16.

[2] Michael Holding was another of the great West Indian fast bowlers. Born in Jamaica in 1954, he played 60 tests between 1975 and 1987, taking 249 wickets at an average of 23.69. He is the 37th highest rating bowler in Table 2.16. His bowling action was smooth and uncomplicated, and he was very fast, often extracting

unexpected bounce and pace. His match figures of 14/149 against England at the Oval in 1976 are still the best by any West Indian bowler. Holding played first-class cricket for Jamaica (1973-89), Derbyshire (1983-89), Lancashire (1981), Tasmania (1982-83) and Canterbury (1987-88). After cricket, Holding has become a successful writer and cricket commentator, and he has taken up several positions with the ICC.

[3] Kapil Dev played 131 tests for India from 1978 to 1994, scoring 5,248 runs at an average of 31.05 and taking 434 wickets at an average of 29.65. Born in Chandigarh in 1959, Kapil Dev played first-class cricket for Haryana (1975-92), Northamptonshire (1981-83) and Worcestershire (1984-85). From 1994 until 1999, he was the leading wicket taker in test cricket. He was a hard-hitting right-hand batsman and an accurate right arm fast-medium bowler. His longevity and stamina made him unique in test cricket. He is the only man to score over 5,000 test runs and take more than 400 test wickets. Kapil Dev was named by Wisden in 2002 as the Indian cricketer of the 20th century. He is the 42nd highest rating bowler in test history (Table 2.16) and the 4th highest rating bowling all-rounder (Table 2.17).

[4] Iqbal Qasim of Pakistan is the highest ranked spin bowler of the decade. He played 50 tests from 1976 to 1988 taking 171 wickets at 28.11. A quicker than average left arm orthodox spin bowler, Iqbal used variations of pace and flight to deceive the batsman. His accuracy made him difficult to score against and he finished his test career with an economy rate of 2.22. His best match figures were 11/115 when he spun Pakistan to victory against Australia at the National Stadium in Karachi in 1980. He took 9/121 against India in Bangalore in 1987 in Sunil Gavaskar's last test match. In India's second innings, he took the prize wickets of Gavaskar, Mohammad Azharuddin, Ravi Shastri and Kapil Dev to set up the win for Pakistan and seal Pakistan's first series win in India.

[5] At the beginning of his long career in the 1980s, Courtney Walsh was an outstanding West Indian fast bowler. He played 132 test matches from 1984 to 2001 and took over 500 test wickets. He is the 16th highest rating bowler of all time (Table 2.16). He made his debut for the West Indies in the first test in Australia in 1984, bowling alongside Michael Holding, Malcolm Marshall and Joel Garner in what was the greatest era for West Indian cricket. West Indies won the 5-test series 3-1 and Walsh became a fixture in the team for the next 17 years. He rated highly enough to be selected in this book in the West Indies national team in three consecutive decades (the 1980s, 1990 and 2000s) — the only bowler to achieve this feat.

[6] Pakistan's Abdul Qadir is the second highest rating spin bowler of the decade. He played 67 tests between 1977 and 1990, taking 236 wickets and an average of 32.81, including best figures of 9/56 in England's first innings at Gaddafi Stadium in Lahore in 1987. In that 3-test series against England, he took 30 wickets at 14.57 to bowl Pakistan to a series win. Abdul Qadir bounded to the crease, with enthusiasm and controlled aggression, and confused batsmen with a variety of deliveries, including the orthodox leg-spinner, a top-spinner, two different googlies and a flipper. He is the 98th highest ranked test bowler (Table 2.16).

Highest Rating All-Rounders:

The 1980s was the decade of the all-rounders. Four of the seven highest rating bowling all-rounders all played against each other in the 1980s, Ian Botham, Imran Khan, Kapil Dev and Richard Hadlee. Ian Botham was the highest rating bowler of the 1970s, but his bowling rating slipped from 142.5 in the 1970s to a still excellent 100.0 in the 1980s. His batting rating however improved from 59.7 to 75.8, elevating him to the position of the highest rating bowling all-rounder in test history (Table 2.17).

Botham was a match winner. In a remarkable display of hitting in England's 2nd innings against Australia at Headingley in 1981, he set England on the way to one of the most remarkable victories in test cricket history. Australia scored 401 in its first innings, with Botham taking 6 wickets. England was than bowled out for 174, with Botham top scoring with a well-made 50. England was forced to follow-on and, at the end of the 3rd day, was precariously poised at 1 wicket for 6 runs. Mid-way through the 4th Day, England had slumped to 7 for 135, still needing a further 92 runs to make Australia bat again. Most Australians on the other side of the world went to bed, thinking that victory was close at hand. Finding unlikely batting support in bowlers Graham Dilley and Chris Old,

Botham smashed 149 not out to lift England's second innings to 356, with Australia requiring just 130 runs for victory. In a devastating display of fast bowling, England's Bob Willis took 8 for 43 and Australia was dismissed for 111.

Highest Rating Wicketkeepers:

The highest rating wicketkeepers in the 1980s are provided in Table 8.4. Jeffrey Dujon (with a rating of 107.9) heads the list, followed by Rod Marsh (Australia, 86.3), Ian Smith (New Zealand, 78.2) and Saleem Yousuf (Pakistan, 78.1).

Ian Smith was the New Zealand wicketkeeper in 63 tests between 1980 and 1992, making 176 dismissals (168 catches and 8 stumpings) and scoring 1,815 runs at an average of 25.56 and a strike rate of 63.17. He was an efficient and reliable wicketkeeper and an aggressive batsman. Smith took a world-record equalling 7 catches in an innings against Sri Lanka at Seddon Park in 1991. A year earlier in 1990 at Eden Park, he scored 173 against India off 136 balls, coming to the crease with New Zealand in trouble at 7 wickets down for just 131. This remains the highest test score for a No. 9 batsman. Smith is the 36th highest rating wicketkeeper in Table 2.18.

Saleem Yousuf played 32 tests matches as wicketkeeper for Pakistan between 1982 and 1990 making 104 dismissals (91 catches and 13 stumpings) and scoring 1,055 runs at 27.05. An excellent keeper to spin bowling, he was the first wicketkeeper to make 3 stumpings in an innings, a feat he achieved against New Zealand in an ODI match in Lahore in 1990. All three stumpings were off the bowling of Saleem Malik and one of the three New Zealand victims was the opposition wicketkeeper Ian Smith. Saleem Yousuf is the 49th highest rating wicketkeeper in Table 2.18.

Table 8.1 Best World team of the 1980s (1980 to 1989, inclusive) — Batting Performances.

Players	Country	Batting style	Matches	Innings	Not outs	100s/ 50s/0s	Highest score	Runs scored	Batting average	Strike rate	Batting rating
1. Gavaskar, SM	India	right	65	106	9	12/20/6	236	4,475	46.13	47.61	101.5
2. Greenidge, CG	W. Indies	right	75	123	12	12/25/7	223	5,094	45.89	49.20	103.6
3. Richards, IVA	W. Indies	right	78	112	8	15/28/7	208	5,113	49.16	66.77	120.7
4. Javed Miandad	Pakistan	right	76	110	7	16/26/3	280	5,642	54.78	49.17	134.0
5. Chappell, GS	Australia	right	33	55	6	9/10/6	235	2,712	55.35	54.67	118.4
6. Border, AR	Australia	left	97	164	30	20/40/4	205	7,386	55.12	42.23	137.3
7. Imran Khan	Pakistan	right	54	71	16	5/13/4	135	2,430	44.18	53.76	80.1
8. Dujon, PJL	W. Indies	right	64	89	9	5/14/5	139	2,885	36.06	47.74	63.9
9. Hadlee, RJ	N. Zealand	left	53	80	14	2/10/7	151	2,040	30.91	58.22	49.7
10. Marshall, MD	W. Indies	right	63	79	7	0/8/10	92	1,430	19.86	52.09	20.3
11. Garner, J	W. Indies	right	49	56	13	0/0/12	46	486	11.30	45.30	6.7
										Total	936.2

Next Best Batsmen:

Lloyd, CH	W. Indies	left	44	61	6	8/17/1	161	2,881	52.38	53.63	111.6
Jones, DM	Australia	right	30	53	7	7/7/4	210	2,370	51.52	48.69	101.7
Gower, DI	England	left	89	157	11	12/32/4	215	6,196	42.44	49.67	101.6
Vengsarkar, DB	India	right	71	112	16	12/22/7	166	4,501	46.89	47.61	100.0
Richardson, RB	W. Indies	right	45	76	7	10/13/3	194	3,320	48.12	46.58	98.2

Table 8.2 Best World team of the 1980s (1980 to 1989, inclusive) — Bowling Performances.

The Team:

Players	Country	Overs	Balls	Maids	Runs against	Bowl style	Wickets	5w/10w	Best	Bowl avge	Strike rate	Econ rate	Bowling rating
1. Gavaskar, SM	India	Less than 100 overs											-
2. Greenidge, CG	England	Less than 100 overs											-
3. Richards, IVA	W Indies	698	4,192	163	1,575	RAO	28	0/0	2/17	56.25	149.7	2.25	38.4
4. Javed Miandad	Pakistan	Less than 100 overs											-
5. Chappell, GS	Australia	228	1,371	69	475	RAM	13	0/0	3/49	36.54	105.5	2.08	37.6
6. Border, AR	W Indies	303	1,824	91	738	LAO	21	1/1	7/46	35.14	86.82	2.43	46.8
7. Imran Khan	England	2,005	12,028	483	4,896	RAF	256	18/5	8/58	19.13	46.98	2.44	157.4
8. Dujon, PJL.	Australia	Wicketkeeper						Did not bowl				-
9. Hadlee, RJ	Australia	2,308	13,852	628	5,574	RAF	289	28/7	9/52	19.29	47.93	2.41	171.4
10. Marshall, MD	England	2,399	14,398	511	6,434	RAF	323	22/4	7/22	19.92	44.58	2.68	160.3
11. Garner, J	W Indies	1,814	10,876	491	4,331	RAF	210	7/0	6/56	20.62	51.79	2.39	127.6
												Total	739.5

Lillee, DK	Australia	1,492	8,961	356	4,117	RAF	171	11/3	7/83	24.08	52.40	2.76	122.5
Holding, M.A.	W. Indies	1,544	9,274	338	4,302	RAF	184	9/1	6/21	23.38	50.40	2.78	118.6
Kapil Dev	India	2,815	16,888	615	8,036	RAFM	272	16/2	9/83	29.54	62.09	2.86	108.2
Iqbal Qasim	Pakistan	1,467	8,809	453	3,274	LAO	131	7/1	7/49	24.99	67.24	2.23	104.8
Walsh, CA	W. Indies	1,102	6.619	240	2.958	RAF	122	4/1	6/62	24.25	54.25	2.68	104.5
Abdul Qadir	Pakistan	2,528	15,175	548	6,980	RAL	216	14/5	9/56	32.31	70.25	2.76	102.1

Table 8.3 Performances of the best all-rounders (1980 to 1989, inclusive).

Player	Country	No. of tests	Years played	Batting style	Runs scored	Batting average	Batting rating	Bowling style	Wickets taken	Bowl avge	Bowl rating	All-rounder Rating
Imran Khan	Pakistan	54	1980-89	right	2,430	44.18	80.1	RAF	256	19.13	157.4	198.9
Botham, IT	England	75	1980-89	right	4,051	33.76	75.8	RAMF	258	32.40	100.0	163.7
Hadlee, RJ	N Zeal.	53	1980-89	left	2,040	30.91	49.7	RAF	289	19.29	171.4	160.3
Kapil Dev	India	80	1980-89	right	3,353	30.76	59.7	RAFM	272	29.54	108.2	143.7

Table 8.4 Wicketkeeping performances (1980 to 1989, inclusive).

Player	Country	No. of tests	Years played	Batting style	Runs scored	Batting average	Batting rating	Catches	Stumpings	Total dismissals	Wicket-keeper rating
Dujon, PJL	W Indies	64	1981-89	right	2,885	36.06	63.9	203	5	208	107.9
Marsh, RW	Australia	41	1980-84	left	1,162	20.03	20.6	142	4	146	86.3
Smith, IDS	N Zeal.	49	1980-89	right	1,376	25.02	32.4	128	7	135	78.2
Saleem Yousuf	Pakistan	25	1982-89	right	878	30.28	35.9	67	11	78	78.1

Note: The ratings are determined from the number of tests played as wicketkeeper.

Chapter 9
The Best World Team — 1990 to 1999

The 1990s saw the two-decade long ban on South Africa lifted and the introduction of Zimbabwe into test cricket. From 1990 to 1999, inclusive, 347 test matches were played. England played in 107 of them, Australia in 108, West Indies in 81, New Zealand in 81, India in 69, Pakistan in 76, Sri Lanka in 67, South Africa in 66 and Zimbabwe in 39. In the top team of the 1990s, Australia had three representatives, West Indies and Pakistan each had two and England, India, Sri Lanka and South Africa had one each.

The Best Team of the 90s

Batting Order:	Country	No. of tests (1990-99)	Period	Batting Rating	Bowling Rating
1. Gooch, GA	England	45	1990-95	120.7	22.2
2. Taylor, MA	Australia	93	1990-99	105.2	-
3. Lara, BC	West Ind.	65	1990-99	133.7	-
4. Tendulkar, SR	India	69	1990-99	143.9	30.3
5. De Silva, PA	Sri Lanka	62	1990-99	107.0	37.4
6. Waugh, SR	Australia	89	1990-99	125.4	74.2
7. Healy, IA (WK)	Australia	102	1990-99	59.2	-
8. Wasim Akram	Pakistan	62	1990-99	39.1	143.6
9. Ambrose, CEL	West Ind.	71	1990-99	9.4	151.1
10. Waqar Younis	Pakistan	56	1990-99	6.6	155.7
11. Donald, AA	South Africa	59	1992-99	6.0	147.2
			Total	856.2	761.7

Notes: 1. Batting and bowling statistics are given in Tables 9.1 and 9.2, respectively.
2. Of the 10 eras considered in this book, the team of the 1990s has the 7th highest batting rating and the 2nd highest bowling rating.

The win/loss/draw results for each of the participating countries are shown below.

Country	No. of tests	England	Australia	West Indies	New Zealand	India	Pakistan	Sri Lanka	South Africa	Zimbabwe	All matches
England	106	-	5/16/6	7/12/7	7/2/7	2/3/4	1/4/3	1/2/0	3/4/9	0/0/2	26/43/38
Australia	108	16/5/6	-	9/9/5	5/2/3	7/3/1	7/2/6	4/1/4	5/3/4	1/0/0	54/25/29
West Indies	80	12/7/7	9/9/5	-	2/2/2	2/1/5	3/4/2	1/0/2	1/5/0	0/0/0	30/28/23
New Zealand	82	2/7/7	2/5/3	2/2/2	-	2/2/8	2/8/0	3/4/5	1/4/2	3/0/5	17/32/32
India	70	3/2/4	3/7/1	1/2/5	2/2/8	-	1/2/0	5/0/8	2/4/4	1/1/1	18/20/31
Pakistan	76	4/1/3	2/7/6	4/3/2	8/2/0	2/1/0	-	5/2/5	1/3/3	6/2/4	32/21/23
Sri Lanka	67	2/1/0	1/4/4	0/1/2	4/3/5	0/5/8	2/5/5	-	0/3/2	5/0/5	14/22/31
South Africa	66	4/3/9	3/5/4	5/1/0	4/1/2	4/2/4	3/1/3	3/0/2	-	3/0/0	29/13/24
Zimbabwe	39	0/0/2	0/1/0	0/0/0	0/3/5	1/1/1	2/6/4	0/5/5	0/3/0	-	3/19/17

The team of the 1990s has a lower total batting rating than the team of the 1980s, but a higher bowling rating. The era of great fast bowlers that had begun in the 1970s continued into the 1990s, with the four top-rating bowlers in the decade all fast bowlers. However, the decade saw the emergence of three of the greatest spin bowlers of all time, Muttiah Muralitharan (Sri Lanka), Shane Warne (Australia) and Anil Kumble (India).

Having rebuilt its test team in the 1980s, Australia was the most successful team in the 1990s, winning 20 of its test series and losing 7. However, after 20 years away from the test scene, South Africa was remarkably successful, winning 15 of its 24 test series and losing only 4. Australia, South Africa, Pakistan and West Indies won more games than they lost, with the ratio of test wins to losses as follows: South Africa 2.23, Australia 2.16, Pakistan 1.52, West Indies 1.07, India 0.90, Sri Lanka 0.64, England 0.60, New Zealand 0.53 and Zimbabwe 0.16. The cricket was a little more attacking than in the previous decades with 35.7% of matches drawn (compared to 45.9% in the 1980s and 42.4% in the 1970s). Australia drew 26.9% of its matches, West Indies 28.4%, Pakistan 30.3%, England 35.5%, South Africa 36.4%, New Zealand 39.5%, Zimbabwe 43.6%, India 44.9%, and Sri Lanka 46.3%.

The six most highly rated batsmen of the decade fill the top six batting places in the best team for the 1990s. England's Graham Gooch, with a batting rating of 120.7, and Australia's Mark Taylor (batting rating 105.2) open the batting. At No. 3 and No.4 are two of the most prolific batsmen of all time, Brian Lara (batting rating 133.7) and Sachin Tendulkar (batting rating 143.9). No one has scored more runs in a single test innings than Brian Lara and no one has scored more test runs or made more test centuries than Sachin Tendulkar. Both feature in the top five of the highest rating batsmen of all time (Table 2.7). At No.5 is Sri Lanka's Aravinda de Silva (batting rating 107.0) and at No. 6 is Stephen Waugh of Australia (batting rating 125.4). The wicketkeeper and No. 7 batsman is Ian Healy of Australia, who was selected ahead of Alec Stewart of England. Healy was a specialist wicketkeeper, outstanding behind the stumps to both spin and pace bowling, and he had a significantly better keeping record than Stewart, who was often used by England as a specialist batsman in the 1990s with Jack Russell keeping wickets. Stewart had a batting rating of 97.5, second only to Graham Gooch in the best English side of the decade and was England's wicketkeeper in 60 test matches. He is unlucky to have missed out on selection.

The bowling attack consists of the four most highly rated bowlers of the decade, the only four with a rating above 140. At No.8 is Pakistan's bowling all-rounder Wasim Akram and at No. 9 is West Indian speedster Curtly Ambrose. The most highly rated bowler of the decade, Pakistan's Waqar Younis is at No. 10 and South Africa's Allan Donald at No. 11 completes the best team of the decade.

The next seven most highly rated batsmen are the two Australians Mark Waugh (101.2) and Michael Slater (98.7), Pakistan's Saeed Anwar (99.9), the three Indians Rahul Dravid (98.8), Sourav Ganguly (97.6) and Mohammad Azharuddin (96.9), and England's Alec Stewart (97.5). The next most highly rated bowlers are: Australian leg-spinner Shane Warne (133.1), Australian fast-medium opening bowlers Glenn McGrath (131.6) and Craig McDermott (113.1), South African paceman Shaun Pollock (126.9), West Indian speedster Courtney Walsh (117.7), Indian leg-spinner Anil Kumble (116.0), Sri Lanka's off-spinner Muttiah Muralitharan (115.0) and England's fast-medium bowler Angus Fraser (108.5). All of these bowlers went on to have great careers, with Muralitharan and Warne rating No. 1 and No.3, respectively, in the list of the highest rating bowlers of all time (Table 2.16). Muralitharan, Warne, Kumble, McGrath and Walsh all took more than 500 test wickets and are 5 of only 9 bowlers who have reached that milestone (up to the end 2024).

The batting and bowling statistics of the World team of the 1990s are presented in Tables 9.1 and 9.2. The performances of the highest rating all-rounders and the wicketkeepers in the decade are provided in Tables 9.3 and 9.4, respectively. The batting and bowling statistics of the eligible players in the best national teams are provided in Appendix J (Tables J.1 to J.9). Of those who played 20 or more test matches in the 1990s, 23 have been inducted subsequently into the ICC's Cricket Hall of Fame. They are:

England:	Graham Gooch
Australia:	Allan Border, Stephen Waugh, Shane Warne, Glenn McGrath, Ricky Ponting
West Indies:	Courtney Walsh, Curtly Ambrose, Brian Lara, Desmond Haynes
Indian:	Kapil Dev, Anil Kumble, Rahul Dravid, Sachin Tendulkar

Pakistan:	Javed Miandad, Wasim Akram, Waqar Younis
New Zealand:	Martin Crowe
Sri Lanka:	Muttiah Muralitharan
South Africa:	Allan Donald, Jacques Kallis, Shaun Pollock
Zimbabwe	Andy Flower

The Top 11 Players:

No. 1: Opening the batting in the top team of the 1990s is England's Graham Gooch. Gooch was somewhat of a late bloomer in test cricket, and like a good wine he got better with age. He started his test career in 1975, playing 73 tests between 1975 and 1989 and scoring 4,724 runs at an average of 36.91. However, from 1990 until his retirement from test cricket in 1995, he played 45 tests, scoring 4,176 runs at an average of 51.56. In 1990, against India at Lords, he became the first man ever to score a triple century and a century in the same test match (a feat only achieved once since by Sri Lanka's Kumar Sangakkara). In the three test home series against India in 1990, he scored 752 runs at an average of 125.33. In 1991, in England's win over the West Indies at Headingley, Gooch carried his bat through England's second innings scoring 154 not out in a total of 252 against a West Indian attack that included Malcolm Marshall, Courtney Walsh, Curtly Ambrose, Patrick Patterson and Carl Hooper. Wisden rated Gooch's innings as the best of all time in England and the third best at any venue. His career statistics rank him the 47th highest rating test batsman (Table 2.7).

Born in Essex, Gooch played first class cricket for that county throughout his career and holds the record of most first-class runs scored for Essex. He played a key role in Essex winning the county championship six times between 1979 and 1992, as well as winning every other major domestic trophy at least once in that period. In his long career (from 1973 until 2000), he scored 67,057 runs in first-class and List A limited overs cricket — more runs than any other player has ever scored.

Gooch captained England in 34 test matches between 1988 and 1993. He led from the front in what was a rather unsuccessful period for the English team. His test batting average as captain was almost double what it had been before he took the reins. At his retirement, he had scored more runs in test cricket for England than anyone else (and remains the second highest test run scorer for England behind Alastair Cook). He also holds the record for the most test runs scored at the home of cricket — Lords. After retirement as a player, Gooch served terms as head coach of Essex and batting coach of the English test side.

No. 2: Partnering Gooch at the top of the order is the left-handed Australian opening batsman Mark Taylor. Affectionately known as "Tubby", he opened the batting for Australia in 104 test matches between 1989 and 1999, scoring 7,525 runs at an average of 43.50, including 19 centuries. Taylor took over the Australian captaincy from Allan Border in 1994 and went on to captain Australia in 50 test matches, winning 26 and losing 13. Widely admired for his positive attitude and boy-next-door public face, Taylor has a sharp cricketing brain, and he is widely considered responsible for the Australian team's success in the 1990s.

Mark Taylor was born in the country town of Leeton in New South Wales, grew up in Wagga Wagga and moved to Sydney as a teenager. He played domestic cricket for New South Wales from 1985 to 1999. He first represented Australia in an under-19 youth international series against Sri Lanka in 1982, with Stephen and Mark Waugh also making their representative debuts in the same series.

After an inauspicious start to his test career against the West Indies early in 1989, Taylor scored 839 runs at an average of 83.9 in the six-test series in England later that year, the second highest aggregate in an Ashes series in England (only surpassed by Bradman's 974 runs in 1930). In the 5th test of that series, Taylor and Geoff Marsh became the first pair to bat for an entire day in a test in England. Taylor made 219 in a partnership of 329. Between 1993 and 1999, Taylor opened the batting 78 times with Michael Slater, and with an opening partnership average of 51.14, they formed the 6th most successful opening combination in history. In 1998, Taylor scored 334 not out against Pakistan to equal Bradman's Australian record. Taylor declared overnight and denied himself the opportunity to take the record from Bradman. He is the 54th highest rating test batsman (Table 2.7).

As well as a fine opening batsman, Taylor was regarded as the best first slip fielder of his day. At the time of his retirement, he had taken 157 catches, then the test cricket record. Among his achievements after cricket, Taylor was named Australian of the Year in 1999, awarded a Centenary Medal in 2001, awarded an Officer of the Order of Australia in 2003 and has continued to be a regular face on Australian television as a cricket commentator for the Nine Network and as a Director of Cricket Australia.

No. 3: West Indian Brian Lara is third in the batting line-up. He is ranked 5th in the list of highest career batting ratings (Table 2.7) and is the highest rating West Indian batsman. Lara played 131 tests between 1990 and 2006 scoring 11,953 runs at an average of 52.89. A magnificent left-hander with an elegant and very correct batting style, Lara made 34 test centuries and passed 200 on 9 occasions. He is affectionately known by his fans as "The Prince of Port of Spain". His ability to concentrate over long periods and make large scores sets him apart. Almost two decades after his retirement, Lara still holds the records for the highest score by an individual in test cricket and the highest individual score in first-class cricket.

In 1993 at the Sydney Cricket Ground, in just his fifth test match, he scored 277 against Australia, his maiden test century. It remains the highest score by any player in a match between Australia and the West Indies. A year later, he broke Sir Garfield Sobers' World Record for the highest individual score in test cricket with his 375 against England at the Antigua Recreation Ground. That record lasted a decade until Matthew Hayden of Australia eclipsed Lara with a score of 380 in 2003. Not to be outdone, Lara regained the record the following year with a score of 400 not out against England, once again at the Antigua Recreation Ground. Lara's world record is yet to be broken, and he remains the only batsman in test history to regain the record after losing it. He is also the only batsman in test history to have passed 350 twice.

Against Australia at Bridgetown in 1999, Lara scored 153 not out in the West Indies' second innings of 9-311, guiding the West Indies to a one wicket win on the 5th day of the match. That innings has since been rated by Wisden as the second-best batting performance in the history of test cricket (behind Bradman's 270 against England at the Melbourne Cricket Ground in 1937). Lara became the all-time top run-scorer in test cricket in 2005 and he held that record until overtaken by Sachin Tendulkar in 2008. Lara also jointly holds the record (with George Bailey of Australia) for the most runs scored off a single over in test cricket - 28 off the bowling of South African spinner Robin Peterson at the New Wanderers Stadium in 2003. He has scored test centuries against all test playing countries.

Despite Lara's exploits with the bat, the fortunes of the West Indian team were on the decline in the late 1990s. He played on the losing side in 63 test matches, a rather unfortunate record at the time of his retirement (but since eclipsed by his teammate Shiv Chanderpaul). He captained the West Indies in 47 test matches between 1997 and 2006, winning just 10 tests and losing 26.

Lara played first-class cricket for Trinidad and Tobago 1987-2008, for Warwickshire 1994-1998 and, in South Africa, for Transvaal 1992-1993. In 1994, playing for Warwickshire against Durham at Edgbaston, Lara scored 501 not out, which remains the highest first-class score of all time. Together with Bill Ponsford of Australia, he is one of only two players in history to have scored two quadruple centuries in first-class cricket. He was named the BBC Overseas Sports Personality of the Year in 1994, one of only 3 cricketers to receive that prestigious award.

After retiring from test cricket, Lara continued to play the shorter forms of the game in the West Indies, India, Bangladesh and Zimbabwe. In 2014, he played for the MCC against a rest-of-the-world team at Lords in a 50 overs celebration match to mark the bicentenary of Lords Cricket Ground. Lara was appointed an honorary member of the Order of Australia in 2009 for service to West Indian and Australian cricket. He is an Ambassador for Sport for Trinidad and Tobago, and in 2017 the Brian Lara Stadium was completed in Tarouba, Trinidad as part of the Brian Lara Cricket Academy.

No. 4: Lara is followed at No. 4 in the team of the 1990s, by India's Sachin Tendulkar — "the Little Master". Tendulkar is the highest rating batsman of the decade and is the 2nd highest rating batsmen of all time (Table 2.7), behind Bradman. Tendulkar's endurance and the total number of runs he amassed during his 25-year test and ODI career are amazing. He played 200 test matches between 1989 and 2013, scoring 15,921 runs at an average of 53.79. No other player has played more than 180 tests and no other player has scored more than 13,400 runs. Tendulkar also played 463 ODI matches (more than anyone else), scoring 18,426 one-day runs (over 4,000 runs more than anyone else). He is the only player to have scored more than 30,000 runs in international cricket. He has scored 51 test centuries (more than anyone else) and 49 ODI centuries (more than anyone else), making him the only player to have scored 100 centuries in international cricket (the next highest is Rickie Ponting of Australia with 71).

In the 1990s, still within the first half of his test career, Tendulkar scored 5,626 runs in 69 tests at an average of 58.00. He also rates high enough in the 2000s and 2010s to make the top Indian national team in three consecutive decades (Tables J.4, K.4 and L.4). Tendulkar made his test debut in 1989 against Pakistan at the age of 16 and played his final test at age 40 in 2013. In 2002, he was ranked by Wisden as the second greatest test batsman behind Sir Donald Bradman. Unlike many of his countrymen, Tendulkar performed just as well, if not better, away from the subcontinent than he did at home. He averaged 54.74 runs per innings away from home (in 106 tests) compared to 52.67 at home (in 94 tests). He scored 29 test centuries away from home, compared to 22 in India.

Tendulkar played domestic cricket in India for Mumbai from 1988 to 2013 and played a season for Yorkshire in 1992. He had a classical batting style, a combination of aggression and grace. His straight drive was textbook perfect, as were most of his other shots. Sir Donald Bradman is said to have considered Tendulkar's batting style similar to his own and Bradman selected Tendulkar in his team of the 20th Century. In addition to his batting, Tendulkar was a handy part-time bowler, often called on to break a partnership. Depending on the wicket and the circumstances of the game, he could bowl medium pace, leg-spin or off-spin. He took 46 test wickets at a bowling average of 54.17. He served two terms as captain of India between 1996 and the end of the decade. His tenure as captain was not successful. In 25 tests at the helm, only 4 were won, 9 were lost and 12 were drawn.

Throughout his career, Tendulkar received numerous sporting and civilian awards and, in 2013 after his retirement from test cricket, he became the youngest recipient of the Bharat Ratna Award, India's highest civilian award. He is the only sportsman to have received this honour. In 2012, he was announced as the winner of the Sir Garfield Sobers Trophy and ICC cricketer of the year, the oldest ever recipient of the trophy. In 2012, Tendulkar was nominated to the Upper House of the Indian Parliament, and, in the same year, he was named an honorary member of the Order of Australia for services to Indian and Australian cricket.

No. 5: Aravinda de Silva makes the top team of the 1990s batting at No.5. He was born in Colombo in 1965 and played 93 tests for Sri Lanka between 1984 and 2002, scoring 6,361 runs at an average of 42.98, including 20 centuries. He is the 80th highest rating test batsman (Table 2.7). He was at his peak in the 1990s, averaging 46.82 in 62 tests, with 14 centuries. He captained Sri Lanka in 6 tests without success, not registering a win and losing 4. Early in his career, he was an aggressive, often reckless batsman, but he settled into a fine attacking player. He was also an effective part-time off-spin bowler, taking 23 wickets in the 1990s at a bowling average of 38.7. In 1991, he made his highest test score of 267 against New Zealand at the Basin Reserve in Auckland and, in 1997, his most productive year of test cricket, he scored 1,220 runs in 11 test matches at an average of 76.26. In that year, he scored centuries in both innings of the test against Pakistan at the Sinhalese Sports Club Ground in Colombo. He repeated the feat at the same ground against India later that year. In his final test match in 2002 (against Bangladesh), he scored 206 in his last test innings, and he took a wicket with his final ball in test cricket.

In addition to his test performances, de Silva represented Sri Lanka in 308 ODI games, most notably helping Sri Lanka to win the final of the 1996 World Cup with a man-of-the-match performance. In doing so, he became the only person ever to score a century and take 3 or more wickets in a World Cup final. After retiring as a player, de Silva has served periods as chairman of Sri Lanka's national selection committee.

No. 6: Stephen Waugh of Australia makes the side at No.6. In his long career, Waugh played 168 test matches between 1985 and 2004 (as of the end of 2024 only Sachin Tendulkar and England's James Anderson have played more). He scored 10,927 runs at an average of 51.06, including 32 test centuries. He sits at No. 20 in Table 2.7. He was also an effective medium pace bowler, taking 92 wickets (including three 5-wicket hauls) at a bowling average of 37.45. He is the 6th highest ranking batting all-rounder in test history (Table 2.17) and the highest rating all-rounder in the 1990s. He performed well enough to earn selection in this book in the best Australian side in three consecutive decades (1980s, 1990s and 2000s). Stephen's twin brother Mark also had an illustrious cricket career for Australia and is the highest rating of the next best batsmen listed in Table 9.1.

Waugh was strong all around the wicket, determined, stubborn and hard to dismiss. He took over the captaincy of the Australian team from Mark Taylor in 1999 and would go on to captain his country in 57 tests, winning 41 and losing just 9. Often regarded as ruthless and uncompromising, he never took a backward step as a batsman or as captain and, with a winning ratio of 72%, he was effective. He led Australia to its world record of 16 consecutive test wins, beginning with the win against Zimbabwe in October 1999 continuing with clean sweep series wins against Pakistan, India, New Zealand and the West Indies and ending with the win against India in February 2001.

Waugh had a slow start to his test career, averaging just 30.12 in his first 24 test matches with a batting rating at the start of 1989 of just 40.0. He had held his position in the side, because of his bowling as much as his batting. He scored his first test century on the 1989 Ashes tour of England, 177 not out in the first test at Headingley, and finished the five-test series with 506 runs at an average of 126.5. The 1990s saw his career blossom, scoring 6,213 runs in 89 tests at an average of 53.1, including 18 centuries. Only Tendulkar scored more test centuries in the 1990s. In Australia's 9-wicket win over South Africa at Newlands in 1994, Waugh scored 86 in Australia's first innings and took a match-winning 5 for 28 in South Africa's second innings. He has scored more test centuries batting at No. 5 than any other player in test history (24) and only England's Ben Stokes has scored more test runs batting at No.6. In July 2003, he scored 153 against Bangladesh to become the first batsman to make a score in excess of 150 against every test playing nation.

Waugh was named the 2004 Australian of the Year for his cricketing achievements and for his charity work, particularly his role in raising funds for a children's leper colony, Udayan Home, outside Kolkata. He was appointed an Officer of the Order of Australia in 2003, and he has been named one of Australia's Living Treasures by the National Trust of Australia.

No. 7: The wicketkeeper and No.7 batsman is Australia's Ian Healy. In a test career from 1988 to 1999, Healy kept wickets for Australia in 119 test matches and made 395 dismals (366 catches and 29 stumpings) in 224 innings as keeper. At the time of his retirement, he had made more dismissals in test cricket than any other wicketkeeper. He passed Rod Marsh's world record number of dismissals (355) when he caught Wasim Akram off the bowling of Colin Miller in the 1st test against Pakistan in 1998 in Rawalpindi. Only South Africa's Mark Boucher and Australia's Adam Gilchrist have since made more test match dismissals behind the stumps. He was a technically superb keeper, with safe hands and nimble footwork. He was also a more than competent batsman, scoring 4,356 test runs at an average of 27.40, including 4 test centuries. He is the 6th highest rating wicketkeeper batsman in test history (Table 2.18).

Healy was a surprise selection for the 1988 tour of Pakistan after just six first-class matches for Queensland and then proceeded to play 119 of the next 120 test matches (missing only one match through injury). He played more test matches in the 1990s than any other player. Healy was a key member of the leadership group responsible for the resurgence of Australia's fortunes in the 1990s. He was selected as the wicketkeeper in the Australian Cricket Board's team of the 20th century.

Since his retirement from all forms of cricket in 1999, Healy has been a cricket commentator and sports presenter on Australian free-to-air television. He is well respected for his knowledge of the game and his critical evaluation of players' performances and team tactics. He is the uncle of Alyssa Healy who is the current wicketkeeper and opening batter for the Australian women's national cricket team. Alyssa is married to the current Australian opening bowler Mitchell Starc, who is one of the next best bowlers in the world team of the 2010s (see Chapter 11).

No. 8: Pakistani bowling all-rounder Wasim Akram was born in Lahore in 1966 and played in 104 test matches between 1985 and 2002, taking 414 wickets (more than any other Pakistani bowler) at a bowling average of 23.62, including 25 five-wicket hauls and 2 hat-tricks. He also took 2 hat-tricks in ODIs and shares the world record (with Sri Lanka's Lasith Malinga) for the most hat-tricks in international cricket. Wasim was a left-arm seam and swing bowler. He bowled both in-swing and out-swing with genuine speed and aggression. Wasim and his fast-bowling partner Waqar Younis were nicknamed "the Sultans of Swing" and, through the 1990s, became one of the most effective and feared fast-bowling partnerships of all-time. Wasim was accurate in both line and length and his mastery of reverse swing meant that he was as effective with the old ball as he was with the new ball. He also possessed a deadly in-swinging yorker that surprised many batsmen, either scattering their stumps or trapping them in front of the wicket. More than half of Wasim's 414 test wickets were either bowled or lbw. He is 18th highest rating test bowler (Table 2.16) and the 16th highest rating bowling all-rounder (Table 2.17).

Wasim scored 2,898 runs in test cricket at a batting average of 22.64, with 3 centuries. He was often criticised for being over aggressive with the bat. In 1996, he scored an unbeaten 257 against Zimbabwe, the highest ever score in test cricket by a No.8 batsman. In that innings, he hit 12 sixes, still the highest number of sixes in a single test innings. Equally successful in ODI cricket, Wasim was man of the match in Pakistan's World Cup Final Win in 1992 against England. He was the first player to take more than 400 wickets in both forms of the game (with only Muttiah Muralitharan since reaching the same milestone). Wasim captained Pakistan in 25 test matches in the 1990s, winning 12, losing 8 and drawing 5. He was an attacking captain, with only 20% of his matches ending in draws.

After retiring from the game, Wasim has become a successfully television commentator. He has also been a successful bowling coach both in Pakistan and for the Kolkata Knight Riders 20-20 franchise in the Indian Premier League.

No. 9: The outstanding West Indian pace bowler Curtly Ambrose earns his place at No.9. Ambrose played 98 test matches for the West Indies from 1988 to 2000, taking 405 wickets at the impressive average of 20.99. He is the 11th highest rating bowler of all time (Table 2.16) and is the 2nd highest rating West Indian bowler, behind Malcolm Marshall. For much of his career he was rated by the ICC as the best bowler in the world and he terrorised many batsmen with his pace, accuracy and hostility. He was selected by a panel of experts in a best of all-time West Indian XI. Standing 2.01 m tall (6 feet 7 inches), he got unexpected bounce, frequently getting even good length balls to pass by the batsman's nose. His accuracy and bounce made it difficult for opposing batsmen to score. Of all the great fast bowlers who have taken more than 250 test wickets, Ambrose has the lowest economy rate and is one of only three with a bowling average of less than 21.

A man of few words, Curtly Ambrose usually let his bowling do the talking, with numerous match-winning performances. He took his best figures of 8 for 45 in the West Indies win against England at Kensington Oval, Barbados in 1990. In the win against Australia by an innings at the WACA in Perth in 1993, Ambrose took 7 wickets in Australia's first innings giving away just a single run in the process. In 1994, at Queens Park Oval in Trinidad, with England needing 193 to win in its 2nd innings, Ambrose took 6 for 24 to bowl England out for 46. His wickets included 5 of the top 6 batsmen.

Born in Antigua in 1963, Ambrose played basketball in his youth and came to cricket relatively late, making his first-class cricket debut in 1985. He played domestic cricket for the Leeward Islands from 1985 to 2000 and county cricket for Northamptonshire from 1989 to 1996. A right arm fast bowler, Ambrose batted left-handed, with a single test 50 and a career batting average of 12.41.

No. 10: Waqar Younis of Pakistan was the highest rating bowler of the decade. A right-arm fast bowler, Waqar is the 14th highest rating test bowler (Table 2.16) and the highest rating Pakistani bowler. He played 87 test matches from 1989 to 2003 and took 373 test wickets at an average of 23.56. For most of his career, he bowled in partnership with Wasim Akram and the pair was largely responsible for Pakistan's success in test matches in the 1990s. Indeed, of all the test wickets taken by Pakistani bowlers in the 1990s, Wasim and Waqar took 47.4% of them. Waqar is well known as the master of reverse swing, and he swung the ball at high speed. He bowled with aggression and hostility and although his economy rate was higher than some contemporary bowlers, he ended his career with the lowest strike rate of any bowler with more than 200 test wickets. Currently, he stands at No. 4 in this list behind South Africans Kagiso Rabada and Dale Steyn and India's Jasprit Bumrah.

Waqar became the youngest test captain for Pakistan in 1993 when he captained his country in a single test against Zimbabwe. He would go on to successfully captain Pakistan again in the early 2000s. Of his 17 tests as captain, Pakistan won 10 and lost 7, with no draws.

Since his retirement as a player, Waqar has been appointed for various terms as the bowling coach of the Pakistan test and limited overs teams, and as head coach of the test team from 2010, stepping down in 2011. He was reappointed as Head coach in 2014 resigning two years later. He has served terms as bowling coach for a number of 20-20 franchises in the Indian Premier League, the Pakistan Super League and in the Bangladesh Premier League. He was reappointed as the bowling coach of the Pakistan team in 2019. Waqar was inducted into the ICC Hall of

Fame in December 2013 to become the 70th male member and the fifth Pakistani, joining Hanif Mohammad and his former teammates Imran Khan, Javid Miandad and Wasim Akram.

No. 11: South African speedster Allan Donald is at No. 11. Born in Bloemfontein in 1966, he commenced his first-class career for Orange Free State in 1985 and was selected to play in South Africa's first test after reinstatement in 1992. He played 72 test matches from 1992 to 2002, taking 330 wickets at a bowling average of 22.25. In 1992, against the West Indies, in South Africa's first test after more than 20 years in the test cricketing wilderness, Donald took 6 wickets. He led the South African attack for the next ten years. At his retirement from test cricket in 2002, he was South Africa's leading wicket taker in test cricket (now passed by Shaun Pollock, Dale Steyn and Makhaya Ntini). He is the 19th highest rated test bowler (Table 2.16).

Donald was a formidable opening bowler, accurate, fast and aggressive and a great competitor. In what was a golden year of test cricket for Donald, in 1998 he took an amazing 80 wickets, including 7 five-wicket hauls and 33 wickets in the 5-test series in England. Donald's career batting average was 10.69, earning him selection at No.11. Unfortunately, he is often remembered for being run out in the semi-final of the 1999 World Cup against Australia. In the last over of that game, South Africa drew level with Australia with 9 wickets down and, with four balls remaining, one more run was needed to progress to the final. Lance Klusener and Donald were batting, with Klusener at the batting end. Klusener drove the ball passed the bowler and set off for what should have been the winning run. Donald was watching the ball and did not run, both batsmen found themselves at the bowler's end. Donald was run out by half the length of the pitch and South Africa's disappointments in World Cups continued.

Donald played first-class cricket in South Africa for Orange Free State from 1985 to 2004, and in England for Warwickshire from 1987 to 2000. Since retirement, he has been a commentator on South African television for home test series. He was appointed bowling consultant for England in 2007 and has served terms as coach for Warwickshire in England, Mountaineers in Zimbabwe, the New Zealand ODI team and the South African test team. He was the bowling consultant to Sri Lanka in the 2017 ICC Champions Trophy, and he became Assistant Coach of Kent in 2018.

Next Best Batsmen:

[1] Mark Waugh played 128 test matches and 244 ODI matches for Australia and finished his career as Australia's leading run-scorer in ODIs. Mark played 99 test matches in the 1990s and is the No. 6 batsman in the highest rating Australian team of the decade (Table J.2). He is the 69th highest rating test batsman (Table 2.7) and the 44th highest rating all-rounder in test cricket (Table 2.17). Mark and Stephen Waugh hold the record for the most international matches in which siblings played together. The two brothers also hold the record for the highest partnership in first-class cricket by two Australians, with their unbroken 5th wicket stand of 464 playing for New South Wales against Western Australia in Perth in December 1990. As schoolboys, both brothers excelled at soccer, as well as cricket, and fortunately both decided to concentrate on cricket. Since retirement as a player, Mark has served terms as an Australian selector and is a popular television commentator on the game.

[2] Saeed Anwar was an attacking left-hand opening batsman who played 55 test matches for Pakistan between 1990 and 2001 scoring 4,052 runs at an average of 45.53 and a strike rate of 55.77, with 11 test centuries. He is ranked 98th in Table 2.7. He had the worst possible start to test cricket, with a duck in both innings of his one and only test in 1990 and was promptly dropped from the side. He was not recalled to play for Pakistan until the 3-test series against New Zealand in 1994, where he scored 169 in the 2nd test and finished the series with an average of 52.2. He scored runs all around the world, with a higher test average away from home than at home. In 1997, he scored 194 in a one-day international match against India, the then highest ever individual score in ODI cricket – a record that stood until 2009. In the test match against India at Eden Gardens in 1999, he guided Pakistan to a 46-run win carrying his bat through Pakistan's 2nd innings and scoring 188 not out. He captained Pakistan in 7 tests in the 1990s, winning just 1 and losing 4.

[3] Rahul Dravid of India made his test debut in 1996 against England at Lords where he made 95 in his first test innings. He played the first 34 of his 164 tests in the 1990s, ending the decade as the 7th most highly rated batsman. Today he is one of only 4 batsmen to have scored more than 13,000 test runs and one of only five batsmen with more than 35 centuries in test cricket. He ranks 8th in the list of the highest rating batsmen of all time (Table 2.7). Known affectionately as "the Wall", he had a great defence and wonderful concentration. By the end of the 1990s, he had announced himself to the cricketing world as a fine defensive batsman and a player to watch. He was a steady accumulator of runs, with a rather modest batting strike rate (38.99) but an impressive batting average (49.96), and he was hard to dismiss. He would go on to improve both his strike rate and his batting average in the 2000s.

[4] Michael Slater opened the batting for Australia in 74 test matches between 1993 and 2001, scoring 5,312 runs at a batting average of 42.84, with 14 centuries. He was a right-handed attacking opener from New South Wales who, with Mark Taylor, formed the 6th most successful opening partnerships in test cricket history. Slater was more prone to the "nervous nineties" than any other test batsman. He passed 90 on 23 occasions but was dismissed nine times before reaching 100. Only Sachin Tendulkar has more 90s, but Tendulkar passed 90 on 61 occasions and converted 51 of those into centuries. Slater made his highest test score of 219 in Australia's win over Sri Lanka at the WACA in Perth in 1995 and, on the way, he participated in an opening stand of 228 with Mark Taylor and a 3rd wicket stand of 156 with Mark Waugh. Since retirement, Slater has become a regular face on Australian television as a popular cricket commentator on the Nine Network and the host or co-host of several cricket and rugby league shows.

[5] Sourav Ganguly was born in Calcutta (now Kolkata) in 1972 and played first-class cricket for Bengal (1990-2010), Lancashire (2000), Glamorgan (2005) Northamptonshire (2006). Affectionately known as *Dada* and the *Prince of Calcutta*, he made his test debut at Lords in the 2nd test of the series against England in 1996, the same match that saw the debut of Rahul Dravid. Ganguly scored 131 in his first test innings and followed this with 136 at Trent Bridge in his next test innings. He was a left-handed stroke-player renowned for his cover drives and his off-side play square of the wicket. Ganguly performed at his best in test cricket in the 1990s playing 32 tests and scoring 2,432 runs at an average of 49.63. By the end of his test career in 2008, he had played 113 tests and scored 7212 runs at 42.18, with 16 centuries. He is the 76th highest rating test batsman (Table 2.7). He had an outstanding career opening the batting for India in ODI cricket with Sachin Tendulkar. In 136 opening partnerships, the pair scored 6,609 runs, still the world record. Ganguly is one of the few ODI players to have scored 10,000 runs, taken 100 wickets and taken 100 catches. He was a better than average right-arm medium pace bowler, taking a total of 32 wickets in test matches. Ganguly took over the test captaincy of the Indian team in 2000 and, over the next 5 years, led India in 49 test matches. He was one of India's most successful captains, with 21 wins, 13 losses and 15 draws. In 2019, Ganguly became president of the Board of Control of Cricket in India.

[6] Alec Stewart was unlucky not to have been included in the top team of the 1990s as wicketkeeper batsman. He played more test matches in the 1990s than any other English player and was England's second highest rating batsman in the decade, frequently opening the innings. Steward played 133 tests between 1990 and 2003, scoring 8,463 runs at 39.55. Through the 1990s, he kept wickets in 41 test matches, with Jack Russell frequently given the task of keeping so that Stewart could concentrate on his batting. In total, he was the English wicketkeeper in 82 of his 133 tests and was responsible for 241 dismissals in his 141 innings as keeper. He is the 11th highest rating wicketkeeper in test history (Table 2.18) and the 2nd highest rating English wicketkeeper. Stewart is the son of former English test cricketer Micky Stewart and, like his father before him, played first-class cricket for Surrey, Micky from 1954 to 1972 and Alec from 1981 to 2003.

[7] Mohammad Azharuddin was a top-order Indian batsman who played 99 test matches between 1984 and 2000, scoring 6,215 runs at an average of 45.04. Born in Hyderabad in 1963, he played domestic cricket for Hyderabad (1981-2000) and county cricket for Derbyshire (1991-94). A wristy, elegant left-handed batsman, he played 64 tests in the 1990s, scoring 3,880 runs at an average of 44.09, with 14 test centuries. He is ranked 68th in Table 2.7. He took over the captaincy of India in 1989 and led India in 47 tests and,

with 14 wins, 14 losses and 19 draws, he was India's most successful captain of the 20th Century. Azharuddin's cricket career came to an abrupt end when he was named in the match-fixing scandal in 2000 and banned from the game. The ban was subsequently lifted in 2012. After cricket, Azharuddin joined the Indian National Congress Party in 2009 and was elected as a member of the Indian Parliament.

Next Best Bowlers:

[1] Shane Warne was a leg-spin bowler who played the first 80 of his 145 test matches for Australia in the 1990s, taking 351 test wickets, more test wickets in the decade than any other player. However, his bowling rating in the 1990s was 133.1, the 5th best for the decade, but significantly less than his career rating of 180.2, and not high enough to force his way into the top team of the 1990s. His rating in the second half of his career in the 2000s did however earn him selection in the top team of that decade. Warne would go on to become the first bowler to take 700 test wickets (in December 2006). He is the 3rd highest rating bowler of all time, behind Muttiah Muralitharan and Sydney Barnes (Table 2.16).

Warne made his debut in first-class cricket for Victoria in 1990 and made a rather inauspicious test debut against India at the Sydney Cricket Ground in 1992 taking 1/150 in India's only innings. He did no better in the next test in Adelaide, finishing with match figures of 0/78. There was little to indicate that he would become Australia's greatest ever bowler. However, in the Ashes series in England in 1993, he was the leading Australian wicket taker with 34, clean bowling Mike Gatting with his first ball of the series. That ball has become known as *"the ball of the century"*. As a batsman, Warne was inconsistent, scoring 1,577 runs in the 1990s at a batting average of 15.61, with four 50s and a top score of 86 against India in 1999. He was also dismissed for a duck 20 times. In addition to his achievements in test cricket, he was also a valuable ODI bowler. In the 1999 World Cup, Warne was 'Man of the Match' in both the semi-final against South Africa and the final against Pakistan. He finished his career as unquestionably the greatest leg-spin bowler of all time.

[2] Glenn McGrath was a right arm fast-medium bowler from New South Wales who made his test debut for Australia in 1993 and played the first 58 of his 124 test matches in the 1990s, taking 266 wickets at the impressive bowling average of 22.88 and at a bowling rating of 131.6. His rating in the second half of his career in the 2000s earned him selection in the top team of that decade and sealed his place as the one of the most successful fast bowlers of all time. He is the 5th highest rating test bowler (Table 2.16). He took his wickets with accurate and persistent line and length and not with extreme pace. Throughout his career, he formed a wonderful bowling combination with Shane Warne; a combination that was largely responsible for the Australian team's successes in the 1990s and 2000s. In the 49 test matches in the 1990s in which McGrath and Warne played together, the pair took 443 wickets out of a total of 777 taken by Australia (57%).

[3] Shaun Pollock was an outstanding bowling all-rounder for South Africa who played 108 test matches between 1995 and 2008, taking 421 wickets at a bowling average of 23.12 and scoring 3,781 runs at a batting average of 32.32. He took 5 wickets in an innings 16 times and scored 2 test centuries. He is the 24th highest rating test bowler (Table 2.16) and the 9th highest rating bowling all-rounder (Table 2.17). He was consistent enough to be rated in this book in the top ten bowlers in the 1990s and in the 2000s. Shaun was destined to be a great cricketer; he is the son of South African fast bowler Peter Pollock and the nephew of South African batsman Graeme Pollock, both of whom made the highest rating world team of the 1960s (Chapter 6). Shaun played domestic cricket for KwaZulu Natal from 1992 to 2004 and county cricket for Warwickshire from 1996 to 2002. He made his test debut against England in 1995 at Centurion and, by the end of the decade, he had played 38 tests and taken 161 wickets at the impressive average of 20.46 and the excellent economy rate of 2.34. He also averaged 31.91 with the bat. He was South Africa's second highest rating bowler of the 1990s (behind Allan Donald).

[4] For a fast bowler, Courtney Walsh's longevity in the game is extraordinary. In his long test career, from 1984 to 2001, he played 132 test matches and took 519 test wickets at an average of 24.44 and an economy rate of 2.54. He is the 16th highest rating bowler of all time (Table 2.16). In the 1990s, he and Curtly Ambrose formed a formidable opening attack. In the second test against New Zealand at the Basin Reserve in Wellington in 1995, Walsh took his career-best figures of 13/55 in 36 overs. He is the only bowler to be selected in this book in his national team in three successive decades.

[5] Anil Kumble is India's highest rating bowler of all time. He played domestic cricket in India for Karnataka from 1988 to 2009, and played county cricket for periods with Surrey, Leicestershire and Northamptonshire. A right arm leg-spinner, he played 132 tests from 1990 to 2008, taking 619 wickets (the 4th highest number of wickets in test history) at a bowling average of 29.65. He took 5 wickets in an innings 35 times and 10 wickets in a match 8 times, including 10/74 in one innings against Pakistan in Delhi in 1999 to win India the match —only the second time anyone has taken all ten wickets in a test innings. He is the 9th highest rating test bowler (Table 2.16). For an over-the-wrist leg-spin bowler, Kumble was not a great turner of the ball, but he was remarkably accurate, relying on subtle variations of pace and bounce, as well as persistent accuracy, to take wickets. He is the only Indian bowler to have taken 5 wickets in an innings more than 30 times and he still holds the record for the most ever caught and bowled dismissals. In 2015, Anil Kumble became the fourth Indian Cricketer to be inducted into the ICC Hall of Fame (after Bishen Bedi, Sunil Gavaskar and Kapil Dev). He captained India in 14 tests from 2007 to 2008, winning 3, losing 5 with 6 draws.

[6] Muttiah Muralitharan of Sri Lanka played the first 48 of his 133 tests in the 1990s, taking 227 wickets at an average of 27.05, with a bowling rating of 115.0. Over the next ten years, from 2000 to 2009, inclusive, he played an additional 84 tests, taking 565 wickets at 20.97, with his bowling rating improving to a bewildering 226.6. Although he is now the highest rating bowler of all time (Table 2.16), his performances in the 1990s were comparatively modest, with nine other bowlers rating more highly and little to indicate the heights he would eventually reach. Relatively early in his career, he was no-balled on several occasions and accused of illegally throwing rather than bowling the ball. Murali's bowling arm has been slightly bent at the elbow since birth, and he has been unable to straighten it completely. His bowling action involves a hyperextension of his more than usually bent bowling arm, with a flinging wristy action that appeared to constitute a throw. However, each time he was accused, he was cleared by the ICC following extensive biomechanical testing. The 1990s saw the beginning of the greatest bowling career in test history.

[7] Craig McDermott played 71 tests from 1984 to 1996 and was the spearhead of the Australian attack for much of that period. A powerfully built opening bowler with deceptive pace and out-swing, he took 291 test wickets at an average of 28.63. He is the 62nd highest rating test bowler (Table 2.16). He played first-class cricket for Queensland from 1983 to 1995. He made his test debut at the age of 19 against the West Indies at the Melbourne Cricket Ground and, because of his youth, he earned the nickname "Billy" after "Billy the kid". Injuries plagued McDermott's career in the 1990s, limiting his opportunities. He scored 940 test runs at an average of 12.21. He was the Australian bowling coach for two terms between 2011 and 2016.

[8] Angus Fraser played first-class cricket for Middlesex from 1984 to 2002 and test cricket for England from 1989 to 1998. A hard-working and accurate fast-medium bowler, he took 177 wickets at 27.32 in 46 test matches. His best test performances were in the West Indies. He took 8/75 in England's famous win in Barbados in 1994 and, four years later in 1998, he took 8/53 at Queen's Park Oval, his best test figures. He is the 84th highest ranked test bowler (Table 2.16). After retiring as a player, Fraser became a journalist and a cricket commentator. He has also served terms as Director of Middlesex County Cricket Club and as a selector for the English cricket team.

Highest Rating All-Rounders:

The highest rating all-rounders in the 1990s and shown in Table 9.3. Steve Waugh heads the list followed by Jacques Kallis. At the beginning of his great career in the 1990s, Jacques Kallis' bowling rating was greater than his batting rating. He would go on to become the leading batting all-rounder in test history (Table 2.17) and the 4th highest rating test batsman (Table 2.7). The ill-fated South African Hansie Cronje is the 3rd highest rating all-rounder of the decade. Cronje was a fine all-round cricketer. He played 64 tests in the decade, captaining South Africa in 49 of them. His test career ended in scandal when he was banned for life for match fixing.

Highest Rating Wicketkeeper:

After Ian Healy, the next two highest rating keepers are England's Alec Stewart and South Africa's Mark Boucher (Table 9.4). As has already been mentioned, Stewart was one of the top ranked batsmen of the decade (see Table 9.1) and unlucky not to have been included in the top team. In just 24 tests in the 1990s, Mark Boucher took 99 catches and made 2 stumpings, a higher number of dismissals per match than any other wicketkeeper in the 1990s. Boucher would go to play more test matches as wicketkeeper than any other player and make more dismissals than any other wicketkeeper. He is the 2nd highest rating custodian in test history (Table 2.18).

Table 9.1 Best World Team of the 1990s (1990 to 1999, inclusive) — Batting Performances.

The Team:

Players	Country	Batting style	Matches	Innings	Not outs	100s/ 50s/0s	Highest score	Runs scored	Batting average	Strike rate	Batting rating
1. Gooch, GA	England	right	45	83	2	12/17/3	333	4,176	51.56	50.99	120.7
2. Taylor, MA	Australia	left	93	166	12	15/35/5	334	6,306	40.95	41.02	105.2
3. Lara, BC	W. Indies	left	65	112	4	13/29/4	375	5,573	51.60	62.05	133.7
4. Tendulkar, SR	India	right	69	109	12	22/21/7	217	5,626	58.00	55.30	143.9
5. De Silva, PA	Sri Lanka	right	62	104	9	14/18/6	267	4,448	46.82	51.99	107.0
6. Waugh, SR	Australia	right	89	143	26	18/28/11	200	6,213	53.10	47.45	125.4
7. Healy, IA (WK)	Australia	right	102	159	21	4/21/15	161	3,949	28.62	51.11	59.2
8. Wasim Akram	Pakistan	left	62	96	10	2/3/7	257	1,956	22.74	51.49	39.1
9. Ambrose, CEL	W. Indies	left	71	104	21	0/1/20	53	1,016	12.24	50.73	9.4
10. Waqar Younis	Pakistan	right	56	76	18	0/0/11	45	607	10.47	46.69	6.6
11. Donald, AA	Sth Africa	right	59	75	27	0/0/13	34	532	11.08	35.54	6.0
										Total	856.2

Next Batters:

Waugh, ME	Australia	right	99	164	11	17/37/15	153	6,371	41.64	51.74	101.2
Saeed Anwar	Pakistan	left	44	75	2	9/21/8	188	3,366	46.11	57.23	99.9
Dravid, R.	India	right	34	58	4	6/16/1	190	2,698	49.96	38.78	98.8
Slater, MJ	Australia	right	58	103	5	13/16/9	219	4,425	45.15	52.64	98.7
Ganguly, SC	India	left	32	54	5	7/12/4	173	2,432	49.63	47.66	97.6
Stewart, AJ	England	right	93	169	12	12/34/7	190	6,407	40.81	47.84	97.5
Azharuddin, Mohd.	India	right	64	94	6	14/12/3	192	3,880	44.09	60.16	96.9

Table 9.2 Best World Team of the 1990s (1990 to 1999, inclusive) — Bowling Performances.

The Team:

Players	Country	Overs	Balls	Maids.	Runs against	Bowl style	Wickets	5w/10w	Best	Bowl avge	Strike rate	Econ rate	Bowling rating
1. Gooch, GA	England	173	1,038	45	447	RAM	9	0/0	3/39	49.67	115.4	2.58	22.2
2. Taylor, MA	Australia					Less than 100 overs							-
3. Lara, BC	W. Indies					Less than 100 overs							-
4. Tendulkar, SR	India	152	912	34	460	RAM	13	0/0	2/7	35.38	70.13	3.03	30.3
5. De Silva, PA	Sri Lanka	308	1,850	50	878	RAO	23	0/0	3/30	38.17	80.44	2.85	37.4
6. Waugh, SR	Australia	585	3,512	170	1374	RAM	47	1/0	5/28	29.23	74.72	2.35	74.2
7. Healy, IA (WK)	Australia		Wicketkeeper				Did not bowl						-
8. Wasim Akram	Pakistan	2,354	14,127	529	6,200	LAF	289	17/3	7/119	21.45	48.88	2.63	143.6
9. Ambrose, CEL	W. Indies	2,689	16,156	730	6,225	RAF	309	21/3	8/45	20.15	52.28	2.31	151.1
10. Waqar Younis	Pakistan	1,862	11,174	375	5,927	RAF	273	21/5	7/76	21.71	40.93	3.18	155.7
11. Donald, AA	S. Africa	2,164	12,995	544	6,200	RAF	284	19/3	8/71	21.83	45.76	2.86	147.2
												Total	761.7

Player	Country	Overs	Balls	Maids.	Runs against	Bowl style	Wickets	5w/10w	Best	Bowl avge	Strike rate	Econ rate	Bowling rating
Warne, SK	Australia	3,762	22,567	1157	9,009	RAL	351	16/4	8/71	25.67	64.29	2.40	133.1
McGrath, GD	Australia	2,325	13,954	642	6,086	RAFM	266	15/1	8/38	22.88	52.46	2.62	131.6
Pollock, SM	S. Africa	1,411	8,460	407	3,294	RAFM	161	10/0	7/87	20.46	52.55	2.34	126.9
Walsh, CA	W Indies	3,012	18,072	624	7,891	RAF	304	13/1	7/37	25.96	59.45	2.62	117.7
Kumble, A	India	3,032	18,206	786	7,341	RAL	264	15/3	10/74	27.81	68.96	2.42	116.0
Muralitharan, M	Sri Lanka	2,479	14,874	625	6,140	RAO	227	17/2	9/65	27.05	65.52	2.48	115.0
McDermott, CJ	Australia	1,926	11,562	450	5,597	RAFM	211	11/2	8/97	26.53	54.79	2.90	113.1
Fraser, ARC	England	1,667	10,015	409	4,513	RAFM	168	13/2	8/53	26.86	59.61	2.70	108.5

Table 9.3 Performances of the best all-rounders (1990 to 1999, inclusive).

Player	Country	No. of tests	Years played	Batting style	Runs scored	Batting average	Batting rating	Bowling style	Wickets taken	Bowl avge	Bowl rating	All-rounder Rating
Waugh, SR	Australia	89	1990-99	right	6,213	53.10	125.4	RAM	47	29.23	74.2	174.0
Kallis, JH	S Africa	32	1995-99	right	1,849	41.09	69.5	RAFM	53	28.45	78.8	143.7
Cronje, WJ	S Africa	64	1992-99	right	3,689	38.03	73.2	RAM	37	32.03	69.5	140.9

Table 9.4 Wicketkeeping performances (1990 to 1999, inclusive).

Player	Country	No. of tests	Years played	Batting style	Runs scored	Batting average	Batting rating	Catches	Stumpings	Total dismissals	Wicketkeeper rating
Healy, IA	Australia	102	1990-99	right	3,949	28.62	59.2	327	27	354	139.3
Stewart, AJ	England	41	1990-99	right	6,407	40.81	97.5	134	8	142	113.5
Boucher, MV	S Africa	24	1997-99	right	844	32.46	47.3	99	2	101	104.6

Note: The ratings are determined from the number of tests while playing as wicketkeeper.

Chapter 10
The Best World Team — 2000 to 2009

The decade 2000-09 saw Bangladesh became the 10th test cricket playing nation and for the first time all of the first ten test playing nations competed against each other. From the beginning of 2000 to the end of 2009, 464 test matches were played; England played 129 of them, Australia 115, West Indies and South Africa each played 108, New Zealand 80, India 103, Pakistan 83, Sri Lanka 96, Zimbabwe 44 and Bangladesh 61.

The Best Team of the 2000s

Batting Order:	Country	No. of tests (2000-09)	Period	Batting Rating	Bowling Rating
1. Hayden, ML	Australia	96	2000-09	151.5	-
2. Sehwag, V.	India	72	2001-09	140.9	37.4
3. Ponting, RT	Australia	107	2000-09	167.7	-
4. Jayawardene, DPMdS	Sri Lanka	95	2000-09	152.2	-
5. Kallis, JH	South Africa	101	2000-09	154.7	85.6
6. Mohammad Yousuf	Pakistan	71	2000-09	147.2	-
7. Gilchrist, AC	Australia	91	2000-08	116.3	-
8. Warne, SR	Australia	65	2000-07	20.8	143.3
9. Muralitharan, M	Sri Lanka	84	2000-09	9.6	213.0
10. Shoaib Akhtar	Pakistan	33	2000-07	6.4	134.9
11. McGrath, GD	Australia	66	2000-07	4.9	145.7
			Total	1072.2	759.9

Note: Batting and bowling statistics are given in Tables 10.1 and 10.2, respectively.

The win/loss/draw results for each of the participating countries are shown below.

Country	No. of tests	England	Australia	West Indies	New Zealand	India	Pakistan	Sri Lanka	South Africa	Zimbabwe	Bangladesh	All matches
England	129	-	6/15/4	15/2/7	8/2/2	2/5/8	5/3/4	5/4/6	7/6/5	3/0/1	4/0/0	55/37/37
Australia	115	15/6/4	-	15/1/2	9/0/4	7/7/6	7/0/0	6/0/1	13/4/1	2/0/0	4/0/0	79/18/18
West Indies	108	2/15/7	1/15/2	-	0/3/4	2/4/6	2/5/3	2/6/1	2/9/5	4/0/2	3/2/1	18/59/31
New Zealand	80	2/8/2	0/9/4	3/0/4	-	2/1/4	2/4/3	2/3/3	1/7/3	4/0/1	7/0/1	23/32/25
India	103	5/2/8	7/7/6	4/2/6	1/2/4	-	4/3/5	6/4/2	3/6/3	6/1/1	4/0/1	40/27/36
Pakistan	83	3/5/4	0/7/0	5/2/3	4/2/3	3/4/5	-	5/6/5	2/5/2	2/0/0	6/0/0	30/31/22
Sri Lanka	96	4/5/6	0/6/1	6/2/1	3/2/3	4/6/2	6/5/5	-	4/5/3	5/0/0	12/0/0	44/31/21
South Africa	108	6/7/5	4/13/1	9/2/5	7/1/3	6/3/3	5/2/2	5/4/3	-	3/0/1	8/0/0	53/32/23
Zimbabwe	44	0/3/1	0/2/0	0/4/2	0/4/1	1/6/1	0/2/0	0/5/0	0/3/1	-	4/1/3	5/30/9
Bangladesh	61	0/4/0	0/4/0	2/3/1	0/7/1	0/4/1	0/6/0	0/12/0	0/8/0	1/4/3	-	3/52/6

Note: Australia also played and won a single test match against the ICC World IX in 2005.

Australia dominated the decade, winning 68.7% of matches, with 79 wins, 18 losses and 18 draws — the most dominant performance by any national side in any era. The next most dominant national sides were the Australian team in the period 1920-1949, winning 57.6% of its matches, and the great West Indian side of the 1980s, winning 52.4 % of its matches.

In the period 2000-2009, Australia, England, India, Sri Lanka and South Africa all won more test matches than they lost. The ratios of wins to losses for the participating nations are Australia 4.39, South Africa 1.66, England

1.49, India 1.48, Sri Lanka 1.42, Pakistan 0.97, New Zealand 0.72, West Indies 0.31, Zimbabwe 0.17 and Bangladesh 0.06. The cricket was significantly more attacking than in the previous decades with 24.6% of matches drawn (compared to 35.7% in the 1990s, 45.9% in the 1980s and 42.4% in the 1970s). England drew 28.7% of its matches, Australia 15.7%, West Indies 28.7%, New Zealand 31.3%, India 35.0%, Pakistan 26.5%, Sri Lanka 21.9%, South Africa 21.3%, Zimbabwe 20.5%, and Bangladesh 9.8%.

Of the 11 players selected in the top team of the 2000s, 5 were Australian, 2 were from Pakistan, 2 from Sri Lanka and 1 each from India and South Africa. With a combined batting rating of 1072.2, the team of the 2000s is the 2nd highest rating batting side, behind only the team containing Bradman in the period 1920 to 1949. With a combined bowling rating of 759.9, the team is the third highest rating bowling side behind the team before World War 1 and the team of the 1990s. The team of the 2000s is without doubt the best all-round team in test cricket history.

Australia's Matthew Hayden with a batting rating of 151.5 and India's Virender Sehwag with a rating of 140.9 were the two most highly rated specialist opening batsmen in the 2000s. Australia's Rickie Ponting (batting rating 167.7) is at No. 3 and is the most highly rated batsman of the decade. He is second only to India's Tendulkar in the most test runs scored by an individual. Mahela Jayawardene of Sri Lanka is at No. 4 and the great South African batting all-rounder Jacques Kallis is at No. 5 and is the second highest rating batsman in the decade. Ponting, Jayawardene and Kallis are all in the top 10 test run scorers and all made in excess of 11,800 career runs. At No. 6 is Pakistan's Mohammad Yousuf. The wicketkeeper is Australia's Adam Gilchrist, perhaps the finest wicketkeeper batsman the game has produced. The bowling attack is arguably the best in the history of the game. With two quick bowlers in Pakistan's Shoaib Akhtar and Australia's Glenn McGrath and the two finest spinners of all time, Sri Lanka's Muttiah Muralitharan and Australia's Shane Warne.

That this is the strongest all-round team of any era is evidenced by the batsmen and bowlers who missed selection. Four of the top seven highest rating batsmen in history did not rate highly enough in the 2000s to make the top 6 batsmen in this side, including Sachin Tendulkar (ranked 2nd in Table 2.7), Sri Lanka's Kumar Sangakkara (ranked 3rd in Table 2.7), West Indian Bran Lara (ranked 5th), and India's Rahul Dravid (ranked 8th). West Indian Shiv Chanderpaul, Pakistan's Inzamam-ul-Haq and Zimbabwe's Andy Flower (ranked 14th, 28th and 60th, respectively) also just missed selection in the top 6. Sangakkara, Lara and Dravid all rated slightly higher than Sehwag, but none were specialist openers in test cricket. Three of the bowlers who just missed selection in the team of the 1990s also just missed selection in the top 11 in the 2000s, namely Anil Kumble (India), Courtney Walsh (West Indies) and Shaun Pollock (South Africa). Other bowlers who just missed selection were the two South African quicks (Dale Steyn and Makhaya Ntini) and Indian spinner Harbhajan Singh.

The batting and bowling statistics of the World team of the 2000s are presented in Tables 10.1 and 10.2, respectively, and the performances of the eligible players in the best national teams are provided in Appendix K (Tables K.1 to K.10). Of those who played 20 or more test matches in the 2000s, 17 have been inducted subsequently into the ICC's Cricket Hall of Fame. They are:

Australia:	Steve Waugh, Shane Warne, Glenn McGrath, Adam Gilchrist, Ricky Ponting.
West Indies:	Courtney Walsh, Brian Lara.
India:	Anil Kumble, Rahul Dravid, Sachin Tendulkar.
Pakistan:	Waqar Younis.
Sri Lanka:	Muttiah Muralitharan, Kumar Sangakkara, Mahela Jayawardene.
South Africa:	Jacques Kallis, Shaun Pollock.
Zimbabwe:	Andy Flower.

The Top 11 Players:

No. 1: Matthew Hayden is the highest rating opening batsman of the decade. He opened the innings for Australia in 103 test matches between 1994 and 2009, scoring 8,625 runs at an average of 50.74. He ranks 19th in the list of the highest rating test batsmen in Table 2.7 and he is the second highest ranked opening batsman behind England's Len Hutton. Hayden was an attacking, hard-hitting, left-hander, strong on both sides of the wicket and hard to contain. He ended his test career with a strike rate of 60.11. He had an equally impressive record in first-class cricket for his home state of Queensland (playing 101 Sheffield Shield matches and scoring 8,831 runs at 54.85) and, in county cricket, for Hampshire and Northamptonshire (scoring 3,461 runs at 55.82). Hayden also opened the batting for Australia in 161 ODI matches forming a successful opening partnership with Adam Gilchrist. He was agile for a big man and an exceptional close-to-the-wicket fielder. He took 128 catches in his test career, many in Australia's slips cordon.

Hayden scored 30 test centuries (29 of them in the 2000s), the 3rd highest number by an opening batsman behind Sunil Gavaskar (India) and Alastair Cook (England). In October 2003, he eclipsed Brian Lara's world record score of 375 when he made 380 against Zimbabwe at the WACA ground in Perth. Hayden's record lasted just 6 months when Lara reclaimed the record with an unbeaten 400 against England in April 2004. Hayden's 380 is still the highest score by an Australian in test cricket and the highest test score in Australia. Hayden is the only Australian to play 10 or more test matches in India and average over 50. His score of 203 against India in Chennai in 2001 is the second highest score by an Australian in India (behind Dean Jones' 210 in the tied test at Chennai in 1986).

Together with Western Australia's Justin Langer, Hayden was part of Australia's most successful opening combination in test cricket. Hayden and Langer opened the batting for Australia in 113 innings between 2001 and 2007 scoring 5,655 runs in partnership at an average of 51.41. This is second only to West Indians Gordon Greenidge and Desmond Haynes who scored 6482 runs in 148 opening partnerships at 46.63. Hayden was the opening batsman in the ICC Test Team of the Year in 2004, 2006 and 2007. He was appointed a member of the order of Australia in 2010 and is currently an Ambassador for the Australian Indigenous Education Foundation. He was inducted into the Australian Cricket Hall of Fame in 2017.

No. 2: Virender Sehwag of India is the next highest rating specialist opener and one of the most destructive attacking batsmen of all time. He opened the batting for India in 104 test matches from 2001 to 2013, scoring 8,586 runs at a batting average of 49.34 and at a strike rate of 82.21. He scored 23 test centuries. For an opening batsman with a batting average of almost 50, Sehwag's strike rate is remarkable. Of all the specialist batsmen who have scored more than 3,000 runs in test cricket, Sehwag has the highest strike rate. He is the 24th highest rating test batsmen (Table 2.7). Sehwag also opened the batting for India in 212 of his 245 ODI matches where he scored 7,518 runs at an average of 36.50 and a strike rate of 104.71. Of the batsmen who have scored in excess of 5,000 runs in one-day internationals, Sehwag's ODI strike rate is second only to Pakistan's Shahid Afridi.

A somewhat unorthodox right-handed batsman, Sehwag was extremely strong through the off side, often backing away to cut the ball with great power, relying on a keen eye rather than nimble footwork. Sehwag played alongside several of India's all-time best batsmen, including Sachin Tendulkar, Rahul Dravid, V.V.S. Laxman and Sourav Ganguly, but his aggression and ability to dominate any bowling attack is without equal and his achievements are astonishing. He holds numerous Indian and world records. Sehwag has made three of the top four highest test scores by an Indian batsman. His 319 against South Africa in Chennai in 2008 is the highest ever by an Indian batsman, reaching 300 off just 278 balls against an attack that included Dale Steyn, Makhaya Ntini and Morne Morkel — the fastest triple century in the history of test cricket.

Against Sri Lanka in Mumbai in 2009, Sehwag hit 293 off an attack that included Muttiah Muralitharan and Rangana Herath, bringing up his 250 off just 207 balls — the fastest 250 in the history of test cricket. His first 200 in this innings was the second fastest double century in test cricket. He scored 284 of these runs in a single day, the most runs in a day in test cricket since World War 2 (and third most in history behind Bradman's 309 in 1930 and Hammond's 295 in 1933). When he was caught and bowled by Muralitharan for 293, he missed by 7 runs becoming the first and only man to ever reach 300 in tests on 3 separate occasions. He has scored more than 200 in test cricket 6 times and is one of only four batsmen who have passed 300 more than once in tests. His 219 against the West Indies in 2011 became the highest ever score in an ODI match (since past by fellow countryman Rohit Sharma and Martin Guptill of New Zealand).

Sehwag was opening batsman in the ICC Test Team of the Year in 2005, 2008 and 2010 and ICC Test Player of the Year in 2010. He was also named the Wisden Leading Cricketer in the World in 2008 and 2009, the only player at that time to have been awarded that honour twice (later equalled by Sri Lanka's Kumar Sangakkara in 2011 and 2014 and surpassed by India's Virat Kohli in 2016, 2017 and 2018).

In addition to his achievements with the bat, Sehwag was a useful off-spin bowler, taking 40 test wickets at an average of 47.35 with best figures of 5-104 against Australia at Delhi in 2008, including the top-order wickets of Matthew Hayden, Rickie Ponting, Michael Hussey and Shane Watson.

No. 3: Ricky Ponting of Australia is the highest rating batsman in the 2000s and he is the 6th highest rating test batsman (Table 2.7). Only Sachin Tendulkar has scored more runs in test cricket than Ponting. He played 168 tests from 1995 to 2012, scoring 13,378 runs at an average of 51.85 and a career strike rate of 58.72. He scored 41 test centuries (only Tendulkar and Kallis have scored more), including 6 double centuries. At his best in the decade 2000-2009, Ponting scored more runs and made more centuries in that decade than any other player, both in test matches and in ODIs, and was voted "Cricketer of the Decade" by a jury of 38 former and current players and cricket writers.

Ponting captained Australia in 77 tests from 2004 to 2011, winning 48 and losing 16, with 13 draws. Only Allan Border has captained Australia in more tests and only Steve Waugh has a higher winning ratio as a captain (with more than 10 matches at the helm). Ponting was aggressive and fiercely competitive, both as a captain and as a player. He captained Australia to a world record equalling 16 consecutive test victories from the Boxing Day test against South Africa at the Melbourne Cricket Ground in 2005 until the 2nd test against India at the Sydney Cricket Ground in January 2008. This equalled the achievement of Steve Waugh's side 5 years earlier (Oct 1999 to February 2001). He also captained Australia in a world record 229 ODI matches winning 76% of them. He played in Australia's winning World Cup side in 1999 and captained Australia to victory in the World Cups of 2003 and 2007. His unbeaten 140 earned him the player of the match award in the 2003 final. He is the 4th highest run-scorer in ODI cricket (behind Tendulkar, Sangakkara and Kohli) and he is the only player in history to have played in 100 test victories. He also holds the record for the most ODI wins, with 262 wins. He was a member of the ICC Test Team of the Year for four consecutive years (2004 to 2007), ICC Player of the Year in 2006, and winner of the ICC Sir Garfield Sobers Trophy in both 2006 and 2007.

Ponting was an attractive right-handed batsman, with shots all around the wicket off both the front and the back foot. For much of his career, he was considered to be the best puller and hooker in the game. He was at his best against pace bowling but was also an excellent player of spin, using his feet to come down the wicket to the pitch of the ball. One of his few blemishes with the bat is his record against spin in India. His batting average in India was 26.48; dismissed by spin bowlers on 17 occasions and by pace bowlers just 6 times. Harbhajan Singh and Anil Kumble have dismissed Ponting 13 and 9 times, respectively, in international cricket.

An excellent close-to- the- wicket fielder, often in the slips cordon, Ponting took 196 catches in test cricket. He has taken more catches as a fielder in World Cup ODI matches than any other player. After retiring from test cricket at the end of 2012, Ponting became a successful television commentator.

No. 4: Mahela Jayawardene of Sri Lanka is the third highest rating batsman of the decade and has been selected at No. 4. He played 149 test matches between his debut in 1997 and his final match in 2014, scoring 11,814 career runs at an average of 49.85. No other Sri Lankan has played more tests and only Kumar Sangakkara has scored more test runs. At his best in the decade 2000-2009, when he played 95 test matches and scored 8,187 runs at 55.32. He is 10th highest rating test batsmen (Table 2.7) and is the second highest rating Sri Lankan batsman (behind Kumar Sangakkara). He is one of only seven players who have scored more than 10,000 runs in both tests and ODIs, the others are Sachin Tendulkar, Ricky Ponting, Jacques Kallis, Rahul Dravid, Kumar Sangakkara and Brian Lara (all of whom are among the highest rating batsmen of the 2000s — Table 10.1).

Born in Colombo in 1977, Jayawardene was a stylish right-handed batsman and a great player of spin bowling. He played first-class cricket domestically in Colombo for the Sinhalese Sports Club from 1995 to 2015, forcing his way into the Sri Lankan national team within two years of his first-class debut. Able to concentrate for long periods, his test career included a triple century, 7 double centuries (only 3 players have scored more doubles) and 34 centuries. In July 2006, at the Sinhalese Sports Club Ground in Columbo (his home ground), he scored 374 against a South African bowling attack that included Dale Steyn and Makhaya Ntini — the highest score ever by a Sri Lankan batsman, the 4th highest ever score in test cricket and the highest score ever by a right-handed batsman. In this same innings, he shared a partnership of 624 for the 3rd wicket with Kumar Sangakkara — the highest partnership for any wicket in the history of test and first-class cricket. In fact, the batting partnership of Jayawardene and Sangakkara is the most productive 3rd wicket combination in history (with 5,890 runs).

Other batting records of Mahela Jayawardene include: the second highest 4th wicket partnership of all time (437 with Thilan Samaraweera against Pakistan in 2009); the highest partnership for the 6th wicket of all time (351 with Prasanna Jayawardene against India in 2009); the Sri Lankan record partnership for the 8th wicket (170 with Chaminda Vaas against South Africa in 2004); and the world record for the highest number of test runs scored by any individual on a single ground (2,291 runs at the Sinhalese Sports Club Ground in Columbo). He was a member of the ICC Test Team of the Year in 2008.

As well as being a great batsman, he was a brilliant close-to-the-wicket fielder, affecting more run outs in ODI cricket than any other fielder. In test cricket, the method of dismissal *caught Jayawardene bowled Muralitharan* is the most common fielder-bowler combination in history. With 205 catches, Jayawardene has taken more catches in test cricket than any other non-wicketkeeping fielder, with the exception of Rahul Dravid of India (210 catches). He is the only non-wicketkeeping cricketer to have taken more than 200 catches in both tests and ODIs. In fact, he is the only fielder with more than 200 catches in ODIs.

Jayawardene took over the captaincy of Sri Lanka in 2006 and captained his country in 38 test matches, winning 18, losing 12 and drawing 8. In 2006, he was named by the International Cricket Council as the best international captain of the year. Since retiring from test cricket, he has had a successful coaching career. He was appointed batting consultant for England in 2015. He successfully coached the Mumbai Indians to victory in the final of the 2017 Indian Premier League and, in that same year, he was appointed head coach of the Khulna Titans franchise in the Bangladesh Premier League.

No. 5: South Africa's Jacques Kallis is the second highest rating batsman of the decade. He was runner up to Ricky Ponting as "player of the decade" and was a member of the ICC Test Team of the Year in six years between 2004 and 2012. He was ICC Test Player of the Year and winner of the ICC Sir Garfield Sobers Trophy in 2005. Kallis is arguably the greatest all-round cricketer to have played the game — statistically the greatest all-rounder in Table 2.17. He was a classical right-handed batsman, good off both the front and back foot on both sides of the wicket, with every shot in the book. He was also an aggressive fast-medium swing bowler who made his first-class cricket debut for Western Provence as an 18-year-old in 1993 and his test debut against England two years later.

Kallis' test statistics are remarkable. He played 166 test matches between 1995 and 2013, scoring 13,289 test runs at an average of 55.37, with 45 test centuries. He also took 292 test wickets at an average of 32.65. He is the only player in test history to have scored more than 10,000 runs and taken more than 250 wickets. Remarkably, he also achieved this feat in ODI cricket, one of only two players to do so the other being Sri Lanka's Sanath Jayasuriya. Kallis was also an outstanding fielder, taking 200 catches in test matches and 131 in ODIs. He is the 4th highest rating test batsman of all time (Table 2.7) — only Sachin Tendulkar and Ricky Ponting have scored more test runs and only Tendulkar has scored more test centuries. He is 39th on the list of bowlers with the most test wickets and only two non-wicketkeeping fielders have taken more test catches. In March 2004, Kallis became only the second batsman in test history (after Sir Donald Bradman 66 years earlier in 1938) to score a century in 5 consecutive test matches. Less than four years later, in late 2007, he scored 5 centuries in 4 consecutive tests. He was man of the match in 23 test matches, more times than any other player.

When discussing the greatest batting all-rounders in test cricket, Sir Garfield Sobers and Jacques Kallis usually head the lists of most informed judges, and they top the list in Table 2.17. Their statistics are remarkably similar. Sobers career batting average (57.78) is a little ahead of Kallis' (55.37); Kallis made 103 scores in excess of fifty in 280 innings (1 in 2.72) a little head of Sobers' 56 scores in excess of fifty in 160 innings (1 in 2.86). Kallis' bowling statistics are a little better than Sobers': Kallis bowled a total of 3,372 overs taking 293 wickets at a strike rate of 69.29 and a bowling average of 32.65, whereas Sobers bowled 3,432 overs taking 235 wickets at a strike rate 91.91 and a bowling average of 34.04. Kallis' career bowling rating was 93.7, compared to Sobers' 89.6. In the field, Kallis took 200 catches in 166 matches (1.21 per match) and Sobers took 109 catches in his 93 tests (1.17 per match).

Little separates these two outstanding cricketers on paper, but on the field, they were entirely different. Sobers was flamboyant, unorthodox and exciting to watch, capable of destroying opposition bowling attacks and the favourite of the crowds wherever he played. Kallis is rarely described in such terms. Although he was capable of fast scoring when necessary; he set a new world record for the fastest 50 in test cricket history when he smashed 54 of just 24 balls against Zimbabwe in 2005 and he scored 97 sixes in test cricket, the 5th highest in history. However, he was generally a methodical, careful batsman, a relentlessly reliable accumulator of runs with an almost impregnable defence. Despite his remarkable statistics, he was often not the crowd's favourite, particularly outside South Africa.

No. 6: Pakistan's Mohammad Yousuf played 90 test matches between 1998 and 2010, scoring 7,530 runs at an average of 52.29, including 24 centuries. In the 2000s, he averaged 58.54 with the bat in 71 test matches (the second highest batting average of the decade behind Kallis). He has the 37th highest career batting rating (Table 2.7). Mohammad Yousuf commenced his test cricket career as Yousuf Youhana, one of the few Christians to have played for Pakistan. In 2005, he converted to Islam and, in so doing, changed his name. In the following year, he broke several world-batting records. In 2006, Mohammad Yousuf scored 1,788 runs in 11 test matches at an average of 99.33, with 9 centuries. This is the most runs in a calendar year in the history of test cricket and the most centuries. In achieving these records, he also equalled Bradman's record of six centuries in successive tests, but Mohammad Yousuf did it in 5 tests (compared to 6 tests for Bradman). Also in 2006, he scored 202 against England at Lords and then became the first player in test history to be dismissed three times in the 190s, with all three dismissals coming in the space of 4 test matches between the beginning of August and the end of November.

A fine player on all types of wickets, Mohammad Yousuf scored centuries against every test playing nation, including centuries on the home soil of all of them. He retired from international cricket in March 2010, after a controversial tour of Australia, but returned to play two final tests matches in England in August 2010. He rates in the top 4 Pakistani batsmen of all time. He was a member of the ICC Test Team of the Year in 2006 and 2007 and the ICC Test Player of the year in 2007.

No. 7: Adam Gilchrist of Australia is the most successful wicketkeeper of the decade, and the highest rating wicketkeeper batsman of all time (Table 2.18). He played 96 test matches between 1999 and 2008, taking 379 catches and affecting 37 stumpings, the second highest number of dismissals by a wicketkeeper in test history (behind Mark Boucher of South Africa). Of the 10 wicketkeepers with the most test dismissals, Gilchrist has the highest rate of dismissals (with an average of 2.18 dismissals per innings).

Gilchrist redefined the role of the wicketkeeper in modern test cricket and demonstrated the importance of the wicketkeeper scoring heavily and quickly at No. 7. He was an outstanding left-hand batsman and the 50th highest ranking batsman in test history (Table 2.7). He scored 5,570 test runs at an average of 47.61 and a strike rate of 81.96. Of all top-order batsman averaging over 40.0, Gilchrist's strike rate is second only to Virender Sehwag. He scored the fourth fastest test century when he took just 57 balls to get to three figures against England at Perth in December 2006. He was the first player to hit 100 sixes in test cricket. He has scored 17 test centuries, more than any other wicketkeeper. Of all the specialist test wicketkeepers, Gilchrist has the highest career batting rating (121.3). He was a member of the ICC Test Team of the Year in 2004 and 2005.

Gilchrist was born in Bellingen, New South Wales in 1971 and began his first-class career as a batsman with New South Wales in 1993. Unable to dislodge the incumbent wicketkeeper in the New South Wales side, Phil Emery, he moved to Western Australia for the 1994-95 season and his career as a wicketkeeper batsman blossomed. He made his international debut in one-day cricket in 1996 and took over from Ian Healy as the Australian test wicketkeeper in 1999. He was the regular vice-captain of the test team under captains Steve Waugh and Ricky Ponting and captained Australia in 6 test matches (with 4 wins, 1 loss and 1 draw). Gilchrist also had a wonderful career in One-Day International cricket. He opened the batting for Australia in 259 of his 279 ODIs, scoring 9,619 runs at an average of 35.89 and a strike rate of 96.95. Behind the stumps in ODIs, he took 417 catches and made 55 stumpings, with the highest rate of dismissals of any keeper in ODI history. Only Kumar Sangakkara has made more ODI dismissals. Gilchrist is one of only three cricketers who have played in the finals of three successive ODI World Cups (1999, 2003 and 2007). He scored over 50 in each final, including 149 off 104 balls against Sri Lanka in the 2007 World Cup final (arguably the best ever innings in a World Cup).

Gilchrist controversially *walked* in the semi-final of the 2003 World Cup against Sri Lanka when the umpire gave him not out. He declared that he felt it was the right thing to do, and he walked on several other occasions. This gained him the respect of many but caused many to shake their heads in dismay. He retired from test and ODI cricket in 2008 but continued to play in the Indian Premier League until 2013 having success with the Deccan Charges and Kings XI Punjab. Post-retirement, Gilchrist has been involved in several charities and is an ambassador for World Vision in India. He took up television commentary work in 2008, became a popular commentator on the game and now has a successful career in the media.

No. 8: Shane Warne played 145 test matches for Australia between 1992 and 2007, taking 708 test wickets with over-the-wrist leg-spin bowling at an average of 25.42. He is the 3rd highest rating bowler of all time, behind Muttiah Muralitharan and Sydney Barnes. He was a member of the ICC Test Team of the Year from 2004 to 2006.

In 2000, a panel of cricket experts selected Warne as one of the five Wisden Cricketers of the Century — the only specialist bowler. His flamboyant personality and immense skill had revived interest in leg-spin bowling, and it introduced an era of great spin bowlers after three decades in which pace bowling had dominated the game. However, it was in the 2000s when Warne was at his best on the field, despite being beset by several scandals off the field. He took 357 wickets in 65 test matches between 2000 and 2007 with a bowling average of 25.17 and taking 5 or more wickets in an innings 21 times and 10 or more wickets in a match on 6 occasions. He missed a full year of test cricket after he was suspended in February 2003 for testing positive to a banned substance, a prescription diuretic. This ban followed an earlier fine imposed on him for allegedly accepting money from a bookmaker. A number of highly publicised personal indiscretions also created controversy. Nevertheless, his on-field performances were not affected. In the two years following his one-year ban, Warne took 166 test wickets, including taking 5 or more wickets in an innings 11 times. In 2005, he took 96 wickets, the most wickets ever taken in a calendar year. He retired from international cricket after the final test of Australia's 5-0 Ashes victory against England in January 2007, at the same time as teammates Glenn McGrath and Justin Langer.

Warne played domestic cricket for his home state of Victoria from 1990 to 2007 and county cricket for Hampshire from 2000 to 2007, captaining Hampshire for his last three seasons with the county. He is one of only two players to have taken more than 500 wickets and scored more than 3,000 runs in test cricket. He was a competent right-hand batsman, often overly aggressive, who could provide valuable runs batting at No. 8 or 9, but who could also get out cheaply. He scored 12 test 50s, including four scores over 85, but no centuries. His top score was 99 against New Zealand in 2001, unfortunately given out on what was later shown on television replay to be a clear no-ball. He holds the dubious distinction of being the only batsman to have scored over 3,000 test runs, without ever scoring a century. In fact, only four other batsmen have scored more than 2000 runs without scoring a century. He has also been dismissed for zero on 34 occasions, to rank 5th in the list of most career test ducks.

After his retirement from test cricket, Warne played one further season for Hampshire and played in the Indian Premier League where he was captain and coach of the Rajasthan Royals leading his team to victory in the 2008 final. Whilst serving his one-year ban in 2003, Warne took on some television commentary work. Since his retirement from cricket, Warne continued as a cricket commentator and became a successful professional poker player. Since 2007, in test series between Australia and Sri Lanka, the teams compete for the Warne-Muralitharan Trophy in honour of the two most successful spin bowlers of all time. Warne passed away suddenly in 2022 at the age of 52.

No. 9: Sri Lanka's Muttiah Muralitharan has taken more wickets in test cricket than any other player and he has bowled more overs. He played domestic cricket in Sri Lanka for Tamil Union Cricket and Athletic Club and county cricket for periods with Kent and Lancashire. He was an off-spin bowler with a unique, sometimes controversial, bowling action that had batsmen bamboozled for the best part of two decades. He played 133 test matches from 1992 to 2010, taking 800 wickets at a bowling average of 22.73 (with Shane Warne's 708 wickets the next most successful) and a career bowling rating of 226.5 making him the highest rating bowler in test history (see Table 2.16). He took 5 wickets in an innings an incredible 67 times (with Shane Warne on 37 the next highest) and 10 wickets in a match 22 times (with Shane Warne next best on 10). He is the only player to have taken 10 wickets in a match against every test cricket playing nation and the only player to take more than 50 wickets against every test cricket playing nation. He also holds the world record for most wickets in ODI matches. His bowling achievements are staggering.

Murali's bowling action is like no other's, he gains off spin and top spin from a wrist spinning action that has consistently fooled even the best of batsman into believing he is bowling leg-breaks. He is also the master of the "doosra", a ball that spins from the leg to the off without any apparent change in bowling action. He uses the doosra to surprise a batsman who has survived long enough to be expecting an off-spinner. Murali was capable of bowling for long periods, usually attacking with every delivery. Although his bowling action has been the subject of much controversy and close scrutiny, he has bowled more deliveries in test cricket than anyone else and is the most successful bowler in history. He was a member of the ICC Test Team of the Year from 2006 to 2008.

In May 2004, Muralitharan took his 520th test wicket to pass Courtney Walsh's world record. The record was taken from Murali by Shane Warne in October the same year, while Murali was out injured. Murali would subsequently reclaim the record on 2nd December 2007 (by bowling England's Paul Collinwood in Kandy) and go on to claim his 800th wicket against India in Galle in 2010 with his last ball in test cricket. He is the only player to have taken 75 or more wickets in each of three different calendar years (2000, 2001 and 2006). In 2006, he took 90 wickets, including 5 or more wickets in an innings 9 times and 10 or more wickets in a match 5 times, at an average of 16.90, a strike rate of 39.24 and an economy rate of 2.58. Like Bradman with the bat, Murali with the ball is simply the best.

No. 10: One of the fastest bowlers of all time, Pakistan's Shoaib Akhtar was a right arm express bowler who earned his place in the team of the 2000s taking 144 wickets in 33 test matches at a bowling average of 22.22 and a strike rate of 39.69. Nicknamed the "Rawalpindi Express", one of his deliveries was officially recorded at 161.3 km/h in a match against England at the 2003 World Cup. Shoaib made his test debut against the West Indies in 1997, but it was not until the 2000s that his performances in tests began to be noticed. In 2002, he took 6 for 11 against New Zealand at Gaddafi Stadium and, in his two best years, 2002 and 2003, he took 72 wickets at an average of 15.08 runs per wicket. He is the 52nd highest rating bowler in tests (Table 2.16). He was also a successful bowler in one-day cricket, playing 163 ODI matches for Pakistan between 1998 and 2011 taking 247 wickets at a bowling average of 24.98 and a strike rate of 31.43.

Shoaib played county cricket for Somerset in 2001, Durham in 2003 and 2004, and for Worcestershire in 2005. Unfortunately, his career was plagued by controversy and injury and the cricket world did not see enough of Shoaib at his best.

No. 11: Glenn McGrath was a right-arm fast-medium bowler who played 124 test matches for Australia between 1993 and 2007, taking 563 test wickets at an average of 21.64. At the end of his career, no other pace bowler in the history of test cricket had taken more wickets than McGrath (overtaken in 2018 by England's James Anderson and in 2022 by England's Stuart Broad). Of the 9 great bowlers who have taken more than 500 test wickets, McGrath has the lowest career bowling average, the second lowest career strike rate and the second lowest career economy rate (behind Muralitharan). He ranks 5th in the list of the highest rating test bowlers (Table 2.16). He was a member of the ICC Test Team of the Year in 2005 and 2006.

McGrath played domestic cricket for New South Wales and county cricket for Worcestershire and Middlesex. He took 80 wickets for Worcestershire in 14 matches at an average of 13.21. He was a consistent, accurate and patient bowler, who could bowl accurate line and length, seemingly hitting the same spot on the pitch ball after ball and denying batsmen the opportunity to score. He formed a wonderful bowling combination with Shane Warne; a combination that was largely responsible for the Australian team's successes in the 1990s and 2000s.

McGrath retired from test cricket in January 2007 after the final test of the 2006/07 Ashes Series at his home ground, the Sydney Cricket Ground, at the same time as his bowling partner Shane Warne. He took James Anderson's wicket with the final ball of his test career. He retired from ODI cricket a few months later following the 2007 World Cup in the West Indies where he took 26 wickets, the highest number in the tournament, and became the highest wicket taker in the history of the World Cup. He was also named Player of the Tournament. In 2002, 21 sportspeople were inducted into the Australian Institute of Sport's "Best of the Best" Hall of Fame, Glenn McGrath was the only cricketer. He was inducted into the ICC Hall of Fame in 2012.

Next Best Batsmen:

After the top 6 batsmen, the next 6 most highly rated batsmen in the 2000s are Kumar Sangakkara (Sri Lanka), Rahul Dravid (India), Bran Lara (West Indies), Inzamam-ul-Haq (Pakistan), Andy Flower (Zimbabwe) and Sachin Tendulkar (India).

[1] Kumar Sangakkara played 134 tests for Sri Lanka from 2000 to 2015 scoring 12,400 runs at an average of 57.41, including 38 test centuries. His career batting rating is the 3rd highest in history, behind Sir Donald Bradman and Sachin Tendulkar (Table 2.7). He was unlucky to have missed selection in the top 11 of the 2000s, but he is the No. 3 batsman in the 2010s team. Sangakkara's batting in the 2000s would have gained him selection in any of the best teams since the Second World War, but not this one. He scored 21 test centuries in the 2000s, six of them double centuries. He scored 287 against South Africa in 2006 at the Sinhalese Sports Club Ground in Columbo and, in doing so, he participated in a still world record partnership of 624 with Mahela Jayawardene. He is all the more unlucky to have missed selection in the top 11 of the 2000s, because he kept wickets for Sri Lanka in 48 of his 88 tests, making 151 dismissals in 90 innings and is the 3rd highest rating wicketkeeper of all time (see Table 2.18). However, Gilchrist was the preferred wicketkeeper, because he kept wickets in all 91 of his tests in the decade and had a significantly better number of dismissals per innings. In an era of great batsmen, Sangakkara has a career batting rating higher than Brian Lara, Jacques Kallis, Ricky Ponting, Rahul Dravid, Mahela Jayawardene, Mohammad Yousuf, Matthew Hayden, Virender Sehwag, Younis Khan, Shiv Chanderpaul, Inzamam-ul-Haque and all the rest, except Sachin Tendulkar. He was a member of the ICC Test Team of the Year seven times from 2006 to 2014.

[2] In his 164 test matches for India from 1996 to 2002, Rahul Dravid scored 13,288 runs (the 4th highest number of runs in test history) at an average of 52.31 and he scored 36 test centuries (the 5th highest number of centuries in test history). In what was a great Indian batting team, he usually batted at No. 3 and often was the backbone of the Indian innings. With attacking stroke players such as Virender Sehwag, Sachin Tendulkar, V.V.S. Laxman and Sourav Ganguly batting at the other end, Dravid's steadiness and reliability provided wonderful balance to the Indian batting order. Sachin Tendulkar is the only Indian batsman who ranks ahead of Dravid in the list of the highest rating batsmen of all time (Table 2.7). Dravid played domestic cricket in India for Karnataka from 1990 to 2012. In the 2000s, he played in 103 test matches, not missing a single test for India, and scored 8,558 runs at 54.86 (more runs than any other Indian batsman), including 22 centuries. This performance would have earned him selection in the top world team in any other era after World War 2. He captained his country in 25 of these matches, winning 8 and losing 6, with 11 draws. He was a member of the ICC Test Team of the year in 2004 and 2006 and he was the inaugural winner of both the ICC Player of the Year and the ICC Sir Garfield Sobers Trophy in 2004.

[3] Brian Lara's batting rating in the 2000s was 142.6, better than the rating of 133.7 that earned him selection in the top team of the 1990s, but not high enough to retain his position in the top team of the 2000s. His career rating however places him the 5th highest rating batsman of all time (Table 2.7). In the 2000s, in the last 7 of his 17 years of test cricket, he scored 6,380 runs in 66 tests at an average of 54.07. This performance would have earned him selection in the top world team in any other era after World War 2. More than a decade after his retirement from test cricket, Lara still holds the records for the highest ever test score (400 not out against England in 2004), the highest ever score in first-class cricket (501 for Warwickshire against Durham in 1994) and the most runs ever scored off a single over in test cricket (28 off a Robin Peterson

over against South Africa in 2003). At his retirement, he had scored more runs in test cricket than anyone else. He was a member of the ICC Test Team of the Year in 2004 and 2005. There have been some great West Indian test batsmen, but Brian Lara is arguably the best of them all.

[4] Inzamam-ul-Haq played 120 test matches for Pakistan between 1992 and 2007 scoring 8,830 runs at an average of 49.61, including 25 test centuries. He was at his best in the 2000s scoring 5113 at an average of 55.58 in 62 test matches. His highest test score was 329 against New Zealand at Gaddafi Stadium in 2002. His career test batting rating is the 28th highest in history (Table 2.7). He captained Pakistan in 31 test matches in the 2000s, winning 11, losing 11 and drawing 9. Inzamam is the third highest run-scorer for Pakistan in test cricket (behind Younis Khan and Javed Miandad) and the highest scorer for Pakistan in ODIs (the 7th highest of all time). He was a member of the ICC Test Team of the Year in 2005. Inzamam is now a member of the Tablighi Jamaat, a Sunni Islamic missionary organisation, and he remains active in cricket administration in Pakistan. He was appointed the chief selector for the Pakistan test team in 2016.

[5] From 1992 to 2002, Andrew Flower played in 63 of Zimbabwe's first 66 test matches. He was an outstanding left-handed wicketkeeper batsman who scored 4,794 runs at an average of 51.55 and he affected 160 dismissals behind the stumps. At his best in the 2000s, he scored 2,214 runs in 24 tests at a batting average of 63.26. He is the 60th highest rating test batsman (Table 2.7), the 17th highest rating wicketkeeper (Table 2.18) and unquestionably Zimbabwe's finest ever test cricketer. In the 1st test against South Africa in 2001 at the Harare Sports Club, Flower scored 142 in the first innings and 199 not out in the second innings, the second highest aggregate score by a batsman in the losing side of a test match. Flower's playing career for Zimbabwe ended after he and teammate Henry Olonga wore black armband during the 2003 world cup in protest at the policies of the Zimbabwean Government of Robert Mugabe. Since then, he has had a successful coaching career, including an extended period as director and coach of the English test team.

[6] Sachin Tendulkar's incredible career continued throughout the 2000s. During the decade, he played 89 test matches and scored 7,129 runs at an average 53.20. His batting rating of 126.0 for the decade was a little down on his rating of 135.9 in the 1990s and was not high enough to force his way into the top 11. However, he cemented his stature as one of the greats of the game and continued to score runs against all oppositions both at home and overseas. For example, he scored 201 against Zimbabwe in India in 2000, 155 against South Africa in South Africa in 2001, 193 against England in 2002 at Headingley, 176 against the West Indies in 2002 in India, 241 against Australia in 2004 at the Sydney Cricket Ground, 194 against Pakistan in 2004 at home, 248 against Bangladesh in 2004, 153 at the Adelaide Oval in 2008 and 160 against New Zealand at Hamilton in 2009. By the end of the decade, he had scored more runs in test cricket than any other player in history, and in ODI cricket as well. He had also scored more centuries in both forms of the game than anyone else. He continues to hold all these records, except that his fellow countryman Virat Kohli has now scored one more century in ODI cricket than Tendulkar. He was a member of the ICC Test Team of the Year in 2004 and from 2009 to 2011 and winner of the ICC Sir Garfield Sobers Trophy in 2010. Sachin Tendulkar is unquestionably the best Indian batsman to have ever played the game.

Next Best Bowlers:

The next 6 most highly rated bowlers are Dale Steyn (South Africa), Makhaya Ntini (South Africa), Harbhajan Singh (India), Anil Kumble (India), Courtney Walsh (West Indies) and Shaun Pollock (South Africa).

[1] Dale Steyn was the 5th highest rated bowler in the 2000s and the highest rating South African. A right arm fast bowler, Steyn played 34 test matches in the 2000s (2004-2009) taking 172 wickets at a bowling average of 23.97 and a strike rate of just 39.98. Steyn went on to earn selection in the team of the 2010s (Chapter 11) and his career bowling rating is the 8th highest in history (Table 2.16). He is widely regarded as one of the best fast bowlers of the 21st century and one of the great attacking fast bowlers of all time. In 2007 and

2008, Steyn took 118 wickets at an average of 19.07 and a strike rate of 33.53 and he was named as the ICC Test Cricketer of the Year in 2008. He has been a member of the ICC Test Team of the Year for a record 8 years between in 2008 and 2016. At the close of the decade, Steyn's strike rate was the lowest of all the bowlers who played 20 or more test matches after World War 1. Mention must be made of New Zealand's Shane Bond whose career was cut short through injury and who played just 18 matches in the 2000s with a strike rate even better than Steyn's of 38.76.

[2] Makhaya Ntini played 101 tests for South Africa between 1998 and 2009 and was the 6th highest rated bowler in the 2000s. He was born in Mdingi, Cape Province in 1977 and played domestic cricket for Border (1995-2004) and Warriors (2004-13) and county cricket for Warwickshire (2005) and Kent (2010). A right arm fast bowler who together with Dale Steyn formed a formidable opening attack for South Africa. Ntini came from a humble background and was the first black South African to play for his country. His career bowling rating is the 38th highest in test history (Table 2.16). He generally bowled from wide of the crease and, consequently, rarely got batsmen out LBW, but his awkward bowling angle made him difficult to play. In 2005, against the West Indies at Queen's Park Oval in Port of Spain, he took 6 for 95 in the West Indies first innings and 7 for 37 in the second innings — the highest number of wickets in a test by a South African bowler.

[3] Harbhajan Singh was born in Chandigarh in 1980 and played first-class cricket for Punjab (1997-2018) and Surrey (2005-07). He was the 7th rated bowler in the 2000s and the highest rated Indian bowler in that decade. He was a right arm off-spinner who played 103 tests between 1998 and 2015. He took 417 test wickets and has the 45th highest bowling rating in test history (Table 2.16). Harbhajan was an attacking bowler with an unusually quick bowling action. He relied on good ball control and variations of length to get his wickets, and he had the ability to get the ball to jump steeply off a good length. His bowling average in India, on home soil, is significantly better than his average away from home. Although he could not be classified as a bowling all-rounded, he was a competent batsman, having scored 2225 test runs (including 2 centuries and 9 half-centuries) at a batting average of 18.24. Harbhajan's career was not without controversy, having had his bowling action reported and subsequently cleared, and having been accused of ill-discipline on several occasions. However, he was fiercely competitive and never took a backward step. His record shows him to be one of India's finest bowlers.

[4] As he did in the 1990s, India's Anil Kumble holds his place as one of the 8 most highly rated bowlers of the decade. In the 2000s, he played his final 74 test matches, taking 355 wickets at an average of 31.03 and a bowling rating of 120.7. On 17th January 2008, against Australia at the WACA Ground, Kumble had Andrew Symonds caught at first slip by Rahul Dravid to become only the third bowler in test history to take 600 test wickets. Only Muttiah Muralitharan and Shane Warne had taken more (James Anderson and Stuart Broad of England have both since reached the 600-wicket milestone in 2020 and 2023, respectively). In his long career, Kumble bowled 6,808 overs, more overs than any other bowler except Muralitharan. His strength was his accuracy and stamina; he could bowl at one end for long periods without relief. He bowled 89 overs in a test match against England in 2001 at Ahmedabad with match figures of 10/233 and 86.5 overs against Australia at the Sydney Cricket Ground in 2004 with match figures of 12/279. In addition to his bowling, Kumble was a competent batsman scoring 2506 runs in his test career at an average of 17.77 with 6 scores in excess of 50, including 1 test century (110 not out against England at the Oval in 2007).

[5] Courtney Walsh's 17-year long test career ended in 2001, playing the last 20 of his 132 tests in the first two years of the decade. In these 20 matches, he took 93 wickets at a bowling average of 19.73, significantly better than his career average of 24.44, and an economy rate of 2.07, significantly better than his career average of 2.54. He took 10 for 117 against England at Lords in 2000 and 6 for 61 against South Africa at Queen's Park Oval in 2001. His performances in just two years were good enough to earn him selection in the best West Indian team for the third successive decade.

[6] Shaun Pollock was born in Port Elizabeth in 1973, three years after the ban was imposed on South Africa that ended the test careers of his father Peter and his uncle Graeme. In the 1990s, he was the 7th highest

rating bowler and, in the 2000s, he was the 10th highest rating bowler. Whilst his teammate Jacques Kallis was the best batting all-rounder of the decade, Pollock was the most successful South African bowling all-rounder (see Table 10.3) and the 9th highest rating bowling all-rounder of all time (Table 2.17). Of all the bowlers who have taken more than 400 wickets in test cricket, only Kapil Dev of India has scored more runs than Pollock. From 2000 until his retirement in 2008, Pollock played 70 test matches taking 260 wickets at a bowling average of 24.77 and an economy rate of 2.43. He also scored 2,377 runs at a batting average of 32.56. He is the 24th highest rating bowler in Table 2.16.

After long-term captain Hansie Cronje was banned from test cricket for life, Shaun was appointed captain of South Africa in 2000 and successfully led the side in 26 test matches, winning 14 and losing 5, with 7 draws. He was removed from the captaincy in 2003 in favour of Graham Smith, after the ODI sides disappointing performance in the 2003 World Cup held in South Africa.

Highest Rating All-Rounders:

After Jacques Kallis, the next highest rating all-rounders in the 2000s were Sri Lanka's Sanath Jayasuriya, New Zealand's Daniel Vettori and England's Andrew Flintoff (see Table 10.3).

[1] Sanath Jayasuriya was a powerful left hand opening batsman and a tidy left-arm orthodox spin bowler. He was born in Matara in 1969, and he played first class cricket in Colombo for Bloomfield (1994-2011) and county cricket for Somerset (2005), Lancashire (2007), Warwickshire (2008) and Worcestershire (2010). From 1991 to 2007, he played 110 tests for Sri Lanka scoring 6,973 runs at an average of 40.07, a strike rate of 65.13 and a top score of 340 (the second highest by a Sri Lankan batsman). He also took 98 wickets at an average of 34.35 and an economy rate of 2.47. He is the 21st highest rating test all-rounder (Table 2.17).

He captained the test team in 38 tests from 1999 to 2003, winning 18 and losing 12. However, he is best known for his aggressive batting and match-winning all-round performances in ODI cricket. He played 445 ODIs for Sri Lanka. He is generally credited with being the first to introduce the strategy of hard-hitting aggression at the top of the order that revolutionised the one-day international game in the mid-1990s. Jayasuriya is the only player to have scored more than 10,000 runs and taken more than 300 wickets in one-day internationals. After retirement as a player, he served a term as the chairman of the Sri Lankan cricket selection committee, and he was elected to the Sri Lankan parliament in 2010.

[2] Daniel Vettori is New Zealand's 2nd highest rating all-rounder (behind Richard Hadlee) and is ranked at No. 23 in Table 2.17. He was a left-hand batsman and left-arm orthodox bowler who played 113 tests from 1997 to 2014 (New Zealand's most capped test player). He took 362 test wickets at a bowling average of 34.37 and scored 4,531 runs at a batting average of 30.01. He captained his country in 32 tests from 2007 to 2011 winning 6 and losing 16. Vettori also had a successful limited overs career playing 295 ODIs (more than any other New Zealand player) and taking more than 300 wickets in ODIs (more than any other New Zealand bowler).

[3] Andrew Flintoff was an attacking right arm fast-bowling all-rounder who played 79 test matches for England from 1998 to 2009. He took 226 test wickets at a bowling average of 32.79 and he hit 3,845 test runs at a batting average of 31.78 and a strike rate of 62.05. He is the 30th highest rating test all-rounder in Table 2.17. He also had a successful career in limited overs cricket. He was named "Man of the Series" in England's 2005 Ashes win against Australia and was awarded the very first Compton-Miller Medal for his efforts. He had a rather unsuccessful period as captain of the English test team in 2006 and 2007, winning just 2 of his 11 test matches at the helm, but he was a crowd favourite, particularly in England. He is one of the few players to be on both the batting and bowling honours boards at Lords. After retiring as a player, Flintoff has had a successful media career and has become a popular television personality and presenter both in England and in Australia.

Highest Rating Wicketkeepers:

After Adam Gilchrist, the next three highest rating wicketkeepers in the 2000s were South Africa's Mark Boucher, Sri Lanka's Kumar Sangakkara and Pakistan's Kamran Akmal (see Table 10.4).

[1] Mark Boucher of South Africa is the second-choice wicketkeeper in the decade behind Adam Gilchrist. Between his test debut in 1997 and his final test in 2012, he played 147 tests and took 532 catches and made 23 stumpings. Over his long career, he kept wickets in 281 test innings (more than any other player) and he took more wickets behind the stumps than any other player. He sits just behind Gilchrist as the 2nd highest rating wicketkeeper of all time (Table 2.18). Born in East London, South Africa in 1976, Boucher played domestic cricket for Border (1996-2003) and Warriors (2004-2012). In the decade of the 2000s, he played 103 tests (compared to Gilchrist's 91 tests) and affected 383 dismissals (compared to Gilchrist's 397 dismissals). He was also a fine right-hand batsman, scoring 5,515 runs in his test career at an average of 30.30 and a strike rate of 50.11, including 5 centuries and 35 half-centuries.

Boucher was also a long-term member of the South African ODI and T20 teams and has played for the Royal Challengers Bangalore and the Kolkata Knight Riders in the Indian Premier League. He was South Africa Player of the Year in 1998, 2000 and 2006. Boucher suffered a serious injury when hit in the eye by a bail while playing against Somerset in July 2012 during South Africa's tour of England. The injury caused him to be ruled out of the tour and led to his retirement from all forms of the game. He was named the Coach of the Year at the 2017 Cricket South Africa's Annual Awards.

[2] Kamran Akmal was born in Lahore in 1982 and was the wicketkeeper for Pakistan in 53 tests from 2002 to 2010, taking 184 catches and affecting 22 stumpings in 99 test innings. He is Pakistan's highest rating wicketkeeper in test cricket and the 18th highest rating wicketkeeper in Table 2.18. He scored 2,648 test runs at a batting average of 30.79, including six centuries. He also had a successful career in limited overs cricket, playing 157 ODI's and making 188 dismissals. Kamran is the older brother of Adnan Akmal and Umar Akmal both of whom have played test and limited overs cricket for Pakistan.

Table 10.1 Best World Team of the 2000s (2000 to 2009, inclusive) — Batting Performances.

Players	Country	Batting style	Matches	Innings	Not outs	100s/50s/0s	Highest score	Runs scored	Batting average	Strike rate	Batting rating
1. Hayden, M.L.	Australia	left	96	172	14	29/29/10	380	8,364	52.94	60.85	151.5
2. Sehwag, V.	India	right	72	123	4	17/19/10	319	6,248	52.50	80.41	140.9
3. Ponting, RT	Australia	right	107	184	22	32/40/8	257	9,458	58.38	62.51	167.7
4. Jayawardene, DPMdS	Sri Lanka	right	95	160	12	25/30/10	374	8,187	55.32	53.46	152.2
5. Kallis, JH	S. Africa	right	101	174	27	27/42/7	189	8,630	58.71	46.51	154.7
6. Mohammad Yousuf	Pakistan	right	71	121	11	23/23/7	223	6,439	58.54	53.03	147.2
7. Gilchrist, AC	Australia	left	91	129	19	16/23/13	204	5,130	46.64	81.97	116.3
8. Warne, SR	Australia	right	65	86	5	0/8/14	99	1,577	19.47	64.48	20.8
9. Muralitharan, M	Sri Lanka	right	84	101	30	0/1/21	67	775	10.92	76.06	9.6
10. Shoaib Akhtar	Pakistan	right	33	49	7	0/0/9	47	474	11.29	42.70	6.4
11. McGrath, GD	Australia	right	66	66	28	0/1/14	61	355	9.34	43.72	4.9
										Total	1072.2

Next Batters

Sangakkara, KC	Sri Lanka	left	88	147	10	21/32/4	287	7,549	55.10	55.53	145.7
Dravid, R.	India	right	103	179	23	22/42/7	270	8,558	54.86	43.49	144.8
Lara, BL	W. Indies	left	66	120	2	21/19/13	400	6,380	54.07	59.24	142.6
Inzamam-ul-Haq	Pakistan	right	62	103	11	17/23/7	329	5,113	55.58	56.06	139.2
Flower, A	Zimbabwe	left	24	42	7	6/11/1	232	2,214	63.26	51.50	138.8
Tendulkar, SR	India	right	89	150	16	21/31/7	248	7,129	53.20	54.36	136.5

Table 10.2 Best World Team of the 2000s (2000 to 2009, inclusive) — Bowling Performances.

Players	Country	Overs	Balls	Maids	Runs against	Bowl style	Wickets	5w/10w	Best	Bowl average	Strike rate	Econ rate	Bowling rating
1. Hayden, M.L.	Australia	\multicolumn{11}{c}{Less than 100 over}	-
2. Sehwag, V.	India	424	2,552	65	1312	RAO	30	1/0	5/104	43.73	85.06	3.08	37.4
3. Ponting, RT	Australia	\multicolumn{11}{c}{Less than 100 over}	-
4. Jayawardene, DPMdS	Sri Lanka	\multicolumn{11}{c}{Less than 100 over}	-
5. Kallis, JH	Sth Africa	2,223	13,348	524	6,561	RAFM	205	4/0	6/54	32.00	65.11	2.95	85.6
6. Mohd Yousuf	Pakistan	\multicolumn{11}{c}{Less than 100 overs}	-
7. Gilchrist, AC	Australia	Wicketkeeper					Did not bowl						-
8. Warne, SR	Australia	3,020	18,129	605	8,986	RAL	357	21/6	7/94	25.17	50.78	2.97	143.3
9. Muralitharan, M	Sri Lanka	4,796	28,783	1159	11,849	RAO	565	49/20	9/51	20.97	50.94	2.47	213.0
10. Shoaib Akhtar	Pakistan	951	5,716	175	3,199	RAF	144	11/2	6/11	22.22	39.69	3.36	134.9
11. McGrath, GD	Australia	2,548	15,293	828	6,100	RAFM	297	14/2	8/24	20.54	51.49	2.39	145.7
												Total	759.9

Next Bowlers

Player	Country	Overs	Balls	Maids	Runs against	Bowl style	Wickets	5w/10w	Best	Bowl average	Strike rate	Econ rate	Bowling rating
Steyn, DW	S. Africa	1,146	6,877	206	4,123	RAF	172	11/3	6/49	23.97	39.98	3.60	133.1
Ntini, M	S. Africa	3,345	20,084	722	10,884	RAF	380	18/4	7/37	28.64	52.85	3.25	126.5
Singh, H	India	3,450	20,706	638	9,763	RAO	322	23/5	8/84	30.32	64.30	2.83	120.0
Kumble, A	India	3,774	22,633	789	11,014	RAL	355	20/5	8/141	31.03	63.76	2.92	120.7
Walsh, CA	W.Indies	887	5,330	280	1,835	RAF	93	5/1	6/61	19.73	57.31	2.07	122.1
Pollock, SM	S. Africa	2,646	15,887	804	6,439	RAFM	260	6/1	6/30	24.77	61.10	2.43	116.5

Table 10.3 Performances of the best all-rounders (2000 to 2009, inclusive).

Player	Country	No. of tests	Years played	Batting style	Runs scored	Batting average	Batting rating	Bowling style	Wickets taken	Bowl avge	Bowl rating	All-rounder Rating
Kallis, J	S Af	101	2000-09	right	8,630	58.71	154.7	RAFM	205	32.00	85.6	205.8
Jayasuriya, ST	Sri Lan	66	2000-07	left	4,222	38.73	87.5	LAO	69	30.48	72.5	152.5
Vettori, DL	N Zeal	69	2000-09	left	3,176	36.09	68.9	LAO	222	33.15	97.0	151.9
Flintoff, A	England	74	2000-09	right	3,695	32.70	68.7	RAF	220	32.38	84.7	145.4
Pollock, SM	S Af	70	2000-08	right	2,377	32.56	50.0	RAFM	260	24.77	116.6	133.3

Table 10.4 Wicketkeeping performances (2000 to 2009, inclusive).

Player	Country	No. of tests	Years played	Batting style	Runs scored	Batting avge	Batting rating	Catches	Stumpings	Total dismissals	Wicket keeper rating
Gilchrist, AC	Australia	91	2000-08	left	5,130	46.64	116.3	362	35	397	178.8
Boucher, MV	S Africa	104	2000-09	right	4,024	30.03	59.7	363	29	383	139.5
Sangakkara, KC	Sri Lanka	64	2000-06	left	5,064	50.64	119.3	146	20	166	113.6
Kamran Akmal	Pakistan	47	2002-09	right	2,525	34.12	63.5	157	22	179	112.4

Note: The ratings are determined from the number of tests while playing as wicketkeeper.

Chapter 11
The Best World Team — 2010 to 2019

All ten test playing nations competed against each other in the period from 2010 until the end of 2019. During this time, 433 test matches were played; England played 126 of them, Australia 112, India 107, Sri Lanka 95, South Africa 90, West Indies 83, New Zealand 83, Pakistan 83, Bangladesh 56 and Zimbabwe 24 (Afghanistan played 4 and Ireland played 3).

The Best Team of the period 2010 to 2019 inclusive

Batting Order:	Country	No. of tests (2010-19)	Period	Batting Rating	Bowling Rating
1. Warner, DA	Australia	83	2011-19	136.1	-
2. Cook, AN	England	111	2010-18	127.8	-
3. Sangakkara, KC	Sri Lanka	46	2010-15	153.5	-
4. Smith, SPD	Australia	72	2010-19	166.7	15.8
5. Kallis, JH	South Africa	33	2010-13	129.6	44.7
6. Kohli, V	India	84	2011-19	132.9	-
7. de Villiers, AB	South Africa	60	2010-18	140.1	WK
8. Ashwin, R	India	70	2011-19	50.4	146.5
9. Herath, HMRKB	Sri Lanka	72	2010-18	13.8	146.5
10. Steyn, DW	South Africa	59	2010-19	9.7	140.5
11. Anderson, JM	England	106	2010-19	5.2	143.3
			Totals	1065.8	637.3

Note: Batting and bowling statistics are given in Tables 11.1 and 11.2.
The win/loss/draw results for each of the participating countries are shown below.

Country	No. of tests	England	Australia	India	Sri Lanka	South Africa	West Indies	New Zealand	Pakistan	Zimbabwe	Bangladesh	All matches
England	126	-	11/14/5	13/7/3	7/2/4	5/6/3	6/4/2	3/3/5	6/9/1	0/0/0	5/1/0	57/46/23
Australia	112	14/11/5	-	8/10/4	6/3/2	5/8/2	6/0/2	9/1/1	8/4/1	0/0/0	1/1/0	57/38/17
India	107	7/13/3	10/8/4	-	7/2/3	9/5/3	11/0/5	6/1/3	0/0/0	0/0/0	5/0/1	56/29/22
Sri Lanka	95	2/7/4	3/6/2	2/7/3	-	5/6/1	3/1/4	2/7/1	7/5/6	3/0/0	4/1/3	31/40/24
South Africa	90	6/5/3	8/5/2	5/9/3	6/5/1	-	4/0/2	5/0/5	7/1/2	2/0/0	2/0/2	45/25/20
West Indies	83	4/6/2	0/6/2	0/11/5	1/3/4	0/4/2	-	3/6/1	3/5/0	3/0/1	7/2/1	22/43/18
New Zealand	83	3/3/5	1/9/1	1/6/3	7/2/1	0/5/5	6/3/1	-	5/3/2	4/0/0	5/0/2	32/31/20
Pakistan	83	9/6/1	4/8/1	0/0/0	5/7/6	1/7/2	5/3/0	3/5/2	-	2/1/0	3/0/1	33/37/13
Zimbabwe	24	0/0/0	0/0/0	0/0/0	0/3/0	0/2/0	0/3/1	0/4/0	1/2/0	-	3/5/0	4/19/1
Bangladesh	56	1/5/0	1/1/0	0/5/1	1/4/3	0/2/2	2/7/1	0/5/2	0/3/1	5/3/0	-	10/36/10

Notes: England and Pakistan each won a test against Ireland;
India and West Indies each won a test against Afghanistan; and
Bangladesh lost a test against Afghanistan

India, South Africa, Australia, England and New Zealand had more wins than losses in this period. The ratios of wins to losses for the participating nations were: India 1.93; South Africa 1.80; Australia 1.50; England 1.24; New Zealand 1.03; Pakistan 0.89; Sri Lanka 0.78; West Indies 0.51; Bangladesh 0.28; and Zimbabwe 0.21. The trend to more attacking cricket in the 2000s continued into the 2010s with 19.6% of matches drawn (compared to 24.6% in the 2000s, 35.7% in the 1990s, 45.9% in the 1980s). Sri Lanka drew 25.3% of its matches, New Zealand

24.1%, South Africa 22.2%, West Indies 21.7%, India 20.6%, England 18.3%, Bangladesh 17.9%, Pakistan 15.7%, Australia 15.2% and Zimbabwe 4.2%.

Of the 11 players selected in the top team of the 2010s, 3 were from South Africa and 2 each from Australia, Sri Lanka, India and England. With a combined batting rating of 1065.8, the team of the 2010s is the 3rd highest rating batting side of any era. However, with a combined bowling rating of 637.3, the bowling attack is not as strong as in the previous three decades. This is not because the four specialist bowlers have lower ratings, but because the bowling contributions from the top seven batsmen are only modest.

Australia's David Warner and England's Alastair Cook are the opening batsmen, with batting ratings of 136.1 and 127.8, respectively. At No. 3 is Kumar Sangakkara of Sri Lanka, at the end of his great career but still has the second highest batting rating of the 2010s. Steven Smith of Australia is at No. 4 and is the highest rating batsman in the decade. At No. 5 is South Africa's Jacques Kallis, holding his place from the team of the 2000s, but with significantly lower ratings. At No. 6 is the current Indian captain Virat Kohli and the wicketkeeper at No.7 is the outstanding South African batsman AB de Villiers. De Villiers was relieved of the wicketkeeping duties for South Africa in 2014 so that he could concentrate on his batting, but he is the 4th highest rating wicketkeeper of all time (Table 2.18) and his selection as wicketkeeper permits the inclusion of another specialist batsman (in this case the all-rounder Jacques Kallis). The bowling attack is well balanced with two outstanding spinners and two outstanding pace bowlers. India's bowling all-rounder Ravi Ashwin, at No. 8, has the second highest career bowling rating of any right arm off-spinner, behind Muttiah Muralitharan. Sri Lanka's Rangana Herath has the highest career rating of any left-arm orthodox bowler in the history of the game and is selected at No.9. South Africa's Dale Steyn and England's James Anderson form a formidable opening bowling combination. Warner, Smith, Kohli, Ashwin and Anderson are still playing test cricket in 2024.

As in the previous decades some great batsmen and bowlers just missed selection in the top 11. The six next most highly rated batsmen are all among the top 42 rated batsmen in test history: Australia's Adam Voges (ranked 42nd in Table 2.7); New Zealand's Kane Williamson (12th in Table 2.7); South Africa's Hashim Amla (38th in Table 2.7); England's Joe Root (7th in Table 2.7); West Indian Shivnarine Chanderpaul (14th in Table 2.7); and Pakistan's Younis Khan (ranked 17th in Table 2.7). Voges, Williamson and Amla all rated higher than Alastair Cook, but none were specialist openers in test cricket. Voges' batting rating in this decade was just higher than that of Kallis, but Kallis' higher bowling rating earned him selection in the top 11.

After the top four bowlers, the next six most highly rated bowlers are: Kagiso Rabada (South Africa — ranked 12th in Table 2.16); Vernon Philander (South Africa — ranked 34th in Table 2.16); Stuart Broad (England — 21st in Table 2.16); Pat Cummins (Australia — 28th in Table 2.16); Mitchell Starc (Australia — 43rd in Table 2.16); Ravi Jadeja (India — ranked 30th in Table 2.16); and Saeed Ajmal (Pakistan — Ranked 82nd in Table 2.16).

The batting and bowling statistics of the World team of the 2010s are presented in Tables 11.1 and 11.2, respectively, and the statistics for the highest rating all-rounders and wicketkeepers are given in Tables 11.3 and 11.4, respectively. The performances of the eligible players in the best national teams are provided in Appendix L (Tables L.1 to L.10).

The Players:

No. 1: Australia's David Warner made his test debut in 2011 against New Zealand, and by the end of the decade, he had played 83 test matches and scored 7,088 runs at an average of 48.22. He is the 39th highest rating batsmen of all time (Table 2.7). He opened the batting for Australia in all but 3 of his 205 test innings. He is an aggressive left-hand batsman, capable of taking apart any bowling attack. He is well known for his powerful cover drives and hits on the leg side high into the outfield. He is also well known for his ability to switch hit, sometimes turning to face the bowler as a right-hand batsman just as the bowler is in his delivery stride — a tactic that he employs more in ODI and T20 cricket than in test cricket. Of all batsmen who have scored in excess of 5,000 test runs, Warner's career strike rate in test cricket of 70.19 is the third highest (behind only Virender Sehwag and Adam Gilchrist). He had a strike rate over 50 in all of his 25 test centuries and a strike rate over 72 in 20 of them. He is also an outstanding fielder, both close to the wicket and in the outfield, and quick across the ground.

After several impressive performances in ODI matches for New South Wales in 2008, Warner was selected in the Australian T20 squad in January 2009, making him the first Australian player since 1877 to represent Australia without having played a first-class match. His first-class debut for New South Wales came later in the 2008-2009 domestic season. Early in his career, he was primarily considered to be an ODI and T20 specialist, but he forced his way into the test team in December 2011 and, until his retirement in 2024, he regularly represented Australia in all forms of the game. He was vice-captain of both the Australian test and ODI teams under captain Steve Smith from 2015 until the beginning of 2018.

In the 1st test against New Zealand at the Brisbane Cricket Ground on 7 November 2015, Warner scored a century in both innings, to become only the third batsman to have achieved that feat three times; the other two being India's Sunil Gavaskar and Australia's Ricky Ponting. Warner followed this up one week later with 253 in the 2nd Test against New Zealand at the WACA Ground in Perth, to make it three consecutive hundreds for the second time in his test career. He became the first person to score a century before lunch on the first morning of a test in Australia when he smashed 118 runs off 95 balls on 2nd January 2017 against Pakistan at the Sydney Cricket Ground. In the second innings of the same match, he hit 50 off just 23 balls, the second fastest half century in test cricket. Only five other players have scored centuries in the first session of a test match; Australians Victor Trumper in 1902, Charlie Macartney in 1926, Don Bradman in 1930, Pakistan's Majid Khan in 1976 and India's Shikhar Dhawan in 2018. Warner finished the decade smashing 335 not out against Pakistan at the Adelaide Oval on 29th and 30th November 2019.

Warner was awarded the Allan Border Medal (the highest individual award in Australian cricket) in 2016, 2017 and 2020 and he was the opening batsman in the ICC Test Team of the Year for 4 consecutive years (2014 to 2017) and the ICC Test Team of the decade (2011-2020). Despite his successes, Warner has been involved in several controversies, both on the field and off the field. He was fined and suspended for a period in 2013 for an off the field altercation with England's Joe Root and, in March 2018, he was suspended for a year from all forms of international cricket for his part in ball tampering in South Africa — a scandal that rocked Australian cricket to the core.

No. 2: England's Alastair Cook is the second opening batsman in the team. Cook has played more tests than any other Englishman, and until overtaken by Joe Root in 2024, he had scored more runs in test cricket than any other Englishman. He sits sixth on the list of the most career runs (behind Tendulkar, Ponting, Kallis, Dravid and Root). He has scored more test runs than any other left-handed batsman and more runs than any other opening batsman. He made a century on his test debut (against India in 2006 in Nagpur) at the age of 21 and a century in his final test innings (also against India at the Oval in September 2018). In total he played 161 test matches and scored 12,472 runs at an average of 45.35, with 33 test centuries (five of them double centuries). He is the youngest player to score 6,000, 7,000, 8,000, 9,000, 10000, 11,000 and 12,000 runs in test cricket. In the nine-year period 2010 to 2018, he played 111 tests, scoring 8,818 runs at 46.41: more tests and more runs than any other player in the 2010s.

Cook was a remarkably consistent opening batsman, with a classically correct technique, a full range of shots and wonderful concentration. His defence was reliable, and he put a high price on his wicket. His 263 runs in 863 minutes against Pakistan in 2015 to ensure a draw was the longest test innings by an Englishman, and the third longest of all time. He is the only Englishman to score over 1,000 runs in his first year of test cricket and he scored centuries in his first test against each of India, Pakistan, West Indies and Bangladesh. Cook's consistent on-field performances and his remarkable durability are evidenced by his longevity in the game. He never missed a test match for England between May 2006 and his retirement in September 2018, breaking Allan Border's world record of 153 consecutive tests in June 2018 and finishing his career with 159 consecutive matches. He captained England in 59 tests between 2010 and 2016, more tests than any other English captain, winning 24, losing 22 and drawing 13. During this period, he became the first Englishman to play in 50 test victories. He is the only test captain to score a century in each of his first five tests at the helm.

Cook was born in Gloucester and has played first-class cricket for Essex since 2003, but his international duties in all forms of the game limited his opportunities in county cricket. Cook was particularly successful batting on the subcontinent. His batting averages in tests in India and in Bangladesh were 51.46 and 61.57, respectively, and against Pakistan in Asia his average was 55.36. Against Pakistan in the United Arab Emirates at the end of 2015, he became the highest non-Asian test run-scorer in Asia.

Cook was the ICC Test Player of the Year in 2011 and opened the batting in the ICC Test Team of the Year in 2011, 2012, 2013, 2015 and 2016, captaining the team in 2013, 2015 and 2016. He was awarded am MBE in 2011 and a CBE in 2016.

No. 3: Sri Lanka's Kumar Sangakkara was the second highest rating batsman in this period and his career batting rating is the 3rd highest of all time, behind Sir Donald Bradman and Sachin Tendulkar (Table 2.7). He is the most successful left-hand batsman in the history of test cricket. He made an inauspicious start to his test career as a wicketkeeper batsman in the 3-test home series against South Africa in 2000. He finished that series with a batting average of just 16.60 and a top score of 25. There was little to indicate that he would finish his career as one of the greatest test batsmen. He played 134 test matches between 2000 and 2015, scoring 12,400 runs at an average of 57.41, with 38 test centuries, including 11 double centuries. Only Sir Donald Bradman (with 12) has scored more double centuries than Kumar Sangakkara. In the last six years of his career (2010-2015), he scored 4,851 runs at 61.41, with a top score of 319. Strong off both the front and the back foot, Sangakkara was a graceful driver in front of the wickets and a powerful cutter and puller of the ball square of the wickets.

Other records in test cricket set by Sangakkara include: the highest batting average of any of the 15 batsman who have scored in excess of 10,000 test runs; the first player to score 150 or more in an innings in four consecutive test matches (in 2007); the fastest to score 8,000 runs (in 152 innings), 9,000 runs (in 172 innings), 11,000 runs (in 208 innings) and 12,000 runs (in 224 innings); the highest partnership in test cricket (624 with Mahela Jayawardene against South Africa at the Sinhalese Sports Club Ground in Colombo in 2006); together with Mahela Jayawardene the pair put on 6,554 runs — the second most productive partnership in test cricket (behind Rahul Dravid and Sachin Tendulkar with 6,920 runs together); the most career runs when batting at No. 3 (11,679); the most centuries when batting at No. 3 (37); the most runs ever by a batsman in a calendar year in all forms of the international game (in 2014, he scored 1,693 test runs, 1,256 ODI runs and 119 T20 runs); second highest run-scorer in international cricket (behind Sachin Tendulkar) with over 28,000 international runs.

Sangakkara captained Sri Lanka in 15 test matches from 2009 to 2011, winning 5, losing 3 and drawing 7. He was included in the ICC Test Team of the Year in seven years from 2006 to 2014; he was the ICC Test Player of the Year in 2012, and winner of the ICC Sir Garfield Sobers Trophy in 2012. He was also the ICC ODI Player of the Year in 2011 and 2013 and a member of the ICC ODI Team of the Year for 2011, 2012, 2013 and 2015. He was Wisden Leading Cricketer in the World in 2011 and 2014 (only the second player to have been awarded that honour twice) and he was inducted into the ICC Cricket Hall of Fame in 2021.

In 2011, Sangakkara was the youngest person, the first Sri Lankan and the first active international cricketer to deliver the MCC Spirit of Cricket Cowdrey Lecture at Lords. The Spirit of Cricket Cowdrey Lecture has been delivered every year since 2001 by some of the leading figures in the cricket world. Sangakkara talked about the history of Sri Lankan cricket, the importance of cricket to the Sri Lankan people and the problems facing cricket in his country. He was widely praised for his oratory skills, honesty and bravery in delivering an important talk that was critical of cricket administration in Sri Lanka. Since his retirement, Sangakkara has become a television commentator on the game.

No. 4: Steven Smith of Australia is the highest rating batsman in the decade. He made his test debut as a bowling all-rounder against Pakistan at Lords in 2010, batting at No. 8 in the first innings and No. 9 in the second innings. His scores of 1 and 12 in that game failed to impress, but he took 3 wickets for 51 in Pakistan's second innings to help bowl Australia to victory. He was not convincing in his first 5 tests and spent a year out of the Australian team until recalled to bat at No.5 in the 3rd test against India in 2012. He impressed with 92 in the first innings in a losing side. In the 2010s, he played 72 test matches scoring 7,164 runs at a batting average of 62.84. In the four years 2014 to 2017, Smith played 44 test matches scoring 5,004 runs at the remarkable average of 75.82.

His batting performances earned him selection in the ICC Test Team of the Year in 2015, 2016, 2017 and 2019, the ICC Test Player of the Year in 2015 and 2017 (the only player to have been awarded this honour twice), the ICC Test Player of the Decade (2011-2020) and the ICC Sir Garfield Sobers Trophy in 2015. At the end of 2017, Smith's ICC Batting Rating was 947, the highest rating ever reached by a batsman (except for the retrospective rating of 961 given to Bradman). In Australia, Smith won the Allan Border Medal in 2015, 2018 and 2021. He was the Australian Test Player of the Year in 2015 and 2018 and was the Australian ODI Player of the Year in 2015 and 2021.

Smith plays domestic first-class cricket for New South Wales and T20 domestic cricket for the Sydney Sixers. He is an unorthodox right-hand batsman who walks across his stumps as the bowler delivers the ball, relying on a great eye and wonderful timing. His backswing is in the direction of gully and his bat swings down to meet the ball in a semi-circular arc. His method is not in the coaching manual, but it is effective. He is also an outstanding slips fielder, having taken 195 catches in his 114 tests (up to the end of 2024), and he is a competent leg spin bowler who has tended to be under-bowled in test cricket, particularly after he took over the captaincy of the Australian team. After captaining Australia in 3 tests against India in 2014-15, Smith was appointed captain to replace Michael Clarke in 2015. He captained Australia in 35 tests, winning 19, losing 10 and drawing 6.

In March 2018, Smith took responsibility for an incident of ball tampering in South Africa in which Australian batsman Cameron Bancroft was caught on camera during a test match using sandpaper to roughen one side of the ball. Smith and vice-captain David Warner were stood down after Smith admitted that the tampering had been a decision of the players' management group. The incident received wide-spread publicity, and the Australian media was baying for blood. Smith, Warner and Bancroft were all suspended by Cricket Australia. Smith was banned from all forms of international and domestic cricket for 1 year (from March 2018) and from any leadership role in Australian cricket for two years until March 2020.

The punishment was harsh and in no way matched the seriousness of the crime. Ball tampering is cheating, it unfairly increases the bowlers' chances of swinging the ball. However, ball tampering has been in the game for many years, probably since the beginning of cricket, and the harshest penalties that had previously been imposed on those found guilty were relatively minor fines and in some extreme cases a one match suspension. The penalties imposed on Smith and Warner were widely seen to be an over-reaction by a cricket administrative body that had overseen a deterioration in the culture of Australian Cricket, and Smith and Warner were the scapegoats. Cricket Australia was prepared to deny the cricketing public around the globe the opportunity to watch two of the best batsmen in the world for a full year perhaps in the false hope that it would take the focus off its own failings.

In December 2021, Smith again took over the captaincy duties when Pat Cummins was ruled out of the 2nd Ashes test match against England at the Adelaide Oval and led Australia to a resounding 275 run victory.

No. 5: South African great batting all-rounder Jacques Kallis ended his test career in 2013, but his performance from 2010 to 2013 earned him selection at No. 5 for the second successive decade. He played his last 33 test matches in the 2010s, scoring 2,810 runs at an average of 58.54 (compared to 58.71 in the 2000s) and a strike rate 53.69 (compared to 46.51 in the previous decade). His bowling in the 2010s was not as effective as it was in the 2000s taking just 34 wickets at a bowling average of 43.12 and a strike rate of over 90. Nevertheless, in a team in which none of his fellow batsmen contributed significantly to the team's bowling rating, it was Kallis' bowling that saw him selected ahead of the next highest rating batsman in the decade (Adam Voges — see Table 11.1).

Kallis ended his 18-year test career with 166 matches, 13,289 test runs and 292 wickets. He is the 4th highest rating test batsman of all time and the highest rating South African batsman (Table 2.7). He is the only player in test history to have scored more than 10,000 runs and taken more than 250 wickets. He is rated here as the greatest all-rounder in test history (Table 2.17). He was selected in the ICC Test Team of the Year in 2010, 2011 and 2012 and, in 2020, he was inducted into the ICC Cricket Hall of Fame.

No. 6: At the end of 2018, India's Virat Kohli was ranked the No. 1 test batsman by the ICC. No other Indian batsman has ever been rated higher by the ICC. A right-hand top-order batsman, he made his test debut in 2011 and, up to the end of 2024, he has played 122 tests and scored 9,207 runs at an average of 47.22, a strike rate of 55.71 and 30 centuries, including 7 double centuries. His career batting rating places him 40th in the list of the highest rating test batsman of all time (Table 2.7). Kohli's batting average climbed from 44.03 at the end of 2015 to 54.98 at the end of 2019.

In 2016 and 2017, he played 22 tests, scoring 2,274 runs at an average of 75.8. Kohli is an outstanding batsman in all forms of the game and holds numerous world and Indian records in ODI cricket. He is the only batsman to have simultaneously averaged over 50 in all forms of international cricket tests, ODIs and T20. His batting average in ODI cricket of 58.18 at the end of 2024 is significantly higher than every other batsman who has played more than 100 innings. Of all the great Indian batsmen, Kohli has scored the most international runs in a calendar year — 2,818 runs in 2017. Kohli also scored 610 runs in the home series against Sri Lanka in November 2017 — the most runs in a 3-test series by an Indian batsman.

He was appointed captain of the Indian test team for the tour to Australia in 2014 and remained the national captain until the tour of South Africa in 2021/22. He captained India in 68 tests, winning 40, losing 17 and drawing 11 — more than anyone else. He is by far India's most successful captain. In the Australian summer of 2018/19, Kohli led India to its first ever series victory in Australia. He is a fierce competitor, both as a batsman and as captain, and never takes a backward step.

In 2018, Kohli was named as one of *Time's* 100 most influential people in the world and, in 2020, he was ranked 66th in the *Forbes* list of the highest-paid athletes in the world. He was selected in the ICC Test Team of the Year in 2017, 2018 and 2019 (captain in 2017). He was the ICC Test Player of the Year in 2018, the ODI Player of the Year in 2012, 2017 and 2018, the winner of the Sir Garfield Sobers Trophy Cricketer of the Year for 2017 and 2018 and the winner of the Sir Garfield Sobers Trophy for Cricketer of the Decade (2011-2020). He is the only player to be named in all three of the ICC teams of the decade — Test, ODI and T20I. He was Wisden's Leading Cricketer in the World in 2016, 2017 and 2018. He received the Polly Umrigar Award for International Indian Cricketer of the Year five times between 2012 and 2018. No other cricketer has received the award more than twice. Kohli plays first–class domestic cricket for Delhi and T20 cricket in the Indian Premier League for the Royal Challenges Bangalore.

No. 7: Abraham Benjamin de Villiers (better known as A.B. de Villiers) is one of the great South African batsmen of the modern era. He was born in Warmbad, Transvaal Provence in 1984 and played domestic first-class cricket for Northerns (2003-04) and the Titans (2004-2018). From his debut against England in Port Elizabeth in 2004 until his final test against Australia in 2018, he has played 114 test matches scoring 8,765 runs at an average of 50.66. He is the 29th highest rating test batsman (Table 2.7). Early in his career and then after the retirement of Mark Boucher, de Villiers kept wickets for South Africa in 45 test innings affecting 106 dismissals at 2.36 dismissals per innings. Because of his batting, he ranks 4th in Table 2.18 and has been selected as the wicketkeeper in the side (ahead of Quinton de Kock of South Africa and New Zealand's B.J. Watling). The team also includes the 3rd highest rating wicketkeeper of all-time — Kumar Sangakkara (Table 2.18), but Sangakkara did not keep wickets in test cricket in the 2010s.

De Villiers played 45 tests and 78 innings before he scored a duck in test cricket — a world record. De Villiers excelled in all formats of the game. He was a member of the ICC Test Team of the Year for five years from 2009 to 2014 and was the ICC ODI Player of the Year in 2010, 2014 and 2015. He was named as one of the five Wisden Cricketers of the Decade in 2019.

De Villiers played domestic first-class cricket for the Titans from 2004 to 2018. As a schoolboy in Pretoria, he excelled at rugby as well as cricket. He is a dashing right-hand batsman and an outstanding fielder in the slips or at cover, as well as being very tidy behind the stumps. He has taken 222 catches in his test career (121 in the field and 101 behind the stumps). He captained the test team in just two matches; the final two home tests against England in January 2016, winning 1 and losing 1. He scored a duck in both innings of the second of these games and did not play test cricket again until December 2017.

De Villiers is an innovative batsman capable of the most unorthodox of shots and he holds a number of records for fast scoring. He scored a century against India in 2010 at Centurion in just 75 balls, the fastest test century by a South African. In ODI cricket, de Villiers has scored the fastest ever 50 (in just 16 balls) and the fastest ever 100 (in 31 balls), both in the same innings against the West Indies in Johannesburg in January 2015. One month later, he smashed the fastest ever 150 in one-day internationals (in just 64 balls) against the same opposition in a World Cup pool match in Sydney. He is the only batsman in ODI history to have scored more than 5,000 runs at an average over 50 and a strike rate over 100.

No. 8: India's bowling all-rounder Ravichandran Ashwin is the equal highest rating bowler in the team. From his debut in 2011 until the end of the decade, he played 70 tests and took 362 wickets with his right-arm off break bowling at an average of 25.37. He also made 2,385 runs at a batting average of 28.73, with 4 test centuries. He has played domestic first-class cricket for Tamil Nadu since 2006 and was first called up for the Indian limit overs side in 2010, following impressive economical bowling performances for the Chennai Super Kings in the Indian Premier League. The following year he made an impressive test debut against the West Indies, taking 3/81 and 6/47 in his maiden test and finishing the series with two 5-wicket hauls, a century and the Player of the Series Award.

Ashwin is the fastest Indian bowler to take 100 wickets in test cricket (in his 18th test), 200 wickets (in his 37th test), 300 wickets (in his 54th test) and 400 wickets (in his 77th test). Only Clarrie Grimmett of Australia in 1936 and Yasir Shah of Pakistan in 2018 reached 200 test wickets faster. In the history of test cricket, the rare feat of scoring a century and taking a 5-wicket haul in the same test has been completed 33 times, and Ashwin has done it three times. He is most effective on home wickets in India, having taken 383 of his 537 wickets in India at an average of 21.44 (up to the end of 2024). In the 2013 series against Australia, he took 28 wickets, the highest number of wickets taken in a 4-match series by an Indian. In 2013, he shared a 280-run partnership with Rohit Sharma against the West Indies at Eden Gardens, Kolkata, India's highest ever 7th wicket partnership. In the home test against Australia at M. Chinnaswamy Stadium in Bengaluru, he became the fastest bowler to take twenty-five 5-wicket hauls in test history, having reached the milestone in his 47th match and in his 89th innings. At the end of 2024, he is the 6th highest rating bowler of all time (Table 2.16) and the 12th highest rating all-rounder (Table 2.17).

Ashwin is a deceptive bowler, with consistently good line and length, typically flighting the ball and relying on dip and spin. His stock ball is the off break, but he has a good arm ball and is one of the few modern bowlers to bowl the carrom ball. He was a member of the ICC Test Team of the Year in 2013, 2015, 2016 and 2017 and was ICC Test Player of the Year in 2016 and winner of the Sir Garfield Sobers Trophy in 2016 (the 3rd Indian to be awarded the Trophy after Rahul Dravid in 2004 and Sachin Tendulkar in 2010).

No. 9: Sri Lanka's Rangana Herath is the equal highest rating bowler of the decade and was a wonderful left arm orthodox spinner. Born in Kurunegala in 1978, he made his test debut against Australia in 1999 and for the first decade of his test career, he played in the shadow of Muttiah Muralitharan. In and out of the Sri Lankan test team in the 2000s, by the end of 2009, he had played just 21 matches, bowled 851 overs and taken 70 wickets at an average of 36.69. His performances improved significantly when Murali retired in 2010. From 2010 to the end of 2018, he played 72 tests, bowled 3,479 overs and took 363 wickets at an average of 26.42. He is the second highest rating left arm orthodox spin bowler in test history (ranked 20th in Table 2.16) and the only left-arm spinner to have taken 400 wickets in test cricket (passing the record of 362 wickets held by New Zealand's Daniel Vettori in March 2017). A few months short of his 40th birthday, in September 2017, Herath became the oldest player to reach the milestone of 400 test wickets and, in March 2018, he took his 415th test wicket to become the most successful left-arm bowler in test history (overtaking Pakistan's Wasim Akram's total of 414 wickets).

Herath's best figures are 9 for 127 against Pakistan in August 2014 at the Sinhalese Sports Club Ground in Colombo. He is the only left-arm bowler to have taken 9 test wickets in an innings. On the 5th August 2016 against Australia at Galle, he dismissed Adam Voges, Peter Nevill and Mitchell Starc in consecutive deliveries to become the oldest player to take a hat-trick in test cricket. In that same series, he took 13 for 145 in Colombo to become only the second player (behind Sri Lanka's Muttiah Muralitharan) to have taken 12 wickets or more in a match five times. On the 8th November 2016, he took 5 for 89 against Zimbabwe, making him only the third bowler to take 5-wicket hauls against all test playing nations (after Muralitharan and South Africa's Dale Steyn). On 6th November 2018, he took his 100th wicket at the Galle International Stadium when he bowled England's Joe Root; only the third bowler to take 100 wickets at the one venue.

Herath captained Sri Lanka in five tests in 2016 and 2017, with 3 wins and 2 losses. He was a member of the ICC Test Team of the Year in 2014 and 2016.

No. 10: South Africa's right arm pace bowler Dale Steyn just missed selection in the team of the 2000s, but consistent performances have earned him selection in the 2010s. In a 93-test career that spans from 2004 to 2019, he was remarkably consistent. In the 2010s, he played 59 tests, bowled 1,953 overs and took 267 wickets at a bowling average of 22.30 and a strike rate of 43.93 Of all the test bowlers who have played 20 or more matches since World War 1, Steyn's career strike rate of 42.39 is the third lowest behind teammate Kagiso Rabada (39.40) and India's Jasprit Bumrah (42.22).

Steyn is an aggressive fast bowler, capable of conventional swing with the new ball and reverse swing with the old ball. He usually bowled around 140 km/hour but is capable of speeds in excess of 150 km/hour. He is a good outfielder with safe hands, and he is a competent, right-hand, lower-order batsman. He was a member of the ICC Test Team of the Year for an unprecedented eight years between 2008 and 2016 and ICC Test Player of the Year in 2008. He was ranked by the ICC as the No. 1 test bowler for a record period of 263 weeks between 2008 and 2014. In total, he has spent over 2,350 days as the top ranked bowler in test cricket: more than any other player since World War 2. A severe shoulder injury kept him out of test cricket for the whole of 2017, but he re-entered the test arena in 2018. On 13th July 2018 against Sri Lanka at Galle International Stadium, Steyn took his 421st test wicket to join Shaun Pollock as the leading South African wicket taker.

Steyn played first-class cricket for the Titans and has had seasons in county cricket in England with Essex, Warwickshire, Glamorgan and Hampshire. He has played ODI and T20 cricket for South Africa throughout his career and has played for various franchises in the Indian Premier League and the Australian and West Indian domestic competitions.

No. 11: England's James Anderson is a right arm fast-medium opening bowler who made his test debut in 2003 and continued to play test cricket until 2024. Anderson stamina and ability to avoid serious injury, saw him remain the spearhead of the English attack throughout the 2010s. He has played 188 test matches, bowled 6,673 overs and taken 704 wickets at an average of 26.46. In the 2010s, he played 106 tests, taking 429 wickets at 24.35. He has taken more test wickets than any other fast bowler, overtaking Australian Glenn McGrath's total of 563 in September 2018 against India at the Oval. He currently sits 3rd on the list of most test wickets, behind Muttiah Muralitharan and Shane Warne.

Anderson has taken more wickets in both tests and ODIs than any other Englishman. Against Pakistan at Old Trafford in July 2016, he became the first bowler to take 50 wickets against each of the other 7 major test playing nations (in Andersons's case, against Australia, South Africa, West Indies, New Zealand, India, Pakistan and Sri Lanka). He has taken more wickets at the home of cricket (Lords) than any other player. He has played first-class cricket for Lancashire since his debut in 2002 and, in 2017, it was announced that the Pavilion End of Lancashire's home ground, Old Trafford, would be renamed the James Anderson End. Off the field, Anderson co-hosts a radio program in Britain, and he is also involved in men's fashion design.

Next Best Batsmen:

After the top 6 batsmen, the next 6 most highly rated batsmen in the 2010s are Adam Voges (Australia), Kane Williamson (New Zealand), Hashim Amla (South Africa), Joe Root (England), Shiv Chanderpaul (West Indies) and Younis Khan (Pakistan).

[1] Adam Voges of Australia played just 20 matches in his test career from June 2015 to November 2016. He made his debut in test cricket four months short of his 36th birthday. He had been playing first-class cricket for his home state of Western Australia since 2002, with stints for English counties Hampshire, Nottinghamshire and Middlesex. He was given his chance in the two-test series against the West Indies in the Caribbean in 2015. He scored an unbeaten century in his maiden test innings to become the oldest player to score a century on debut. He finished 2015, after 12 tests, with 1,028 runs at a batting average of 85.67, with 4 centuries and 3 half-centuries. He was just the third test batsman to score over 1,000 runs in his debut year (behind Australian Mark Taylor's 1,219 in 1989 and Alastair Cook's 1,013 in 2006).

In the first test against the West Indies in the home series in December 2015 at Bellerive Oval in Hobart, Voges and Shaun March put on a then world record 4th wicket partnership 449 in Australia's first innings. It is the second highest partnership in test cricket by a pair of Australians behind the 2nd wicket partnership of 451 by Bradman and Bill Ponsford against England at the Oval in 1934. Voges finished that innings with an unbeaten 269, the highest test score at Bellerive and the first Australian over 35 to make a score in excess of 250. After scores of 269 not out, and 106 not out in his last two innings of 2015 he scored 239 in his next test innings on 14th February 2016, to pass Sachin Tendulkar's world record for the most runs between dismissals in test cricket (614). He finished his short test career with a batting average 61.88, the second highest batting average in history, behind Sir Donald Bradman (Table 2.2). He was selected in the ICC Test Team of the Year in 2016.

[2] Kane Williamson made his test debut against India in 2010 scoring 131 in his first test innings. At the end of 2024, he had played 105 tests and scored 9,276 runs at an average of 54.89, including 33 test centuries. His batting rating is the 12th highest in the history of test cricket and the highest by a New Zealander. He was born in Tauranga in 1990 and has played domestic first-class cricket for Northern Districts since December 2007 and county cricket in England for Gloucestershire 2011-12 and Yorkshire 2013-2018. Williamson scored 1,172 runs in 2015 to break the New Zealand record for the most test runs in a calendar year. He captained New Zealand in 41 test matches between 2016 and 2022, with 22 wins and 11 losses — by far New Zealand's most successful test captain.

[3] South Africa's Hashim Amla was born in Durban in 1983 and made his test debut against India at Eden Gardens in 2004. By the end of his test career in 2019, he had played 124 test matches and scored 9,282 runs at an average of 46.64, with 28 centuries. He is the 38th highest rating test batsman (Table 2.7). He is a right-hand batsman who has excelled in all formats of the game. Against England at the Oval in 2012, he scored an unbeaten 311 to become the only South African to score a triple century in test cricket. During that innings, he shared a 259-run partnership with Graeme Smith and a 379 run unbroken partnership with Jacques Kallis. He was a versatile batsman, capable of scoring runs on all types of wickets. His batting averages on the slow wickets in India, on the seaming pitches in England and on the bouncier wickets in Australia are 62.73, 60.37 and 45.88, respectively. He has made test centuries against all test playing nations other than Zimbabwe. He was a member of the ICC Test team of the Year for 4 consecutive years (2010 to 2013).

[4] England's Joe Root made his test debut against India in 2012 and by the end 2024, he had played 152 tests and scored 12,972 runs at an average of 50.87, with 36 centuries and a high score of 262. He is the 7th highest rating test batsman and the highest rating English batsman (Table 2.7). Of all the batsmen still playing test cricket at the end of 2024, Root has the highest batting rating. He plays domestic cricket for his home county of Yorkshire. After a relatively slow start to his test career, he had a batting average of 57.56 in the four-year period 2014 to 2017 and was selected in the ICC Test Team of the Year in 2014, 2015 and 2016. Root was appointed as the 80th test captain of England in 2017 after Alastair Cook stepped down. He captained England in 64 matches between February 2017 and March 2022, winning 27, losing 26 and drawing 11.

[5] Shivnarine Chanderpaul hails from Guyana and is one of the great West Indian batsmen. In a 21-year test career from 1994 to 2015, he played 164 tests (more than any other West Indian) and scored 11,867 runs (including 30 test centuries) at a batting average of 51.37. He performed well enough to make the best West Indian team in three consecutive decades. His batting improved with age. In the last six years of his long career (2010-2015), he played 41 tests and scored 3,198 runs at a batting average of 60.34 — significantly higher than his career average. Of all West Indian batsmen, only Brain Lara has scored more test runs and made more test centuries. His career batting rating is the 14th highest in test history (Table 2.7).

As his career progressed, Chanderpaul adopted an unorthodox, front-on batting stance and, towards the end of his career, both feet pointed directly down the wicket as he prepared to face the bowler. Despite looking awkward, his stance was obviously effective. Playing for most of his career in relatively weak West Indies batting sides, he was a careful and often defensive batsman, a steady accumulator of runs and the mainstay of the West Indies batting, particularly after Brian Lara retired. His performances in the two calendar years 2007 and 2008 were particularly impressive, playing 13 tests and scoring 1467 runs at an average of 104.8. As a result, he was selected in the ICC Test Team of the Year in 2008 and was the winner of the ICC Sir Garfield Sobers Trophy in that same year.

[6] Younis Khan was born in Mardan in 1977 and played domestic cricket for Peshawar (1998-2005) and Habib Bank Limited (1999-2018), county cricket in England for Nottinghamshire (2005), Yorkshire (2007) and Surrey (2010) and Sheffield Shield cricket for South Australia (2008-09). He was a right-hand top-order batsman who played 118 test matches for Pakistan between 2000 and 2017, making 10,099 runs at an average of 52.06. He scored 34 test centuries, including 6 double centuries and one triple century. He is the only test cricketer to have scored a century in all of the 11 countries that have hosted test cricket up until the end of his career (i.e., the ten test playing nations plus the UAE). He has scored more test runs and made more test centuries than any other player from Pakistan. He is the highest rating batsman from Pakistan and the 17th highest rating test batsman (Table 2.7). Younis Khan captained Pakistan in 9 test matches in the 2000s, winning 1, losing 3 and drawing 5. He is a fine player of spin bowling, particularly strong on the leg side, and an excellent close-to-the-wicket fielder, with 139 catches in test matches.

Next Best Bowlers:

The next 6 most highly rated bowlers are Kagiso Rabada (South Africa), Vernon Philander (South Africa), Stuart Broad (England), Pat Cummins (Australia), Mitchell Starc (Australia), Ravindra Jadeja (India) and Saeed Ajmal (Pakistan).

[1] South Africa has produced some outstanding fast bowlers in recent years and Kagiso Rabada is yet another one — potentially one of the greats. He is an aggressive and intelligent fast bowler with intimidating pace and presence and remarkable control. Born in Johannesburg in 1995, he made his test debut against India 2015, and at the end of 2024, he had played 69 tests and taken 321 wickets at an average 21.89 and a strike rate of 39.43. Of all the bowlers who have played 20 or more tests since World War 1, Rabada has the lowest strike rate. By January 2018, still only 22 years old, he was the ICC's top ranked bowler in both ODI and test cricket. On 13th July 2018, Rabada took his 150th test wicket at the age of just 23 to become the youngest bowler ever to reach that milestone. At the end of 2024, Rabada is the 12th highest rating test bowlers (Table 2.16).

[2] Vernon Philander is another of South Africa's outstanding fast bowlers and the 34th highest rating bowler in test history (Table 2.16). He made his test debut against Australia in 2011 and, up until the end of his career in 2020, he had played 64 tests and taken 224 wickets at a bowling average of 22.32. He also scored 1,779 runs at a batting average of 24.04. An aggressive right-arm fast-medium bowler, Philander had an explosive start to his test career. He took four 5-wicket hauls in his first three test matches, including 5 for 15 in his maiden test — a 'Man of the Match' performance that helped bowl Australia out for 47 (Australia's worst performance in over 100 years). He finished the 2-test series against Australia with 14 wickets at an average of 13.92 and was named 'Man of the Series'. In his next test against Sri Lanka, he took two 5-wicket hauls finishing with 10 for 102. By the end of 2013, he had played 20 test matches and taken 105 wickets at 18.01. He took his 100th test wicket in his 19th test to become the fastest South African to reach that milestone. He was selected in the ICC Test Team of the Year in 2012 and 2013.

[3] England's Stuart Broad is a right arm fast-medium seam bowler who has shared England's opening bowling attack with James Anderson for much of the last 16 years. He made his test debut in 2007, and by the end of his test career in 2023, he had played 167 tests and taken 604 wickets at an average of 27.68, with 20 five-wicket hauls. Only four other bowlers have taken more test wickets. On 30 July 2011, he took a hat-trick against India at Trent Bridge. He is the 21st highest rating test bowler (Table 2.16). Broad is also an

aggressive left-handed batsman who has scored 3,662 runs in tests at a batting average of 18.04 and an impressive strike rate of 65.31. He scored 169 against Pakistan at Lords on 28 August 2010, his only test century and the second highest score by a No. 9 batsman in test cricket history. He was selected in the ICC Test Team of the Year on four occasions, 2009, 2011, 2012 and 2014. He plays county cricket for Nottinghamshire, following in the footsteps of his father Chris Broad, who opened the batting for England in the 1980s (Appendix I —Table I.2).

[4] Pat Cummins of Australia is a right arm fast bowler and useful lower order batsman. He made his test debut in November 2011 against South Africa at the Wanderers Stadium at the age of 18. In what was only his fourth first class match, he impressed by taking 6/79 in the second innings and hitting the winning runs in a Man of the Match' performance. After a single test match, a series of injuries, including stress fractures of his back, kept him out of test cricket until March 2017. Since his return to the test team, Cummins has cemented his place in Australian Cricket. In 2019, he was awarded the Allan Border Medal as best Australian cricketer of the year and was named the ICC Test cricketer of the year. From 2019 to 2022, he was ranked as the ICC's No. 1 test bowler. He was appointed captain of the Australian test team for the 2021 home Ashes Series. By the end of 2024, he had played 66 tests and taken 289 wickets at a bowling average of 22.55 and a strike rate of 46.48. He is currently the 28th highest rating test bowler (Table 2.16).

[5] Mitchell Starc is a left-arm fast bowler who has played 93 test matches for Australia. from his debut against New Zealand in December 2011 until the end of 2024. He has taken 373 test wickets at a bowling average of 27.78 and strike rate of 48.81. He also has scored 2,189 runs at a batting average of 20.27 and a top score of 99. Starc is a deceptively quick fast bowler. On 15th November 2015, one of his deliveries was measured at 160.4 km/hr and it is considered one of the fastest balls ever bowled in test cricket. In 2017, playing for New South Wales against Western Australia, Starc became the first bowler to take a hat-trick in each innings of a first-class match. Starc is married to Alyssa Healy, the opening batsman, wicketkeeper and current captain of the Australian women's test cricket team.

[6] India's Ravindra Jadeja is a bowling all-rounder who is a left-arm orthodox spin bowler and a left-hand batsman. He was born in Jamnagar in 1988 and has played domestic first-class cricket for Saurashtra since 2006 and T20 cricket in the Indian Premier League for the Rajasthan Royals (2008-09), Kochi Tuskers Kerala (2011), Chennai Super Kings (2012-15 and 2018-22) and Gujarat Lions (2016-17). He made his test debut for India in December 2012 against England and has played 79 test matches up to the end of 2024, taking 323 wickets at 24.05, including fifteen 5-wicket hauls and best figures in the 2010s of 7 for 48 against England at MA. Chidambaram Stadium in December 2016. He has also scored 3,331 runs at a batting average of 35.06, including 3 centuries and 19 half-centuries. He is the 30th highest rating test bowler (Table 2.16), the 5th highest rating bowling all-rounder (Table 2.17) and the 4th highest rating all-rounder in the decade (Table 11.3). He was selected in the ICC ODI Team of the Year in 2013 and 2016 and was the top ranked test all-rounder in 2021. Test cricket has yet to see the best of Ravi Jadeja with the bat. He is one of only two batsmen who has participated in two partnerships in first-class cricket of over 500 runs (the other is West Indian Frank Worrell) and he is one of only eight players (and the only Indian) to have scored three first-class triple centuries. (the others are Don Bradman, Brian Lara, Bill Ponsford, Wally Hammond, WG Grace, Graeme Hick and Mike Hussey).

[7] Saeed Ajmal of Pakistan is a right arm off break bowler and right-hand tail end batsman. Born in Faisalabad in 1977, he played 35 test matches from 2009 to 2014, taking 178 wickets at a bowling average of 28.11. He played first-class cricket for Faisalabad from 1996 but did not make his test debut until he was almost 32 years old. He was the fastest Pakistani bowler to take 100 test wickets, reaching that milestone in just his 19th match in 2012. Ajmal's record was broken by Yasir Shah in October 2016 who took his 100th wicket in his 17th test match. He was selected in the ICC Test Team of the Year in 2012, Ajmal also excelled in the limited overs format of the game, being selected in the ICC ODI Team of the Year in 2012 and 2013.

Highest Rating All-Rounders:

[1] Shakib Al Hasan of Bangladesh is the top-rating test all-rounder in the decade (see Table 11.3) and the 3rd highest rating bowling all-rounder in test history (Table 2.17). A left-hand batsman and slow left-arm orthodox bowler, he is the only bowling all-rounder with a batting rating in excess of 85. In 2015, Shakib became the first and only player to be ranked by the ICC as the best-all-rounder in all three formats of the game, tests, ODIs and T20s. Born in Magura in 1987, he has played domestic first-class cricket for Khulna Division (2004-24) and county cricket for Worcestershire (2010-11). He played 71 test matches between 2007 and the end of 2024, scoring 4,609 runs at a batting average of 37.78, with 5 test centuries, including the then highest ever test score by a Bangladeshi batsman (217 against New Zealand in January 2017). He has also taken 256 test wickets at a bowling average of 31.72. He holds the unique position of being his country's highest rating bowler and its second highest rating batsman.

[2] The second highest rating all-rounder in the decade is England's Ben Stokes. He made his test debut against Australia in 2013, and by the end of 2024, he had played 110 test matches, scoring 6,719 runs at an average of 35.55 and taking 210 wickets at an average of 32.37. Born in New Zealand, Stokes moved to England with his family at the age of 12 and made his first-class debut for Durham in 2010. He is a left-hand middle-order batsman and a right arm fast-medium bowler. Like Shakib Al Hasan, Stokes is one of only 6 test all-rounders who have career batting and bowling ratings both in excess of 80. He holds the world record for the highest score in an innings by a No. 6 batsman (258 against South Africa at Newlands in 2016) and he has scored more sixes in test cricket than any other batsman. In the 3rd Ashes test of 2019 at Headingley, England was bowled out for 67 in its first innings and required a record run chase of 359 for victory in the 2nd innings. In what has been rated by Wisden as the greatest century of the 2010s, Stokes remained unbeaten on 135 in England's 2nd innings score of 9 for 362, smashing England to a remarkable victory with 11 fours and 8 sixes.

Highest Rating Wicketkeepers:

After de Villiers, the 2nd and 3rd highest rating wicketkeepers in the 2010s are South Africa's Quinton de Kock and New Zealand's B.J. Watling.

[1] Quinton de Kock was born in Johannesburg in 1992 and played domestic cricket for the Highveld Lions (2009-15) and Titans (2015-22). He made his test debut against Australia in 2014 and took over the wicketkeeping duties from A.B. de Villiers in his 2nd test match. By his retirement in 2021, he had played 54 test matches and made 232 dismissals in 98 innings behind the stumps — 221 catches and 11 stumpings. In the history of test cricket, 33 wicketkeepers have taken 150 or more wickets and de Kock has the highest rate of dismissals of them all (2.37 per innings) and he made his 150th dismissal in only his 35th test, fewer tests than anyone else. His wicketkeeper rating is the 5th highest in Table 2.18. De Kock is also an aggressive left-hand batsman who has scored 3,300 runs at an average of 38.82 and a strike rate of 70.94, with 6 centuries. He has an impressive record in ODI and T20 cricket, both with the bat and behind the stumps. He scored a fifty off just 17 deliveries against England at Kingsmead in 2020 to become the fastest South African batsman to reach 50 in T20 cricket.

[2] B.J. Watling (Bradley-John Watling) is New Zealand's highest rating wicketkeeper and the 9th highest rating wicketkeeper in test history (see Table 2.18). Born in Durban in South Africa, Watling moved to Hamilton in New Zealand when he was 10 years old. He played first-class cricket for Northern Districts from 2004 until 2021 and he made his test debut as an opening batsman in 2009. It was not until his 7th test match that he took up the role of wicketkeeper (against Zimbabwe in 2012) and moved to the middle-order in the batting line-up. By his retirement from test cricket in 2021, Watling had played 75 tests making 265 dismissals (257 catches and 8 stumpings) in 127 innings behind the stumps. He scored 3,790 runs at an

average of 37.52, including 8 centuries and 19 fifties. He has been involved in the highest 6th and 7th wicket partnerships for New Zealand in tests — an unbroken stand of 365 for the 6th wicket with Kane Williamson against Sri Lanka at the Basin Reserve in 2015 and 261 for the 7th wicket with Mitchell Santner against England at the Bay Oval in 2019. After Santner was dismissed in that record 7th wicket stand, Watling became the first and only New Zealand wicketkeeper to score a double century in test cricket (205).

Table 11.1 Best World Team of the 2010s (2010 to 2019, inclusive) — Batting Performances.

The Team:

Players	Country	Batting style	Matches	Innings	Not outs	100s/50s/0s	Highest score	Runs scored	Batting average	Strike rate	Batting rating
1. Warner, DA	Australia	left	83	153	6	23/30/9	335	7,088	48.22	73.04	136.1
2. Cook, AN	England	left	111	201	11	23/37/6	294	8,818	46.41	46.94	127.8
3. Sangakkara, KC	Sri Lanka	left	46	86	7	17/20/7	319	4,851	61.41	52.22	153.5
4. Smith, SPD	Australia	right	72	130	16	26/28/4	239	7,164	62.84	55.60	166.7
5. Kallis, JH	Sth Africa	right	33	55	7	13/6/6	224	2,810	58.54	53.69	129.6
6. Kohli, V	India	right	84	141	10	27/22/10	254	7,202	54.98	57.82	132.9
7. de Villiers, AB	Sth Africa	right	60	98	10	13/27/7	278	5,059	57.49	55.65	140.1
8. Ashwin, R	India	right	70	96	13	4/11/3	124	2,385	28.73	54.68	50.4
9. Herath, HMRKB	Sri Lanka	left	72	117	24	0/3/14	80	1,492	16.04	54.00	13.8
10. Steyn, DW	Sth Africa	right	59	76	19	0/1/8	58	808	14.18	44.54	9.7
11. Anderson, JM	England	left	106	152	61	0/1/25	81	729	8.01	41.68	5.2
										Total	1065.8

Next Batters

Voges, AC	Australia	right	20	31	7	5/04/2	269	1,485	61.88	55.68	129.7
Williamson, K	N.Zealand	right	78	137	13	21/31/9	242	6,379	51.44	51.55	129.4
Amla, HM	Sth Africa	right	85	146	12	21/27/7	311	6,695	49.96	50.48	128.3
Root, JE	England	right	89	164	12	17/45/8	254	7,359	48.41	54.38	127.5
Chanderpaul, S	W. Indies	right	41	70	17	9/13/2	203	3,198	60.34	44.62	127.1
Younis Khan	Pakistan	right	55	101	12	18/12/7	218	4,839	54.37	50.48	123.6

Table 11.2 Best World Team of the 2010s (2010 to 2019, inclusive) – Bowling Performances.

The Team:

Players	Country	Overs	Balls	Maids	Runs against	Bowl style	Wkts	5w/10w	Best	Avge	Strike rate	Econ rate	Bowling rating
1. Warner, DA	Australia					Less than 100 overs							-
2. Cook, AN	England					Less than 100 overs							-
3. Sangakkara, KC	Sri Lanka					Less than 100 overs							-
4. Smith, SPD	Australia	230	1380	25	960	RAL	17	0/0	3/18	56.47	81.20	4.17	15.8
5. Kallis, JH	S. Africa	515	3,090	122	1,466	RAFM	34	0/0	3/35	43.12	90.88	2.85	44.7
6. Kohli, V	India					Less than 100 overs							-
7. de Villiers, AB	S. Africa	Wicketkeeper				Did not bowl							-
8. Ashwin, R	India	3,234	19,412	671	9,183	RAO	362	27/7	7/59	25.37	53.63	2.84	146.5
9. Herath, HMRKB	Sri Lanka	3,479	20,879	661	9,589	LAO	363	30/9	9/127	26.42	57.49	2.76	146.5
10. Steyn, DW	S. Africa	1,953	11,729	454	5,954	RAF	267	15/2	7/51	22.30	43.93	3.05	140.5
11. Anderson, JM	England	3,927	23,568	1,057	10,448	RAFM	429	20/3	7/42	24.35	54.94	2.66	143.3
												Total	637.3

Next Bowlers

Rabada, K	S. Africa	1,267	7,604	258	4,289	RAF	190	9/4	7/112	22.57	40.02	3.38	139.5
Philander, VD	S. Africa	1,830	10,986	489	4,838	RAFM	220	13/2	6/21	21.99	49.90	2.64	132.1
Broad, SCJ	England	3,807	22,850	911	11,146	RAMF	403	14/2	8/15	27.66	56.68	2.93	125.1
Cummins, PJ	Australia	1,094	6,563	258	3,048	RAF	139	5/1	6/23	21.93	47.22	2.79	121.2
Starc, MA	Australia	1,927	11,573	382	6,501	LAF	240	13/2	6/50	27.09	48.22	3.37	117.2
Jadeja, RA	India	2,135	12,822	542	5,200	LAO	211	9/1	7/48	24.64	60.75	2.43	113.3
Saeed Ajmal	Pakistan	1,661	9,968	343	4,242	RAO	160	10/4	7/55	26.51	62.30	2.55	111.9

Table 11.3 Performances of the best all-rounders (2010 to 2019, inclusive).

Player	Country	No. of tests	Years played	Batting style	Runs scored	Batting avge	Batting rating	Bowl style	Wkts taken	Bowl avge	Bowl rating	All-rounder Rating
Shakib Al Hasan	Bangladesh	42	2010-19	left	3,147	42.53	91.0	LAO	162	31.94	91.9	182.5
Stokes, BA	England	60	2013-19	left	3,787	35.73	78.4	RAFM	139	33.14	76.2	153.5
Ashwin, R	India	70	2011-19	right	2,385	28.73	50.4	RAO	362	25.37	146.5	148.9
Jadeja, RA	India	48	2012-19	left	1,844	35.46	59.2	LAO	211	24,64	113.3	145.5

Table 11.4 Wicketkeeping performances (2010 to 2019, inclusive).

Player	Country	No. of tests	Years played	Batting style	Runs scored	Batting avge	Batting rating	Catches	Stumpings	Total dismissals	Wicket keeper rating
De Villiers, AB	S Africa	45	2010-18	right	5,059	57.49	140.1	101	5	106	142.6
De Kock, Q	S Africa	79	2014-19	left	2,683	38.88	78.2	176	11	187	130.3
Watling, BJ	N Zealand	112	2010-19	right	3,538	39.31	76.8	228	8	236	129.3

Note: The ratings are determined from the number of tests while playing as wicketkeeper.

Chapter 12
The Best World Team — 2020 to 2024

All ten test playing nations competed against each other in the period from 2020 until the end of 2024. During this time, 196 test matches were played; England played 64 of them, Australia 41, India 48, Sri Lanka 36, South Africa 35, West Indies 37, New Zealand 39, Pakistan 35, Bangladesh 33, Zimbabwe 12, Afghanistan 7 and Ireland 6). In this five-year period, there were fewer tests played than in the previous decades and therefore fewer players played 20 or more test matches.

The Best Team of the period 2020 to 2024 inclusive

Batting Order:	Country	No. of tests	Period	Batting Rating	Bowling Rating
1. Khawaja, UT	Australia	33	2022-24	96.7	-
2. Karunaratne, D	Sri Lanka	34	2020-24	97.7	-
3. Williamson, KS	N Zealand	27	2020-24	148.9	-
4. Root, JE	England	63	2020-24	136.3	44.0
5. Brook. HC	England	24	2022-24	150.3	-
6. Labuschagne, M	Australia	41	2020-24	94.3	-
7. Pant, RR	India	31	2020-24	80.2	WK
8. Ashwin, R	India	36	2020-24	25.8	131.9
9. Rabada, K	S Africa	28	2020-24	8.1	132.6
10. Hazlewood, JR	Australia	21	2020-24	4.8	121.6
11. Bumrah, JJ	India	32	2020-24	4.3	136.5
			Totals	847.4	566.6

Note: Batting and bowling statistics are given in Tables 12.1 and 12.2.

The win/loss/draw results for each of the participating countries are shown below.

Country	No. of tests	England	Australia	India	Sri Lanka	South Africa	West Indies	New Zealand	Pakistan	Zimbabwe	Bangladesh	All matches
England	64	-	2/6/2	4/9/1	4/1/0	5/1/0	5/2/2	6/3/1	5/2/2	0/0/0	0/0/0	32/24/8
Australia	41	6/2/2	-	5/5/3	1/1/0	2/0/1	3/1/0	3/0/0	4/0/2	0/0/0	0/0/0	24/9/8
India	48	9/4/1	5/5/3	-	2/0/0	2/3/0	1/0/1	1/6/1	0/0/0	0/0/0	4/0/0	24/18/6
Sri Lanka	36	1/4/0	1/1/0	0/2/0	-	0/4/0	2/0/2	2/2/0	1/3/0	1/0/1	4/0/2	15/16/5
South Africa	35	1/5/0	0/2/1	3/2/0	4/0/0	-	5/0/1	1/3/0	1/2/0	0/0/0	4/0/0	19/14/2
West Indies	37	2/5/2	1/3/0	0/1/1	0/2/2	0/5/1	-	0/2/0	1/1/0	1/0/1	5/1/0	10/20/7
New Zealand	39	3/6/1	0/3/0	6/1/1	2/2/0	3/1/0	2/0/2	-	2/0/2	0/0/0	2/2/0	20/15/4
Pakistan	35	2.5.2	0/4/2	0/0/0	3/1/0	2/1/0	1/1/0	0/2/2	-	2/0/0	3/2/0	13/16/6
Zimbabwe	12	0/0/0	0/0/0	0/0/0	0/1/1	0/0/0	0/1/1	0/0/0	0/2/0	-	0/2/0	1/8/3
Bangladesh	33	0/0/0	0/0/0	0/4/0	0/4/2	0/4/0	1/5/0	2/2/0	2/3/0	2/0/0	-	9/22/2

Notes: Ireland played six tests, losing four and winning two, with wins against Afghanistan and Zimbabwe and losses to Bangladesh, England and Sri Lanka (2). Afghanistan played six tests, losing one each to Bangladesh, Zimbabwe, Sri Lanka and Ireland and winning one against Zimbabwe, with one draw.

Australia, England, India, South Africa and New Zealand had more wins than losses in this period. The ratios of wins to losses for the participating nations were Australia 2.67, South Africa 1.36, New Zealand 1.33, England 1.33, India 1.33, Sri Lanka 0.94, Pakistan 0.81, West Indies 0.50, Bangladesh 0.41 and Zimbabwe 0.13. The trend to more attacking cricket continued into the 2020s with 13.4% of matches drawn (compared to 19.6% in the 2010s, 24.6% in the 2000s, 35.7% in the 1990s, 45.9% in the 1980s).

Of the 11 players selected in the top team of the 2020s, 3 were from Australia, 3 from India, 2 from England and 1 each from South Africa, Sri Lanka and New Zealand. Because the players in this five-year period did not have the opportunity to play many test matches, it is not reasonable to compare the team's batting and bowling ratings with the ratings from other eras. However, as in the 2010s, the team's total bowling rating was low because six of the top seven batsmen did not contribute.

Australia's Usman Khawaja and Sri Lanka's Dimuth Karunaratne are the opening batsmen. At No. 3 is New Zealand's Kane Williamson, the highest rating batsman of the period. At Nos. 4, 5 and 6 are Joe Root and Harry Brook of England and Australia's Manus Labuschagne, respectively. The wicketkeeper at No.7 is India's Rishabh Pant. India's right arm off-spinner Ravi Ashwin retains his place from the team of the 2010s at No. 8. At Nos. 9, 10 and 11 are the three pace bowlers, Kagiso Rabada of South Africa, Josh Hazlewood of Australia and Jasprit Bumrah of India, respectively.

The batting and bowling statistics of the World team of the period 2020 to 2024 are presented in Tables 12.1 and 12.2, respectively, and the statistics for the highest rating all-rounders and wicketkeepers are given in Tables 12.3 and 12.4, respectively. The performances of the eligible players in the best national teams are provided in Appendix M (Tables M.1 to M.10).

The Players:

No. 1: Australia's left-handed opening batsman Usman Khawaja was born in Islamabad Pakistan in 1986 and his family emigrated to Australia when he was four years old. He played first-class domestic cricket for New South Wales (2008 to 2011) and for Queensland (2012 to 2024) and county cricket for Derbyshire (2011 and 2012), Lancashire (2014) and Glamorgan (2018). He made his test debut in January 2011 against England at the Sydney Cricket Ground. Up until the end of 2024, he had played 77 tests and scored 5,592 runs at an average of 44.38. He is the 95th highest rating test batsman (Table 2.7). After an average home series against India in December 2019, he was dropped from the Australian test team but made a triumphant return in 2022. He was the second highest scoring batsman in the 2021-2023 ICC World Test Championship, and in 2023, he won the ICC Test Cricketer of the year award. Khawaja is one of the next best batsmen in the highest rating Australian team of the 2010s (Table L.2).

No. 2: Sri Lanka's Dimuth Karunaratne is a left-handed opening batsman for Sri Lanka. He is a member of the top Sri Lankan team of all time (Table 13.22), as well as the top Sri Lankan team for the 2010s (Table L.7). He was born in Colombo in 1988 and has played domestic cricket for the Sinhalese Sports Club since 2008 and County cricket for Yorkshire in 2022. From his test debut in 2012 until the end of 2024, he had played 98 tests and scored 7,168 runs at an average of 39.81, including 16 centuries. He is the 86th highest rating test batsman (Table 2.7). He captained Sri Lanka in 30 tests from 2019 to 2023, with 12 wins, 12 losses and 6 draws.

No. 3: Kane Williamson of New Zealand is one of the next best batsmen in the top world team of the 2010s (Chapter 11) and he is the highest rating batsman in the top New Zealand team of all time (Table 13.16).

No. 4: England's Joe Root is one of the next best batsmen in the top world team of the 2010s (Chapter 11) and a member of the highest rating English team of all time (Table 13.4).

No. 5: Harry Brook of England was born in Keighley, West Yorkshire in 1999 and is a right-hand batsman and a useful right arm medium bowler. He has played domestic first-class cricket for Yorkshire since 2016. He made his test debut against South Africa in 2022 and, up until the end of 2024, he had played 24 tests and scored 2,281 test runs at an average of 58.49, including 8 centuries, and a strike rate of 88.38. He scored 317 against Pakistan at the Multan Cricket Stadium in October 2024 sharing a world record 4th wicket partnership with Joe Root of 454. Brook has had an outstanding start to his test career, and at the end of 2024, he is the 15th highest rating batsman in the history of test cricket (see Table 2.7) and he has a higher strike rate than any other test batsman.

No. 6: Manus Labuschagne of Australia was born in Klerksdorp, South Africa in 1994. His family moved to Australia when he was ten years old, and he grew up in Brisbane. A classical right-hand batsman, strong on both sides of the wicket, he plays domestic first-class cricket for Queensland (2014/15 to present) and County cricket for Glamorgan (2019-present). He made his test debut against Pakistan in Dubai in October 2018, and by the end of

2024, he had played 54 tests and scored 4,338 runs at an average of 48.20, with 11 centuries. He was named in the ICC Men's Test Team of the Year in 2019, 2021 and 2022.

No. 7: India's Rishabh Pant is the highest rating wicketkeeper batsman for this four-year period. He was born in Roorkee in 1997 and played domestic cricket for Delhi (2015-Present). An aggressive left-handed batsman, he made his test debut against England at Trent Bridge in 2018 and since that time has played 42 test matches and scored 2,847 test runs at an average of 41.87 and a strike rate of 73.51. In 83 innings as wicketkeeper in test cricket, he has taken 147 catches and made 15 stumpings. He is the 16th highest rating test wicketkeeper (Table 2.18). In the first test against Australia at the Adelaide Oval in December 2018, Pant took 11 catches, the most catches by an Indian wicketkeeper in a test match. On 30 December 2022, Pant was injured in a car accident when the vehicle he was driving collided with a road barrier near Roorkee. He did not play cricket for India again in any format until June 2024.

No. 8: Ravichandran Ashwin of India is the highest rating bowler in the team and retains the same position he held in the highest rating world team of the 2010s (see Chapter 11).

No. 9: South Africa's Kagiso Rabada is the 5th highest rating bowler in the best world team of the 2010s (see Chapter 11) and the opening bowler in the best South African team of all time (Table 13.26).

No. 10: Australia's Josh Hazlewood is a tall right arm fast-medium bowler. He was born in Tamworth in New South Wales in 1991 and made his first-class debut for New South Wales in the summer of 2008/09 at the age of 17. Since that time he has been one of the opening bowlers for new South Wales whenever his test duties permit. He made his test debut in 2014 against India in Brisbane, and up until the end of 2024, he has played 72 tests and taken 279 wickets at an average of 24.58. He was the ICC Men's Emerging Cricketer of the Year in 2015 and a member of the ICC Men's Test Team in that same year.

No. 11: Jasprit Bumrah of India is the 22nd highest rating test bowler (Table 2.16) and the highest rating Indian pace bowler. Bumrah is a right-arm fast-medium bowler with a distinctive slinging action. He has played first-class cricket for Gujarat since 2013 and made his test debut against South Africa in 2018. Up to the end of 2024, he had played 44 tests, taking 203 wickets at a bowling average of 19.43 and a strike rate of 42.22 — the lowest career test bowling average of any bowler with 20 or more matches since World War 1 and the second lowest strike rate. He is one of the opening bowlers in the highest rating Indian team of all time (Table 13.14).

Next Best Batsmen:

After the top 6 batsmen, the next 6 most highly rated batsmen in the five years 2020 to 2024 are Angelo Mathews (Sri Lanka), Ben Duckett (England), Dinesh Chandimal (Sri Lanka), Travis Head (Australia), Babar Azam (Pakistan) and Steven Smith (Australia).

[1] Sri Lanka's Angelo Mathews is a hard-hitting right-hand batsman and a member of the top Sri Lankan team of all time (Table 13.22) and one of the highest- ranking Sri Lankan batsmen in the 2010s (Table L.7). He was born in Colombo in 1987 and made his test debut against Pakistan in 2009. Up to the end 2024, he has played 116 tests and scored 8,042 runs at an average of 44.93, with 16 centuries. He is Sri Lanka's 3rd highest rating test batsman. He captained Sri Lanka in 34 tests between 2013 and 2017, winning 13, losing 15 and drawing 6.

[2] Ben Duckett of England was born in London in 1994. He is a left-hand opening batsman who has played first-class cricket for Northamptonshire (2013—2018) and Nottinghamshire (2018-present). He made his test debut against Bangladesh in 2016, but after 4 tests averaging just 15.71 with the bat, he spent the next 5 years out of the English test team. Recalled in 2022, his performance improved, and by the end of 2024 he has played 32 tests and scored 2,270 runs at an average of 39.82. He is the 173rd highest rating test batsman (Table A.1).

[3] Dinesh Chandimal is a right-hand middle order Sri Lankan batsman and former wicket-keeper. Born in Balapitiya, he has played first-class cricket for Nondescripts Cricket Club (2009-2019) and Sri Lankan

Army (1919- Present). He made his test debut against South Africa in 2011, and by the end of 2024, he has played 86 tests and scored 6,019 runs at an average of 43.30. He is the 90th highest rating test batsman (Table 2.7). He has been selected primarily as a batsman in recent years, but he has kept wickets for Sri Lanka in 50 innings, taking 63 catches and 10 stumpings at 1.46 dismissals per innings. He is the 29th highest rating wicket-keeper (Table 2.18).

[4] Travis Head of Australia is an aggressive left-hand top-order batsman. Born in Adelaide in 1993, he has played domestic first-class cricket for South Australia (2011/12 to present) and County cricket for Yorkshire (2016), Worcestershire (2018) and Sussex (2021). He made his test debut against Pakistan in 2018, and up to the end of 2024, he has played 53 tests and scored 3,583 runs at 43.17. He is the 128th highest rating test batsman (Table A.1). He was the player of the match in the 2023 ICC World Test Championship final against India at the Oval, with a score of 163 in the first innings of the match.

[5] Pakistan's Babar Azam was born in 1994 in Lahore and grew up playing cricket in the streets of Lahore, inspired by his older first cousins Kamran, Umar and Adnan Akmal — all having previously represent Pakistan in test cricket. Babar made his test debut against the West Indies in Dubai in 2016. By the end of 2024, he had played 56 tests and scored 4,051 runs at an average of 43.56. He had also played 123 ODI matches and scored 5,957 runs at the impressive average of 56.73. He is an outstanding right-hand batsman; the only batsman at the end of 2023 to be ranked by the ICC in the top five batsmen in all formats of the game. He was named as the ICC Cricketer of the year for 2022 and the winner of the Sir Garfield Sobers Trophy. He has captained Pakistan in all formats of the game, captaining the test team in 20 tests from 2021 to 2023, with 10 wins, 6 losses and 4 draws.

[6] Australia's Steve Smith is the highest rating batsman in the best world team of the 2010s (Chapter 10) and one of the next best batsmen in the best world team of all time (Table 13.1).

Next Best Bowlers:

The next 7 most highly rated bowlers are Pat Cummings (Australia), Ravindra Jadeja (India), Stuart Broad (England), Nathan Lyon (Australia), Oli Robinson (England) and James Anderson (England).

[1] Australia's Pat Cummins is one of the next best bowlers in the highest rating world team of the 2010s (see Chapter 11) and the best Australian team of all time (Table 13.8).

[2] India's Ravindra Jadeja is one of the next best bowlers and one of the best all-rounders in the highest rating world team of the 2010s (see Chapter 11) and one of the next best bowlers in the best Indian team of all time (Table 13.14).

[3] England's Stuart Broad is one of the next best bowlers in the highest rating world team of the 2010s (see Chapter 11) and the best English team of all time (Table 13.5).

[4] Nathan Lyon of Australia is an off-spin bowler who made his test debut in 2011 and by the end of 2024 had played 133 test matches and taken 538 test wickets at an average of 30.42. He is the 27th highest rating test bowler (Table 2.16). Lyon has played domestic cricket for South Australia (2010-2013) and for his home state of New South Wales (2013-Present). He was a member of the ICC Test Team of the Year in 2018, 2019 and 2022 and the Australian Test Player of the Year 2019. He is one of the next best bowlers in the highest rating Australian team of all time (Table 13.8).

[5] Ollie Robinson of England is a tall right arm medium-fast bowler. He was born in Margate in Kent in 1993 and played first-class cricket for Yorkshire (2013-14) and Sussex (2015-24). He made his test debut in 2021 against New Zealand at Lords, and up until the end of 2024, he has played 20 tests and taken 76 wickets at an average of 22.92.

[6] James Anderson of England is one of the opening bowlers in the highest rating world team of the 2010s (see Chapter 11) and the best English team of all time (Table 13.5).

Highest Rating All-Rounders:

The three highest rating all-rounders are Ben Stokes (England), Joe Root (England) and Ravi Jadeja (India). Jadeja and Root have already been introduced. England's Ben Stokes is the highest rating all-rounder in the highest rating world team of the 2010s (Chapter 11).

Highest Rating Wicketkeepers:

After Rishabh Pant, the next highest rating wicketkeepers in the period 2020 to 2024 are Alex Carey (Australia), Joshua Da Silva (West Indies) and Litton Das (Bangladesh).

[1] Alex Carey is the current Australian wicketkeeper and is the 22th highest rating test wicketkeeper (Table 2.18). He was born in Loxton, South Australia and plays domestic first-class cricket for South Australia (2012/13 to present) and County cricket for Sussex (2019). He made his test debut in December 2021 against England at the Brisbane Cricket Ground, and by the end of 2024, he had played 36 test matches scoring 1,534 runs at 31.96 and making 151 dismissals in 68 test innings behind the stumps.

[2] Joshua Da Silva is the current West Indian wicketkeeper and is the 35th highest rating test wicketkeeper (Table 2.18). He was born in Port of Spain and plays domestic first-class cricket for Trinidad and Tobago (2018 to present) and made his test debut against New Zealand at the Basin Reserve in December 2020. At the end of 2024, he had played 33 tests scoring 1,238 runs at a batting average of 24.76 and making 127 test dismissals.

[3] Bangladesh's Litton Das is a right-hand opening batsman and wicketkeeper. Born in Dinajpur in 1994, he has played first-class cricket for North Zone (Bangladesh) since 2012 and test cricket since his test debut in 2015 against India. By the end of 2024, he had played 48 tests and scored 2,788 runs at 34.00. At No.31 in Table 2.18, he is Bangladesh's second highest rating wicketkeeper having kept wickets in 62 test innings, with 108 test dismissals. He is the opening batsman in Bangladesh's highest rating team of all time (Table 13.31).

Table 12.1 Best World Team of the 2020s (2020 to 2024, inclusive) — Batting Performances.

The Team:

Players	Country	Batting style	Matches	Innings	Not outs	100s/50s/0s	Highest score	Runs scored	Batting average	Strike rate	Batting rating
1. Khawaja, UT	Australia	left	33	62	7	7/13/4	195	2,705	49.18	45.85	96.7
2. Karunaratne, D	Sri Lanka	left	34	63	3	7/15/0	244	2,744	45.73	56.21	97.7
3. Williamson, KS	N Zealand	right	27	49	4	12/6/2	251	2,897	64.38	52.30	148.9
4. Root, JE	England	right	63	114	11	19/20/5	262	5,613	54.50	62.13	136.3
5. Brook. HC	England	right	24	40	1	8/10/2	317	2,281	58.49	88.38	150.3
6. Labuschagne, M	Australia	right	41	76	7	8/16/3	215	3,153	45.70	50.89	94.3
7. Pant, RR	India	right	31	55	6	4/12/2	146	2,093	41.04	74.54	80.2
8. Ashwin, R	India	right	36	55	2	2/3/6	113	1,118	21.09	54.25	25.8
9. Rabada, K	S Africa	left	28	45	9	0/0/9	47	438	12.17	57.11	8.1
10. Hazlewood, JR	Australia	left	21	26	16	0/0/2	22	108	10.80	39.71	4.8
11. Bumrah, JJ	India	right	32	50	14	0/0/19	34	292	8.11	48.67	4.3
										Total	847.4

Next Batters

Mathews, AD	Sri Lanka	right	32	55	6	7/10/4	200	2,338	47.71	46.76	92.1
Duckett, BM	England	left	28	53	3	4/12/3	182	2,160	43.20	88.06	91.2
Chandimal, LD	Sri Lanka	right	31	54	8	5/12/4	206	2,173	47.24	52.36	91.0
Head, TM	Australia	left	37	61	3	7/10/5	175	2,502	43.14	77.61	89.5
Babar Azam	Pakistan	right	31	55	2	5/14/2	196	2,344	44.23	53.56	87.4
Smith, SPD	Australia	right	41	72	9	8/13/7	200	2,798	44.41	48.93	86.7

Table 12.2 Best World Team of the 2020s (2020 to 2024, inclusive) — Bowling Performances.

Players	Country	Overs	Balls	Maids	Runs against	Bowl style	Wkts	5w/10w	Best	Average	Strike rate	Econ rate	Bowling rating
1. Khawaja, UT	Australia	Less than 100 overs											-
2. Karunaratne, D	Sri Lanka	Less than 100 overs											-
3. Williamson, KS	N Zealand	Less than 100 overs											-
4. Root, JE	England	589	3,539	86	1,983	RAO	47	1/0	5/8	42.19	75.31	3.36	44.0
5. Brook, HC	England	Less than 100 overs											-
6. Labuschagne, M	Australia	Less than 100 overs											-
7. Pant, RR	India	Wicketkeeper					Did not bowl						-
8. Ashwin, R	India	1,300	7,806	236	3,656	RAO	175	10/1	7/71	20.89	44.61	2.81	131.9
9. Rabada, K	S Africa	841	5,051	164	2,737	RAF	131	7/0	6/46	20.89	38.56	3.25	132.6
10. Hazlewood, JR	Australia	633	3,799	169	1,748	RAFM	84	5/0	5/8	20.81	45.22	2.76	121.6
11. Bumrah, JJ	India	976	5,857	234	2,751	RAF	141	8/0	6/45	19.51	41.54	2.82	136.5
												Total	566.6
Next Bowlers													
Cummins, PJ	Australia	1,144	6,870	231	3,468	RAF	150	8/1	6/91	23.12	45.80	3.03	119.8
Jadeja, RA	India	930	5,580	186	2,569	LAO	112	6/2	7/42	22.94	49.82	2.76	114.9
Broad, SCJ	England	1,025	6,149	237	3,064	RAMF	128	3/1	6/31	23.94	48.04	2.99	110.5
Lyon, NM	Australia	1,529	9,180	307	4,163	RAO	158	8/3	6/65	26.35	58.10	2.72	107.0
Robinson, OE	England	632	3,794	159	1,742	RAMF	76	3/0	5/49	22.92	49.93	2.75	106.3
Anderson, JM	England	1,246	7,474	357	3,020	RAFM	127	5/0	6/40	23.78	58.85	2.42	104.9

Table 12.3 Performances of the best all-rounders (2020 to 2024, inclusive).

Player	Country	No. of tests	Years played	Batting style	Runs scored	Batting avge	Batting rating	Bowling style	Wickets taken	Bowl avge	Bowl rating	All-rounder Rating
Stokes, BA	England	50	2020-24	left	2,932	35.33	69.2	RAFM	71	30.86	72.8	140.2
Root, JE	England	63	2020-24	right	5,613	54.50	136.3	RAO	47	42.19	44.0	134.2
Jadeja, RA	India	31	2020-24	left	1,487	34.58	52.7	LAO	112	22.94	105.0	131.6

Table 12.4 Wicketkeeping performances (2020 to 2024, inclusive).

Player	Country	No. of tests	Years played	Batting style	Runs scored	Batting avge	Batting rating	Catches	Stumpings	Total dismissals	Wicket Keeper Rating
Pant, RR	India	31	2020-24	left	2,093	41.04	80.2	97	13	110	105.5
Carey, A	Australia	36	2021–24	left	1,534	31.96	47.9	137	14	151	100.1
Da Silva, J	W Indies	33	2020–23	right	1,238	24.76	28.3	120	7	127	91.8
Litton Das	Bangladesh	30	2020–24	right	2,044	39.31	73.7	77	12	89	90.5

Notes: 1. The ratings are determined from the number of tests while playing as wicketkeeper.

Chapter 13
The Best World and National
Teams of All Time — 1877 to 2024

From the first test played in 1877 until the conclusion of the Boxing Day test between Australia and India on 30th December 2024, 2,574 test matches have been played between the various test playing nations. England played 1083 of them, Australia 870, West Indies 582, India 588, Pakistan 462, New Zealand 478, South Africa 471, Sri Lanka 323, Bangladesh 150 and Zimbabwe 119. Afghanistan played 10 tests (between June 2018 and December 2024) and Ireland played 9 tests (between May 2018 and July 2024).

The total numbers of players who have represented their counties in test cricket up to the end of 2024 are shown in the table below, together with the much fewer numbers who have played 20 or more matches. Of this select group, the numbers of batsmen with a career batting average greater than 30, the number of bowlers who have bowled more than 3000 balls and who have a career bowling average less than 40, and the numbers of specialist wicketkeepers who have been selected are also shown.

Country	Total Number of Players	Players with 20 or more test matches			
		Total Number	Batsmen with Batting Average ≥ 30	Bowlers with Bowling Average ≤ 40	Specialist Wicketkeepers
England	718	173	85	71	18
Australia	468	151	86	60	15
South Africa	367	66	42	24	8
West Indies	340	95	43	39	13
New Zealand	288	85	37	34	7
India	314	97	49	41	10
Pakistan	257	86	42	38	9
Sri Lanka	167	52	23	16	8
Zimbabwe	129	20	6	5	3
Bangladesh	106	22	7	3	3
Afghanistan	35	0	-	-	-
Ireland	29	0	-	-	-
Totals	3,218	847	420	331	94

The win/loss/draw results for each of the test playing countries over the 146-year history of test cricket are shown on the next page. Only England, Australia, South Africa and Pakistan have won more test matches than they have lost. In total, 1,702 tests have been won and lost, 782 have been drawn and 2 ended in a tie. Almost one third of all test matches have ended in a draw.

Win/Loss/Draw Results for all test matches before the end of 2024

Country	No of tests	England	Australia	West Indies	New Zealand	India	Pakistan	Sri Lanka	South Africa	Zimbabwe	Bangladesh	All Nations
England [3]	1083	-	112/152/97	55/59/53	55/14/47	51/35/50	30/23/39	19/9/11	66/35/55	3/0/3	9/1/0	400/328/355
Australia [1,2]	871	152/112/97	-	61/33/25	36/8/18	47/33/30	37/15/20	20/5/8	54/26/21	3/0/0	5/1/0	416/233/219
W. Indies [1,5]	582	59/54/53	33/61/25	-	13/17/19	30/23/47	18/21/15	4/11/9	3/23/8	8/0/4	15/5/2	184/215/182
N. Zealand	478	14/54/47	8/36/18	17/13/19	-	16/22/27	14/25/23	18/11/11	7/26/16	11/0/6	14/2/3	119/189/170
India [1,4]	589	35/51/50	33/47/30	23/30/47	22/16/27	-	9/12/38	22/7/17	16/18/10	7/2/2	13/0/2	181/183/223
Pakistan [9]	463	23/30/39	15/37/20	21/18/15	25/14/23	12/9/38	-	23/17/19	6/16/7	12/3/4	12/2/1	150/146/166
Sri Lanka [6]	323	9/19/11	5/20/8	11/4/9	11/18/11	7/22/17	17/23/19	-	9/18/6	14/0/6	20/1/5	106/125/92
Sth. Africa	471	35/66/55	26/54/21	23/3/8	26/7/16	18/16/10	16/6/7	18/9/6	-	8/0/1	14/0/2	184/161/126
Zimbabwe [8]	119	0/3/3	0/3/0	0/8/4	0/11/6	2/7/2	3/12/4	0/14/6	0/8/1	-	7/8/3	13/76/30
Bangladesh [7]	150	1/9/0	1/5/0	5/15/2	2/14/3	0/13/2	2/12/1	1/20/5	0/14/2	8/7/3	-	22/110/18

1. Australia played two tied test matches, India and West Indies each played one tied test (not included in the win/loss/draw numbers above)
2. Australia also played and won a single test match against the ICC World XI in 2005.
3. England played and won two tests against Ireland, one in 2018 and one in 2023.
4. India played and won a single test against Afghanistan in 2018.
5. West Indies played and won a single test against Afghanistan in 2019.
6. Sri Lanka played and won two tests against Ireland in 2023 and won a single test against Afghanistan in 2024.
7. Bangladesh played two tests against Afghanistan, losing in 2019 and winning in 2023.
8. Zimbabwe played three tests against Afghanistan – winning one and losing one in 2021 and drawing one in 2024. Zimbabwe also played and lost one test against Ireland in 2024.
9. Pakistan won a single test against Ireland in 2018.

The Best World Team of All Time:

The highest rating team of all time is shown below, together with the next seven highest rating batsmen, the next seven highest rating bowlers and the two next highest rating wicketkeepers. These are arguably the greatest 27 players in test cricket history: 4 Englishmen, 7 Australians, 4 South Africans, 4 West Indians, 4 Indians, 3 Sri Lankans and 1 New Zealander. The batting and bowling statistics and ratings of each of the players are shown in Tables 13.1 and 13.2, respectively, and the wicketkeeping statistics are provided in Table 13.3.

All of these players were in the top teams in the eras in which they played, and their achievements have been presented and discussed in previous chapters as follows:

- Chapter 3 (1877-1914): One of the top 27 players was a member of the best team before World War 1 — England's Sydney Barnes.

Top 11 Players:	Country	Playing period	No. of tests	Next best batsmen:	Country	Playing period	No. of tests
1. Hutton, L	Eng	1937-55	79	Lara, BC	W.Indies	1990-06	131
2. Hayden, ML	Aust	1994-09	103	Ponting, RT	Aust	1995-12	168
3. Bradman, DG	Aust	1928-48	52	Root, JE [1]	Eng	2012-24	152
4. Sangakkara, K	S.Lanka	2000-15	134	Dravid, R	India	1996-12	164
5. Tendulkar, SR	India	1989-13	200	Smith, SPD [1]	Aust	2010-24	113
6. Kallis, JH	S.Africa	1995-13	166	Jayawardene, DPMdS	S.Lanka	1997-14	149
7. Gilchrist, AC (W-K)	Aust	1998-08	96	Sobers, GSA	W.Indies	1954-74	93
8. Hadlee, RJ	N.Zealand	1973-90	86				
10. Muralitharan, M	S.Lanka	1992-10	133	Next best bowlers:			
11. Barnes, SF	Eng	1901-14	27	McGrath, GD	Aust	1993-07	124
				Ashwin, R [1]	India	2011-23	95
Next Best Wicketkeepers:				Anderson, JM	Eng	2003-23	183
Boucher, MV	S.Africa	1997-12	147	Steyn, DW	S.Africa	2004-19	93
De Villiers, AB	S.Africa	2004-18	114	Kumble, A	India	1990-08	132
				Marshall, MD	W.Indies	1978-91	81
				Ambrose, CEL	W.Indies	1988-00	98

Note: 1. Smith, Root and Ashwin are still playing at the end of 2024.

- Chapter 4 (1920-1949): Two were in the best team from 1920 to 1949 — England's Sir Len Hutton and Australian Sir Donald Bradman.
- Chapter 5 (1950-1959): Two were in the best team of the 1950s — England's Sir Len Hutton and West Indian Sir Garfield Sobers,
- Chapter 6 (1960-1969): Only one of the top 27 played in the 1960s — West Indian Sir Garfield Sobers.
- Chapter 7 (1970-1969): None of the top 27 were members of the best team of the 1970s.
- Chapter 8 (1980-1989): Two were in the best team of the 1980s — New Zealand's Sir Richard Hadlee and West Indian Malcolm Marshall.
- Chapter 9 (1990-1999): Eight of the top 27 were selected either in the best team of the 1990s or in the next best batters or bowlers — West Indians Brain Lara and Curtly Ambrose, Indians Sachin Tendulkar, Rahul Dravid and Anil Kumble, Australians Shane Warne and Glenn McGrath, and Sri Lankan Muttiah Muralitharan.
- Chapter 10 (2000-2010): Fifteen of the top 27 were selected either in the best team of the 2000s or in the next best batters or bowlers — as in the previous decade West Indian Brain Lara, Indians Sachin Tendulkar, Rahul Dravid and Anil Kumble, Australians Shane Warne and Glenn McGrath, and Sri Lanka's Muttiah Muralitharan. In addition, Australians Matthew Hayden, Rickie Ponting and Adam Gilchrist, Sri Lanka's Kumar Sangakkara and Mahela Jayawardene, and South Africans Jacques Kallis, Dale Steyn and Mark Boucher. No other era has seen so many of the all-time greats playing test cricket.
- Chapter 11 (2010-2019): Eight of the top 27 were selected either in the best team of the 2010s or in the next best batters or bowlers — England's James Anderson and Joe Root, Sri Lanka's Kumar Sangakkara, Australia's Steve Smith, India's Ravi Ashwin and South Africans Dale Steyn, Jacques Kallis and AB de Villiers.
- Chapter 12 (2020-2024): Four of the top 27 were selected either in the best team of the 2020s or in the next best batters or bowlers — England's James Anderson and Joe Root, Australia's Steve Smith and India's Ravi Ashwin.

The squad of 27 players contains the 11 highest rating batsmen in the history of test cricket (Table 2.7), the two highest rating opening batsmen, the 11 highest rating bowlers (Table 2.16) and the 4 highest rating wicketkeepers (Table 2.18). It also contains the 2 highest rating batting all-rounders (see Table 2.17).

Top 11 Players:

No. 1 and No. 2: Len Hutton and Matthew Hayden are the highest rating specialist opening batsmen in history, and they rank 16th and 17th, respectively, in the list of the highest rating batsmen of all time (Table 2.7). Len Hutton played for England from 1937 to 1955 and was one of the opening batsmen in both the best world team of the period 1920 to 1949 (Chapter 4) and best team of the 1950s (Chapter 5). Matthew Hayden played for Australia in the 1990s and 2000s and was the top ranked opening batsman in the best world team of the 2000s (Chapter 10).

The next highest rating specialist opening batsmen are India's Sunil Gavaskar (21st in Table 2.7), England's Alastair Cook (22nd in Table 2.7), India's Virender Sehwag (24th in Table 2.7), and England's Herbert Sutcliffe (25th in Table 2.7).

No. 3, No.4, No. 5 and No. 6: After the two openers come the four highest rating batsmen of all time. The greatest batsman of them all, Sir Donald Bradman, is an automatic selection at No. 3 in the best ever world team. He played test cricket from 1928 until 1948 (Chapter 4). His test batting average of 99.94 is more than 60% higher than the next best. With Bradman filling the No. 3 position, Kumar Sangakkara is selected at No.4 even though he played 207 of his 233 test innings at No. 3 for Sri Lanka and averaged 60.83 runs per innings in that batting position. He is one of the top six rated batsmen in the world teams of the 2000s (Chapter 10) and the 2010s (Chapter 11).

Sachin Tendulkar is selected at No. 5. He is the top-rated batsman in the best world team of the 1990s (see Chapter 9) and one of the top-rating batsmen in the 2000s (Chapter 10). He rated highly enough to make the top-rating Indian test teams in three decades (1990s, 2000s and 2010s). At No. 6 is South Africa's Jacques Kallis, arguably the greatest batting all-rounder in the history of the game. He is the No.5 batsman in the top world teams of the 2000s (Chapter 10) and 2010s (Chapter 11).

No. 7: Adam Gilchrist of Australia is the finest wicketkeeper batsman in the history of the game and was a member of the best world team of the 2000s (Chapter 10).

No. 8, No. 9, No. 10 and No. 11: The four specialist bowlers are the four highest rating bowlers in test history. New Zealand's Sir Richard Hadlee is the top-rating bowler in the top world team of the 1980s (Chapter 8). Shane Warne of Australia is selected at No. 8. He is one of the top-rating bowlers of the 1990s (Chapter 9) and the highest rating leg spin bowler in history.

Muttiah Muralitharan is unquestionably the greatest bowler in the history of cricket and one of the highest rating bowlers of the 2000s (Chapter 10) and one of the top-rating bowlers of the 1990s (Chapter 9). Sydney Barnes played for England between 1901 and 1914, and he led the bowling attack in the top-rating world team before World War 1 (Chapter 3). His career bowling rating of 190.8 positions him second behind Muralitharan in Table 2.16.

The Next 7 Highest Rating Batsmen:

[1] West Indian Brian Lara is the highest rating West Indian test batsman and the 5th highest rating batsman of all time (Table 2.7). He is selected at No. 3 in the top team of the 1990s (Chapter 9) and is one of the next six batsmen for the top team of the 2000s (Chapter 10).

[2] Ricky Ponting of Australia has the 6th highest career batting rating and is the highest ranked batsman in the top team of the 2000s (Chapter 10).

[3] Joe Root is the 7th highest rating batsman of all-time and the highest rating English batsman (Table 2.7). He is one of the next best batsmen in the world team of the 2010s (Chapter 11) and the highest rating batsman still playing in 2024 (Chapter 12).

[4] India's Rahul Dravid is the 8th highest rating batsman of all time (Table 2.7). He is one of the highest rated batsmen in the top world teams of the 1990s (Chapter 9) and 2000s (Chapter 10).

[5] Steven Smith of Australia is the 9th highest rating batsman in Table 2.7. He is selected at No. 4 in the top team of the 2010s (Chapter 11) and is one of the highest rated batsmen in the top team of the 2020s (Chapter 12).

[6] Mahela Jayawardene is the 2nd highest rating Sri Lankan batsman (ranked 10th in Table 2.7) and is selected at No. 4 in the best world team of the 2000s (Chapter 10).

[7] Sir Garfield Sobers is the No. 6 batsman in the top world teams of the 1950s (Chapter 5) and 1960s (Chapter 6) and his career batting rating is the 11th highest in history (Table 2.7).

The Next 7 Highest Rating Bowlers:

[1] Glenn McGrath of Australia is one of the top-rating bowlers of the 1990s (see Chapter 9) and the 2000s (Chapter 10) and he is the 5th highest rated bowler of all time (Table 2.16).

[2] India's Ravi Ashwin is the 6th highest rated bowler in test cricket (Table 2.16) and is one of the top four bowlers in the top teams of the 2010s (Chapters 11) and the 2020s (Chapter 12).

[3] England's James Anderson is the 7th highest rated bowler (Table 2.16) and one of the opening bowlers in the top world team of the 2010s (Chapter 11) and one of the highest rating bowlers of the 2020s (Chapter 12).

[4] South Africa's Dale Steyn is the 8th highest rated bowler (Table 2.16) and one of the opening bowlers in the top world team of the 2010s (Chapter 11).

[5] India's Anil Kumble is the 9th highest rated bowler in test cricket (Table 2.16) and is one of the top-rated bowlers in the 1990s (Chapter 9) and the 2000s (Chapter 10).

[6] West Indian Malcolm Marshall is the 10th highest rating test bowler (Table 2.16) and a member of the top world team of the 1980s (Chapter 8).

[7] West Indian Curtly Ambrose is the 11th highest rating test bowler (Table 2.16) and a member of the top world team of the 1990s (Chapter 9).

The Next Highest Rating Wicketkeepers:

After Gilchrist, the next highest rating wicketkeeper in Table 2.18 is Mark Boucher. He was the 2nd highest ranking wicketkeeper in the 1990s (Chapter 9) and in the 2000s (Chapter 10).

Although playing as specialist batsmen for most of their careers, Kumar Sangakkara (Sri Lanka) and A.B. de Villiers (South Africa) are the 3rd and 4th highest rating wicketkeepers. Both kept wickets for more than 40 test innings and both were outstanding glovemen.

Table 13.1 Batting statistics of the all-time best World team.

Player	Batting style	No. of Innings	100s	50s	0s	High score	Runs scored	Batting Avge	Strike rate	Batting Rating
1. Hutton, L	right	138	19	33	5	364	6,971	56.67	50	149.2
2. Hayden, ML	left	184	30	29	14	380	8,625	50.74	60.11	146.4
3. Bradman, DG	right	80	29	13	7	334	6,996	99.94	54.95	310.0
4. Sangakkara, K	left	233	38	52	11	319	12,400	57.41	54.19	177.8
5. Tendulkar, SR	right	329	51	68	14	248	15,921	53.79	54.12	183.7
6. Kallis, JH	right	280	45	58	16	224	13,289	55.37	45.98	170.9
7. Gilchrist, AC	left	137	17	26	14	204	5,570	47.61	81.96	121.3
8. Hadlee, RJ	left	134	2	15	12	151	3,124	27.17	56.08	50.7
9. Warne, SR	right	199	0	12	34	99	3,154	17.33	57.66	21.0
10. Muralitharan, M	right	164	0	1	33	67	1,261	11.68	70.29	11.3
11. Barnes, SF	right	39	0	0	8	38	242	8.07	49.59	4.2
									Total	1,346.5
Next Batsmen:										
Lara, BC	left	232	34	48	17	400	11,953	52.89	60.52	168.4
Ponting, RT	right	287	41	62	17	257	13,378	51.85	58.72	168.2
Root, JE [1]	right	278	36	65	13	262	12,927	50.87	57.48	163.4
Dravid, R	right	286	36	63	8	270	13,288	52.31	42.51	163.1
Smith, SPD [1]	right	185	32	40	9	239	9,472	58.11	53.55	162.4
Jayawardene, DPMdS	right	252	34	50	15	374	11,814	49.85	51.47	157.0
Sobers, GSA	left	160	26	30	12	365	8,032	57.78	50	156.50
Next Wicketkeeper Batsmen:										
Boucher, MV	right	206	5	35	17	125	5515	30.30	50.11	71.1
De Villiers, AB	right	191	22	46	8	278	8,765	50.66	54.53	140.4

Note: 1. Root and Smith are still playing at the end of 2024.

Table 13.2 Bowling statistics of the all-time best World team.

Player	Bowling style	Overs	Maidens	Runs against	Wickets	5w 10w	Best	Bowling Avge	Strike rate	Economy rate	Bowling Rating
1. Hutton, L				Less than 100 overs							-
2. Hayden, ML				Less than 100 overs							-
3. Bradman, DG				Less than 100 overs							-
4. Sangakkara, K				Less than 100 overs							-
5. Tendulkar, SR	RAM	706	83	2,492	46	0/0	3/10	54.17	92.17	3.53	29.6
6. Kallis, JH	RAFM	3,372	848	9,535	292	5/0	6/54	32.65	69.29	2.83	93.7
7. Gilchrist, AC	Did not bowl		Wicketkeeper							-
8. Hadlee, RJ	RAF	3,461	809	9,611	431	36/9	9/52	22.3	50.85	2.63	170.3
9. Warne, SR	RAL	6,784	1762	17,995	708	37/10	8/71	25.42	57.49	2.65	180.2
10. Muralitharan, M	RAO	7,340	1792	18,180	800	67/22	9/51	22.73	55.05	2.48	226.5
11. Barnes, SF	RAMF	1,312	356	3,106	189	24/7	9/103	16.43	41.66	2.37	190.8
										Total	891.1
Next Bowlers:											
McGrath, GD	RAFM	4,874	1,470	12,186	563	29/3	8/24	21.64	51.95	2.50	170.1
Ashwin, R [1]	RAO	4,536	907	12,839	537	37/8	7/59	23.91	50.68	2.83	169.2
Anderson, JM	RAFM	6,673	1,721	18,627	704	32/3	7/42	26.46	56.87	2.79	163.9
Steyn, DW	RAF	3,101	660	10,077	439	26/5	7/51	22.95	42.39	3.25	161.5
Kumble, A	RAL	6,808	1,575	18,355	619	35/8	10/74	29.65	65.99	2.70	157.7
Marshall, MD	RAF	2,930	613	7,876	376	22/4	7/22	20.95	46.77	2.69	156.5
Ambrose, CEL	RAF	3,684	1,001	8502	405	22/3	8/45	20.99	54.58	2.31	153.9

Note: 1. Ashwin is still playing at the end of 2024.

Table 13.3 Wicketkeeping statistics of the best of all-time.

Wicketkeeper	Country	Career span	No. of Innings	Dismissals Catches	Dismissals Stumpings	Dismissals Total	Dismissals/ Innings	Wicket-keeper rating
Gilchrist, AC	Australia	1999-08	191	379	37	416	2.18	176.3
Boucher, MV	S. Africa	1997-12	281	532	23	555	1.98	170.9
Sangakkara, KC	Sri Lanka	2000-15	90	131	20	151	1.68	144.1
de Villiers, AB	S. Africa	2004-18	45	101	5	106	2.36	142.7

The Best English Team of All Time:

The highest rating English team of all time is shown below, together with the next seven highest rating batsmen, the next seven highest rating bowlers and the next two highest rating wicketkeepers. The batting, bowling and wicketkeeping statistics and ratings of each of the players are shown in Table 13.4, 13.5 and 13.6, respectively.

Top 11 Players	Playing period	No. of tests	Batting style	Bowling style
1. Hutton, L	1937-55	79	right	< 100 overs
2. Cook, AN	2006-18	161	left	< 100 overs
3. Root, JE [1]	2012-24	135	right	RAO
4. Hammond, WR	1927-47	85	right	RAMF
5. Barrington, KF	1955-68	82	right	RAL
6. Brook, HC [1]	2022-24	24	right	< 100 overs
7. Stewart, AJ	1990-03	133	right	W-K
8. Botham, IT	1977-92	102	right	RAMF
9. Briggs, J	1884-99	33	right	LAO
10. Anderson, JM	2003-24	183	left	RAMF
11. Barnes, SF	1901-14	27	right	RAMF

Next Best Wicketkeepers:

Bairstow, JM [1]	2012-24	95	right	DNB
Prior, MJ	2007-14	79	right	DNB

Next best batsmen:	Playing period	No. of tests	Batting style	Bowling style
Sutcliffe, H	1924-35	54	right	DNB
Hobbs, JB	1908-30	61	right	< 100 overs
Pietersen, KP	2005-14	104	right	RAO
Boycott, G	1964-82	108	right	RAM
Gooch, GA	1975-95	118	right	RAM
Compton, DCS	1937-57	78	right	LAWS
Paynter, E	1931-39	20	left	DNB

Next best bowlers:

Broad, SCJ	2007-23	167	left	RAMF
Trueman, FS	1952-65	67	right	RAF
Peel, R	1884-96	20	left	LAO
Underwood, DL	1966-82	86	right	LAO
Laker, JC	1948-59	46	right	RAO
Barnes, W	1880-90	21	right	RAM
Bedser, AV	1946-55	51	right	RAFM

Note: 1. Root, Brook and Bairstow are still playing at the end of 2024.

Top 11 Player:

The team is a strong one, with the 3rd highest total batting rating out of the 10 top-rating national teams and the highest total bowling rating. The batting ratings of all six top-order batsmen are in the top 22 of all time (Table 2.7) and the bowling ratings of the top 10 specialist bowlers for England are all in the top 36 in Table 2.16. Four of the top eleven members of the team played test cricket before World War 2, two of them before World War 1. Six members of the top team and only eleven of the 27 individuals listed above played test cricket after 1982. Four of these Englishmen feature in the 25 members of the top world team of all time (Len Hutton, Sydney Barnes, Joe Root and James Anderson).

Six of the top eleven rating English batsmen were specialist openers, with Yorkshireman Len Hutton and Essex's Alastair Cook selected to open the batting.

[1] and [2] Hutton is the highest rating opener of all time and was selected at No. 1 in the top world team (Table 13.1). Cook is one of the openers in the top world team of the 2010s (Chapter 11). At his retirement in 2018 he had played more tests, scored more test runs and more test centuries than any other Englishman.

[3] Joe Root is selected at No.3 one of the next best batsmen in the top world team of the 2010s (see Chapter 11) and the No. 4 batsman in the top team of the 2020s (Chapter 12). He has scored more runs and more test centuries than any other Englishmen.

[4] Wally Hammond is one of the next best batsmen in the all-time top world team (Table 12.1) and the No 4 batsman in the top team of the period 1920 to 1949 (Chapter 4).

[5] Ken Barrington is the No. 4 batsman in the top world team of the 1960s (Chapter 6). Of all the batsmen who played more than 40 test matches, Barrington's batting average is the 2nd highest by an Englishman and the 4th highest of all time (Table 2.2).

[6] Harry Brook played his first test in 2022 and, after just 24 tests, he is the 3rd highest rating English batsman. He is the No. 5 batsman in the world team of the 2020s (Chapter 12).

[7] Alec Stewart is selected as the wicketkeeper batsman. He is the 2nd highest-ranking English wicketkeeper in Table 2.18 behind Jonny Bairstow, but his significantly better batting rating won him selection. He is one of the next best batsmen and the 2nd ranked wicketkeeper in the top world team of the 1990s (Chapter 9).

[8] Sir Ian Botham is England's finest all-rounder and the highest rating bowling all-rounder in test history (Table 2.17). Botham is the highest rated bowler in the top world team of the 1970s (Chapter 7) and one of the two highest rating all-rounders in the 1980s (Chapter 8). He has been selected at No. 8, ahead of Stuart Broad and Fred Trueman, the 4th and 5th highest rating English bowlers.

[9] Johnny Briggs is a member of the top world team in the *golden age* of cricket before World War 1 (Chapter 3). He is the 12th highest rating test bowler and the 3rd highest rating English bowler (Table 2.16).

[10] James Anderson is the 2nd highest rating English bowler. He was the opening bowler in the top team of the 2010s (Chapter 11) and one of the next best bowlers in the top team of the 2020s (Chapter 12). He is one of the next best bowlers in the top team of all time (Table 13.2).

[11] Sydney Barnes is the top-rating English bowler at No. 2 in Table 2.16. He is in the top world team before World War 1 (see Chapter 3) and the top world team of all time (Tables 13.1 and 13.2).

The Next 7 Highest Rating English Batsmen:

[1] Herbert Sutcliffe of Yorkshire was an outstanding opening batsman for England between the two world wars. Sutcliffe opened the batting with Hutton in the top world team for the period 1920 to 1949 (Chapter 4). He has the highest batting average by an English batsman.

[2] Jack Hobbs is the highest rating batsman in the top world team before World War 1 (Chapter 3) and he is unlucky to just miss selection in the top team of the era 1920-1949 (Chapter 4). With 61,760 runs in first-class cricket and 199 first-class centuries, he is the leading first-class run scorer and century-maker of all-time.

[3] Kevin Pietersen made his first-class debut for Natal in South Africa in 1997. After moving to the UK, he played first-class cricket for Nottinghamshire (2001-2004), Hampshire (2005-2010) and Surrey (2010-2017). He played 104 test matches for England between 2005 and 2014 scoring 8,181 runs at an average of 47.29 and a strike rate of 61.72. He was an aggressive right-hand batsman and occasional off-spin bowler. He made the top-rated English team in both the 2000s and 2010s (Tables K.1 and L.1, respectively). He is the 43rd highest rating batsman in test history (Table 2.7).

[4] Geoffrey Boycott is one of the opening batsmen of the top world team of the 1970s (Chapter 7). He is one of the opening batsmen in the top-rating English teams of the 1960s, 1970s and 1980s (Tables G.1, H.1 and I.1, respectively).

[5] Graham Gooch is one of the opening batsmen in the top world team of the 1990s (Chapter 9). He is a member of the top English sides of the 1980s and 1990s (Tables I.1 and J.1, respectively).

[6] Denis Compton is a member of the top-rating world team of the period 1920 to 1949 (Chapter 4) and also a member of the top-rating English team in the 1950s (Table F.1).

[7] Eddie Paynter is one of the next batters in the top world team of the period 1920 to 1949 (see Chapter 4).

The Next 7 Highest Rating English Bowlers:

[1] Stuart Broad is the 4th highest rating English bowler but made way in the top 11 for the all-round skills of Ian Botham. He is one of the next best bowlers in the world teams of the 2010s (Chapter 11) and 2020s (Chapter 12).

[2] Fred Trueman was the highest rating bowler in the best world team of the 1960s (Chapter 6) and was one of the next best bowlers in the world team of the 1950s (Chapter 5).

[3] Robert Peel is one of the next best bowlers in the best world team before World War 1 (Chapter 3).

[4] Derek Underwood was the top-rating spin bowler of the 1970s and a member of the top world team of that decade (Chapter 7).

[5] Jim Laker is the top-rated bowler in the best world team of the 1950s (Chapter 5). He has the best match figures in history — 19/90 against Australia at Old Trafford in 1956.

[6] William Barnes is one of the next best bowlers in the best world team before World War 1 (Chapter 3).

[7] Alec Bedser is one of the opening bowlers in the best world team of the 1950s (Chapter 5).

The Next Highest Rating English Wicketkeepers:

[1] The highest rating English wicketkeeper is Yorkshireman Jonny Bairstow who is still playing test cricket at the end of 2024 as a specialist batsman. Bairstow is the wicketkeeper in the top English team of the 2010s (Tables L.1) and is ranked 7th in Table 2.18.

[2] After Bairstow and Stewart, the next highest rating keeper is Sussex's Matthew Prior ranked 13th in Table 2.18. Prior is the wicketkeeper in the top English team of the 2000s (Tables K.1).

[3] The 4th highest rating English wicketkeeper is Kent's Alan Knott (1967-81) and one of the next highest rating wicketkeepers of the 1970s (see Chapter 7).

Table 13.4 Batting statistics of the best English team of all time.

The team

Player	No. of Innings	Not outs	100s	50s	0s	High score	Runs scored	Avge	Strike rate	Batting Rating
1. Hutton, L	138	15	19	33	5	364	6,971	56.67	50	149.2
2. Cook, AN	291	16	33	57	9	294	12,472	45.35	46.96	146.0
3. Root, JE [1]	278	23	36	65	13	262	12,972	50.87	57.48	163.4
4. Hammond, WR	140	16	22	24	4	336	7,249	58.46	49.53	152.0
5. Barrington, KF	131	15	20	35	5	256	6,806	58.67	48.86	150.2
6. Brook, HC [1]	40	1	8	10	2	317	2,281	58.49	88.38	150.3
7. Stewart, AJ (W-K)	235	21	15	45	14	190	8,463	39.55	48.67	106.6
8. Botham, IT	161	6	14	22	14	208	5,200	33.55	60.71	81.8
9. Briggs, J	50	5	1	2	10	121	815	18.11	50	14,9
10. Anderson, JM	256	110	0	1	31	81	1,340	9.18	39.67	7.5
11. Barnes, SF	39	9	0	0	8	38	242	8.07	49,59	4.2
									Total	1111.2

Next Batsmen:

Sutcliffe, H	84	9	16	23	2	194	4,555	60.73	46.77	144.7
Hobbs, JB	102	7	15	28	4	211	5,410	56.95	49.69	136.5
Pietersen, KP	181	8	23	35	10	227	8,181	47.29	61.72	128.4
Boycott, G	193	23	22	42	10	246	8,114	47.73	38.17	123.8
Gooch, GA	215	6	20	46	13	333	8,900	42.58	49.24	123.0
Compton, DCS	131	15	17	28	10	278	5,807	50.06	50.12	122.0
Paynter, E	31	5	4	7	3	243	1,540	59.23	50	120.0
Gower, DI	204	18	18	39	7	215	8,231	44.25	50.60	116.6

Next Wicketkeepers:

Bairstow, JM [1]	168	12	12	26	16	167	5,804	37.21	58.40	87.2
Prior, MJ	123	21	7	28	13	131	4,099	40.19	61.67	84.3
Knott, APE	149	15	5	30	8	135	4,389	32.75	47.44	68.8

Table 13.5 Bowling statistics of the best English team of all time.

The team

Player	Overs	Maidens	Runs against	Wickets	5w/10w	Best	Bowling Average	Strike rate	Economy rate	Bowling Rating
1. Hutton, L				Less than 100 overs						-
2. Cook, AN				Less than 100 overs						-
3. Root, JE [1]	975	159	3,221	71	1/0	5/8	45.37	82.41	3.30	43.5
4. Hammond, W	1,278	300	3,138	83	2/0	5/36	37.81	95.99	2.36	60.1
5. Barrington, KF	437	102	1,300	29	0/0	3/4	44.83	93.62	2.87	39.9
6. Brook, HC				Less than 100 overs						-
7. Stewart, AJ	Wicketkeeper			Less than 100 overs						-
8. Botham, IT	3,550	788	10,878	383	27/4	8/34	28.40	56.96	2.99	130.4
9. Briggs, J	1,052	385	2,094	118	9/4	8/11	17.75	45.19	2.36	153.4
10. Anderson, JM [1]	6,536	1,691	18,234	690	32/3	7/42	26.43	56.84	2.79	162.8
11. Barnes, SF	1,312	356	3,106	189	24/7	9/103	16.43	41.66	2.37	190.8
									Total	780.9

Next Bowlers:

Broad, SCJ [1]	5,616	1304	16,719	604	20/3	8/15	27.68	55.79	2.98	146.1
Trueman, FS	2,447	522	6,625	307	17/3	8/31	21.58	49.44	2.62	143.3
Peel, R	1,073	444	1,715	101	5/1	7/31	16.98	51.64	1.97	141.6
Underwood, DL	3,464	1,239	7,674	297	17/6	8/51	25.84	73.61	2.11	131.9
Laker, JC	1,913	674	4,101	193	9/3	10/53	21.25	62.32	2.05	130.4
Barnes, W	568	271	793	51	3/0	6/28	15.55	44.88	2.08	128.4
Bedser, AV	2,425	574	5,876	236	15/5	7/44	24.90	67.45	2.21	125.5

Notes: 1. Root and Brook are still playing at the end of 2024.

Table 13.6 Highest rating English wicketkeepers.

Wicketkeeper	Career span	No. of Innings	Dismissals Catches	Dismissals Stumpings	Dismissals Total	Dismissals/ Innings	Wicketkeeper Rating
Bairstow, JM [1]	2012-24	104	209	14	223	2.14	132.5
Stewart, AJ	1990-03	141	227	14	241	1.71	130.1
Prior, MJ	2007-14	146	243	13	256	1.75	124.7
Knott, APE	1967-81	174	250	19	269	1.55	114.2

Note: 1. Bairstow is still playing in 2024.

The Best Australian Team of All Time:

The highest rating Australian team of all time is shown below, together with the next seven highest rating batsmen, the next seven highest rating bowlers and the next two highest rating wicketkeepers. The batting, bowling and wicketkeeping statistics and ratings of each of the players are shown in Table 13.7, 13.8 and 13.9, respectively.

Top 11 Players:	Playing period	No. of tests	Batting style	Bowling style
1. Hayden, ML	1994-09	103	left	< 100
2. Warner, DA [1]	2011-24	112	left	< 100
3. Bradman, DG	1928-48	52	right	< 100
4. Ponting, RT	1995-12	168	right	< 100
5. Smith, SPD [1]	2010-24	113	right	RAL
6. Waugh, SR	1985-04	168	right	RAM
7. Gilchrist, AC	1998-08	96	left	W-K
8. Warne, SR	1992-07	145	right	RAL
9. Lillee, DK	1971-84	70	right	RAF
10. Grimmett, CV	1925-36	37	right	RAL
11. McGrath, GD	1993-07	124	right	RAMF

Next Best Wicketkeepers:

Healy, IA	1988-99	119	right	W-K
Marsh, RW	1970-84	96	left	W-K
Haddin, BJ	2008-15	66	right	W-K

Next best batsmen:	Playing period	No. of tests	Batting style	Bowling style
Border, AR	1978-94	156	left	LAO
Chappell, GS	1970-84	87	right	RAM
Clarke, MJ	2004-15	115	right	LAO
Voges, AC	2015-16	20	right	< 100
Hussey, MEK	2005-13	79	left	< 100
Langer, JL	1993-07	105	left	< 100
Taylor, MA	1989-99	104	left	< 100

Next best bowlers:

Lyon, NM [1]	2011-24	133	right	RAO
Cummins, PJ [1]	2011-24	66	right	RAF
Davidson, AK	1953-63	44	left	LAFM
Trumble, H	1890-04	32	right	RAO
O'Reilly, WJ	1932-46	27	left	RAL
Starc, MA [1]	2011-24	84	left	LAF
Hazlewood, JR [1]	2014-24	72	left	RAFM

Note: 1. Warner, Smith, Lyon, Cummins, Starc and Hazlewood are still playing in 2024.

Top 11 Players:

The Australian team has the highest total batting rating out of the 10 top-rating national teams and the 4th highest total bowling rating. The first seven batsmen in the top team and the next seven highest rating batsmen all have career ratings in the top 54 in history (Table 2.7). The career bowling ratings of the four specialist bowlers in the team and the next seven specialist bowlers all rank in the top 46 in Table 2.16. Of the 28 individuals listed above, four played before World War 2 and only one of them played before World War 1. Seventeen played test cricket in the 21st century. Seven of these Australians feature in the 24 members of the top world team of all time (Don Bradman, Adam Gilchrist, Shane Warne, Steve Smith, Ricky Ponting, Matthew Hayden and Glenn McGrath).

[1] and [2] Matthew Hayden and David Warner are the two highest rating specialist Australian opening batsmen. Hayden is opening batsman in the top world team in test history (see Table 13.1) and the top world team of the 2000s (Chapter 10). Warner is the opening batsman in the top team of the 2010s (Chapter 11).

[3] Sir Donald Bradman is the No.3 batsman for the top world team of all time (Table 13.1) and the top world team of the period 1920-1949 (Chapter 4). He is the highest rating batsman in test history (Table 2.7).

[4] Ricky Ponting is the highest-ranking batsman in the top team of the 2000s (Chapter 10) and is one of the 13 batsmen listed in the top team of all-time (Table 13.1).

[5] Steve Smith is also one of the 13 batsmen listed in the top team of all time (Table 13.1). He is the highest rating batsman in the world team of the 2010s (Chapter 11) and one of the next best batsmen in the world team of the 2020s (Chapter 12).

[6] Steve Waugh is the No. 6 batsman in the top world team of the 1990s (Chapter 9) and a member of Australia's top test team for three consecutive decades, the 1980s, 1990s and 2000s (Tables I.2, J.2 and K.2).

[7] Adam Gilchrist is the highest rating wicketkeeper batsman in test history. He is the wicketkeeper in the top world team of all time (Table 13.1) and the top world team of the 2000s (Chapter 10).

[8] Shane Warne is the top-rating bowler in the Australian team and the 3rd highest ranked bowler in test history. He is one of the two spinners in the top world team of the 2000s (Chapter 10) and the all-time top world team shown in Tables 13.1 and 13.2.

[9] Dennis Lillee is the third highest rating Australian bowler, behind Shane Warne and Glen McGrath. He is a member of the top world team in the 1970s (Chapter 7) and one of the next best bowlers in the top world team of the 1980s (Chapter 8).

[10] Clarrie Grimmett is the highest rating bowler in the world team of the period from 1920 to 1949 (Chapter 4).

[11] Glenn McGrath is Australia's highest rating pace bowler in Table 2.16. He is one of the next best bowlers in the top team of all time (Table 13.2). He is a member of the top world team of the 2000s (Chapter 10) and one of the next best bowlers in the top world team of the 1990s (Chapter 9).

The Next 7 Highest Rating Australian Batsmen:

[1] Allan Border is the highest rating batsman in the 1980s and the No. 6 batsman in the world team of the 1980s (Chapter 8).

[2] Greg Chappell is one of the six top-order batsmen in the best world teams of both the 1970s (Chapter 7) and the 1980s (Chapter 8).

[3] Michael Clarke played first-class cricket for New South Wales (2000-15) and Hampshire (2004), and test cricket from 2004 to 2015. He is in the best Australian teams of both the 2000s and 2010s (Tables K.2 and L.2, respectively). He was a right-hand No. 4 or No.5 batsman and a useful left-arm orthodox spinner. He played 115 tests and scored 8,643 runs at an average of 49.11 and a strike rate of 55.92. He is the 32nd

highest rating test batsman. He captained Australia in 47 test matches between January 2011 and his final test in 2015, winning 24, losing 16 and drawing 7. He won the ICC's Sir Garfield Sobers Trophy in 2013

[4] Adam Voges is the 42nd highest rating batsman in Table 2.7 and a member of the top world team of the 2010s (Chapter 11).

[5] Michael Hussey made his first-class debut for Western Australia as a left-hand opening batsman in the 1994-95 domestic season but had to wait for another decade before breaking into the national test and ODI teams. He played first-cricket for Western Australia (1994-2013), Northamptonshire (2001-03), Gloucestershire (2004) and Durham (2005). He is one of only eight batsmen to have scored three triple centuries in first-class cricket. While playing for Northamptonshire, he scored three triples in two seasons causing the Australian test selectors to sit up and take notice. He played 79 test matches between 2005 and 2013, mainly as a No. 4, 5 or 6 batsman, scoring 6,235 runs at an average of 51.53, including 19 centuries. Affectionately known as "*Mr Cricket*", he is the 46th highest rating test batsman (Table 2.7). He is a member of the best Australian teams of the 2000s and 2010s (Tables K.2 and L.2, respectively).

[6] Justin Langer played first-class cricket for Western Australia from 1991 to 2008, with stints in county cricket for Middlesex (1998-2000) and Somerset (2006-2009). He played test cricket from 1993 to 2007 and scored 7,696 runs in 105 test matches at an average of 45.27. He is placing at No. 53 in Table 2.7. Langer opened the Australian innings 113 times with his great friend Matthew Hayden. Theirs was the most successful Australian opening batting combination totalling 5,655 runs. After retirement as a player, Langer has had a successful coaching career, including a four-year term as the Australian coach from 2018 to 2022.

[7] Mark Taylor is the opening batsman in the highest rating world team of the 1990s (Chapter 9).

The Next 7 Highest Rating Australian Bowlers:

[1] Nathan Lyon is an off-spin bowler who is one of the next best bowlers in the highest rating world team of the 2020s (Chapter 12).

[2] Pat Cummins is one of the next best bowlers in the top world team of the 2010s (Chapter 11) and the 2020s (Chapter 12).

[3] Alan Davidson is one of the next best bowlers in the top world teams of the 1950s (Chapter 5) and a member of the top Australian team of the 1950s (Table F.2).

[4] Hugh Trumble is one of the next best bowlers in the top world team before the first world war (Chapter 3) and was Australia's highest rating spin bowler of that era (Table D.2).

[5] Bill O'Reilly is a member of the highest rating world team of the era from 1920 to 1949 (Chapter 4).

[6] Mitchell Starc was one of the next best bowlers in the world team of the 2010s (Chapter 11).

[7] Josh Hazlewood made his first-class debut for New South Wales in the summer of 2008/09 and his test debut in 2024 against India. Up until the end of 2024, he has played 72 tests taking 279 wickets at an average of 24.58 and a strike rate of 53.11. He is a right-arm fast-medium bowler and the 46^h highest rating test bowler (Table 2.16). Hazlewood is a member of the top Australian team of the 2010s (Table L.2). He was the ICC's Men's Emerging Cricketer of the Year in 2015 and a member of the ICC Men's Test Team of that same year.

Next Best Australian Wicketkeepers:

[1] Ian Healy is the next best wicketkeeper after Gilchrist and is the wicketkeeper for the top world team of the 1990s (Chapter 9).

[2] Rod Marsh is the 3rd highest rating Australian wicketkeeper. He is the wicketkeeper for the top world team of the 1970s (Chapter 7).

[3] The 4th highest rating Australian wicketkeeper is New South Welshman Brad Haddin, who ranks 11th in Table 2.18. Haddin is the wicketkeeper in the best Australian team of the 2010s (Table L.2).

Table 13.7 Batting statistics of the best Australian team of all time.

Player	No. of Innings	Not outs	100s	50s	0s	Highest score	Runs scored	Batting Avge	Strike rate	Batting Rating
1. Hayden, ML	184	14	30	29	14	380	8,625	50.74	60.11	146.4
2. Warner, DA [1]	207	8	26	37	13	335	8,786	44.60	70.19	134.0
3. Bradman, DG	80	10	29	13	7	334	6,996	99.94	54.95	310.0
4. Ponting, RT	287	29	41	62	17	257	13,378	51.85	58.72	168.2
5. Smith, SPD [1]	202	25	34	41	11	239	9,962	56.28	53.54	159.6
6. Waugh, SR	260	46	32	50	22	200	10,927	51.06	48.65	146.3
7. Gilchrist, AC	137	20	17	26	14	204	5,570	47.61	81.96	121.3
8. Warne, SR	199	17	0	12	34	99	3154	17.33	57.66	16.5
9. Lillee, DK	90	24	0	1	10	73	905	13.71	41.37	10.3
10. Grimmett, CV	50	10	0	1	7	50	557	13.93	50	10.1
11. McGrath, GD	138	51	0	1	35	61	641	7.37	40.83	5.7
									Total	1228.4

Next Batsmen:

Border, AR	265	44	27	63	11	205	11,174	50.56	40.98	145.1
Chappell, GS	151	19	24	31	12	247	7,110	53.86	51.52	138.2
Clarke, MJ	198	22	28	27	9	329	8,643	49.11	55.92	137.5
Voges, AC	31	7	5	4	2	269	1,485	61.88	55.68	129.7
Hussey, MEK	137	16	19	29	12	195	6,235	51.53	50.13	123.7
Langer, JL	182	12	23	30	11	250	7,696	45.27	54.23	119.8
Taylor, MA	186	13	19	40	5	334	7,525	43.50	41.48	117.3

Next Wicketkeepers:

Healy, IA	182	23	4	22	18	161	4,356	27.40	49.73	59.8
Marsh, RW	150	13	3	16	12	132	3,633	26.62	44.82	50.4
Haddin, BJ	112	13	4	18	8	169	3,266	32.99	58.46	64.1

Note: 1. Warner and Smith are still playing in 2024.

Table 13.8 Bowling statistics of the best Australian team of all time.

Player	Overs	Maidens	Runs against	Wickets	5w/10w	Best	Bowling Avge	Strike rate	Economy rate	Bowling Rating
1. Hayden, ML				Less than 100 overs						-
2. Warner, DA [1]				Less than 100 overs						-
3. Bradman, DG				Less than 100 overs						-
4. Ponting, RT				Less than 100 overs						-
5. Smith, SPD [1]	245	28	1008	19	0/0	3/18	53.05	77.37	4.11	18.7
6. Waugh, SR	1,301	332	3,445	92	3/0	5/28	37.45	84.84	2.65	61.9
7. Gilchrist, AC		Did not bowl				Wicketkeeper				-
8. Warne, SR	6,784	1762	17,995	708	37/10	8/71	25.42	57.49	2.65	180.2
9. Lillee, DK	2,836	652	8,493	355	23/7	7/83	23.92	52.00	2.76	149.5
10. Grimmett, CV	2,408	736	5,231	216	21/7	7/40	24.22	67.19	2.16	141.7
11. McGrath, GD	4,874	1470	12,186	563	29/3	8/24	21.64	51.95	2.50	170.1
									Total	722.1

Next Bowlers:

Lyon, NM [1]	5,577	1061	16,365	538	24/5	8/50	30.42	62.20	2.93	136.7
Cummins, PJ [1]	2,239	489	6,516	289	13/2	6/23	22.55	46.48	2.91	136.6
Davidson, AK	1,665	431	3,819	186	14/2	7/93	20.53	62.30	1.98	130.3
Trumble, H	1,431	452	3,072	141	9/3	8/65	21.79	57.44	2.28	126.4
O'Reilly, WJ	1,588	585	3,254	144	11/3	7/54	22.60	69.61	1.95	125.9
Starc, MA [1]	3,034	579	10,363	373	15/2	6/50	27.78	48.81	3.42	124.8
Hazlewood, JR	2,469	635	6,857	279	12/0	6/67	24.58	53.11	2.78	121.6

Note: 1. Warner, Smith, Lyon, Cummins, Starc and Hazlewood are still playing in 2024.

Table 13.9 Highest rating Australian wicketkeepers.

Wicketkeeper	Career span	No. of Innings	Dismissals Catches	Dismissals Stumpings	Dismissals Total	Dismissals/ Innings	Wicketkeeper Rating
Gilchrist, AC	1999-08	191	379	37	416	2.18	176.3
Healy, IA	1988-99	224	366	29	395	1.76	136.1
Marsh, RW	1970-84	182	343	12	355	1.95	131.9
Haddin, BJ	2008-15	128	262	8	270	2.11	129.4

The Best West Indian Team of All Time:

The highest rating West Indian team of all time is shown below, together with the next seven highest rating batsmen, the next seven highest rating bowlers and the next two highest rating wicketkeepers. The batting and bowling statistics and ratings of each of the players are shown in Tables 13.10, 13.11 and 132.12, respectively.

Top 11 Players:	Playing period	No. of tests	Batting style	Bowling style
1. Greenidge, G	1974-91	108	right	< 100
2. Gayle, CH	2000-14	103	left	RAO
3. Richards, IVA	1974-91	121	right	RAO
4. Lara, BC	1990-06	131	left	< 100
5. Chanderpaul, S	1994-15	164	left	RAL
6. Sobers, GSA[1]	1954-74	93	left	LAO
7. Dujon, PJL	1981-91	93	right	W-K
8. Marshall, MD	1978-91	81	right	RAF
9. Garner, J	1977-87	58	right	RAF
10. Ambrose, CEL	1988-00	98	left	RAF
11. Walsh, CA	1984-01	132	right	RAF

Next Best Wicketkeepers:

Jacobs, RD	1998-04	65	left	W-K
Ramdin, D	2005-16	74	right	W-K

Next best batsmen:	Playing period	No. of tests	Batting style	Bowling style
Weekes, EDC	1948-58	48	right	< 100
Headley, GA	1930-54	22	right	< 100
Walcott, CL	1948-60	44	right	RAFM
Lloyd, CH	1966-84	110	left	RAM
Kanhai, RB	1957-74	79	right	< 100
Worrell, FMM	1948-63	51	right	LAO
Haynes, DL	1978-94	116	right	< 100

Next best bowlers

Holding, MA	1975-87	60	right	RAF
Gibbs, LR	1958-76	79	right	RAO
Roberts, AME	1974-83	47	right	RAF
Roach, KAJ[2]	2009-24	84	right	RAFM
Croft, CEH	1977-82	27	right	RAF
Bishop, IR	1989-98	43	right	RAF
Hall, WW	1958-69	48	right	RAF

Notes: 1. Sobers bowled left arm orthodox, left arm chinaman and left arm medium fast.
2. Roach is still playing in 2024.

The West Indian team has the 7th highest total batting rating out of the 10 top-rating national teams and the 2nd highest total bowling rating. The top six batsmen in the team and the next seven highest rating batsmen all have career ratings in the top 82 of all time (Table 2.7). The career bowling ratings of the four specialist bowlers in the team and the next seven specialist bowlers all rank in the top 86 in history (Table 2.16). Of the 27 individuals listed above, 1 played before World War 2, 9 played in the period 1945 to 1974, 16 played in the period 1975 to 1995 and 8 played test cricket in the 21st century. Four of the West Indians listed above where among the 27 members of the top world team of all time (Brain Lara, Sir Garfield Sobers, Malcolm Marshall and Curtly Ambrose). Ten of the top 27 West Indian players were born in Barbados — perhaps the most fertile 432 km^2 on the planet for world class cricketers.

Top 11 Players:

[1] One of the top two highest rating West Indian opening batsmen is Gordon Greenidge. He is one of the opening batsmen in the top world team of the 1980s (Chapter 8) and is also a member of the top West Indian team of the 1970s and 1980s (Tables H3 and I.3). He is the 11th highest rating West Indian batsman.

[2] The second opening batsman is Chris Gayle, an aggressive left-hand batsman who is selected in the top West Indian teams of the 2000s and 2010s (Tables K.3 and L.3). Born in Kingston, Jamaica in 1971, Gayle played first-class cricket for Jamaica from 1998 to 2018 and test cricket from 2000 to 2015. In 103 test matches, he scored 7,214 runs at an average of 42.19 and a strike rate over 60. He is one of only four batsmen who have score two triple centuries in test cricket — the others are Don Bradman, Brian Lara and Virender Sehwag. Gayle captained the West Indies in 20 test matches between 2007 and 2010, winning 3, losing 9 and drawing 8.

[3] Sir Vivian Richards is the No. 3 batsman in the top world teams of the 1970s (Chapter 7) and 1980s (Chapter 8). At his attacking best, Viv Richards was arguably the most attractive batsman to watch in the history of the game.

[4] Brian Lara is one of the 27 members of the top world team in Table 13.1 and a member of the top world teams of the 1990s (Chapter 9) and 2000s (Chapters 10). He is highest rating West Indian batsman of all time.

[5] Shivnarine Chanderpaul is selected at No. 5 in the best ever West Indian team. He is one of the next best batsmen in the world team of the 2010s (Chapter 11). He is the only West Indian to have won the ICC's Sir Garfield Sobers Trophy.

[6] Sir Garfield Sobers is one of the 27 members of the top world team of all time (Table 13.1) and he is a member of the top-rating world teams of the 1950s (Chapter 5) and the 1960s (Chapter 6). He is the 11th highest rating test batsman (Table 2.7) and the 2nd highest rating all-rounder (Table 2.17).

[7] Jeffrey Dujon is the wicketkeeper in the top world team of the 1980s (Chapter 8) and the highest rating West Indian wicketkeeper. He is placed at 15th Table 2.18.

[8] Malcolm Marshall is a member of the world top team of the 1980s (Chapter 8) and one of the 27 members of the top world team of all time (Table 13.1).

[9] Curtly Ambrose is also one of the 27 members of the top world team of all time (Table 13.1) and is a member of the top world team of the 1990s (Chapter 9).

[10] Joel Garner is a member of the top world team of the 1980s (Chapter 8) and the 31st highest rating test bowler (Table 2.16).

[11] Courtney Walsh is one of the next six bowlers in the top world teams of the 1980s (Chapter 8), 1990s (Chapter 9) and 2000s (Chapter 10).

The Next 7 Highest Rating West Indian Batsmen:

[1] Everton Weekes is the 5th highest rating West Indian batsman, but as none of the top 5 batsmen were specialist openers, he is a surprise omission from the top West Indian 11. He is the No. 4 batsman in the top world team of the 1950s (Chapter 5) and the highest rating of the 'Three Ws' (Worrell, Weekes and Walcott).

[2] George Headley was the second highest rating batsman (behind Bradman) in the top world team of the era from 1920 to 1949 (Chapter 4) and the 6th highest rating West Indian batsman.

[3] Clyde Walcott was the youngest of the 'Three Ws' and he is the No. 5 batsman in the top world team of the 1950s (Chapter 5).

[4] Clive Lloyd is one of the next batsmen in the top world teams of the 1970s (Chapter 7) and the 1980s (Chapter 8).

[5] Rohan Kanhai is one of the next batsmen in the top world team of the 1960s (Chapter 6) and he also features in the best West Indian national teams for the 1950s, 1960s and 1970s (Tables F.3, G.3 and H.3).

[6] Frank Worrell is the eldest of the 'Three Ws' and one of the next batsmen in the top world team of the 1950s (Chapter 5).

[7] Desmond Haynes was born in Barbados in 1956 and played first-class cricket for Barbados (1976-1995), Middlesex (1989-1994) and Western Provence (1994-1997) and test cricket for the West Indies (1978-1994). A powerful right-hand opening batsman, he scored 7,487 runs in 116 tests at an average of 42.30 and he is 82nd in Table 2.7. Between 1978 and 1991, Haynes and Gordon Greenidge formed the most successful opening batting combination in test history scoring 6,482 runs at an average of 46.63 runs per partnership.

The Next 7 Highest Rating West Indian Bowlers:

[1] Michael Holding is one of the next best bowlers in the world top team of the 1980s (Chapter 8) and a member of the best West Indian team of the 1980s (Table I.3).

[2] Lance Gibbs is a member of the top world team of the 1960s (Chapter 6) and the top West Indian teams of the 1960s and 1970s (Tables G.3 and H.3).

[3] Andy Roberts is a right arm fast bowlers in the top world team of the 1970s (Chapter 7) and features in the top West Indian teams of the 1970s and 1980s (Tables H.3 and I. 3).

[4] Kemar Roach was born in Barbados in 1988 and commenced his first-class career for Barbados in 2006/2007. A right arm fast-medium bowler who has played 84 tests from his debut in 2009 until the end of 2024. He has taken 282 wickets at a bowling average of 27.32. Roach is the 60th highest rating test bowler (Table 2.16).

[5] Colin Croft was a right arm fast bowler who played first-class cricket for Guyana (1972-82) and Lancashire (1977-82) and test cricket from 1977 to 1982. In 27 test matches, he took 125 wickets at an average of 23.30. He was part of the four-pronged pace attack that saw the West Indies dominate test cricket during his career. Croft is 78th in Table 2.16.

[6] Ian Bishop was a right arm fast bowler who played first-class cricket for Trinidad and Tobago (1986-2000) and Derbyshire (1989-93) and test cricket from 1989 to 1998. He took 161 wickets in 43 tests at an average of 24.29 and is 80th in Table 2.16. Born in Trinidad in 1967, he is a member of the best West Indies team of the 1990s (Table J.3). Bishop's career was shortened by injuries, but when fit he was part of a formidable bowling attack alongside Curtly Ambrose and Coutney Walsh. Bishop is now a well-regarded cricket commentator.

[7] Wesley Hall was a right arm fast bowler who led the West Indian attack for much of the 1960s (Chapter 6). Born in Barbados in 1937, he played first-class cricket for Barbados (1955-71) and Queensland (1961-63) and test cricket from 1958 to 1969. In 48 tests, he took 192 wickets at an average of 26.39 and he sits at No. 86 in Table 2.16. He was a charismatic fast bowler, a favourite of the cricketing public wherever he played. After cricket, Hall entered politics, with terms in the Barbadian Senate and House of Assembly and a stint as the Minister of Tourism. He also was heavily involved with the administration of West Indian cricket, serving terms as selector, team manager and President of the West Indies Cricket Board.

Next Best West Indian Wicketkeepers:

[1] After Jeffrey Dujon, Ridley Jacobs is the next highest rating West Indian wicketkeeper, with the 23rd highest rating in Table 2.18. He was born in Antigua in 1967 and played first-class cricket for the Leeward Islands (1991-2005). He was the wicketkeeper in the best West Indian side of the 2000s (Table K.3). In 65 tests, he made 219 dismissals at 1.80 dismissals per innings.

[2] Denesh Ramdin is the 3rd highest rating West Indian wicketkeeper and a member of the best West Indian team of the 2010s (Table L.3). Born in Trinidad of Indian descent, he played first-class cricket for Trinidad and Tobago (2004-18) and test cricket from 2005 to 2016. In 74 tests, he made 217 dismissals at 1.66 dismissals per innings and is positioned 24th in Table 2.18.

Table 13.10 Batting statistics of the best West Indian team of all time

Player	No. of Innings	Not outs	100s	50s	0s	Highest score	Runs scored	Batting Avge	Strike rate	Batting Rating
1. Greenidge, G	185	16	19	34	11	226	7,558	44.72	50.09	114.7
2. Gayle, CH	182	11	15	37	15	333	7,214	42.19	60.27	115.0
3. Richards, IVA	182	12	24	45	10	291	8,540	50.24	60.82	142.4
4. Lara, BC	232	6	34	48	17	400	11,953	52.89	60.52	168.4
5. Chanderpaul, S	280	49	30	66	15	203	11,867	51.37	43.32	151.3
6. Sobers, GSA[1]	160	21	26	30	12	365	8,032	57.78	49.62	156.5
7. Dujon, PJL	115	11	5	16	8	139	3,322	31.94	46.43	58.5
8. Marshall, MD	107	11	0	10	15	92	1,810	18.85	51.91	19.7
9. Ambrose, CEL	145	29	0	1	26	53	1,439	12.41	46.72	10.4
10. Garner, J	68	14	0	1	17	60	672	12.44	48.42	8.3
11. Walsh, CA	185	61	0	0	43	30	936	7.55	44.83	5.7
									Total	950.9

Next Batsmen:

Player	No. of Innings	Not outs	100s	50s	0s	Highest score	Runs scored	Batting Avge	Strike rate	Batting Rating
Weekes, EDC	81	5	15	19	6	207	4,455	58.62	50.00	136.9
Headley, GA	40	4	10	5	2	270	2,190	60.83	50.00	136.5
Walcott, CL	74	7	15	14	1	220	3,798	56.69	50.00	130.6
Lloyd, CH	175	14	19	39	4	242	7,515	46.68	51.22	122.1
Kanhai, RB	137	6	15	28	7	256	6,227	47.53	49.93	115.1
Worrell, FMM	87	9	9	22	11	261	3,860	49.49	49.72	107.8
Haynes, DL	202	25	18	39	10	184	7,487	42.30	45.22	107.1

Next Wicketkeepers:

Player	No. of Innings	Not outs	100s	50s	0s	Highest score	Runs scored	Batting Avge	Strike rate	Batting Rating
Jacobs, RD	112	21	3	14	12	118	2,577	28.32	47.79	46.8
Ramdin, D	126	14	4	15	9	166	2,898	25.88	48.75	49.4

Table 13.11 Bowling statistics of the best West Indian team of all time.

The team

Player	Overs	Maidens	Runs against	Wickets	5w/10w	Best	Bowling Avge	Strike rate	Economy rate	Bowling Rating
1. Greenidge, G				Less than 100 overs						-
2. Gayle, CH	1,185	227	3,120	73	2/0	5/34	42.74	97.38	2.63	49.8
3. Richards, IVA	856	203	1,964	32	0/0	2/17	61.38	161.6	2.28	37.2-
4. Lara, BC				Less than 100 overs						-
5. Chanderpaul, S	290	50	883	9	0/0	1/2	98.11	193.3	3.04	16.4
6. Sobers, GSA	3,432	974	7,999	235	6/0	6/73	34.04	91.91	2.22	79.9
7. Dujon, PJL				Did not bowl Wicketkeeper						-
8. Marshall, MD	2,930	613	7,876	376	22/4	7/22	20.95	46.77	2.69	156.5
9. Ambrose, CEL	3,684	1001	8,502	405	22/3	8/45	20.99	54.58	2.31	153.9
10. Garner, J	2,195	575	5,433	259	7/0	6/56	20.98	50.85	2.48	130.7
11. Walsh, CA	5,003	1144	12,684	519	22/3	7/37	24.44	57.84	2.54	148.9
									Total	736.1

Next Bowlers:

Player	Overs	Maidens	Runs against	Wickets	5w/10w	Best	Bowling Avge	Strike rate	Economy rate	Bowling Rating
Holding, MA	2,067	459	5,898	249	13/2	8/92	23.69	50.92	2.79	126.7
Gibbs, LR	4,208	1313	8,989	309	18/2	8/38	29.09	87.75	1.99	120.0
Roberts, AME	1,779	382	5,174	202	11/2	7/54	25.61	55.12	2.79	113.9
Roach, KAJ[1]	2,483	539	7,705	282	11/1	6/48	27.32	52.84	3.10	113.2
Croft, CEH	1,027	211	2,913	125	3/0	8/29	23.30	49.32	2.84	107.6
Bishop, IR	1,411	288	3,911	161	6/0	6/40	24.29	52.59	2.77	107.1
Hall, WW	1,658	312	5,066	192	9/1	7/69	26.39	54.28	2.92	106.3

Note: 1. Roach is still playing in 2024.

Table 13.12 Highest rating West Indian wicketkeepers.

Wicketkeeper	Career span	No. of Innings	Dismissals Catches	Dismissals Stumpings	Dismissals Total	Dismissals/ Innings	Wicket-keeper Rating
Dujon, PJL	1981-91	150	265	5	270	1.80	117.9
Jacobs, RD	1998-04	122	207	12	219	1.80	105.4
Ramdin, D	2005-16	131	205	12	217	1.66	102.0

The Best Indian Team of All Time:

The highest rating Indian team of all-time is shown below, together with the next seven highest rating batsmen, the next seven highest rating bowlers and the two next highest rating wicketkeepers. The batting and bowling statistics and ratings of each of the players are shown in Tables 13.13 and 13.14, respectively, and the wicketkeeping statistics are provided in Table 13.15.

Top 11 Players:	Playing period	No. of tests	Batting style	Bowling style
1. Sehwag, V	2001-13	104	right	RAO
2. Gavaskar, SM	1971-87	125	right	< 100
3. Dravid, R	1996-12	164	right	< 100
4. Tendulkar, SR [1]	1989-13	200	right	RAM
5. Kohli, V [2]	2011-24	122	right	< 100
6. Laxman, VVS	1996-12	134	right	< 100
7. Dhoni, MS	2005-14	90	right	W-K
8. Kapil Dev	1978-94	131	right	RAFM
9. Ashwin, R [2]	2011-24	106	right	RAO
10. Kumble, A	1990-08	132	right	RAL
11. Bumrah, JJ [2]	2018-24	44	right	RAF

Next Best Wicketkeepers:

Pant, RR [2]	2018-24	42	left	W-K
Kirmani, SMH	1976-86	88	right	W-K

Next batsmen:	Playing period	No. of tests	Batting style	Bowling style
Mohd. Azharuddin	1984-00	99	right	< 100
Pujara, CA	2010-23	103	right	< 100
Ganguly, SC	1996-08	113	left	RAM
Vengsarkar, DB	1976-92	116	right	< 100
Viswanath, GR	1969-83	91	right	< 100
Hazare, VS	1946-53	30	right	RAM
Sharma, RG [2]	2013-24	55	right	< 100

Next bowlers:

Jadeja, R [2]	2012-24	67	left	LAO
Harbhajan Singh	1998-15	103	right	RAO
Bedi, BS	1966-79	67	right	LAO
Chandrasekhar, BS	1964-79	58	right	RAL
Mohammed Shami	2013-23	64	right	RAF
Sharma, I	2007-21	105	right	RAFM
Zaheer Khan	2000-14	92	right	LAFM

Notes: 1. Tendulkar bowled right arm medium and right arm leg spin.
2. Kohli, Ashwin, Bumrah, Pant, Sharma RG and Jadeja are still playing in 2024.

The Indian team has the 2nd highest total batting rating out of the 10 top-rating national teams and the 6th highest bowling rating. The top six batsmen in the team all have career batting ratings in the top 44 of all time (Table 2.7). The top six rated bowlers all have career ratings in the top 45 in history (Table 2.16). Of the 27 individuals listed above, only 1 played before 1960, 7 played in the period 1960 to 1980, 12 played between 1980 and 2000 and 18 played test cricket in the 21st century. Four of these Indian cricketers feature in the 27 members of the top world team of all time (Sachin Tendulkar, Rahul Dravid, Anil Kumble and Ravi Ashwin).

Top 11 Players:

[1] and [2] India's two highest rating specialist openers are Virender Sehwag and Sunil Gavaskar. Sehwag is the opening batsman in the top world team of the 2000s (Chapter 10) and the top Indian teams of the 2000s and 2010s (Tables K.4 and L.4). Sunil Gavaskar is the opening batsman in the top world teams of the 1970s (Chapter 7) and the 1980s (Chapter 8).

[3] Rahul Dravid is a member of the top world team of all time (see Table 13.1) and one of the top-rating batsmen in the world teams of the 1990s (Chapter 9) and the 2000s (Chapter 10). He is the 8th highest rating test batsman (Table 2.7).

[4] Sachin Tendulkar is a member of the top world team of all time (see Table 13.1) and one of the top-rating batsmen in the world teams of the 1990s (Chapter 9) and the 2000s (Chapter 10). He is the 2nd highest rating test batsman (Table 2.7).

[5] Virat Kohli is widely regarded as the best Indian batsman currently playing test cricket. He is the No. 6 batsman in the top world team of the 2010s (Chapter 11).

[6] Stylish right-hand batsman, V.V.S. Laxman is at No. 6. He was born in Hyderabad in 1974 and played first-class cricket for Hyderabad (1992-2012) and county cricket for Lancashire (2007, 2009). He played 134 tests from 1996 to 2012 and scored 8,781 runs at an average of 45.97, with 17 centuries. He was known for his match-winning and match saving-innings. With India trailing by 274 on the first innings against Australia at Eden Gardens in 2001, Laxman scored 281 in India's 2nd innings to win the game for India in what was one of the great test innings. Laxman is the 44th highest rating test batsman (Table 2.7).

[7] The wicketkeeper and hard-hitting left-hand No. 7 batsman is Mahendra Singh (MS) Dhoni. He was born in Ranchi in 1981 and played first-class cricket for Bihar (1999-2004) and Jharkhand (2004-18) and test cricket from 2005 to 2014. In 90 test matches, he made 294 dismissals (256 catches and 38 stumpings) — the most dismissals by an Indian wicketkeeper and the 5th highest in test history. He was the wicketkeeper in the top Indian teams in the 2000s and 2010s (Tables K.4 and L.4, respectively). He also scored 4,876 runs at an average of 38.09, with six test centuries. He has the 8th highest wicketkeeper rating of all time (see Table 2.18). In ODI cricket, Dhoni played 350 matches and made 444 dismissals (only Sangakkara and Gilchrist have made more). Of the wicketkeepers who have made over 150 dismissals in ODIs, he is the only one to average in excess of 50 with the bat.

[8] India's great bowling all-rounder Kapil Dev is at No.8. He is one of the next best bowlers in the world team of the 1980s (see Chapter 8).

[9] Ravi Ashwin is a member of the top world team of all time (see Table 13.1) and one of the top four bowlers in the best world teams of the 2010s (Chapter 11) and 2020s (Chapter 12).

[10] Anil Kumble is a member of the top world team of all time (see Table 13.1) and one of the top-rating bowlers in the best world teams of the 1990s (Chapter 9) and 2000s (Chapter 10).

[11] Jasprit Bumrah is the highest rating Indian pace bowler and is selected at No. 11. Bumrah is the highest rated bowler in the highest rating world team of the 2020s (Chapter 12).

The Next 6 Highest Rating Indian Batsmen:

[1] Mohammad Azharuddin is one of the next best batsmen in the top world team of the 1990s (Chapter 9).

[2] Cheteshwar Pujara (No. 74 in Table 2.7) is a member of the top Indian team of the 2010s (Table L.4). He was born in Rajkot in 1988 and has played first-cricket for Saurashtra (2005-18), Derbyshire (2014), Yorkshire (2015, 2018) and Nottinghamshire (2017). He is a right-hand batsman who played 103 tests from 2010 to 2023, batting most often at No. 3 and scoring 7,195 runs at an average of 43.61, with 19 test centuries.

[3] Sourav Ganguly is one of the next best batsmen in the highest rating world team of the 1990s (Chapter 9).

[4] Dillip Vengsarkar is one of the next best batsmen in the highest rating world team of the 1980s (Chapter 8).

[5] Gundappar Viswanath is one of the next best batsmen in the highest rating world team of the 1970s (Chapter 7).

[6] Vijay Hazare was born in 1915 in Sangli, in the then Bombay Presidency of British India. He was a right-hand batsman who played 30 test matches from 1946 to 1953, scoring 2,192 runs at an average of 47.65,

including 7 test centuries. He captained India in 14 tests. He is the 136th highest rating test batsman (Table A.1).

[7] Rohit Sharma is the opening batsman in the best Indian team of the 2010s (Table L.4). He has played first-class cricket for Mumbai since 2006, and he made his test debut against the West Indies in 2013. Up until the end of 2024, he had played 67 tests and scored 4,301 runs at an average of 40.58 and a strike rate of 57.06. Sharma is best known as an outstanding opening batsman in ODI cricket. His 264 against Sri Lanka in 2014 remains the highest ever individual score in an ODI match and he is the only batsman ever to score three ODI double centuries. He is the 137th highest rating test batsman (Table A.1).

The Next 6 Highest Rating Indian Bowlers:

[1] Ravindra Jadeja is one of the next best bowlers in the highest rating world teams of the 2010s (Chapter 11) and 2020s (Chapter 12). He is the 4th highest rating Indian bowler (Table 2.16).

[2] Harbhajan Singh is one of the next best bowlers in the highest rating world team of the 2000s (Chapter 10) and the 5th highest rating Indian bowler (Table 2.16).

[3] Bishen Bedi is one of the next best bowlers in the highest rating world team of the 1970s (Chapter 7).

[4] Bhagwat Chandrasekhar is one of the next best bowlers in the highest rating world team of the 1970s (Chapter 7).

[5] Mohammed Shami is a right arm fast bowler who made his first-class debut for Bengal in 2010 and his test debut against the West Indies in 2013. He played 64 tests from 2013 to 2023 and took 229 wickets at a bowling average of 27.71. He bowls consistently at about 140 km/h, with the ability to swing the bowl both ways and deviate the ball off the seam. He is the 94th highest rating test bowler (Table 2.16).

[6] Ishant Sharma was born in Delhi in 1988 and made his test debut against Bangladesh in 2007. He is a tall right-arm fast-medium bowler with good control and accurate line and length. Between 2007 and 2021, Sharma played 105 test matches and took 311 wickets at an average of 32.41.

[7] Zaheer Khan is a left-arm fast-medium bowler who made his test debut against Bangladesh in 2000 and, by his retirement from test cricket in 2014, he had played 92 test and taken 311 wickets at an average of 32.95. The career test bowling statistics for Ishant Sharma and Zaheer Khan are remarkably similar as the comparison in the final two rows of Table 13.14 clearly shows. They are the 107th and 108th highest rating test bowlers (Table A.2).

The Next Highest Rating Indian Wicketkeepers:

[1] The next highest rating Indian wicketkeeper is Rishabh Pant who is a member of the best Indian team of the 2010s and wicketkeeper in the highest rating world team of the 2020s (Chapter 12).

[2] The 3rd highest rating Indian wicketkeeper is Syed Kirmani, who is a member of the best Indian teams of the 1970s and 1980s (Tables H.4 and I.4, respectively). He played 88 test matches taking 160 catches and making 38 stumpings at 1.311 dismissals per innings. He is the 42nd highest rating wicketkeeper in Table 2.18.

Table 13.13 Batting statistics of the best Indian team of all-time.

The team

Player	No. of Innings	Not outs	100s	50s	0s	Highest score	Runs scored	Batting Avge	Strike rate	Batting Rating
1. Sehwag, V	180	6	23	32	16	319	8,586	49.34	82.21	144.7
2. Gavaskar, SM	214	16	34	45	12	236	10,122	51.12	48.03	146.0
3. Dravid, R	286	32	36	63	8	270	13,288	52.31	42.51	163.1
4. Tendulkar, SR	329	33	51	68	14	248	15,921	53.79	54.12	183.7
5. Kohli, V [1]	207	13	30	31	15	254	9,202	47.43	55.78	133.0
6. Laxman, VVS	225	34	17	56	14	281	8,781	45.97	49.37	127.9
7. Dhoni, MS	144	16	6	33	10	224	4,876	38.09	59.11	88.0
8. Kapil Dev	184	15	8	27	16	163	5,248	31.05	54.87	72.8
9. Ashwin, R [1]	151	15	6	14	9	124	3,503	25.76	54.54	52.1
10. Kumble, A	173	32	1	5	17	110	2,506	17.77	38.82	17.8
11. Bumrah, JJ [1]	67	22	0	0	24	34	310	6.89	43.00	3.4
									Total	1,132.5

Next Batsmen:

Mohd. Azharuddin	147	9	22	21	5	199	6,215	45.04	54.64	110.7
Pujara, CA	176	11	19	35	12	206	7195	43.61	44.37	108.9
Ganguly, SC	188	17	16	35	13	239	7,212	42.18	51.26	108.0
Vengsarkar, DB	185	22	17	35	15	166	6,868	42.13	47.76	102.5
Viswanath, GR	155	10	14	35	10	222	6,080	41.93	48.33	101.7
Hazare, VS	52	6	7	9	3	164	2,192	47.65	48.59	90.2
Sharma, RG [1]	116	10	12	18	6	212	4,301	40.58	57.06	89.8

Next Wicketkeepers:

Pant, RR	72	5	6	14	3	159	2,817	42.04	74.74	86.6
Kirmani, SMH	124	22	2	12	7	102	2,759	27.05	48.20	44.5

Note: 1. Kohli, Ashwin, Bumrah and Sharma RG are still playing in 2024.

Table 13.14 Bowling statistics of the best Indian team of all-time.

The team:

Player	Overs	Maidens	Runs against	Wickets	5w/10w	Best	Bowling Avge	Strike rate	Economy rate	Bowling Rating
1. Sehwag, V	622	78	1,894	40	1/0	5/104	47.35	93.28	3.05	36.5
2. Gavaskar, SM				Less than 100 overs						-
3. Dravid, R				Less than 100 overs						-
4. Tendulkar, SR	706	83	2,492	46	0/0	3/10	54.17	92.17	3.53	29.6
5. Kohli, V [1]				Less than 100 overs						-
6. Laxman, VVS				Less than 100 overs						-
7. Dhoni, MS		Did not bowl				Wicketkeeper				-
8. Kapil Dev	4,623	1,060	12,867	434	23/2	9/83	29.65	63.92	2.78	125.2
9. Ashwin, R [1]	4,536	907	12,839	537	37/8	7/59	23.91	50.68	2.83	169.2
10. Kumble, A	6,808	1,575	18,355	619	35/8	10/74	29.65	65.99	2.70	157.7
11. Bumrah, JJ [1]	1,428	344	3.944	203	13/0	6/27	19.43	42.22	2.76	144.0
									Total	662.2

Next Bowlers:

Jadeja, R [1]	3,068	728	7,769	323	15/3	7/42	24.05	56.99	2.53	131.5
Harbhajan Singh	4,763	869	13,537	417	25/5	8/84	32.46	68.54	2.84	122.5
Bedi, BS	3,441	1,096	7,637	266	14/1	7/98	28.71	80.32	2.14	111.7
Chandrasekhar, BS	2,549	584	7,199	242	16/2	8/79	29.75	65.96	2.71	106.6
Mohammed Shami [1]	1,919	364	6,346	229	6/0	6/56	27.71	50.30	3.31	103.7
Sharma, I	3,193	640	10,078	311	11/1	7/74	32.41	61.61	3.16	99.5
Zaheer Khan	3,131	624	10,247	311	11/1	7/87	32.95	60.40	3.27	99.0

Notes: 1. Kohli, Ashwin, Bumrah and Jadeja are still playing in 2024.

Table 13.15 Highest rating Indian wicketkeepers.

Wicketkeeper	Career span	No. of Innings	Dismissals Catches	Dismissals Stumpings	Dismissals Total	Dismissals/ Innings	Wicketkeeper Rating
Dhoni, MS	2005-14	166	256	38	294	1.77	132.4
Pant, RR	2018-22	83	147	15	162	1.95	117.5
Kirmani, SMH	1976-86	151	160	38	198	1.31	86.8

The Best New Zealand Team of All Time:

The highest rating New Zealand team of all time is shown below, together with the next highest rating batsmen and bowlers and the next highest rating wicketkeepers. The batting and bowling statistics and ratings of each of the players are shown in Table 13.16 and 13.17, respectively, and the wicketkeeping statistics are given in Table 13.18.

Top 11 Players:	Playing period	No. of tests	Batting style	Bowling style
1. Latham, TWM [1]	2014-24	88	left	DNB
2. Turner, GM	1969-83	41	right	< 100
3. Williamson, KS [1]	2010-24	105	right	RAO
4. Taylor, LRPL	2007-22	112	right	< 100
5. Fleming, SP	1994-08	111	left	DNB
6. Crowe, MD	1982-95	77	right	RAM
7. McCullum, BB	2004-16	101	right	W-K
8. Vettori, DL	1997-14	113	left	LAO
9. Hadlee, RJ	1973-90	86	left	RAF
10. Southee, TG [1]	2008-24	107	right	RAMF
11. Boult, TA	2011-22	78	right	LAFM

Next Best Wicketkeepers:

Watling, BJ	2009-21	75	right	W-K
Parore, AC	1990-02	78	right	W-K

Next batsmen:	Playing period	No. of tests	Batting style	Bowling style
Mitchell, DJ [1]	2019-24	31	right	RAM
Astle, NJ	1996-06	81	right	RAM
Richardson, MH	2000-04	38	left	< 100
Wright, JG	1978-93	82	left	< 100
Jones, AH	1987-95	39	right	< 100
Sutcliffe, B	1947-65	42	left	< 100
McMillan, CD	1997-05	55	right	RAM

Next best bowlers:

Wagner, N	2012-24	64	left	LAMF
Cairns, CL	1989-04	62	right	RAFM
Taylor, BR	1965-73	30	left	RAFM
Martin, CS	2000-13	71	right	RAFM
Nash, DJ	1992-01	32	right	RAM
Doull, SB	1992-00	32	right	RAFM
Collinge, RO	1965-78	35	right	LAFM

Note: 1. Latham, Williamson, Southee and Mitchell are still playing at the end of 2024.

The New Zealand team has the 8th highest total batting rating out of the 10 top-rating national teams and the 8th highest bowling rating. Of the 27 individuals listed above, only one played before 1950, 6 played in the period 1950 to 1980, 13 played between 1980 and 2000 and 19 played test cricket in the 21st century. Only Sir Richard Hadlee is a member of the top world team of all time (Tables 13.1 and 13.2). Despite only two New Zealanders featuring in the top 60 highest rating test batsmen (Kane Williamson at No. 12 and Ross Taylor at No.51 in Table 2.7), the team has a surprising high batting rating, with the wicketkeeper Brendan McCullum having a rating in excess of 100 and each of the first two specialist bowlers (Daniel Vettori and Richard Hadlee) being highly rated bowling all-rounders (Table 2.17) with career batting ratings in excess of 50.

Top 11 Players:

[1] New Zealand's highest rating specialist opening batsman is Tom Latham. Born in Christchurch in 1992, he has played domestic first-class cricket for Canterbury since his debut in 2010. He made his test debut against India in 2014 and, up until the end 2024, he had played 88 tests and scored 5,834 runs at an average of 38.38. Tom Latham is the son of former New Zealand test batsman Rod Latham and is the 127th highest rating test batsman (Table A.1).

[2] The second highest rating opening batsman is Glenn Turner. He was born in Dunedin in 1947 and played first-class cricket for Otago (1964-76; 1978/83), Worcestershire (1967-82) and Northern Districts (1976-77). Turner played 41 tests for New Zealand from 1969 to 1983, scoring 2,991 runs at a batting average of 44.64. He played 455 first-class games, scoring 34,346 runs at 49.70, including 103 first-class centuries. He is one of only four non-English batsmen to have scored over 100 first-class centuries, the others being, Don Bradman (Aus), Zaheer Abbas (Pak) and Viv Richards (WI). He scored 141 not out in Worcestershire's completed innings of 169 against Glamorgan in 1977. This remains the highest percentage (83.4%) of runs scored by an individual batsman in any completed innings in first-class cricket. Turner is a member of the best New Zealand side in the 1970s (Table H.5).

[3] Kane Williamson is New Zealand's highest rating test batsman (No. 12 in Table 2.7) and the top-rating batsman in the world team of the 2020s (Chapter 12). He is one of the next best batsmen in the world team of the 2010s (Chapter 11).

[4] Ross Taylor is New Zealand's 2nd highest rating batsman and the 51st highest rating batsman in Table 2.7. He was born in Wellington in 1984 and has played domestic first-class cricket for Central Districts since 2002 and for English counties Durham (2010), Sussex (2016-17), Nottinghamshire (2018) and Middlesex (2019). He also played for Victoria in the Australian summer of 2009-10. He played in 112 tests from 2007 to 2022, scoring 7,683 runs at an average of 44.67. He is a member of New Zealand's top teams of the 2000s (Table K.5) and the 2010s (Table L.5).

[5] Stephen Fleming is a native of Christchurch and played domestic cricket for Canterbury (1991-2000) and Wellington (2000-09) and county cricket for Middlesex (2001), Yorkshire (2003) and Nottinghamshire (2005-07). He played 111 test matches from 1994 to 2008, scoring 7,172 runs at a batting average 40.07. He is a member of New Zealand's top team of the 1990s (Table J.5) and is the top-rating batsman in the top New Zealand team of the 2000s (Table K.5). Fleming captained his country in 80 test matches between 1997 and 2006 (more tests as captain than any other New Zealander).

[6] Martin Crowe was born in Auckland in 1962 and played domestic cricket for Auckland (1979-83), Central Districts (1983-90) and Wellington (1990-95) and county cricket for Somerset (1984-88). He played test cricket from 1982 to 1995 scoring 5,444 in 77 tests at an average of 45.37. He scored 299 against Sri Lanka at the Basin Reserve in 1991 and this remained the highest score by a New Zealand batsman until Brendan McCullum's 302 against India in 2014. He captained New Zealand in 16 tests from 1990 to 1993 winning 2 and losing 7. At the time of his retirement, he had scored more runs in test cricket and more runs in ODI cricket than any other New Zealander and was widely regarded as New Zealand's finest batsman. He is New Zealand's highest rating batsman in the 1980s (Table I.5) and in the 1990s (Table J.5). Martin Crowe's brother Jeff also played test cricket for New Zealand (39 tests) and also captained his country in 2 tests. The Crowe brothers are first cousins of academy award winning actor Russell Crowe.

[7] Brendon McCallum is the hard-hitting wicketkeeper batsman in the top New Zealand teams of the 2000s (Table K.5) and 2010s (Table L.5). McCullum was born in Dunedin in 1981 and played domestic cricket for Otago (1999-2003; 2007-15) and Canterbury (2003-06) and seasons overseas with Glamorgan (2006), Sussex (2010), Warwickshire (2015), Middlesex (2016) and New South Wales (2009). He played 101 tests from 2004 to 2016 scoring 6,453 runs at an average of 38.64 and a strike rate of 64.60. As wicketkeeper, he made 179 dismissals in 95 innings at 1.884 dismissals per innings. He is the 14th highest rating wicketkeeper of all time (Table 2.18). Although BJ Watling has a higher wicketkeeper rating than McCullum, McCullum's batting saw him selected in the top New Zealand side ahead of Watling. McCullum's score of 302 against India at Wellington in 2015 is the highest score, and only triple century, by a New Zealander. He has hit 4 double centuries in test cricket and at the time of his retirement he had hit more sixes in test cricket (107) than any other batsman. He captained New Zealand in 31 tests from 2013 to 2016, winning 11 and losing 11.

[8] Daniel Vettori is a left-arm orthodox bowling all-rounder. He was born in Auckland in 1979 and played first-class cricket for Northern Districts (1996-2015) and county cricket for Nottinghamshire (2003) and

Warwickshire (2006). He played 113 tests from 1997 to 2014, the most capped New Zealander in history, and took 362 wickets at a bowling average of 34.37. Only Richard Hadlee has taken more test wickets for New Zealand. He also made 4,531 test runs at a batting average of 30.01. Vettori is the 14th highest rating bowling all-rounder of all time (Table 2.17). He was a member of the best New Zealand team of the 2000s (Table K.5) and one of the next best bowlers in the best New Zealand team of the 1990s (Table J.5).

[9] Sir Richard Hadlee is the 4th highest rating bowler in the history of the game. He is a member of the top world team of the 1980s (see Chapter 8) and the top world team of all time (Table 13.1).

[10] Tim Southee is right arm medium-fast bowler who was born in Whangarei near the top of the north island of New Zealand in 1988. He played domestic first-class cricket for Northern Districts (2006-18), county cricket for Essex (2011) and Middlesex (2017) and test cricket since 2008. By the end of 2024, he had played 107 tests and taken 391 wickets at a bowling average of 30.26. He is also a swash buckling lower order batsman with a batting average of 16.32, but a strike rate of 83.12, the fourth highest batting strike rate in test history. He is a member of the best New Zealand team of the 2010s (Table L.5).

[11] Trent Boult is a left-arm fast-medium swing bowler who, together with Tim Southee, has spearheaded the New Zealand attack since 2011. He was born in Rotorua in 1989 and has played first-class cricket for Northern districts since 2008. He made his test debut against Australia in 2011 and went on to play 78 tests and take 317 wickets at a bowling average of 27.50. Boult is a member of the top New Zealand team of the 2010s (Table L.5) and he is the 4th highest wicket taker for New Zealand behind Richard Hadlee, Daniel Vettori and Tim Southee.

The Next 6 Highest Rating New Zealand Batsmen:

[1] Daryl Mitchell was born in Hamilton in 1991 and has played domestic cricket for Northern Districts (2012-2019) and Canterbury (2020-2024) and county cricket for Middlesex (2021) and Lancashire (2023). He made his test debut against England in November 2019 and, up until the end of 2024, he had played 31 test matches scoring 2,059 runs at an average of 43.81. In the three-test series in England in 2022, Mitchell became the 5th New Zealand batsman to score a century in three consecutive tests against England. His total of 482 runs in that series is a record for the most runs by a New Zealander in a test series against England. He is the son of former New Zealand rugby union player and coach John Mitchell.

[2] Nathan Astle was born in Christchurch in 1971 and played domestic cricket for Canterbury (1991-2007) and county cricket for Nottinghamshire (1997), Durham (2005) and Lancashire (2006). He played test cricket from 1996 to 2006 and scored 4,702 runs in 81 tests at a batting average of 37.02. He was a useful medium pace bowler who took 51 test wickets at an average of 42.02. He batted predominantly at No.5 and was a member of the best New Zealand teams of the 1990s (Table J.5) and 2000s (Table K.5). He is the 53rd highest rating all-rounder in Table 2.17.

[3] Mark Richardson was born in Hastings in 1971 and played domestic cricket for Auckland (1989-92; 2001-05) and Otago (1992-2001). Richardson was a dour left-hand opening batsman who played 38 test matches from 2000 to 2004, scoring 2,776 runs at an average of 44.77 and a strike rate of 37.67. He was a member of the best New Zealand side of the 2000s (Table K.5). Since retiring from cricket Richardson is a popular, if controversial, TV personality and cricket commentator.

[4] John Wright was a gritty left-hand opening batsman who was a member of the best New Zealand team of the 1980s (Table I.5). He was born in Darfield (just outside Christchurch) in 1954 and played domestic cricket for Northern Districts (1975-84), Canterbury (1984-89) and Auckland (1989-93) and county cricket for Derbyshire (1977-88). He played 82 tests from 1978 to 1993) and scored 5,334 runs at an average of 37.83. After retirement as a player, Wright has had a successful coaching career, including coaching the Indian test team from 2000 to 2005.

[5] Andrew Jones was the No. 3 batsman in the best New Zealand side of the 1990s (Table J.5). He was born in Wellington in 1959 and played domestic cricket for Central Districts, Otago and Wellington. He played 39 tests from 1987 to 1995 scoring 2,922 runs at an average of 44.27, with 7 centuries. Against Sri Lanka at the Basin Reserve in Wellington in 1991, Jones and Martin Crowe shared a partnership of 467 which at that time was a test record partnership for any wicket and is still the 3rd highest test partnership. Jones is the only New Zealand batsman to have scored three centuries in consecutive test innings.

[6] Bert Sutcliffe was New Zealand's highest rating batsman of the 1950s (Table F.6). Born in Auckland, he played domestic cricket for Otago after serving in World War 2 and test cricket from 1947 to 1965. He opened the batting in 41 of his 76 test innings and scored 2,727 runs at a batting average of 40.10 with 5 test centuries. In first-class cricket, Sutcliffe scored two triple centuries batting for Otago. His 385 against Canterbury in 1952/53 remained the highest score by a left-hand batsman in first-class cricket until 1994 when Brian Lara scored 501 for Warwickshire against Durham at Edgbaston.

[7] Craig McMillan was a right-hand batsman and a useful medium pace bowler. He generally batted at No. 6 for New Zealand. He was born in Christchurch in 1976 and played first-class cricket for Canterbury from 1994 to 2010, with seasons of county cricket for Gloucestershire and Hampshire. He played 55 tests for New Zealand from 1997 to 2004 and scored 3,116 runs at a batting average of 38.47, with six test centuries.

The Next 6 Highest Rating New Zealand Bowlers:

[1] Neil Wagner was born in Pretoria, South Africa in 1986. He is a left-arm medium-fast bowler who played for Northerns (2005-08) in South Africa before moving to New Zealand. He has played domestic cricket in New Zealand for Otago (2008-18) and Northern Districts (2018-2022) and county cricket for Lancashire (2016) and Essex (2017-2022). He made his test debut for New Zealand in 2012 and played his final test in 2024. He played 64 tests and taken 260 wickets at a bowling average of 27.57. He is a member of the best New Zealand team of the 2010s (Table L.5).

[2] The right arm fast-medium bowling all-rounder Chris Cairns was born in Picton on the South Island of New Zealand in 1970. He played domestic first-class cricket for Northern Districts (1998-99) and Canterbury (1990-2006). In 62 tests from 1989 to 2004, he took 218 wickets at an average of 29.40 and he scored 3,320 runs at an average of 33.54. He is the 24th highest rated all-rounder in test history (Table 2.17) and the 95th highest rating bowler (Table 2.16). Cairns is the son of Lance Cairns who was a member of New Zealand's best side of the 1980s (Table I.5). Chris Cairns hit 87 sixes in his test career (the 11th highest by an individual in test history).

[3] Bruce Taylor was a right-arm fast-medium bowler and left-hand batsman who played 30 test matches for New Zealand from 1965 to 1973, taking 111 wickets at a bowling average of 26.60. Taylor was born at Timaru on the South Island of New Zealand in 1943 and played first-class cricket for Canterbury and Wellington. Taylor is the only test cricketer to score a century and take 5-wickets in an innings on his test debut (against India in March 1965).

[4] Chris Martin is a member of the best New Zealand team of the 2000s (Table K.5). He was born in Christchurch in 1974 and played first-class domestic cricket for Canterbury and Auckland and county cricket for Warwickshire and Essex. A right-arm fast-medium bowler, he played 71 tests from 2000 to 2013 and took 233 wickets at a bowling average of 33.64. An effective bowler, but a true batting bunny, he scored a duck in 36 of his 104 test innings (the third most in test history and the highest frequency). He finished his career with just 123 test runs at a batting average of 2.37 and a top score of 12. Of all who played 20 or more test matches, Martin has the lowest batting average and the lowest career batting rating.

[5] Dion Nash was born in Haast on the west coast of the South Island of New Zealand and played domestic cricket for Norther Districts (1990-92; 1994-98), Otago (1992-94) and Auckland (1998-2002) and county cricket for Middlesex (1995-96). He played test cricket from 1992 to 2001 and, in 32 tests, he took 93

wickets at a bowling average of 28.48. He was a right-arm medium pace bowler and a useful lower-order batsman. He is a member of the best New Zealand team of the 1990s (Table J.5).

[6] Simon Doull was born in Pukekohe on the north island of New Zealand and played domestic first-class cricket for Northern Districts (1989-2002). He was a right-arm fast-medium bowler, who played 32 tests from 1992 to 2000 and took 98 wickets at an average of 29.31. He is a member of the best New Zealand team of the 1990s (Table J.5). Since retiring from cricket, Doull has become a radio personality and cricket commentator.

[7] Richard Collinge was a left-arm fast-medium bowler who played 35 test matches between 1965 and 1978 and took 116 wickets at an average of 29.25. Born in Wellington in 1946, ne played first-class cricket for Central Districts (1964-1969), Wellington (1968-1975) and Northern Districts (1975-1978).

The Next Highest Rating New Zealand Wicketkeepers:

[1] The highest rating New Zealand wicketkeeper is BJ Watling, the 9th highest rating test wicketkeeper (Table 2.18). Watling is one of the next best wicketkeepers in the best world team of the 2010s (see Chapter 11). Although having a higher wicketkeeper rating than Brendon McCallum, McCullum was preferred in the top New Zealand team because of his superior batting rating. Nevertheless, Watling is a fine batsman and, with a career batting rating of 74.9, he is the 13th highest rating New Zealand batsman.

[2] The 3rd highest rating New Zealand wicketkeeper is Adam Parore (No. 26 in Table 2.18). Parore was born in Auckland and played first-class domestic cricket for Auckland and Northern Districts. He played 78 tests from 1990 to 2002, making 201 dismissals in 121 innings as wicketkeeper. He scored 2,865 runs at an average of 26.28. Parore has made the second most dismissals by a New Zealand wicketkeeper, after BJ Watling.

Table 13.16 Batting statistics of the best New Zealand team of all time.

The team

Player	No. of Innings	Not outs	100s	50s	0s	Highest score	Runs scored	Batting Avge	Strike rate	Batting Rating
1. Latham, TWM [1]	134	6	13	27	11	264	5201	40.63	47.06	95.4
2. Turner, GM	73	6	7	14	1	259	2,991	44.64	45.14	90.4
3. Williamson, KS [1]	186	17	33	37	11	251	9,276	54.89	51.78	153.0
4. Taylor, LRPL	196	24	19	35	14	290	7,683	44.67	59.28	120.9
5. Fleming, SP	189	10	9	46	16	274	7,172	40.07	45.83	103.0
6. Crowe, MD	131	11	17	18	9	299	5,444	45.37	44.66	106.5
7. McCullum, BB	176	9	12	31	14	302	6,453	38.64	64.60	102.1
8. Vettori, DL	174	23	6	23	20	140	4,531	30.01	58.19	65.4
9. Hadlee, RJ	134	19	2	15	12	151	3,124	27.17	56.08	50.7
10. Southee, TG [1]	137	11	0	6	17	73	2059	16.34	83.12	19.7
11. Boult, TA	94	46	0	1	13	52	759	15.81	60.00	12.6
									Total	919.7

Next Batsmen:

Mitchell, DJ [1]	52	5	5	14	1	190	2,059	43.81	53.382	86.6
Astle, NJ	137	10	11	24	11	222	4,702	37.02	49.60	83.2
Richardson, MH	65	3	4	19	1	145	2,776	44.77	37.67	83.0
Wright, JG	148	7	12	23	7	185	5,334	37.83	35.54	82.2
Jones, AH	74	8	7	11	2	186	2,922	44.27	39.26	1.7
Sutcliffe, B	76	8	5	15	5	230	2,727	40.10	49.88	77.2
McMillan, CD	91	10	6	19	7	142	3,116	38.47	54.93	74.1

Next Wicketkeepers:

Watling, BJ	117	16	8	19	10	205	3,790	37.52	42.61	74.9
Parore, AC	128	19	2	14	6	110	2,865	26.28	38.72	43.9

Note: 1. Latham, Williamson, Mitchell and Southee are still playing in 2024.

Table 13.17 Bowling statistics of the best New Zealand team of all time.

The team

Player	Overs	Maidens	Runs against	Wickets	5w/10w	Best	Bowling Avge	Strike rate	Economy rate	Bowling Rating
1. Latham, TWM[1]	Did not bowl									-
2. Turner, GM	Less than 100 overs									-
3. Williamson, KS[1]	358	48	1,207	30	0/0	4/44	40.23	71.70	3.37	37.9
4. Taylor, LRPL	Less than 100 overs									-
5. Fleming,	Did not bowl									
6. Crowe, MD	229	52	676	14	0/0	2/25	48.29	98.36	2.95	24.4
7. McCullum, BB	Wicketkeeper			Less than 100 overs						-
8. Vettori, DL	4,802	1197	12,441	362	20/3	7/87	34.37	79.60	2.59	111.0
9. Hadlee, RJ	3,461	809	9,611	431	36/9	9/52	22.30	50.85	2.63	170.3
10. Southee, TG[1]	3,915	893	11,832	391	15/1	7/64	30.26	60.08	30.2	115.6
11. Boult, TA	2,903	656	8,717	317	10/1	6/30	27.50	54.94	3.00	115.2
									Total	574.4

Next Bowlers:

Wagner, N[1]	2,287	473	7,169	260	9/0	7/39	27.57	52.79	3.13	108.1
Cairns, CL	1,949	414	6,410	218	13/1	7/27	29.40	53.66	3.29	103.7
Taylor, BR	999	206	2,953	111	4/0	7/74	26.60	57.06	2.80	92.3
Martin, CS	2,337	486	7,839	233	10/1	6/26	33.64	60.20	3.35	90.6
Nash, DJ	1,032	312	2,649	93	3/1	6/27	28.48	66.62	2.57	87.7
Doull, SB	1,009	251	2,872	98	6/0	7/65	29.31	61.77	2.85	85.4
Collinge, RO	1,116	228	3,393	116	3/0	6/63	29.25	66.28	2.65	81.6

Note: 1. Latham, Williamson and Southee and Wagner are still playing at the end of 2024.

Table 13.18 Highest rating New Zealand wicketkeepers.

Wicketkeeper	Career span	No. of Innings	Dismissals Catches	Dismissals Stumpings	Dismissals Total	Dismissals/ Innings	Wicketkeeper Rating
McCullum, BB	2004-16	95	168	11	179	1.88	124.2
Watling, BJ	2009-21	127	257	8	265	2.09	132.3
Parore, AC	1990-02	121	194	7	201	1.66	97.5

The Best Pakistan Team of All Time:

The highest rating Pakistani team of all time is shown below, together with the next six highest rating batsmen, the next six highest rating bowlers and the next two highest rating wicketkeepers. The batting and bowling statistics and ratings of each of the players are shown in Table 13.19 and 13.20, respectively, and the wicketkeeping statistics are provided in Table 13.21.

Top 11 Players	Playing period	No. of tests	Batting style	Bowling style
1. Saeed Anwar	1990-01	55	left	< 100
2. Hanif Mohammad	1952-69	55	right	< 100
3. Younis Khan	2000-17	118	right	RAL
4. Javed Miandad	1976-93	124	right	RAL
5. Inzamam-ul-Haq	1992-07	120	right	< 100
6. Mohd. Yousuf	1998-10	90	right	< 100
7. Imran Khan	1971-92	88	right	RAF
8. Kamran Akmal	2002-10	53	right	W-K
9. Wasim Akram	1985-02	104	left	LAF
10. Fazal Mahmood	1952-62	34	right	RAFM
11. Waqar Younis	1989-03	87	right	RAF

Next Best Wicketkeepers:

Sarfaraz Ahmed	2010-19	49	right	W-K
Mohammad Rizwan [1]	2016-24	36	right	W-K
Rashid Latif	1992-03	37	right	W-K

Next best batsmen:	Playing period	No. of tests	Batting style	Bowling style
Azhar Ali	2010-22	97	right	RAL
Misbah-ul-Haq	2001-17	75	right	DNB
Saleem Malik	1982-99	103	right	RAO
Zaheer Abbas	1969-85	78	right	< 100
Babar Azam [1]	2016-24	56	right	< 100
Shoaib Mohd.	1983-95	45	right	< 100
Asad Shafiq	2010-20	77	right	< 100

Next best bowlers:

Shoaib Akhtar	1997-07	46	right	RAF
Mohammad Abbas [1]	2017-24	26	right	RAF
Mohammad Asif	2005-10	23	right	RAFM
Saeed Ajmal	2009-14	35	right	RAO
Yasir Shah	2014-22	48	right	RAL
Saqlain Mushtaq	1995-04	49	right	RAO
Abdul Qadir	1977-90	67	right	RAL

Note: 1. Babar Azam, Mohammad Abbas and Mohammad Rizwan are still playing in 2024.

The best Pakistani team has the 6th highest total batting rating out of the 10 top-rating national teams and the 7th highest bowling rating. Four of the top six batsmen in the team all have career batting ratings in the top 37 of all time (see Table 2.7). The 4 specialist bowlers all have career ratings in the top 48 in history (Table 2.16), 3 of them in the top 18. Of the 28 individuals listed above, 2 played before 1960, 6 played in the period 1960 to 1980, 14 played in the period 1980 to 2000, and 20 played test cricket in the 21st century.

Top 11 Players:

[1] Saeed Anwar was born in Karachi in 1968. He was one of the next best batsmen in the world team of the 1990s (Chapter 9). He scored runs all around the world, with a higher test average away from home than at home.

[2] Hanif Mohammad was born in Junagadh in 1936 and made his first-class debut for Pakistan against the MCC in 1951. The first of the great Pakistani batsmen, Hanif opened the batting in Pakistan's very first test match and was one of the opening batsmen in the best world team of the 1950s (Chapter 5).

[3] At No. 3 is Pakistan's highest rating test batsman, Younis Khan. He is one of the next best batsmen in the world team of the 2010s (Chapter 11) and a member of the best Pakistani team of the 2000s and 2010s (Tables K.6 and L.6, respectively).

[4] Javed Miandad is the top-rating batsmen in the best world teams of the 1970s (Chapter 7) and 1980s (Chapter 8).

[5] Inzamam-ul-Haq was born in Multan, Punjab in 1970 and is one of the next best batsmen in the top world team of the 2000s (Chapter 10). He is a member of the top Pakistan teams of the 1990s and 2000s (Tables J.6 and K.6, respectively).

[6] Mohammad Yousuf is one of the top six batsmen in the best world team of the 2000s (Chapter 10).

[7] The great bowling all-rounder Imran Khan is a member of the best world team of the 1980s (Chapter 8) and also a member of the best Pakistani teams of the 1970s and 1980s (Tables H.6 and I.6).

[8] The wicketkeeper is Kamran Akmal who was one of the next best keepers in the top world team of the 2000s (Chapter 10).

[9] Wasim Akram is another of Pakistan's great bowling all-rounders. He is a member of the top world team of the 1990s (Chapter 9).

[10] Fazal Mahmood is a member of the highest rating world team of the 1950s (Chapter 5).

[11] Waqar Younis is Pakistan's highest rating bowler and a member of the best world team of the 1990s (Chapter 9).

Every member of this team, except Kamran Akmal, captained Pakistan: Saeed Anwar was captain for 7 tests; Hanif Mohammad for 11; Younis Khan for 9; Javed Miandad for 34; Inzamam-ul-Haq for 31; Mohammad Yousuf for 9; Imran Khan for 48; Wasim Akram for 25; Waqar Younis for 17; and Fazal Mahmood for 10.

The Next 6 Highest Rating Pakistani Batsmen:

[1] Azhar Ali is the 71st highest rating test batsman (Table 2.7) and the No. 3 batsman in the best Pakistani team of the 2010s (Table L.6). He was born in Lahore in 1985 and played 97 tests from 2010 to the end of 2022 and scored 7,142 runs at an average of 42.26. He scored 302 not out against the West Indies in October 2016 to become the first batsman to score a century, a double century and a triple century in day/night test matches.

[2] Misbah-ul-Haq is the No. 5 batsman in the best Pakistani team of the 2010s (Table L.6) and the 88th highest rating test batsman (Table 2.7). Born in Mianwali in 1974, he made his first-class cricket debut for Sargodha in 1998 at the age of 24 and his test debut against New Zealand in 2001. He played 75 tests from 2001 to 2017 and scored 5,222 runs at 46.63. He captained Pakistan in 56 tests from 2011 to 2017, winning 26 and losing 19. Misbah holds the world record for the fastest 50 in test cricket (in just 21 balls against Australia in 2014) and the 2nd fastest 100 (in just 56 balls in the same innings against Australia).

[3] Saleem Malik is the No.6 batsman in the best Pakistani teams of the 1980s (Table I.6) and 1990s (Table J.6). He ranks 89th in Table 2.7. Saleem was born in Lahore in 1963 and played first-class cricket in Pakistan for Lahore (1981-99), Habib Bank Limited (1982-2000) and Sargodha (1991-92) and county cricket for Essex (1991-92). He played 103 tests from 1982-99 and scored 5,768 runs at 43.70, with 15 centuries.

[4] Zaheer Abbas is one of the specialist batsmen in the top Pakistani teams of the 1970s and 1980s (Table H.6 and I.6, respectively) and the 96th highest rating test batsman (Table 2.7). He was born in Sialkot in 1947 and played domestic cricket for a variety of teams, including Dawood, Karachi and PIA, and county cricket for Gloucestershire (1972-84). He finished his career with a first-class average of 51.54 and 108 first-class centuries — the first Asian batsman to score 100 first-class centuries. He played test cricket from 1969 to 1985 scoring 5,062 runs in 78 tests at a batting average of 44.80.

[5] Babar Azam is the No. 5 batsman in the best Pakistan team of the 2010s (Table L.6) and is ranked 122nd in Table A.1. Born in Lahore in 1994, he made his test debut in 2016, and by the end of 2024, he has played 56 tests and scored 4,051 runs at an average of 43.56. After a slow start to his test career, his test batting performances up until 2023 were steadily improving. Babar's batting in ODI and T20 cricket is outstanding, and in 2022, he was the only player in the world to be ranked by the ICC in the top 5 batsmen in all formats of the game.

[6] Shoaib Mohammad is the No. 3 batsman in the best Pakistan team of the 1980s (Table I.6). Born in Karachi in 1962, Shoaib was a right-hand batsman who played 45 tests from 1983 to 1995 and scored 2,705 runs at an average of 44.34. He opened the batting in 40 of his 68 test innings. He is the 169th highest rating test batsman (Table A.1). He is the son of Hanif Mohammad and nephew of Mushtaq, Sadiq and Wasir Mohammad (all former test players for Pakistan).

[7] Asad Shafiq is the No.6 batsman in the best Pakistan team of the 2010s (Table L.6). He was born in Karachi in 1986 and played 77 tests from 2010 to 2020 scoring 4,660 runs at an average of 38.20. He is the 175th highest rating test batsman (Table A.1).

The Next 6 Highest Rating Pakistani Bowlers:

[1] Shoaib Akhtar was the opening bowler in the best world team of the 2000s (Chapter 10) and is the 52nd highest rating bowler in test history (Table 2.16).

[2] Mohammad Abbas was born in Sialkot (Punjab) in 1990 and made his test debut in 2017 against the West Indies. He is a right arm fast bowler who played 25 tests from 2017 to 2024 and taken 97 wickets at an average of 22.73 and a strike rate of 55.43. He is the 65th highest rating test bowler (Table 2.16).

[3] Mohammad Asif was a right arm fast bowler who played 23 test matches for Pakistan between 2005 and 2010 and took 106 wickets at an average of 24.45 and a strike rate of 48.83. His cricket career was interrupted when he tested positive in 2006 for a performance enhancing substance and abruptly terminated when he was found guilty of charges related to spot-fixing of matches. Despite his off-field problems, he is the 67th highest rating test bowler (Table 2.16).

[4] Saeed Ajmal is one of the next best bowlers in the world team of the 2010s (Chapter 11) and he sits at No. 82 in Table 2.16.

[5] Yasir Shah is a leg break bowler who was born in Swabi in 1986 and ranks at No. 89 in Table 2.16. He made his test debut in 2014 and played 48 tests up until the end of 2022. He has taken 244 wickets at 31.38. In just his 33rd test in December 2018 against New Zealand, Yasir Shah took his 200th test wicket to become the fastest bowler to reach that milestone in the history of test cricket. The previous record holder was Clarrie Grimmett, also an outstanding leg-spin bowler, who took his 200th wicket 82 years earlier in 1936.

[6] Saqlain Mushtaq was born in Lahore in 1976. He was a right-arm off break bowler who played 49 tests from 1995 to 2004 and took 208 wickets at an average of 29.84. He ranks 93rd in Table 2.16. He is a member of the highest rating Pakistani team of the 1990s (Table J.6). After retiring as a player, Saqlain has had a successful coaching career and at the end of 2022 he was the head coach of the Pakistan national team.

[7] Abdul Qadir was one of the next best bowlers in the highest rating world team of the 1980s (Chapter 8).

The Next Highest Rating Pakistani Wicketkeepers:

[1] After Kamran Akmal, the 2nd most highly rated Pakistani wicketkeeper is Sarfaraz Ahmed. He was born in Karachi in 1987, and he played 53 tests and took 160 catches and made 23 stumpings. He is the keeper in the top Pakistan team of the 2010s (Table L.6) and rated No. 21 in Table 2.18. Sarfaraz captained Pakistan in 13 tests from 2017 to 2019, winning 4 and losing 8.

[2] and [3] The next most highly rated wicketkeepers for Pakistan are the current incumbent Mohammad Rizwan (2016-2024) and Rashid Latif (1992-2003) who rank No. 33 and No. 34 respectively in Table 2.18. After retiring as a player, Rashid Latif forged a career as a coach and was appointed to coach the Pakistan national team in 2016.

Table 13.19 Batting statistics of the best Pakistan team of all time.

The team:

Player	No. of Innings	Not outs	100s	50s	0s	Highest score	Runs scored	Batting Avge	Strike rate	Batting Rating
1. Saeed Anwar	91	2	11	25	8	188	4,052	45.53	55.77	102.1
2. Hanif Mohammad	97	8	12	15	5	337	3,915	43.99	48.01	99.2
3. Younis Khan	213	19	34	33	19	313	10,099	52.06	52.12	150.0
4. Javed Miandad	189	21	23	43	6	280	8,832	52.57	48.36	143.0
5. Inzamam-ul-Haq	200	22	25	46	15	329	8,830	49.61	54.02	141.2
6. Mohd. Yousuf	156	12	24	33	11	223	7,530	52.29	52.40	135.3
7. Imran Khan	126	25	6	18	8	136	3,807	37.69	49.29	71.7
8. Kamran Akmal	92	6	6	12	14	158	2,648	30.79	63.12	57.0
9. Wasim Akram	147	19	3	7	17	257	2,898	22.64	51.95	39.1
10. Fazal Mahmood	50	6	0	1	10	60	620	14.09	50.00	9.6
11. Waqar Younis	120	21	0	0	21	45	1,010	10.20	47.96	7.7
									Total	955.9

Next Batsmen:

Azhar Ali	180	11	19	35	19	302	7,142	42.26	41.93	109.4
Misbah-ul-Haq	132	20	10	39	9	161	5,222	46.63	44.53	104.1
Saleem Malik	154	22	15	29	12	237	5,768	43.70	50.28	104.0
Zaheer Abbas	124	11	12	20	10	274	5,062	44.80	52.66	102.3
Babar Azam [1]	102	9	9	27	8	196	4,051	43.56	54.49	95.5
Shoaib Mohammad	68	7	7	13	6	203	2,705	44.34	40.52	83.5
Asad Shafiq	128	6	12	27	13	137	4,660	38.20	48.60	82.5

Next Wicketkeepers:

Sarfaraz Ahmed	86	13	3	18	4	112	2,657	36.40	70.99	68.7
Mohammed Rizwan [1]	59	9	3	10	4	171	2,039	40.78	54.36	70.1
Rashid Latif	57	9	1	7	4	150	1,381	28.77	47.42	41.8

Note: 1. Babar Azam and Mohammad Rizwan are still playing in 2024.

Table 13.20 Bowling statistics of the best Pakistan team of all time.

The team

Player	Overs	Maidens	Runs against	Wickets	5w/10w	Best	Bowl Avge	Strike rate	Econ rate	Bowling Rating
1. Saeed Anwar	Less than 100 overs									-
2. Hanif Mohammad	Less than 100 overs									-
3. Younis Khan	134	18	491	9	0/0	2/23	54.56	89.33	3.66	13.0
4. Javed Miandad	201.	32	682	17	0/0	3/74	40.12	86.47	2.78	30.5
5. Inzamam-ul-Haq	Did not bowl									-
6. Mohd. Yousuf	Less than 100 overs									-
7. Imran Khan	3,107	727	8,258	362	23/6	8/58	22.81	53.75	2.55	148.6
8. Kamran Akmal	Wicketkeeper				Did not bowl					-
9. Wasim Akram	3,771	871	9,779	414	25/5	7/119	23.62	54.65	2.59	148.3
10. Fazal Mahmood	1,639	563	3,434	139	13/4	7/42	24.71	70.75	2.10	119.9
11. Waqar Younis	2,704	516	8,788	373	22/5	7/76	23.56	43.50	3.25	150.4
									Total	610.7

Next Bowlers:

Shoaib Akhtar	1,357	238	4,574	178	12/2	6/11	25.7	45.75	3.37	117.4
Mohammad Abbas [1]	896	271	2,205	97	5/1	6/54	22.73	55.43	2.46	111.5
Mohammad Asif	862	196	2,592	106	7/1	6/41	24.45	48.83	3.00	111.2
Saeed Ajmal	1,932	386	5,003	178	10/4	7/55	28.11	65.15	2.59	107.0
Yasir Shah	2,376	359	7,657	244	16/3	8/41	31.38	58.42	3.22	105.1
Saqlain Mushtaq	2,345	541	6,206	208	13/3	8/164	29.84	67.64	2.65	103.9
Abdul Qadir	2,811	608	7,742	236	15/5	9/56	32.81	72.57	2.71	102.3

Note: 1. Mohammad Abbas is still playing in 2024.

Table 13.21 Highest rating Pakistan wicketkeepers.

Wicketkeeper	Career span	No. of Innings	Dismissals Catches	Dismissals Stumpings	Dismissals Total	Dismissals/ Innings	Wicketkee per Rating
Kamran Akmal	2002-10	99	184	33	206	2.08	116.1
Sarfaraz Ahmed	2010-19	94	146	21	167	1.78	105.8
Mohammad Rizwan [1]	1016-24	60	92	7	99	1.65	92.4
Rashid Latif	1992-03	69	119	11	130	1.88	91.8

Note: 1. Mohammad Rizwan is still playing in 2024.

The Best Sri Lankan Team of All Time:

The highest rating Sri Lankan team of all time is shown below, together with the next seven highest rating batsmen and the next seven highest rating bowlers. Two of the next best wicketkeepers are shown, but Dinesh Chandimal has also kept wickets for Sri Lanka, and he is already listed as one of the next best batsmen. The batting and bowling statistics and ratings of each of the players are shown in Table 13.22 and 13.23, respectively, and the wicketkeeping statistics are provided in Table 13.24.

Players	Playing period	No. of tests	Batting style	Bowling style
1. Jayasuriya, ST	1991-07	110	left	LAO
2. Karunaratne, FDM [1]	2012-24	98	left	< 100
3. Sangakkara, K	2000-15	134	left	W-K
4. Jayawardene DPMD	1997-14	149	right	< 100
5. Samaraweera, TT	2001-13	81	right	RAO
6. de Silva, PA	1984-02	93	right	RAO
7. Mathews, AD [1]	2009-24	116	right	RAFM
8. Vaas, WPUJC	1994-09	111	left	LAFM
9. Herath, HMRKB	1999-18	93	left	LAO
10. Muralitharan, M	1992-10	133	right	RAO
11. Malinga, SL	2004-10	30	right	RAF

Next best wicketkeeper:

Dickwella, N	2014-23	54	left	W-K
Jayawardene, HAPW	2000-15	58	right	W-K

Next batsmen:	Playing period	No. of tests	Batting style	Bowling style
Chandimal, LD [1,2]	2011-24	76	right	DNB
Dilshan, TM	1999-13	87	right	RAM
Tillakaratne, HP	1989-04	83	left	< 100
Atapattu, MS	1990-07	90	right	< 100
Dhananjaya de Silva [1]	2016-24	61	right	RAO
Mendis, BKG [1]	2015-24	69	right	< 100
Ranatunga, A	1982-00	93	left	RAM

Next best bowlers:

Perera, MDK	2014-21	43	right	RAO
Lakmal, RAS	2010-22	70	right	RAMF
Ratnayake, RJ	1983-92	23	right	RAFM
Zoysa, DNT	1997-04	30	left	LAFM
Prasad, KTGD	2008-15	25	right	RAFM
Ratnayeke, JR	1982-89	22	left	RAFM
Fernando, CRD	2000-12	40	right	RAFM

Notes: 1. Karunaratne, Mathews, Chandimal, Dhananjaya de Silva and Mendis are still playing in 2024.
2. Chandimal is the 3rd highest rating wicketkeeper for Sri Lanka.

The top-rating Sri Lankan team has the 5th highest total batting rating out of the 10 top-rating national teams and the 3rd highest bowling rating. The six highest rating batsmen in the team have career batting ratings in the top

80 of all time, two in the top 9 (Table 2.7). Three of the specialist bowlers have career ratings in the top 61 in history, two in the top 20 (Table 2.16). Twenty-four of the 27 individuals listed above played at least some of their test cricket in the 21st century. Five played in the 1980s (Sri Lanka's first decade of test cricket) and 12 played in the 1990s.

Top 11 Players:

[1] Jayasuriya was a hard-hitting left-hand batsman and left-arm orthodox bowler who was one of the highest rating all-rounders of the 2000s (Chapter 10) and a member of the top Sri Lankan teams of the 1990s and 2000s (Tables J.7 and K.7, respectively).

[2] Dimuth Karunaratne is the current left-hand opening batsmen for Sri Lanka and a member of the highest rating world team of the 2020s (Chapter 12) and the top Sri Lankan teams for the 2010s (Table L.7). He is the highest rating Sri Lankan batsman in the 2020s (Table M.7).

[3] At No. 3 and wicketkeeper is Kumar Sangakkara. He is a member of the top world team of all time (Table 13.1) and the top world teams of the 2000s (Chapter 10) and the 2010s (Chapter 11).

[4] Mahela Jayawardene is a member of the best world team of the 2000s (Chapter 10) and the 10th highest rating test batsman (Table 2.7).

[5] Thilan Samaraweera is at No. 5. He started his career as an off-spin bowler, but developed into a fine right-hand batsman. He is the 4th highest rating Sri Lankan batsman (No. 67 in Table 2.7). Samaraweera was born in Colombo in 1976 and played test cricket for Sri Lanka from 2001 to 2013. In 81 test matches, he scored 5,462 at an average of 48.77, with 14 centuries. Against Pakistan at the National Stadium in Karachi in 2009, he scored 231 and shared a 4th wicket partnership of 437 with Mahela Jayawardene (the third highest 4th wicket partnership of all time). He is a member of the best Sri Lankan teams of the 2000s and 2010s (Tables K.7 and L.7, respectively).

[6] Aravinda de Silva is a member of the top world team of the 1990s (Chapter 9) and Sri Lanka's most successful batsman of the 20th Century.

[7] With Sangakkara taking the wicketkeeping duties, there is room for a 7th batsman in Angelo Mathews. He was one of the next best batsmen in the World team of the 2020s (Chapter 12) and a member of the top Sri Lankan team of the 2010s (Table L.7) and 2020s (Table M.7). Six of the top 7 batsmen captained their country: Jayasuriya in 38 tests; Jayawardene in 38; Mathews in 34; Karunaratne in 30; Sangakkara in 15; and de Silva in 6.

[8] Chaminda Vaas is Sri Lanka's most successful fast bowler. He is a member of Sri Lanka's top teams of the 1990s and 2000s (see Tables J.7 and K.7 respectively) and is ranked 61st in Table 2.16. He was born in Wattala in 1974 and played domestic cricket for the Colts Cricket Club from 1990 to 2012 and county cricket for Hampshire (2003), Worcestershire (2005), Middlesex (2007) and Northamptonshire (2010-12). A left-arm swing bowler who was highly regarded for his accuracy of line and length, he played 111 test matches from 1994 to 2009, taking 355 wickets at a bowling average of 29.58. In 2004, he was selected in both the World Test and ODI teams at the inaugural ICC awards. With a career test batting rating of 42.9, he is the 58th highest rating all-rounder in Table 2.17. Only 3 bowlers have taken more ODI wickets than Chaminda Vaas.

[9] Rangana Herath is the highest rating bowler in the best world team of the 2010s (Chapter 11).

[10] Muttiah Muralitharan is the highest rating bowler in test history. He is a member of the top world team of all time (Tables 13.1 and 13.2) and the top world teams of the 1990s (Chapter 9) and 2000s (Chapters 10).

[11] Lasith Malinga is Sri Lanka's second highest rating pace bowler. He was born in Galle in 1983 and played first-class cricket for Nondescripts (2004-18). More successful in ODI and Twenty20 cricket than in test cricket, Malinga was an intimidating right-arm fast bowler, with a slinging motion and a deadly yorker. He is the only player to have taken three hat-tricks in ODI cricket and the only player ever to take 4 wickets in

four consecutive balls in international cricket (in the ICC World Cup against South Africa at Providence Stadium, Guyana in March 2007). He played 30 test matches from 2004 to 2010 and took 101 wickets at an average of 33.16.

The Next 6 Highest Rating Sri Lankan Batsmen:

[1] Dinesh Chandimal is a member of the top-rating team of the 2020s (Chapter 12) and the highest rating Sri Lankan teams of the 2010s (Table L.7) and 2020s (M.7).

[2] Tillakaratne Dilshan was born in Kalutara in 1976 and played 87 tests matches from 1999 to 2013, scoring 5,492 runs at an average of 40.99 and a strike rate of 65.55, with 16 test centuries. He was a member of the top Sri Lankan teams of the 2000s and 2010s (Tables K.7 and L.7, respectively). As his strike rate suggests, he was an explosive batsman, who, like Jayasuriya, excelled at ODI cricket as well as test cricket.

[3] Hashan Tillakaratne is a member of Sri Lanka's top teams of the 1990s and 2000s (Tables J.7 and K.7, respectively). He was a left-hand middle-order batsman, most often batting at No. 6. Born in 1967 in Colombo, he played domestic cricket for Nondescript Cricket Club (1987-2006) and test cricket from 1989 to 2004. He played 83 tests scoring 4,545 runs at 42.88, with 11 centuries.

[4] Marvan Atapattu is a member of Sri Lanka's top teams of the 2000s (Table K.7). He was born in Kalutara in 1970 and played domestic first-class cricket for the Sinhalese Sports Club (1990-2007). He opened the batting for most of his test career and, in 90 tests from 1990 to 2007, he scored 5,502 runs at an average of 39.02, including 16 centuries, 6 of them were double centuries. He had perhaps the worst start to his test career of any specialist batsman, scoring 5 ducks and just 1 run in his first 6 test innings. After 9 tests, he had scored 182 runs at an average of just 10.7. In his 10th test and 7 years after his test debut, he scored a century and cemented himself into the test team for the next decade.

[5] Dhananjaya de Silva was born in Hambantota in 1991, and he plays domestic cricket for Tamil Union and test cricket for Sri Lanka. He is a top-order right-hand batsman who made his test debut against Australia in 2016, and by the end of 2024, he had played 61 tests and scored 4,011 runs at an average of 40.11. Against Bangladesh in 2021, de Silva and captain Dimuth Karunaratne put on 345 runs in a record partnership for any wicket in a test match in Kandy.

[6] Kusal Mendis was born in Moratuwa in 1995 and played domestic first-class cricket for Bloomfield C&AC (2015-17) and Colombo Cricket Club (2017-2022). Up to the end of 2024, he has played 69 test matches and scored 4,478 runs at an average of 36.11. He is one of the highest-ranking Sri Lankan batsmen in the 2010s (Table L.7) and 2020s (Table M.7).

[7] Arjuna Ranatunga was Sri Lanka's highest rating batsman of the 1980s (Table I.7) and a member of Sri Lanka's top team of the 1990s (Table J.7). He was born in Gampaha in 1963 and played domestic cricket for the Sinhalese Sports Club (1982-2001). He played in Sri Lanka's first ever test match and scored 54 in his first test innings. He went on to play 93 tests from 1982 to 2000 scoring 5,105 runs at an average of 35.70. He is the only person in history to have played for his country in its 1st and in its 100th test match. He captained Sri Lanka in 56 tests from 1989 to 1999, more matches as captain than any other Sri Lankan. After retiring as a player, he held a number of administrative positions in Sri Lanka, including a term as President of Sri Lanka Cricket (2008-09). He entered the Sri Lankan parliament after the 2001 elections and has since had a colourful political career. In December 2018, he was appointed as Sri Lanca's Minister for Transport and Civil Aviation.

The Next 6 Highest Rating Sri Lankan Bowlers:

[1] Dilruwan Perera is a right-arm off break bowler who is a member of the top-rating Sri Lankan team of the 2010s (Table L.7). He was born in Panadura in 1982 and played domestic cricket for Panadura Sports Club

(2000-07) and Colts Cricket Club (2007-2021). He played 43 test matches from 2014 to 2021 taking 161 wickets at a bowling average of 35.90. He was unlucky to miss selection in the top team as he is the fourth highest rating Sri Lankan bowler, but with Muralitharan and Herath in the side, a second pace bowler (Malinga) was preferred to balance the team.

[2] Suranga Lakmal is right arm medium-fast bowler and a member of the top Sri Lankan team of the 2010s (see Table L.7). He was born in Matara in 1987 and, from 2010 to the end of his test career in 2022, he played 70 tests, taking 171 wickets at 36.44.

[3] Rumesh Ratnayake was born in Colombo in 1964 and made his test debut at the age of 19 against New Zealand in 1983. He was a right-arm fast-medium bowler who played 23 test matches between 1983 and 1992, taking 74 wickets at a bowling average of 34.64. His career was affected by injury, but when fit, Ratnayake was capable of generating considerable pace and was an efficient swing bowler. Since retirement, he has had a successful coaching career including terms as Interim Coach of the Sri Lankan test team.

[4] Nuwan Zoysa was a left-arm fast-medium bowler who played 30 tests from 1997 to 2004 and took 64 wickets at an average of 33.70. He was born in Colombo in 1978 and played domestic cricket for the Sinhalese Sports Club (1996-2011). He is one of the next bowlers in the top Sri Lankan side of the 2000s (Table K.7).

[5] Dhammika Prasad was a right-arm fast-medium bowler who is a member of the Sri Lankan team of the 2010s (Table L.7). Born in Ragama in 1983, he played domestic cricket for the Sinhalese Sports Club (2002-18). He played 25 tests between 2008 and 2015 and took 75 wickets at 35.97.

[6] Ravi Ratnayeke was a right-arm fast medium fast bowler and a handy left-hand lower order batsman. He played 22 tests for Sri Lanka from 1982 to 1989, taking 55 wickets at 35.85. He took 7 for 83 against Pakistan at Jinnah Stadium in October 1985, the best test figures by a Sri Lankan bowler at that time.

[7] Dilhara Fernando was a right arm fast-medium bowler who played 40 tests from 2000 to 2012 and took 100 wickets at an average of 37.84. He was born in Colombo in 1979 and played domestic cricket for the Sinhalese Sports Club (1997-2018) and county cricket for Worcestershire in 2008. He is a member of the top Sri Lankan team of the 2000s (Table K.7).

The Next Highest Rating Sri Lankan Wicketkeeper:

[1] Niroshan Dickwella is the next highest rating Sri Lankan wicketkeeper behind Sangakkara. He was born in Kandy in 1993 and has played domestic cricket for Nondescripts Cricket Club since 2012. He is a left-handed batsman who kept wickets for Sri Lanka from his test debut against South Africa in 2014 until 2023. He has played 54 tests and made 160 wicketkeeping dismissals (133 catches and 27 stumpings) at 1.67 dismissals per innings. With the bat, he has made 2,757 runs at 30.98.

[2] Prasanna Jayawardene is the 4th highest rating Sri Lankan wicketkeeper (Table 13.24). He was born in Colombo in 1979 and kept wickets for Sri Lanka in 58 tests between 2000 and 2015, taking 124 catches and making 32 stumpings. He is the 39th highest rating test wicketkeeper (Table 2.18).

Table 13.22 Batting statistics of the best Sri Lankan team of all time.

The team

Player	No. of Innings	Not outs	100s	50s	0s	High score	Runs scored	Avge	Strike rate	Batting Rating
1. Jayasuriya, ST	188	14	14	31	15	340	6,973	40.07	65.13	109.8
2. Karunaratne, FDM [1]	187	76	16	39	12	244	7,165	39.81	51.56	104.8
3. Sangakkara, K	233	17	38	52	11	319	12,400	57.41	54.19	177.8
4. Jayawardene, DPMdS	252	15	34	50	15	374	11,814	49.85	51.47	157.0
5. Samaraweera, TT	132	20	14	30	11	231	5,462	48.77	46.92	113.0
6. de Silva, PA	159	11	20	22	7	237	6,361	42.98	50.94	107.6
7. Mathews, A [1]	206	27	16	44	6	200	8,042	44.93	48.43	116.4
8. Vaas, WPUJC	162	35	1	13	12	100	3,089	24.32	43.92	42.9
9. Herath, HMRKB	144	28	0	3	23	80	1,699	14.65	49.90	13.3
10. Muralitharan, M	164	56	0	1	33	67	1,261	11.68	70.29	11.3
11. Malinga, SL	37	13	0	1	9	64	275	11.46	44.43	6.1
									Total	960.0

Next Batsmen:

Player	No. of Innings	Not outs	100s	50s	0s	High score	Runs scored	Avge	Strike rate	Batting Rating
Chandimal, LD [1,2]	154	15	16	30	8	206	6,019	43.30	50.18	103.9
Dilshan, TM	145	11	16	23	14	193	5,492	40.99	65.55	98.6
Tillakaratne, HP [2]	131	25	11	20	9	204	4,545	42.88	40.35	89.1
Atapattu, MS	156	15	16	17	22	249	5,502	39.02	44.48	88.9
Dhananjaya de Silva [1]	108	8	12	19	9	173	4,011	40.11	58.28	86.8
Mendis, BKG [1]	129	5	10	19	14	245	4,478	36.11	57.92	81.1
Ranatunga, A	155	12	4	38	12	135	5,105	35.70	49.74	77.8

Next Wicketkeeper:

Player	No. of Innings	Not outs	100s	50s	0s	High score	Runs scored	Avge	Strike rate	Batting Rating
Dickwella, N	96	7	0	22	4	96	2,757	30.98	66.47	56.5
Jayawardene, HAPW	83	11	4	5	9	154	2,124	29.50	48.70	45.0

Notes: 1. Karunaratne, Mathews, Chandimal, Dhananjaya de Silva and Mendis are still playing in 2024.
2. Chandimal and Tillakaratne have also kept wickets for Sri Lanka.

Table 13.23 Bowling statistics of the best Sri Lankan team of all time.

The team

Player	Overs	Maidens	Runs against	Wickets	5w/10w	Best	Bowling Avge	Strike rate	Economy rate	Bowling Rating
1. Jayasuriya, ST	1,364	323	3,366	98	2/0	5/34	34.35	83.55	2.47	67.1
2. Karunaratne, FDM [1]	Less than 100 overs									-
3. Sangakkara, K	Wicketkeeper				Less than 100 overs					-
4. Jayawardene DPMdS	Less than 100 overs									-
5. Samaraweera, TT	221	36	689	15	0/0	4/49	45.93	88.47	3.12	23.7
6. de Silva, PA	432	77	1,208	29	0/0	3/30	41.66	89.48	2.79	40.6
7. Mathews, A [1]	663	161	1,798	33	0/0	4/44	54.48	120.6	2.71	37.0
8. Vaas, WPUJC	3,906	895	10,501	355	12/2	7/71	29.58	66.02	2.69	113.0
9. Herath, HMRKB	4,332	816	12,157	433	34/9	9/127	28.08	60.03	2.81	146.5
10. Muralitharan, M	7,340	1,792	18,180	800	67/22	9/51	22.73	55.05	2.48	226.5
11. Malinga, SL	868	112	3,349	101	3/0	5/34	33.16	51.57	3.86	74.6
									Total	729.0

Next Bowlers:

Player	Overs	Maidens	Runs against	Wickets	5w/10w	Best	Bowling Avge	Strike rate	Economy rate	Bowling Rating
Perera, MDK	1,801	239	5,780	161	8/2	6/32	35.90	67.11	3.21	77.4
Lakmal, RAS	2,074	438	6,232	171	4/0	5/47	36.44	72.77	3.01	72.0
Ratnayake, RJ	827	136	2,563	74	5/0	6/66	34.64	67.04	3.10	66.6
Zoysa, DNT	737	160	2,157	64	1/0	5/20	33.70	69.09	2.93	64.6
Prasad, KTGD	721	96	2,696	75	1/0	5/50	35.95	57.69	3.74	61.6
Ratnayeke, JR	639	118	1,972	55	4/0	7/83	35.85	69.69	3.09	61.5
Fernando, CRD	1,030	143	3,784	100	3/0	5/60	37.84	61.81	3.67	60.8

Note: 1. Karunaratne and Mathews is still playing in 2024.

Table 13.24 Highest rating Sri Lankan wicketkeepers.

Wicketkeeper	Career span	No. of Innings	Dismissals Catches	Dismissals Stumpings	Dismissals Total	Dismissals/ Innings	Wicketkeeper Rating
Sangakkara, K	2000-15	90	131	20	151	1.68	144.1
Dickwella, N [1]	2014-22	96	133	27	160	1.67	96.6
Chandimal, LD [1]	2011-23	50	63	10	73	1.46	94.6
Jayawardene, HAPW	2000-15	102	124	32	156	1.53	87.3

The Best South African Team of All Time:

The highest rating South African team of all time is shown below, together with the next seven highest rating batsmen, the next seven highest rating bowlers and the next two highest rating wicketkeepers. The batting and bowling statistics and ratings of each of the players are shown in Table 13.25 and 13.26, respectively, and the wicketkeeping statistics are provided in Table 13.27.

Players	Playing period	No. of tests	Batting style	Bowling style
1. Smith, GC	2002-14	117	left	RAM
2. Kirsten, G	1993-04	101	left	< 100
3. Amla, HM	2005-19	124	right	< 100
4. Pollock, RG	1963-70	23	left	< 100
5. Kallis, JH	1995-13	166	right	RAFM
6. de Villiers, AB	2004-18	114	right	< 100
7. Boucher, MV	1997-12	147	right	W-K
8. Pollock, SM	1995-08	108	right	RAFM
9. Steyn, DW	2004-19	93	right	RAF
10. Rabada, K [1]	2015-23	61	right	RAF
11. Donald, AA	1992-02	72	right	RAF

Next Best Wicketkeeper:

De Kock, Q [2]	2014-21	54	left	W-K
Richardson, DJ	1992-98	42	right	W-K

Next batsmen:	Playing period	No. of tests	Batting style	Bowling style
Nourse, AD	1935-51	34	right	< 100
Mitchell, B	1929-49	42	right	RAL
Cullinan, DJ	1993-01	70	right	< 100
Gibbs, HH	1996-08	90	right	< 100
Barlow, EJ	1961-70	30	right	RAM
Bland, KC	1961-66	21	right	< 100
Elgar, D [1]	2012-23	85	left	LAO
Next best bowlers:				
Philander, VD	2011-18	55	right	RAFM
Ntini, M	1998-09	101	right	RAF
Tayfield, HJ	1949-60	37	right	RAO
Morkel, M	2006-18	86	left	RAF
Pollock, PM	1961-70	28	right	RAF
Adcock, NAT	1953-62	26	right	RAF
Goddard, TL	1955-70	41	left	LAM

Note: 1. Rabada is still playing at the end of 2024.
2. de Kock is the 3rd highest rating South African wicketkeeper behind Boucher and de Villiers.

The best South African team has the 4th highest total batting rating out of the 10 top-rating national teams and the 5th highest bowling rating. The top seven rated batsmen all have career batting ratings in the top 61 of all time (Table 2.7). The ten highest rating bowlers have career ratings in the top 72 of all time (Table 2.16). Of the 27 individuals listed above, three played before 1950, eight played between 1950 and the ban in 1970 and eighteen played after South Africa's reinstatement in 1992. This team includes three members of the same family, brothers Graeme and Peter Pollock and Peter's son Shaun.

Top 11 Players:

[1] Graeme Smith was a tall left-hand opening batsman and an occasional right-arm medium pace bowler. Born in Johannesburg in 1981, he played first-class domestic cricket for Gautang (1999-2000), Western Province (2000-04) and Cape Cobras (2004-14) and county cricket for Hampshire (2000), Somerset (2005) and Surrey (2013-14). He made his test debut against Australia at Newlands in February 2002 and played his final test also against Australia at Newlands in March 2014. He played a total of 117 tests and scored 9,265 runs at an average of 48.26, including 27 centuries (5 of them double centuries). He was an imposing and determined leader who quickly gained the respect of his peers and the selectors. He was appointed captain

of South Africa in April 2003 in just his 9th test match at the age of 22. He went on to captain South Africa in 109 tests until his retirement, winning 53 and losing 29. No other captain has led his country in more than 100 tests and no other captain has had more than 50 test victories. As well as having an unrivalled record as captain, he was also a fine batsman with the 31st highest career batting rating in Table 2.7. In the history of test cricket, there have been 15 opening partnerships in excess of 300. Smith features in 4 of them, including the world record opening stand of 415 with Neil McKenzie against Bangladesh in 2008. His other 3 opening stands over 300 were all with his long-time opening partner Herschelle Gibbs.

[2] Gary Kirsten was a gritty left-handed opening batsman with a reputation for patience and reliability. He was born in Cape Town in 1967 and played first-class domestic cricket for Western Province from 1987 to 2004. From his test debut against Australia in the Boxing Day test at the Melbourne Cricket Ground in 1993 until his final test against New Zealand at the Basin Reserve in 2004, he played 101 tests and scored 7,289 at an average of 45.27, including 21 centuries. At the time of his retirement, he had scored more test runs and more test centuries than any other South African, but both records were to be broken within a year by Jacques Kallis. He scored 275 in a marathon innings of over 14 hours to salvage a draw for South Africa against England at Durban in 1999, in what is thought to be the second longest innings (in terms of duration) in test history. His 188 against the United Arab Emirates in the 1996 World Cup is still the highest ODI score by a South African batsman. After retiring as a player, Kirsten has had a successful coaching career. He was coach of the Indian team from 2008 to 2011 and the South African team from 2011 to 2013. He successfully coached India to victory in the 2011 World Cup.

[3] Hashim Amla is one of the next best batsmen in the best World team of the 2010s (Chapter 11). He ranks 38th in Table 2.7.

[4] Graeme Pollock is the No. 3 batsman in the best World team of the 1960s (Chapter 6). He ranks 33rd in Table 2.7.

[5] Jacques Kallis is the No. 6 batsman in the top World team of all time (Table 13.1) and a member of the top world teams of the 2000s (Chapter 10) and 2010s (Chapter 11). He is the 4th highest rating test batsman (Table 2.7) and the highest rating all-rounder (Table 2.17).

[6] A.B. de Villiers is a member of the highest rating world team of the 2010s (Chapter 11), and although he spent much of his test career as a specialist batsman, he is the 2nd highest rating South African wicketkeeper after Mark Boucher (Table 2.18).

[7] Mark Boucher was the second-choice wicketkeeper in the 2000s behind Adam Gilchrist (Chapter 10) and one of the top three wicketkeepers in the 1990s (Chapter 9). He sits just behind Gilchrist as the 2nd highest rating test wicketkeeper of all time (Table 2.18).

[8] Shaun Pollock is one of the next best bowlers in the top-ranking World teams of the 1990s (Chapter 9) and 2000s (Chapter 10).

[9] Dale Steyn is the top-rating South African bowler of all time (8th in Table 2.16) and one of the next best bowlers in the top-rating world team of all-time (Table 13.2). He is also one of the next best bowlers in the top world team of the 2000s (Chapter 10) and one of the four specialist bowlers in the top world team of the 2010s (Chapter 11).

[10] Kagiso Rabada is the 5th highest rating bowler in the best world team of the 2010s (Chapter 11) and one of the four specialist bowlers in the top world team of the 2020s (Chapter 12).

[11] Allan Donald is one of the four fast bowlers in the highest rating world team of the 1990s (Chapter 9).

The Next 6 Highest Rating South African Batsmen:

[1] Arthur Dudley Nourse is one of the next best batsmen in the highest rating World team for the period 1920 to 1949 (Chapter 4).

[2] Bruce Mitchell is the opening batsman in the top-rating South African team from 1920 to 1949 (Table E.3). He was born in Johannesburg in 1909 and played first-class cricket for Transvaal. He made his test debut against England in 1929 at Edgbaston and played his final test at Port Elizabeth, also against

England, in 1949, never missing a test in that period. A fine batsman whose performances improved with age, and a handy leg-spin bowler, he played 42 consecutive tests scoring 3,471 runs at an average 48.89, including 8 centuries. He scored two 50s in his first test (88 and 61 not out) and two more in his final test (99 and 56). He is the 92nd highest rating test batsman (Table 2.7).

[3] Daryll Cullinan is the No. 5 batsman in the top-rating South African team of the 1990s (Table J.8). He was born in Kimberley, Cape Province in 1967 and played test cricket from 1993 to 2001. He played 70 tests and scored 4,554 runs at an average of 44.21. His top score of 275 against New Zealand at Eden Park in 1999 was, at the time, the highest test score by a South African. He is the 102nd highest rating test batsman (Table A.1).

[4] Herschelle Gibbs is the No. 3 batsman in the top-rating South African team of the 2000s (TableK.8). He opened the batting in 116 of his 154 test innings for South Africa. He was born in Cape Town in 1974 and played domestic first-class cricket for Western Province (1990-2004) and Cape Cobras (2004-06) and county cricket for Glamorgan (2008) and Yorkshire (2010). He played 90 test matches from 1996 to 2008, scoring 6,167 runs at an average of 41.95, with 14 centuries. He featured in three test opening partnerships in excess of 300 (all with Graeme Smith) and he and Jacques Kallis hold the record for the highest second wicket partnership for South Africa in tests (an unbroken 315 runs against New Zealand at AMI Stadium in 1999). He is the 104th highest rating test batsman (Table A.1).

[5] Eddie Barlow is the third highest rating South African batsman of the 1960s (Table G.5) and the 36th highest rating test all-rounder (Table 2.17). He was born in Pretoria in 1940 and played domestic cricket for Transvaal, Eastern Province (1959-68) and Western Province (1968-81) and county cricket for Derbyshire (1976-78). Another of the talented cricketers whose test career was ended by the boycott on South Africa in 1970, Barlow played 30 tests from 1961 to 1970, scoring 2,516 runs at an average of 45.75 and taking 40 wickets at 34.05.

[6] Colin Bland is the second highest rating South African batsman of the 1960s (Table G.5) and generally regarded as the finest cover fieldsman of his day. He was born in Bulawayo in 1938 and played domestic first-class cricket for Rhodesia (1956-68) and later for eastern Province and Orange Free State. He played 21 test matches from 1961 until injury ended his career in 1966, scoring 1,669 runs at an average of 49.09.

[7] Dean Elgar was born in Orange Free State Provence in 1987 and played domestic first-class cricket for Free State (2005-2012) and Titans (2014-2024). He is a left-hand opening batsman in the best South African teams of the 2010s (Table L.8) and one of the highest rating South African batsmen in the 2020s (Table M.8). He has played 86 test matches from his debut in 2012 until his final test in January 2024 and scored 5,347 runs at an average of 37.92. He is the 163rd highest rating test batsman (Table A.1).

The Next 6 Highest Rating South African Bowlers:

[1] Vernon Philander is one of the next best bowlers in the highest rating World team for the 2010s (Chapter 11).

[2] Makhaya Ntini is one of the next best bowlers in the highest rating World team for the 2000s (Chapter 10).

[3] Hugh Tayfield is one of the next best bowlers in the highest rating World team of the 1950s (Chapter 5) and the highest rating South African bowler of the decade (Table F.5).

[4] Morne Morkel is a tall right-arm fast bowler and a member of the highest rating South African team of the 2010s (Table L.8). Born in Transvaal in 1984, Morkel played 86 tests for South Africa between 2006 and 2018, taking 309 wickets at an average of 27.67. He is the 66th highest rating test bowler (Table 2.16). By 2012, together with Dale Steyn and Vernon Philander, Morkel was a member of what South African bowling coach Alan Donald called the finest pace attack that South Africa had ever produced. After his retirement from international cricket, Morkel became a permanent resident of Australia in 2020.

[5] Peter Pollock is one of opening bowlers in the highest rating World team of the 1960s (Chapter 6).

[6] Neil Adcock is the 2nd highest rating South African bowler of the 1950s (Table F.5). A tall right-arm fast bowler, Adcock was born in Cape Town in 1931 and made his test debut against New Zealand at Kingsmead

in 1953. He played 26 tests and took 104 wickets at the impressive average of 21.11. He is the 72nd highest rating test bowler (Table 2.16).

[7] Trevor Goddard was one of the next best bowlers in the top world team of the 1960s (Chapter 6).

The Next Highest Rating South African Wicketkeeper:

After Mark Boucher and AB de Villiers, the next highest rating South African wicketkeepers are Quinton de Kock and Dave Richardson.

[1] Quinton de Kock one of the back-up wicketkeepers in the highest rating world team of the 2010s (Chapter 11).

[2] Dave Richardson was born in Johannesburg in 1959 and played domestic first-class cricket for Eastern Province (1977-83 and 1984-98) and Northern Transvaal (1983/84). He was the permanent South African wicketkeeper for the first 7 years after South Africa's reinstatement in 1992, playing 42 tests and making 152 dismissals (150 catches and 2 stumpings). He also scored 1,359 runs at an average of 24.27. Since retirement as a player Richardson has served terms as general manager and chief executive officer of the ICC.

Table 13.25 Batting statistics of the best South African team of all time.

The team

Player	No. of Innings	Not outs	100s	50s	0s	Highest score	Runs scored	Batting Avge	Strike rate	Batting Rating
1. Smith, GC	205	13	27	38	11	277	9,265	48.26	59.69	138.1
2. Kirsten, G	176	15	21	34	13	275	7,289	45.27	43.43	116.4
3. Amla, HM	215	16	28	41	13	311	9,282	46.64	49.97	134.1
4. Pollock, RG	41	4	7	11	1	274	2,256	60.97	50.83	137.5
5. Kallis, JH	280	40	45	58	16	224	13,289	55.37	45.98	170.9
6. de Villiers, AB	191	18	22	46	8	278	8,765	50.66	54.53	140.4
7. Boucher, MV	206	24	5	35	17	125	5,515	30.30	50.11	71.1
8. Pollock, SM	156	39	2	16	9	111	3,781	32.32	52.53	59.8
9. Steyn, DW	119	27	0	2	14	76	1,251	13.60	44.39	10.6
10. Rabada, K [1]	105	19	0	0	20	47	1,024	11.91	50.12	9.1
11. Donald, AA	94	33	0	0	17	37	652	10.69	35.07	6.1
									Total	994.1

Next Batsmen:

Nourse, AD	62	7	9	14	3	231	2,960	53.82	50.00	115.7
Mitchell, B	80	9	8	21	3	189	3,471	48.89	50.00	103.0
Cullinan, DJ	115	12	14	20	10	275	4,554	44.21	48.97	100.6
Gibbs, HH	154	7	14	26	11	228	6,167	41.95	50.26	99.8
Barlow, EJ	57	2	6	15	3	201	2,516	45.75	48.00	91.3
Bland, KC	39	5	3	9	2	144	1,669	49.09	50.00	87.6
Elgar, D [1]	152	11	14	23	13	199	5,347	37.92	47.78	86.5

Next Wicketkeeper:

de Kock, Q [2]	59	5	3	13	4	129	1,970	36.48	71.82	67.4
Richardson, DJ	64	8	1	8	7	109	1,359	24.27	43.27	30.7

Note: 1. Rabada ia still playing at the end of 2024.

2. de Kock is the 3rd highest rating South African wicketkeeper behind Boucher and de Villiers.

Table 13.26 Bowling statistics of the best South African team of all time.

The team

Player	Overs	Maidens	Runs against	Wickets	5w/10w	Best	Bowling Avge	Strike rate	Economy rate	Bowling Rating
1. Smith, GC	236	28	885	8	0/0	2/145	110.63	177.25	3.74	10.6
2. Kirsten, G	Less than 100 overs									-
3. Amla, HM	Less than 100 overs									-
4. Pollock, RG	Less than 100 overs									-
5. Kallis, JH	3,372	848	9,535	292	5/0	6/54	32.65	69.29	2.83	93.7
6. de Villiers, AB	Less than 100 overs									-
7. Boucher, MV	Wicketkeeper					Did not bowl				-
8. Pollock, SM	4,059	1,211	9,733	439	16/1	7/87	23.12	57.85	2.40	141.9
9. Steyn, DW	3,101	660	10,077	424	26/5	7/51	22.95	42.39	3.25	161.5
10. Rabada, K [1]	2,109	422	7,026	321	16/4	7/112	21.89	39.43	3.33	153.8
11. Donald, AA	2,586	661	7,344	330	20/3	8/71	22.25	47.03	2.84	147.7
									Total	709.2

Next Bowlers:

Player	Overs	Maidens	Runs against	Wickets	5w/10w	Best	Bowling Avge	Strike rate	Economy rate	Bowling Rating
Philander, VD	1,898	507	5,000	224	13/2	6/21	22.32	50.85	2.63	130.3
Ntini, M	3,472	759	11,242	390	18/4	7/37	28.83	53.42	3.24	126.5
Tayfield, HJ	1,852	602	4,405	170	14/2	9/113	25.91	79.81	1.95	113.8
Morkel, M	2,749	605	8,550	309	8/0	6/23	27.67	53.39	3.11	111.3
Pollock, PM	1,034	270	2,806	116	9/1	6/38	24.19	56.22	2.58	110.1
Adcock, NAT	918	218	2,195	104	5/0	6/43	21.11	61.45	2.06	109.2
Goddard, TL	1,768	706	3,226	123	5/0	6/53	26.23	95.41	1.65	98.7

Note: 1. Rabada is still playing at the end of 2024.

Table 13.27 Highest rating South African wicketkeepers.

Wicketkeeper	Career span	No. of Innings	Dismissals - Catches	Dismissals - Stumpings	Dismissals - Total	Dismissals/ Innings	Wicketkeeper Rating
Boucher, MV	1997-12	281	532	23	555	1.98	170.9
de Villiers, AB	2004-18	45	101	5	106	2.36	142.7
De Kock, Q	2014-21	98	221	11	232	2.37	138.3
Richardson, DJ	1992-98	77	150	2	152	1.97	94.3

The Best Zimbabwe Team of All Time:

The highest rating Zimbabwe team of all time is shown below, together with the next five highest rating batsmen and the next highest rating bowler. At the end of 2024, only 20 players from Zimbabwe had played more than 20 test matches. The batting and bowling statistics and ratings of each of the players are shown in Tables 13.28 and 13.29, respectively, and the statistics of highest rating wicketkeepers are shown in Table 13.30.

Players	Playing period	No. of tests	Batting style	Bowling style	Next best batsmen:	Playing period	No. of tests	Batting style	Bowling style
1. Flower, G	1992-04	67	right	LAO	Goodwin, MW	1998-00	19	right	< 100 overs
2. Masakadza, H	2001-18	38	right	RAL	Ervine, CR [1]	2011-24	22	left	DNB
3. Taylor, BRM	2004-21	34	right	< 100 overs	Sikandar Raza	2014-21	17	right	RAM
4. Houghton, DL	1992-97	22	right	< 100 overs	Taibu, T	2001-12	28	right	< 100 overs
5. Flower, A	1992-02	63	left	W-K	Campbell, ADR	1992-02	60	left	< 100 overs
6. Whittall, GJ	1993-02	46	right	RAFM	Carlisle, SV	1995-05	37	right	DNB
7. Streak, HH	1993-05	65	right	RAFM	Blignaut, AM	2001-05	19	left	RAFM
8. Strang, PA	1994-01	24	right	RAL					
9. Strang, BC	1995-01	26	right	LAFM					
10. Price, RW	1999-13	22	right	LAO					
11. Olonga, HW	1995-02	30	right	RAFM					

Note: 1. Ervine is still playing at the end of 2024.

The best Zimbabwe team has the lowest total batting rating out of the 10 top-rating national teams and the 2nd lowest bowling rating. Only one of the batsmen has a career batting rating in the top 100 of all time, Andrew Flower at No. 60 in Table 2.7. There are no bowlers from Zimbabwe with career bowling ratings in the top 100 shown in Table 2.16. Of the 18 individuals listed above, all but 6 commenced their careers in the 1990s (the decade Zimbabwe entered test cricket) and only 1 is still playing at the end of 2024. Three of the top six batsmen played in Zimbabwe's first ever test match in October 1992, David Houghton and the two Flower brothers, Grant and Andrew. The team includes a second set of two brothers, Paul and Bryan Strang.

Top 11 Players:

[1] Grant Flower was Zimbabwe's third highest rating batsmen of the 1990s (Table J.9) and the younger of two brothers in the highest rating Zimbabwe team. He was born in Salisbury, Rhodesia in 1970 and played 67 test matches from 1992 to 2004, scoring 3,457 runs at an average of 29.55. He was a steady right-hand batsman and a slow left-arm orthodox bowler. He has played more test matches than any other Zimbabwean. He opened the batting for Zimbabwe in its first ever test match, scoring 82 in his first test innings. He carried his bat in an ODI match against England at the Sydney Cricket Ground in December 1994 and, just over three years later in March 1998, he carried his bat in Zimbabwe's first innings of the test against Pakistan at the Queens Sports Club in Bulawayo. He finished that innings with an unbeaten 156 and became the only batsman to have carried his bat in both test and ODI cricket.

[2] Hamilton Masakadza is a right-hand batsman, occasional right-arm leg-break bowler. He was born in Harare in 1983 and has played domestic cricket for Manicaland (2000-05), Easterns (2007-09) and Mountaineers (2009-18). He made his test debut 13 days before his 18th birthday against the West Indies in Harare in 2001, scoring a century in Zimbabwe's second innings and becoming the youngest test player to score a century on debut (a record since beaten by Bangladesh's Mohammad Ashraful). From 2001 until his final test in 2018, Masakadza played 38 tests and scored 2,223 runs at an average of 30.04.

[3] Brendan Taylor is Zimbabwe's highest rating batsman of the 2010s (Table L.9). He was born in Harare in 1986 and has played first-class domestic cricket since 2003 for Mashonaland, Northerns and, Mid-West Rhinos and county cricket for Nottinghamshire (2015-17). He played 34 tests from 2004 to 2021, scoring 2,320 runs at an average of 36.25. Taylor has scored centuries in both innings of a test match on two occasions, against Bangladesh in Harare in April 2013 and again against Bangladesh at Shere Bangla National Stadium in November 2018. He captained Zimbabwe in 16 tests between 2011 and 2021.

[4] David Houghton is the 2nd highest rating Zimbabwean batsman of all time. He was born in Bulawayo in 1957 and played for Zimbabwe's national cricket team from 1983 to 1997. He also represented his country in field hockey. He captained Zimbabwe in its first 4 test matches. He scored 121 in his maiden test innings

in Zimbabwe's first ever test match against India at Harare in 1992, to become the first player from Zimbabwe to score a test century. He played 22 tests from 1992 to 1997 and scored 1,464 runs at an average 43.06. He scored 266 against Sri Lanka in October 1994 at the Queens Sports Club in Bulawayo against a Sri Lankan attack that included Chaminda Vaas and Muttiah Muralitharan. This remains the highest test score by a Zimbabwean batsman. Houghton holds the record for scoring the most runs in a test career without ever making a duck.

[5] Andy Flower is the highest rating batsman ever to play for Zimbabwe. He is also the highest rating wicketkeeper from Zimbabwe. Born in Cape Town in 1968, he played domestic first-class cricket for Mashonaland (1993-2003), county cricket for Essex (2002-06) and a season for South Australia (2003/04). He played 63 tests from 1992 to 2002 and scored 4,794 runs at an average of 51.55. No Zimbabwean batsman has a higher batting average in test cricket or has scored more runs. He is the 60th highest rating test batsman (Table 2.7). He also kept wickets for Zimbabwe throughout his career, and with 151 dismissals (142 catches and 9 stumpings) at 1.57 dismissals/innings, he is the 17th highest rating test wicketkeeper (Table 2.18). He captained Zimbabwe in 20 tests between 1993 and 2000. During the 2003 World Cup, Andy Flower and teammate Henry Olonga publicly criticised the Zimbabwean Government policies and actions on human rights. After the World Cup, neither player ever represented Zimbabwe again. Andy Flower had a successful period as head coach of the England cricket team from 2009 to 2014 and in 2011 he was appointed an Officer of the Order of the British Empire (OBE) for services to sport.

[6] Guy Whittall was a right-hand batsman and right-arm medium-fast bowler. He was born in Chipinge in 1972 and played first-class cricket for Matabeleland (1993-99) and Manicaland (1999-2003). He played 46 test matches from 1993 to 2002, scoring 2,207 runs at 29.43 and taking 51 wickets at 40.94. He scored a test double century in 1997 at the Queens Sports Club in Bulawayo against a New Zealand attack that included Chris Cairns and Daniel Vettori. He was preferred to bat at No.6 here ahead of Craig Ervine because of his superior bowling rating.

[7] Heath Streak is Zimbabwe's highest rating bowler and the only Zimbabwean bowler to take over 200 test wickets. In fact, he is also the only Zimbabwean bowler to take over 100 test wickets. Born in Bulawayo in 1974, he played domestic first-class cricket for Matabeleland (1993-2004) and county cricket for Hampshire (1995) and Warwickshire (2004-07). He played 65 tests from 1993 to 2005, taking 216 wickets at a bowling average of 28.14 and scoring 1,990 runs at 22.36. He captained Zimbabwe in 21 tests. As captain, his career batting average was 36.18. After retirement, Streak has held several elite coaching positions, including head coach of the Zimbabwe national team and bowling coach of the Kolkata Knight Riders in the Indian Premier League.

[8] Paul Strang is the No.8 batsman and the older brother of Bryan Strang who is selected at No.9. Paul was born in Bulawayo in 1970 and was a right-arm leg break bowler and right-handed batsman. He played domestic, first-class cricket for Mashonaland (1993-2001) and Manicaland (2001-04) and county cricket for Kent (1997) and Nottinghamshire (1998). He played 24 tests from 1994 to 2001 and took 70 wickets at 36.03 and made 839 runs at 27.06.

[9] Bryan Strang was born in Bulawayo in 1972 and was a left-arm fast medium bowler, who took 56 wickets in 26 tests at an average of 39.34. He was an accurate, nagging bowler and, with a career economy rate of 2.43, he was difficult to get away.

[10] Ray Price is Zimbabwe's second highest rating test bowler. He was born in Salisbury, Rhodesia in 1976 and played first-class domestic cricket for Midlands (1999-2004), Mashonaland (2007-08) and Mashonaland eagles (2009-18) and county cricket for Worcestershire (2007-08). A left-arm orthodox spinner, he played 22 tests from 1999 to 2013 and took 80 wickets at a bowling average of 36.06. He is the nephew of Zimbabwean professional golfer Nick Price.

[11] Henry Olonga was born in Lusaka, Zambia in 1976 and became the youngest player to represent Zimbabwe when he made his debut against Pakistan in 1995 at the age of 18 years and 213 days. He was also the first ethnically black man to play for Zimbabwe. A right arm fast bowler, he played domestic cricket for Matabeleland (1993-99), Mashonaland A (2001-02) and Manicaland (2002-03). He played 30 tests from

1995 to 2002 and took 68 wickets at 38.53. In 2003 during the World Cup, and while still in his cricketing prime, his international career ended after he, and teammate Andy Flower, publicly protested against human rights abuses in Zimbabwe. He was forced to live in England after the World Cup following death threats and accusations of treason in Zimbabwe. Olonga and Flower were awarded honorary life memberships of the MCC later in 2003.

The Next 5 Highest Rating Zimbabwe Batsmen:

[1] Murray Goodwin is Zimbabwe's 3rd highest rating test batsman, but he only played 19 test matches and so is not eligible for inclusion in the top 11. Born in Salisbury, Rhodesia in 1972, his family emigrated to Western Australia where Goodwin grew up. He played domestic cricket for Western Australia between 1994 and 2007, for Mashonaland (1998-99) and county cricket for Sussex (2001-12) and Glamorgan (2013-14). He moved back to Zimbabwe to play test cricket for three years from 1998 to 2000, making 1,414 runs at an average of 42.85, with a top score of 166 not out against Pakistan in 1998 against an attack that included Waqar Younis, Shoaib Akhtar and Saqlain Mushtaq. Regularly at the top of the lists of run scorers for Western Australia and Sussex in first-class cricket, Goodwin remained the highest individual scorer for Sussex when he scored 344 not out against Somerset in 2009 beating his own previous record of 335 set six years earlier.

[2] Craig Ervine is a left-handed batsman who was born in Harare in 1985. He is unlucky not to be selected as the No. 6 batsman in the top 11, but Guy Whittall was preferred because of his bowling contribution. Ervine has played domestic first-class for Southern Rocks (2009-2011) and Matabeleland Tuskers 92011-2018). He made his test debut in 2011, and at the end of 2024, he has played 22 tests and scored 1,470 runs at an average of 35.85.

[3] Sikandar Raza was born in Sialkot in the Punjab, Pakistan in 1986 and emigrated to Zimbabwe with his family in 2002. He has played 17 tests for Zimbabwe, usually as a middle-order batsman, and has scored 1,187 runs at a batting average of 35.97. He is a handy medium pace bowler having taken 34 test wickets at a bowling average of 42.38.

[4] Tatenda Taibu was a wicketkeeper batsman who played domestic first-class cricket for Mashonaland (2000-05), Namibia (2006-07) and Northerns (2007-09). Born in Harare in 1983, he made his first-class debut at the age of 16 and his test debut at the age of 18. He played 28 test matches from 2001 to 2012 and scored 1,546 runs at 30.31. Behind the stumps, he took 55 catches and made 5 stumpings. He captained Zimbabwe in 10 test matches in 2004 and 2005 and he became the youngest test captain when he led the national team in a test against Sri Lanka in Harare in May 2004, a week before his 21st birthday.

[5] Alistair Campbell was a left-hand top-order batsman who played in Zimbabwe's first ever test match against India in 1992, batting at No.3. He captained his country in 21 tests, leading Zimbabwe to a rare series win against Pakistan in 1998/99. Born in Salisbury, Rhodesia in 1972, he played 60 tests from 1992 to 2002, scoring 2,858 test runs at an average of 27.22.

[6] Stuart Carlisle was a right-hand batsman who played 37 tests for Zimbabwe from 1995 to 2005, scoring 1,615 runs at 26.92. He was born in Salisbury Rhodesia in 1972 and captained his country in six tests in 2001 and 2002. He scored the first of his two test centuries against Australia at the Sydney Cricket Ground in October 2002.

The Next Highest Rating Zimbabwe Bowler:

[1] Andy Blignaut was a right-arm medium fast bowler and the 4th highest rating bowler from Zimbabwe, but he only played 19 tests and so was ineligible for selection in the top 11. He was also a hard-hitting lower-order left-hand batsman. He took 53 test wickets at an average of 37.06 and scored 886 runs at 26.85. Blignaut took 5/73 on his debut in 2001 against Bangladesh at Queens Sports Club and he is the only

Zimbabwean to take a hat-trick in test cricket (also against Bangladesh on 22 February 2004 at Harare). He played his final test in September 2005 against India (it would be Zimbabwe's final test for the next six years).

Table 13.28 Batting statistics of the best Zimbabwe team of all time [1]

The team

Player	No. of Innings	Not outs	100s	50s	0s	Highest score	Runs scored	Batting Avge	Strike rate	Batting Rating
1. Flower, G	123	6	6	15	16	201	3,457	29.55	34.53	55.5
2. Masakadza, H	76	2	5	8	10	158	2,223	30.04	44.38	48.3
3. Taylor, BRM	68	4	6	12	3	171	2,320	36.26	56.07	68.5
4. Houghton, DL	36	2	4	4	0	266	1,464	43.06	45.45	77.2
5. Flower, A	112	19	12	27	5	232	4,794	51.55	45.07	116.2
6. Whittall, GJ	82	7	4	10	6	203	2,207	29.43	41.08	49.9
7. Streak, HH	107	18	1	11	15	127	1,990	22.36	37.06	32.4
8. Strang, PA	41	10	1	2	3	106	839	27.06	43.74	28.1
9. Strang, BC	45	9	0	1	8	53	465	12.92	54.77	8.6
10. Price, RW	38	8	0	0	6	36	261	8.70	31.79	3.6
11. Olonga, HW	45	11	0	0	14	24	184	5.41	23.50	1.7
									Total	490.0

Next Batsmen:

Goodwin, MW [2]	37	4	3	8	4	166	1,414	42.85	46.32	72.1
Ervine, CR	44	3	4	5	2	160	1,470	35.85	50.67	58.1
Sikandar Raza [2]	33	0	1	8	3	127	1,187	35.97	55.16	55.2
Taibu, T	54	3	1	12	5	153	1,546	30.31	41.43	45.5
Campbell, ADR	109	4	2	18	10	103	2,858	27.22	41.77	45.5
Carlisle, SV	66	6	2	8	7	118	1,615	26.92	37.28	35.8

Notes: 1. Only 20 cricketers have played more than 20 matches for Zimbabwe.
2. Goodwin and Sikandar Raza played less than 20 matches and were therefore not considered for the top 11.

Table 13.29 Bowling statistics of the best Zimbabwe team of all time [1].

The team

Player	Overs	Maidens	Runs against	Wickets	5w/10w	Best	Bowling Avge	Strike rate	Economy rate	Bowling Rating
1. Flower, G	563	122	1,537	25	0/0	4/41	61.48	135.1	2.73	31.8
2. Masakadza, H	194	49	489	16	0/0	3/24	30.56	72.75	2.52	41.1
3. Taylor, BRM				Less than 100 overs						-
4. Houghton, DL				Less than 100 overs						-
5. Flower, A	Wicketkeeper					Less than 100 overs				-
6. Whittall, GJ	781	208	2,088	51	0/0	4/18	40.94	91.88	2.67	51.1
7. Streak, HH	2,260	595	6,079	216	7/0	6/73	28.14	62.77	2.69	99.7
8. Strang, PA	953	211	2,522	70	4/1	8/109	36.03	81.71	2.65	66.2
9. Strang, BC	905	304	2,203	56	1/0	5/101	39.34	97.00	2.43	58.2
10. Price, RW	1,022	242	2,885	80	5/1	6/73	36.06	76.69	2.82	69.5
11. Olonga, HW	750	129	2,620	68	2/0	5/70	38.53	66.21	3.49	55.9
									Total	473.5

Next Bowler:

Blignaut, AM [2]	529	99	1,964	53	3/0	5/73	37.06	59.89	3.70	61.1

Notes: 1. Only 20 cricketers have played more than 20 matches for Zimbabwe.
2. Blignaut played less than 20 matches and was therefore not considered for the top 11.

Table 13.30 Highest rating Zimbabwe wicketkeepers.

Wicketkeeper	Career span	No. of Innings	Catches	Stumpings	Total	Dismissals/ Innings	Wicketkeeper Rating
Flower, A	1992-02	96	142	9	151	1.57	116.3
Taibu, T	2001-12	40	55	5	60	1.50	72.2

The Best Bangladesh Team of All Time:

The highest rating Bangladesh team of all time is shown below, together with the next three highest rating batsmen, the next highest rating bowler and the next highest rating wicketkeeper. At the end of 2024, only 23 players from Bangladesh have played more than 20 test matches. The batting and bowling statistics and ratings of each of the players are shown in Tables 13.31, 13.32 and 13.33, respectively.

Players	Playing period	No. of tests	Batting style	Bowling style
1. Tamim Iqbal	2008-23	70	left	< 100
2. Litton Das	2015-24	48	right	W-K
3. Mominul Haque	2013-24	69	left	< 100
4. Habibul Bashar	2000-08	50	right	< 100
5. Shakib Al Hasan	2007-24	71	Left	LAO
6. Mushfiq Rahim	2005-24	94	right	W-K
7. Mahmudullah	2009-21	50	right	RAO
8. Mehidy Hasan	2016-24	51	right	RAO
9. Mashrafe Mortaza	2001-09	36	right	RAFM
10. Shahadat Hosain	2005-15	38	right	RAMF
11. Taijul Islam	2014-24	51	left	LAO

Next best batsmen:	Playing period	No. of tests	Batting style	Bowling style
Mohd. Ashraful	2001-13	61	right	RAL
Shahriar Nafees	2005-13	24	left	< 100
Imrul Kayes	2008-19	39	left	< 100

Next best bowler:

Mohd. Rafique	2000-08	33	left	LAO

Next best wicketkeeper:

Khaled Mashud	2000-07	44	right	W-K

The best Bangladesh team has the 2nd lowest total batting rating out of the 10 top-rating national teams and the lowest bowling rating. There are no Bangladesh batsmen in the top 100 of all time in Table 2.7 and no bowlers in the top 100 shown in Table 2.16. Shakib Al Hasan is the 5th highest rating all-rounder in Table 2.17, with career batting and bowling ratings both above 85. Of the top 11 players in the best ever team, 6 are still playing in 2024.

Top 11 Players:

[1] Tamim Iqbal opened the batting for Bangladesh in 70 test matches, from 2008 until 2023, and he scored 5,134 runs at an average of 38.89 and a strike rate of 58.00. He is Bangladesh's highest rating batsman. Born in Chittagong in 1989, he has played first-class domestic cricket for Chittagong Division from 2004 to 2023 and county cricket for Nottinghamshire (2011) and Essex (2017). He is the second highest run-scorer for Bangladesh in test cricket. No other batsman from Bangladesh has scored more international runs (tests, ODIs and T20s) and more centuries than Tamim Iqbal. He is the only batsman from Bangladesh to have reached the milestones of 15,000 international runs and 25 international centuries.

[2] Litton Das is one of the next best wicketkeepers in the highest rating world team of the 2020s (Chapter 12) and is the highest ranked wicketkeeper from Bangladesh (No. 31 in Table 2.18).

[3] Mominul Haque was born in Cox's Bazar in 1991, and he played domestic first-class cricket for Dhaka Division (2008-09) and Chittagong Division (2009-23). He made his test debut against Sri Lanka in 2013, and in 69 tests (up to the end of 2024), he scored 4,412 runs at an average of 37.08. No other Bangladesh batsman has scored more test centuries than Mominul Haque. He is the only batsman from Bangladesh to score a century in both innings of a test match, a feat he achieved against Sri Lanka at Chittagong on 4th February 2018.

[4] Habibul Bashar made his test debut in Bangladesh's first ever test match in November 2000 and played his final test against South Africa in 2008. In 50 tests, he scored 3,026 runs at an average of 30.88. He was born

in Nagakanda in 1972 and played domestic cricket for Biman Bangladesh Airlines and Khulna Division. He captained Bangladesh in 18 tests from 2004 to 2007, including Bangladesh's first ever test victory (against Zimbabwe in January 2005).

[5] Shakib Al Hasan is arguably the best current all-rounder in test cricket and the highest rating all-rounder in the world top team of the 2010s (see Chapter 11).

[6] Mushfiqur Rahim is the second highest rating Bangladeshi wicketkeeper and the 44th highest rating wicketkeeper of all time (Table 2.18). Born in Bogra in 1987, he plays domestic, first-class cricket for Rajshahi Division (2006-24) and made his test debut against England at Lords in 2005. At the end of 2024, he had played 94 tests and scored 6,007 runs at 37.78. He has scored more test runs for Bangladesh than any other batsman. In 99 innings as wicketkeeper, he has taken 98 catches and made 15 stumpings. In November 2018, he scored 219 against Zimbabwe in Dhaka to pass the previous highest score by a Bangladeshi batsman and to become the first wicketkeeper in test history to score two double centuries. On 24 February 2020, he scored his third double century also against Zimbabwe.

[7] Mohammad Mahmudullah is a right-hand middle-order batsman and a right arm off-spin bowler. Born in Mymensingh in 1986, Mahmudullah played domestic first-class cricket for Dhaka Division (2004-23) and played 50 test matches from 2009 to 2021. He has scored 2,914 runs at 33.49 and taken 43 wickets at 45.53. He has scored 5 centuries in test cricket and 3 ODI centuries. On 9th March 2015 he became the first Bangladeshi batsman to score a century in a World Cup match when he hit 102 against England at the Adelaide Oval. Four days later, against New Zealand at Seddon Park, he hit his 2nd World Cup century with 128 not out.

[8] Mehidy Hasan is a right arm off break bowler and a handy right-hand batsman. Born in Khulna in 1997, he has played first-class cricket for Khulna Division since 2015. He made his test debut against England in 2016, and by the end of 2024, he had played 51 tests, taken 190 wickets at 33.59 and scored 1,952nruns at 23.52. Against the West Indies in November 2018, Mehidy Hasan took 12 wickets for 117 runs, the best ever match figures for Bangladesh in test cricket.

[9] Mashrafe Mortaza was a right-arm fast-medium bowler who played test cricket from 2001 to 2009. He was born in Narail in 1983 and played first-class domestic cricket for Khulna Division. He made his debut in test cricket in November 2001 against Zimbabwe without ever having played a first-class match. He played 36 test matches and took 78 wickets at a bowling average of 41.53. Knee and back injuries led to his early retirement from test cricket. In December 2018, he was elected to a seat in the Bangladesh Parliament.

[10] Shahadat Hosain was a right-arm medium-fast bowler who played 38 test matches from 2005 to 2015 and took 72 wickets at 51.82. He was born in Narayanganj in 1986 and played domestic cricket for Dhaka Division (2005-21). Although Shahadat Hosain is not one of the top four highest rating Bangladeshi bowlers, he has been selected in the top 11 to ensure that the team has two pace bowlers.

[11] Taijul Islam is a left-arm orthodox spinner who made his test debut against the West Indies at the Arnos Vale Ground in St Vincent in September 2014, taking 5 wickets in the West Indies first innings. Born in Natore in 1992, he has played domestic cricket for Rajshahi Division and North Zone. By the end of 2024, he had played 51 tests and taken 217 test wickets at 31.74. He is Bangladesh's 2nd highest rating bowler. In only his 3rd test match, against Zimbabwe in November 2014 at the Shere Bangla National Stadium in Dhaka, he took 8 for 39, the best figures ever by a Bangladesh bowler.

The Next Highest Rating Bangladesh Batsmen:

[1] Mohammad Ashraful was a right-arm batsman and a right-arm leg break bowler, who played 61 test matches between 2001 and 2013, captaining his country in 13 test matches from 2007 to 2009. He was born in Brahmanbaria in 1984 and played first-class cricket for Dhaka Metropolis (2000-01 and 2011-23) and Dhaka Division (2001-11). He scored 2,737 runs at a batting average of 24.01 and took 20 test wickets at a bowling average of 62.45.

[2] Shahriar Nafees was a left-hand batsman who opened the batting in 20 of his 48 test innings between 2005 and 2013. He was born in Dhaka in 1985 and played domestic cricket for Barisal Blazers (2005-23). He played 24 test matches and scored 1,267 runs at 26.40.

[3] Imrul Kayes is a left-hand batsman who played 39 test matches between his debut against South African in 2008 and his final test against India in 2019. He was born in Meherpur in 1987 and played domestic cricket for Khulna Division (2006-23). He scored 1,797 test runs at a batting average of 24.28.

The Next Highest Rating Bangladesh Bowler:

[1] Mohammad Rafique is a left-arm orthodox bowler and left-hand batsman. He was born in Dhaka in 1970 and played domestic cricket for Dhaka Division (2000-08). He made his test debut against India in November 2000, in Bangladesh's first ever test match, and played his final test against South Africa in February 2008. In 33 tests, he took 100 wickets at a bowling average of 40.76. He was the first Bangladesh bowler to take 100 test wickets.

The Next Highest Rating Bangladesh Wicketkeeper:

[1] Khaled Mashud is the next highest rating Bangladesh wicketkeeper after Mushfiqur Rahim and Litton Das. He kept wickets for Bangladesh in its first ever test match and in 44 of its first 45 tests. Born in Rajshahi in 1976, he played domestic cricket for Rajshahi Division (1997-2011). A right-hand batsman, he played 44 test matches between 2000 and 2007, scored 1,409 test runs at an average of 19.04 and made 78 catches and 9 stumpings. He is the 69th highest rating test wicketkeeper (Table 2.18).

Table 13.31 Batting statistics of the best Bangladesh team of all time [1].

Batting Performances

Player	No. of Innings	Not outs	100s	50s	0s	Highest score	Runs scored	Batting Avge	Strike rate	Batting Rating
1. Tamim Iqbal	134	2	10	31	11	206	5,134	38.89	58.00	91.2
2. Litton Das [1]	84	2	4	17	2	141	2,788	34.00	58.82	64.4
3. Mominul Haque [1]	129	10	13	21	18	181	4,412	37.08	54.16	81.0
4. Habibul Bashar	99	1	3	24	7	113	3,026	30.88	60.28	59.8
5. Shakib Al Hasan [1]	130	8	5	31	6	217	4,609	37.78	61.68	86.1
6. Mushfiqur Rahim [1]	174	15	11	27	13	219	6,007	37.78	48.47	89.2
7. Mahmudullah	94	7	5	16	11	150	2,914	33.49	53.41	61.2
8. Mehidy Hasan [1]	93	10	1	9	6	103	1,952	23.52	49.80	34.2
9. Mashrafe Mortaza	67	5	0	3	12	79	797	12.85	67.20	10.6
10. Shahadat Hossain	69	17	0	0	10	40	521	10.02	45.94	6.0
11. Taijul Islam [1]	88	11	0	0	13	47	772	10.03	36.96	6.2
									Total	589.9

Next Batsmen:

Mohammad Ashraful	119	5	6	8	16	190	2,737	24.01	46.23	44.6
Shahriar Nafees	48	0	1	7	4	138	1,267	26.40	55.86	37.2
Imrul Kayes	76	2	3	4	4	150	1797	24.48	48.02	35.9

Next Wicketkeeper:

Khaled Mashud	84	10	1	3	11	103	1409	19.04	34.07	15.1

Notes: 1. Only 22 cricketers have played more than 20 matches for Bangladesh.
2. Litton Das, Mominul Haque, Shakib al Hasan, Mushfiqur Rahim, Mehidy Hasan and Taijul Islam are still playing in 2024.

Table 13.32 Bowling statistics of the best Bangladesh team of all time [1].

Bowling Performances:

Player	Overs	Maids	Runs against	Wkts	5w/10w	Best	Bowling Avge	Strike rate	Economy rate	Bowling Rating
1. Tamim Iqbal	Less than 100 overs									-
2. Litton Das [1]	Did not bowl									-
3. Mominul Haque [1]	147	11	562	10	0/0	3/4	56.20	88.30	3.82	11.6
4. Habibul Bashar	Less than 100 overs									-
5. Shakib Al Hasan [1]	2,612	485	7,804	246	19/2	7/36	31.72	63.72	2.99	101.4
6. Mushfiqur Rahim [1]	Wicketkeeper				Did not bowl					-
7. Mahmudullah	570	56	1,958	43	1/0	5/51	45.53	79.60	3.43	37.7
8. Mehidy Hasan [1]	2,011	299	6,382	190	10/2	7/58	33.59	63.52	3.17	86.7
9. Mashrafe Mortaza	998	202	3,239	78	0/0	4/60	41.53	76.79	3.24	50.6
10. Shahadat Hossain	896	92	3,731	72	4/0	6/27	51.82	74.72	4.16	37.0
11. Taijul Islam [1]	2,261	403	6,888	217	15/2	8/39	31.74	62.53	3.05	98.2
									Total	423.2

Next Bowler:

Mohd. Rafique	1,457	301	4,076	100	7/0	6/122	40.76	87.44	2.80	60.8

Notes: 1. Only 22 cricketers have played more than 20 matches for Bangladesh.

2. Litton Das, Mominul Haque, Shakib al Hasan, Mushfiqur Rahim, Mehidy Hasan and Taijul Islam are still playing in 2024.

Table 13.33 Highest rating Bangladesh wicketkeepers.

| Wicketkeeper | Career span | No. of Innings | Dismissals | | | Dismissals/ Innings | Wicketkeeper Rating |
			Catches	Stumpings	Total		
Mushfiqur Rahim	2005-23	99	98	15	113	1.14	86.4
Litton Das	2015-24	62	94	14	108	1.74	94.2
Khaled Mashud	2000-07	61	78	9	87	1.43	61.9

Appendix A
The Highest Rating Test Batsmen and Bowlers

The career batting details for the 377 batsmen who played more than 20 test matches before the end of 2024 and whose batting rating exceeded 50 are given in Table A.1 and the career bowling details for the 353 bowlers who played more than 20 tests and whose bowling rating exceeded 50 are given in Table A.2. The tables include the data from all test matches played before the end of 2024.

Of the 377 highest rating batsmen:

(i) 79 represented Australia, 78 England, 41 India, 37 West Indies, 38 South Africa, 39 Pakistan, 33 New Zealand, 22 Sri Lanka, 7 Bangladesh and 4 Zimbabwe. One batsman, Kepler Wessels, represented both Australia and South Africa at different times.

(ii) 269 were right handers and 108 batted left-handed.

(iii) 18 played some of their matches before World War 1 (i.e., 1877-1914); 50 played in the period 1920-1949; 50 in the 1950s; 67 in the 1960s; 71 in the 1970s; 85 in the 1980s; 100 in the 1990s; 124 in the 2000s; and 121 in the 2010s.

Of course, many of these batsmen played in more than one of these time periods.

Of the 350 highest rating bowlers:

(i) 75 represented England, 66 Australia, 42 India, 41 West Indies, 37 Pakistan, 34 New Zealand, 28 South Africa, 18 Sri Lanka, 6 Zimbabwe and 5 Bangladesh.

(ii) 276 were right-arm bowlers and 77 were left-arm bowlers.

(iii) 57 were right arm fast bowlers, 112 were right arm fast medium or medium fast bowlers, 30 bowled right arm medium pace, 46 were right arm off-break bowlers, 30 bowled right arm leg breaks, 5 were left-arm fast bowlers, 26 bowled left-arm medium, medium fast or fast medium and 44 were left-arm orthodox spin bowlers.

(iv) 23 played some of their matches before World War 1, 41 played in the period 1920-1949, 48 in the 1950s, 65 in the 1960s, 83 in the 1970s, 80 in the 1980s, 98 in the 1990s, 113 in the 2000s, and 98 in the 2010s. Of course, many of these bowlers played in more than one of these time periods.

Table A.1 Batsmen with a career test batting rating of 50 or more (20 or more matches up to 2024).

Batsman	Country	Career	Mat.	Inn.	N.O.	100s	50s	0s	H.S.	Runs	Avge	S.R.	Rating
1 Bradman, DG	Australia	1928-48	52	80	10	29	13	7	334	6996	99.94	54.95	310.0
2 Tendulkar, SR	India	1989-13	200	329	33	51	68	14	248	15921	53.79	54.12	183.7
3 Sangakkara, KC	S. Lanka	2000-15	134	233	17	38	52	11	319	12400	57.41	54.19	177.8
4 Kallis, JH	S Africa	1995-13	166	280	40	45	58	16	224	13289	55.37	45.98	170.9
5 Lara, BC	W Indies	1990-06	131	232	6	34	48	17	400	11953	52.89	60.52	168.4
6 Ponting, RT	Australia	1995-12	168	287	29	41	62	17	257	13378	51.85	58.72	168.2
7 Root, JE [1]	England	2012-24	152	278	23	36	65	13	262	12972	50.87	57.48	163.4
8 Dravid, R	India	1996-12	164	286	32	36	63	8	270	13288	52.31	42.51	163.1

Batsman	Country	Career	Mat.	Inn.	N.O.	100s	50s	0s	H.S.	Runs	Avge	S.R.	Rating
9 Smith, SPD [1]	Australia	2010-24	113	202	25	34	41	11	239	9962	56.28	53.54	159.6
10 Jayawardene, DPMD	S Lanka	1997-14	149	252	15	34	50	15	374	11814	49.85	51.47	157.0
11 Sobers, GStA	W Indies	1954-74	93	160	21	26	30	12	365	8032	57.78	49.62	156.5
12 Williamson, KS [1]	N Zeal.	2010-24	105	186	17	33	37	11	251	9276	54.89	51.78	153.0
13 Hammond, WR	England	1927-47	85	140	16	22	24	4	336	7249	58.46	49.53	152.0
14 Chanderpaul, S	W Indies	1994-15	164	280	49	30	66	15	203	11867	51.37	43.32	151.4
15 Brook, HC	England	2022-24	24	40	1	8	10	2	317	2281	58.49	88.38	150.3
16 Barrington, KF	England	1955-68	82	131	15	20	35	5	256	6806	58.67	48.86	150.2
17 Younis Khan	Pakistan	2000-17	118	213	19	34	33	19	313	10099	52.06	52.12	150.0
18 Hutton, L	England	1937-55	79	138	15	19	33	5	364	6971	56.67	50.00	149.2
19 Hayden, ML	Australia	1994-09	103	184	14	30	29	14	380	8625	50.74	60.11	146.4
20 Waugh, SR	Australia	1985-04	168	260	46	32	50	22	200	10927	51.06	48.65	146.3
21 Gavaskar, SM	India	1971-87	125	214	16	34	45	12	236	10122	51.12	48.03	146.0
22 Cook, AN	England	2006-18	161	291	16	33	57	9	294	12472	45.35	46.96	146.0
23 Border, AR	Australia	1978-94	156	265	44	27	63	11	205	11174	50.56	40.98	145.1
24 Sehwag, V	India	2001-13	104	180	6	23	32	16	319	8586	49.34	82.21	144.7
25 Sutcliffe, H	England	1924-35	54	84	9	16	23	2	194	4555	60.73	46.77	144.7
26 Javed Miandad	Pakistan	1976-93	124	189	21	23	43	6	280	8832	52.57	48.36	143.0
27 Richards, IVA	W Indies	1974-91	121	182	12	24	45	10	291	8540	50.24	60.82	142.4
28 Inzamam-ul-Haq	Pakistan	1992-07	120	200	22	25	46	15	329	8830	49.61	54.02	141.2
29 De Villiers, AB	Sth Africa	2004-18	114	191	18	22	46	8	278	8765	50.66	54.53	140.4
30 Chappell, GS	Australia	1970-84	87	151	19	24	31	12	247	7110	53.86	51.52	138.2
31 Smith, GC	Sth Africa	2002-14	117	205	13	27	38	11	277	9265	48.26	59.69	138.1
32 Clarke, MJ	Aust.	2004-15	115	198	22	28	27	9	329	8643	49.11	55.92	137.5
33 Pollock, RG	Sth Africa	1963-70	23	41	4	7	11	1	274	2256	60.97	50.83	137.5
34 Weekes, E	W Indies	1948-58	48	81	5	15	19	6	207	4455	58.62	50.00	136.9
35 Hobbs, JB	England	1908-30	61	102	7	15	28	4	211	5410	56.95	49.69	136.5
36 Headley, GA	W Indies	1930-54	22	40	4	10	5	2	270	2190	60.83	50.00	136.5
37 Mohammad Yousuf	Pakistan	1998-10	90	156	12	24	33	11	223	7530	52.29	52.4	135.3
38 Amla, HM	Sth Africa	2004-19	124	215	16	28	41	13	311	9282	46.64	49.97	134.1
39 Warner, DA [1]	Australia	2011-24	112	205	8	26	37	13	335	8786	44.60	70.19	134.0
40 Kohli, V [1]	India	2011-24	122	208	13	30	31	15	254	9207	47.22	55.71	132.5
41 Walcott, CL	W Indies	1948-60	44	74	7	15	14	1	220	3798	56.69	50.00	130.6
42 Voges, AC	Australia	2015-16	20	31	7	5	4	2	269	1485	61.88	55.68	129.7
43 Pietersen, KP	England	2005-14	104	181	8	23	35	10	227	8181	47.29	61.72	128.4
44 Laxman, VVS	India	1996-12	134	225	34	17	56	14	281	8781	45.97	49.37	127.9
45 Boycott, G	England	1964-82	108	193	23	22	42	10	246	8114	47.73	38.17	123.8
46 Hussey, MEK	Australia	2005-13	79	137	16	19	29	12	195	6235	51.53	50.13	123.7
47 Gooch, GA	England	1975-95	118	215	6	20	46	13	333	8900	42.58	49.24	123.0
48 Lloyd, CH	W Indies	1966-84	110	175	14	19	39	4	242	7515	46.68	51.22	122.1
49 Compton, DCS	England	1937-57	78	131	15	17	28	10	278	5807	50.06	50.12	122.0
50 Gilchrist, AC	Australia	1999-08	96	137	20	17	26	14	204	5570	47.61	81.96	121.3
51 Taylor, LRPL	N Zeal.	2007-22	112	196	24	19	35	14	290	7683	44.67	59.28	120.9
52 Paynter, E	England	1931-39	20	31	5	4	7	3	243	1540	59.23	50.00	120.0
53 Langer, JL	Australia	1993-07	105	182	12	23	30	11	250	7696	45.27	54.23	119.8
54 Taylor, MA	Australia	1989-99	104	186	13	19	40	5	334	7525	43.5	41.48	117.3
55 Harvey, RN	Australia	1948-63	79	137	10	21	24	7	205	6149	48.42	50.00	117.2
56 Walters, KD	Australia	1965-81	74	125	14	15	33	4	250	5357	48.26	49.56	116.9
57 Gower, DI	England	1978-92	117	204	18	18	39	7	215	8231	44.25	50.6	116.6
58 Mathews, AD [1]	S Lanka	2009-24	116	206	27	16	44	6	200	8042	44.93	48.43	116.4
59 Kirsten, G	S Africa	1993-04	101	176	15	21	34	13	275	7289	45.27	43.43	116.4
60 Flower, A	Zimb	1992-02	63	112	19	12	27	5	232	4794	51.55	45.07	116.2
61 Nourse, AD	S Africa	1935-51	34	62	7	9	14	3	231	2960	53.82	50.00	115.7
62 Bell, IR	England	2004-15	118	205	24	22	46	14	235	7727	42.69	49.46	115.7
63 Kanhai, RB	W Indies	1957-74	79	137	6	15	28	7	256	6227	47.53	49.93	115.1
64 Gayle, CH	W Indies	2000-14	103	182	11	15	37	15	333	7214	42.19	60.27	115.0
65 Greenidge, CG	W Indies	1974-91	108	185	16	19	34	11	226	7558	44.72	50.09	114.7
66 Cowdrey, MC	England	1954-75	114	188	15	22	38	9	182	7624	44.07	47.51	113.5
67 Samaraweera, TT	S Lanka	2001-13	81	132	20	14	30	11	231	5462	48.77	46.92	113.0
68 Azharuddin, M	India	1984-00	99	147	9	22	21	5	199	6215	45.04	54.64	110.7
69 Waugh, ME	Australia	1991-02	128	209	17	20	47	19	153	8029	41.82	52.27	110.4
70 Jayasuriya, ST	S Lanka	1991-07	110	188	14	14	31	15	340	6973	40.07	65.13	109.8
71 Azhar Ali	Pakistan	2010-22	97	180	11	19	35	19	302	7142	42.29	41.93	109.4
72 Thorpe, GP	England	1993-05	100	179	28	16	39	12	200	6744	44.66	45.90	109.2
73 Simpson, RB	Australia	1957-78	62	111	7	10	27	8	311	4869	46.82	49.23	109.0
74 Pujara, CA	India	2010-23	103	176	11	19	35	12	206	7195	43.61	44.37	108.9
75 Boon, DC [1]	Australia	1984-96	107	190	20	21	32	16	200	7422	43.66	40.97	108.2
76 Ganguly, SC	India	1996-08	113	188	17	16	35	13	239	7212	42.18	51.26	108.0
77 Worrell, FMM	W Indies	1948-63	51	87	9	9	22	11	261	3860	49.49	49.72	107.8

Batsman	Country	Career	Mat.	Inn.	N.O.	100s	50s	0s	H.S.	Runs	Avge	S.R.	Rating
78 May, PBH	England	1951-61	66	106	9	13	22	8	285	4537	46.77	50.00	107.8
79 Labuschagne, M [1]	Australia	2018-24	54	97	7	11	23	4	215	4338	48.20	52.01	107.8
80 De Silva, PA	S Lanka	1984-02	93	159	11	20	22	7	267	6361	42.98	50.94	107.6
81 Lawry, WM	Australia	1961-71	67	123	12	13	27	6	210	5234	47.15	47.11	107.2
82 Haynes, DL	W Indies	1978-94	116	202	25	18	39	10	184	7487	42.30	45.22	107.1
83 Stewart, AJ	England	1990-03	133	235	21	15	45	14	190	8463	39.55	48.67	106.6
84 Crowe, MD	N Zeal.	1982-95	77	131	11	17	18	9	299	5444	45.37	44.66	106.5
85 Dexter, ER	England	1958-68	62	102	8	9	27	6	205	4502	47.89	49.71	105.4
86 Karunaratne, FDM [1]	Sri Lanka	2012-24	98	187	7	16	39	12	244	7165	39.81	51.56	104.8
87 Trescothick, ME	England	2000-06	76	143	10	14	29	12	219	5825	43.8	54.52	104.3
88 Misbah-ul-Haq	Pakistan	2001-17	75	132	20	10	39	9	161	5222	46.63	44.53	104.1
89 Saleem Malik	Pakistan	1982-99	103	154	22	15	29	12	237	5768	43.70	50.28	104.0
90 Chandimal, LD [1]	S Lanka	2011-24	86	154	15	16	30	8	206	6019	43.3	50.18	103.9
91 Richardson, RB	W Indies	1983-95	86	146	12	16	27	8	194	5949	44.40	47.78	103.8
92 Mitchell, B	S Africa	1929-49	42	80	9	8	21	3	189	3471	48.89	50.00	103.0
93 Fleming, SP	N Zeal.	1994-08	111	189	10	9	46	16	274	7172	40.07	45.83	103.0
94 Vengsarkar, DB	India	1976-92	116	185	22	17	35	15	166	6868	42.13	47.76	102.5
95 Khawaja, UT [1]	Australia	2011-24	77	139	13	15	27	8	195	5592	44.38	48.17	102.4
96 Zaheer Abbas	Pakistan	1969-85	78	124	11	12	20	10	274	5062	44.80	52.66	102.3
97 McCullum, BB	N Zeal.	2004-16	101	176	9	12	31	14	302	6453	38.64	64.6	102.1
98 Saeed Anwar	Pakistan	1990-01	55	91	2	11	25	8	188	4052	45.53	55.77	102.1
99 Viswanath, GR	India	1969-83	91	155	10	14	35	10	222	6080	41.93	48.33	101.7
100 Strauss, AJ	England	2004-12	100	178	6	21	27	15	177	7037	40.91	48.92	101.5
101 Martyn, DR	Australia	1992-06	67	109	14	13	23	7	165	4406	46.38	51.41	101.4
102 Cullinan, DJ	S Africa	1993-01	70	115	12	14	20	10	275	4554	44.21	48.97	100.6
103 Edrich, JH	England	1963-76	77	127	9	12	24	6	310	5138	43.54	41.05	100.5
104 Gibbs, HH	S Africa	1996-08	90	154	7	14	26	11	228	6167	41.95	50.26	99.8
105 Sarwan, RR	W Indies	2000-11	87	154	8	15	31	12	291	5842	40.01	46.8	99.5
106 Hanif Mohammad	Pakistan	1952-69	55	97	8	12	15	5	337	3915	43.99	48.01	99.2
107 Hendren, EH	England	1920-35	51	83	9	7	21	4	205	3525	47.64	47.97	98.7
108 Dilshan, TM	S Lanka	1999-13	87	145	11	16	23	14	193	5492	40.99	65.55	98.6
109 Ryder, J	Australia	1920-29	20	32	5	3	9	1	201	1394	51.63	47.50	98.4
110 Graveney, TW	England	1951-69	79	123	13	11	20	8	258	4882	44.38	48.62	98.4
111 Slater, MJ	Australia	1993-01	74	131	7	14	21	9	219	5312	42.84	53.3	98.4
112 Morris, AR	Australia	1946-55	46	79	3	12	12	4	206	3533	46.49	49.12	97.9
113 McCabe, SJ	Australia	1930-38	39	62	5	6	13	4	232	2748	48.21	54.15	97.6
114 Atherton, MA	England	1989-01	115	212	7	16	46	20	185	7728	37.7	37.32	97.5
115 Katich, SM	Australia	2001-10	56	99	6	10	25	4	157	4188	45.03	49.38	96.6
116 Vaughan, MP	England	1999-08	82	147	9	18	18	9	197	5719	41.44	51.13	96.5
117 Chappell, IM	Australia	1964-80	75	136	10	14	26	11	196	5345	42.42	48.22	96.4
118 Stokes, BA [1]	England	2013-24	110	198	9	13	35	15	258	6719	35.55	59.72	95.8
119 Jones, DM	Australia	1984-92	52	89	11	11	14	11	216	3631	46.55	48.89	95.7
120 Ponsford, W	Australia	1924-34	29	48	4	7	6	1	266	2122	48.23	48.36	95.7
121 Hassett, AL	Australia	1938-53	43	69	3	10	11	1	198	3073	46.56	49.09	95.7
122 Babar Azam [1]	Pakistan	2016-24	56	102	9	9	27	8	196	4051	43.56	54.49	95.5
123 Kallicharran, AI	W Indies	1972-80	66	109	10	12	21	10	187	4399	44.43	49.21	95.3
124 Nurse, SM	W Indies	1960-69	29	54	1	6	10	3	258	2523	47.60	50.00	95.1
125 Cowper, RM	Australia	1964-68	27	46	2	5	10	3	307	2061	46.84	50.00	94.9
126 Amiss, DL	England	1966-77	50	88	10	11	11	10	262	3612	46.31	43.00	94.3
127 Latham, TWM [1]	N Zeal.	2014-24	88	158	6	13	31	13	264	5834	38.38	47.5	93.9
128 Head, TM	Australia	2018-23	53	88	5	9	17	7	175	3583	43.17	67.02	92.4
129 Smith, RA	England	1988-96	62	112	15	9	28	8	175	4236	43.67	45.65	92.3
130 Redpath, IR	Australia	1964-76	66	120	11	8	31	9	171	4737	43.46	42.64	92.1
131 Trott, IJL	England	2009-15	52	93	6	9	19	8	226	3835	44.08	47.18	92.0
132 Hunte, CC	W Indies	1958-67	44	78	6	8	13	5	260	3245	45.07	47.58	91.7
133 Barlow, EJ	S Africa	1961-70	30	57	2	6	15	3	201	2516	45.75	48.00	91.3
134 Tamim Iqbal	Bangladesh	2008-23	70	134	2	10	31	11	206	5134	38.89	58	91.2
135 Turner, GM	N Zeal.	1969-83	41	73	6	7	14	1	259	2991	44.64	45.14	90.4
136 Hazare, VS	India	1946-53	30	52	6	7	9	4	164	2192	47.65	48.59	90.2
137 Sharma, RG [1]	India	2013-24	67	116	10	12	18	6	212	4301	40.58	57.06	89.8
138 Gambhir, G	India	2004-16	58	104	5	9	22	7	206	4154	41.96	51.49	89.8
139 Jackson, FS	England	1893-05	20	33	4	5	6	3	144	1415	48.79	50	89.8
140 Leyland, M	England	1928-38	41	65	5	9	10	6	187	2764	46.07	46.94	89.6
141 Fredericks, RC	W Indies	1968-77	59	109	7	8	26	7	169	4334	42.49	49.35	89.6
142 Umrigar, PR	India	1948-62	59	94	8	12	14	5	223	3631	42.22	50.00	89.5
143 Lehmann, DS	Australia	1998-04	27	42	2	5	10	2	177	1798	44.95	61.81	89.3
144 Mushfiqur Rahim	Bangla	2005-24	94	174	15	11	27	13	219	6007	37.78	48.47	89.2
145 Tillakaratne, HP	S Lanka	1989-04	83	131	25	11	20	9	204	4545	42.88	40.35	89.1
146 Atapattu, MS	S Lanka	1990-07	90	156	15	16	17	22	249	5502	39.02	44.48	88.9

Batsman	Country	Career	Mat.	Inn.	N.O.	100s	50s	0s	H.S.	Runs	Avge	S.R.	Rating
147 Amarnath, M	India	1969-88	69	113	10	11	24	12	138	4378	42.50	49.41	88.8
148 Hooper, CL	W Indies	1987-02	102	173	15	13	27	13	233	5762	36.47	50.27	88.4
149 Brown, WA	Australia	1934-48	22	35	1	4	9	1	206	1592	46.82	42.44	88.3
150 Hussain, N	England	1990-04	96	171	16	14	33	14	207	5764	37.19	40.39	88.2
151 Rowe, LG	W Indies	1972-80	30	49	2	7	7	2	302	2047	43.55	49.05	88.0
152 Dhoni, MS	India	2005-14	90	144	16	6	33	10	224	4876	38.09	59.11	88.0
153 Hardstaff, J (Jnr)	England	1935-48	23	38	3	4	10	4	205	1636	46.74	47.71	88.0
154 O'Neill, NC	Australia	1958-65	42	69	8	6	15	6	181	2779	45.56	49.47	87.6
155 Bland, KC	S Africa	1961-66	21	39	5	3	9	2	144	1669	49.09	50.00	87.6
156 Bairstow, JM [1]	England	2012-24	100	178	12	12	26	17	167	6042	36.4	59.07	86.8
157 Dhananjaya de Silva [1]	S Lanka	2016-24	61	108	8	12	19	9	173	4011	40.11	58.28	86.8
158 Rahane, AM	India	2013-23	85	144	12	12	26	10	188	5077	38.46	49.5	86.7
159 Woodfull, WM	Australia	1926-34	35	54	4	7	13	6	161	2300	46.00	39.73	86.6
160 Mitchell, DJ [1]	N Zeal	2019-24	31	52	5	5	14	1	190	2059	43.81	53.38	86.6
161 Butcher, BF	W Indies	1958-69	44	78	6	7	16	3	209	3104	43.11	49.71	86.6
162 Elgar, D	S Africa	2012-24	86	152	11	14	23	13	199	5347	37.92	47.78	86.5
163 Shakib Al Hasan	Bangla	2007-24	71	130	8	5	31	6	217	4609	37.78	61.68	86.1
164 Pant, RR [1]	India	2018-24	42	73	5	6	14	3	159	2847	41.87	73.51	85.9
165 Collingwood, PD	England	2003-11	68	115	10	10	20	6	206	4259	40.56	46.66	85.7
166 Rogers, CJL	Australia	2008-15	25	48	1	5	14	1	173	2015	42.87	50.6	84.4
167 Prior, MJ	England	2007-14	79	123	21	7	28	13	131	4099	40.19	61.67	84.3
168 du Plessis, F	S Africa	2012-21	69	118	14	10	21	9	199	4163	40.03	46.33	83.8
169 Shoaib Mohammad	Pakistan	1983-95	45	68	7	7	13	6	203	2705	44.34	40.52	83.5
170 Sidhu, NS	India	1983-99	51	78	2	9	15	9	201	3202	42.13	44.39	83.5
171 Astle, NJ	N Zeal.	1996-06	81	137	10	11	24	11	222	4702	37.02	49.6	83.2
172 Richardson, MH	N Zeal.	2000-04	38	65	3	4	19	1	145	2776	44.77	37.67	83.0
173 Duckett, BM [1]	England	2016-24	32	60	3	4	13	4	182	2270	39.82	85.89	82.6
174 McGlew, DJ	S Africa	1951-62	34	64	6	7	10	4	255	2440	42.07	50.00	82.6
175 Asad Shafiq	Pakistan	2010-20	77	128	6	12	27	13	137	4660	38.2	48.6	82.5
176 Wright, JG	N Zeal.	1978-93	82	148	7	12	23	7	185	5334	37.83	35.54	82.2
177 Mushtaq Mohammad	Pakistan	1959-79	57	100	7	10	19	4	201	3643	39.17	46.32	81.8
178 Botham, IT	England	1977-92	102	161	6	14	22	14	208	5200	33.55	60.71	81.8
179 Jones, AH	N Zealand	1987-95	39	74	8	7	11	2	186	2922	44.27	39.26	81.8
180 Washbrook, C	England	1937-56	37	66	6	6	12	2	195	2569	42.82	50.00	81.7
181 de Kock, Q	Sth Africa	2014-21	54	91	6	6	22	7	141	3300	38.82	70.94	81.3
182 Taylor, HW	Sth Africa	1912-32	42	76	4	7	17	2	176	2936	40.78	50.00	81.2
183 Mendis, BKG [1]	Sri Lanka	2015-24	69	129	5	10	19	14	245	4478	36.11	57.92	81.1
184 Mominul Haque [1]	Bangladesh	2013-24	69	129	10	13	21	18	181	4412	37.08	54.16	81.0
185 Pullar, G	England	1959-63	28	49	4	4	12	3	175	1974	43.87	50.00	80.9
186 Yallop, GN	Australia	1976-84	39	70	3	8	9	3	268	2756	41.13	44.10	80.9
187 Rowan, EAB	S Africa	1935-51	26	50	5	3	12	4	236	1965	43.67	50.00	80.8
188 Brathwaite, KC	W Indies	2011-23	96	185	10	12	30	18	212	5851	33.43	40.65	80.5
189 Mudassar Nazar	Pakistan	1976-89	76	116	8	10	17	7	231	4114	38.09	45.80	80.3
190 Greig, AW	England	1972-77	58	93	4	8	20	5	148	3599	40.44	46.54	80.3
191 Prince, AG	S Africa	2002-11	66	104	16	11	11	7	162	3665	41.65	43.71	80.1
192 Jardine, DR	England	1928-34	22	33	6	1	10	2	127	1296	48.00	44.81	79.7
193 Macartney, CG	Australia	1907-26	35	55	4	7	9	1	170	2131	41.78	52.04	79.5
194 Hill, C	Australia	1896-12	49	89	2	7	19	9	191	3412	39.22	53.67	79.4
195 Hughes, KJ	Australia	1977-84	70	124	6	9	22	10	213	4415	37.42	42.79	79.0
196 Vijay, M	India	2008-18	61	105	1	12	15	8	167	3982	38.29	46.3	78.4
197 Fletcher, KWR	England	1968-82	59	96	14	7	19	6	216	3272	39.90	41.34	78.4
198 Mohammad Hafeez	Pakistan	2003-18	55	105	8	10	12	8	224	3652	37.65	56.01	78.3
199 Lamb, AJ	England	1982-92	79	139	10	14	18	9	142	4656	36.09	51.4	78.2
200 Bardsley, W	Australia	1909-26	41	66	5	6	14	6	193	2469	40.48	53.53	78.0
201 Trumper, VT	Australia	1899-12	48	89	8	8	13	7	214	3163	39.05	54.55	77.9
202 Dhawan, S	India	2013-18	34	58	1	7	5	4	190	2315	40.61	66.95	77.8
203 Ranatunga, A	S Lanka	1982-00	93	155	12	4	38	12	135	5105	35.70	49.74	77.8
204 Majid Khan	Pakistan	1964-83	63	106	5	8	19	9	167	3931	38.92	48.07	77.7
205 Wessels, KC	Aust/S Af	1982-94	40	71	3	6	15	5	179	2788	41	46.48	77.6
206 Agarwal, MA	India	2018-22	21	36	0	4	6	1	243	1488	41.33	53.49	77.2
207 Sutcliffe, B	N Zeal.	1947-65	42	76	8	5	15	5	230	2727	40.10	49.88	77.2
208 Houghton, DL	Zimb	1992-97	22	36	2	4	4	0	266	1464	43.06	45.45	77.2
209 Edrich, WJ	England	1938-55	39	63	2	6	13	3	219	2440	40.00	46.47	77.2
210 Asif Iqbal	Pakistan	1964-80	58	99	7	11	12	9	175	3575	38.86	49.18	77.1
211 Ijaz Ahmed	Pakistan	1987-01	60	92	4	12	12	7	211	3315	37.67	45.37	77.0
212 Saeed Ahmed	Pakistan	1958-72	41	78	4	5	16	2	172	2991	40.42	49.11	76.7
213 Stollmeyer, JB	W Indies	1939-55	32	56	5	4	12	2	160	2159	42.33	50.00	76.3
214 Booth, BC	Australia	1961-66	29	48	6	5	10	5	169	1773	42.21	49.61	76.1
215 Gatting, MW	England	1978-95	79	138	14	10	21	16	207	4409	35.56	45.16	75.5

Batsman	Country	Career	Mat.	Inn.	N.O.	100s	50s	0s	H.S.	Runs	Avge	S.R.	Rating
216 McDonald, CC	Australia	1952-61	47	83	4	5	17	2	170	3107	39.33	50.00	75.3
217 Adams, JC	W Indies	1992-01	54	90	17	6	14	7	208	3012	41.26	37.57	75.0
218 Watling, BJ	N Zeal.	2009-21	75	117	16	8	19	10	205	3790	37.52	42.61	74.9
219 Manjrekar, VL	India	1951-65	55	92	10	7	15	11	189	3208	39.12	50.00	74.7
220 McMillan, CD	N Zeal.	1997-05	55	91	10	6	19	7	142	3116	38.47	54.93	74.1
221 Gomes, HA	W Indies	1976-87	60	91	11	9	13	5	143	3171	39.64	43.86	74.1
222 Taufeeq Umar	Pakistan	2001-14	44	83	5	7	14	6	236	2963	37.99	44.71	74.1
223 Bravo, DM	W Indies	2010-20	56	102	5	8	17	5	218	3538	36.47	44.86	74.0
224 Faulkner, GA	S Africa	1906-24	25	47	4	4	8	2	204	1754	40.79	52.16	73.0
225 Nicholls, HM	N Zeal.	2016-23	56	87	7	9	12	6	200	2973	37.16	50.2	73.0
226 Kapil Dev	India	1978-94	131	184	15	8	27	16	163	5248	31.05	54.87	72.8
227 D'Oliveira, BL	England	1966-72	44	70	8	5	15	4	158	2484	40.06	46.10	72.8
228 Stackpole, KR	Australia	1966-74	43	80	5	7	14	5	207	2807	37.43	48.78	72.7
229 Shahid Afridi	Pakistan	1998-10	27	48	1	5	8	6	156	1716	36.51	86.97	72.1
230 Shastri, RJ	India	1981-92	80	121	14	11	12	9	206	3830	35.79	42.26	71.8
231 Imran Khan	Pakistan	1971-92	88	126	25	6	18	8	136	3807	37.69	49.29	71.7
232 Samuels, MN	W Indies	2000-16	71	127	7	7	24	14	260	3917	32.64	47.66	71.7
233 Symonds, A	Australia	2004-08	26	41	5	2	10	4	162	1462	40.61	64.81	71.6
234 Bavuma, T [1]	S Africa	2014-24	62	107	13	3	24	10	172	3500	37.23	48.97	71.3
235 Butcher, MA	England	1997-04	71	131	7	8	23	10	173	4288	34.58	42.02	71.3
236 Ames, LEG	England	1929-39	47	72	12	8	7	5	149	2434	40.57	46.33	71.3
237 Watson, SR	Australia	2005-15	59	109	3	4	24	6	176	3731	35.2	52.59	71.2
238 Boucher, MV	S Africa	1997-12	147	206	24	5	35	17	125	5515	30.30	50.11	71.1
239 Sardesai, DN	India	1961-72	30	55	4	5	9	4	212	2001	39.24	49.29	71.0
240 Pope, OJD [1]	England	2018-24	55	97	5	7	15	4	205	3130	34.02	63.68	70.9
241 Matthews, GRJ	Australia	1983-93	33	53	8	4	12	2	130	1849	41.09	44.26	70.6
242 McKenzie, ND	S Africa	2000-09	58	94	7	5	16	9	226	3253	37.39	42.01	70.3
243 Rahul, KL [1]	India	2014-24	57	98	4	8	17	8	199	3240	34.47	52.86	70.3
244 Parfitt, PH	England	1961-72	37	52	6	7	6	5	131	1882	40.91	46.83	70.2
245 Mohammed Rizwan [1]	Pakistan	2016-24	36	59	9	3	10	4	171	2039	40.78	54.36	70.1
246 Jadeja, RA [1]	India	2012-24	79	116	21	4	22	8	175	3331	35.06	55.89	69.8
247 Cronje, WJ	S Africa	1992-00	68	111	9	6	23	11	135	3714	36.41	44.64	69.7
248 Woolley, FE	England	1909-34	64	98	7	5	23	13	154	3283	36.08	50.66	69.3
249 Mohsin Khan	Pakistan	1978-86	48	79	6	7	9	3	200	2709	37.11	49.67	69.2
250 Markram, AK [1]	S Africa	2017-24	44	80	1	7	13	6	152	2826	35.77	59.49	68.9
251 Knott, APE	England	1967-81	95	149	15	5	30	8	135	4389	32.75	47.44	68.8
252 Sarfaraz Ahmed	Pakistan	2010-19	49	86	13	3	18	4	112	2657	36.40	70.99	68.7
253 Taylor, BRM	Zimb	2004-21	34	68	4	6	12	3	171	2320	36.25	56.07	68.5
254 Miller, KR	Australia	1946-56	55	87	7	7	13	5	147	2958	36.98	50.01	68.5
255 Armstrong, WW	Australia	1902-21	50	84	10	6	8	6	159	2863	38.69	51.52	68.0
256 Flintoff, A	England	1998-09	79	130	9	5	26	17	167	3845	31.78	62.05	67.4
257 Cairns, CL	N Zeal.	1989-04	62	104	5	5	22	7	158	3320	33.54	57.08	67.3
258 Edwards, R	Australia	1972-75	20	32	3	2	9	4	170	1171	40.38	45.94	67.3
259 Broad, BC	England	1984-89	25	44	2	6	6	3	162	1661	39.55	37.86	67.3
260 Pataudi, MAK	India	1961-75	46	83	3	6	16	7	203	2793	34.91	48.21	67.3
261 Burge, PJP	Australia	1955-66	42	68	8	4	12	5	181	2290	38.17	50.05	67.3
262 Aamir Sohail	Pakistan	1992-00	47	83	3	5	13	6	205	2823	35.29	55.32	67.0
263 Conway, DP [1]	N Zeal.	2021-24	27	51	1	4	11	4	200	1836	36.72	51.52	66.8
264 Denness, MH	England	1969-75	28	45	3	4	7	2	188	1667	39.69	41.35	66.5
265 Borde, CG	India	1958-69	55	97	11	5	18	13	177	3061	35.59	50.00	66.3
266 de Grandhomme, C	N Zeal.	2016-22	29	44	7	2	8	6	120	1432	38.70	80.45	66.2
267 Gurusinha, AP	S Lanka	1985-96	41	70	7	7	8	3	143	2452	38.92	38.33	66.1
268 Reid, JR	N Zeal.	1949-65	58	108	5	6	22	5	142	3428	33.28	49.71	65.9
269 Coney, JV	N Zeal.	1974-87	52	85	14	3	16	3	174	2668	37.58	42.57	65.9
270 Vettori, DL	N Zeal.	1997-14	113	174	23	6	23	20	140	4531	30.01	58.19	65.4
271 Richardson, PE	England	1956-63	34	56	1	5	9	1	126	2061	37.47	49.94	64.7
272 Litton Das [1]	Bangla	2015-24	48	84	2	4	17	2	141	2,788	34.00	58.82	64.4
273 Crawley, Z [1]	England	2019-24	53	97	2	4	16	9	267	2899	30.52	65.72	64.3
274 Rudolph, JA	S Africa	2003-12	48	83	9	6	11	8	222	2622	35.43	43.82	64.3
275 Abdullah Shafique [1]	Pakistan	2021-24	22	42	3	5	5	6	201	1504	38.56	44.17	64.3
276 Wasim Raja	Pakistan	1973-85	57	92	14	4	18	8	125	2821	36.17	50.67	64.2
277 Catterall, RH	S Africa	1922-31	24	43	2	3	11	3	120	1555	37.93	50.00	64.2
278 Haddin, BJ	Australia	2008-15	66	112	13	4	18	8	169	3266	32.99	58.46	64.1
279 McCosker, RB	Australia	1975-80	25	46	5	4	9	5	127	1622	39.56	42.21	63.9
280 Burns, JA	Australia	2014-20	23	40	1	4	7	6	180	1442	36.97	56.39	63.8
281 McMillan, BM	S Africa	1992-98	38	62	12	3	13	3	113	1968	39.36	42.86	63.7
282 Congdon, BE	N Zeal	1965-78	61	114	7	7	19	9	176	3448	32.22	44.47	63.6
283 Patil, SM	India	1980-84	29	47	4	4	7	4	174	1588	36.93	57.18	63.3
284 Manjrekar, SV	India	1987-96	37	61	6	4	9	3	218	2043	37.15	38.97	62.9

Batsman	Country	Career	Mat.	Inn.	N.O.	100s	50s	0s	H.S.	Runs	Avge	S.R.	Rating
285 Ballance, GS	England	2014-17	23	42	2	4	7	3	156	1498	37.45	47.17	62.2
286 Jaffer, W	India	2000-08	31	58	1	5	11	6	212	1944	34.11	48.06	62.2
287 Hinds, WW	W Indies	2000-05	45	80	1	5	14	6	213	2608	33.01	47.77	62.1
288 Sadiq Mohammad	Pakistan	1969-80	41	74	2	5	10	6	166	2579	35.82	47.97	62.0
289 Blewett, G.S	Australia	1995-00	46	79	4	4	15	6	214	2552	34.03	41.27	61.6
290 Logie, AL	W Indies	1983-91	52	78	9	2	16	8	130	2470	35.80	57.66	61.5
291 Hick, GA	England	1991-01	65	114	6	6	18	11	178	3383	31.32	48.89	61.4
292 Wood, GM	Australia	1978-88	59	112	6	9	13	9	172	3374	31.83	42.49	61.3
293 Mohd. Mahmudullah	Bangla	2009-21	50	94	7	5	16	11	150	2914	33.49	53.41	61.2
294 Petersen, AN	S Africa	2010-15	36	64	4	5	8	3	182	2093	34.88	51.76	60.9
295 Rhodes, JN	S Africa	1992-00	52	80	9	3	17	4	117	2532	35.66	46.31	60.9
296 Imam-ul-Haq	Pakistan	2018-23	24	46	4	3	9	4	157	1568	37.33	46.06	60.5
297 Styris, SB	N Zeal.	2002-07	29	48	4	5	6	5	170	1586	36.05	51.34	60.5
298 Shubman Gill [1]	India	2020-24	31	57	5	5	7	5	128	1860	35.77	60.39	60.5
299 Sheppard, DS	England	1950-63	22	33	2	3	6	2	119	1172	37.81	50.00	60.4
300 Campbell, SL	W Indies	1995-02	52	93	4	4	18	7	208	2882	32.38	40.26	60.4
301 Healy, IA	Australia	1988-99	119	182	23	4	22	18	161	4356	27.4	49.73	59.8
302 Habibul Bashar	Bangla	2000-08	50	99	1	3	24	7	113	3026	30.88	60.28	59.8
303 Pollock, SM	S Africa	1995-08	108	156	39	2	16	9	111	3781	32.32	52.53	59.8
304 Qasim Omar	Pakistan	1983-86	26	43	2	3	5	2	210	1502	36.63	50.00	59.7
305 Vincent, L	N Zeal.	2001-07	23	40	1	3	9	4	224	1332	34.15	47.15	59.7
306 Dias, RL	S Lanka	1982-87	20	36	1	3	8	2	109	1285	36.71	48.55	59.6
307 Blundell, TA [1]	N Zeal	2017-24	40	69	7	5	11	6	138	2138	34.48	53.28	59.4
308 Marsh, SE	Australia	2011–19	38	68	2	6	10	10	182	2265	34.32	43.85	59.2
309 Fowler, G	England	1982-85	21	37	0	3	8	3	201	1307	35.32	38.88	58.8
310 Randall, DW	England	1977-84	47	79	5	7	12	14	174	2470	33.38	43.91	58.7
311 Shoaib Malik	Pakistan	2001-15	35	60	6	3	8	6	245	1898	35.15	45.68	58.7
312 Dujon, PJL	W Indies	1981-91	81	115	11	5	16	8	139	3322	31.94	46.43	58.5
313 Vandort, MG	S Lanka	2001-08	20	33	2	4	4	3	140	1144	36.9	47.25	58.5
314 Oram, JDP	N Zeal.	2002-09	33	59	10	5	6	4	133	1780	36.33	50.38	58.2
315 Kippax, AF	Australia	1925-34	22	34	1	2	8	1	146	1192	36.12	46.09	58.1
316 Singh, Y	India	2003-12	40	62	6	3	11	7	169	1900	33.93	57.98	57.7
317 Kelleway, C	Australia	1910-28	26	42	4	3	6	1	147	1422	37.42	42.17	57.7
318 Goddard, TL	S Africa	1955-70	41	78	5	1	18	4	112	2516	34.47	49.08	57.5
319 Buttler, JC	England	2014-22	57	100	9	2	18	9	152	2907	31.95	54.18	57.3
320 Barber, RW	England	1960-68	28	45	3	1	9	1	185	1495	35.60	51.75	57.2
321 Kamran Akmal	Pakistan	2002-10	53	92	6	6	12	14	158	2648	30.79	63.12	57.0
322 Robinson, RT	England	1984-89	29	49	5	4	6	5	175	1601	36.39	41.63	56.9
323 North, MJ	Australia	2009-10	21	35	2	5	4	5	128	1171	35.48	48.15	56.7
324 Gregory, JM	Australia	1920-28	24	34	3	2	7	3	119	1146	36.97	51.53	56.7
325 Holder, JO [1]	W Indies	2014-24	69	123	20	3	14	11	202	3073	29.83	54.92	56.7
326 Ramiz Raja	Pakistan	1984-97	57	94	5	2	22	7	122	2833	31.83	47.85	56.6
327 Dickwella, DPDN	S Lanka	2014-23	54	96	7	0	22	4	96	2757	30.98	66.47	56.5
328 Hayward, T	England	1896-09	35	60	2	3	12	7	137	1999	34.47	50.00	56.4
329 MacLaren, AC	England	1894-09	35	61	4	5	8	4	140	1931	33.88	50.00	56.3
330 Klusener, L	Sth Africa	1996-04	49	69	11	4	8	4	174	1906	32.86	59.81	56.3
331 Ransford, VS	Australia	1906-12	20	38	6	1	7	2	143	1211	37.84	50.67	56.2
332 Marsh, GR	Australia	1985-92	50	93	7	4	15	3	138	2854	33.19	35.13	56.2
333 Hudson, AC	Sth Africa	1992-98	35	63	3	4	13	7	163	2007	33.45	39.13	55.8
334 Flower, GW	Zimbabwe	1992-04	67	123	6	6	15	16	201	3457	29.55	34.53	55.5
335 Dowling, GT	N Zealand	1961-72	39	77	3	3	11	6	239	2306	31.16	48.29	55.4
336 Taylor, JM	Australia	1920-26	20	28	0	1	8	1	108	997	35.61	49.02	55.1
337 Howarth, GP	N Zeal.	1975-85	47	83	5	6	11	7	147	2531	32.45	40.07	55.0
338 Green, C [1]	Australia	2021-24	28	43	5	2	6	3	174	1377	36.24	48.57	54.9
339 Young, BA	N Zeal.	1993-99	35	68	4	2	12	5	267	2034	31.78	38.91	54.9
340 Crawley, JP	England	1994-03	37	61	9	4	9	4	156	1800	34.62	39.28	54.7
341 Duminy, JP	S Africa	2008-17	46	74	10	6	8	9	166	2103	32.86	46.28	54.6
342 Endean, WR	S Africa	1951-58	28	52	4	3	8	3	162	1630	33.96	50.00	54.6
343 Duff, RA	Australia	1902-05	22	40	3	2	6	0	146	1317	35.59	50.00	54.6
344 Mankad, MH	India	1946-59	44	72	5	5	6	7	231	2109	31.48	49.62	54.4
345 Shrewsbury, A	England	1881-93	23	40	4	3	4	1	164	1277	35.47	48.65	54.3
346 Roy, P	India	1951-60	43	79	4	5	9	14	173	2442	32.56	50.00	54.2
347 Burke, JW	Australia	1951-59	24	44	7	3	5	0	189	1280	34.59	45.01	54.2
348 Imran Farhat	Pakistan	2001-13	40	77	2	3	14	3	128	2400	32	48.29	54.1
349 Burgess, MG	N Zeal.	1968-80	50	92	6	5	14	5	119	2684	31.21	45.94	54.1
350 Blackwood, J.	W Indies	2014-23	56	102	6	3	18	7	112	2898	30.19	53.94	53.9
351 Mendis, LRD	S Lanka	1982-88	24	43	1	4	8	2	124	1329	31.64	54.96	53.7
352 Guptill, MJ	N Zeal.	2009-16	47	89	1	3	17	10	189	2586	29.39	46.61	53.2
353 Ritchie, GM	Australia	1982–87	30	53	5	3	7	1	146	1690	35.21	38.73	53.2

Batsman	Country	Career	Mat.	Inn.	N.O.	100s	50s	0s	H.S.	Runs	Avge	S.R.	Rating
354 Waite, JHB	S Africa	1951-65	50	86	7	4	16	9	134	2405	30.44	50.00	53.0
355 Yasir Hameed	Pakistan	2003-10	25	49	3	2	8	1	170	1491	32.41	57.61	53.0
356 Luckhurst, BW	England	1970-74	21	41	5	4	5	4	131	1298	36.06	35.73	52.7
357 Ali, MM	England	2014-23	68	118	8	5	15	15	155	3094	28.13	51.8	52.5
358 Simpson, RT	England	1948-55	27	45	3	4	6	6	156	1401	33.36	50.00	52.5
359 Mahanama, RS	S Lanka	1986-98	52	89	1	4	11	7	225	2576	29.27	41.94	52.4
360 Nash, BP	W Indies	2008-11	21	33	0	2	8	0	114	1103	33.42	43.29	52.3
361 Engineer, FM	India	1961-75	46	87	3	2	16	7	121	2611	31.08	50.91	52.2
362 Ashwin, R [1]	India	2011-24	106	151	15	6	14	9	124	3503	25.76	54.54	52.1
363 Barnett, CJ	England	1933-48	20	35	4	2	5	1	129	1098	35.42	49.55	51.9
364 Moin Khan	Pakistan	1990-04	69	104	8	4	15	5	137	2741	28.55	51.12	51.7
365 Das, SS	India	2000-02	23	40	2	2	9	3	110	1326	34.89	38.92	51.4
366 Tharanga, WU	Sri Lanka	2005-17	31	58	3	3	8	6	165	1754	31.89	54.61	51.1
367 Hughes, PJ	Australia	2009–13	26	49	2	3	7	6	160	1535	32.66	53.56	51.1
368 Hookes, DW	Australia	1977–85	23	41	3	1	8	4	143	1306	34.37	53.52	51.0
369 Bravo, DJ	W Indies	2004-10	40	71	1	3	13	6	113	2200	31.43	48.59	50.9
370 Hadlee, RJ	N Zeal.	1973-90	86	134	19	2	15	12	151	3124	27.17	56.08	50.7
371 Perera, MDKJ	Sri Lanka	2015-21	22	41	3	2	7	5	153	1177	30.97	72.25	50.5
372 Tyldesley, JT	England	1899-09	31	55	1	4	9	4	138	1661	30.76	50.00	50.5
373 Marsh, RW	Australia	1970-84	96	150	13	3	16	12	132	3633	26.52	44.82	50.4
374 Elliott, MTG	Australia	1996–04	21	36	1	3	4	5	199	1172	33.49	44.44	50.3
375 Rhodes, W	England	1899-30	58	98	21	2	11	6	179	2325	30.19	49.20	50.3
376 Imtiaz Ahmed	Pakistan	1952-62	41	72	1	3	11	9	209	2079	29.28	50.00	50.1
377 Smith, OG	W Indies	1955-59	26	42	0	4	6	8	168	1331	31.69	50.00	50.0

[1] Still playing in 2024

Table A.2 Bowlers with a career test bowling rating of 50 or more (20 or more matches before 2024)

Batsman	Country	Career	Style[3]	Tests	n_{balls}	n_{overs}	n_{maids}	Runs	Wkts	n_5/n_{10}	w_{avge}	w_{sr}	w_{ecom}	Bowl rating
1 Muralitharan, M	S.L.	1992–10	RAO	133	43,984	7340	1792	18,180	800	67/22	22.73	55.05	2.48	226.5
2 Barnes, SF	Eng	1901-14	RAMF	27	7,863	1312	356	3,106	189	24/7	16.43	41.66	2.37	190.8
3 Warne, SK	Aust	1992–07	RAL	145	40,743	6784	1762	17,995	708	37/10	25.42	57.49	2.65	180.2
4 Hadlee, RJ	N.Z.	1973–90	RAF	86	21,926	3461	809	9,611	431	36/9	22.3	50.85	2.63	170.3
5 McGrath, GD	Aust	1993–07	RAFM	124	29,246	4874	1470	12,186	563	29/3	21.64	51.95	2.50	170.1
6 Ashwin, R [1]	India	2011-24	RAO	106	27,220	4536	907	12,839	537	37/8	23.91	50.68	2.83	169.2
7 Anderson, JM	Eng	2003-24	RAFM	188	40,058	6672	1721	18,627	704	32/3	26.46	56.87	2.79	163.9
8 Steyn, DW	S.A.	2004–19	RAF	93	18,604	3101	660	10,077	439	26/5	22.95	42.39	3.25	161.5
9 Kumble, A	India	1990-08	RAL	132	40,789	6808	1575	18,355	619	35/8	29.65	65.99	2.7	157.7
10 Marshall, MD	W.I.	1978-91	RAF	81	17,567	2930	613	7,876	376	22/4	20.95	46.77	2.69	156.5
11 Ambrose, CEL	W.I.	1988-00	RAF	98	22,083	3683	1001	8,502	405	22/3	20.99	54.58	2.31	153.9
12 Rabada, K [1]	S.A.	2015-24	RAF	69	12,659	2109	422	7,026	321	16/4	21.89	39.43	3.33	153.8
13 Briggs, J	Eng	1884-99	LAO	33	5,324	1051	385	2,094	118	9/4	17.75	45.19	2.36	153.4
14 Waqar Younis	Pak	1989–03	RAF	87	16,224	2704	516	8,788	373	22/5	23.56	43.5	3.25	150.4
15 Lillee, DK	Aust	1971–84	RAF	70	18,463	2836	652	8,493	355	23/7	23.92	52.00	2.76	149.5
16 Walsh, CA	W.I.	1984-01	RAF	132	29,962	5003	1144	12,684	519	22/3	24.44	57.84	2.54	148.9
17 Imran Khan	Pak	1971–92	RAF	88	19,431	3107	727	8,258	362	23/6	22.81	53.75	2.55	148.6
18 Wasim Akram	Pak	1985-02	LAF	104	22,654	3771	871	9,779	414	25/5	23.62	54.65	2.59	148.3
19 Donald, AA	S.A.	1992-02	RAF	72	15,515	2586	661	7,344	330	20/3	22.25	47.03	2.84	147.7
20 Herath, HMRKB	S.L.	1999–18	LAO	93	25,958	4332	816	12,157	433	34/9	28.08	60.03	2.81	146.5
21 Broad, SCJ	Eng	2007-23	RAFM	167	33,662	5616	1304	16,719	604	20/3	27.68	55.79	2.98	146.1
22 Bumrah, JJ [1]	India	2018-24	RAF	44	8,574	1428	344	3,944	203	13/0	19.43	42.22	2.76	144.0
23 Trueman, FS	Eng	1952-65	RAF	67	15,172	2448	522	6,625	307	17/3	21.58	49.44	2.62	143.3
24 Pollock, SM	S. A.	1995–08	RAFM	108	24,333	4058	1211	9,733	421	16/1	23.12	57.85	2.4	141.9
25 Grimmett, CV	Aust	1925–36	RAL	37	14,531	2408	736	5,231	216	21/7	24.22	67.19	2.16	141.7
26 Peel, R	Eng	1884-96	LAO	20	5,223	1072	444	1,715	101	5/1	16.98	51.64	1.97	141.6
27 Lyon, NM [1]	Aust	2011–24	RAO	133	33,512	5576	1061	16,365	538	24/5	30.42	62.20	2.93	136.7
28 Cummins, PJ [1]	Aust	2011–24	RAF	66	13,435	2239	489	6,516	289	13/2	22.55	46.48	2.91	136.6
29 Underwood, DL	Eng	1966-82	LAO	86	21,822	3464	1239	7,674	297	17/6	25.84	73.61	2.11	131.9
30 Jadeja, RA [1]	India	2012-24	LAO	79	18,425	3067	728	7,769	323	15/3	24.05	56.99	2.53	131.5
31 Garner, J	W.I.	1977-87	RAF	58	13,144	2194	575	5,433	259	7/0	20.98	50.85	2.48	130.7
32 Laker, JC	Eng	1948-59	RAO	46	12,003	1913	674	4,101	193	9/3	21.25	62.32	2.05	130.4
33 Botham, IT	Eng	1977-92	RAMF	102	21,829	3550	788	10,878	383	27/4	28.40	56.96	2.99	130.4
34 Philander, VD	S.A.	2011–20	RAFM	64	11,407	1898	507	5,000	224	13/2	22.32	50.85	2.63	130.3
35 Davidson, AK	Aust	1953–63	LAFM	44	11,573	1665	431	3,819	186	14/2	20.53	62.30	1.98	130.3
36 Barnes, W	Eng	1880-90	RAM	21	2,288	568	271	793	51	3/0	15.55	44.88	2.08	128.4

Batsman	Country	Career	Style[3]	Tests	n_{balls}	n_{overs}	n_{maids}	Runs	Wkts	n_5/n_{10}	w_{avge}	w_{sr}	w_{ecom}	Bowl rating
37 Holding, MA	W.I.	1975-87	RAF	60	12,684	2067	459	5,898	249	13/2	23.69	50.92	2.79	126.7
38 Ntini, M	S.A.	1998–09	RAF	101	20,819	3472	759	11,242	390	18/4	28.83	53.42	3.24	126.5
39 Trumble, H	Aust	1890-04	RAO	32	8,084	1431	452	3,072	141	9/3	21.79	57.44	2.28	126.4
40 O'Reilly, WJ	Aust	1932-46	RAL	27	10,012	1588	585	3,254	144	11/3	22.60	69.61	1.95	125.9
41 Bedser, AV	Eng	1946-55	RAMF	51	15,953	2425	574	5,876	236	15/5	24.90	67.45	2.21	125.5
42 Kapil Dev	India	1978-94	RAFM	131	27,771	4623	1060	12,867	434	23/2	29.65	63.92	2.78	125.2
43 Starc, MA [1]	Aust	2011–24	LAF	93	18,181	3034	579	10,363	373	15/2	27.78	48.81	3.42	124.8
44 Willis, RGB	Eng	1971-84	RAF	90	17,364	2700	554	8,190	325	16/0	25.20	53.41	2.83	123.3
45 Singh, H	India	1998-15	RAO	103	28,599	4,763	869	13537	417	25/5	32.46	68.54	2.84	122.5
46 Hazlewood, JR	Aust	2014–24	RAFM	72	14,799	2,469	635	6857	279	12/0	24.58	53.11	2.78	121.6
47 Gibbs, LR	W.I.	1958-76	RAO	79	27,103	4,207	1313	8989	309	18/2	29.09	87.75	1.99	120.0
48 Fazal Mahmood	Pak	1952–62	RAFM	34	9,811	1,639	563	3434	139	13/4	24.71	70.75	2.1	119.9
49 Wardle, JH	Eng	1948-57	LAO/WS	28	6,603	1,030	403	2080	102	5/1	20.39	64.68	1.89	119.3
50 Johnson, MG	Aust	2007-15	LAF	73	16,020	2,666	514	8891	313	12/3	28.41	51.12	3.33	117.8
51 Lindwall, RR	Aust	1946-60	RAF	61	13,639	1,971	419	5251	228	12/0	23.03	59.87	2.31	117.6
52 Shoaib Akhtar	Pak	1997-07	RAF	46	8,144	1,357	238	4574	178	12/2	25.7	45.75	3.37	117.4
53 Southee, TG [1]	N.Z.	2008-24	RAMF	107	23,507	3,915	893	11832	391	15/1	30.26	60.08	3.02	115.6
54 Boult, TA	N.Z.	2011–22	LAMF	78	17,434	2,902	656	8717	317	10/1	27.5	54.94	3	115.2
55 Statham, JB	Eng	1951-65	RAF	70	16,054	2,495	595	6261	252	9/1	24.85	63.71	2.34	114.1
56 Benaud, R	Aust	1952-64	RAL	63	19,064	2,729	805	6704	248	16/1	27.03	77.05	2.11	114.0
57 Lock, GAR	Eng	1952-68	LAO	49	13,156	2,140	819	4451	174	9/3	25.58	75.56	2.03	114.0
58 Roberts, AME	W.I.	1974-83	RAF	47	11,127	1,778	382	5174	202	11/2	25.61	55.12	2.79	113.9
59 Tayfield, HJ	S.A.	1949–60	RAO	37	13,554	1,852	602	4405	170	14/2	25.91	79.81	1.95	113.8
60 Roach, KAJ [1]	W.I.	2009–24	RAFM	84	14,913	2,483	539	7705	282	11/1	27.32	52.84	3.10	113.2
61 Vaas, WPUJC	S.L.	1994–09	RAFM	111	23,422	3,906	895	10501	355	12/2	29.58	66.02	2.69	113.0
62 McDermott, CJ	Aust	1984-96	RAFM	71	16,609	2,764	583	8332	291	14/2	28.63	57.00	3.01	112.9
63 Gillespie, JN	Aust	1996-06	RAF	71	14,253	2,372	630	6770	259	8/0	26.14	54.96	2.85	112.3
64 Bedi, BS	India	1966-79	LAO	67	21,412	3,441	1096	7637	266	14/1	28.71	80.32	2.14	111.7
65 Mohammed Abbas [1]	Pak	2017-24	RAF	26	5,378	896	271	2205	97	5/1	22.73	55.43	2.46	111.5
66 Morkel, M	S.A.	2006–18	RAF	86	16,495	2,749	605	8550	309	8/0	27.67	53.39	3.11	111.3
67 Mohammad Asif	Pak	2005–10	RAFM	23	5,184	862	196	2592	106	7/1	24.45	48.83	3	111.2
68 Miller, KR	Aust	1946-56	RAF	55	10,463	1,497	337	3906	170	7/1	22.98	61.54	2.24	111.0
69 Vettori, DL	N.Z.	1997-14	LAO	113	28,821	4,802	1197	12441	362	20/3	34.37	79.6	2.59	111.0
70 Pollock, PM	S.A.	1961–70	RAF	28	6,526	1,034	270	2806	116	9/1	24.19	56.22	2.58	110.1
71 Swann, GP	Eng	2008-13	RAO	60	15,335	2,558	493	7642	255	17/3	29.97	60.19	2.99	109.3
72 Adcock, NAT	S.A,	1953–62	RAF	26	6,393	917	218	2195	104	5/0	21.11	61.45	2.06	109.2
73 Harris, RJ	Aust	2010–15	RAFM	27	5,737	956	258	2658	113	5/0	23.52	50.76	2.78	109.2
74 Ulyett, G	Eng	1877-90	RAF	25	2,627	653	299	1020	50	10/0	20.40	52.54	2.33	108.9
75 Verity, H	Eng	1931-39	LAO	40	11,202	1,693	604	3510	144	5/2	24.38	77.59	1.88	108.8
76 Noble, MA	Aust	1898–09	RAO	42	7,118	1,213	361	3025	121	9/2	25.00	58.75	2.55	108.7
77 Wagner, N	N.Z.	2012–24	RAFM	64	13,742	2,287	473	7169	260	9/0	27.57	52.79	3.13	108.1
78 Croft, CEH	W.I.	1977-82	RAF	27	6,154	1,027	211	2913	125	3/0	23.3	49.32	2.84	107.6
79 McKenzie, GD	Aust	1961–71	RAF	60	17,658	2,630	547	7328	246	16/3	29.79	71.87	2.49	107.5
80 Bishop, IR	W.I.	1989-98	RAF	43	8,471	1,411	288	3911	161	6/0	24.29	52.59	2.77	107.1
81 Reid, BA	Aust	1985-92	LAFM	27	6,233	10,404	244	2784	113	5/2	24.64	55.26	2.68	107.1
82 Saeed Ajmal	Pak	2009-14	RAO	35	11,590	1,932	386	5003	178	10/4	28.11	65.15	2.59	107.0
83 Alderman, TM	Aust	1981-91	RAFM	41	10,182	1,696	432	4616	170	14/1	27.15	59.89	2.72	107.0
84 Fraser, ARC	Eng	1989-98	RAFM	46	10,867	1,812	439	4836	177	13/2	27.32	61.45	2.67	107.0
85 Chandrasekhar, BS	India	1964-79	RAL	58	15,939	2,549	584	7199	242	16/2	29.75	65.96	2.71	106.6
86 Hall, WW	W.I.	1958-69	RAF	48	10,410	1,658	312	5066	192	9/1	26.39	54.28	2.92	106.3
87 Robinson, OE [1]	Eng	2021-24	RAMF	20	3,801	632	159	1742	76	3/0	22.92	49.95	2.75	106.3
88 MacGill, SCG	Aust	1998-08	RAL	44	11,249	1,872	365	6037	208	12/2	29.02	54.02	3.22	106.2
89 Yasir Shah	Pak	2014-22	RAL	48	14,268	2,375	359	7657	244	16/3	31.38	58.42	3.22	105.1
90 Johnston, WA	Aust	1947–55	LAFM	40	11,037	1,517	372	3826	160	7/0	23.91	69.05	2.08	104.9
91 Snow, JA	Eng	1965-76	RAF	49	12,016	1928	415	5,387	202	8/1	26.67	59.51	2.69	104.6
92 Lee, B	Aust	1999-08	RAF	76	16,522	2755	547	9,555	310	10/1	30.82	53.33	3.47	104.1
93 Saqlain Mushtaq	Pak	1995-04	RAO	49	14,051	2345	541	6,206	208	13/3	29.84	67.64	2.65	103.9
94 Mohammed Shami	India	2013-23	RAF	64	11,503	1919	364	6,346	229	6/0	27.71	50.28	3.31	103.7
95 Cairns, CL	N.Z.	1989-04	RAFM	62	11,690	1949	414	6,410	218	13/1	29.4	53.66	3.29	103.7
96 Gough, D	Eng	1994-03	RAF	58	11,824	1970	368	6,503	229	9/0	28.40	51.62	3.30	103.1
97 Caddick, AR	Eng	1993-03	RAFM	62	13,546	2259	500	6,999	234	13/1	29.91	57.94	3.10	102.5
98 Abdul Qadir	Pak	1977-90	RAL	67	17,141	2810	608	7,742	236	15/5	32.81	72.57	2.71	102.3
99 Tate, MW	Eng	1924-35	RAMF/O	39	12,541	1982	581	4,055	155	7/1	26.16	80.79	1.94	101.8
100 Hughes, MG	Aust	1985-94	RAF	53	12,280	2047	499	6,017	212	7/1	28.38	57.95	2.94	101.8
101 Shakib Al Hasan	Bangla	2007-24	LAO/MF	71	15,660	2612	485	7,804	246	19/2	31.72	63.72	2.99	101.4
102 Iqbal Qasim	Pak	1976-88	LAO	50	12,992	2084	649	4,807	171	8/2	28.11	76.13	2.22	101.0
103 Clark, SR	Aust	2006-09	RAFM	24	5,137	857.	230	2,243	94	2/0	23.86	54.74	2.62	100.8
104 Thomson, JR	Aust	1973-85	RAF	51	10,535	1590	300	5,601	200	8/0	28.01	52.68	3.19	100.6
105 Ramadhin, S	W.I.	1950-60	RAO/L	43	13,946	2233	813	4,579	158	10/1	28.98	88.22	1.97	100.2

Batsman	Country	Career	Style[3]	Tests	n_{balls}	n_{overs}	n_{maids}	Runs	Wkts	n_5/n_{10}	w_{avge}	w_{sr}	w_{ecom}	Bowl rating
106 Streak, HH	Zimb	1993–05	RAFM	65	13,559	2259	595	6,079	216	7/0	28.14	62.77	2.69	99.7
107 Sharma, I	India	2007–21	RAFM	105	19,135	3193	640	10,078	311	11/1	32.41	61.61	3.16	99.5
108 Khan, Z	India	2000–14	LAFM	92	18,802	3130	624	10,247	311	11/1	32.95	60.4	3.27	99.0
109 Hoggard, MJ	Engl	2000–08	RAFM	67	13,921	2318	492	7,564	248	7/1	30.50	56.08	3.26	98.8
110 Goddard, TL	S.A.	1955–70	LAM	41	11,731	1768	706	3,226	123	5/0	26.23	95.41	1.65	98.7
111 Giffen, G	Aust	1882–96	RAM	31	6,392	1287	435	2,791	103	7/1	27.10	62.05	2.62	98.7
112 Srinath, J	India	1991–02	RAFM	67	15,097	2517	599	7,196	236	10/1	30.49	64	2.86	98.4
113 Gupte, SP	India	1951-61	RAL	36	11,290	1880	608	4,403	149	12/1	29.55	75.73	2.34	98.2
114 Taijul Islam [1]	Bang	2014–24	LAO	51	13,550	2261	403	6,888	217	15/2	31.74	62.53	3.05	98.2
115 Valentine, AL	W.I.	1950–62	LAO	36	12,969	2030	789	4,215	139	8/2	30.32	93.19	1.95	98.0
116 Woakes, CR	Eng	2013–24	RAFM	57	10,123	1688	380	5,112	181	5/1	28.24	55.98	3.03	97.6
117 Prasanna, EAS	India	1962-78	RAO	49	14,355	2262	602	5,742	189	10/2	30.38	75.94	2.4	97.4
118 Maharaj, KA[1]	S.A.	2016–24	LAO	56	11,049	1838	351	5,727	193	11/1	29.67	57.16	3.11	97.4
119 Pattinson, JL	Aust	2011–20	RAFM	21	3,962	660.	142	2,133	81	4/0	26.33	48.93	3.23	96.7
120 Lawson, GF	Aust	1980–89	RAFM	46	11,113	1853	386	5,501	180	11/2	30.56	61.77	2.97	96.3
121 Hasan Ali [1]	Pak	2017–24	RAMF	24	4,298	715	164	2,185	80	6/1	27.31	53.69	3.05	95.7
122 Siddle, PM	Aust	2008–19	RAFM	67	13,925	2317	615	6,777	221	8/0	30.67	62.93	2.92	94.7
123 Rhodes, W	Eng	1899-30	LAO	58	8,220	1396	365	3,425	127	6/1	26.97	64.81	2.50	94.6
124 Danish Kaneria	Pak	2000–10	RAL	61	17,692	2949	517	9,082	261	15/2	34.8	67.8	3.08	94.5
125 Kumar, B	India	2013-18	RAM	21	3,344	558	141	1,644	63	4/0	26.1	53.14	2.95	93.9
126 Shaheen Afridi [1]	Pak	2018-24	LAM	31	6,162	1027	206	3,235	116	4/1	27.89	53.12	3.15	93.9
127 Kallis, JH	S.A.	1995–13	RAFM	166	20,216	3372	848	9,535	292	5/0	32.65	69.29	2.83	93.7
128 Mankad, MH	India	1946-59	LAO	44	14,680	2389	777	5,236	162	8/2	32.32	90.65	2.14	92.7
129 Harmison, SJ	Eng	2002-09	RAF	63	13,360	2229	431	7,192	226	8/1	31.82	59.18	3.23	92.6
130 Walker, MHN	Aust	1973–77	RAFM	34	10,112	1449	380	3,792	138	6/0	27.48	73.14	2.25	92.4
131 Hogg, RM	Aust	1978–84	RAF	38	7,643	1175	232	3,503	123	6/2	28.48	62.06	2.75	92.3
132 Taylor, BR	N.Z.	1965–73	RAFM	30	6,328	999	206	2,953	111	4/0	26.6	57.06	2.80	92.3
133 Fleming, DW	Aust	1994–01	RAFM	20	4,132	688	153	1,942	75	3/0	25.89	55.05	2.82	92.2
134 Faulkner, GA	S.A.	1906–24	RAL	25	4,233	704	124	2,180	82	4/0	26.59	51.55	3.09	92.0
135 Reiffel, PR	Aust	1992–98	RAFM	35	6,397	1067	280	2,804	104	5/0	26.96	61.57	2.63	91.5
136 Nadkarni, RG (Bapu)	India	1955-68	LAO	41	9,139	1503	665	2,559	88	4/1	29.08	104.15	1.68	91.5
137 Mushtaq Ahmed	Pak	1990–03	RAL	52	12,534	2087	405	6,100	185	10	32.97	67.71	2.92	90.6
138 Martin, CS	N.Z.	2000–13	RAFM	71	14040	2337.4	486	7839	233	10/1	33.64	60.2	3.35	90.6
139 Voce, B	Eng	1930-47	LAFM	27	6356	991.4	211	2733	98	3/2	27.89	64.90	2.58	89.9
140 Sobers, GSA	W.I.	1954-74	LAMF/ LAO	93	21619	3432.5	974	7999	235	6/0	34.04	91.91	2.22	89.6
141 Holder, JO	W.I.	2014–23	RAMF/O	69	11315	1883.3	484	4922	162	8/1	30.38	69.76	2.61	89.6
142 Old, CM	Eng	1972-81	RAFM	46	8868	1407	311	4020	143	4/0	28.11	61.94	2.72	89.5
143 Lever, JK	Eng	1976-86	LAFM	21	4434	683.3	140	1951	73	3/1	26.73	60.73	2.64	89.4
144 Sidebottom, RJ	Eng	2001-10	LAFM	22	4815	802	188	2231	79	5/1	28.24	60.91	2.78	89.1
145 Mallett, AA	Aust	1968–80	RAO	38	9975	1464	419	3940	132	6/1	29.85	75.68	2.37	88.9
146 Dymock, G	Aust	1974–80	LAMF	21	5544	815.3	179	2116	78	5/1	27.13	71.09	2.29	88.8
147 Cotter, A	Aust	1904–12	RAF	21	4635	772.1	86	2549	89	7/0	28.64	52.06	3.30	87.9
148 Yadav, UT	India	2011-23	RAF	57	8971	1496.3	245	5263	170	3/1	30.96	52.82	3.52	87.7
149 Nash, DJ	N.Z.	1992–01	RAM	32	6184	1032.4	312	2649	93	3/1	28.48	66.62	2.57	87.7
150 Arnold, GG	Eng	1967-75	RAMF	34	7656	1211.2	284	3254	115	6/0	28.30	66.52	2.55	87.7
151 Ojha, PP	India	2009-13	LAO	24	7628	1272.1	298	3420	113	7/1	30.27	67.55	2.69	87.5
152 Titmus, F	Eng	1955-75	RAO	53	14942	2302.2	763	4931	153	7/0	32.23	97.71	1.98	87.2
153 Bailey, TE	Eng	1949-59	RAMF	61	9721	1497.2	379	3856	132	5	29.21	73.58	2.38	87.0
154 Dilley, GR	Eng	1979-89	RAF	41	8187	1365.2	279	4107	138	6/0	29.76	59.36	3.01	86.7
155 Mehidy Hasan [1]	Bangla	2016–24	RAO	51	12079	2011.3	299	6382	190	10/2	33.59	63.52	3.17	86.7
156 Allen, GOB	Eng	1930-48	RAF	25	4392	688.2	116	2379	81	5/1	29.37	54.15	3.25	86.6
157 Finn, ST	Eng	2010-16	RAFM	36	6404	1068.4	190	3800	125	5/0	30.40	51.30	3.56	86.6
158 Schwarz, RO	S.A.	1906–12	RAO	20	2640	439.5	66	1417	55	2/0	25.76	47.98	3.22	86.4
159 Hendrick, M	Eng	1974-81	RAFM	30	6216	959.2	249	2248	87	0/0	25.84	71.36	2.17	86.2
160 Cork, DG	Eng	1995-02	RAFM	37	7684	1279.4	264	3906	131	5/0	29.82	58.61	3.05	85.7
161 Panesar, MS	Eng	2006-13	LAO	50	12467	2079.1	468	5797	167	12/2	34.71	74.70	2.79	85.6
162 Larwood, H	Eng	1926-33	RAF	21	4971	828.1	167	2212	78	4/1	28.36	63.71	2.67	85.5
163 Allen, DA	Eng	1960-66	RAO	39	11281	1816.3	685	3779	122	4/0	30.98	92.60	2.01	85.4
164 Doull, SB	N.Z.	1992–00	RAFM	32	6046	1008.5	251	2872	98	6/0	29.31	61.77	2.85	85.4
165 Pathan, IK	India	2003-08	LAMF	29	5883	980.4	212	3226	100	7/2	32.26	58.84	3.29	85.3
166 Snooke, SJ	S.A.	1906–23	RAFM	26	1620	270	62	702	35	1/1	20.06	46.29	2.60	85.1
167 Griffith, CC	W.I.	1960-69	RAF	28	5629	884.1	177	2683	94	5/0	28.54	59.90	2.86	85.0
168 Gomez, GE	W.I.	1939-54	RAFM	29	5242	838.2	289	1590	58	1/1	27.41	90.28	1.82	84.8
169 Hilfenhaus, BW	Aust	2009–12	RAFM	27	6069	1013	258	2822	99	2/0	28.51	61.39	2.79	84.4
170 Yardley, B	Aust	1978–83	RAO	33	8924	1415.5	379	3986	126	6/1	31.63	70.71	2.68	84.4
171 Flintoff, A	Eng	1998-09	RAF	79	14970	2491.5	506	7410	226	3/0	32.79	66.15	2.97	84.4
172 Stokes, BA [1]	Eng	2013-24	RAFM	110	12247	2042	359	6797	210	4/0	32.37	58.34	3.33	84.4
173 Hawke, NJN	Aust	1963–68	RAFM	27	6983	1034.2	238	2677	91	6/1	29.42	76.64	2.30	84.3

Batsman	Country	Career	Style[3]	Tests	n_{balls}	n_{overs}	n_{maids}	Runs	Wkts	n_5/n_{10}	w_{avge}	w_{sr}	w_{ecom}	Bowl rating
174 Gabriel, ST	W.I.	2012–23	RAFM	59	9382	1563.1	269	5348	165	6/1	32.41	56.84	3.42	84.3
175 Benjamin, KCG	W.I.	1992–98	RAFM	26	5126	855.2	158	2785	92	4/1	30.27	55.78	3.26	84.0
176 Illingworth, R	Eng	1958-73	RAO	61	11774	1893	702	3807	122	3/0	31.20	96.59	1.94	83.8
177 Wood, MA [1]	Eng	2015-24	RAFM	37	6544	1090.4	196	3621	119	5/0	30.43	54.99	3.32	83.7
178 Doshi, DR	India	1979-83	LAO	33	9339	1553.4	456	3502	114	6/0	30.72	81.77	2.25	83.0
179 Sarfraz Nawaz	Pak	1969–84	RAFM	55	13971	2110.2	485	5798	177	4/1	32.76	78.81	2.49	82.9
180 Greig, AW	Eng	1972-77	RAMF	58	9801	1557.2	338	4541	141	6/2	32.21	69.52	2.78	82.9
181 Raju, SLV	India	1990-01	LAO	28	7619	1267	359	2857	93	5/1	30.72	81.74	2.25	82.5
182 Johnson, IW	Aust	1946–56	RAO	45	8798	1231.2	330	3182	109	3/0	29.19	80.55	2.17	82.0
183 Connolly, AN	Aust	1963-71	RAFM	29	7810	1164	289	2981	102	4/0	29.23	76.65	2.29	81.8
184 Mohammad Amir	Pak	2009-19	LAFM	36	7617	1269	297	3618	119	4	30.4	63.98	2.85	81.7
185 Macartney, CG	Aust	1907–26	LAM	35	3,560	592	176	1,240	45	2/1	27.56	79.00	2.09	81.7
186 Collinge, RO	N.Z.	1965–78	LAFM	35	7,682	1116	228	3,393	116	3/0	29.25	66.28	2.65	81.6
187 Benjamin, WKM	W.I.	1987-95	RAF	21	3,690	615	136	1,648	61	0/0	27.02	60.56	2.68	81.5
188 Patterson, BP	W.I.	1986-92	RAF	28	4,830	804	109	2,874	93	5/0	30.90	51.92	3.57	80.9
189 Cairns, BL	N.Z.	1974–85	RAFM	43	10,609	1676	447	4,279	130	6/1	32.92	81.75	2.42	80.8
190 Brown, DJ	Eng	1965-69	RAFM	26	5,103	813	182	2,237	79	2/0	28.32	64.53	2.63	80.7
191 Nel, A	S.A.	2001–08	RAFM	36	7,634	1271	280	3,919	123	3/1	31.86	62.03	3.08	80.5
192 Chatfield, EJ	N.Z.	1975–89	RAMF	43	10,370	1683	487	3,958	123	3/1	32.18	84.23	2.29	80.2
193 Ahmed, G	India	1949-59	RAO	22	5,648	941	254	2,052	68	4/1	30.18	83.09	2.18	80.0
194 Abdur Rehman	Pak	2007–14	LAO	22	6,901	1148	256	2,910	99	2/0	29.39	69.62	2.53	79.2
195 Adams, PR	S.A.	1995–04	LAO	45	8,839	1475	339	4,405	134	4/1	32.87	66.04	2.99	79.1
196 Morrison, DK	N.Z.	1987–97	RAFM	48	10,059	1677	313	5,549	160	10/0	34.68	62.9	3.31	79.1
197 Boyce, KD	W.I.	1971-76	RAF	21	3,497	541	99	1,801	60	2/1	30.02	58.35	3.09	78.7
198 Asif Iqbal	Pak	1964–80	RAM	58	3,868	615	181	1,502	53	2/0	28.34	72.91	2.33	78.3
199 Mohammed Siraj [1]	India	2020-24	RAMF	35	5,212	869.2	161	3,023	96	3/0	31.49	54.33	3.48	78.1
200 Mailey, AA	Aust	1920-26	RAL	21	6,124	938	115	3,358	99	6/2	33.92	61.81	3.29	78.0
201 Mushtaq Mohammad	Pak	1959–79	RAL	57	5,268	797	177	2,309	79	3/0	29.23	66.58	2.63	77.9
202 Harper, RA	W.I.	1983-93	RAO	25	3,620	602	183	1,291	46	1/0	28.07	78.59	2.14	77.6
203 Motz, RC	N.Z.	1961–69	RAF	32	7,022	1142	279	3,148	100	5/0	31.48	70.34	2.69	77.5
204 Perera, MDK	S.L.	2014–21	RAO	43	10,804	1800	239	5,780	161	8/2	35.90	67.11	3.21	77.4
205 Venkataraghavan, S	India	1965-83	RAO	57	14,892	2448	696	5,634	156	3/1	36.12	95.37	2.27	77.2
206 Collymore, CD	W.I.	1999–07	RAFM	30	6,346	1056	245	3,004	93	4/1	32.3	68.14	2.84	76.9
207 Umar Gul	Pak	2003–13	RAFM	47	9,602	1599	256	5,553	163	4/0	34.07	58.89	3.47	76.4
208 Foster, NA	Eng	1983-93	RAFM	29	6,262	1043	239	2,891	88	5/1	32.85	71.15	2.77	75.6
209 Edmonds, PH	Eng	1975-87	LAO	51	12,037	1938	613	4,273	125	2/0	34.18	96.22	2.13	75.5
210 De Freitas, PAJ	Eng	1986-95	RAFM	44	9,826	1639	367	4,700	140	04	33.57	70.27	2.87	75.3
211 Tauseef Ahmed	Pak	1980-93	RAO	34	7,763	1296	359	2,950	93	3/0	31.72	83.63	2.28	75.0
212 Ali, MM	Eng	2014-23	RAO	68	12,617	2101	293	7,612	204	5/1	37.31	61.81	3.62	74.7
213 Kasprowicz, MS	Aust	1996–06	RAFM	38	7,146	1190	245	3,716	113	4/0	32.88	63.19	3.12	74.7
214 Cronje, WJ	S.A.	1992–00	RAM	68	3,807	633	243	1,288	43	0/0	29.95	88.37	2.03	74.6
215 Malinga, SL	S.L.	2004–10	RAFM	30	5,206	868	112	3,349	101	3/0	33.16	51.57	3.86	74.6
216 Hirst, GH	Eng	1897–09	LAF	24	3,992	672	146	1,770	59	3/0	30.00	67.75	2.66	74.5
217 Intikhab Alam	Pak	1959–77	RAL	47	10,492	1637	383	4,494	125	5/2	35.95	83.79	2.57	74.4
218 Emburey, JE	Eng	1978-95	RAO	64	15,398	2517	741	5,646	147	6/0	38.41	104.70	2.20	74.4
219 Junaid Khan	Pak	2011–15	LAMF	22	4,598	767	157	2,253	71	5/0	31.73	64.86	2.94	74.3
220 Tuffey, DR	N.Z.	2000–10	RAFM	26	4,874	812	209	2,445	77	2/0	31.75	63.34	3.01	74.1
221 Gregory, JM	Aust	1920–28	RAF	24	5,575	861	138	2,648	85	4/0	31.15	65.67	2.85	73.8
222 Taylor, JE	W.I.	2003–16	RAF	46	7,746	1292	258	4,480	130	4/0	34.46	59.67	3.47	73.6
223 Tufnell, PCR	Eng	1990-01	LAO	42	11,259	1880	505	4,560	121	5/2	37.69	93.24	2.43	73.6
224 Prasad, BKV	India	1996-01	RAMF	33	7,049	1173	274	3,360	96	7/1	35.00	73.34	2.86	73.5
225 Edwards, F	W.I.	2003–12	RAF	55	9,614	1601	184	6,249	165	12/0	37.87	58.22	3.9	73.1
226 Vincent, CL	S.A.	1927–35	LAO	25	5,868	977	194	2,631	84	3/0	31.32	69.8	2.69	73.0
227 Holder, VA	W.I.	1969–79	RAFM	40	9,105	1460	367	3,627	109	3/0	33.28	83.44	2.39	72.6
228 Reid, JR	N.Z.	1949-65	RAFM	58	7,732	1240	445	2,835	85	1/0	33.35	90.88	2.2	72.4
229 Ghavri, KD	India	1974-81	lAFM	39	7,031	1151	233	3,656	109	4/0	33.54	64.55	3.12	72.3
230 Lakmal, RAS	S.L.	2010–22	RAFM	70	12,423	2073	438	6,232	171	4/0	36.44	72.77	3.01	72.0
231 Dillon, MV	W.I.	1997–04	RAFM	38	8,709	1450	269	4,398	131	2/0	33.57	66.44	3.03	71.9
232 Higgs, JD	Aust	1978–81	RAL	22	4,747	726	176	2,057	66	2/0	31.17	72.00	2.60	71.9
233 MacGibbon, AR	N.Z.	1951-58	RAFM	26	5,659	886	228	2,160	70	1/0	30.86	80.84	2.29	71.8
234 Malcolm, DE	Engl	1989-97	RAF	40	8,479	1413	252	4,748	128	5/2	37.09	66.25	3.36	71.8
235 Walters, KD	Aust	1965–81	RAM	74	3,301	448	79	1,425	49	1/0	29.08	67.24	2.59	71.7
236 Armstrong, WW	Aust	1902–21	RAL	50	8,008	1337	407	2,923	87	3/0	33.60	92.21	2.19	71.5
237 Miller, G	Eng	1976-84	RAO	34	5,140	764	219	1,859	60	1/0	30.98	85.82	2.17	71.3
238 Sinclair, JH	S.A.	1896–11	RAF	25	3,607	620	110	1,996	63	1/0	31.68	57.19	3.32	71.1
239 Bracewell, JG	N.Z.	1980-90	RAO	41	8,398	1400	361	3,653	102	4/1	35.81	82.38	2.61	70.2
240 Woolley, FE	Eng	1909-34	LAO	64	6,496	1045	250	2,815	83	4/1	33.92	78.25	2.60	69.7
241 Boock, SL	N.Z.	1978-89	LAO	30	6,603	1053	327	2,564	74	4/0	34.65	89.16	2.33	69.5

Batsman	Country	Career	Style[3]	Tests	n_{balls}	n_{overs}	n_{maids}	Runs	Wkts	n_5/n_{10}	w_{avge}	w_{sr}	w_{ecom}	Bowl rating
242 Price, RW	Zimb	1999–13	LAO	22	6,138	1022	242	2,885	80	5/1	36.06	76.69	2.82	69.5
243 Franklin, JEC	N.Z.	2001-13	LAFM	31	4,762	794	143	2,786	82	3/0	33.98	58.13	3.51	69.4
244 Durani, SA	India	1960-73	LAO	29	6,454	1074	317	2,657	75	3/1	35.43	85.95	2.47	69.4
245 Atkinson, DSE	W.I.	1948–58	RAM	22	5,201	862	311	1,647	47	3/0	35.04	110.66	1.90	69.3
246 Bresnan, TT	Eng	2009-13	RAMF	23	4,667	779	185	2,357	72	1/0	32.74	64.92	3.03	69.3
247 O'Brien, I	N.Z.	2005-09	RAM	22	4,390	732	158	2,429	73	1/0	33.27	60.19	3.32	68.9
248 Maninda Singh	India	1982-93	LAO	35	8,220	1369	359	3,288	88	3/2	37.36	93.39	2.4	68.9
249 Collins, PT	W.I.	1999–06	LAFM	32	6,970	1160	221	3,671	106	3/0	34.63	65.7	3.16	68.6
250 Knight, BR	Eng	1961-69	RAFM	29	5,378	858	204	2,223	70	0/0	31.76	76.81	2.48	68.3
251 Brown, FR	Eng	1931-53	RAL / M	22	3,264	507	117	1,398	45	1/0	31.07	72.44	2.57	68.3
252 Gleeson, JW	Aust	1967-72	RAO / L	29	8,861	1283	378	3,367	93	3/0	36.20	95.24	2.28	68.1
253 May, TBA	Aust	1987-95	RAO	24	6,570	1096	322	2,606	75	3/0	34.75	87.69	2.38	68.1
254 Mackay, KD	Aust	1956–63	RAM	37	5,801	859	267	1,721	50	2/0	34.42	115.84	1.78	68.1
255 Yadav, NS	India	1979-87	RAO	35	8,358	1393	341	3,580	102	3/0	35.10	81.96	2.57	68.1
256 Watson, SR	Aust	2005–15	RAFM	59	5,491	915	238	2,526	75	3/0	33.68	73.27	2.76	68.0
257 Amarnath, L	India	1933-52	RAM	24	4,231	664	195	1,481	45	2/0	32.91	94.24	2.10	67.1
258 Jayasuriya, S	S.L.	1991–07	LAO	110	8,177	1364	323	3,366	98	2/0	34.35	83.55	2.47	67.1
259 Cowper, RM	Aust	1964-68	RAO	27	3,011	459	138	1,139	36	0/0	31.64	83.47	2.27	66.8
260 Bishoo, D	W.I.	2011–18	RAL	36	8,056	1344	174	4,350	118	5/1	36.86	68.36	3.24	66.8
261 Sharma, C	India	1984-89	RAFM	23	3,470	578	61	2,163	61	4/1	35.46	56.89	3.74	66.7
262 Oram, JDP	N.Z.	2002-09	RAM	33	4,958	826	240	1,975	60	0/0	32.92	82.63	2.39	66.6
263 Goddard, JDC	W.I.	1948–57	RAM	27	2,930	474	148	1,050	33	1/0	31.82	88.82	2.15	66.6
264 Shastri, RJ	India	1981-92	LAO	80	15,727	2625	657	6,186	151	2/0	40.97	104.31	2.36	66.6
265 Ratnayake, RJ	S.L.	1983–92	RAFM	23	4,961	826	136	2,563	74	5/0	34.64	67.04	3.10	66.4
266 Strang, PA	Zimb	1994–01	RAL	24	5,710	953	211	2,522	70	4/1	36.03	81.71	2.65	66.2
267 Kumara, CBRLS [1]	S.L.	2016-24	RAF	33	5,770	961	135	3,712	104	1/0	35.69	55.46	3.86	66.1
268 Howarth, HJ	N.Z.	1969-77	LAO	30	8,828	1326	393	3,178	86	2/0	36.95	102.7	2.16	66.1
269 Wahab Riaz	Pakistan	2010-18	LAF	27	5,025	836	118	2,864	83	2/0	34.51	60.46	3.42	65.3
270 Smith, OG (Collie)	W.I.	1955-59	RAO	26	4,432	738	229	1,625	48	1/0	33.85	92.31	2.20	65.2
271 McMillan, BM	S.A.	1992–98	RAMF	38	6,065	1009	255	2,537	75	0/0	33.83	80.72	2.51	65.1
272 Kelleway, CE	Aust	1910–28	RAFM	26	4,371	670	146	1,683	52	1/0	32.37	83.90	2.31	64.9
273 Zoysa, DNT	S.L	1997-04	LAFM	30	4,417	737	160	2,157	64	1/0	33.70	69.09	2.93	64.6
274 Binny, RMH	India	1979-87	RAFM	27	2,867	478	76	1,534	47	2/0	32.64	61.06	3.21	64.4
275 Sikander Bakht	Pak	1976-83	RAFM	26	4,873	74	147	2,412	67	3/1	36.00	72.69	2.97	64.2
276 Sammy, DJG	W.I.	2007–13	RAMF	38	6,221	1035	216	3,007	84	4/0	35.80	73.99	2.90	64.2
277 de Grandhomme, C	N.Z.	2016-22	RAFM	29	4,054	675	163	1,615	49	1/0	32.96	82.73	2.39	64.2
278 Wright, DVP	Eng	1938-51	RAL	34	8,123	1151	177	4,224	108	6/1	39.11	75.32	3.12	63.4
279 Giles, AF	Eng	1998-06	LAO	54	12,180	2030	397	5,806	143	5/0	40.60	85.17	2.86	63.0
280 Harris, PL	S.A.	2007–11	LAO	37	8,799	1468	336	3,901	103	3/0	37.87	85.52	2.66	62.8
281 Phadkar, DG	India	1947-59	RAO/M	31	5,987	979	277	2,285	62	3/0	36.85	96.68	2.29	62.5
282 Hadlee, D	N.Z.	1969-79	RAFM	26	4,876	691	114	2,389	71	0/0	33.65	68.77	2.94	62.5
283 Prabhakar, MM	India	1984-95	RAM	39	7,486	1245	274	3,581	96	3/0	37.30	77.86	2.87	62.4
284 Pringle, DR	Eng	1982-92	RAMF	30	5,283	881	192	2,518	70	3/0	35.97	75.53	2.86	62.0
285 Waugh, SR	Aust	1985–04	RAM	168	7,800	1300	332	3,445	92	3/0	37.45	84.78	2.65	61.9
286 Sreesanth, S	India	2006-11	RAM	27	5,422	903	162	3,271	87	3/0	37.60	62.29	3.62	61.8
287 Bright, RJ	Aust	1977-86	LAO	25	5,542	923	298	2,180	53	4/1	41.13	104.6	2.36	61.8
288 Prasad, KTDG	S.L.	2008–15	RAFM	25	4,325	721	96	2,696	75	3/0	35.95	57.69	3.74	61.6
289 Ratnayeke, JR	S.L.	1982–89	RAFM	22	3,829	638	118	1,972	55	4/0	35.85	69.69	3.09	61.5
290 Barlow, EJ	S.A.	1961–70	RAM	30	3,015	488	115	1,362	40	1/0	34.05	75.53	2.71	61.1
291 Abdul Razzaq	Pak	1999–06	RAFM	46	7,014	1168	219	3,694	100	1/0	36.94	70.08	3.16	60.9
292 Lewis, CC	Eng	1990-96	RAFM	32	6,843	1142	220	3,490	93	3/0	37.53	73.68	3.06	60.9
293 Douglas, JWHT	Eng	1911-25	RAFM	23	2,813	461	66	1,486	45	1/0	33.02	62.49	3.17	60.9
294 Aaqib Javed	Pak	1989-98	RAFM	22	3,918	653	136	1,874	54	1/0	34.70	72.56	2.87	60.8
295 Mohammad Rafique	Bang	2000–08	LAO	33	8,734	1457	301	4,076	100	7/0	40.76	87.44	2.80	60.8
296 Fernando, CRD	S.L.	2000–12	RAFM	40	6,186	1030	143	3,784	100	3/0	37.84	61.81	3.67	60.8
297 Benn, SJ	W.I.	2008–15	LAO	26	7,316	1220	229	3,402	87	6/0	39.10	84.15	2.79	60.6
298 Dexter, ER	Eng	1958-68	RAM	62	5,322	854	186	2,306	66	0/0	34.94	80.56	2.60	60.5
299 Klusener, L	S.A.	1996–04	RAFM	49	6,893	1147	318	3,033	80	1/0	37.91	86.09	2.64	60.2
300 Hammond, WR	Eng	1927-47	RAMF	85	7,978	1278	300	3,138	83	2/0	37.81	95.99	2.36	60.1
301 D'Oliveira, B	Eng	1966-72	RAM	44	5,720	912	318	1,859	47	0/0	39.55	121.4	1.95	60.0
302 Mishra, A	India	2008-16	RAL	22	5,107	850	123	2,715	76	1/0	35.72	67.14	3.19	59.7
303 Mohammad Hafeez	Pak	2003–18	RAO	55	4,063	677	118	1,808	53	0/0	34.11	76.74	2.67	59.0
304 Congdon, B	N.Z	1965-78	RAM	61	5,619	823	197	2,154	59	1/0	36.51	95.25	2.30	58.8
305 Worrell, FMM	W.I.	1948–63	LAO/MF	51	7,125	1116	275	2,672	69	2/0	38.72	103.5	2.25	58.6
306 Nasim-ul-Ghani	Pak	1958-73	LAO	29	4,402	733	204	1,959	52	2/0	37.67	84.73	2.67	58.3
307 Strang, BC	Zimb	1995–01	LAFM	26	5,440	905	304	2,203	56	1/0	39.34	97.00	2.43	58.2
308 Desai, RB	India	1959-68	RAFM	28	5,597	928	178	2,761	74	2/0	37.31	75.64	2.96	58.2
309 Curran, SM	Eng	2018-21	LAMF	24	3,091	515	96	1,669	47	0/0	35.51	65.77	3.24	57.9

Batsman	Country	Career	Style[3]	Tests	n_{balls}	n_{overs}	n_{maids}	Runs	Wkts	n_5/n_{10}	w_{avge}	w_{sr}	w_{ecom}	Bowl rating
310 White, C	Eng	1994-02	RAFM	30	3,964	659	119	2,220	59	3/0	37.63	67.10	3.36	57.6
311 Julien, B	W.I.	1973-77	LAMF	24	4,538	719	192	1,868	50	1/0	37.36	90.84	2.47	57.5
312 O'Keeffe, KJ	Aust	1971-77	RAL	24	5,381	727	189	2,018	53	1/0	38.08	101.6	2.25	57.3
313 Coney, JV	N.Z	1974-87	RAM	52	2,841	447	135	966	27	0/0	35.78	105.0	2.04	57.3
314 Croft, RDB	Eng	1996-01	RAO	21	4,620	769	195	1,825	49	1/0	37.24	94.27	2.37	57.3
315 Umrigar, PR	India	1948-62	RAM	59	4,726	787	262	1,473	35	2/0	42.09	135.0	1.87	57.1
316 Wasim Raja	Pak	1973-85	RAL	57	4,088	643	134	1,826	51	0/0	35.80	80.04	2.68	56.8
317 Border, AR	Aust	1978-94	LAO	156	4,013	651	197	1,525	39	2/1	39.10	102.8	2.28	56.8
318 Pushpakumara, KR	S.L.	1994-01	RAFM	23	3,789	632	99	2,242	58	4/0	38.66	65.38	3.55	56.6
319 Snedden, MC	N.Z	1981-90	RAM	25	4,780	795	194	2,199	58	1/0	37.91	82.33	2.76	56.4
320 Shahid Afridi	Pak	1998-10	RAL	27	3,194	532	69	1,709	48	1/0	35.60	66.54	3.21	56.3
321 Mahmood Hussain	Pak	1952-62	RAFM	27	5,906	985	213	2,628	68	2/0	38.65	86.91	2.67	56.3
322 Hopkins, AJY	Aust	1902-09	RAM	20	1,326	221	49	696	26	0/0	26.77	51.04	3.15	56.2
323 Cunis, RS	N.Z	1964-72	RAFM	20	4,256	659	140	1,887	51	1/0	37.00	83.33	2.66	56.0
324 Olonga, HK	Zimb	1995-02	RAFM	30	4,504	750	129	2,620	68	2/0	38.53	66.21	3.49	55.9
325 Azhar Mahmood	Pak	1997-01	RAFM	21	3,015	502	111	1,402	39	0/0	35.95	77.31	2.79	55.8
326 Bracewell, DAJ	N.Z	2011-16	RAM	27	4,978	830	147	2,796	72	2/0	38.83	69.22	3.37	55.6
327 Braund, LC	Eng	1901-08	RAL/MF	23	3,797	633	144	1,810	47	3/0	38.51	80.91	2.86	55.6
328 Astle, NJ	N.Z	1996-06	RAM	81	5,845	948	317	2,143	51	0/0	42.02	111.5	2.20	55.5
329 Mudassar Nazar	Pakistan	1976-89	RAM	76	5,958	984	217	2,532	66	1/0	38.36	90.41	2.55	55.5
330 Bravo, DJ	W.I.	2004-10	RAM	40	6,464	1077	213	3,426	86	2/0	39.84	75.19	3.18	55.4
331 Hooper, C	W.I.	1987-02	RAO	102	13,800	2299	531	5,635	114	4/0	49.43	121.0	2.45	55.4
332 Alabaster, J	N.Z	1955-72	RAL	21	3,992	665	178	1,863	49	0/0	38.02	81.47	2.80	55.1
333 Madan Lal, S	India	1974-86	RAFM	39	5,992	951	188	2,846	71	4/0	40.08	84.46	2.85	54.9
334 Chauhan, RK	India	1993-98	RAO	21	4,741	791	238	1,857	47	0/0	39.51	101.0	2.35	54.8
335 Chappell, GS	Aust	1970-84	RAM	87	5,339	786	208	1,913	47	1/0	40.70	113.3	2.15	54.3
336 Boje, N	S.A.	2000-06	LAO	43	8,616	1436	292	4,265	100	3/0	42.65	86.20	2.97	54.1
337 Kulasekara, KMDN	S.L.	2005-14	RAFM	21	3,564	594	120	1,794	48	0/0	37.38	74.31	3.02	53.8
338 Veivers, TR	Aust	1963-67	RAO	21	4,188	644	195	1,375	33	0/0	41.67	127.0	1.97	53.8
339 Rahat Ali	Pak	2013-18	LAFM	21	4,232	704	127	2,264	58	2/0	39.03	72.88	3.21	53.7
340 Dharmasena, HDPK	S.L.	1993-04	RAO	31	6,952	1156	265	2,920	69	3/0	42.32	100.6	2.52	53.6
341 Wickramasinghe, GP	S.L.	1991-01	RAFM	40	7,263	1210	249	3,559	85	3/0	41.87	85.41	2.94	53.5
342 Saleem Altaf	Pak	1967-78	RAFM	21	4,008	606	122	1,710	46	0/0	37.17	86.98	2.56	53.5
343 Patel, DN	N.Z	1987-97	RAO	37	6,594	1099	254	3,154	75	3/0	42.05	87.92	2.87	53.3
344 Simpson, RB	Aust	1957-78	RAL	62	6,873	1011	253	3,001	71	2/0	42.27	96.92	2.62	52.8
345 Nourse, AW	S.A.	1902-24	RAMF	45	3,235	539	120	1,553	41	0/0	37.88	78.88	2.88	52.7
346 Holford, DAJ	W.I.	1966-77	RAL	24	4,822	757	164	2,009	51	1/0	39.39	94.43	2.5	52.6
347 Pocock, PI	Eng	1968-85	RAO	25	6,638	1108	281	2,976	67	3/0	44.42	99.25	2.69	51.6
348 Whittall, GJ	Zimb	1993-02	RAFM	46	4,692	781	208	2,088	51	0/0	40.94	91.88	2.67	51.1
349 Best, TL	W.I.	2003-13	RAFM	25	3,715	619	81	2,291	57	2/0	40.19	65.19	3.7	50.9
350 Mashrafe Mortaza	Bang	2001-09	RAFM	36	5,998	998	202	3,239	78	0/0	41.53	76.79	3.24	50.6
351 Marsh, MR	Aust	2014-19	RAM	32	2,856	475	83	1,623	42	1/0	38.64	67.93	3.41	50.6
352 Welegedara, UWMBCA	S.L.	2007-14	LAFM	21	3,799	633	114	2,273	55	2/0	41.33	69.07	3.59	50.3
353 Tahir, MI	S.A.	2011-15	RAL	20	3,921	654	86	2,294	57	2/0	40.25	68.86	3.51	50.3
Lohmann GA [2]	Eng	1886-96	RAM	18	3825	800	364	1205	112	9/5	10.76	34.12	1.89	219.5
Spofforth FR [2]	Aust	1877-87	RAMF	18	4188	1045	416	1731	94	7/4	18.41	44.52	2.48	154.7

[1] Still playing in 2024
[2] Only 18 matches played
[3] RAO — Right arm off break RAL — Right arm leg break RAM — Right arm medium
RAF — Right arm fast RAFM — Right arm fast medium RAMF — Right arm medium fast
LAO — Left arm ortodox LAF — Left arm fast LAFM — Left arm fast medium
LAMF — Left arm medium fast LAM — Left arm medium

Appendix B
Modes of Dismissing a Batsman and Test Venues

B.1 Modes of Dismissal

The most common ways that a batsman can be dismissed are bowled, caught, leg before wicket (LBW), stumped and run out. Other modes of dismissal are hit-wicket, hit the ball twice, obstructing the field, retired out and timed out, but these rarely occur. The bowler only gets credit for the wicket when the batsman is either bowled, caught, LBW, stumped, or hit-wicket. However, if one of these modes of dismissal occurs from a no-ball, the batsman is not out. If the batsman is dismissed by run out, by hitting the ball twice or obstructing the field, the bowler is not credited with the wicket and the batsman is out, even if the delivery is a no-ball. None of the bowlers get credit if a batsman is retired out or timed out.

Bowled: If a legitimate delivery hits the stumps either directly or after deflecting off the batsman, and at least one bail is dislodged and falls from the stumps, the batsman is out *bowled*. The batsman is not out bowled, if the ball hits a fieldsman (including the wicketkeeper) or the umpire before hitting the stumps.

Caught: A batsman is out *caught,* if the ball hits the bat (or the batsman's glove when it is in contact with the bat) and the ball is caught by one of the 11 fielders before it hits the ground. When the catcher is the wicketkeeper, the batsman is said to be *caught behind* or *caught at the wicket*. When the catcher is the bowler of the delivery, the batsman is said to be *caught and bowled*.

Leg before wicket (LBW): If the ball from a legitimate delivery strikes the batsman (without hitting the bat or glove first) and the umpire considers that the ball would have gone on to hit the stumps, then the batsman is out *LBW*, provided: (i) the ball does not strike the batsman outside the line of the off stump (this can be waived if the batsman has not played a shot at the ball); and (ii) the ball does not pitch outside the line of the leg stump.

Stumped: After facing a legitimate delivery and provided he is not attempting to take a run, a batsman may be out *stumped*, if the part of the batsman's body or his bat is not grounded behind the popping crease and the wicketkeeper removes the bails with the ball, or with his gloved hand holding the ball.

Run out: If a batsman is running between the wickets and has not yet grounded his bat behind the popping crease, he is run-out if a fielder uses the ball to remove the bails from the stumps at that end of the pitch. Either the striker or the non-striker can be dismissed depending on who is nearest the end where the bails have been removed and not yet behind the popping crease.

Hit-wicket: If a batsman in the process of playing a shot or attempting his first run, dislodges the bails at the striker's end with his bat or part of his body or part of his protective equipment, he is out hit-wicket.

Hit the ball twice: If a batsman intentionally hits the ball a second time he may be given out. No batsman has ever been dismissed in this way in test cricket.

Obstructing the field: If a batsman distracts a fielder who is attempt a dismissal, the batsman may be given out obstructing the field.

Retired out: A batsman is *retired out* if he fails to resume his innings after leaving the field of play (without the umpire's consent) for any reason other than injury or illness. If a player retires hurt and is unable to resume his innings, he is considered not out.

Timed out: If an incoming batsman takes more than 3 minutes to reach the pitch and be ready to start play or if a not out batsman is not ready to start play after a scheduled break, he may be timed out if the fielding side appeals.

Table B.1 shows a breakdown of the dismissals made by the twenty-seven bowlers who have taken more than 350 test wickets. Clearly "caught" in the field is the most common mode of dismissal.

Table B.1 Modes of dismissal for the 26 highest wicket takers in test cricket up to the end of 2024.

Name	Number of Dismissal						
	Bowled	Caught in the field	Caught behind	LBW	Stumped	Hit-wicket	Total
Muralitharan, M (SL)	167	388	47	150	47	1	800
Warne, SK (Aus)	115	345	73	139	36	0	708
Anderson, JM (Eng)	137	270	199	98	0	0	704
Kumble, A (Ind)	94	313	32	156	24	0	619
Broad, SCJ (Eng)	101	254	148	101	0	0	604
McGrath, GD (Aus)	76	221	152	113	0	1	563
Lyon, NM (Aus) [1]	66	317	45	84	27	0	539
Ashwin, R. (Ind) [1]	109	248	50	116	14	0	537
Walsh, CA (WI)	92	238	111	76	0	2	519
Steyn, DW (SA)	90	176	109	64	0	0	439
Kapil Dev, N (Ind)	87	136	96	112	0	3	434
Herath, HMRKB (SL)	82	168	40	108	35	0	433
Hadlee, RJ (NZ)	92	176	80	83	0	0	431
Pollock, SM (SA)	59	175	97	90	0	0	421
Harbhajan Singh (Ind)	47	256	31	68	15	0	417
Wasim Akram (Pak)	102	123	70	119	0	0	414
Ambrose, CEL (WI)	83	173	96	52	0	1	405
Ntini, M (SA)	72	205	89	24	0	0	390
Botham, IT (Eng)	58	148	95	81	0	1	383
Marshall, MD (WI)	73	144	83	76	0	0	376
Starc, MA (Aus) [1]	89	138	98	50	0	1	376
Waqar Younis (Pak)	102	96	65	110	0	0	373
Imran Khan (Pak)	96	117	68	80	0	1	362
Vettori, DL (NZ)	42	195	36	76	13	0	362
Lillee, DK (Aus)	54	142	97	62	0	0	355
Vaas, WPUJC (SL)	37	130	88	100	0	0	355
Totals	2,222	5,292	2,195	2,388	211	11	12,319
% of total dismissals	18.0	43.0	17.8	19.4	1.7	0.1	100.0

[1] Still playing at the end of 2024

B.2 Test Cricket Venues

England: 556 tests have been played in England up until the end of 2024 at 9 venues, including: 147 tests at Lords Cricket Ground in London (the "home of cricket"); 107 tests at Kennington Oval in London ("the Oval"); 85 tests at Old Trafford in Manchester; 81 tests at Headingley in Leeds; 66 tests at Trent Bridge in Nottingham; and 56 tests at Edgbaston in Birmingham. England has also played test matches at the Riverside Ground in County Durham (6), The Rose Bowl in Southampton (7); and Bramall Lane in Sheffield (1).

Australia: To the end of 2024, Australia has hosted 449 test matches at 11 different venues. The test cricketing venues in Australia and the number of tests played at each are: Melbourne Cricket Ground (MCG) (117); Sydney Cricket Ground (SCG) (112); Adelaide Oval (83); Brisbane Cricket Ground (GABBA) (67); WACA Ground in Perth

(44); Bellerive Oval in Hobart (14); Perth Stadium in Perth (5); Cazaly's Stadium in Cairns (2); Exhibition Ground in Brisbane (2); Marrara Cricket Ground in Darwin (2); and Manuka Oval in Canberra (1).

South Africa: 253 tests have been played to date in South Africa at 11 different venue: Newlands in Cape Town (60); Kingsmead in Durban (46); New Wanderers Stadium in Johannesburg (44); St George's Park in Port Elizabeth (33); SuperSport Park in Centurion (30); Old Wanderers in Johannesburg (22); Ellis Park in Johannesburg (6); Mangaung Oval in Bloemfontein (5); Lord's (SAF) in Durban (4); Senwes Park in Potchefstroom (2); and Buffalo Park in East London (1).

West Indies: The West Indies have played 267 tests in the Caribbean at 12 different venues: Queen's Park Oval in Trinidad (63); Kensington Oval in Barbados (55); Sabina Park in Jamaica (55); Bourda in Guyana (30); Antigua Recreation Ground at St. John's (22); Sir Vivian Richards Stadium in Antigua (13); Darren Sammy National Cricket Stadium in St. Lucia (10); Windsor Park in Dominica (6); National Cricket Stadium in Granada (4); Warner Park in St Kitts (3); Arnos Vale Ground in St Vincent (3); and Providence Stadium in Guyana (3).

New Zealand: In New Zealand, 235 home test matches have been played at 9 different venues: Basin Reserve in Wellington (69); Eden Park in Auckland (50); AMI Stadium in Christchurch (40); Seddon Park in Hamilton (29); Hagley Oval in Christchurch (14); McLean Park in Napier (10); Carisbrook in Dunedin (10); University Oval in Dunedin (8); and Bay Oval in Mount Maunganui (5).

India: India has used 29 different venues to host its 296 home tests up until the end of 2024. Two additional venues in India were used to host Afghanistan's two "home" tests in 2019. The 27 venues for India's home tests are: Eden Gardens in Kolkata (42); Feroz Shah Kotla (renamed Arun Jaitley Stadium in 2019) in Delhi (35); MA Chidambaram Stadium in Chennai (35); Wankhede Stadium in Mumbai (27); M Chinnaswamy Stadium in Bengaluru (25); Green Park in Kanpur (24); Brabourne Stadium in Mumbai (18); Punjab Cricket Association IS Bindra Stadium in Mohali (14); Narendra Modi Stadium in Ahmedabad (15); Vidarbha Cricket Association Ground in Nagpur (9); Nehru Stadium in Chennai (9); Vidarbha Cricket Association Stadium in Nagpur (7); Rajiv Gandhi International Stadium in Hyderabad (6); Lal Bahadur Shastri Stadium in Hyderabad (3); Barabati Stadium in Cuttack (2); Dr YS Rajasekhara Reddy Cricket Stadium in Visakhapatnam (3); JSCA International Stadium Complex in Ranchi (3); Maharashtra Cricket Association Stadium in Pune (3); Saurashtra Cricket Association Stadium in Khandheri (3); Holkar Cricket Stadium in Indore (3); Gandhi Stadium in Jalandhar (1); Gymkhana Ground in Mumbai (1); Himachal Pradesh Cricket Association Stadium in Dharamsala (2); KD Singh "Babu" Stadium in Lucknow (1); Sawai Mansingh Stadium in Jaipur (1); Sector 16 Stadium in Chandigarh (1); and University Ground in Lucknow (1). In 2019, Afghanistan played two home tests in India: Rajiv Gandhi International Cricket Stadium in Dehra Dun (1) and Bharat Ratna Shri Atal Bihari Vajpayee Ekana Cricket Stadium in Lucknow (1).

Pakistan: For security reasons, no tests were played in Pakistan between March 2009 and December 2019 (when Pakistan played Sri Lanka in two test matches). To the end of 2024, a total of 162 tests have been played in Pakistan at 16 different venues: National Stadium in Karachi (47); Gaddafi Stadium in Lahore (41); Iqbal Stadium in Faisalabad (24); Rawalpindi Cricket Stadium in Rawalpindi (16); Arbab Niaz Stadium in Peshawar (6); Multan Cricket Stadium in Multan (8); Niaz Stadium in Hyderabad (5); Jinnah Stadium in Sialkot (4); Bagh-e-Jinnah in Lahore (3); Sheikhupura Stadium in Sheikhupura (2); Bahawal Stadium in Bahawalpur (1); Defence Housing Authority Stadium in Karachi (1); Ibn-e-Qasim Bagh Stadium in Multan (1); Jinnah Stadium in Gujranwala (1); Peshawar Club Ground in Peshawar (1); and Pindi Club Ground in Rawalpindi (1).

Sri Lanka: Sri Lanka has hosted 159 home test matches to date at 8 different venues: Sinhalese Sports Club Ground in Colombo (45); Galle International Stadium in Galle (46); P Sara Oval in Colombo (22); Asgiriya Stadium in Kandy (21); R Premadasa Stadium in Colombo (9); Pallekele International Cricket Stadium in Pallekele (9); Tyronne Fernando Stadium in Moratuwa (4); and Colombo Cricket Club Ground in Colombo (3).

Zimbabwe: Up to the end of 2024, 66 home test matches have been played at 3 different venues in Zimbabwe: Harare Sports Club in Harare (39); Queen's Sports Club in Bulawayo (26); and Bulawayo Athletic Club in Bulawayo (1).

Bangladesh: There have been 87 tests in Bangladesh at 8 different grounds: Shere Bangla National Stadium in Dhaka (28); Zahur Ahmed Chowdhury Stadium in Chittagong (25); Bangabandhu National Stadium in Dhaka (17); MA Aziz Stadium in Chittagong (8); Sheikh Abu Naser Stadium in Khulna (3); Sylhet Stadium in Sylhet (3); Khan Shaheb Osman Ali Stadium in Futullah (2); and Shaheed Chandu Stadium in Bogra (1).

United Arab Emirates: The UAE has hosted 38 tests at four venues: Sheikh Zayed Stadium in Abu Dhabi (15); Dubai International Cricket Stadium in Dubai (13); Sharjah Cricket Stadium in Sharjah (9); and Tolerance Oval in Abu Dhabi (1).

Wales: Three tests have been played at Sophia Gardens in Cardiff (3).

Ireland: Tests have been played at two venues in Ireland: The Village in Dublin (1); and the Civil Service Cricket Club in Belfast.

Appendix C
The Distribution of Batting Averages – Top-Order Batsmen

Up until the end of 2024, 847 cricketers have played 20 or more test matches for at least one of the ten test playing nations. Of these, 541 were top- or middle-order batsmen who regularly batted in the top 7. The distribution of the batting averages of these players is shown in the bar chart of Figure C.1. The mean is 36.76 and the standard deviation is 9.17. The dashed line in the figure corresponds to a normal distribution with the same mean and standard deviation as the batting averages. This batting data is not normally distributed, but a normal distribution is a reasonable approximation.

The data in Figure C.1 represents the specialist batsmen who were good enough and performed well enough to be selected for more than 20 test matches — the best of the best. Don Bradman's average at 99.94 is 6.89 standard deviations above the mean. If the data is assumed to be normally distributed, the chance of such an event is less than 1 in 100,000,000,000.

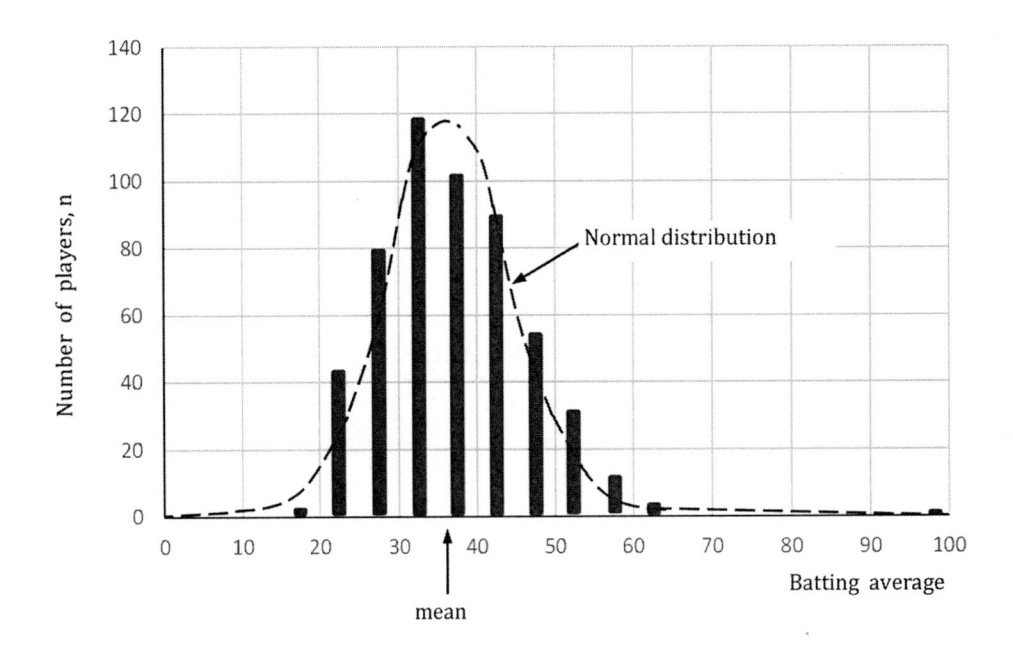

Figure C.1 Distribution of batting averages (top-order batsmen with 20 or more tests).

Appendix D
Best National Teams Before World War 1 — 1877-1914

Table D.1 The highest rating English team before World War 1

Batting Performances

Player	Tests	Innings	Not outs	Years played	Batting style	100s/50s/0s	HS	Runs scored	Batting Average	Strike rate	Batting Rating
1. Hobbs, JB	28	49	6	1908-14	right	5/16/3	187	2,465	57.33	50.49	120.1
2. Shrewsbury, A	23	40	4	1881-93	right	3/4/1	164	1,277	35.47	48.65	54.3
3. Hayward, T	35	60	2	1896-09	right	3/12/7	137	1,999	34.47	50	56.4
4. MacLaren, AC	35	61	4	1894-09	right	5/8/4	140	1,931	33.88	50	56.3
5. Jackson, FS	20	33	4	1893-05	right	5/6/3	144	1,415	48.79	50	89.8
6. Rhodes, W	47	77	16	1899-14	right	2/10/5	179	1,965	32.21	49.87	51.6
7. Lilley, AFA	35	52	8	1896-09	right	0/4/10	84	903	20.52	50	18.8
8. Briggs, J	33	50	5	1884-99	right	1/2/10	121	815	18.11	50	14.9
9. Peel, R	20	33	4	1884-96	left	0/3/8	83	427	14.72	50	9.8
10. Lohmann, GA	18	26	2	1886-96	right	0/1/7	62	213	8.88	50	4.6
11. Barnes, SF	27	39	9	1901-14	right	0/0/8	38	242	8.07	49.59	4.2
										Total	480.8

Next Batters:

Grace, WB	22	36	2	1880-99	right	2/5/2	170	1,098	32.29	50.07	48.2
Woolley, FE	22	32	3	1909-14	left	1/8/3	133	937	32.31	50.92	48.1
Barnes, W	21	33	2	1880-90	right	1/5/3	134	725	23.39	49.45	30.0

Bowling Performances:

Player	Overs	Balls	Maids	Runs against	Bowl style	Wkts	5w/10w	Best	Bowl Avge	Strike rate	Econ rate	Bowling Rating
1. Hobbs, JB				Less than 100 overs								-
2. Shrewsbury, A				Less than 100 overs								-
3. Hayward, T	158	886	41	514	RAM	14	0/0	4/22	36.71	63.36	3.48	30.4
4. MacLaren, AC				Did not bowl								-
5. Jackson, FS	291	1,587	77	799	RAM	24	1/0	5/52	33.29	66.13	3.02	46.5
6. Rhodes, W	995	5,833	231	2,615	LAO	105	6/1	8/68	24.90	55.55	2.69	101.3
8. Lilley, AFA	Less than 100 overs				Wicketkeeper							-
9. Briggs, J	1,052	5,324	385	2,094	LAO	118	9/4	8/11	17.75	45.19	2.36	153.4
9. Peel, R	1,073	5,223	444	1,715	LAO	101	5/1	7/31	16.98	51.64	1.97	141.6
10. Lohmann, GA	801	3,825	364	1,205	RAM	112	9/5	9/28	10.76	34.12	1.89	219.5
11. Barnes, SF	1,312	7,863	356	3,106	RAMF	189	24/7	9/103	16.43	41.66	2.37	190.8
											Total	883.5

Next Bowlers:

Barnes, W	569	2,288	271	793	RAM	51	3/0	6/28	15.55	44.88	2.08	128.3
Woolley, FE	329	1,974	71	923	LAO	39	3/1	5/20	23.67	50.62	2.81	82.3
Grace, WB	146	665	65	236	RAL	9	0/0	2/12	26.22	73.90	2.13	39.3

Note: A total of 180 different individuals represented England in this period before World War 1, with only 18 of them playing more than 20 test matches. Because of George Lohmann's phenomenal bowling record in his 18 test matches, he was included in an expanded group of 19 players, from which the best English team was selected.

Table D.2 The highest rating Australian team before World War 1.

Batting Performances

Player	Tests	Innings	Not outs	Years played	Batting style	100s/50s/0s	HS	Runs scored	Batting Average	Strike rate	Batting Rating
1. Trumper, VT	48	89	8	1899-12	right	8/13/7	214	3,163	39.05	54.55	77.9
2. Bardsley, W	20	33	0	1909-12	left	5/7/4	164	1,490	45.15	55.60	85.8
3. Hill, C	49	89	2	1896-12	left	7/19/9	191	3,412	39.22	53.67	79.4
4. Ransford, VS	20	38	6	1907-12	left	1/7/2	143	1,211	37.84	50.67	56.2
5. Armstrong, W	40	71	8	1902-12	right	3/7/4	159	2,247	35.67	50.76	56.9
6. Noble, MA	42	73	7	1898-09	right	1/16/4	133	1,997	30.26	50	49.5
7. Giffen, G	31	53	0	1881-96	right	1/6/5	161	1,238	23.36	50	31.8
8. Carter, H	20	36	6	1907-12	right	0/4/2	72	655	21.83	50	22.3
9. Trumble, H	32	57	14	1890-04	right	0/4/7	70	851	19.79	50	19.4
10. Cotter, A	21	37	2	1904-12	right	0/0/6	45	457	13.06	64.65	10.3
11. Spofforth FR	18	29	6	1877-87	right	0/1/6	50	217	9.43	50	4.9
										Total	494.5

Next Batters:

Player	Tests	Innings	Not outs	Years played	Batting style	100s/50s/0s	HS	Runs scored	Batting Average	Strike rate	Batting Rating
Duff, RA	22	40	3	1902-05	right	2/6/0	146	1,317	35.59	50	54.5
Gregory, SE	58	100	7	1890-12	right	4/8/12	201	2,282	24.54	50	43.1
Macartney, CG	21	34	1	1907-12	right	1/6/1	137	879	26.64	54.29	38.1

Bowling Performances:

Player	Overs	Balls	Maids	Runs against	Bowl style	Wkt	5w/10w	Best	Bowl Avge	Strike rate	Econ rate	Bowling Rating
1. Trumper, VT					Less than 100 overs							-
2. Bardsley, W					Did not bowl							-
3. Hill, C					Did not bowl							-
4. Ransford, VS					Less than 100 overs							-
5. Armstrong, W	1,106	6,643	330	2,507	RAL	70	3/0	6/35	35.81	94.89	2.26	65.5
6. Noble, MA	1,213	7,118	361	3,025	RAO	121	9/2	7/17	25.00	58.75	2.55	108.7
7. Giffen, G	1,289	6,392	435	2,791	RAM	103	7/1	7/117	27.10	62.05	2.62	98.7
8. Carter, H			Wicketkeeper					Did not bowl				-
9. Trumble, H	1,431	8,084	452	3,072	RAO	141	9/3	8/65	21.79	57.44	2.28	126.4
10. Cotter, A	772	4,635	86	2,549	RAF	89	7/0	7/148	28.64	52.06	3.30	87.9
11. Spofforth FR	1,046	4,188	416	1,731	RAFM	94	7/4	7/44	18.41	44.52	2.48	154.7
											Total	641.9

Next Bowler:

Player	Overs	Balls	Maids	Runs against	Bowl style	Wkt	5w/10w	Best	Bowl Avge	Strike rate	Econ rate	Bowling Rating
Macartney, CG	401	2,404	98	884	LAM	34	1/1	7/58	26.00	70.70	2.21	83.8

Notes: 1. A total of 105 different individuals represented Australia in test cricket before World War 1, but only 19 of them played more than 20 test matches.

2. Because of his fine record as a fast bowler, Fred Spofforth, who only played 18 matches, was added to the pool.

3. Charles Turner was a right arm fast-medium bowler who played 17 test matches between 1887 and 1895. He took 101 wickets at an average of 16.53, a strike rate of 51.44 and an economy rate of 1.93.

Table D.3 The eligible South African players before World War 1.

Batting Performances

Player	Tests	Innings	Not outs	Years played	Batting style	100s/50s/0s	HS	Runs scored	Batting Average	Strike rate	Batting Rating
Sinclair, JH.	25	47	1	1896-11	right	3/3/7	106	1,069	23.24	50.90	28.9
Nourse, AW	32	60	7	1902-14	left	0/11/3	93	1,512	28.53	48.77	39.3
Faulkner, GA	24	45	4	1906-14	right	4/8/2	204	1,717	41.88	52.20	75.6
Schwarz, RO	20	35	8	1906-12	right	0/1/6	61	374	13.85	50.95	9.2
Snooke, SJ (Tip)	23	41	0	1906-12	right	1/5/1	103	954	23.27	48.26	28.9

Bowling Performances:

Player	Overs	Balls	Maids	Runs against	Bowl style	Wkts	5w/10w	Best	Bowl Avge	Strike rate	Econ rate	Bowling Rating
Sinclair, JH.	621	3,607	110	1,996	RAF	63	1/0	6/26	31.68	57.19	3.32	69.0
Nourse, AW	393	2,358	92	1,113	LAMF	36	0/0	4/25	30.92	65.50	2.83	58.8
Faulkner, GA	687	4,125	124	2,093	RAL	82	4/0	7/84	25.52	50.31	3.04	96.3
Schwarz, RO	440	2,640	66	1,417	RAO	55	2/0	6/47	25.76	47.98	3.22	85.9
Snooke, SJ (Tip)	215	1,290	49	594	RAFM	29	1/1	8/70	20.48	44.48	2.76	77.9

Note: A total of 94 different individuals represented South Africa in test cricket before World War 1, but only the above 5 played more than 20 test matches before the war.

Appendix E
Best National Teams — 1920 To 1949

Table E.1 The highest rating English team from 1920 to 1949 (inclusive).

Batting Performances

Player	Tests	Innings	Not outs	Years played	Batting style	100s/50s/0s	HS	Runs scored	Batting Average	Strike rate	Batting Rating
1. Hobbs, JB	33	53	1	1920-30	right	10/12/1	211	2,945	56.63	49.03	125.3
2. Sutcliffe, H	54	84	9	1924-35	right	16/23/2	194	4,555	60.73	46.77	144.6
3. Hutton, L	41	72	5	1937-49	right	11/17/3	364	3,788	56.54	50	134.0
4. Hammond, WR	85	140	16	1927-47	right	22/24/4	336	7,249	58.46	49.53	152.0
5. Compton, DCS	36	60	8	1937-49	right	13/12/2	208	3,132	60.23	50.22	137.5
6. Paynter, E	20	31	5	1931-39	right	4/7/3	243	1,540	59.23	50	120.0
7. Ames, LEG	47	72	12	1929-39	right	8/7/5	149	2,434	40.57	46.33	71.3
8. Tate, MW	39	52	5	1924-35	right	1/5/5	100	1,198	25.49	50	30.4
9. Allen, GOB	25	33	2	1930-48	right	1/3/1	122	750	24.19	47.32	28.3
10. Verity, H	40	44	12	1931-39	right	0/3/4	66	669	20.91	49.59	19.2
11. Voce, W	27	38	15	1930-47	right	0/1/6	66	308	13.39	50	8.1
										Total	970.7

Next Batters:

Hendren, EH	51	83	9	1920-35	right	7/21/4	205	3,525	47.64	47.97	98.7
Leyland, M	41	65	5	1928-38	left	9/10/6	187	2,764	46.07	44.11	88.8
Hardstaff, J (Jnr)	23	38	3	1935-48	right	4/10/4	205	1,636	46.74	47.71	88.0
Washbrook, C	26	48	6	1937-49	right	6/12/2	195	2,569	47.12	50	87.8
Woolley, FE	42	66	4	1920-34	left	4/15/10	154	2,346	37.84	50.55	66.6

Bowling Performances:

Player	Overs	Balls	Maids	Runs against	Bowl style	Wkts	5w/10w	Best	Bowl Avge	Strike rate	Econ rate	Bowling Rating
1. Hobbs, JB					Less than 100 overs							-
2. Sutcliffe, H					Did not bowl							-
3. Hutton, L					Less than 100 overs							-
4. Hammond, WR	1,278	7,978	300	3,138	RAFM	83	2/0	5/36	37.81	95.99	2.36	60.1
5. Compton, DCS	315	2,132	60	1,031	LAWS	20	1/0	5/70	51.55	106.6	2.90	28.8
6. Paynter, E					Did not bowl							-
7. Ames, LEG			Wicketkeeper					Did not bowl				-
8. Tate, MW	1,982	12,541	581	4,055	RAMF	155	7/1	6/42	26.16	80.79	1.94	101.8
9. Allen, GOB	688	4,392	116	2,379	RAF	81	5/1	7/80	29.37	54.15	3.25	86.6
10. Verity, H	1,692	11,202	604	3,510	LAO	144	5/2	8/43	24.38	77.59	1.88	108.8
11. Voce, W	991	6,356	211	2,733	LAF	98	3/2	7/70	27.89	64.90	2.58	89.9
											Total	476.0

Next Bowlers:

Larwood, H	828	4,971	167	2,212	RAF	78	4/1	6/32	28.36	63.71	2.67	85.5
Bedser, AV	1,107	7,548	231	2,959	RAMF	89	2/2	7/49	33,25	84.81	2.35	74.5
Woolley, FE	717	5,421	179	1,892	LAO	44	1/0	7/76	43.00	102.8	2.51	48.6

Note: A total of 174 different individuals represented England in this 30-year period, with 28 of them playing more than 20 test matches. Only 10 players who commenced their careers before World War 1 continued to play test cricket after the war, including Jack Hobbs, Wilfred Rhodes and Frank Woolley who were all included in the best English team before the war (Table D.1).

Table E.2 The highest rating Australian team from 1920 to 1949 (inclusive).

Batting Performances

Player	Tests	Innings	Not outs	Years played	Batting style	100s/50s/0s	HS	Runs scored	Batting Average	Strike rate	Batting Rating
1. Ponsford, WH	29	48	4	1924-34	right	7/6/1	266	2,122	48.23	48.36	95.7
2. Brown, WA	22	35	1	1934-48	right	4/9/1	206	1,592	46.82	42.44	88.3
3. Bradman, DG	52	80	10	1928-48	right	29/13/7	334	6,996	99.94	54.95	310.0
4. McCabe, SJ	39	62	5	1930-38	right	6/13/4	232	2,748	48.21	54.15	97.6
5. Hassett, AL	21	30	2	1938-49	right	4/4/1	198	1,361	48.61	47.99	87.9
6. Ryder, J	20	32	5	1920-29	right	3/9/1	201	1,394	51.63	47.50	98.4
7. Miller, KR	18	23	3	1946-49	right	1/6/1	141	878	43.90	49.69	71.3
8. Lindwall, RR	17	19	1	1946-49	right	1/1/3	100	450	25.00	55.42	26.1
9. Oldfield, WAS	54	80	17	1920-37	right	0/4/9	65	1,427	22.65	43.79	24.9
10. Grimmett, CV	37	50	10	1925-36	right	0/1/7	50	557	13.93	39.90	8.3
11. O'Reilly, WJ	27	39	7	1932-46	left	0/1/6	56	410	12.81	46.43	7.6
										Total	916.1

Next Batters:

Woodfull, WM	35	54	4	1926-34	right	7/13/6	161	2,300	46.00	39.73	86.6
Gregory, JM	24	34	3	1920-28	left	2/7/3	119	1,146	36.97	51.53	56.7

Bowling Performances:

Player	Overs	Balls	Maids	Runs against	Bowl style	Wkts	5w/10w	Best	Bowl Avge	Strike rate	Econ rate	Bowling Rating
1. Ponsford, WH				Did not bowl								-
2. Brown, WA				Did not bowl								-
3. Bradman, DG				Less than 100 overs								-
4. McCabe, SJ	610	3,748	127	1,543	RAFM	36	0/0	4/13	42.86	104.1	2.47	45.5
5. Hassett, AL				Less than 100 overs								-
6. Ryder, J	303	1,897	71	743	RAFM	17	0/0	2/20	43.71	111.6	2.35	35.0
7. Miller, KR	393	2,852	81	1,028	RAF	48	2/0	7/60	21.42	59.42	2.16	97.2
8. Lindwall, RR	521	3,688	110	1,342	RAF	70	5/0	7/38	19.17	52.69	2.18	118.0
9. Oldfield, WAS		Wicketkeeper					Did not bowl					-
10. Grimmett, CV	2,409	14,531	736	5,231	RAL	216	21/7	7/40	24.22	67.19	2.16	141.7
11. O'Reilly, WJ	1,588	10,012	585	3,254	RAL	144	11/3	7/54	22.60	69.61	1.95	125.9
											Total	563.3

Next Bowler:

Gregory, JM	861	5,575	138	2,648	RAF	85	4/0	7/69	31.15	65.67	2.85	73.8

Note: A total of 83 different individuals represented Australia in this 30-year period (less than half the number of players who represented England in the same period), with only 15 of them playing 20 or more tests in the period. To increase the number of players eligible for inclusion in the best team between 1920 and 1949, the minimum number of test matches required for eligibility was decreased to 17, thereby expanding the number of eligible players by 5 and permitting the inclusion of the great opening bowling combination of Lindwall and Miller (both in the early stages of their test careers).

Table E.3 The highest rating South African team from 1920 to 1949 (inclusive).

Batting Performances

Player	Tests	Innings	Not outs	Years played	Batting style	100s/50s/0s	HS	Runs scored	Batting Average	Strike rate	Batting Rating
1. Mitchell, B	42	80	9	1929-49	right	8/21/3	189	3,471	48.89	50	103.0
2. Taylor, HW	31	55	3	1921-32	right	6/13/1	176	2,234	42.96	50	83.7
3. Catterall, RH	24	43	2	1922-32	right	3/11/3	120	1,555	37.93	50	64.2
4. Nourse, AD	26	49	7	1935-49	right	8/12/3	231	2,469	58.79	50	128.0
5. Rowan, EAB	18	35	4	1935-49	right	1/8/2	156	1,208	38.97	50	60.8
6. Cameron, HB	26	45	4	1927-35	right	0/10/3	90	1,239	30.22	50	41.3
7. Siedle, IJ	18	34	0	1928-36	right	1/5/3	141	977	28.74	50	38.1
8. Viljoen, KG	27	50	2	1930-49	right	2/9/5	124	1,365	28.44	50	42.0
9. Morkel, DPB	16	28	1	1927-32	right	0/4/3	88	663	24.56	50	25.6
10. Vincent, CL	25	38	12	1927-35	left	0/2/4	60	526	20.23	50	16.5
11. Bell, AJ	16	23	12	1929-35	right	0/0/6	26	69	6.27	50	2.7
										Total	605.8

Bowling Performances:

Player	Overs	Balls	Maids	Runs against	Bowl style	Wkts	5w/10w	Best	Bowl Avge	Strike rate	Econ rate	Bowling Rating
1. Mitchell, B	361	2,517	26	1,380	RAL	27	1/0	5/87	51.11	93.3	3.29	26.6
2. Taylor, HW				Less than 100 overs								-
3. Catterall, RH				Less than 100 overs								-
4. Nourse, AD				Did not bowl								-
5. Rowan, EAB				Less than 100 overs								-
6. Cameron, HB			Wicketkeeper					Did not bowl				
7. Siedle, IJ				Less than 100 overs								-
8. Viljoen, KG				Less than 100 overs								-
9. Morkel, DPB	284	1,704	55	821	RAFM	18	0/0	4/93	45.61	94.67	2.89	28.6
10. Vincent, CL	977	5,868	194	2,631	LAO	84	3/0	6/51	31.32	69.80	2.69	73.0
11. Bell, AJ	557	3,346	89	1,567	RAF	48	4/0	6/99	32.65	69.63	2.81	66.8
											Total	195.0

Note: A total of 93 different individuals represented South Africa in this 30-year period, with only 7 of them playing 20 or more tests in the period. To form the above team, the minimum number of test matches required for eligibility has been decreased to 16, thereby expanding the number of eligible players by 5.

Table E.4 Other eligible players from 1920 to 1949 (inclusive).

Batting Performances

Player	Tests	Innings	Not outs	Years played	Batting style	100s/50s/0s	HS	Runs scored	Batting Average	Strike rate	Batting Rating
Constantine, L (WI)	18	33	0	1928-39	right	0/4/4	90	635	19.24	50	18.1
Headley, GA (WI)	21	38	4	1930-49	right	10/5/2	270	2,173	63.91	50	146.3

Bowling Performances:

Player	Overs	Balls	Maids	Runs against	Bowl style	Wkts	5w/10w	Best	Bowl Avge	Strike rate	Econ rate	Bowling Rating
Constantine, L (WI)	573	3,588	125	1,746	RAF	58	2/0	5/75	30.10	61.78	2.92	74.1
Headley, GA (WI)	Less than 100 overs											-

Notes: 1. A total of 69 different individuals represented West Indies in test cricket between their first test in 1928 and the end of 1949, but only the above 2 played more than 18 test matches in that period.

2. A total of 50 different individuals represented New Zealand in test cricket between their first test in 1930 and the end of 1949, but none played more than 20 test matches in that period.

3. A total of 52 different individuals represented India in test cricket between their first test in 1932 and the end of 1949, but none played more than 20 test matches in that period.

Appendix F
Best National Teams — 1950 To 1959

Table F.1 The highest rating English team of the 1950s.

Batting Performances

Player	Tests	Innings	Not outs	Years played	Batting style	100s/ 50s/0s	HS	Runs scored	Batting Average	Strike rate	Batting Rating
1. Hutton, L	38	66	10	1950-55	right	8/16/2	205	3,183	56.84	50	121.8
2. Richardson, PE	25	40	0	1956-59	left	5/7/1	126	1,623	40.58	50	71.6
3. May, PBH	59	93	8	1951-59	right	13/20/6	285	4,182	49.20	50	113.0
4. Compton, DCS	42	71	7	1950-57	right	4/16/8	278	2,675	41.80	50	81.7
5. Cowdrey, MC	39	61	3	1954-59	right	6/16/3	160	2,440	42.07	46.59	81.0
6. Graveney, TW	48	76	10	1951-59	right	4/11/7	258	2,590	39.24	50	72.2
7. Evans, TG	64	93	7	1950-59	right	2/6/15	104	1,693	19.69	50	20.4
8. Trueman, FS	31	34	9	1952-59	right	0/0/6	39	401	16.04	50	10.6
9. Laker, JC	38	49	13	1950-59	right	0/0/4	48	453	12.58	49.08	7.8
10. Lock, GAR	31	39	6	1952-59	right	0/0/5	25	375	11.36	44.53	6.3
11. Bedser, AV	28	36	9	1950-55	right	0/0/6	30	263	9.74	50	5.3
										Total	591.8

Next Batters:

Bailey, TE	57	86	12	1950-59	right	1/8/7	134	2,071	27.99	49.06	40.6
Wardle, JH [2]	27	39	7	1950-57	left	0/2/5	66	647	20.22	50	16.4

Bowling Performances:

Player	Overs	Balls	Maids	Runs against	Bowl style	Wkts	5w/ 10w	Best	Bowl Avge	Strike rate	Econ rate	Bowling Rating
1. Hutton, L				Less than 100 overs								-
2. Richardson, PE				Did not bowl								-
3. May, PBH				Did not bowl								-
4. Compton, DCS				Less than 100 overs								-
5. Cowdrey, MC				Less than 100 overs								-
6. Graveney, TW				Less than 100 overs								-
7. Evans, TG		Wicketkeeper				Did not bowl						-
8. Trueman, FS	1,003	6,200	232	2,685	RAF	128	5/0	8/31	20.98	48.44	2.60	119.3
9. Laker, JC	1,539	9,783	578	2,992	RAO	162	8/3	10/53	18.47	60.39	1.84	139.7
10. Lock, GAR	1,302	8,117	524	2,554	LAO	123	8/3	7/35	20.76	65.99	1.89	127.9
11. Bedser, AV	1,318	8,370	343	2,917	RAMF	147	13/3	7/44	19.84	56.94	2.09	136.8
											Total	523.7

Next Bowlers:

Bailey, TE	1,339	8,764	357	3,257	RAMF	116	3/1	7/34	28.08	75.55	2.23	87.3
Wardle, JH [2]	1,026	6,579	403	2,071	LAO[2]	102	5/1	7/36	20.30	64.50	1.89	119.8
Statham, JB	1540	9,995	379	3,737	RAF	159	5/0	7/39	23.50	62.86	2.24	105.6

Notes: 1. A total of 74 different individuals represented England in this 10-year period, with 16 of them playing more than 20 test matches. Two of the team who were selected in the 1919 to 1949 team, also made the best team of the 1950s, Sir Len Hutton and Denis Compton.

2. In addition to left arm orthodox, Wardle also bowled left arm chinamen.

Table F.2 The highest rating Australian team of the 1950s.

Batting Performances

Player	Tests	Innings	Not outs	Years played	Batting style	100s/50s/0s	HS	Runs scored	Batting Average	Strike rate	Batting Rating
1. Morris, AR	30	54	0	1950-55	left	5/8/3	206	2,059	38.13	49.84	68.6
2. McDonald, CC	36	64	4	1952-59	right	5/13/2	170	2,590	43.17	50	80.8
3. Harvey, RN	56	99	8	1950-59	left	15/19/5	205	4,573	50.25	49.99	113.5
4. Hassett, AL	22	39	1	1950-53	right	6/7/0	167	1,712	45.05	50	86.3
5. Miller, KR	37	64	4	1950-56	right	6/7/4	147	2,080	34.67	50.14	58.9
6. Burke, JW	24	44	7	1951-59	right	3/5/0	189	1,280	34.59	45.01	54.2
7. Benaud, R	42	63	4	1952-59	right	3/4/6	122	1,440	24.41	48.98	33.0
8. Davidson, AK	27	36	3	1953-59	left	0/3/0	76	788	23.88	48.34	24.6
9. Lindwall, RR	42	63	11	1950-59	right	1/4/6	118	1,041	20.02	51.59	23.7
10. Langley, GRA	26	37	12	1951-56	right	0/1/3	53	374	14.96	50.07	9.6
11. Johnston, WA	29	39	20	1950-55	left	0/0/7	28	179	9.42	50.56	4.9
										Total	558.0

Next Batters:

| Mackay, KD | 21 | 28 | 4 | 1956-59 | left | 0/7/4 | 83 | 804 | 33.50 | 50 | 43.4 |
| Johnson, IW | 30 | 47 | 10 | 1950-56 | right | 0/4/6 | 77 | 725 | 19.59 | 50.03 | 16.8 |

Bowling Performances:

Player	Overs	Balls	Maids	Runs against	Bowl style	Wkts	5w/10w	Best	Bowl Avge	Strike rate	Econ rate	Bowling Rating
1. Morris, AR				Less than 100 overs								-
2. McDonald, CC				Less than 100 overs								-
3. Harvey, RN				Less than 100 overs								-
4. Hassett, AL				Less than 100 overs								-
5. Miller, KR	1,104	7,609	256	2,878	RAF	122	5/1	6/107	23.59	62.37	2.27	104.0
6. Burke, JW	111	814	41	230	RAO	8	0/0	4/37	28.75	101.8	1.70	37.9
7. Benaud, R	1,633	11,201	476	3,952	RAL	165	11/1	7/72	23.95	67.88	2.12	112.7
8. Davidson, AK	894	6,273	249	1,886	LAFM	92	5/1	7/93	20.50	68.19	1.80	112.5
9. Lindwall, RR	1,367	9,470	286	3,687	RAF	152	7/0	7/43	24.26	62.30	2.34	102.9
10. Langley, GRA		Wicketkeeper						Did not bowl				-
11. Johnston, WA	1,051	7,935	243	2,826	LAFM	106	5/0	6/62	26.66	74.86	2.14	89.1
											Total	559.1

Next Bowlers:

| Mackay, KD | 355 | 2,406 | 124 | 595 | RAM | 20 | 1/0 | 6/42 | 29.75 | 120.3 | 1.48 | 66.8 |
| Johnson, IW | 762 | 5,394 | 202 | 1,945 | RAO | 68 | 2/0 | 7/44 | 28.60 | 79.32 | 2.16 | 78.1 |

Note: A total of 45 different individuals represented Australia in this 10-year period, with 13 of them playing more than 20 test matches. Three of the team who were selected in the 1919 to 1950 team, also made the best team of the 1950s, Lindsay Hassett, Keith Miller and Ray Lindwall.

Table F.3 The highest rating West Indian team of the 1950s.

Batting Performances

Player	Tests	Innings	Not outs	Years played	Batting style	100s/50s/0s	HS	Runs scored	Batting Average	Strike rate	Batting Rating
1. Stollmeyer, JB	23	42	4	1950-55	right	3/7/1	152	1,520	40.00	50	66.0
2. Worrell, FMM[2]	29	53	3	1950-57	right	7/10/4	261	2,397	47.94	50	97.4
3. Kanhai, RB	18	32	2	1957-59	right	2/4/4	256	1,317	43.90	50	72.2
4. Weekes, EDC	39	68	5	1950-58	right	10/17/6	207	3,383	53.70	50	116.7
5. Walcott, CL	33	57	6	1950-58	right	13/11/1	220	3,129	61.35	50	141.8
6. Sobers, GStA	27	46	7	1954-59	left	6/7/1	365	2,213	56.74	50	121.2
7. Smith, OG	26	42	0	1955-59	right	4/6/8	168	1,331	31.69	50	50.0
8. Atkinson, DStE	18	29	4	1950-58	right	1/5/2	219	843	33.72	50	50.9
9. Gomez, GE	18	30	4	1950-54	right	0/5/3	74	733	28.19	50	31.9
10. Ramadhin, S	37	50	14	1950-59	right	0/0/12	44	299	8.31	50	4.5
11. Valentine, AL	29	39	12	1950-58	right	0/0/11	14	102	3.78	50	1.6
										Total	754.1

Next Batter:

Goddard, JDC	18	26	7	1950-57	left	0/4/5	83	547	28.79	50	29.7

Bowling Performances:

Player	Overs	Balls	Maids	Runs against	Bowl style	Wkts	5w/10w	Best	Bowl Avge	Strike rate	Econ rate	Bowling Rating
1. Stollmeyer, JB	106	636	18	327	RAL	8	0/0	2/12	40.88	79.50	3.08	19.4
2. Worrell, FMM[2]	682	4,269	153	1,701	LAO[2]	47	2/0	7/70	36.19	90.88	2.39	58.2
3. Kanhai, RB					Did not bowl							-
4. Weekes, EDC					Less than 100 overs							-
5. Walcott, CL	176	1,056	68	326	RAFM[3]	10	0/0	3/50	32.60	105.6	1.85	39.1
6. Sobers, GStA	661	3,967	218	1,444	LAMF	31	0/0	4/26	46.58	128.0	2.18	48.8
7. Smith, OG	739	4,432	229	1,625	RAO	48	1/0	5/90	33.85	92.31	2.20	65.2
8. Atkinson, DStE	768	4,637	294	1,423	RAM	42	3/0	7/53	33.88	110.4	1.84	71.9
9. Gomez, GE	572	3,640	193	1,105	RAFM	41	1/1	7/55	26.95	88.71	1.82	84.5
10. Ramadhin, S	1,946	12,154	726	3,950	RAO	138	10/1	7/49	28.62	88.06	1.95	99.7
11. Valentine, AL	1,787	11,157	708	3,568	LAO	123	8/2	8/104	29.01	90.71	1.92	100.4
											Total	587.2

Next Bowler:

Goddard, JDC	188	1,208	58	412	RAM	13	0/0	4/25	31.69	92.92	2.05	40.7

Notes:
1. A total of 53 different individuals represented the West Indies in this 10-year period, with 8 of them playing more than 20 test matches. By reducing the eligible number of matches to 18, the pool of players increased to 12 permitting the above selections.
2. Worrell was not a specialist opening batsman but has been elevated to that position because there were no other qualified openers. In addition to left arm orthodox, Worrell also bowled left arm medium.
3. Walcott is selected as the wicketkeeper.
4. In addition to left arm medium fast, Sobers also bowled left arm orthodox and chinaman.
5. In addition to right arm off break, Ramadhin also bowled right arm leg break.

Table F.4 The highest rating Indian team of the 1950s.

Batting Performances

Player	Tests	Innings	Not outs	Years played	Batting style	100s/50s/0s	HS	Runs scored	Batting Average	Strike rate	Batting Rating
1. Roy, P	39	72	4	1951-59	right	5/8/14	173	2,280	33.53	50	54.7
2. Mankad, MH	31	48	5	1951-59	right	3/5/3	231	1,536	35.72	50	58.2
3. Contractor, NJ	16	28	1	1955-59	left	0/7/2	92	821	30.41	50	40.1
4. Umrigar, PR	43	70	6	1951-59	right	7/11/4	223	2,520	39.38	50	75.9
5. Hazare, VS	17	27	3	1951-53	right	3/5/4	164	1,097	45.71	50	77.8
6. Manjrekar, VL	32	54	6	1951-59	right	4/7/7	177	1,682	35.04	50	56.5
7. Ramchand, GS	30	48	5	1952-59	right	2/5/5	109	1,124	26.14	50	33.5
8. Phadkar, DG	23	30	4	1951-58	right	1/4/2	115	675	25.96	50	31.8
9. Tamhane, NS	19	25	5	1955-59	right	0/1/7	54	222	11.10	50	6.1
10. Ghulam Ahmed	19	26	7	1952-58	right	0/1/8	50	161	8.47	50	4.2
11. Gupte, SP	31	39	12	1951-59	right	0/0/4	21	182	6.74	50	3.2
										Total	442.1

Bowling Performances:

Player	Overs	Balls	Maids	Runs against	Bowl style	Wkts	5w/10w	Best	Bowl Avge	Strike rate	Econ rate	Bowling Rating
1. Roy, P	\multicolumn{12}{c}{Less than 100 overs}	-
2. Mankad, MH	1,803	97.1	664	3570	LAO	122	7/2	8/52	29.26	88.69	1.98	97.1
3. Contractor, NJ				Less than 100 overs								-
4. Umrigar, PR	383	43.6	110	776	RAM	18	1/0	6/74	43.11	127.4	2.03	43.6
5. Hazare, VS	199	29.9	61	400	RAM	9	0/0	2/13	44.44	132.7	2.01	29.9
6. Manjrekar, VL				Less than 100 overs								-
7. Ramchand, GS	766	52.6	234	1,747	RAM	41	1/0	6/49	42.61	112.2	2.28	52.6
8. Phadkar, DG[2]	781	57.4	242	1,620	RAO	40	2/0	5/64	40.50	117.1	2.08	57.4
9. Tamhane, NS			Wicketkeeper					Did not bowl				-
10. Ghulam Ahmed	812	85.4	239	1,691	RAO	60	4/1	7/49	28.18	81.23	2.08	85.4
11. Gupte, SP	1,636	97.6	523	3,903	RAL	134	11/1	9/102	29.13	73.30	2.38	97.6
											Total	463.6

Notes: 1. A total of 60 different individuals represented India in this 10-year period, with 7 of them playing more than 20 test matches. By reducing the eligible number of matches to 16, the pool of players increased to 11 permitting the above selections.

2. In addition to right arm off break, Phadkar also bowled right arm medium fast.

Table F.5 South African players with more than 15 test matches in the 1950s.

Batting Performances

Player	Tests	Innings	Not outs	Years played	Batting style	100s/50s/0s	HS	Runs scored	Batting Average	Strike rate	Batting Rating
McGlew, DJ	24	45	3	1951-58	right	5/9/3	255	1,825	43.45	50	83.8
Goddard, TL	15	29	1	1955-58	left	0/6/2	90	852	30.43	50	38.1
Endean, WR	28	52	4	1951-58	right	3/8/3	162	1,630	33.96	50	54.6
McLean, RA	28	51	2	1951-58	right	3/7/8	142	1,420	28.98	50	42.6
Waite, JHB	31	57	5	1951-58	right	3/8/7	134	1,518	29.19	50	43.6
Cheetham, JE	21	37	6	1950-55	right	0/5/1	89	788	25.42	50	29.0
Funston, KJ	18	33	1	1952-58	right	0/5/2	92	824	25.75	50	29.2
van Ryneveld, CB	19	33	6	1951-58	right	0/3/2	83	724	26.81	50	27.3
Tayfield, HJ	30	48	8	1950-58	right	0/1/4	66	674	16.85	50	12.2
Adcock, NAT	19	28	8	1953-58	right	0/0/8	17	80	4.00	50	1.6

Bowling Performances:

Player	Overs	Balls	Maids	Runs against	Bowl style	Wkts	5w/10w	Best	Bowl Avge	Strike rate	Econ rate	Bowling Rating
McGlew, DJ				Less than 100 overs								-
Goddard, TL	720	5,130	298	1,315	LAM	47	2/0	5/31	27.98	109.2	1.54	85.3
Endean, WR				Did not bowl								-
McLean, RA				Less than 100 overs								-
Waite, JHB		Wicketkeeper			Did not bowl							-
Cheetham, JE				Less than 100 overs								-
Funston, KJ				Did not bowl								-
van Ryneveld, CB	199	1,554	27	671	RAL	17	0/0	4/67	39.47	91.41	2.59	31.5
Tayfield, HJ	1,593	11,875	526	3,686	RAO	153	14/2	9/113	24.09	77.61	1.86	119.1
Adcock, NAT	573	4,321	111	1,460	RAF	69	3/0	6/43	21.16	62.62	2.03	101.8

Note: A total of 38 different individuals represented South Africa in this 10-year period, with only 6 of them playing more than 20 test matches so a full eligible South Africa team could not be selected. Performances of all players with more than 15 test matches are shown.

Table F.6 Eligible New Zealand players in the 1950s

Batting Performances

Player	Tests	Innings	Not outs	Years played	Batting style	100s/50s/0s	HS	Runs scored	Batting Average	Strike rate	Batting Rating
Sutcliffe, B	29	54	5	1951-59	left	3/7/4	230	1,854	37.84	49.83	64.3
Reid, JR	32	58	3	1951-59	right	3/8/3	135	1,487	27.04	49.34	41.7
MacGibbon, AR	26	46	5	1951-58	right	0/3/7	66	814	19.85	50	15.8

Bowling Performances:

Player	Overs	Balls	Maids	Runs against	Bowl style	Wkts	5w/10w	Best	Bowl Avge	Strike rate	Econ rate	Bowling Rating
Sutcliffe, B				Less than 100 overs								-
Reid, JR	725	4,636	246	1,649	RAMF	47	0/0	4/34	35.09	98.64	2.13	63.4
MacGibbon, AR	886	5,659	228	2,160	RAFM	70	1/0	5/64	30.86	80.84	2.29	71.8

Note: 1. A total of 50 different individuals represented New Zealand in test cricket in the 1950s, but only the above 3 played 20 or more matches.

Table F.7 Eligible Pakistan players in the 1950s.

Batting Performances

Player	Tests	Innings	Not outs	Years played	Batting style	100s/50s/0s	HS	Runs scored	Batting Average	Strike rate	Batting Rating
Hanif Mohammad	27	48	3	1952-59	right	5/9/2	337	1,937	43.04	50	86.9
Imtiaz Ahmed	29	48	0	1952-62	right	2/7/6	209	1,320	27.50	50	42.6
Abdul Kardar	23	37	3	1952-58	left	0/5/1	93	847	24.91	50	28.5
Fazal Mahmood	26	39	6	1952-59	right	0/1/8	60	541	16.39	50	11.4
Wazir Mohammad	20	33	4	1952-59	right	2/3/8	189	801	27.62	50	35.5

Bowling Performances:

Player	Overs	Balls	Maids	Runs against	Bowl style	Wkts	5w/10w	Best	Bowl Avge	Strike rate	Econ rate	Bowling Rating
Hanif Mohammad					Less than 100 overs							-
Imtiaz Ahmed					Less than 100 overs							-
Abdul Kardar	452	2,713	139	954	LAM	21	0/0	3/35	45.43	129.1	2.11	45.5
Fazal Mahmood	1,302	7,815	452	2,765	RAFM	125	12/4	7/42	22.12	62.52	2.12	130.6
Wazir Mohammad					Less than 100 overs							-

Note: 1. A total of 35 different individuals represented Pakistan in test cricket in the 1950s, but only the above 5 played 20 or more matches.

Appendix G
Best National Teams — 1960 To 1969

Table G.1 The highest rating English team of the 1960s.

Batting Performances

Player	Tests	Innings	Not outs	Years played	Batting style	100s/50s/0s	HS	Runs scored	Batting Average	Strike rate	Batting Rating
1. Boycott, G	41	70	9	1964-69	right	6/13/6	246	2,609	42.77	45.81	82.0
2. Edrich, JH	40	63	4	1963/69	left	8/10/3	310	2,711	45.95	49.00	95.8
3. Dexter, ER	55	92	8	1960-68	right	8/26/4	205	4,232	50.38	49.69	110.2
4. Barrington, KF	75	122	15	1960-68	right	20/31/4	256	6,397	59.79	48.79	151.6
5. Cowdrey, MC	65	110	12	1960-69	right	16/21/6	182	4,788	48.86	49.67	110.1
6. Graveney, TW	31	47	3	1962-69	right	7/9/1	165	2,292	52.09	47.15	103.0
7. Parks, JM	45	67	7	1960-68	right	2/9/3	108	1,947	32.45	49.59	48.3
8. Titmus, FJ	47	64	11	1962-68	right	0/9/2	84	1,272	24.00	46.48	31.0
9. Trueman, FS	36	51	5	1960-65	right	0/0/5	38	580	12.61	50	8.3
10. Snow, JA	25	33	11	1965-69	right	0/1/8	59	273	12.41	44.25	6.7
11. Statham, JB	23	30	11	1960-65	right	0/0/4	26	246	12.95	50	7.5
										Total	754.5

Next Batter:

| Pullar, G | 25 | 45 | 4 | 1960-63 | left | 3/11/3 | 175 | 1,732 | 42.24 | 50 | 74.9 |
| D'Oliveira, BL | 25 | 38 | 6 | 1966-69 | right | 3/8/3 | 158 | 1,390 | 43.44 | 49.08 | 73.7 |

Bowling Performances:

Player	Overs	Balls	Maids	Runs against	Bowl style	Wkts	5w/10w	Best	Bowl Avge	Strike rate	Econ rate	Bowling Rating
1. Boycott, G	123	784	36	339	RAM	7	0/0	3/47	48.43	112.0	2.59	20.2
2. Edrich, JH				Less than 100 overs								-
3. Dexter, ER	792	4,939	168	2,186	RAM	60	0/0	4/10	36.43	82.32	2.66	56.8
4. Barrington, KF	390	2,433	95	1,165	RAL	24	0/0	3/4	48.54	101.4	2.87	34.3
5. Cowdrey, MC				Less than 100 overs								-
6. Graveney, TW				Less than 100 overs								-
7. Parks, JM		Wicketkeeper				Did not bowl						-
8. Titmus, FJ	2,147	13,773	723	4,470	RAO	145	7/0	7/79	30.83	94.99	1.95	89.2
9. Trueman, FS	1,443	8,978	290	3,940	RAF	179	12/3	7/44	22.01	50.16	2.63	130.7
10. Snow, JA	996	5,977	215	2,724	RAF	99	4/1	7/49	27.52	60.37	2.73	90.9
11. Statham, JB	955	6,061	216	2,524	RAF	93	4/1	6/63	27.14	65.17	2.50	90.5
											Total	512.7

Next Bowlers:

D'Oliveira, BL	555	3,330	191	1,146	RAM	0	0/0	2/38	45.84	133.2	2.06	49.9
Allen, DA	1,817	11,281	685	3,779	RAO	122	4/0	5/30	30.98	92.60	2.01	85.4
Illingworth, R	1,099	6,679	430	2,162	RAO	79	2/0	6/29	27.37	84.54	1.94	87.3

Note: 1. A total of 71 different individuals represented England in this 10-year period, with 20 of them playing more than 20 test matches.

Table G.2 The highest rating Australian team of the 1960s.

Batting Performances

Player	Tests	Innings	Not outs	Years played	Batting style	100s/50s/0s	HS	Runs scored	Batting Average	Strike rate	Batting Rating
1. Simpson, RB	46	84	6	1960-68	right	8/23/6	311	3,995	51.22	49.66	115.7
2. Lawry, WM	58	105	10	1960-69	left	13/23/5	210	4,717	49.65	50	112.0
3. Cowper, RM	27	46	2	1964-68	left	5/10/3	307	2,061	46.84	50	94.9
4. O'Neill, NC	32	53	3	1960-65	right	5/12/5	181	2,219	44.38	50	83.1
5. Walters, KD	21	34	4	1965-69	right	7/11/3	242	1,992	66.40	46.79	152.9
6. Burge, PJP	30	50	6	1960-66	right	4/10/3	181	1,931	43.89	50.17	78.9
7. Benaud, R	21	34	3	1960-64	right	0/5/2	90	761	24.55	50	27.4
8. Hawke, NJN	27	37	15	1963-68	right	0/0/6	45	365	16.59	46.44	10.6
9. McKenzie, GD	54	78	9	1961-69	right	0/2/14	76	886	12.84	50	9.4
10. Grout, ATW	37	50	5	1960-66	right	0/1/10	50	538	11.96	49.68	7.6
11. Connolly, AN	24	35	18	1963-69	right	0/0/8	37	163	9.59	50	4.9
										Total	697.4

Next Batters:

Booth, BC	29	48	6	1961-66	right	5/10/5	169	1,773	42.21	49.61	76.1
Chappell, IM	27	46	4	1964-69	right	4/8/3	165	1,675	39.88	49.88	68.3
Davidson, AK[2]	17	25	4	1960-63	left	0/2/1	80	540	25.71	50	24.9

Bowling Performances:

Player	Overs	Balls	Maids	Runs against	Bowl style	Wkts	5w/10w	Best	Bowl Avge	Strike rate	Econ rate	Bowling Rating
1. Simpson, RB	845	5,757	226	2,352	RAL	60	2/0	5/57	39.20	95.95	2.45	56.6
2. Lawry, WM				Less than 100 overs								-
3. Cowper, RM	459	3,011	138	1,139	RAO	36	0/0	4/48	31.64	83.47	2.27	66.8
4. O'Neill, NC	182	1,226	41	583	RAL	16	0/0	4/41	36.44	76.63	2.85	33.6
5. Walters, KD	133	1,010	21	432	RAM	11	0/0	4/53	39.27	91.82	2.57	25.6
6. Burge, PJP				Did not bowl								-
7. Benaud, R	1,095	7,907	329	2,752	RAL	83	5/0	6/70	33.16	95.27	2.09	75.3
8. Hawke, NJN	1,034	6,983	238	2,677	RAFM	91	6/1	7/105	29.42	76.64	2.30	84.3
9. McKenzie, GD	2,408	16,132	512	6,644	RAF	238	16/3	8/71	27.92	67.78	2.47	112.4
10. Grout, ATW		Wicketkeeper					Did not bowl					-
11. Connolly, AN	922	6,316	229	2,378	RAFM	81	2/0	5/72	29.36	77.97	2.26	77.3
											Total	532.1

Next Bowler:

Davidson, AK[2]	770	5,314	182	1,933	LAFM	94	9/1	6/53	20.56	56.53	2.18	122.1

Notes: 1. A total of 49 different individuals represented Australia in this 10-year period, with 15 of them playing more than 20 test matches.

2. Davidson only played 17 matches and was therefore ineligible for selection.

Table G.3 The highest rating West Indian team of the 1960s.

Batting Performances

Player	Tests	Innings	Not outs	Years played	Batting style	100s/50s/0s	HS	Runs scored	Batting Average	Strike rate	Batting Rating
1. Hunte, CC	33	59	5	1960-67	right	5/12/1	182	2,386	44.19	46.77	82.3
2. Nurse. SM	29	54	1	1960-69	right	6/10/3	258	2,523	47.60	50	95.1
3. Kanhai, RB	43	76	1	1960-69	right	10/18/2	153	3,739	49.85	50.06	105.9
4. Butcher, BF	36	65	4	1960-69	right	5/12/3	209	2,485	40.74	49.64	76.3
5. Lloyd, CH	18	33	3	1966-69	left	3/5/0	129	1,159	38.63	50	62.0
6. Sobers, GStA	49	86	10	1960-69	left	15/19/7	226	4,563	60.04	49.62	140.4
7. Solomon, JS	20	35	4	1960-65	right	0/5/6	96	831	26.81	42.64	26.9
8. Hendriks, JL	20	32	8	1962-69	right	0/2/4	64	447	18.63	50	13.9
9. Hall, WW	40	57	12	1960-69	right	0/2/4	50	764	16.98	51.07	13.0
10. Griffith, CC	28	42	10	1960-69	right	0/1/5	54	530	16.56	50.09	11.5
11. Gibbs, LR	42	62	22	1961-69	right	0/0/11	18	226	5.65	47.78	2.7
										Total	630.1

Bowling Performances:

Player	Overs	Balls	Maids	Runs against	Bowl style	Wkts	5w/10w	Best	Bowl Avge	Strike rate	Econ rate	Bowling Rating
1. Hunte, CC	\multicolumn{11}{c}{Less than 100 overs}	-
2. Nurse. SM	Less than 100 overs											-
3. Kanhai, RB	Less than 100 overs											-
4. Butcher, BF	Less than 100 overs											-
5. Lloyd, CH	Less than 100 overs											-
6. Sobers, GStA	2,066	13,399	514	5,232	LAMF	162	6/0	6/73	32.30	82.71	2.34	82.6
7. Solomon, JS	Less than 100 overs											-
8. Hendriks, JL	Wicketkeeper				Did not bowl							-
9. Hall, WW	1,336	8,486	229	4,249	RAF	146	6/0	7/69	29.10	58.12	3.00	88.4
10. Griffith, CC	884	5,629	177	2,683	RAF	94	5/0	6/36	28.54	59.90	2.86	85.0
11. Gibbs, LR	2,375	15,483	733	5,124	RAO	184	12/2	8/38	27.85	84.15	1.99	107.5
											Total	363.6

Notes: 1. A total of 42 different individuals represented the West Indies in this 10-year period, with 10 of them playing more than 20 test matches. By reducing the eligible number of matches to 18, the pool of players increased to 11 permitting the above selections.

2. In addition to left arm medium fast, Sobers also bowled left arm orthodox and left arm chinaman.

Table G.4 The highest rating Indian team of the 1960s.

Batting Performances

Player	Tests	Innings	Not outs	Years played	Batting style	100s/50s/0s	HS	Runs scored	Batting Average	Strike rate	Batting Rating
1. Engineer, FM	30	57	1	1961-69	right	1/8/3	109	1,607	28.70	50	39.8
2. Jaisimha, ML [2]	35	64	4	1960-69	right	3/12/7	129	2,004	33.40	50	53.9
3. Sardesai, DN	21	39	3	1961-69	right	2/7/4	200	1,190	33.06	50	52.2
4. Manjrekar, VL	23	38	4	1960-65	right	3/8/4	189	1,526	44.88	50	78.4
5. Pataudi, MAK [3]	39	71	2	1961-69	right	6/14/7	203	2,552	36.99	50	70.4
6. Borde, CG	45	79	10	1960-69	right	4/15/8	177	2,562	37.13	50	66.4
7. Surti, RF [4]	26	48	4	1960-69	left	0/9/5	99	1,263	28.70	50	37.0
8. Nadkarni, RG	33	52	11	1960-68	left	1/5/6	122	1,063	25.93	50	31.3
9. Durani, SA	23	40	2	1960-66	left	1/5/3	104	935	24.61	50	29.9
10. Desai, RB	21	30	8	1960-68	right	0/1/4	85	373	16.95	48.44	11.2
11. Prasanna, EAS	22	38	6	1962-69	right	0/0/6	26	362	11.31	50	6.7
										Total	477.1

Next Batter:

Wadekar, AL	21	42	2	1966-69	left	1/10/4	143	1,364	34.10	50	52.1

Bowling Performances:

Player	Overs	Balls	Maids	Runs against	Bowl style	Wkts	5w/10w	Best	Bowl Avge	Strike rate	Econ rate	Bowling Rating
1. Engineer, FM	\multicolumn{4}{Wicketkeeper}		\multicolumn{6}{Did not bowl}	-
2. Jaisimha, ML [2]	323	1,947	105	757	RAO	9	0/0	2/54	84.11	216.3	2.33	25.3
3. Sardesai, DN					Less than 100 overs							-
4. Manjrekar, VL					Less than 100 overs							-
5. Pataudi, MAK [3]					Less than 100 overs							-
6. Borde, CG	751	4,507	201	1,831	RAL	44	1/0	5/88	41.61	102.4	2.44	51.1
7. Surti, RF [4]	606	3,872	115	1,962	LAO	42	1/0	5/74	46.71	92.14	3.04	40.5
8. Nadkarni, RG	1,254	7,676	587	1,975	LAO	76	4/1	6/43	25.99	101.0	1.54	98.7
9. Durani, SA	990	5,942	298	2,437	LAO	71	3/1	6/73	34.32	83.69	2.46	71.8
10. Desai, RB	655	3,958	125	1,867	LAFM	57	1/0	6/56	32.75	69.44	2.83	64.9
11. Prasanna, EAS	1,194	7,556	344	3,057	RAO	113	8/1	6/74	27.05	66.87	2.43	99.3
											Total	451.6

Next Bowler:

Bedi, BS [5]	897	5,540	341	1,798	LAO	70	4/0	7/98	25.69	79.15	1.95	93.2

Notes: 1. A total of 54 different individuals represented India in this 10-year period, with 12 of them playing more than 20 test matches.

2. In addition to right arm off break, Jaisimna also bowled right arm medium.

3. Pataudi, MAK was also known as the Nawab of Pataudi Jr. and was the son of the las ruler of the state of Pataudi in the British Raj.

4. In addition to left arm orthodox, Surti also bowled left arm medium.

5. Bedi only played 19 games and was excluded from the top 11.

Table G.5 South African players with more than 17 test matches in the 1960s.

Player	Tests	Innings	Not outs	Years played	Batting style	100s/50s/0s	HS	Runs scored	Batting Average	Strike rate	Batting Rating
Barlow, EJ	26	50	2	1961-67	right	4/14/3	201	2,156	44.92	50	86.6
Goddard, TL	23	44	4	1960-67	left	1/12/2	112	1,606	40.15	50	64.7
Pollock, RG	19	34	4	1963-67	left	6/8/1	209	1,739	57.97	50	122.5
Bland, KC	21	39	5	1961-66	right	3/9/2	144	1,669	49.09	50	87.6
Waite, JHB	19	29	2	1960-65	right	1/8/2	101	887	32.85	50	48.9
Pollock, PM	24	34	10	1961-67	right	0/2/2	75	533	22.21	50	19.5
Lindsay, DT	17	27	1	1963-67	right	3/4/1	182	1,021	39.27	50	66.2

Bowling Performances:

Player	Overs	Balls	Maids	Runs against	Bowl style	Wkts	5w/10w	Best	Bowl Avge	Strike rate	Econ rate	Bowling Rating
Barlow, EJ	395	2,457	88	1,105	RAM	29	1/0	5/85	38.10	84.72	2.70	46.8
Goddard, TL	921	5,847	350	1,708	LAM	67	3/0	6/53	25.49	87.27	1.75	91.7
Pollock, RG				Less than 100 overs								-
Bland, KC				Less than 100 overs								-
Waite, JHB		Wicketkeeper					Less than 100 overs					-
Pollock, PM	919	5,832	231	2,548	RAF	101	8/1	6/38	25.23	57.74	2.62	104.3
Lindsay, DT		Wicketkeeper					Did not bowl					-

Notes: 1. A total of 41 different individuals represented South Africa in this 10-year period, with only 4 of them playing more than 20 test matches.

2. John Waite and Graeme Pollock (RG) only played 19 matches in the 1960s, and Denis Lindsay only 17.

3. Not included in the above figures are the statistics from the 4 tests played in 1970 (all won by South Africa) before the apartheid induced ban that ended South Africa's participation in test cricket. Barry Richards played just the 4 test matches in 1970 averaging 72.57 with the bat and Mike Procter played 7 matches from 1967 until 1970 with a bowling average of 15.02. Both played no additional test cricket.

Table G.6 Eligible New Zealand players in the 1960s.

Batting Performances

Player	Tests	Innings	Not outs	Years played	Batting style	100s/50s/0s	HS	Runs scored	Batting Average	Strike rate	Batting Rating
Reid, JR	24	46	2	1961-65	right	3/12/2	142	1,768	40.18	50	70.7
Dowling, GT	35	69	2	1961-69	right	3/10/6	239	2,163	32.28	50	56.6
Sinclair, BW	21	40	1	1963-68	right	3/3/5	138	1,148	29.44	50	40.3
Congdon, BE	29	58	2	1965-69	right	1/10/4	104	1,513	27.02	50	38.3
Taylor, BR	20	37	5	1965-69	left	2/2/6	124	712	22.25	49.86	24.7
Pollard, V	27	50	5	1965-69	right	0/5/4	81	848	18.84	50	18.1
Motz, RC	32	56	3	1961-69	right	0/3/12	60	612	11.55	50	7.6
Cameron, FJ	19	30	20	1961-65	right	0/0/4	27	116	11.60	50	6.1

Bowling Performances:

Player	Overs	Balls	Maids	Runs against	Bowl style	Wkts	5w/10w	Best	Bowl Avge	Strike rate	Econ rate	Bowling Rating
Reid, JR	513	3,078	199	1,172	RAMF	38	1/0	6/60	30.84	80.99	2.28	73.4
Dowling, GT				Less than 100 overs								-
Sinclair, BW				Less than 100 overs								-
Congdon, BE	151	907	49	374	RAM	11	0/0	3/33	34.00	82.42	2.48	33.0
Taylor, BR	582	3,614	123	1,664	RAFM	62	2/0	5/26	26.84	58.30	2.76	85.0
Pollard, V	631	3,893	183	1,637	RAO	36	0/0	3/3	45.47	108.1	2.52	46.2
Motz, RC	1,143	7,022	279	3,148	RAF	100	5/0	6/63	31.48	70.34	2.69	77.5
Cameron, FJ	762	4,565	220	1,849	RAFM	61	3/0	5/34	30.31	74.92	2.43	76.1

Note: 1. A total of 45 different individuals represented New Zealand in test cricket in the 1960s, but only 7 played 20 or more matches.

Table G.7 Pakistani players with more than 17 tests in the 1960s.

Batting Performances

Player	Tests	Inn	Not outs	Years played	Batting style	100s/50s/0s	HS	Runs scored	Batting Average	Strike rate	Batting Rating
Hanif Mohammad	28	49	5	1960-69	right	7/6/3	203	1,978	44.95	46.20	83.4
Saeed Ahmed	27	51	3	1960-69	right	3/9/2	172	1,792	37.33	49.49	62.7
Javed Burki	25	48	4	1960-69	right	3/4/3	140	1,341	30.48	47.86	43.2
Mushtaq Mohammad	21	37	4	1960-69	right	2/7/1	101	1,176	35.64	46.89	52.8
Asif Iqbal	17	29	1	1964-69	right	1/5/3	146	872	31.14	49.46	42.5
Intikhab Alam	25	42	8	1960-69	right	0/4/4	61	748	22.00	47.86	21.5
Nasim-ul-Ghani	18	31	4	1960-67	left	1/1/2	101	562	20.81	48.45	19.4

Bowling Performances:

Player	Overs	Balls	Maids	Runs against	Bowl style	Wkts	5w/10w	Best	Bowl Avge	Strike rate	Econ rate	Bowling Rating
Hanif Mohammad				Less than 100 overs								-
Saeed Ahmed	281	1,703	82	677	RAO	20	0/0	4/64	33.85	85.14	2.39	45.2
Javed Burki				Less than 100 overs								-
Mushtaq Mohammad	157	939	41	382	RAL	14	0/0	4/80	27.29	67.04	2.44	42.2
Asif Iqbal	428	2,610	134	962	RAO	40	2/0	5/48	24.05	65.25	2.21	86.1
Intikhab Alam	832	5,010	189	2,143	RAL	46	2/1	5/91	46.59	108.9	2.57	48.9
Nasim-ul-Ghani	397	2,392	113	1081	LAO	18	0/0	3/32	60.06	132.9	2.71	30.4

Note: 1. A total of 42 different individuals represented Pakistan in test cricket in the 1960s, but only 5 played 20 or more matches.

Appendix H
Best National Teams — 1970 To 1979

Table H.1 The highest rating English team of the 1970s.

Player	Tests	Innings	Not outs	Years played	Batting style	100s/ 50s/0s	HS	Runs scored	Batting Average	Strike rate	Batting Rating
1. Boycott, G	44	77	9	1970-79	right	12/21/2	191	3,806	55.97	34.97	121.5
2. Amiss, DL	45	80	9	1971-77	right	11/11/8	262	3,487	49.11	43.72	101.5
3. Edrich, JH	37	64	5	1970-76	left	4/14/3	175	2,427	41.14	34.76	71.5
4. Denness, MH	27	43	2	1972-75	right	4/6/2	188	1,610	39.27	41.79	65.1
5. Fletcher, KWR	46	76	10	1970-77	right	7/15/5	216	2,748	41.64	41.62	79.9
6. Greig, AW	58	93	4	1972-77	right	8/20/5	148	3,599	40.44	46.54	80.3
7. Botham, IT	22	30	1	1977-79	right	4/3/2	137	1,068	36.83	52.80	59.7
8. Knott, APE	71	112	10	1970-77	right	5/23/6	135	3,509	34.40	48.12	66.5
9. Underwood, DL	59	83	23	1970-79	right	0/0/13	43	661	11.02	37.71	6.5
10. Willis, RGD	51	70	35	1971-79	right	0/0/8	24	441	12.60	27.01	6.0
11. Hendrick, M.	25	28	9	1974-79	right	0/0/8	15	98	5.16	26.56	1.4
										Total	659.9

Next Batters:

Luckhurst, BW	21	41	5	1970-74	right	4/5/4	131	1,298	36.06	35.73	52.8
Randall, DW	26	43	4	1977-79	right	2/6/7	174	1,100	28.21	38.62	38.0

Bowling Performances:

Player	Overs	Balls	Maids	Runs against	Bowl style	Wkts	5w/10w	Best	Bowl Avge	Strike rate	Econ rate	Bowling Rating
1. Boycott, G					Less than 100 overs							-
2. Amiss, DL					Did not bowl							-
3. Edrich, JH					Did not bowl							-
4. Denness, MH					Did not bowl							-
5. Fletcher, KWR					Less than 100 overs							-
6. Greig, AW	1,557	9,807	338	4,541	RAMF	141	6/2	8/86	32.21	69.55	2.78	82.9
7. Botham, IT	811	5,386	191	2,274	RAMF	118	12/2	8/34	19.27	45.64	2.53	142.5
8. Knott, APE		Wicketkeeper					Did not bowl					-
9. Underwood, DL	2,383	15,374	787	5,587	LAO	202	10/4	8/51	27.66	76.11	2.18	110.9
10. Willis, RGD	1,460	9,917	280	4,511	RAF	182	11/0	7/78	24.79	54.49	2.73	109.1
11. Hendrick, M	770	5,074	200	1,766	RAFM	78	0/0	4/28	22.64	65.05	2.09	96.2
											Total	541.6

Next Bowlers:

Snow, JA	932	6,041	200	2,663	RAF	103	4/0	7/40	25.85	58.65	2.64	93.6
Old, CM	1,223	7,749	256	3,594	RAFM	129	4/0	7/50	27.86	60.07	2.78	89.0
Arnold, GG	1,125	7,136	257	3,077	RAMF	107	5/0	6/45	28.76	66.70	2.59	84.7

Note: 1. A total of 63 different individuals represented England in this 10-year period, with 21 of them playing more than 20 test matches.

Table H.2 The highest rating Australian team of the 1970s.

Batting Performances

Player	Tests	Innings	Not outs	Years played	Batting style	100s/50s/0s	HS	Runs scored	Batting Average	Strike rate	Batting Rating
1. Redpath, IR	33	64	7	1970-76	right	7/18/3	171	2,861	50.19	39.09	99.8
2. Stackpole, KR	26	50	2	1970-74	right	5/10/4	207	1,868	38.92	48.18	71.5
3. Chappell, IM	45	84	5	1970-76	right	10/17/8	196	3,512	44.46	47.50	91.5
4. Chappell, GS	54	96	13	1970-79	right	15/21/6	247	4,398	52.99	49.76	122.6
5. Walters, KD	47	82	8	1970-77	right	7/19/1	250	2,968	40.11	52.23	84.9
6. McCosker, RB	23	42	5	1975-79	right	4/9/5	127	1,545	41.76	43.08	69.1
7. Marsh, RW	55	88	9	1970-79	left	3/12/6	132	2,471	31.28	45.17	50.6
8. Walker, MHN	34	43	13	1972-77	right	0/1/5	78	586	19.53	42.31	13.6
9. Lillee, DK	35	45	14	1971-79	right	0/1/6	73	497	16.03	44.81	10.3
10. Thomson, JR	34	46	9	1972-79	right	0/0/11	49	433	11.70	50.41	7.2
11. Mallett, AA	28	36	8	1970-76	right	0/0/7	31	294	10.5	35.90	4.9
										Total	626.1

Next Batters:

Edwards, R	20	32	3	1972-75	right	2/9/4	170	1,171	40.38	45.94	67.3
Hughes, KJ	20	38	3	1977-79	right	3/8/2	130	1,426	40.74	39.24	65.1
Yallop, GN	21	41	3	1976-79	left	4/6/1	167	1,488	39.16	43.32	64.9

Bowling Performances:

Player	Overs	Balls	Maids	Runs against	Bowl style	Wkts	5w/10w	Best	Bowl Avge	Strike rate	Econ rate	Bowling Rating
1. Redpath, IR	\multicolumn{6}{Less than 100 overs}							-
2. Stackpole, KR	149	1,077	36	412	RAL	5	0/0	2/75	82.4	215.5	2.29	16.5
3. Chappell, IM	122	841	31	362	RAL	9	0/0	1/4	40.22	93.47	2.58	24.6
4. Chappell, GS	558	3,958	139	1,438	RAM	34	1/0	5/61	42.29	116.4	2.18	50.2
5. Walters, KD	301	2,200	54	946	RAM	38	1/0	5/66	24.89	57.90	2.58	73.3
6. McCosker, RB	Did not bowl											-
7. Marsh, RW	Wicketkeeper				Did not bowl							-
8. Walker, MHN	1,449	10,112	380	3,792	RAFM	138	6/0	8/143	27.48	73.14	2.25	92.4
9. Lillee, DK	1,343	9,515	296	4,376	RAF	184	12/4	6/26	23.78	51.71	2.76	127.8
10. Thomson, JR	1,086	7,513	210	3,892	RAF	152	6/0	6/46	25.61	49.43	3.11	104.7
11. Mallett, AA	943	6,841	246	2,709	RAO	91	3/0	8/59	29.77	75.17	2.38	79.0
											Total	568.5

Next Bowlers:

O'Keeffe, KJ	727	5,381	189	2,018	RAL	53	1/0	5/101	38.08	101.6	2.25	57.3

Note: 1. A total of 75 different individuals represented Australia in this 10-year period, with 15 of them playing more than 20 test matches.

Table H.3 The highest rating West Indian team of the 1970s.

Batting Performances

Player	Tests	Innings	Not outs	Years played	Batting style	100s/ 50s/0s	HS	Runs scored	Batting Average	Strike rate	Batting Rating
1. Fredericks, RC	49	90	7	1971-77	left	8/22/5	169	3,809	45.89	50	95.2
2. Greenidge, CG	21	40	3	1974-79	right	5/9/4	134	1,732	46.81	53.89	87.1
3. Richards, IVA	30	49	2	1974-79	right	9/9/2	291	2,736	58.21	50.96	130.0
4. Rowe, LG	26	41	2	1972-79	right	6/6/2	302	1,785	45.77	49.31	91.4
5. Kallicharran, AI	53	89	9	1972-79	left	11/20/7	187	3,956	49.45	50	106.2
6. Lloyd, CH	48	81	5	1971-79	left	8/17/3	242	3,475	45.72	49.76	96.1
7. Murray, DL	43	65	5	1973-79	right	0/10/4	91	1,553	25.88	49.52	34.8
8. Boyce, KD	21	30	3	1971-76	right	0/4/4	95	657	24.33	55.58	25.2
9. Holder, VA	37	53	11	1971-79	right	0/0/6	42	602	14.33	50	9.7
10. Roberts, AME	29	38	5	1974-79	right	0/1/5	54	290	8.79	51.06	4.8
11. Gibbs, LR	29	36	17	1971-76	right	0/0/2	25	151	7.95	47.04	3.7
										Total	684.3

Next Batter:

Sobers, GStA [2]	17	28	4	1971-74	left	5/4/4	178	1,256	52.33	48.95	98.1
Kanhai, RB [2]	18	29	3	1971-74	right	3/6/1	158	1,171	45.04	49.45	78.8
Julien, BD	24	34	6	1973-77	right	2/3/0	121	866	30.93	54.57	42.7

Bowling Performances:

Player	Overs	Balls	Maids	Runs against	Bowl style	Wkts	5w/ 10w	Best	Bowl Avge	Strike rate	Econ rate	Bowling Rating
1. Fredericks, RC	189	1,187	41	548	LAWS	7	0/0	1/12	78.29	169.6	2.77	15.4
2. Greenidge, CG				Less than 100 overs								-
3. Richards, IVA	102	644	27	235	RAO	4	0/0	2/34	58.75	160.9	2.19	12.0
4. Rowe, LG				Less than 100 overs								-
5. Kallicharran, AI				Less than 100 overs								-
6. Lloyd, CH	192	1,186	56	419	RAM	6	0/0	2/13	69.83	197.7	2.12	20.8
7. Murray, DL		Wicketkeeper				Did not bowl						-
8. Boyce, KD	542	3,497	99	1,801	RAF	60	2/1	6/77	30.02	58.35	3.09	78.7
9. Holder, VA	1,312	8,205	315	3,292	RAFM	100	3/0	6/28	32.92	82.05	2.41	71.8
10. Roberts, AME	1,145	7,331	234	3,521	RAF	140	9/2	7/54	25.15	52.36	2.88	112.1
11. Gibbs, LR	1,540	9,878	488	3,232	RAO	100	5/0	7/98	32.32	98.78	1.96	79.4
												390.3

Holding, MA [2]	522	3,411	121	1,596	RAF	65	4/1	8/92	24.55	52.48	2.81	103.0
Sobers, GStA [2]	706	4,232	242	1,323	LAO	42	0/0	4/64	31.5	100.8	1.88	70.0
Julien, BD	720	4,538	192	1,868	RAMF	50	1/0	5/57	37.36	90.84	2.47	57.4

Notes: 1. A total of 54 different individuals represented West Indies in this 10-year period, with 12 of them playing more than 20 test matches.

2. Sobers, Kanhai and Holding all played less than 20 matches in the decade and were therefore not considered for selection in the top 11.

Table H.4 The highest rating Indian team of the 1970s.

Batting Performances

Player	Tests	Inn	Not outs	Years played	Batting style	100s/50s/0s	HS	Runs scored	Batting Average	Strike rate	Batting Rating
1. Gavaskar, SM	60	108	7	1971-79	right	22/25/6	221	5,647	55.91	48.36	138.4
2. Chauhan, CPS	29	47	1	1973-79	right	0/13/5	93	1,501	32.63	48.64	47.6
3. Amarnath, M	25	43	2	1976-79	right	2/9/5	101	1,450	35.37	49.54	52.8
4. Vengsarkar, DB	34	56	6	1976-79	right	5/10/6	157	1,997	39.94	49.37	69.5
5. Viswanath, GR	62	108	8	1971-79	right	10/28/5	179	4,611	46.11	48.97	101.3
6. Gaekwad, AD	21	37	3	1974-79	right	1/5/1	102	1,089	32.03	47.91	41.6
7. Kapil Dev	23	31	3	1978-79	right	1/5/2	126	893	31.89	50	42.9
8. Kirmani, SMH	39	57	9	1976-79	right	1/6/3	101	1,360	28.33	48.18	36.0
9. Ghavri, KD	32	45	11	1974-79	left	0/2/1	86	777	22.85	47.73	21.8
10. Bedi, BS	48	69	20	1971-79	right	0/1/16	50	452	9.22	51.42	5.6
11. Chandrasekhar, BS	42	57	27	1971-79	right	0/0/18	20	95	3.17	31.46	1.0
										Total	558.5

Next Batter:

Solkar, ED	22	39	4	1971-77	left	1/6/0	102	877	25.06	43.03	32.0

Bowling Performances:

Player	Overs	Balls	Maids	Runs against	Bowl style	Wkts	5w/10w	Best	Bowl Avge	Strike rate	Econ rate	Bowling Rating
1. Gavaskar, SM					Less than 100 overs							-
2. Chauhan, CPS					Less than 100 overs							-
3. Amarnath, M	346	28.5	61	1,109	RAM	21	0/0	4/63	52.81	110.5	2.87	28.5
4. Vengsarkar, DB					Less than 100 overs							-
5. Viswanath, GR					Less than 100 overs							-
6. Gaekwad, AD					Less than 100 overs							-
7. Kapil Dev	793	90.1	170	2,413	RAFM	87	5/0	6/63	27.74	54.66	3.04	90.1
8. Kirmani, SMH			Wicketkeeper					Did not bowl				-
9. Ghavri, KD	936	68.3	195	2,925	LAFM	87	2/0	5/33	33.62	66.02	3.06	68.3
10. Bedi, BS	2,544	99.0	755	5,839	LAO	196	10/1	6/71	29.79	80.68	2.22	99.0
11. Chandrasekhar, BS	1,773	99.9	362	5,257	RAL	180	14/1	8/79	29.21	62.28	2.81	99.9
											Total	385.7

Next Bowler:

Prasanna, EAS	1,068	6,795	258	2,685	RAO	76	2/1	8/76	35.33	89.41	2.37	67.0

Note: 1. A total of 39 different individuals represented India in this 10-year period, with 15 of them playing more than 20 test matches.

Table H.5 The highest rating New Zealand team in the 1970s.

Batting Performances:

Player	Tests	Innings	Not outs	Years played	Batting style	100s/50s/0s	HS	Runs scored	Batting Average	Strike rate	Batting Rating
1. Turner, GM	30	52	4	1971-77	right	6/11/0	259	2,370	49.38	43.63	99.2
2. Parker, JM	30	52	2	1973-79	right	3/3/2	121	1,316	26.32	36.14	33.6
3. Congdon, BE	32	56	5	1971-78	right	6/9/5	176	1,935	37.94	41.17	65.9
4. Howarth, GP	17	32	3	1975-79	right	4/3/4	123	1,040	35.86	38.99	51.9
5. Burgess, MG	33	59	3	1971-79	right	4/9/2	111	1,815	32.41	43.26	50.8
6. Hastings, BF	20	35	3	1972-76	right	3/3/4	110	890	27.81	46.07	36.4
7. Wadsworth, KJ	24	36	4	1971-76	right	0/5/3	80	886	27.69	47.81	26.7
8. Hadlee, RJ	26	47	5	1973-79	left	0/3/4	87	844	20.10	48.90	19.0
9. Howarth, HJ	21	28	11	1971-77	left	0/1/6	61	248	14.59	37.69	7.7
10. Collinge, RO	22	32	11	1971-78	right	0/1/8	68	284	13.52	40.80	7.3
11. Hadlee, DR	18	29	3	1973-78	right	0/0/6	37	323	12.42	32.14	6.0
										Total	404.4

Bowling Performances:

Player	Overs	Balls	Maids	Runs against	Bowl style	Wkts	5w/10w	Best	Bowl Avge	Strike rate	Econ rate	Bowling Rating
1. Turner, GM					Less than 100 overs							-
2. Parker, JM					Less than 100 overs							-
3. Congdon, BE	672	4,716	148	1,780	RAM	48	1/0	5/65	37.08	98.24	2.26	56.2
4. Howarth, GP					Less than 100 overs							-
5. Burgess, MG					Less than 100 overs							-
6. Hastings, BF					Less than 100 overs							-
7. Wadsworth, KJ		Wicketkeeper				Did not bowl						-
8. Hadlee, RJ	871	6,374	125	3,225	RAF	107	6/2	7/23	30.14	59.57	3.04	87.3
9. Howarth, HJ	889	6,213	229	2,324	LAO	50	0/0	4/46	46.48	124.3	2.24	48.4
10. Collinge, RO	696	5,167	126	2,249	LAFM	79	3/0	6/63	28.47	65.41	2.61	79.6
11. Hadlee, DR	475	3,581	60	1,876	RAFM	44	0/0	4/42	42.64	81.39	3.14	41.9
											Total	313.5

Note: 1. A total of 39 different individuals represented New Zealand in this 10-year period, with 9 of them playing more than 20 test matches. To form a team, the minimum number of matches for consideration was reduced to 17 and this permitted the inclusion of Geoff Howarth and Dale Hadlee.

Table H.6 The highest rating Pakistan team in the 1970s.

Batting Performances:

Player	Tests	Inn	Not outs	Years played	Batting style	100s/ 50s/0s	HS	Runs scored	Batting Average	Strike rate	Batting Rating
1. Majid Khan	38	69	2	1971-79	right	7/11/4	167	2,884	43.04	49.25	81.1
2. Sadiq Mohammad	33	59	2	1971-79	left	5/9/4	166	2,271	39.84	48.39	69.7
3. Zaheer Abbas	36	64	4	1971-79	right	6/9/5	274	2,563	42.72	50.47	82.6
4. Javed Miandad	25	43	11	1976-79	right	6/10/2	206	2,059	64.34	50	137.3
5. Mushtaq Mohammad	35	61	3	1971-79	right	8/12/3	201	2,449	42.22	46.03	83.2
6. Asif Iqbal	39	66	5	1971-79	right	10/7/6	175	2,644	43.34	48.99	82.7
7. Wasim Raja	28	47	6	1973-79	left	2/10/4	117	1,575	38.41	48.70	59.9
8. Intikhab Alam	21	33	2	1971-77	right	1/4/5	138	739	23.84	49.86	28.2
9. Imran Khan	25	42	5	1971-79	right	0/1/2	59	832	22.49	48.26	19.8
10. Wasim Bari	45	68	18	1971-79	right	0/5/14	85	892	17.84	45.88	13.3
11. Sarfraz Nawaz	33	47	8	1972-79	right	0/2/5	53	626	16.05	49.96	11.3
										Total	669.1

Next Batter:

Mudassar Nazar	15	26	1	1976-79	right	2/3/0	126	786	31.44	43.21	43.9

Bowling Performances:

Player	Overs	Balls	Maids	Runs against	Bowl style	Wkts	5w/ 10w	Best	Bowl Avge	Strike rate	Econ rate	Bowling Rating
1. Majid Khan	277	1,910	66	771	RAO	15	0/0	4/45	51.4	127.3	2.42	30.1
2. Sadiq Mohammad				Less than 100 overs								-
3. Zaheer Abbas				Less than 100 overs								-
4. Javed Miandad	166	1,255	29	556	RAL	17	0/0	3/74	32.71	73.80	2.66	37.6
5. Mushtaq Mohammad	634	4,285	136	1893	RAL	65	3/0	5/28	29.12	65.93	2.65	77.1
6. Asif Iqbal	187	1,252	47	540	RAM	13	0/0	3/37	41.54	96.31	2.59	29.1
7. Wasim Raja	257	1,766	53	795	RAL	26	0/0	4/68	30.58	67.94	2.70	50.7
8. Intikhab Alam	780	5,309	189	2,289	RAL	76	3/1	7/52	30.12	69.86	2.59	80.1
9. Imran Khan	1,003	6,831	222	3,125	RAF	98	5/1	6/63	31.89	69.70	2.74	79.2
10. Wasim Bari		Wicketkeeper				Less than 100 overs						-
11. Sarfraz Nawaz	1,215	8,576	270	3,591	RAFM	120	4/1	9/86	29.93	71.47	2.51	83.9
											Total	467.8

Next Bowlers:

Sikander Bakht	504	3,398	101	1,631	RAFM	57	3/1	8/69	28.61	59.62	2.88	83.9
Iqbal Qasim	617	4,206	196	1,533	LAO	40	1/1	6/40	38.33	105.2	2.19	61.8
Saleem Altaf	479	3,237	88	1,440	RAFM	37	0/0	4/11	38.92	87.50	2.67	48.9

Note: 1. A total of 34 different individuals represented Pakistan in this 10-year period with only 11 of them playing more than 20 test matches. The next best batters and bowlers all played under 20 matches in the decade.

Appendix I
Best National Teams — 1980 To 1989

Table I.1 The highest rating English team of the 1980s.

Batting Performances:

Player	Tests	Innings	Not outs	Years played	Batting style	100s/50s/0s	HS	Runs scored	Batting Average	Strike rate	Batting Rating
1. Boycott, G	23	46	5	1980-82	right	4/8/2	137	1,699	41.44	36.30	66.8
2. Broad, BC	25	44	2	1984-89	left	6/6/3	162	1,661	39.55	37.86	67.3
3. Gooch, GA	56	105	2	1980-89	right	8/23/7	196	3,970	38.54	49.50	81.3
4. Gower, DI	89	157	11	1980-89	left	12/32/4	215	6,196	42.44	49.67	101.6
5. Gatting, MW	66	114	14	1980-89	right	9/18/12	207	3,859	38.59	46.75	78.2
6. Botham, IT	75	124	4	1980-89	right	10/19/12	208	4,051	33.76	64.04	75.8
7. Emburey, JE	55	81	17	1980-89	right	0/8/13	75	1,471	22.98	38.39	26.2
8. Taylor, RW (WK)	34	55	9	1980-84	right	0/1/8	54	652	14.17	30.54	8.0
9. Dilley, GR	40	56	18	1980-89	left	0/2/10	56	467	12.29	36.60	6.6
10. Foster, NA	28	43	7	1983-89	right	0/0/9	39	410	11.39	37.55	5.9
11. Willis, RGD	39	58	20	1980-84	right	0/0/4	28	399	10.50	38.40	5.4
										Total	523.1

Next Batters:

Randall, DW	21	36	1	1980-84	right	5/6/7	164	1,370	39.14	49.33	67.1
Lamb, AJ	57	100	9	1982-89	right	9/12/6	137	3,098	34.04	48.50	63.8
Fowler, G	21	37	0	1982-85	left	3/8/3	201	1,307	35.32	38.88	58.8

Bowling Performances:

Player	Overs	Balls	Maids	Runs against	Bowl style	Wkts	5w/10w	Best	Bowl Avge	Strike rate	Econ rate	Bowling Rating
1. Boycott, G					Less than 100 overs							-
2. Broad, BC					Less than 100 overs							-
3. Gooch, GA	227	1,359	67	529	RAM	13	0/0	2/12	40.69	104.5	2.34	32.9
4. Gower, DI					Less than 100 overs							-
5. Gatting, MW	124	744	29	316	RAM	4	0/0	1/14	79.00	186.0	2.55	12.9
6. Botham, IT	2,649	15,896	571	8,359	RAMF	258	15/2	8/103	32.40	61.61	3.16	100.0
7. Emburey, JE	2,148	12,890	636	4,759	RAO	120	6/0	7/78	39.66	107.4	2.22	69.7
8. Taylor, RW (WK)		Wicketkeeper				Did not bowl						-
9. Dilley, GR	1,329	7,975	275	4,010	RAF	135	6/0	6/38	29.70	59.08	3.02	86.9
10. Foster, NA	1,014	6,084	235	2,797	RAFM	88	5/1	8/107	31.78	69.14	2.76	78.4
11. Willis, RGD	1,240	7,447	274	3,679	RAF	143	5/0	8/43	25.73	52.08	2.96	101.6
											Total	482.4

Next Bowlers

Edmonds, PH	1,324	7,338	417	3,022	LAO	76	0/0	4/31	39.76	104.6	2.28	59.1
Pringle, DR	624	3,752	133	1,807	RAMF	48	2/0	5/95	37.65	78,16	2.89	51.8

Notes: 1. A total of 81 different individuals represented England in this 10-year period, with 20 of them playing more than 20 test matches.

2. Despite a lower batting rating than Downton, Taylor was the preferred wicketkeeper with significantly more dismissals per match.

Table I.2 The highest rating Australian team of the 1980s.

Batting Performances:

Player	Tests	Innings	Not outs	Years played	Batting style	100s/50s/0s	HS	Runs scored	Batting Average	Strike rate	Batting Rating
1. Boon, DC	45	82	7	1984-89	right	8/14/5	200	3,119	41.59	42.39	80.2
2. Wessels, KC	24	42	1	1982-85	left	4/9/3	179	1,761	42.95	50.90	77.8
3. Jones, DM	30	53	7	1984-89	right	7/9/4	216	2,370	51.52	48.69	101.7
4. Chappell, GS	33	55	6	1980-84	right	9/10/6	235	2,712	55.35	54.67	118.4
5. Border, AR	97	164	30	1980-89	left	20/40/4	205	7,386	55.12	42.23	137.3
6. Waugh, SR	35	54	10	1985-89	right	3/13/6	177	1,889	42.93	49.63	75.5
7. Marsh, RW	41	62	4	1980-84	left	0/4/6	91	1,162	20.03	44.10	20.6
8. Hughes, MG	20	24	3	1985-89	right	0/2/4	72	401	19.10	50.82	14.5
9. Lawson, GS	46	68	12	1980-89	right	0/4/6	74	894	15.96	50.11	13.2
10. Lillee, DK	35	45	10	1980-84	right	0/0/4	40	408	11.66	31.93	5.7
11. Alderman, TM	33	42	18	1981-89	right	0/0/10	23	163	6.79	27.72	2.3
										Total	647.2

Next Batters:

Yallop, GN [3]	18	29	0	1980-84	left	4/3/2	268	1,268	43.72	45.04	78.2
Hughes, KJ	50	86	3	1980-84	right	6/14/8	213	2,989	36.01	44.72	67.7
Matthews, GRJ	21	34	6	1983-86	left	3/4/1	130	1,031	36.82	44.61	54.7
Phillips, WB [2]	27	48	2	1983-86	left	2/7/1	159	1,485	32.28	43.41	48.3

Bowling Performances:

Player	Overs	Balls	Maids	Runs against	Bowl style	Wkts	5w/10w	Best	Bowl Avge	Strike rate	Econ rate	Bowling Rating
1. Boon, DC					Less than 100 overs							-
2. Wessels, KC					Less than 100 overs							-
3. Jones, DM					Less than 100 overs							-
4. Chappell, GS	229	1,371	69	475	RAM	13	0/0	3/49	36.54	105.5	2.08	37.6
5. Border, AR	304	1,824	91	738	LAO	21	1/1	7/46	35.14	86.82	2.43	46.8
6. Waugh, SR	603	3,617	139	1,787	RAM	42	2/0	5/69	42.55	86.11	2.96	47.7
7. Marsh, RW		Did not bowl					Wicketkeeper					-
8. Hughes, MG	749	4,495	172	2,332	RAF	72	4/1	8/87	32.39	62.43	3.11	77.3
9. Lawson, GS	1,853	11,113	386	5,501	RAFM	180	11/2	8/112	30.56	61.77	2.97	96.3
10. Lillee, DK	1,492	8,961	356	4,117	RAF	171	11/3	7/83	24.08	52.40	2.76	122.5
11. Alderman, TM	1,395	8,376	356	3,810	RAFM	136	11/1	6/128	28.01	61.59	2.73	99.7
											Total	527.9

Next Bowlers:

Yardley, B [3]	896	5,382	251	2,549	RAO	89	6/1	7/98	28.64	60.47	2.84	92.9
McDermott, CJ	838	5,030	133	2,735	RAFM	80	3/0	8/141	34.19	62.87	3.26	66.6
Hogg, RM	651	3,911	112	2,003	RAF	59	1/0	6/77	33.95	66.29	3.07	62.5
Matthews, GRJ	583	3,499	139	1,707	RAO	39	2/1	5/103	43.77	89.71	2.93	49.9

Notes: 1. A total of 67 different individuals represented Australia in this 10-year period, with 21 of them playing more than 20 test matches.

2. Wayne Phillips took over as wicketkeeper for Australia following the retirement of Rod Marsh.

3. Yallop and Yardley only played in 18 and 19 matches, respectively, and were therefore not eligible for inclusion in the top 11.

Table I.3 The highest rating West Indian team of the 1980s.

Batting Performances:

Player	Tests	Innings	Not outs	Years played	Batting style	100s/50s/0s	HS	Runs scored	Batting Average	Strike rate	Batting Rating
1. Greenidge, CG	75	123	12	1980-89	right	12/25/7	223	5,094	45.89	49.20	103.6
2. Haynes, DL	81	139	16	1980-89	right	12/28/7	184	5,074	41.25	43.92	91.4
3. Richards, IVA	78	112	8	1980-89	right	15/28/7	208	5,113	49.16	66.77	120.7
4. Richardson, RB	45	76	7	1983-89	right	10/13/3	194	3,320	48.12	46.58	98.2
5. Gomes, HA	49	72	11	1980-87	left	7/9/3	143	2,490	40.82	42.51	71.1
6. Lloyd, CH	44	61	6	1980-84	left	8/17/1	161	2,881	52.38	53.63	111.6
7. Dujon, PJL	64	89	9	1981-89	right	5/14/5	139	2,885	36.06	47.74	63.9
8. Marshall, MD	63	79	7	1980-89	right	0/8/10	92	1,430	19.86	52.09	20.3
9. Holding, MA	45	54	8	1980-87	right	0/5/12	73	685	14.89	61.60	11.8
10. Garner, J	49	56	13	1980-87	right	0/0/12	46	486	11.30	45.30	6.7
11. Walsh, CA	34	43	16	1984-89	right	0/0/8	30	277	10.26	46.71	5.4
										Total	704.7

Next Batter:

| Logie, AL | 37 | 56 | 6 | 1983-89 | right | 2/9/8 | 130 | 1,707 | 34.14 | 56.35 | 51.8 |

Bowling Performances:

Player	Overs	Balls	Maids	Runs against	Bowl style	Wkts	5w/10w	Best	Bowl Avge	Strike rate	Econ rate	Bowling Rating
1. Greenidge, CG				Less than 100 overs								-
2. Haynes, DL				Less than 100 overs								-
3. Richards, IVA	698	4,192	163	1,575	RAO	28	0/0	2/17	56.25	149.7	2.25	38.4
4. Richardson, RB				Less than 100 overs								-
5. Gomes, HA	368	2,210	74	831	RAM	14	0/0	2/20	59.36	157.9	2.26	28.6
6. Lloyd, CH				Less than 100 overs								-
7. Dujon, PJL		Wicketkeeper				Dis not bowl						-
8. Marshall, MD	2,399	14,398	511	6,434	RAF	323	22/4	7/22	19.92	44.58	2.68	160.3
9. Holding, MA	1,544	9,274	338	4,302	RAF	184	9/1	6/21	23.38	50.40	2.78	118.6
10. Garner, J	1,814	10,876	491	4,331	RAF	210	7/0	6/56	20.62	51.79	2.39	127.6
11. Walsh, CA	1,102	6,619	240	2,958	RAF	122	4/1	6/62	24.25	54.25	2.68	104.5
											Total	578.1

Next Bowlers:

Harper, RA	577	3,168	171	1,252	RAF	45	1/0	6/57	27.82	70.40	2.37	78.9
Croft, CEH	666	3,997	138	1,793	RAF	73	2/0	6/74	24.56	54.75	2.69	94.5
Roberts, AME	632	3,793	148	1,653	RAF	62	2/0	5/39	26.66	61.18	2.61	85.3
Patterson, BP	474	2,848	62	1,759	RAF	59	3/0	5/24	29.81	48.26	3.71	79.9

Notes: 1. A total of 40 different individuals represented the West Indies in this 10-year period, with 13 of them playing more than 20 test matches.

2. Croft, Roberts and Patterson all played less than 20 matches in the decade.

Table I.4 The highest rating Indian team of the 1980s.

Batting Performances:

Player	Tests	Innings	Not outs	Years played	Batting style	100s/50s/0s	HS	Runs scored	Batting Average	Strike rate	Batting Rating
1. Gavaskar, SM	65	106	9	1980-87	right	12/20/6	236	4,475	46.13	47.61	101.5
2. Srikkanth, K	39	64	3	1981-89	right	2/12/6	123	1,927	31.59	51.40	49.6
3. Amarnath, M	43	68	7	1982-88	right	9/15/6	138	2,912	47.74	49.34	95.0
4. Vengsarkar, DB	71	112	16	1980-89	right	12/22/7	166	4,501	46.89	47.61	100.0
5. Azharuddin, M	34	51	3	1984-89	right	7/9/2	199	2,224	46.33	51.42	91.2
6. Shastri, RJ	69	104	14	1981-89	right	8/11/9	142	3,036	33.73	43.88	60.2
7. Kapil Dev	80	118	9	1980-89	right	5/17/11	163	3,353	30.76	54.85	59.7
8. Kirmani, SMH (WK)	49	67	13	1980-86	right	1/6/4	102	1,399	25.91	48.22	32.8
9. Sharma, C	23	27	9	1984-89	right	0/1/2	54	396	22.00	51.43	17.3
10. Yadav, NS	26	31	9	1980-87	right	0/0/2	43	325	14.77	33.93	7.8
11. Doshi, DR	23	29	8	1980-83	left	0/0/11	14	86	4.10	27.65	1.1
										Total	616.2

Next Batters:

Player	Tests	Innings	Not outs	Years played	Batting style	100s/50s/0s	HS	Runs scored	Batting Average	Strike rate	Batting Rating
Patil, SM	29	47	4	1980-84	right	4/7/4	174	1,588	36.93	57.18	63.3
Sharma, Y	24	40	7	1980-83	right	1/5/2	140	1,015	30.76	44.11	39.7

Bowling Performances:

Player	Overs	Balls	Maids	Runs against	Bowl style	Wkts	5w/10w	Best	Bowl Avge	Strike rate	Econ rate	Bowling Rating
1. Gavaskar, SM				Less than 100 overs								-
2. Srikkanth, K				Less than 100 overs								-
3. Amarnath, M	194	1,170	29	621	RAM	9	0/0	2/34	69.00	130.0	3.19	13.5
4. Vengsarkar, DB				Less than 100 overs								-
5. Azharuddin, M				Less than 100 overs								-
6. Shastri, RJ	2,420	14,526	629	5,573	LAO	141	2/0	5/75	39.52	103.0	2.30	67.5
7. Kapil Dev	2,815	16,888	615	8,036	RAFM	272	16/2	9/83	29.54	62.09	2.86	108.2
8. Kirmani, SMH (WK)		Wicketkeeper				Less than 100 overs						-
9. Sharma, C	578	3,470	61	2,163	RAFM	61	4/1	6/58	35.46	56.89	3.74	66.7
10. Yadav, NS	1,063	6,388	264	2,710	RAO	70	3/0	5/76	38.71	91.25	2.55	59.0
11. Doshi, DR	1,084	6,501	317	2,542	LAO	74	4/0	6/102	34.35	87.86	2.35	69.8
											Total	384.6

Next Bowlers:

Player	Overs	Balls	Maids	Runs against	Bowl style	Wkts	5w/10w	Best	Bowl Avge	Strike rate	Econ rate	Bowling Rating
Singh, M	1,302	7,817	347	3,143	LAO	81	3/2	7/27	38.80	96.51	2.41	66.2
Binny, RMH	405	2,433	63	1,265	RAMF	38	2/0	6/56	33.29	64.04	3.12	56.4

Note: 1. A total of 55 different individuals represented India in this 10-year period, with 18 of them playing more than 20 test matches.

Table I.5 The highest rating New Zealand team in the 1980s.

Batting Performances:

Player	Tests	Innings	Not outs	Years played	Batting style	100s/50s/0s	HS	Runs scored	Batting Average	Strike rate	Batting Rating
1. Wright, JG	56	100	4	1980-89	left	7/13/4	141	3,271	34.07	35.29	60.6
2. Edgar, BA	33	57	4	1980-86	left	2/11/5	161	1,662	31.36	32.11	46.6
3. Howarth, GP	30	51	2	1980-85	right	2/8/3	147	1,491	30.43	40.86	44.3
4. Crowe, MD	45	76	7	1982-89	right	10/11/7	188	3,127	45.32	42.61	87.9
5. Crowe, JJ	38	64	4	1983-89	right	3/6/6	128	1,592	26.53	34.49	35.6
6. Coney, JV	45	73	14	1980-87	right	3/14/3	174	2,303	39.03	43.09	66.9
7. Hadlee, RJ	53	80	14	1980-89	left	2/10/7	151	2,040	30.91	58.22	49.7
8. Smith, IDS (WK)	49	70	15	1980-89	right	1/5/7	113	1,376	25.02	58.63	32.4
9. Bracewell, JG	35	54	10	1980-89	right	1/4/11	110	925	21.02	39.86	20.2
10. Cairns, BL	29	40	3	1980-85	right	0/1/5	64	581	15.70	64.34	12.4
11. Chatfield, EJ	39	47	30	1982-89	right	0/0/10	21	149	8.76	22.54	2.8
										Total	459.5

Next Batter:

Reid, JF [2]	18	29	3	1981-86	left	6/2/3	180	1,277	49.12	35.41	86.6

Bowling Performances:

Player	Overs	Balls	Maids	Runs against	Bowl style	Wkts	5w/10w	Best	Bowl Avge	Strike rate	Econ rate	Bowling Rating
1. Wright, JG					Less than 100 overs							-
2. Edgar, BA					Less than 100 overs							-
3. Howarth, GP					Less than 100 overs							-
4. Crowe, MD	206	1,239	46	607	RAM	13	0/0	2/25	46.69	95.28	2.94	24.0
5. Crowe, JJ					Less than 100 overs							-
6. Coney, JV	372	2,238	116	800	RAM	24	0/0	3/28	33.33	93.24	2.14	53.8
7. Hadlee, RJ	2,308	13,852	628	5,574	RAF	289	28/7	9/52	19.29	47.93	2.41	171.4
8. Smith, IDS (WK)	Wicketkeeper				Less than 100 overs							-
9. Bracewell, JG	1,170	7,025	302	3,057	RAO	82	3/1	6/32	37.28	85.67	2.61	65.0
10. Cairns, BL	1,222	7,330	344	3,025	RAFM	101	5/1	7/74	29.95	72.58	2.48	85.3
11. Chatfield, EJ	1,551	9,312	471	3,473	RAMF	115	3/1	6/73	30.20	80.98	2.24	84.2
											Total	483.8

Next Bowlers:

Boock, SL	798	4,792	236	2,008	LAO	57	3/0	7/87	35.23	84.08	2.51	65.3
Snedden, MC [2]	537	2,354	133	1,534	RAM	44	1/0	5/68	34.86	73.27	2.85	53.4

Notes: 1. A total of 41 different individuals represented New Zealand in this 10-year period, with 12 of them playing more than 20 test matches.

2. Reid and Snedden both played less than 20 matches in the 1980s.

Table I.6 The highest rating Pakistan team in the 1980s.

Batting Performances:

Player	Tests	Innings	Not outs	Years played	Batting style	100s/50s/0s	HS	Runs scored	Batting Average	Strike rate	Batting Rating
1. Mudassar Nazar	61	90	7	1980-89	right	8/14/7	231	3,328	40.10	46.46	79.5
2. Mohsin Khan	42	69	6	1981-86	right	7/9/3	200	2,427	38.52	51.82	72.4
3. Shoaib Mohammad	26	37	3	1983-89	right	4/8/4	203	1,543	45.38	44.55	81.6
4. Javed Miandad	76	110	7	1980-89	right	16/26/3	280	5,642	54.78	49.17	134.0
5. Zaheer Abbas	41	58	7	1980-85	right	6/11/5	215	2,460	48.24	55.19	95.1
6. Saleem Malik	56	77	13	1982-89	right	7/14/6	119	2,642	41.28	49.64	75.2
7. Imran Khan	54	71	16	1980-89	right	5/13/4	135	2,430	44.18	53.76	80.1
8. Saleem Yousuf (WK)	25	34	5	1982-89	right	0/5/2	91	878	30.28	51.53	35.9
9. Wasim Akram	29	34	6	1985-89	left	0/2/8	66	468	16.71	50.16	11.4
10. Abdul Qadir	57	66	9	1980-89	right	0/3/6	61	914	16.04	45.13	12.1
11. Iqbal Qasim	32	34	8	1980-88	left	0/1/4	56	421	16.19	44.83	10.3
										Total	687.6

Next Batters:

Player	Tests	Innings	Not outs	Years played	Batting style	100s/50s/0s	HS	Runs scored	Batting Average	Strike rate	Batting Rating
Qasim Omar	26	43	2	1983-86	right	3/5/2	210	1,502	36.63	50	59.7
Wasim Raja	29	45	8	1980-85	left	2/8/4	125	1,246	33.68	53.39	50.5
Ramiz Raja	29	46	3	1984-89	right	2/9/2	122	1,379	32.07	49.60	49.1

Bowling Performances:

Player	Overs	Balls	Maids	Runs against	Bowl style	Wkts	5w/10w	Best	Bowl Avge	Strike rate	Econ rate	Bowling Rating
1. Mudassar Nazar	844	5,063	181	2169	RAM	56	1/0	6/32	38.73	90.41	2.57	53.5
2. Mohsin Khan				Less than 100 overs								-
3. Shoaib Mohammad				Less than 100 overs								-
4. Javed Miandad				Less than 100 overs								-
5. Zaheer Abbas				Less than 100 overs								-
6. Saleem Malik				Less than 100 overs								-
7. Imran Khan	2,005	12,028	483	4,896	RAF	256	18/5	8/58	19.13	46.98	2.44	157.4
8. Saleem Yousuf (WK)		Wicketkeeper				Did not bowl						-
9. Wasim Akram	1,034	6,199	240	2,649	LAF	94	5/1	6/91	28.18	65.95	2.56	88.1
10. Abdul Qadir	2,528	15,175	548	6,980	RAL	216	14/5	9/56	32.31	70.25	2.76	102.1
11. Iqbal Qasim	1,468	8,809	453	3,274	LAO	131	7/1	7/49	24.99	67.24	2.23	104.8
											Total	505.8

Next Bowlers:

Player	Overs	Balls	Maids	Runs against	Bowl style	Wkts	5w/10w	Best	Bowl Avge	Strike rate	Econ rate	Bowling Rating
Tausif Ahmed	1,162	6,974	334	2,573	RAO	87	3/0	6/45	29.57	80.17	2.21	79.8
Sarfraz Nawaz	861	5,168	209	2,129	RAFM	57	0/0	4/42	37.35	90.67	2.47	56.4

Note: 1. A total of 53 different individuals represented Pakistan in this 10-year period, with 17 of them playing more than 20 test matches.

Table I.7 Sri Lankan players with more than 20 test matches in the 1980s.

Batting Performances

Player	Tests	Innings	Not outs	Years played	Batting style	100s/50s/0s	HS	Runs scored	Batting Average	Strike rate	Batting Rating
Dias, RL	20	36	1	1982-87	right	3/8/2	109	1,285	36.71	48.55	59.6
Madugalle, RS	21	39	4	1982-88	right	1/7/4	103	1,029	29.40	44.97	37.8
Mendis, LRD	24	43	1	1982-88	right	4/8/2	124	1,329	31.64	54.96	53.7
Ranatunga, A	26	46	2	1982-89	left	2/12/3	135	1,621	36.84	48.92	61.0
Wettimuny, S	23	43	1	1982-87	right	2/6/5	190	1,221	29.07	43.39	42.1
Ratnayeke, JR	22	38	6	1982-89	left	0/5/5	93	807	25.22	47.17	26.1
De Mel, ALF	17	28	5	1982-86	right	0/0/5	34	326	14.17	51.42	8.9
De Silva, PA	17	31	2	1984-89	right	3/3/0	167	974	33.59	49.24	52.2

Bowling Performances:

Player	Overs	Balls	Maids	Runs against	Bowl style	Wkts	5w/10w	Best	Bowl Avge	Strike rate	Econ rate	Bowling Rating
Dias, RL				Less than 100 overs								-
Madugalle, RS				Less than 100 overs								-
Mendis, LRD				Did not bowl								-
Ranatunga, A	259	1,554	78	688	RAM	11	0/0	2/17	62.55	141.3	2.66	23.7
Wettimuny, S				Less than 100 overs								-
Ratnayeke, JR	639	3,829	118	1,972	RAFM	55	4/0	7/83	35.85	69.65	3.09	61.5
De Mel, ALF	586	3,516	92	2,180	RAFM	59	3/0	6/109	36.95	59.66	3.72	60.9
De Silva, PA				Less than 100 overs								-

Note: 1. A total of 45 different individuals represented Sri Lanka in this 10-year period, but only the above 8 players played more than 17 matches.

Appendix J
Best National Teams — 1990 To 1999

Table J.1 The highest rating English team of the 1990s.

Batting Performances:

Player	Tests	Inn	Not outs	Years played	Batting style	100s/50s/0s	HS	Runs scored	Batting Average	Strike rate	Batting Rating
1. Gooch, GA	45	83	2	1990-95	right	12/17/3	333	4,176	51.56	50.99	120.7
2. Atherton, MA	91	168	6	1990-99	right	13/38/18	185	6,217	38.38	37.21	90.1
3. Hussain, N	45	81	8	1990-99	right	8/13/9	207	2,918	39.97	39.73	74.8
4. Smith, RA	54	96	13	1990-96	right	7/24/6	175	3,538	42.63	44.63	85.7
5. Thorpe, GP	57	105	13	1993-99	left	6/24/8	138	3,599	39.12	46.19	75.8
6. Lamb, AJ	22	39	1	1990-92	right	5/6/3	142	1,558	41.00	58.33	73.5
7. Stewart, AJ (WK)	93	169	12	1990-99	right	12/34/7	190	6,407	40.81	47.84	97.5
8. Caddick, AR	28	44	5	1993-99	right	0/0/8	48	508	13.03	33.27	7.0
9. Gough, D	34	51	8	1994-99	right	0/2/10	65	514	11.95	41.35	6.9
10. Fraser, ARC	43	62	15	1990-98	right	0/0/9	32	341	7.26	28.00	3.0
11. Tufnell, PCR	40	55	28	1990-99	right	0/0/13	22	144	5.33	21.40	1,5
										Total	636.6

Next Batter:

Hick, GA	54	94	6	1991-99	right	5/17/6	178	3,005	34.15	51.34	65.1
Crawley, JP	29	47	5	1994-99	right	3/7/3	156	1,329	31.64	38.50	47.1
Ramprakash, MR	38	67	6	1991-99	right	1/10/10	154	1,701	27.89	34.37	37.7

Bowling Performances:

Player	Overs	Balls	Maids	Runs against	Bowl style	Wkts	5w/10w	Best	Bowl Avge	Strike rate	Econ rate	Bowling Rating
1. Gooch, GA	173	1,038	45	447	RAM	9	0/0	3/39	49.67	115.4	2.58	22.2
2. Atherton, MA				Less than 100 overs								-
3. Hussain, N				Less than 100 overs								-
4. Smith, RA				Less than 100 overs								-
5. Thorpe, GP				Less than 100 overs								-
6. Lamb, AJ				Did not bowl								-
7. Stewart, AJ (WK)		Wicketkeeper					Less than 100 overs					-
8. Caddick, AR	1,077	6,462	251	3,132	RAFM	106	7/0	7/46	29.55	60.96	2.91	86.6
9. Gough, D	1,230	7,382	242	3,925	RAF	135	6/0	6/42	29.07	54.68	3.19	90.4
10. Fraser, ARC	1,667	10,015	409	4,513	RAFM	168	13/2	8/53	26.86	59.61	2.70	108.5
11. Tufnell, PCR	1,800	10,812	493	4,289	LAO	119	5/2	7/47	36.04	90.85	2.38	76.4
											Total	384.1

De Freitas, PAJ	1,186	7,122	270	3,404	RAFM	114	3/0	7/70	29.86	62.47	2.87	82.0
Cork, DG	993	5,964	193	3,118	RAFM	98	5/0	7/43	31.82	60.86	3.14	77.2
Malcolm, DE	1,369	8,215	250	4,582	RAF	127	5/2	9/57	36.08	64.69	3.35	74.1

Note: A total of 84 different individuals represented England in this 10-year period, with 19 of them playing more than 20 test matches.

Table J.2 The highest rating Australian team of the 1990s.

Batting Performances

Player	Tests	Inn	Not outs	Years played	Batting style	100s/ 50s/0s	HS	Runs scored	Batting Average	Strike rate	Batting Rating
1. Taylor, MA	93	166	12	1990-99	left	15/35/5	334	6,306	40.95	41.02	105.2
2. Slater, MJ	58	103	5	1993-99	right	13/16/9	219	4,425	45.15	52.64	98.7
3. Boon, DC	62	108	13	1990-96	right	13/18/11	164	4,303	45.29	40.00	92.4
4. Ponting, RT	33	52	5	1995-99	right	6/10/3	197	2,092	44.51	48.99	84.5
5. Waugh, SR	89	143	26	1990-99	right	18/28/11	200	6,213	53.10	47.45	125.4
6. Waugh, ME	99	164	11	1991-99	right	17/37/15	153	6,371	41.64	51.74	101.2
7. Healy, IA (WK)	102	159	21	1990-99	right	4/21/15	161	3,949	28.62	51.11	59.2
8. Warne, SK	80	113	12	1992-99	right	0/4/20	86	1,577	15.61	54.38	14.2
9. Hughes, MG	33	46	5	1990-94	right	0/0/6	45	631	15.39	43.85	10.1
10. McDermott, CJ	47	57	10	1991-96	right	0/0/8	42	601	12.79	58.57	9.2
11. McGrath, GD	58	72	23	1993-99	right	0/0/21	39	286	5.84	37.93	2.6
										Total	703.2

Next Batters:

Border, AR	45	73	11	1990-94	left	4/17/6	200	2,686	43.32	39.90	79.1
Blewett, G.S	43	74	4	1995-99	right	4/15/5	214	2,483	35.47	42.20	64.5
Jones, DM	22	36	4	1990-92	right	4/5/7	150	1,261	39.41	49.28	62.4
Langer, JL	29	48	1	1993-99	left	5/9/4	179	1,702	36.21	42.23	63.0

Bowling Performances:

Player	Overs	Balls	Maids	Runs against	Bowl style	Wkts	5w/ 10w	Best	Bowl Avge	Strike rate	Econ rate	Bowling Rating
1. Taylor, MA												-
2. Slater, MJ												-
3. Boon, DC												-
4. Ponting, RT												-
5. Waugh, SR	585	3,512	170	1,374	RAM	47	1/0	5/28	29.23	74.72	2.35	74.2
6. Waugh, ME	677	4,060	147	1,984	RAO	50	1/0	5/40	39.68	81.21	2.93	51.1
7. Healy, IA (WK)	Wicketkeeper				Did not bowl							-
8. Warne, SK	3,762	22,567	1157	9,009	RAL	351	16/4	8/71	25.67	64.29	2.40	133.1
9. Hughes, MG	1,298	7,794	327	3,685	RAF	140	3/0	5/64	26.32	55.67	2.84	97.3
10. McDermott, CJ	1,926	11,562	450	5,597	RAFM	211	11/2	8/97	26.53	54.79	2.90	113.1
11. McGrath, GD	2,325	13,954	642	6,086	RAFM	266	15/1	8/38	22.88	52.46	2.62	131.6
											Total	600.5

Next Bowlers:

| Reiffel, PR | 1,067 | 6,397 | 280 | 2,804 | RAFM | 104 | 5/0 | 6/71 | 26.96 | 61.57 | 2.63 | 91.5 |
| Fleming, DW[2] | 632 | 3,796 | 140 | 1,772 | RAFM | 73 | 2/0 | 5/30 | 24.27 | 52.00 | 2.80 | 97.8 |

Notes: 1. A total of 56 different individuals represented Australia in this 10-year period, with 17 of them playing more than 20 test matches.

2. Fleming only played 18 matches in the 1990s and was not considered for selection in the top 11.

Table J.3 The highest rating West Indian team of the 1990s.

Batting Performances

Player	Tests	Innings	Not outs	Years played	Batting style	100s/50s/0s	HS	Runs scored	Batting Average	Strike rate	Batting Rating
1. Haynes, DL	31	56	8	1990-94	right	6/8/3	167	2,147	44.73	47.52	80.4
2. Campbell, SL	36	63	3	1995-99	right	4/12/6	208	2,184	36.40	41.11	63.3
3. Richardson, RB	41	70	5	1990-95	right	6/14/5	182	2,629	40.45	49.39	76.4
4. Lara, BC	65	112	4	1990-99	left	13/29/4	375	5,573	51.60	62.05	133.7
5. Hooper, CL	64	110	12	1990-99	right	8/15/10	178	3,514	35.86	52.81	70.6
6. Adams, JC	39	63	12	1992-99	left	5/11/4	208	2,326	45.61	40.08	81.9
7. Murray, JR (WK)	31	42	4	1993-99	right	1/3/7	101	917	24.13	55.61	25.6
8. Ambrose, CEL	71	104	21	1990-99	left	0/1/20	53	1,016	12.24	50.73	9.4
9. Bishop, IR	39	58	8	1990-98	right	0/0/9	48	577	11.54	36.22	6.4
10. Benjamin, KCG	26	36	8	1992-98	right	0/0/8	43	222	7.93	41.57	3.6
11. Walsh, CA	78	110	36	1990-99	right	0/0/27	30	557	7.53	46.47	4.6
										Total	555.9

Next Batters:

Chanderpaul, S	37	62	7	1994-99	left	2/18/4	137	2,234	40.62	40.75	69.6
Arthurton, KLT	28	42	3	1992-95	left	2/8/7	157	1,277	32.74	42.42	47.4

Bowling Performances:

Player	Overs	Balls	Maids	Runs against	Bowl style	Wkts	5w/10w	Best	Bowl Avge	Strike rate	Econ rate	Bowling Rating
1. Haynes, DL	\multicolumn{11}{c}{Did not bowl}	-
2. Campbell, SL	\multicolumn{11}{c}{Did not bowl}	-
3. Richardson, RB	\multicolumn{11}{c}{Less than 100 overs}	-
4. Lara, BC	\multicolumn{11}{c}{Less than 100 overs}	-
5. Hooper, CL	1,544	4,337	354	3,851	RAO	86	4/0	5/26	44.78	107.8	2.49	49.9
6. Adams, JC	284	1,707	54	845	LAO	19	1/0	5/17	44.47	89.82	2.97	30.2
7. Murray, JR (WK)	Wicketkeeper				Did not bowl							-
8. Ambrose, CEL	2,689	16,156	730	6,225	RAF	309	21/3	8/45	20.15	52.28	2.31	151.1
9. Bishop, IR	1,273	7,647	250	3,541	RAF	145	5/0	6/40	24.42	52.74	2.78	104.2
10. Benjamin, KCG	855	5,126	158	2,785	RAFM	92	4/1	6/66	30.27	55.78	3.26	84.0
11. Walsh, CA	3,012	18,072	624	7,891	RAF	304	13/1	7/37	25.96	59.45	2.62	117.7
											Total	537.1

Note: 1. A total of 55 different individuals represented the West Indies in this 10-year period, with 15 of them playing more than 20 test matches.

Table J.4 The highest rating Indian team of the 1990s.

Batting Performances

Player	Tests	Inn	Not outs	Years played	Batting style	100s/50s/0s	HS	Runs scored	Batting Average	Strike rate	Batting Rating
1. Sidhu, NS	38	56	0	1990-99	right	7/12/6	201	2,517	44.95	43.90	86.8
2. Prabhakar, MM	33	48	5	1990-95	right	1/8/3	120	1,346	31.30	38.28	41.6
3. Dravid, R	34	58	4	1996-99	right	6/16/1	190	2,698	49.96	38.78	98.8
4. Tendulkar, SR	69	109	12	1990-99	right	22/21/7	217	5,626	58.00	55.30	143.9
5. Azharuddin, M	64	94	6	1990-99	right	14/12/3	192	3,880	44.09	60.16	96.9
6. Ganguly, SC	32	54	5	1996-99	left	7/12/4	173	2,432	49.63	47.66	97.6
7. Kapil Dev	28	35	3	1990-94	right	2/5/3	129	1,002	31.31	60.18	46.2
8. Mongia, NR	40	61	6	1994-99	right	1/6/5	152	1,343	24.42	37.82	31.2
9. Kumble, A	58	75	14	1990-99	right	0/3/8	88	1,079	17.69	40.29	13.1
10. Srinath, J	43	62	16	1991-99	right	0/4/5	76	771	16.76	52.53	14.3
11. Venkatapathy Raju, SL	27	33	10	1990-98	right	0/0/3	31	236	10.26	32.87	4.4
										Total	674.8

Next Batters:

Kambli, VG [2]	17	21	1	1993-95	left	4/3/3	227	1,084	54.20	59.46	109.6
Manjrekar, SV	28	46	4	1990-96	right	1/6/2	104	1,259	29.98	36.14	36.7
More, K	21	26	5	1990-93	right	0/5/2	73	587	27.95	36.89	30.5

Bowling Performances:

Player	Overs	Balls	Maidens	Runs against	Bowl style	Wickets	5w/10w	Best	Bowling Avge	Strike rate	Econ rate	Bowling Rating
1. Sidhu, NS					Did not bowl							
2. Prabhakar, MM	1,035	6,212	244	2,937	RAM	79	1/0	5/101	37.18	78.63	2.84	59.6
3. Dravid, R					Less than 100 overs							
4. Tendulkar, SR	152	912	34	460	RAM	13	0/0	2/7	35.38	70.13	3.03	30.3
5. Azharuddin, M					Less than 100 overs							
6. Ganguly, SC	192	1,154	38	628	RAM	19	0/0	3/28	33.05	60.73	3.27	38.4
7. Kapil Dev	1,014	6,079	275	2,418	RAFM	75	2/0	5/97	32.24	81.06	2.39	70.9
8. Mongia, NR			Wicketkeeper					Did not bowl				
9. Kumble, A	3,033	18,206	786	7,341	RAL	264	15/3	10/74	27.81	68.96	2.42	116.0
10. Srinath, J	1,695	10,182	382	4,892	RAFM	162	6/1	8/86	30.20	62.85	2.88	90.1
11. Venkatapathy Raju, SL	1,231	7,397	354	2,741	LAO	92	5/1	6/12	29.79	80.40	2.22	84.8
											Total	490.2

Prasad, BKV	1,015	6,092	235	2,864	RAMF	84	6/1	6/33	34.10	72.53	2.82	73.7
Chauhan, RK	791	4,741	238	1,857	RAO	47	0/0	4/48	39.51	101.0	2.35	54.8

Notes: 1. A total of 52 different individuals represented India in this 10-year period, with 15 of them playing more than 20 test matches.

2. Kambli played only 17 matches and was not therefore eligible for selection in the top 11.

Table J.5 The highest rating New Zealand team in the 1990s.

Batting Performances:

Player	Tests	Inn	Not outs	Years played	Batting style	100s/50s/0s	HS	Runs scored	Batting Average	Strike rate	Batting Rating
1. Horne, MJ	24	45	2	1997-99	right	3/5/1	157	1,453	33.79	43.21	50.8
2. Young, BA	35	68	4	1993-99	right	2/12/5	267	2,034	31.78	38.91	54.9
3. Jones, AH	29	55	7	1990-95	right	6/7/1	186	2,171	45.23	39.47	80.1
4. Crowe, MD	32	55	4	1990-95	right	7/7/2	299	2,317	45.43	47.76	90.5
5. Fleming, SP	48	84	6	1994-99	left	2/23/7	174	2,984	38.26	41.94	69.9
6. Astle, NJ	34	60	5	1996-99	right	5/9/4	125	2,020	36.73	46.61	60.7
7. Cairns, CL	43	72	3	1991-99	right	2/17/5	126	2,026	29.36	50.36	49.9
8. Parore, AC (WK)	58	98	10	1990-99	right	1/13/4	100	2,249	25.56	38.81	38.4
9. Nash, DJ	30	43	13	1992-99	right	0/3/5	89	642	21.40	33.72	17.0
10. Doull, SB	30	46	10	1992-99	right	0/0/10	46	501	13.92	63.82	10.4
11. Morrison, DK	39	60	23	1990-97	right	0/0/18	42	332	8.97	23.46	3.5
										Total	526.2

Next Batters:

Player	Tests	Inn	Not outs	Years played	Batting style	100s/50s/0s	HS	Runs scored	Batting Average	Strike rate	Batting Rating
Wright, JG [2]	18	33	3	1990-93	left	5/7/2	185	1,662	55.40	36.73	105.5
McMillan, CD [2]	19	32	3	1997-99	right	3/7/2	142	1,256	43.31	58.92	76.8
Rutherford, KR	40	72	5	1990-95	right	2/16/8	105	2,097	31.30	48.28	50.0

Bowling Performances:

Player	Overs	Balls	Maids	Runs against	Bowl style	Wkts	5w/10w	Best	Bowl Avge	Strike rate	Econ rate	Bowling Rating
1. Horne, MJ	\multicolumn{11}{l}{Less than 100 overs}	-
2. Young, BA	\multicolumn{11}{l}{Did not bowl}	-
3. Jones, AH	\multicolumn{11}{l}{Less than 100 overs}	-
4. Crowe, MD	\multicolumn{11}{l}{Less than 100 overs}	-
5. Fleming, SP	\multicolumn{11}{l}{Did not bowl}	-
6. Astle, NJ	405	2,427	114	1,013	RAM	22	0/0	2/26	46.05	110.3	2.50	39.2
7. Cairns, CL	1,364	8,186	307	4,335	RAFM	150	9/1	7/27	28.90	54.57	3.18	97.5
8. Parore, AC (WK)	Wicketkeeper				Did not bowl							-
9. Nash, DJ	968	5,814	287	2,503	RAM	92	3/1	6/27	27.21	63.20	2.58	91.8
10. Doull, SB	960	5,766	239	2,730	RAFM	97	6/0	7/65	28.14	59.44	2.84	89.3
11. Morrison, DK	1,397	8,383	265	4,600	RAFM	139	9/0	7/89	33.09	60.31	3.29	81.0
											Total	398.7

Next Bowlers:

Player	Overs	Balls	Maids	Runs against	Bowl style	Wkts	5w/10w	Best	Bowl Avge	Strike rate	Econ rate	Bowling Rating
Vettori, DL	1,247	7,483	354	3,161	LAO	91	3/0	6/64	34.74	82.23	2.53	69.3
Patel, DN	1,028	6,166	237	2,944	RAO	74	3/0	6/50	39.78	83.33	2.86	56.6

Notes: 1. A total of 57 different individuals represented New Zealand in this 10-year period, with 15 of them playing more than 20 test matches.

2. Wright and MacMillan played less than 20 matches and were not eligible for selection in the top 11.

Table J.6 The highest rating Pakistan team in the 1990s.

Batting Performances

Player	Tests	Innings	Not outs	Years played	Batting style	100s/50s/0s	HS	Runs scored	Batting Average	Strike rate	Batting Rating
1. Saeed Anwar	44	75	2	1990-99	left	9/21/8	188	3,366	46.11	57.23	99.9
2. Aamir Sohail	45	79	3	1992-98	left	5/13/4	205	2,777	36.54	55.99	69.9
3. Ijaz Ahmed	44	71	4	1990-99	right	11/10/5	211	2,815	42.01	46.18	84.6
4. Inzamam-ul-Haq	58	97	11	1992-99	right	8/23/8	200	3,717	43.22	51.45	90.6
5. Javed Miandad	23	36	3	1990-93	right	1/7/1	153	1,131	34.27	43.50	49.7
6. Saleem Malik	47	77	9	1990-99	right	8/15/6	237	3,126	45.97	50.68	94.2
7. Moin Khan (WK)	50	77	6	1990-99	right	3/13/5	117	2,049	28.86	50.17	47.1
8. Wasim Akram	62	96	10	1990-99	left	2/3/7	257	1,956	22.74	51.49	39.1
9. Saqlain Mushtaq	24	38	7	1995-99	right	0/2/9	79	402	12.97	22.64	5.9
10. Mushtaq Ahmed	43	63	13	1990-99	right	0/2/12	59	606	12.12	35.86	6.9
11. Waqar Younis	56	76	18	1990-99	right	0/0/11	45	607	10.47	46.69	6.6
										Total	594.5

Next Batters:

| Ramiz Raja | 28 | 48 | 2 | 1990-97 | right | 0/13/5 | 98 | 1,454 | 31.61 | 46.29 | 45.2 |
| Shoaib Mohammad[2] | 19 | 31 | 4 | 1990-95 | right | 3/5/2 | 203 | 1,162 | 43.04 | 36.19 | 69.9 |

Bowling Performances:

Player	Overs	Balls	Maids	Runs against	Bowl style	Wkts	5w/10w	Best	Bowl Avge	Strike rate	Econ rate	Bowling Rating
1. Saeed Anwar				Less than 100 overs								-
2. Aamir Sohail	355	2,130	71	950	LAO	20	0/0	4/54	47.5	106.5	2.68	31.9
3. Ijaz Ahmed				Less than 100 overs								-
4. Inzamam-ul-Haq				Less than 100 overs								-
5. Javed Miandad				Did not bowl								-
6. Saleem Malik				Less than 100 overs								-
7. Moin Khan (WK)		Wicketkeeper					Did not bowl					-
8. Wasim Akram	2,354	14,127	529	6,200	LAF	289	17/3	7/119	21.45	48.88	2.63	143.6
9. Saqlain Mushtaq	1,159	6,962	281	3,119	RAO	107	9/2	6/46	29.15	65.06	2.69	95.5
10. Mushtaq Ahmed	1,797	10,780	361	5,152	RAL	172	10/3	7/56	29.95	62.68	2.87	98.4
11. Waqar Younis	1,862	11,174	375	5,927	RAF	273	21/5	7/76	21.71	40.93	3.18	155.7
											Total	525.0

Next Bowler:

| Aaqib Javed | 605 | 3,632 | 130 | 1,714 | LAFM | 54 | 1/0 | 5/84 | 31.74 | 67.27 | 2.83 | 68.1 |

Notes: 1. A total of 63 different individuals represented Pakistan in this 10-year period, with 15 of them playing more than 20 test matches.

2. Shoaib Mohammad played less than 20 matches and was not eligible for selection in the top 11.

Table J.7 The highest rating Sri Lankan team in the 1990s.

Batting Performances

Player	Tests	Innings	Not outs	Years played	Batting style	100s/50s/0s	HS	Runs scored	Batting Average	Strike rate	Batting Rating
1. Jayasuriya, ST	44	74	9	1991-99	left	5/14/9	340	2,751	42.32	64.23	89.6
2. Mahanama, RS	46	79	1	1990-98	right	4/10/7	225	2,333	29.91	42.17	52.1
3. Gurusinha, AP	32	55	5	1990-96	left	6/8/2	143	2,038	40.76	36.91	68.9
4. De Silva, PA	62	104	9	1990-99	right	14/18/6	267	4,448	46.82	51.99	107.0
5. Ranatunga, A	60	97	8	1990-99	left	2/22/9	131	3,074	34.54	49.76	62.0
6. Tillakaratne, HP	55	89	14	1990-99	left	6/16/7	126	2,966	39.55	39.22	69.3
7. Kaluwitharana, RS	33	50	3	1992-99	right	3/7/3	132	1,432	30.47	60.93	48.6
8. Dharmasena, HDPK	20	35	5	1993-98	right	0/2/3	62	660	22.00	33.33	16.8
9. Vaas, WPUJC	34	47	7	1994-99	left	0/2/5	57	680	17.00	37.40	11.0
10. Muralitharan, M	48	62	25	1992-99	right	0/0/12	39	481	13.00	62.88	9.4
11. Wickramasinghe, GP	36	56	5	1991-99	right	0/1/12	51	528	10.35	50.19	6.5
										Total	541.2

Next Batter:

| Atapattu, MS | 29 | 51 | 5 | 1990-99 | right | 3/3/10 | 223 | 1,447 | 31.46 | 43.44 | 44.3 |
| Jayawardene, DPMdS | 15 | 22 | 1 | 1997-99 | right | 2/5/1 | 242 | 933 | 44.43 | 46.44 | 79.7 |

Bowling Performances:

Player	Overs	Balls	Maids	Runs against	Bowl style	Wkts	5w/10w	Best	Bowl Avge	Strike rate	Econ rate	Bowling rating
1. Jayasuriya, ST	477	2,867	105	1,263	LAO	29	0/0	4/40	43.55	98.87	2.64	42.4
2. Mahanama, RS				Less than 100 overs								-
3. Gurusinha, AP	192	1,154	42	509	RAM	13	0/0	2/7	39.15	88.80	2.65	29.1
4. De Silva, PA	308	1,850	50	878	RAO	23	0/0	3/30	38.17	80.44	2.85	37.4
5. Ranatunga, A	134	806	35	339	RAM	5	0/0	2/60	67.80	161.2	2.52	15.3
6. Tillakaratne, HP				Less than 100 overs								-
7. Kaluwitharana, RS		Wicketkeeper					Did not bowl					-
8. Dharmasena, HDPK	791	4,746	193	1,893	RAO	50	3/0	6/72	37.86	94.92	2.39	58.3
9. Vaas, WPUJC	1,224	7,352	269	3,166	LAFM	108	4/1	6/87	29.31	68.07	2.58	84.4
10. Muralitharan, M	2,479	14,874	625	6,140	RAO	227	17/2	9/65	27.05	65.52	2.48	115.0
11. Wickramasinghe, GP	1,091	6,549	219	3,202	RAFM	75	3/0	6/60	42.69	87.32	2.93	51.2
											Total	433.1

Next Bowler:

| Pushpakumara, KR | 530 | 3,180 | 74 | 1,932 | RAFM | 52 | 4/0 | 7/116 | 37.15 | 61.16 | 3.64 | 59.6 |

Notes: 1. A total of 51 different individuals represented Sri Lanka in this 10-year period, with 13 of them playing more than 20 test matches.

2. Jayawardene and Pushpakumara played less than 20 matches.

Table J.8 The highest rating South African team in the 1990s.

Batting Performances

Player	Tests	Innings	Not outs	Years played	Batting style	100s/50s/0s	HS	Runs scored	Batting Average	Strike rate	Batting Rating
1. Kirsten, G	56	100	9	1993-99	left	10/18/8	275	3,792	41.67	41.28	88.0
2. Hudson, AC	35	63	3	1993-98	right	4/13/7	163	2,007	33.45	39.13	55.8
3. Cronje, WJ	64	106	9	1992-99	right	6/23/8	135	3,689	38.03	44.84	73.2
4. Kallis, JH	32	51	6	1995-99	right	5/10/3	148	1,849	41.09	36.18	69.5
5. Cullinan, DJ	53	87	8	1993-99	right	9/16/10	275	3,354	42.46	50.2	89.2
6. Rhodes, JN	48	73	8	1992-99	right	3/15/4	117	2,321	35.71	46.30	59.5
7. McMillan, BM	38	62	12	1992-98	right	3/13/3	113	1,968	39.36	42.86	63.7
8. Boucher, MV (WK)	24	30	4	1997-99	right	3/4/3	125	844	32.46	45.94	47.3
9. Pollock, SM	38	56	12	1995-99	right	0/8/2	92	1,404	31.91	50.18	42.1
10. Donald, AA	59	75	27	1992-99	right	0/0/13	34	532	11.08	35.54	6.0
11. Adams, PR	28	31	8	1995-99	right	0/0/6	29	139	6.04	38.29	2.3
										Total	596.6

Next Batters:

Klusener, L	25	33	5	1996-99	left	2/3/2	174	954	34.07	68.14	52.8
Gibbs, HH [2]	17	30	1	1996-99	right	2/3/2	211	969	33.41	42.76	48.4
Richardson, DJ (WK)	42	64	8	1992-98	right	1/8/7	109	1,359	24.27	43.27	30.7

Bowling Performances:

Player	Overs	Balls	Maids	Runs against	Bowl style	Wkts	5w/10w	Best	Bowl Avge	Strike rate	Econ rate	Bowling Rating
1. Kirsten, G					Less than 100 overs							-
2. Hudson, AC					Did not bowl							-
3. Cronje, WJ	591	3,550	226	1,185	RAM	37	0/0	3/14	32.03	95.94	2.00	69.5
4. Kallis, JH	633	3,800	202	1,508	RAFM	53	1/0	5/90	28.45	71.69	2.38	78.8
5. Cullinan, DJ					Less than 100 overs							-
6. Rhodes, JN					Less than 100 overs							-
7. McMillan, BM	1,009	6,065	255	2,537	RAMF	75	0/0	4/65	33.83	80.72	2.51	65.1
8. Boucher, MV (WK)		Wicketkeeper						Did not bowl				-
9. Pollock, SM	1,411	8,460	407	3,294	RAFM	161	10/0	7/87	20.46	52.55	2.34	126.9
10. Donald, AA	2,164	12,995	544	6,200	RAF	284	19/3	8/71	21.83	45.76	2.86	147.2
11. Adams, PR	949	5,698	249	2,560	LAWS	86	1/0	6/55	29.77	66.26	2.70	77.9
											Total	565.4

Next Bowlers:

Klusener, L	713	4,281	184	1,996	RAFM	52	1/0	8/64	38.38	82.33	2.80	55.5
De Villiers, PS [2]	801	4,812	221	2,061	RAFM	85	5/2	6/23	24.25	56.53	2.57	109.0
Matthews, CR [2]	663	3,988	231	1,502	RAFM	52	2/0	5/42	28.88	76.54	2.26	79.6

Notes: 1. A total of 39 different individuals represented South Africa in this 10-year period, with 14 of them playing more than 20 test matches.

2. Gibbs, De Villiers and Matthews all played less than 20 matches and were not eligible for selection in the top 11.

Table J.9 Zimbabwean players with more than 20 test matches in the 1990s.

Batting Performances

Player	Matches	Inn	Not outs	Years played	Batting style	100s/50s/0s	HS	Runs scored	Batting Average	Strike rate	Batting Rating
Flower, A	39	70	12	1992-99	left	6/16/4	156	2,580	44.48	40.71	82.1
Flower, GW	38	70	3	1992-99	right	5/8/8	201	2,230	33.28	35.43	54.2
Campbell, ADR	39	70	2	1992-99	left	0/11/6	99	1,773	26.07	41.76	34.6
Houghton, DL	22	36	2	1992-97	right	4/4/0	266	1,464	43.06	45.45	77.2
Streak, HH	27	43	7	1993-99	right	0/2/9	53	536	14.89	33.73	8.5
Whittall, GJ	31	54	4	1993-99	right	2/7/4	203	1,368	27.36	38.71	40.6
Strang, PA	20	34	7	1994-98	right	1/2/2	106	747	27.67	44.92	29.4

Bowling Performances:

Player	Overs	Balls	Maids	Runs against	Bowl style	Wkts	5w/10w	Best	Bowl Avge	Strike rate	Econ rate	Bowling Rating
Flower, A	\multicolumn{4}{c}{Wicketkeeper}		\multicolumn{6}{c}{Did not bowl}	-
Flower, GW	198	1,191	41	525	LAO	6	0/0	1/8	87.50	198.5	2.64	14.9
Campbell, ADR	\multicolumn{11}{c}{Less than 100 overs}	-
Houghton, DL	\multicolumn{11}{c}{Less than 100 overs}	-
Streak, HH	1,027	6,168	255	2,726	RAFM	111	4/0	6/90	24.56	55.57	2.65	100.8
Whittall, GJ	634	3,811	162	1,706	RAFM	42	0/0	4/18	40.62	90.73	2.69	49.9
Strang, PA	809	4,859	182	2,154	RAL	57	3/0	5/106	37.79	85.24	2.66	58.1

Note: 1. A total of 43 different individuals represented Zimbabwe in this 10-year period, but only the above 7 players played more than 20 matches.

Appendix K
Best National Teams — 2000 To 2009

Table K.1 The highest rating English team of the 2000s.

Batting Performances

Player	Tests	Innings	Not outs	Years played	Batting style	100s/50s/0s	HS	Runs scored	Batting Average	Strike rate	Batting Rating
1. Trescothick, ME	76	143	10	2000-06	left	14/29/12	219	5,825	43.80	54.52	104.3
2. Strauss, AJ	69	126	5	2004-09	left	18/18/9	177	5,367	44.36	49.71	100.6
3. Vaughan, MP	80	143	9	2000-08	right	18/18/9	197	5,631	42.02	51.87	97.7
4. Pietersen, KP	56	100	4	2005-09	right	16/16/4	226	4,799	49.99	62.50	118.4
5. Thorpe, GP	43	74	15	2000-05	left	10/15/4	200	3,145	53.31	45.58	110.9
6. Collingwood, PD	55	96	10	2003-09	right	9/18/4	206	3,732	43.40	45.96	89.1
7. Prior, MJ (WK)	25	40	7	2007-09	right	2/11/5	131	1,390	42.12	63.61	73.6
8. Flintoff, A	74	122	9	2000-09	right	5/26/15	167	3,695	32.70	61.92	68.7
9. Sidebottom, RJ	21	29	11	2001-09	right	0/0/2	31	298	16.56	33.87	9.1
10. Gough, D	24	35	10	2000-03	right	0/0/4	39	341	13.64	47.10	8.1
11. Hoggard, MJ	67	92	27	2000-08	right	0/0/19	38	473	7.28	22.63	3.2
										Total	783.7

Next Batters:

Cook, AN	50	90	5	2006-09	left	10/20/3	160	3,654	42.99	47.01	89.1
Bell, IR	51	91	9	2004-09	right	9/21/7	199	3,291	40.13	50.27	83.8
Butcher, MA	46	83	6	2000-04	left	6/19/5	173	3,115	40.45	45.26	78.0
Stewart, AJ	40	66	9	2000-03	right	3/11/7	124	2,056	36.07	49.06	57.1

Bowling Performances:

Player	Overs	Balls	Maids	Runs against	Bowl style	Wkts	5w/10w	Best	Bowl Avge	Strike rate	Econ rate	Bowling Rating
1. Trescothick, ME					Less than 100 overs							-
2. Strauss, AJ					Did not bowl							-
3. Vaughan, MP	147	882	19	497	RAO	6	0/0	2/71	82.83	147.0	3.38	9.3
4. Pietersen, KP	124	747	9	525	RAO	4	0/0	1/0	131.3	186.8	4.22	3.9
5. Thorpe, GP					Did not bowl							-
6. Collingwood, PD	268	1,610	40	891	RAM	15	0/0	3/23	59.40	107.4	3.32	18.1
7. Prior, MJ (WK)		Wicketkeeper					Did not bowl					-
8. Flintoff, A	2,393	14,363	486	7,124	RAF	220	3/0	5/58	32.38	65.29	2.98	84.7
9. Sidebottom, RJ	771	4,625	182	2,133	RAFM	77	5/1	7/47	27.70	60.07	2.77	90.9
10. Gough, D	740	4,440	126	2,578	RAF	94	3/0	5/61	27.43	47.23	3.48	93.3
11. Hoggard, MJ	2,318	13,921	492	7,564	RAFM	248	7/1	7/61	30.5	56.08	3.26	98.8
											Total	398.8

Next Bowlers:

Caddick, AR	1,181	7,099	249	3,867	RAFM	128	6/1	0	30.21	55.46	3.27	89.7
Harmison, SJ	2,229	13,360	431	7,192	RAF	226	8/1	7/12	31.82	59.18	3.23	92.6
Panesar, M	1,506	9,047	308	4,331	LAO	126	8/1	6/37	34.37	71.80	2.87	77.1
Anderson, JM	1,497	8,992	307	5,159	RAFM	148	7/0	7/43	34.86	60.75	3.44	76.9

Note: 1. A total of 72 different individuals represented England in this 10-year period, with 24 of them playing more than 20 test matches.

Table K.2 The highest rating Australian team of the 2000s.

Batting Performances

Player	Tests	Innings	Not outs	Years played	Batting style	100s/50s/0s	HS	Runs scored	Batting Average	Strike rate	Batting Rating
1. Hayden, ML	96	172	14	2000-09	left	29/29/10	380	8,364	52.94	60.85	151.5
2. Langer, JL	76	134	11	2000-07	left	18/21/7	250	5,994	48.73	58.98	119.5
3. Ponting, RT	107	184	22	2000-09	right	32/40/8	257	9,458	58.38	62.51	167.7
4. Hussey, MEK	46	79	9	2005-09	left	10/19/7	182	3,638	51.97	48.22	108.8
5. Clarke, MJ	56	91	12	2004-09	right	12/17/5	151	3,926	49.70	53.23	105.6
6. Waugh, SR	44	63	10	2000-04	right	11/9/5	157	2,825	53.30	51.61	109.2
7. Gilchrist, AC	91	129	19	2000-08	left	16/23/13	204	5,130	46.64	81.97	116.3
8. Warne, SK	65	86	5	2000-07	right	0/8/14	99	1,577	19.47	64.48	20.8
9. Lee, B	75	89	18	2000-08	right	0/5/14	64	1,424	20.06	53.29	24.0
10. Gillespie, JN	57	71	19	2000-06	right	1/2/10	201	985	18.94	32.73	18.1
11. McGrath, GD	66	66	28	2000-07	right	0/1/14	61	355	9.34	43.72	4.9
										Total	946.4

Next Batters:

Martyn, DR	60	97	13	2000-06	right	13/20/6	165	4,089	48.68	52.15	105.7
Lehmann, DS	22	34	2	2002-04	left	5/8/1	177	1,570	49.06	62.62	100.3
Katich, SM	47	81	5	2001-09	left	8/20/3	157	3,392	44.63	49.94	91.3

Bowling Performances:

Player	Overs	Balls	Maids	Runs against	Bowl style	Wkts	5w/10w	Best	Bowl Avge	Strike rate	Econ rate	Bowling Rating
1. Hayden, ML				Less than 100 overs								-
2. Langer, JL				Less than 100 overs								-
3. Ponting, RT				Less than 100 overs								-
4. Hussey, MEK				Less than 100 overs								-
5. Clarke, MJ	257	1,541	42	755	LAO	19	1/0	6/9	39.74	81.12	2.94	32.5
6. Waugh, SR	112	673	23	284	RAM	3	0/0	1/2	94.67	224.2	2.53	10.9
7. Gilchrist, AC		Wicketkeeper					Did not bowl					-
8. Warne, SK	3,020	18,129	605	8,986	RAL	357	21/6	7/94	25.17	50.78	2.97	143.3
9. Lee, B	2,717	16,312	539	9,477	RAF	303	9/0	5/30	31.28	53.84	3.49	101.7
10. Gillespie, JN	2,001	12,006	524	5,662	RAF	209	5/0	6/40	27.09	57.45	2.83	102.2
11. McGrath, GD	2,548	15,293	828	6,100	RAFM	297	14/2	8/24	20.54	51.49	2.39	145.7
											Total	536.2

Next Bowlers:

Clark, SR	857	5,137	230	2,243	RAFM	94	2/0	5/32	23.86	54.74	2.62	100.8
Johnson, MG	1,198	7,189	221	3,843	LAF	137	4/1	8/61	28.05	52.48	3.21	95.3
MacGill, SCG	1,404	8,420	271	4,661	RAL	149	9/1	8/108	31.28	56.51	3.32	90.9

Note: 1. A total of 50 different individuals represented Australia in this 10-year period, with 21 of them playing more than 20 test matches.

Table K.3 The highest rating West Indian team of the 2000s.

Batting Performances

Player	Tests	Innings	Not outs	Years played	Batting style	100s/50s/0s	HS	Runs scored	Batting Average	Strike rate	Batting Rating
1. Gayle, CH	85	150	6	2000-09	left	12/31/14	317	5,848	40.61	58.28	102.9
2. Hinds, WW	45	80	1	2000-05	left	5/14/6	213	2,608	33.01	47.77	62.1
3. Sarwan, RR	83	146	8	2000-09	right	15/31/10	291	5,759	41.73	47.02	103.1
4. Lara, BL	66	120	2	2000-06	left	21/19/13	400	6,380	54.07	59.24	142.6
5. Chanderpaul, S	86	148	25	2000-09	left	19/35/9	203	6,435	52.32	43.64	126.2
6. Hooper, CL	22	37	2	2001-02	right	4/9/0	233	1,609	45.97	48.64	89.2
7. Jacobs, RD	54	91	17	2000-04	left	3/11/12	118	2,071	27.99	48.92	42.8
8. Dillon, MV	31	55	2	2000-04	right	0/0/20	43	465	8.77	37.59	4.6
9. Collymore, CD	29	50	26	2003-07	right	0/0/11	16	180	7.50	30.93	2.8
10. Collins, PT	29	42	7	2001-06	right	0/0/11	24	221	6.31	35.36	2.5
11. Walsh, CA	20	32	9	2000-01	right	0/0/8	22	102	4.43	36.30	1.5
										Total	680.3

Next Batters:

Bravo, DJ	34	63	1	2004-09	right	3/11/5	113	2,009	32.40	49.41	51.4
Samuels, MN	29	53	4	2000-08	right	2/9/4	105	1,408	28.73	44.39	40.6
Ganga, D	44	80	2	2000-08	right	3/9/8	135	2,085	26.73	39.59	40.0

Bowling Performances:

Player	Overs	Balls	Maids	Runs against	Bowl style	Wkts	5w/10w	Best	Bowl Avge	Strike rate	Econ rate	Bowling Rating
1. Gayle, CH	1,138	6,832	220	2,988	RAO	71	2/0	5/34	42.08	96.22	2.62	50.6
2. Hinds, WW	187	1,124	41	590	RAM	15	0/0	3/79	39.33	74.87	3.15	29.1
3. Sarwan, RR	337	2,023	33	1,163	RAL	23	0/0	4/37	50.57	87.91	3.45	23.9
4. Lara, BL	Did not bowl											-
5. Chanderpaul, S	Less than 100 overs											-
6. Hooper, CL	566	3,398	142	1,263	RAO	21	0/0	2/32	60.14	161.8	2.23	36.5
7. Jacobs, RD	Wicketkeeper			Did not bowl								-
8. Dillon, MV	1,215	7,302	236	3,656	RAFM	110	1/0	5/71	33.24	66.38	3.00	70.1
9. Collymore, CD	1,015	6,094	238	2,895	RAFM	92	4/1	7/57	31.47	66.24	2.85	79.1
10. Collins, PT	1,047	6,287	202	3,309	LAFM	98	3/0	6/53	33.77	64.15	3.16	70.0
11. Walsh, CA	887	5,330	280	1,835	RAF	93	5/1	6/61	19.73	57.31	2.07	122.1
											Total	481.4

Next Bowlers:

Taylor, JE	822	4,937	150	2,923	RAF	82	3/0	5/11	35.65	60.21	3.55	65.6
Edwards, FH	1,210	7,264	142	4,811	RAF	122	8/0	7/87	39.43	59.54	3.97	63.9
Bravo, DJ	950	5,704	177	3,090	RAM	81	2/0	6/55	38.15	70.42	3.25	57.7

Note: 1. A total of 75 different individuals represented the West Indies in this 10-year period, with 19 of them playing more than 20 test matches.

Table K.4 The highest rating Indian team of the 2000s.

Batting Performances

Player	Tests	Innings	Not outs	Years played	Batting style	100s/50s/0s	HS	Runs scored	Batting Average	Strike rate	Batting Rating
1. Sehwag, V	72	123	4	2001-09	right	17/19/10	319	6,248	52.50	80.41	140.9
2. Gambhir, G	27	48	3	2004-09	left	8/10/1	206	2,553	56.73	53.11	122.1
3. Dravid, R	103	179	23	2000-09	right	22/42/7	270	8,558	54.86	43.49	144.8
4. Tendulkar, SR	89	150	16	2000-09	right	21/31/7	248	7,129	53.20	54.36	136.5
5. Ganguly, SC	81	134	12	2000-08	left	9/23/9	239	4,780	39.18	53.30	87.6
6. Laxman, VVS	92	150	24	2000-09	right	14/37/9	281	6,291	49.93	50.05	123.5
7. Dhoni, MS	40	62	8	2005-09	right	3/16/3	148	2,176	40.30	62.24	75.5
8. Pathan, IK	29	40	5	2003-08	left	1/6/5	102	1,105	31.57	53.23	40.9
9. Singh, H	72	100	14	2001-09	right	0/7/12	66	1,494	17.37	65.35	18.1
10. Kumble, A	74	98	18	2000-08	right	1/2/9	110	1,427	17.84	38.58	14.8
11. Zaheer Khan	68	89	22	2000-09	right	0/3/18	75	903	13.48	50.93	10.0
										Total	914.7

Next Batters:

Jaffer, W	31	58	1	2000-08	right	5/11/6	212	1944	34.11	48.06	62.2
Singh, Y	31	48	6	2003-09	left	3/8/6	169	1545	36.79	58.50	60.9
Das, SS	23	40	2	2000-02	right	2/9/3	110	1326	34.89	38.92	51.4

Bowling Performances:

Player	Overs	Balls	Maids	Runs against	Bowl style	Wkts	5w/10w	Best	Bowl Avge	Strike rate	Econ rate	Bowling Rating
1. Sehwag, V	424	2,552	65	1312	RAO	30	1/0	5/104	43.73	85.06	3.08	37.4
2. Gambhir, G				Did not bowl								-
3. Dravid, R				Less than 100 overs								-
4. Tendulkar, SR	506	3,039	46	1813	RAM	31	0/0	3/10	58.48	98.02	3.58	23.7
5. Ganguly, SC	327	1,962	72	1053	RAM	13	0/0	2/20	81.00	150.9	3.22	18.4
6. Laxman, VVS				Less than 100 overs								-
7. Dhoni, MS			Wicketkeeper					Less than 100 overs				-
8. Pathan, IK	980	5,883	212	3,226	LAMF	100	7/2	7/59	32.26	58.84	3.29	85.3
9. Singh, H	3,450	20,706	638	9,763	RAO	322	23/5	8/84	30.32	64.30	2.83	120.0
10. Kumble, A	3,774	22,633	789	11,014	RAL	355	20/5	8/141	31.03	63.76	2.92	120.7
11. Zaheer Khan	2,263	13,584	458	7,472	LAFM	220	8/0	5/29	33.96	61.75	3.30	85.2
											Total	490.5

Next Bowlers:

Srinath, J	821	4,928	217	2,304	RAFM	74	4/0	6/76	31.14	66.59	2.81	76.6
Sharma, I [2]	572	3,433	103	1,859	RAFM	54	1/0	5/118	34.43	63.57	3.25	62.2

Notes: 1. A total of 58 different individuals represented India in this 10-year period, with 18 of them playing more than 20 test matches.

2. Ishant Sharma played only 19 matches.

Table K.5 The highest rating New Zealand team in the 2000s.

Batting Performances

Player	Tests	Innings	Not outs	Years played	Batting style	100s/50s/0s	HS	Runs scored	Batting Average	Strike rate	Batting Rating
1. Richardson, MH	38	65	3	2000-04	left	4/19/1	145	2,776	44.77	37.67	83.0
2. Vincent, L	23	40	1	2001-07	right	3/9/4	224	1,332	34.15	47.15	59.7
3. Fleming, SP	63	105	4	2000-08	left	7/23/9	274	4,188	41.47	49.07	89.8
4. Taylor, LRPL	22	40	1	2007-09	right	4/8/0	154	1,644	42.15	59.61	78.1
5. Astle, NJ	47	77	5	2000-06	right	6/15/7	222	2,682	37.25	52.13	72.7
6. Styris, SB	29	48	4	2002-07	right	5/6/5	170	1,586	36.05	51.34	60.5
7. McCullum, BB	49	81	4	2004-09	right	3/15/8	143	2,474	32.13	61.91	57.5
8. Vettori, DL	69	104	16	2000-09	left	5/17/9	140	3,176	36.09	62.36	68.9
9. Franklin, JEC	26	36	6	2001-09	left	1/2/6	122	644	21.47	38.65	19.2
10. Tuffey, DR	24	33	8	2000-09	right	0/1/5	80	349	13.96	40.44	7.8
11. Martin, CS	53	77	40	2000-09	right	0/0/27	12	83	2.24	20.30	0.5
										Total	597.8

Next Batters:

Cairns, CL [2]	18	30	2	2000-04	right	3/5/2	158	1,265	45.18	73.68	84.0
McMillan, CD	36	59	7	2000-05	right	3/12/5	142	1,860	35.77	52.53	59.8
Oram, JDP	33	59	10	2002-09	left	5/6/4	133	1,780	36.33	50.38	58.2

Bowling Performances:

Player	Overs	Balls	Maids	Runs against	Bowl style	Wkts	5w/10w	Best	Bowl Avge	Strike rate	Econ rate	Bowling Rating
1. Richardson, MH				Less than 100 overs								-
2. Vincent, L				Less than 100 overs								-
3. Fleming, SP				Did not bowl								-
4. Taylor, LRPL				Less than 100 overs								-
5. Astle, NJ	543	3,261	203	1,130	RAM	29	0/0	3/27	38.97	112.4	2.08	57.9
6. Styris, SB	328	1,967	76	1,023	RAM	20	0/0	3/28	51.15	98.30	3.12	27.6
7. McCullum, BB		Wicketkeeper					Did not bowl					-
8. Vettori, DL	2,758	16,556	650	7,359	LAO	222	15/3	7/87	33.15	74.56	2.67	97.0
9. Franklin, JEC	732	4,402	134	2,612	LAFM	80	3/0	6/119	32.65	55.03	3.56	73.9
10. Tuffey, DR	760	4,565	195	2,279	RAFM	74	2/0	6/54	30.80	61.68	3.00	76.5
11. Martin, CS	1,745	10,471	373	5,917	RAFM	176	8/1	6/54	33.62	59.49	3.39	85.2
											Total	418.1

Next Bowlers:

Bond, SE [2]	562	3,372	113	1,922	RAF	87	5/1	6/51	22.09	38.76	3.42	127.4
Cairns, CL [2]	572	3,438	105	2,015	RAFM	68	4/0	7/53	29.63	50.55	3.52	84.5
O'Brien, IE	732	4,390	158	2,429	RAM	73	1/0	6/75	33.27	60.19	3.32	68.9

Notes: 1. A total of 57 different individuals represented New Zealand in this 10-year period, with 15 of them playing more than 20 test matches.

2. Cairns and Bond played less than 20 matches and were not eligible for selection in the top 11. Bond's strike rate is lower than any other test player with 18 or more matches since World War 1.

Table K.6 The highest rating Pakistan team in the 2000s.

Batting Performances

Player	Tests	Innings	Not outs	Years played	Batting style	100s/50s/0s	HS	Runs scored	Batting Average	Strike rate	Batting Rating
1. Taufeeq Umar	25	46	2	2001-06	left	4/9/3	135	1,729	39.30	44.88	65.7
2. Shahid Afridi	20	35	1	2000-06	right	4/7/4	156	1,329	39.09	92.16	79.3
3. Younis Khan	63	112	7	2000-09	right	16/21/12	313	5,260	50.10	53.73	120.9
4. Inzamam-ul-Haq	62	103	11	2000-07	right	17/23/7	329	5,113	55.58	56.06	139.2
5. Mohammad Yousuf	71	121	11	2000-09	right	23/23/7	223	6,439	58.54	53.03	147.2
6. Abdul Razzaq	45	75	9	2000-06	right	3/7/4	134	1,933	29.29	41.33	42.9
7. Kamran Akmal	47	80	6	2002-09	right	6/12/10	158	2,525	34.12	63.41	63.5
8. Saqlain Mushtaq	25	40	7	2000-04	right	1/0/4	101	525	15.91	28.73	9.3
9. Shoaib Akhtar	33	49	7	2000-07	right	0/0/9	47	474	11.29	42.70	6.4
10. Waqar Younis	29	42	3	2000-03	right	0/0/9	39	399	10.23	51.28	6.1
11. Danish Kaneria	56	75	32	2000-09	right	0/0/24	29	293	6.81	48.35	3.5
										Total	684.2

Next Batters:

Yasir Hameed	23	45	3	2003-07	right	2/8/0	170	1,450	34.52	57.68	57.5
Imran Farhat	31	59	2	2001-09	left	3/12/2	128	1,944	34.11	48.88	56.8
Shoaib Malik	28	46	6	2001-09	right	2/7/4	148	1,440	36.00	44.16	52.7

Bowling Performances:

Player	Overs	Balls	Maids	Runs against	Bowl style	Wkts	5w/10w	Best	Bowl Avge	Strike rate	Econ rate	Bowling Rating
1. Taufeeq Umar					Less than 100 overs							-
2. Shahid Afridi	404	2,423	45	1,313	RAL	36	0/0	4/95	36.47	67.31	3.25	46.4
3. Younis Khan					Less than 100 overs							-
4. Inzamam-ul-Haq					Did not bowl							-
5. Mohammad Yousuf					Less than 100 overs							-
6. Abdul Razzaq	1,150	6,904	216	3,628	RAFM	100	1/0	5/35	36.28	69.04	3.15	62.3
7. Kamran Akmal					Wicketkeeper Did not bowl							-
8. Saqlain Mushtaq	1,185	7,109	260	3,087	RAO	101	4/1	8/164	30.56	70.38	2.61	81.3
9. Shoaib Akhtar	951	5,716	175	3,199	RAF	144	11/2	6/11	22.22	39.69	3.36	134.9
10. Waqar Younis	783	4,702	137	2,624	RAF	94	1/0	6/55	27.91	50.02	3.35	87.6
11. Danish Kaneria	2,751	16,510	499	8,291	RAL	245	14/2	7/77	33.84	67.39	3.01	94.9
											Total	507.3

Next Bowler:

Umar Gul	846	5,076	133	3,060	RAFM	91	4/0	6/135	33.63	55.78	3.62	72.6

Notes: 1. A total of 66 different individuals represented Pakistan in this 10-year period, with 19 of them playing more than 20 test matches.

Table K.7 The highest rating Sri Lankan team in the 2000s.

Batting Performances

Player	Tests	Inn	Not outs	Years played	Batting style	100s/50s/0s	HS	Runs scored	Batting Average	Strike rate	Batting Rating
1. Jayasuriya, ST	66	114	5	2000-07	left	9/17/6	253	4,222	38.73	65.73	87.5
2. Atapattu, MS	61	105	10	2000-07	right	13/14/12	249	4,055	42.68	44.86	90.2
3. Sangakkara, KC	88	147	10	2000-09	left	21/32/4	287	7,549	55.10	55.53	145.7
4. Jayawardene, DPMdS	95	160	12	2000-09	right	25/30/10	374	8,187	55.32	53.46	152.2
5. Samaraweera, TT	57	90	13	2001-09	right	11/21/6	231	3,938	51.14	47.65	112.0
6. Tillakaratne, HP	27	40	11	2001-04	left	5/4/1	204	1,573	54.24	42.88	98.7
7. Dilshan, TM	57	91	9	2000-09	right	10/13/9	168	3,482	42.46	65.72	88.0
8. Vaas, WPUJC	77	115	28	2000-09	left	1/11/7	100	2,409	27.69	46.19	42.2
9. Muralitharan, M	84	101	30	2000-09	right	0/1/21	67	775	10.92	76.06	9.6
10. Malinga SL	28	34	13	2004-07	right	0/0/9	42	192	9.14	38.17	4.0
11. Fernando, CRD	33	40	13	2000-09	right	0/0/7	36	198	7.33	31.68	2.8
										Total	833.0

Next Batters:

Player	Tests	Inn	Not outs	Years played	Batting style	100s/50s/0s	HS	Runs scored	Batting Average	Strike rate	Batting Rating
Vandort, MG	20	33	2	2001-08	left	4/4/3	140	1,144	36.90	47.25	58.5
Jayawardene, HAPW	30	40	6	2000-09	right	2/2/5	154	1,044	30.71	48.38	38.5
Arnold, RP	32	50	1	2000-04	left	1/7/5	109	1,186	24.20	46.62	30.6

Bowling Performances:

Player	Overs	Balls	Maids	Runs against	Bowl style	Wkts	5w/10w	Best	Bowl Avge	Strike rate	Econ rate	Bowling Rating
1. Jayasuriya, ST	886	5,325	218	2103	LAO	69	2/0	5/34	30.48	77.17	2.37	72.5
2. Atapattu, MS	Did not bowl											-
3. Sangakkara, KC	Wicketkeeper Less than 100 overs											
4. Jayawardene, DPMdS	Less than 100 overs											-
5. Samaraweera, TT	215	1,290	36	679	RAO	14	0/0	4/49	48.5	92.14	3.16	21.7
6. Tillakaratne, HP	Less than 100 overs											-
7. Dilshan, TM	154	925	31	471	RAM	13	0/0	4/10	36.23	71.17	3.05	29.1
8. Vaas, WPUJC	2,680	16,084	626	7,335	LAFM	247	8/1	7/71	29.70	65.12	2.74	99.3
9. Muralitharan, M	4,796	28,783	1159	11,849	RAO	565	49/20	9/51	20.97	50.94	2.47	213.0
10. Malinga SL	796	4,780	106	3,076	RAFM	91	2/0	5/68	33.80	52.52	3.86	71.0
11. Fernando, CRD	854	5,125	129	3,072	RAFM	88	3/0	5/42	34.91	58.24	3.60	66.9
											Total	573.6

Next Bowler:

Player	Overs	Balls	Maids	Runs against	Bowl style	Wkts	5w/10w	Best	Bowl Avge	Strike rate	Econ rate	Bowling Rating
Zoysa, DNT	569	3,416	126	1,706	LAFM	49	1/0	5/20	34.82	69.71	3.00	61.0
Herath, HMRKB [2]	782	4,692	139	2,373	LAO	64	4/0	5/99	37.08	73.31	3.03	59.9

Notes: 1. A total of 56 different individuals represented Sri Lanka in this 10-year period, with 16 of them playing more than 20 test matches.
2. Herath played only 19 matches in this 10-year period.

Table K.8 The highest rating South African team in the 2000s.

Batting Performances

Player	Tests	Innings	Not outs	Years played	Batting style	100s/50s/0s	HS	Runs scored	Batting Average	Strike rate	Batting Rating
1. Smith, GC	79	139	9	2002-09	left	18/26/10	277	6,451	49.62	60.58	126.0
2. Kirsten, G	45	76	6	2000-04	left	11/16/5	220	3,497	49.96	46.01	106.7
3. Gibbs, HH	73	124	6	2000-08	right	12/23/9	228	5,198	44.05	51.96	100.0
4. Kallis, JH	101	174	27	2000-09	right	27/42/7	189	8,630	58.71	46.51	154.7
5. Prince, AG	50	81	12	2002-09	left	11/8/4	162	3,137	45.46	44.46	86.9
6. De Villiers, AB	54	93	8	2004-09	right	9/19/1	217	3,706	43.60	53.05	93.4
7. Boucher, MV	104	152	18	2000-09	right	2/26/13	122	4,024	30.03	50.52	59.7
8. Pollock, SM	70	100	27	2000-08	right	2/8/7	111	2,377	32.56	54.02	50.0
9. Steyn, DW	34	43	8	2004-09	right	0/1/6	76	443	12.66	43.86	7.4
10. Ntini, M	97	111	41	2000-09	right	0/0/20	32	690	9.86	49.08	6.6
11. Nel, A	36	42	8	2001-08	right	0/0/11	34	337	9.91	46.87	5.4
										Total	796.8

Next Batters:

Player	Tests	Innings	Not outs	Years played	Batting style	100s/50s/0s	HS	Runs scored	Batting Average	Strike rate	Batting Rating
Amla, HM	39	69	4	2004-09	right	7/14/6	176	2,587	39.80	48.70	75.9
McKenzie, ND	58	94	7	2000-09	right	5/16/9	226	3,253	37.39	42.01	70.3
Rudolph, JA	35	63	7	2003-06	left	5/8/8	222	2,028	36.21	42.96	61.4

Bowling Performances:

Player	Overs	Balls	Maids	Runs against	Bowl style	Wkts	5w/10w	Best	Bowl Avge	Strike rate	Econ rate	Bowling Rating
1. Smith, GC	220	1,319	28	801	RAM	8	0/0	2/145	100.1	164.8	3.64	9.5
2. Kirsten, G					Less than 100 overs							-
3. Gibbs, HH					Less than 100 overs							-
4. Kallis, JH	2,223	13,348	524	6,561	RAFM	205	4/0	6/54	32.00	65.11	2.95	85.6
5. Prince, AG					Less than 100 overs							-
6. De Villiers, AB					Less than 100 overs							-
7. Boucher, MV		Wicketkeeper				Less than 100 overs						-
8. Pollock, SM	2,646	15,887	804	6,439	RAFM	260	6/1	6/30	24.77	61.10	2.43	116.5
9. Steyn, DW	1,146	6,877	206	4,123	RAF	172	11/3	6/49	23.97	39.98	3.60	133.1
10. Ntini, M	3,345	20,084	722	10,884	RAF	380	18/4	7/37	28.64	52.85	3.25	126.5
11. Nel, A	1,271	7,643	280	3,919	RAFM	123	3/1	6/32	31.86	62.03	3.08	80.5
											Total	551.7

Next Bowlers:

Player	Overs	Balls	Maids	Runs against	Bowl style	Wkts	5w/10w	Best	Bowl Avge	Strike rate	Econ rate	Bowling Rating
Harris, PL	947	5,685	196	2,635	LAO	79	3/0	6/127	33.35	71.96	2.78	65.2

Note: 1. A total of 48 different individuals represented South Africa in this 10-year period, with 19 of them playing more than 20 test matches.

Table K.9 Zimbabwean players with more than 20 test matches in the 2000s

Batting Performances

Player	Tests	Innings	Not outs	Years played	Batting style	100s/50s/0s	HS	Runs scored	Batting Average	Strike rate	Batting Rating
Flower, A	24	42	7	2000-02	left	6/11/1	232	2,214	63.26	51.50	138.8
Taibu, T	24	46	3	2001-05	right	1/9/5	153	1,273	29.60	40.93	41.5
Campbell, ADR	21	39	2	2000-02	left	2/7/4	103	1,085	29.32	41.78	39.8
Carlisle, SV	31	56	5	2000-05	right	2/7/5	118	1,440	28.24	37.57	37.1
Streak, HH	38	64	11	2000-05	right	1/9/6	127	1,454	27.43	38.46	36.1
Flower, G	29	53	3	2000-04	right	1/7/8	106	1,227	24.54	33.00	27.7
Ebrahim, DD	29	55	1	2001-05	right	0/10/7	94	1,226	22.70	39.35	27.5

Bowling Performances:

Player	Overs	Balls	Maids	Runs against	Bowl style	Wkts	5w/10w	Best	Bowl Avge	Strike rate	Econ rate	Bowling Rating
Flower, A					Less than 100 overs							-
Taibu, T					Less than 100 overs							-
Campbell, ADR					Less than 100 overs							-
Carlisle, SV					Did not bowl							-
Streak, HH	1,231	7,399	340	3,353	RAFM	105	3/0	6/73	31.93	70.46	2.72	76.4
Flower, G	364	2,188	81	1,012	LAO	19	0/0	4/41	53.26	115.2	2.77	29.3
Ebrahim, DD					Did not bowl							-

Note; 1. Zimbabwe player no test cricket in the years 2006 to 2009. Nevertheless, a total of 50 different individuals represented Zimbabwe in the first 6 years of the decade, with only the above 7 playing more than 20 test matches.

Table K.10 Bangladeshi players with more than 20 matches in the 2000s.

Batting Performances

Player	Tests	Innings	Not outs	Years played	Batting style	100s/50s/0s	HS	Runs scored	Batting Average	Strike rate	Batting Rating
Habibul Bashar	50	99	1	2000-08	right	3/24/7	113	3,026	30.88	60.28	59.8
Mohammad Ashraful	50	97	4	2001-09	right	5/7/15	158	2,149	23.11	46.05	37.9
Javed Omar	40	80	2	2001-07	right	1/9/5	119	1,743	22.35	38.55	31.1
Rajin Saleh	24	46	2	2003-08	right	0/7/8	89	1,141	25.93	35.87	27.2
Mohammad Rafique	33	63	6	2000-08	left	1/4/8	111	1,059	18.58	64.93	19.7
Khaled Mashud	44	84	10	2000-07	right	1/3/11	103	1,409	19.04	34.07	15.1
Mashrafe Mortaza	36	67	5	2001-09	right	0/3/12	79	797	12.85	67.20	10.6
Tapash Baisya	21	40	6	2002-05	right	0/2/9	66	384	11.29	49.81	6.7
Shahadat Hossain	23	43	13	2005-09	right	0/0/7	33	231	7.70	38.69	3.4

Bowling Performances:

Player	Overs	Balls	Maids	Runs against	Bowl style	Wkts	5w/10w	Best	Bowl Avge	Strike rate	Econ rate	Bowling Rating
Habibul Bashar				Less than 100 overs								-
Mohammad Ashraful	247	1,483	11	1,092	RAL	18	0/0	2/42	60.67	82.38	4.42	12.4
Javed Omar				Less than 100 overs								-
Rajin Saleh				Less than 100 overs								-
Mohammad Rafique	1,457	8,734	301	4,076	LAO	100	7/0	6/77	40.76	87.44	2.80	60.8
Khaled Mashud		Wicketkeeper					Did not bowl					-
Mashrafe Mortaza	998	5,998	202	3,239	RAFM	78	0/0	4/60	41.53	76.79	3.24	50.6
Tapash Baisya	563	3,374	93	2,137	RAFM	36	0/0	4/72	59.36	93.78	3.80	26.2
Shahadat Hossain	557	3,346	58	2,316	RAMF	53	2/0	6/27	43.70	63.13	4.15	45.0

Note: 1. A total of 56 different individuals represented Bangladesh in this 10-year period, but only the above 9 played more than 20 matches.

Appendix L
Best National Teams — 2010 To 2019

Table L.1 The highest rating English team of the 2010s.

Batting Performances

Player	Tests	Innings	Not outs	Years played	Batting style	100s/50s/0s	HS	Runs scored	Batting Average	Strike rate	Batting Rating
1. Cook, AN	111	201	11	2010-18	left	23/37/6	294	8,818	46.41	46.94	127.8
2. Root, JE	89	164	12	2012-19	right	17/45/8	254	7,359	48.41	54.38	127.5
3. Trott, IJL	49	88	6	2010-15	right	8/18/8	226	3,560	43.41	47.51	88.8
4. Bell, IR	67	114	15	2010-15	right	13/25/7	235	4,436	44.81	48.88	101.3
5. Pietersen, KP	48	81	4	2010-14	right	7/19/6	227	3,382	43.92	60.64	93.9
6. Prior, MJ	54	83	14	2010-14	right	5/17/8	126	2,709	39.26	60.71	73.2
7. Stokes, BA	60	110	4	2013-19	left	8/20/12	258	3,787	35.73	57.97	78.4
8. Ali, MM	60	104	8	2014-19	left	5/14/14	155	2,782	28.98	51.12	52.1
9. Broad, SCJ	111	165	23	2010-19	left	1/7/33	169	2,354	16.58	65.61	22.2
10. Swann, GP	46	59	10	2010-13	right	0/1/4	56	907	18.51	73.80	17.6
11. Anderson, JM	106	152	61	2010-19	left	0/1/25	81	729	8.01	44.00	5.3
										Total	788.0

Next Batters:

Bairstow, JM	70	123	7	2012-19	right	5/17/8	167	4,030	34.74	55.08	69.0
Ballance, GS	23	42	2	2014-17	left	4/7/3	156	1,498	37.45	47.17	62.2
Buttler, JC	38	68	6	2014-19	right	5/13/10	105	2,046	33.00	57.41	56.4
Woakes, CR	32	51	11	2013-19	right	1/4/6	137	1,145	27.26	49.91	33.0

Bowling Performances:

Player	Overs	Balls	Maids	Runs against	Bowl style	Wkts	5w/10w	Best	Bowl Avge	Strike rate	Econ rate	Bowling Rating
1. Cook, AN				Less than 100 overs								-
2. Root, JE	384	2,313	73	1,238	RAO	24	0/0	2/9	51.58	96.38	3.21	28.4
3. Trott, IJL	112	672	11	372	RAM	5	0/0	1/5	74.4	134.5	3.32	8.0
4. Bell, IR				Did not bowl								-
5. Pietersen, KP				Less than 100 overs								-
6. Prior, MJ							Did not bowl					-
7. Stokes, BA	1,377	8,265	248	4,606	RAFM	139	4/0	6/22	33.14	59.45	3.34	76.2
8. Ali, MM	1,828	10,972	265	6,624	RAO	181	5/1	6/53	36.60	60.62	3.62	74.5
9. Broad, SCJ	3,807	22,850	911	11,146	RAFM	403	14/2	8/15	27.66	56.68	2.93	125.1
10. Swann, GP	1,939	11,638	366	5,818	RAO	193	13/3	6/65	30.15	60.29	3.00	101.9
11. Anderson, JM	3.927	23,568	1,057	10,448	RAFM	429	20/3	7/42	24.35	54.94	2.66	143.3
											Total	557.5

Next Bowlers:

Finn, ST	1,068	6,412	190	3,800	RAFM	125	5/0	6/79	30.4	51.30	3.56	86.6
Woakes, CR	921	5,528	201	2,849	RAFM	92	3/1	6/17	30.97	60.10	3.09	80.2
Bresnan, TT	748	4,488	178	2,260	RAMF	69	1/0	5/48	32.75	65.05	3.02	69.0

Notes: 1. A total of 68 different individuals represented England in this period, with 18 of them playing more than 20 test matches.

2. Joe Root is not a specialist opening batsman, but he has had some experience as an opener and the next highest specialist opener for England had a significantly inferior batting rating to any in the top 6.

3. Moeen Ali was preferred over Steven Finn and Chris Woakes because of his better batting rating.

Table L.2 The highest rating Australian team of the 2010s.

Batting Performances

Player	Tests	Innings	Not outs	Years played	Batting style	100s/50s/0s	HS	Runs scored	Batting Average	Strike rate	Batting Rating
1. Warner, DA	83	153	6	2011-19	left	23/30/9	335	7,088	48.22	73.04	136.1
2. Rogers, CJL	24	46	1	2013-15	left	5/14/1	173	1,996	44.36	50.47	88.2
3. Smith, SPD	72	130	16	2010-19	right	26/28/4	239	7,164	62.84	55.60	166.7
4. Hussey, MEK	33	58	7	2010-13	left	9/10/5	195	2,597	50.92	53.06	104.2
5. Voges, AC	20	31	7	2015-16	right	5/4/2	269	1,485	61.88	55.68	129.7
6. Clarke, MJ	59	107	10	2010-15	right	16/10/4	329	4,717	48.63	58.37	115.2
7. Haddin, BJ	43	74	9	2010-15	right	2/13/7	136	1,862	28.65	58.92	47.2
8. Starc, MA	56	84	17	2011-19	left	0/10/11	99	1,493	22.28	68.23	31.9
9. Harris, RJ	27	39	11	2010-15	right	0/3/2	99	603	21.54	63.14	22.5
10. Cummins, PJ	29	43	6	2011-19	right	0/2/7	63	639	17.27	38.31	11.2
11. Lyon, NM	95	122	38	2011-19	right	0/0/15	47	1,025	12.20	47.12	9.1
										Total	862.0

Next Batters:

Khawaja, UT	44	77	6	2011-19	left	8/14/4	174	2887	40.66	50.55	79.5
Burns, JA	20	34	0	2014-19	right	4/6/5	180	1321	38.85	57.07	68.4
Ponting, RT	28	51	2	2010-12	right	3/12/6	221	1828	37.31	54.03	67.7
Watson, SR	44	84	2	2010-15	right	3/17/5	176	2758	33.63	53.41	62.3

Bowling Performances:

Player	Overs	Balls	Maids	Runs against	Bowl style	Wkts	5w/10w	Best	Bowl Avge	Strike rate	Econ rate	Bowling Rating
1. Warner, DA					Less than 100 overs							-
2. Rogers, CJL					Did Not Bowl							-
3. Smith, SPD	230	1,380	25	960	RAL	17	0/0	3/18	56.47	81.20	4.17	15.8
4. Hussey, MEK					Less than 100 overs							-
5. Voges, AC					Less than 100 overs							-
6. Clarke, MJ	149	894	20	429	LAO	12	1/0	5/86	35.75	74.52	2.88	27.6
7. Haddin, BJ			Wicketkeeper					Did not bowl				-
8. Starc, MA	1,927	11,563	382	6,501	LAF	240	13/2	6/50	27.09	48.20	3.37	117.2
9. Harris, RJ	956	5,736	258	2,658	RAFM	113	5/0	7/117	23.52	50.73	2.78	109.2
10. Cummins, PJ	1,094	6.564	258	3,048	RAF	139	5/1	6/23	21.93	47.21	2.79	121.2
11. Lyon, NM	4,047	24,282	754	12,202	RAO	380	16/2	8/50	32.11	63.91	3.01	110.9
											Total	502.0

Next Bowlers

Johnson, MG	1,468	8,814	293	5,049	LAF	176	8/2	7/40	28.68	50.07	3.44	103.8
Hazlewood, JR	1,836	11,019	466	5,109	RAFM	195	7/0	6/67	26.20	56.51	2.78	105.0
Siddle, PM	1,751	10,512	472	5,038	RAFM	167	6/0	6/54	30.17	69.93	2.88	85.9
Watson, SR	664	3,991	192	1,738	RAFM	52	3/0	6/33	33.42	76.72	2.61	67.2

Note: 1. A total of 61 different individuals represented Australia in this period, with 24 of them playing more than 20 test matches.

Table L.3 The highest rating West Indian team of the 2010s.

Batting Performances

Player	Tests	Innings	Not outs	Years played	Batting style	100s/50s/0s	HS	Runs scored	Batting Average	Strike rate	Batting Rating
1. Gayle, CH [2]	18	32	5	2010-14	left	3/6/1	333	1,366	50.59	70.59	106.0
2. Brathwaite, KC	59	112	7	2011-19	right	8/17/12	212	3,496	33.30	40.77	65.9
3. Bravo, DM	54	98	5	2010-19	left	8/17/5	218	3,506	37.70	44.95	76.2
4. Samuels, MN	42	74	3	2011-16	right	5/15/10	260	2,509	35.34	49.71	68.4
5. Chanderpaul, S	41	70	17	2010-15	left	9/13/2	203	3,198	60.34	44.62	127.1
6. Chase, RL	32	58	4	2016-19	right	5/7/6	137	1,695	31.39	48.39	50.0
7. Holder, JO	40	69	11	2014-19	right	3/8/3	202	1,898	32.72	59.72	56.2
8. Ramdin, D	35	58	7	2010-16	right	3/7/3	126	1,479	29.00	49.12	43.1
9. Bishoo, D	36	61	15	2011-18	left	0/0/10	45	707	15.37	37.15	9.7
10. Roach, KAJ	51	80	14	2010-19	right	0/0/12	41	844	12.79	39.68	8.4
11. Gabriel, ST	45	66	24	2012-19	right	0/0/17	20	200	4.76	37.45	1.9
										Total	612.9

Next Batters:

Blackwood, J.	28	49	4	2014-19	right	1/10/5	112	1,362	30.27	59.01	45.0
Dowrich, SO (W-K)	31	56	8	2015-19	right	3/8/6	125	1,444	30.08	46.51	43.9
Powell, KOA	40	76	1	2011-17	left	3/6/7	134	2,011	26.81	51.17	40.1

Bowling Performances:

Player	Overs	Balls	Maids	Runs against	Bowl style	Wkts	5w/10w	Best	Bowl Avge	Strike rate	Econ rate	Bowling Rating
1. Gayle, CH [2]				Less than 100 overs								-
2. Brathwaite, KC	315	1,890	26	1,025	RAO	18	1/0	6/29	56.94	105.4	3.24	19.6
3. Bravo, DM				**Less than 100 overs**								-
4. Samuels, MN	466	2,796	43	1,556	RAO	34	0/0	4/13	45.76	82.23	3.34	34.1
5. Chanderpaul, S				**Less than 100 overs**								-
6. Chase, RL	726	4,356	81	2,500	RAO	59	2/0	8/60	42.37	73.86	3.44	45.5
7. Holder, JO	1,089	6,534	294	2,796	RAFM	106	6/1	6/59	26.38	61.71	2.56	96.5
8. Ramdin, D		Wicketkeeper					Did not bowl					-
9. Bishoo, D	1,344	8,064	174	4,350	RAL	118	5/1	8/49	36.86	68.36	3.24	66.8
10. Roach, KAJ	1,489	8,934	331	4,652	RAFM	173	8/1	5/8	26.89	51.63	3.13	105.1
11. Gabriel, ST	1,205	7,230	216	4,075	RAFM	132	5/1	8/62	30.87	54.80	3.38	85.9
											Total	453.6

Next Bowlers:

Sammy, DJG	792	4,753	172	2,258	RAMF	57	1/0	5/29	39.61	83.35	2.85	52.4

Notes: 1. A total of 53 different individuals represented the West Indies in this period, with 15 of them playing more than 20 test matches.

2. Gayle played only 18 matches but was included because no other specialist openers played more than 20 matches during the decade.

Table L.4 The highest rating Indian team of the 2010s.

Batting Performances

Player	Tests	Inn	Not outs	Years played	Batting style	100s/50s/0s	HS	Runs scored	Batting Average	Strike rate	Batting Rating
1. Sehwag, V	32	57	2	2010-13	right	6/13/6	173	2,338	42.51	87.43	91.4
2. Sharma, RG	32	53	7	2013-19	right	6/10/4	212	2,141	46.54	59.26	91.9
3. Pujara, CA	75	124	8	2010-19	right	18/24/7	206	5,740	49.48	46.69	106.9
4. Tendulkar, SR	38	64	5	2010-13	right	8/14/0	214	2,951	50.02	53.75	103.8
5. Kohli, V	84	141	10	2011-19	right	27/22/10	254	7,202	54.98	57.82	132.9
6. Rahane, AM	63	105	11	2013-19	right	11/22/6	188	4,112	43.74	50.66	90.6
7. Dhoni, MS	50	82	8	2010-14	right	3/17/7	224	2,700	36.49	56.81	69.3
8. Ashwin, R	70	96	13	2011-19	right	4/11/3	124	2,385	28.73	54.68	50.4
9. Jadeja, RA	48	69	17	2012-19	left	1/14/4	100	1,844	35.46	63.61	59.2
10. Kumar, B	21	29	4	2013-18	right	0/3/4	63	552	22.08	45.06	20.5
11. Mohammed Shami	47	60	19	2013-19	right	0/1/13	51	453	11.05	75.38	9.9
										Total	848.9

Next Batters:

Laxman, VVS	26	47	8	2010-12	right	3/14/2	176	1,864	47.79	50.76	90.1
Dravid, R	27	49	5	2010-12	right	8/5/0	191	2,032	46.18	43.94	87.1
Dhawan, S	34	58	1	2013-18	left	7/5/4	190	2,315	40.61	66.95	77.8
Vijay, M	59	102	1	2010-18	right	12/14/8	167	3,821	37.83	45.78	76.7

Bowling Performances:

Player	Overs	Balls	Maids	Runs against	Bowl style	Wkts	5w/10w	Best	Bowl Avge	Strike rate	Econ rate	Bowling Rating
1. Sehwag, V	196	1,180	13	582	RAO	10	0/0	3/51	58.20	117.8	2.96	14.6
2. Sharma, RG				Less than 100 overs								-
3. Pujara, CA				Less than 100 overs								-
4. Tendulkar, SR				Less than 100 overs								-
5. Kohli, V				Less than 100 overs								-
6. Rahane, AM				Did not bowl								-
7. Dhoni, MS		Wicketkeeper				Did not bowl						-
8. Ashwin, R	3,234	19,412	671	9,183	RAO	362	27/7	7/59	25.37	53.63	2.84	146.5
9. Jadeja, RA	2,135	12,822	542	5,200	LAO	211	9/1	7/48	24.64	60.75	2.43	113.3
10. Kumar, B	558	3,344	141	1,644	RAM	63	4/0	6/82	26.10	53.14	2.95	93.9
11. Mohammed Shami	1,432	8,602	265	4,742	RAF	175	5/0	6/56	27.10	49.18	3.31	100.9
											Total	469.2

Next Bowlers:

Ojha, PP	1,187	7,122	277	3,162	LAO	104	7/1	6/47	30.40	68.49	2.66	86.5
Sharma, I	2,429	14,578	492	7,685	RAFM	238	9/1	7/74	32.29	61.25	3.16	92.6
Yadav, UT	1,198	7,191	200	4,297	RAF	142	3/1	6/88	30.26	50.63	3.59	88.8
Zaheer Khan	866	5,199	166	2,775	LAFM	91	3/1	7/87	30.49	57.14	3.20	82.3

Note: 1. A total of 53 different individuals represented India in this period, with 23 of them playing more than 20 test matches.

Table L.5 The highest rating New Zealand team of the 2010s.

Batting Performances

Player	Tests	Inn	Not outs	Years played	Batting style	100s/50s/0s	HS	Runs scored	Batting Average	Strike rate	Batting Rating
1. Latham, TWM	49	86	3	2014-19	left	11/16/8	264	3,554	42.82	46.73	91.8
2. McCullum, BB	52	95	5	2010-16	right	9/16/6	302	3,979	44.21	66.39	101.0
3. Williamson, KS	78	137	13	2010-19	right	21/31/9	242	6,379	51.44	51.55	129.4
4. Taylor, LRPL	76	133	19	2010-19	right	15/25/14	290	5,486	48.12	60.10	117.2
5. Nicholls, HM	31	47	5	2016-19	left	5/9/4	162	1,711	40.74	49.81	72.4
6. Watling, BJ	66	104	14	2010-19	right	8/17/9	205	3,538	39.31	42.51	76.8
7. de Grandhomme, C	21	32	4	2016-19	right	1/7/4	105	1,044	37.29	84.19	62.0
8. Santner, MJ	22	29	0	2015-19	left	1/2/2	126	741	25.55	42.37	27.6
9. Southee, TG	65	94	8	2010-19	right	0/4/7	68	1,535	17.85	86.97	21.1
10. Boult, TA	65	80	38	2011-19	right	0/1/13	52	615	14.64	54.71	10.5
11. Wagner, N	46	60	16	2012-19	left	0/0/11	47	554	12.59	44.75	7.7
										Total	717.7

Next Batters:

Guptill, MJ	39	75	1	2010-16	right	3/16/8	189	2257	30.50	46.20	54.2
Raval, JA	23	37	1	2016-19	left	1/7/3	132	1100	30.56	42.39	41.4

Bowling Performances:

Player	Overs	Balls	Maids	Runs against	Bowl style	Wkts	5w/10w	Best	Bowl Avge	Strike rate	Econ rate	Bowling Rating
1. Latham, TWM					Did not bowl							-
2. McCullum, BB					Less than 100 overs							-
3. Williamson, KS	350	2,103	47	1,178	RAO	29	0/0	4/44	40.62	72.47	3.36	36.9
4. Taylor, LRPT					Less than 100 overs							-
5. Nicholls, HM					Did not bowl							-
6. Watling, BJ		Wicketkeeper				Did not bowl						-
7. de Grandhomme, C	535.5	3,215	123	1,292	RAMF	42	1/0	6/41	30.76	76.57	2.41	68.1
8. Santner, MJ	623.8	3,746	128	1,744	LAO	39	0/0	3/53	44.72	96.05	2.79	42.4
9. Southee, TG	2,463	14,787	561	7,352	RAFM	256	8/1	7/64	28.83	58.00	2.98	104.2
10. Boult, TA	2,407	14,448	545	7,171	LAFM	255	8/1	6/30	28.01	56.44	2.98	106.8
11. Wagner, N	1,729	10,382	361	5,330	LAFM	201	9/0	7/39	26.52	51.63	3.08	107.2
											Total	465.5

Next Bowlers:

Bracewell, DAJ	830	4,978	147	2,796	RAM	72	2/0	6/40	38.83	69.22	3.37	55.6

Notes: 1. A total of 50 different individuals represented New Zealand in this period, with 14 of them playing more than 20 test matches.

2. Santner was selected ahead of Bracewell to provide a spin option and due to his better batting rating.

Table L.6 The highest rating Pakistan team of the 2010s.

Batting Performances

Player	Tests	Innings	Not outs	Years played	Batting style	100s/50s/0s	HS	Runs scored	Batting Average	Strike rate	Batting Rating
1. Mohammad Hafeez	44	84	7	2010-18	right	8/9/8	224	2,975	38.64	59.14	76.0
2. Azhar Ali [3]	77	146	8	2010-19	right	16/31/14	302	5,885	42.64	41.83	104.4
3. Younis Khan	55	101	12	2010-17	right	18/12/7	218	4,839	54.37	50.48	123.6
4. Misbah-ul-Haq	57	101	17	2010-17	right	8/35/6	135	4,225	50.30	46.16	108.3
5. Babar Azam	25	47	7	2016-19	right	4/13/6	127	1,707	42.68	55.82	77.4
6. Asad Shafiq	73	122	6	2010-19	right	12/26/13	137	4,528	39.03	48.62	83.5
7. Sarfaraz Ahmed	49	86	13	2010-19	right	3/18/4	112	2,657	36.40	70.99	68.7
8. Yasir Shah	38	57	6	2014-19	left	1/0/9	113	702	13.76	46.55	9.9
9. Mohammad Amir	29	53	8	2010-19	right	0/0/6	48	598	13.29	40.35	8.0
10. Saeed Ajmal	30	43	7	2010-14	right	0/1/7	50	422	11.72	42.42	6.6
11. Junaid Khan	22	28	11	2011-15	right	0/0/5	17	122	7.18	39.87	2.8
										Total	669.3

Next Batters:

Taufeeq Umar [4]	19	37	3	2016-18	left	3/5/3	236	1,234	36.29	44.49	59.1
Adnan Akmal	21	29	5	2010-13	right	0/3/2	64	591	24.63	44.07	23.3

Bowling Performances:

Player	Overs	Balls	Maids	Runs against	Bowl style	Wkts	5w/10w	Best	Bowl Avge	Strike rate	Econ rate	Bowling Rating
1. Mohammad Hafeez	553	3,317	95	1,489	RAO	49	0/0	4/16	30.39	67.72	2.69	67.7
2. Azhar Ali	142	845	8	611	RAL	8	0/0	2/35	76.38	105.6	4.34	5.5
3. Younis Khan				Less than 100 overs								-
4. Misbah-ul-Haq				Did not bowl								-
5. Babar Azam				Did not bowl								-
6. Asad Shafiq				Less than 100 overs								-
7. Sarfaraz Ahmed				Wicketkeeper Did not bowl								
8. Yasir Shah	1,995	11,975	310	6,361	RAL	209	16/3	8/41	30.44	57.29	3.19	106.5
9. Mohammad Amir	1,042	6,258	248	2,871	LAFM	101	3/0	6/44	28.43	61.99	2.75	84.9
10. Saeed Ajmal	1,661	9,968	343	4,242	RAO	160	10/4	7/55	26.51	62.25	2.56	111.9
11. Junaid Khan	768	4,598	157	2,253	LAMF	71	5/0	5/38	31.73	64.86	2.94	74.3
											Total	450.7

Next Bowlers:

Abdur Rehman	1,023	6,142	235	2,558	LAO	88	2/0	6/25	29.07	69.73	2.50	79.2
Wahab Riaz	836	5,025	118	2,864	LAF	83	2/0	5/63	34.51	60.46	3.42	65.3
Umar Gul	754	4,523	123	2,493	RAFM	72	0/0	4/61	34.63	62.82	3.31	62.0

Notes: 1. A total of 67 different individuals represented Pakistan in this period, with 16 of them playing more than 20 test matches.

2. Azhar Ali batted most often at No. 3 but opened the batting in 37 of his 146 test innings.

3. Taufeeq Umar played 19 matches in this time period.

Table L.7 The highest rating Sri Lankan team of the 2010s.

Batting Performances

Player	Tests	Inn	Not outs	Years played	Batting style	100s/50s/0s	HS	Runs scored	Batting Average	Strike rate	Batting Rating
1. Dilshan, TM	27	50	1	2010-13	right	5/10/4	193	1,801	36.76	67.86	71.8
2. Karunaratne, FDM	64	124	4	2012-19	left	9/24/12	196	4,421	36.84	49.05	79.2
3. Sangakkara, KC	46	86	7	2010-15	left	17/20/7	319	4,851	61.41	52.22	153.5
4. Jayawardene, DPMdS	39	70	2	2010-14	right	7/15/4	203	2,694	39.62	47.83	78.2
5. Mathews, AD	77	140	20	2010-19	right	9/32/2	160	5,325	44.38	48.55	98.3
6. Samaraweera, TT	24	42	7	2010-13	right	3/9/5	137	1,524	43.54	45.14	71.2
7. Chandimal, LD	55	100	7	2011-19	right	11/18/4	164	3,846	41.35	49.02	85.9
8. Perera, MDK	41	73	8	2014-19	right	0/6/13	95	1,208	18.58	47.26	15.7
9. Herath, HMRKB	72	117	24	2010-18	left	0/3/17	80	1,492	16.04	52.39	14.1
10. Prasad, KTGD	21	35	2	2010-15	right	0/0/8	47	410	12.42	53.45	7.9
11. Lakmal, RAS	59	93	23	2010-19	right	0/0/18	42	804	11.49	48.49	8.0
										Total	683.8

Next Batters:

Mendis, BKG	42	82	3	2015-19	right	6/10/7	196	2,777	35.15	56.47	65.6
Dickwella, DPDN	35	64	4	2014-19	left	0/14/3	80	1,857	30.95	68.05	50.2

Bowling Performances:

Player	Overs	Balls	Maids	Runs against	Bowl style	Wkts	5w/10w	Best	Bowl Avge	Strike rate	Econ rate	Bowling Rating
1. Dilshan, TM	410	2,459	52	1,240	RAM	26	0/0	3/56	47.69	94.57	3.03	30.7
2. Karunaratne, FDM				Less than 100 overs								-
3. Sangakkara, KC				Less than 100 overs								-
4. Jayawardene, DPMdS				Less than 100 overs								-
5. Mathews, AD	557	3,342	144	1,443	RAFM	28	0/0	4/44	51.54	119.4	2.59	39.3
6. Samaraweera, TT				Less than 100 overs								-
7. Chandimal, LD		Wicketkeeper				Did not bowl						-
8. Perera, MDK	1,707	10,246	230	5,512	RAO	156	8/2	6/32	35.33	65.68	3.23	78.5
9. Herath, HMRKB	3,479	20,879	661	9,589	LAO	363	30/9	9/127	26.42	57.49	2.76	146.5
10. Prasad, KTGD	599	3,593	89	2,129	RAFM	62	1/0	5/50	34.34	57.98	3.55	64.0
11. Lakmal, RAS	1,762	10,577	338	5,500	RAMF	141	3/0	5/54	39.01	75.00	3.12	63.1
											Total	422.1

Next Bowler:

Pradeep, N	845	5,075	130	3,003	RAFM	70	1/0	6/132	42.90	72.53	3.55	47.0

Note: 1. A total of 57 different individuals represented Sri Lanka in this period, with 20 of them playing more than 20 test matches.

Table L.8 The highest rating South African team of the 2010s.

Batting Performances

Player	Tests	Innings	Not outs	Years played	Batting style	100s/50s/0s	HS	Runs scored	Batting Average	Strike rate	Batting Rating
1. Smith, GC	38	66	4	2010-14	left	9/12/1	234	2,814	45.39	57.76	96.8
2. Elgar, D	60	104	9	2012-19	left	12/13/10	199	3,666	38.59	46.03	78.3
3. Amla, HM	85	146	12	2010-19	right	21/27/7	311	6,695	49.96	50.48	128.3
4. Kallis, JH	33	55	7	2010-13	right	13/6/6	224	2,810	58.54	53.69	129.6
5. de Villiers, AB	60	98	10	2010-18	right	13/27/7	278	5,059	57.49	55.65	140.1
6. du Plessis, F	62	106	14	2012-19	right	9/21/9	137	3,799	41.29	45.99	81.5
7. de Kock, Q	44	74	5	2014-19	left	5/18/5	129	2,683	38.88	72.79	78.2
8. Philander, VD	61	88	19	2011-19	right	0/8/8	74	1,700	24.64	45.17	31.5
9. Steyn, DW	59	76	19	2010-19	right	0/1/8	58	808	14.18	44.54	9.7
10. Rabada, K	41	60	10	2015-19	left	0/0/11	34	586	11.72	45.93	7.3
11. Morkel, M	67	78	21	2010-18	left	0/0/18	40	608	10.67	55.37	7.3
										Total	788.7

Next Batter:

Markram, AK	20	37	0	2017-19	right	4/6/5	154	1,424	38.49	63.57	67.3
Petersen, AN	36	64	4	2010-15	right	5/8/3	182	2,093	34.88	51.76	60.9
Duminy, JP	38	60	8	2010-17	left	5/5/8	155	1,643	31.60	48.35	48.5

Bowling Performances:

Player	Overs	Balls	Maids	Runs against	Bowl style	Wkts	5w/10w	Best	Bowl Avge	Strike rate	Econ rate	Bowling Rating
1. Smith, GC				Less than 100 overs								-
2. Elgar, D	169	1019	12	653	LAO	15	0/0	4/22	43.53	67.86	3.85	21.3
3. Amla, HM				Less than 100 overs								-
4. Kallis, JH	515	3,090	122	1,466	RAFM	34	0/0	3/35	43.12	90.97	2.84	44.7
5. de Villiers, AB				Less than 100 overs								-
6. du Plessis, F				Less than 100 overs								-
7. de Kock, Q		Wicketkeeper				Did not bowl						-
8. Philander, VD	1,830	10,986	489	4,838	RAFM	220	13/2	6/21	21.99	49.90	2.64	132.1
9. Steyn, DW	1,953	11,729	454	5,954	RAF	267	15/2	7/51	22.30	43.93	3.05	140.5
10. Rabada, K	1,267	7,604	258	4,289	RAF	190	9/4	7/112	22.57	40.02	3.38	139.5
11. Morkel, M	2,161	12,977	531	6,446	RAF	248	7/0	6/23	25.99	52.32	2.98	111.8
											Total	589.8

Next Bowlers:

Maharaj, KA	984	5,910	174	3,243	LAO	102	5/1	9/129	31.79	57.98	3.29	80.8
Imran Tahir	654	3,921	86	2,294	RAL	57	2/0	5/32	40.25	68.86	3.51	50.3
Duminy, JP	380	2,283	40	1,363	LAMF	36	0/0	4/47	37.86	63.43	3.58	43.6

Note: 1. A total of 54 different individuals represented South Africa in this period, with 17 of them playing more than 20 test matches.

Table L.9 Zimbabwe players with more than 15 test matches in the 2010s.

Player	Tests	Innings	Not outs	Years played	Batting style	100s/50s/0s	HS	Runs scored	Batting Average	Strike rate	Batting Rating
Masakadza, H	23	46	1	2011-18	right	4/5/5	158	1,438	31.96	44.90	48.6
Taylor, BRM	18	36	4	2011-18	right	6/5/2	171	1,418	44.31	53.59	83.0
Ervine, CR	15	30	2	2011-17	left	2/3/2	160	941	33.61	48.88	47.4

Bowling Performances:

Player	Overs	Balls	Maids	Runs against	Bowl style	Wkts	5w/10w	Best	Bowl Avge	Strike rate	Econ rate	Bowling Rating
Masakadza, H	173	1,038	45	450	RAL	14	0/0	3/24	32.14	74.20	2.60	36.7
Taylor, BRM					Did not bowl							-
Ervine, CR					Did not bowl							-

Note: 1. During the decade, 50 individuals represented Zimbabwe. Only one played more than 20 matches.

Table L.10 The Bangladesh players with more than 20 test matches in the 2010s.

Batting Performances

Player	Tests	Innings	Not outs	Years played	Batting style	100s/50s/0s	HS	Runs scored	Batting Average	Strike rate	Batting Rating
Tamim Iqbal	46	90	1	2010-19	left	8/25/6	206	3,719	41.79	58.73	92.4
Imrul Kayes	33	64	2	2010-19	left	3/4/4	150	1,636	26.39	49.19	38.2
Mominul Haque	38	71	4	2013-19	left	8/13/8	181	2,657	39.66	56.32	78.0
Mohd. Mahmudullah	46	87	5	2010-19	right	4/16/10	146	2,694	32.85	54.01	58.8
Shakib Al Hasan	42	79	5	2010-19	left	5/21/2	217	3,147	42.53	64.39	91.0
Mushfiqur Rahim	53	98	7	2010-19	right	6/17/8	219	3,531	38.80	48.12	76.4
Mehidy Hasan Miraz	22	42	6	2016-19	right	0/2/2	68	638	17.72	51.79	14.5
Taijul Islam	27	45	6	2014-19	left	0/0/5	39	374	9.59	39.75	4.9
Rubel Hossain	24	42	17	2010-18	right	0/0/7	45	254	10.16	48.85	5.5

Bowling Performances:

Player	Overs	Balls	Maids	Runs against	Bowl style	Wkts	5w/10w	Best	Bowl Avge	Strike rate	Econ rate	Bowling Rating
Tamim Iqbal					Less than 100 overs							-
Imrul Kayes					Less than 100 overs							-
Mominul Haque	100	598	8	376	LAO	4	0/0	3/27	94.00	150.3	3.75	5.1
Mohd. Mahmudullah	502	2,971	47	1,752	RAO	31	0/0	3/70	56.52	97.11	3.49	25.1
Shakib Al Hasan	1,667	10,029	283	5,175	LAO	162	13/2	6/33	31.94	61.91	3.10	91.9
Mushfiqur Rahim		Wicketkeeper					Did not bowl					-
Mehidy Hasan Miraz	884	5,306	107	2,981	RAO	90	7/2	7/58	33.12	58.96	3.37	80.5
Taijul Islam	1,086	6,490	159	3,475	LAO	106	7/1	8/39	32.78	61.23	3.21	78.7

Note: 1. A total of 53 different individuals represented Bangladesh in this period, but only the above 9 played more than 20 matches.

Appendix M
Highest Rating National Players - 2020 To 2024

In this shorter time frame of just five years, relatively few players in each nation played more than 20 matches and it was not possible to form national teams from the available eligible players. In the following tables, the statistics of the highest rating batsmen and bowlers from each nation are presented.

Table M.1 The highest rating English players (2020-2024, inclusive).

Highest rating batsmen:

Player	Tests	Innings	Not outs	Years played	Batting style	100s/50s/0s	HS	Runs scored	Batting Average	Strike rate	Batting Rating
Brook, HC	24	40	1	2022-24	right	8/10/2	317	2281	58.49	88.38	150.3
Root, JE	28	53	3	2020-24	right	19/20/5	262	5613	54.50	62.13	136.3
Duckett, BM	28	53	3	2022-24	left	4/12/3	182	2160	43.20	88.06	91.2
Bairstow, JM	30	55	5	2021-24	right	6/5/7	162	2012	40.24	69.12	73.0
Pope, OJD	51	91	5	2020-24	right	7/14/4	205	2966	34.49	65.41	71.4
Stokes, BA	50	88	5	2020-24	left	5/15/3	176	2932	35.33	62.14	69.2
Crawley, Z	52	96	2	2020-24	right	4/16/9	267	2898	30.83	65.79	64.8

Highest rating bowlers:

Player	Tests	Overs	Maids	Runs against	Bowl style	Wkts	5w/10w	Best	Bowl Avge	Striker rate	Econ rate	Bowling Rating
Broad, SCJ	32	1025	237	3,064	RAMF	128	3/1	6/31	23.94	48.04	2.99	110.5
Robinson, OE	20	632	159	1,742	RAMF	76	3/0	5/49	22.92	49.93	2.75	106.3
Anderson, JM	38	1246	357	3,020	RAFM	127	5/0	6/40	23.78	58.85	2.42	104.9
Woakes, CR	25	767	179	2,263	RAFM	89	2/0	5/50	25.43	51.75	2.95	96.2
Wood, MA	24	688	101	2,276	RAF	83	4/0	6/37	27.42	49.83	3.30	90.1
Stokes, BA	50	664	111	2,191	RAFM	71	0/0	4/33	30.86	56.21	3.29	72.8
Leach, MJ	29	1221	247	3,851	LAO	108	4/1	5/66	35.66	67.88	3.15	70.8

Note: A total of 47 different individuals represented England in this period, with 14 of them playing more than 20 test matches.

Table M.2 The highest rating Australian players (2020-2024, inclusive).

Highest rating batsmen:

Player	Tests	Innings	Not outs	Years played	Batting style	100s/50s/0s	HS	Runs scored	Batting Average	Strike rate	Batting Rating
Khawaja, UT	33	62	7	2022-24	left	7/13/4	195	2705	49.18	45.85	96.6
Labuschagne, M	41	76	7	2020-24	right	8/16/3	215	3153	45.70	50.89	94.3
Head, TM	37	61	3	2020-24	left	7/10/5	175	2502	43.14	77.61	89.5
Smith, SPD	41	72	9	2020-24	right	8/3/7	200	2798	44.41	48.93	86.7
Warner, DA	29	52	2	2020-24	left	3/7/4	200	1698	33.96	60.36	57.7
Green, C	28	43	5	2021-24	right	2/6/3	174	1377	36.24	48.57	54.9

Highest rating bowlers:

Player	Tests	Overs	Maids	Runs against	Bowl style	Wkts	5w/10w	Best	Bowl Avge	Strike rate	Econ rate	Bowling Rating
Hazlewood, JR	21	633	169	1,748	RAFM	84	5/0	5/8	20.81	45.22	2.76	121.6
Cummins, PJ	37	1,144	231	3,468	RAF	150	8/1	6/91	23.12	45.80	3.03	119.8
Lyon, NM	38	1,529	307	4,163	RAO	158	8/3	6/65	26.35	58.10	2.72	107.0
Starc, MA	37	1,105	197	3862	LAF	133	2/0	6/48	29.04	49.86	3.49	89.2
Green, C	28	365	62	1,237	RAFM	35	1/0	5/27	35.34	62.57	3.39	49.7

Note: A total of 29 different individuals represented Australia in this period, with 11 of them playing more than 20 test matches in the period.

Table M.3 The highest rating West Indian players (2020-2024, inclusive).

Highest rating batsmen:

Player	Tests	Innings	Not outs	Years played	Batting style	100s/50s/0s	HS	Runs scored	Batting Average	Strike rate	Batting Rating
Brathwaite, KC	37	73	3	2020-24	right	4/13/6	182	2,355	33.64	40.47	57.7
Blackwood, J.	28	53	2	2020-23	right	2/8/2	104	1,536	30.12	50.11	43.8

Highest rating bowlers:

Player	Tests	Overs	Maids	Runs against	Bowl style	Wkts	5w/10w	Best	Bowl Avge	Strike rate	Econ rate	Bowling Rating
Roach, KAJ	28	813	169	2,467	RAFM	89	2/0	5/47	27.72	54.89	3.03	86.3
Joseph, AS	28	790	100	3,064	RAFM	86	1/0	5/81	35.63	55.16	3.88	64.2
Holder, J0	29	792	190	2,126	RAMF	56	2/1	6/42	37.96	84.92	2.68	56.8

Table M.4 The highest rating Indian players (2020-2024, inclusive).

Highest rating batsmen:

Player	Tests	Innings	Not outs	Years played	Batting style	100s/50s/0s	HS	Runs scored	Batting Average	Strike rate	Batting Rating
Pant, R	31	55	4	2020-22	left	4/12/2	146	2093	41.04	74.54	80.2
Sharma, RG	35	63	3	2020-23	right	6/8/2	161	2160	36.00	55.03	64.8
Shubman Gill	31	57	5	2020-23	left	5/7/5	128	1860	35.77	60.39	60.5
Jadeja, RA	31	47	4	2020-23	right	3/8/4	175	1487	34.58	48.58	55.9
Kohli, V	38	67	3	2020-23	right	3/9/5	186	2005	31.33	49.26	51.5
Rahul, KL	21	39	2	2020-23	right	3/6/3	129	1234	33.35	47.81	50.5

Highest rating bowlers:

Player	Tests	Overs	Maids	Runs against	Bowl style	Wkts	5w/10w	Best	Bowl Avge	Strike rate	Econ rate	Bowling Rating
Bumrah, JJ	32	976	234	2,751	RAF	141	8/0	6/45	19.51	41.54	2.82	136.5
Ashwin, R	36	1300	236	3,656	RAO	175	10/1	7/71	20.89	44.61	2.81	131.9
Jadeja, RA	31	930	186	2,569	LAO	112	6/2	7/42	22.94	49.82	2.76	114.9
Mohammed Siraj	35	868	161	3,023	RAMF	96	3/0	6/15	31.49	54.37	3.48	78.1

Note: A total of 39 different individuals represented India in this period, with 11 of them playing more than 20 test matches.

Table M.5 The highest rating New Zealand players (2020-2024, inclusive).

Highest rating batsmen:

Player	Tests	Innings	Not outs	Years played	Batting style	100s/50s/0s	HS	Runs scored	Batting Average	Strike rate	Batting Rating
Williamson, KS	27	49	4	2020-24	right	12/6/2	251	2,897	64.38	52.30	148.9
Mitchell, DJ	30	51	5	2020-24	right	5/13/1	190	1,986	43.17	53.70	84.5
Conway, DP	27	51	1	2021-24	left	4/11/4	200	1,836	36.72	51.52	66.8
Latham, TWM	39	72	3	2020-24	left	2/15/5	252	2,280	33.04	48.75	60.8
Nicholls, HM	25	40	2	2020-24	left	4/3/2	200	1,262	33.21	50.75	53.6
Blundell, TA	37	64	6	2020-24	right	3/11/6	138	1,866	32.17	52.64	52.1

Highest rating bowlers:

Player	Tests	Overs	Maids	Runs against	Bowl style	Wkts	5w/10w	Best	Bowl Avge	Strike rate	Econ rate	Bowling Rating
Southee, TG	36	1247	293	3779	RAMF	121	6/0	6/43	31.23	61.87	3.03	82.3

Note: A total of 30 different individuals represented New Zealand in this period, with 8 of them playing more than 20 test matches.

Table M.6 The highest rating Pakistan players (2020-2024, inclusive).

Highest rating batsmen:

Player	Tests	Innings	Not outs	Years played	Batting style	100s/50s/0s	HS	Runs scored	Batting Average	Strike rate	Batting Rating
Babar Azam	31	55	2	2020-24	right	5/14/2	196	2344	44.23	53.56	87.4
Mohammad Rizwan	31	51	7	2020-24	right	3/9/2	171	1824	41.45	53.48	71.4
Abdullah Shafique	22	42	3	2021-24	right	5/5/6	201	1504	38.56	44.17	64.3
Azhar Ali	20	34	3	2020-24	right	3/4/5	185	1257	40.55	42.43	61.9

Highest rating bowlers:

Player	Tests	Overs	Maids	Runs against	Bowl style	Wkts	5w/10w	Best	Bowl Avge	Strike rate	Econ rate	Bowling Rating
Shaheen Afridi	24	796	163	2,488	LAF	91	3/1	6/51	27.34	52.54	3.12	93.4

Note: A total of 35 different individuals represented Pakistan in this period, with 4 of them playing more than 20 test matches.

Table M.7 The highest rating Sri Lankan players (2020-2024, inclusive).

Highest rating batsmen:

Player	Tests	Innings	Not outs	Years played	Batting style	100s/50s/0s	HS	Runs scored	Batting Average	Strike rate	Batting Rating
Karunaratne, FDM	24	44	2	2020-23	left	7/10/0	244	2,210	52.62	55.85	113.9
Mathews, AD	22	37	5	2020-23	right	6/6/3	200	1,657	51.78	46.04	99.4
Dhananjaya de Silva	22	36	4	2020-23	right	4/8/1	166	1,543	48.22	58.14	92.2
Chandimal, D	21	37	8	2020-23	right	3/7/1	206	1,449	49.97	51.31	91.0
Mendis, BKG	18	31	1	2020-23	right	3/7/5	245	1,211	40.37	58.08	74.3

Highest rating bowlers:

Player	Tests	Overs	Maids	Runs against	Bowl style	Wkts	5w/10w	Best	Bowl Avge	Strike rate	Econ rate	Bowling Rating
Fernando, MVT	20	530	76	1850	LAMF	58	1/0	5/101	31.90	54.90	3.49	70.1

Notes: 1. A total of 35 different individuals represented Sri Lanka in this period, with 7 of them playing more than 20 test matches.

Table M.8 The highest rating South African players (2020-2024, inclusive).

Highest rating batsmen:

Player	Tests	Innings	Not outs	Years played	Batting style	100s/50s/0s	HS	Runs scored	Batting Average	Strike rate	Batting Rating
Bavuma, T	23	42	6	2020-24	right	2/11/3	172	1688	46.89	49.85	82.7
Elgar, D	26	48	2	2020-24	left	2/10/3	185	1681	36.54	52.37	61.4
Markram, AK	24	43	1	2020-24	right	3/7/1	115	1402	33.38	55.85	53.4

Highest rating bowlers:

Player	Tests	Overs	Maids	Runs against	Bowl style	Wkts	5w/10w	Best	Bowl Avge	Strike rate	Econ rate	Bowling Rating
Rabada, K	28	841	164	2,737	RAF	131	7/0	6/46	20.89	38.56	3.25	132.6
Maharaj, KA	28	853	177	2,484	LAO	91	6/0	7/32	27.30	56.25	2.91	90.9

Note: A total of 46 different individuals represented South Africa in this period, with 6 of them playing more than 20 test matches.

Table M.9 The highest rating Zimbabwe players (2020-2024, inclusive).

A total of 40 different individuals represented Zimbabwe in this four-year period, but no one played more than 20 matches.

Table M.10 The highest rating Bangladesh players (2020-2024, inclusive).

Highest rating batsmen:

Player	Tests	Innings	Not outs	Years played	Batting style	100s/ 50s/0s	HS	Runs scored	Batting Average	Strike rate	Batting Rating
Mushfiqur Rahim	25	45	6	2020-24	right	5/6/2	203	1797	46.08	51.79	84.2
Litton Das	30	53	1	2020-24	right	4/13/1	141	2044	39.31	59.20	73.7
Mominul Haque	31	58	6	2020-24	left	5/8/10	132	1755	33.75	51.19	53.8

Highest rating bowlers:

Player	Tests	Overs	Maids	Runs against	Bowl style	Wkts	5w/ 10w	Best	Bowl Avge	Strike rate	Econ rate	Bowling Rating
Taijul Islam	24	1179	244	3,413	LAO	111	8/1	7/116	30.75	63.76	2.89	87.0
Mehidy Hasan	29	1127	192	3,401	RAO	100	3/0	5/61	34.01	67.61	3.02	68.1

Note: A total of 31 different individuals represented Bangladesh in this period, with 6 of them playing more than 20 test matches.

Indexes

A'Beckett, EL 70
Aamir Sohail 210, 261
Aaqib Javed 216, 261
Abdul Kardar 235
Abdul Qadir 41, 47, 94, 100, 102, 105, 106, 108, 184, 186, 188, 213, 254
Abdul Razzaq 51, 216, 270
Abdur Rehman 215, 280
Adams, JC 210, 258
Adams, PR 215, 263
Adcock, NAT 37, 46, 193, 195, 197, 213, 234
Adnan Akmal 52, 134, 153, 280
Alderman, TM 46, 213, 250
Ali, MM 51, 212, 215, 275
Allen, DA 214, 236
Allen, GOB 66, 67, 68, 71, 214, 226
Amarnath, L 216
Amarnath, M 209, 246, 252
Ambrose, CEL 37, 38, 41, 43, 45, 47, 100, 109, 110, 111, 115, 119, 120, 121, 158, 160, 161, 170, 171, 172, 173, 212, 219, 258
Ames, LEG 52, 62, 65, 66, 67, 69, 71, 210, 226
Amiss, DL 91, 95, 97, 208, 243
Amla, HM 31, 34, 137, 143, 144, 148, 193, 194, 196, 197, 207, 272, 282
Anderson, JM 30, 38, 41, 43, 45, 113, 129, 132, 136, 137, 143, 145, 148, 153, 155, 158, 160, 161, 162, 163, 165, 212, 219, 265, 275, 284
Armstrong, W 48, 50, 56, 57, 59, 210, 215, 224
Arnold, GG 214, 243
Arnold, RP 271
Arthurton, KLT 258
Asad Shafiq 184, 185, 187, 209, 280
Ashwin, R 38, 39, 40, 41, 42, 43, 45, 50, 87, 136, 137, 142, 148, 149, 150, 151, 152, 154, 155, 158, 160, 161, 174, 175, 177, 212, 219, 278, 286
Asif Iqbal 48, 50, 209, 215, 242, 248
Astle, NJ 50, 178, 180, 182, 209, 217, 260, 269

Atapattu, MS 31, 32, 188, 190, 192, 208, 262, 271
Atherton, MA 208, 256
Atkinson, DStE 51, 216, 232
Azhar Ali 35, 184, 185, 187, 207, 280, 287
Azharuddin, M 35, 106, 110, 117, 118, 120, 174, 175, 177, 207, 252, 259

Babar Azam 152, 153, 154, 184, 185, 187, 208, 280, 287
Bailey, GJ 112
Bailey, TE 51, 65, 214, 230
Bairstow, JM 49, 51, 162, 163, 164, 165, 166, 209, 275, 284
Ballance, GS 211, 275
Bancroft, CT 140
Bardsley, W 53, 54, 59, 60, 209, 224
Barlow, EJ 50, 91, 193, 195, 196, 208, 216, 240
Barlow, RG 59
Barnes, SF 36, 38, 39, 40, 41, 45, 47, 53, 54, 56, 59, 60, 66, 78, 118, 128, 157, 158, 159, 161, 162, 163, 165, 212, 223
Barnes, W 36, 45, 53, 57, 60, 162, 164, 166, 212, 223
Barrington, KF 27, 34, 75, 81, 82, 83, 88, 162, 163, 165, 207, 236
Bavuma, T 210, 287
Bedi, BS 38, 43, 46, 91, 95, 96, 98, 119, 174, 176, 177, 213, 239, 246
Bedser, AV 41, 45, 62, 66, 72, 73, 76, 79, 80, 162, 164, 166, 213, 226, 230
Bedser, EA 76
Bell, AJ 228
Bell, IR 34, 207, 265, 275
Benaud, R 43, 44, 46, 73, 74, 77, 78, 80, 82, 213, 231, 237
Benjamin, KCG 215, 258
Benjamin, WKM 215
Binny, RMH 216, 252
Bishoo, D 216, 277
Bishop, IR 46, 170, 172, 173, 213, 258

Blackwood, J.	211, 277, 285
Bland, KC	193, 195, 196, 209, 240
Blewett, G.S	211, 257
Blundell, TA	51, 211, 286
Bond, SE	132, 269
Boock, SL	215, 253
Boon, DC	35, 207, 250, 257
Booth, BC	209, 237
Borde, CG	51, 210, 239
Border, AR	27, 28, 31, 34, 50, 99, 100, 101, 102, 107, 108, 110, 111, 125, 132, 134, 138, 140, 146, 166, 167, 169, 207, 217, 250, 257
Botham, IT	29, 38, 41, 42, 43, 45, 48, 49, 90, 91, 93, 94, 96, 97, 98, 100, 101, 103, 106, 107, 108, 162, 163, 164, 165, 209, 212, 219, 243, 249
Boucher, MV	49, 51, 114, 120, 121, 127, 134, 135, 141, 158, 160, 161, 162, 193, 194, 196, 197, 210, 263, 272
Boult, TA	38, 46, 178, 180, 182, 183, 213, 279
Bowes, WE	67
Boyce, KD	215, 245
Boycott, G	25, 34, 82, 90, 91, 92, 97, 98, 101, 162, 163, 165, 207, 236, 243, 249
Bracewell, DAJ	217, 279
Bracewell, JG	215, 253
Bradman, DG	27, 28, 30, 31, 33, 41, 61, 62, 63, 64, 65, 66, 67, 68, 70, 71, 74, 75, 76, 77, 83, 84, 111, 112, 113, 123, 124, 126, 127, 129, 130, 138, 139, 140, 144, 146, 158, 159, 161, 166, 167, 169, 171, 179, 206, 222, 227
Brathwaite, KC	209, 277, 285
Bravo, DJ	212, 217, 267
Bravo, DM	210, 277
Bresnan, TT	216, 275
Briggs, J	36, 41, 45, 53, 56, 57, 59, 60, 162, 163, 165, 212, 223
Broad, BC	146, 210, 249
Broad, SCJ	29, 30, 38, 43, 45, 129, 132, 137, 145, 148, 153, 155, 162, 163, 164, 166, 212, 219, 275, 284
Brockwell, W	59
Brook, HC	27, 28, 29, 33, 34, 150, 151, 154, 155, 162, 163, 165, 166, 207, 284
Brown, DJ	215
Brown, FR	67, 216
Brown, WA	62, 79, 209, 227
Browne, CO	52
Bumrah, JJ	36, 37, 39, 40, 45, 115, 143, 150, 151, 152, 154, 155, 174, 175, 177, 212, 286
Burge, PJP	210, 237
Burgess, MG	211, 247
Burke, JW	76, 211, 231
Burns, JA	210, 276
Butcher, BF	209, 238
Butcher, MA	210, 265
Buttler, JC	51, 211, 275
Caddick, AR	47, 213, 256, 265
Cairns, BL	181, 215, 253
Cairns, CL	47, 48, 50, 178, 181, 183, 199, 210, 213, 260, 269
Cameron, FJ	241
Cameron, HB	228
Campbell, ADR	198, 200, 201, 264, 273
Campbell, SL	211, 258
Carey, A	29, 51, 154, 155
Carlisle, SV	198, 200, 201, 273
Carter, H	57, 58, 60, 224
Catterall, RH	210, 228
Chanderpaul, S	25, 27, 28, 31, 34, 112, 123, 130, 137, 143, 144, 148, 170, 171, 173, 207, 258, 267, 277
Chandimal, LD	33, 35, 51, 152, 154, 188, 190, 192, 193, 208, 281, 287
Chandrasekhar, BS	46, 91, 95, 96, 98, 174, 176, 177, 213, 246
Chappell, GS	27, 34, 50, 90, 91, 92, 97, 98, 99, 100, 101, 102, 107, 108, 166, 167, 169, 207, 217, 244, 250
Chappell, IM	82, 91, 208, 237, 244
Chase, RL	277
Chatfield, EJ	215, 253
Chauhan, CPS	246
Chauhan, RK	217, 259
Cheetham, JE	234
Clark, SR	213, 266
Clarke, MJ	28, 31, 34, 44, 50, 140, 166, 167, 169, 207, 266, 276
Collinge, RO	178, 182, 183, 215, 247
Collingwood, PD	209, 265
Collins, PT	216, 267
Collymore, CD	215, 267
Compton, DCS	27, 28, 34, 61, 62, 64, 65, 68, 70, 71, 73, 133, 162, 164, 165, 207, 226, 230
Coney, JV	51, 210, 217, 253

Congdon, BE	51, 210, 216, 241, 247	Dhoni, MS	49, 51, 174, 175, 177, 178, 209, 268, 278
Connolly, AN	215, 237	Dias, RL	211, 255
Constantine, L (WI)	62, 229	Dickwella, DPDN	29, 51, 188, 191, 192, 193, 211, 281
Contractor, NJ	233		
Conway. DP	210, 286	Dilley, GR	106, 214, 249
Cook, AN	28, 30, 34, 64, 111, 124, 136, 137, 138, 139, 143, 144, 148, 159, 162, 165, 207, 265, 275	Dillon, MV	30, 215, 267
		Dilshan, TM	29, 188, 190, 192, 208, 271, 281
Cork, DG	214, 256	Donald, AA	37, 38, 39, 40, 41, 45, 109, 110, 111, 116, 118, 120, 121, 193, 194, 195, 196, 197, 212, 263
Cotter, A	57, 214, 224		
Cowdrey, MC	35, 73, 76, 77, 82, 86, 88, 139, 207, 230, 236		
		Doshi, DR	215, 252
Cowper, RM	48, 50, 87, 89, 208, 216, 237	Doull, SB	178, 182, 183, 214, 260
Crawley, JP	211, 256	Dowling, GT	211, 241
Crawley, Z	29, 210, 284	Dowrich, SO	52, 277
Croft, CEH	46, 94, 170, 172, 173, 213, 251	Dravid, R	25, 27, 28, 30, 33, 110, 117, 120, 123, 124, 125, 126, 130, 132, 134, 138, 139, 142, 158, 159, 161, 174, 175, 177, 206, 259, 268, 278
Croft, RDB	217		
Cronje, WJ	48, 50, 120, 121, 133, 210, 215, 263		
Crowe, JJ	179, 253	du Plessis, F	209, 282
Crowe, MD	35, 101, 111, 178, 179, 181, 182, 183, 208, 253, 260	Duckett, BM	28, 29, 152, 154, 209, 284
		Duckworth, G	67, 69, 71
Crowe, RI	179	Duff, RA	211, 224
Cullinan, DJ	193, 195, 196, 208, 263	Dujon, PJL	49, 51, 99, 100, 103, 107, 108, 170, 171, 172, 173, 174, 211, 251
Cummins, PJ	37, 38, 39, 40, 45, 137, 140, 145, 146, 148, 153, 155, 166, 168, 169, 212, 276, 285		
		Duminy, JP	211, 282
		Durani, SA	216, 239
D'Oliveira, BL	50, 210, 216, 236		
Da Silva, J	52, 154, 155	Ebrahim, DD	273
Danish Kaneria	38, 214, 270	Edgar, BA	253
Das, SS	212, 268	Edmonds, PH	215, 249
Davidson, AK	37, 41, 45, 73, 77, 78, 80, 82, 93, 166, 168, 169, 212, 231, 237	Edrich, JH	208, 236, 243
		Edrich, WJ	51, 209
de Freitas, PAJ	215, 256	Edwards, FH	215, 267
de Grandhomme, C	28, 29, 50, 210, 216, 279	Edwards, R	210, 244
de Kock, Q	28, 29, 49, 51, 141, 147, 149, 193, 196, 197, 209, 282	Elgar, D	193, 195, 196, 209, 282, 287
		Emburey, JE	215, 249
de Mel, ALF	255	Endean, WR	211, 234
de Silva, DM	188, 190, 192, 209, 287	Engineer, FM	52, 94, 212, 239
de Silva, PA	35, 109, 110, 113, 120, 121, 188, 189, 192, 208, 255, 262	Ervine, CR	198, 199, 200, 201, 283
		Evans, TG	52, 69, 71, 72, 73, 75, 79, 80, 84, 230
de Villiers, AB	27, 34, 49, 51, 136, 137, 141, 147, 148, 149, 158, 160, 161, 162, 193, 194, 196, 197, 207, 272, 282		
		Fairfax, AG	70
		Faulkner, GA	48, 50, 53, 54, 55, 58, 59, 60, 210, 214, 225
de Villiers, PS	263		
Denness, MH	210, 243	Fazal Mahmood	41, 46, 72, 73, 75, 79, 80, 84, 184, 185, 187, 213, 235
Desai, RB	216, 239		
Dexter, ER	35, 50, 82, 86, 88, 208, 216, 236	Ferguson, W	67
Dharmasena, HDPK	217, 262	Fernando, CRD	188, 191, 192, 216, 271
Dhawan, S	29, 138, 209, 278	Fernando, MVT	287

291

Finn, ST 214, 275
Fleming, DW 214, 257
Fleming, SP 35, 178, 179, 182, 208, 260, 269
Fletcher, KWR 209, 243
Flintoff, A 29, 48, 50, 133, 135, 210, 214, 265
Flower, A 27, 34, 49, 51, 111, 123, 130, 131, 134, 198, 199, 200, 201, 202, 207, 264, 273
Flower, GW 198, 201, 211, 264, 273
Foster, NA 215, 249
Fowler, G 211, 249
Franklin, JEC 216, 269
Fraser, ARC 46, 110, 119, 121, 213, 256
Fredericks, RC 208, 245
Fry, CB 59
Funston, KJ 234

Gabriel, ST 215, 277
Gaekwad, AD 246
Gambhir, G 208, 268
Ganga, D 267
Ganguly, SC 35, 110, 117, 120, 124, 130, 174, 175, 177, 207, 259, 268
Garner, J 37, 38, 39, 40, 45, 94, 99, 100, 101, 104, 106, 107, 108, 170, 171, 173, 212, 251
Gatting, MW 118, 209, 249
Gavaskar, SM 27, 28, 30, 34, 86, 90, 91, 94, 95, 96, 97, 98, 99, 100, 101, 106, 107, 108, 119, 124, 138, 159, 174, 177, 207, 246, 252
Gayle, CH 29, 31, 34, 50, 170, 171, 173, 207, 267, 277
Ghavri, KD 215, 246
Ghulam Ahmed 233
Gibbs, HH 28, 193, 194, 195, 196, 208, 263, 272
Gibbs, LR 38, 43, 46, 78, 81, 82, 85, 86, 88, 91, 95, 170, 172, 173, 213, 238, 245
Giffen, G 214, 224
Gilchrist, AC 28, 29, 34, 49, 51, 114, 122, 123, 124, 127, 128, 130, 134, 135, 137, 158, 159, 160, 161, 162, 166, 167, 168, 169, 170, 175, 194, 207, 266
Gillespie, JN 38, 46, 213, 266
Goddard, JDC 216, 232
Goddard, TL 39, 50, 82, 87, 88, 89, 193, 196, 197, 211, 214, 234, 240
Gomes, HA 210, 251
Gomez, GE 39, 214, 232
Gooch, GA 34, 50, 101, 109, 110, 111, 120, 121, 162, 163, 165, 207, 249, 256
Gough, D 39, 40, 47, 213, 256, 265

Gower, DI 34, 100, 101, 104, 105, 107, 165, 207, 249
Grace, WB 54, 58, 59, 76, 146, 223
Graveney, TW 73, 82, 86, 88, 208, 230, 236
Green, C 211, 285
Greenidge, CG 34, 91, 99, 100, 101, 104, 107, 108, 124, 170, 171, 172, 173, 207, 245, 251
Gregory, JM 50, 69, 71, 211, 215, 227
Gregory, SE 224
Greig, AW 48, 50, 96, 98, 209, 215, 243
Griffith, CC 214, 238
Grimmett, CV 20, 41, 42, 45, 61, 62, 66, 67, 69, 70, 71, 76, 142, 166, 167, 169, 186, 212, 227
Grout, ATW 52, 82, 87, 88, 89, 237
Gunn, W 59
Gupte, SP 214, 233
Guptill, MJ 124, 211, 279
Gurusinha, AP 210, 262

Habibul Bashar 29, 202, 204, 205, 211, 274
Haddin, BJ 49, 51, 166, 168, 169, 170, 210, 276
Hadlee, BG 104
Hadlee, KA 103
Hadlee, RJ 37, 38, 39, 40, 41, 42, 43, 45, 50, 91, 92, 99, 100, 101, 103, 104, 106, 107, 108, 133, 158, 159, 161, 178, 180, 182, 183, 212, 219, 247, 253
Hadlee, WA 104
Hadlee. DR 104, 216, 247
Hall, WW 46, 82, 170, 172, 173, 213, 238
Hammond, WR 27, 28, 31, 34, 49, 61, 62, 64, 65, 67, 69, 70, 71, 75, 86, 124, 146, 162, 163, 165, 207, 216, 226
Hanif Mohammad 72, 73, 74, 79, 80, 82, 96, 116, 184, 185, 187, 208, 235, 242
Hardstaff, J (Jnr) 209, 226
Harmison, SJ 214, 265
Harper, RA 215, 251
Harris, PL 216, 272
Harris, RJ 46, 213, 276
Harvey, MR 74
Harvey, RN 34, 72, 73, 74, 79, 80, 207, 231
Hassett, AL 62, 76, 77, 79, 208, 227, 231
Hastings, BF 247
Hawke, NJN 214, 237
Hayden, ML 27, 29, 31, 34, 112, 122, 123, 124, 125, 130, 134, 135, 158, 159, 161, 166, 167, 168, 169, 207, 266
Haynes, DL 35, 101, 110, 124, 170, 172, 173, 208, 251, 258

Hayward, T	56, 57, 59, 211, 223
Hazare, VS	174, 175, 177, 208, 233
Hazlewood, JR	38, 46, 150, 151, 152, 154, 155, 166, 168, 169, 213, 276, 285
Head, TM	29, 152, 153, 154, 208, 285
Headley, DW	64
Headley, GA	27, 34, 61, 62, 64, 70, 71, 170, 171, 173, 207, 229
Headley, RGA	64
Healy, AJ	114, 146
Healy, IA	49, 51, 109, 110, 114, 120, 121, 127, 166, 168, 169, 170, 211, 257
Hearne, JT	59
Hendren, EH	64, 208, 226
Hendrick, M.	214, 243
Herath, HMRKB	38, 41, 43, 45, 124, 136, 137, 142, 148, 188, 189, 191, 192, 212, 219, 271, 281
Hick, GA	146, 211, 256
Hill, C	53, 54, 57, 59, 60, 209, 224
Hinds, WW	211, 267
Hirst, GH	59, 215
Hobbs, JB	27, 34, 53, 54, 55, 59, 60, 62, 63, 64, 67, 68, 70, 73, 84, 162, 163, 165, 207, 223, 226
Hogg, RM	214, 250
Hoggard, MJ	214, 265
Holder, JO	50, 211, 214, 277, 285
Holder, VA	215, 245
Holding, MA	39, 40, 45, 94, 95, 100, 101, 105, 106, 108, 170, 172, 173, 213, 245, 251
Hooper, CL	50, 111, 209, 217, 258, 267
Horne, MJ	260
Hornibrook, PM	70
Houghton, DL	198, 199, 201, 209, 264
Howard, T	70
Howarth, GP	211, 247, 253
Howarth, HJ	216, 247
Hudson, AC	211, 263
Hughes, KJ	209, 244, 250
Hughes, MG	47, 213, 250, 257
Hughes, PJ	212
Hunte, CC	208, 238
Hurwood, A	70
Hussain, N	209, 256
Hussey, MEK	27, 34, 125, 146, 166, 168, 169, 207, 266, 276
Hutton, L	27, 34, 61, 62, 63, 64, 70, 71, 72, 73, 75, 77, 79, 80, 124, 158, 159, 161, 162, 163, 165, 207, 226, 230
Ijaz Ahmed	209, 261
Illingworth, R	215, 236
Imran Farhat	211, 270
Imran Khan	37, 38, 41, 42, 44, 45, 48, 49, 74, 91, 93, 99, 100, 101, 102, 103, 106, 107, 108, 116, 184, 185, 187, 210, 212, 219, 248, 254
Imrul Kayes	202, 204, 283
Imtiaz Ahmed	52, 212, 235
Intikhab Alam	215, 242, 248
Inzamam-ul-Haq	31, 34, 123, 130, 131, 134, 184, 185, 187, 207, 261, 270
Iqbal Qasim	100, 105, 106, 108, 213, 248, 254
Jackson, AA	70
Jackson, FS	51, 53, 55, 59, 60, 208, 223
Jacobs, RD	51, 170, 172, 173, 174, 267
Jadeja, RA	38, 44, 45, 48, 49, 137, 145, 146, 148, 149, 153, 154, 155, 174, 176, 177, 210, 212, 278, 286
Jaffer, W	211, 268
Jaisimha, ML	239
Jardine, DR	12, 63, 65, 66, 67, 68, 209
Javed Burki	242
Javed Miandad	25, 27, 31, 34, 74, 90, 91, 92, 93, 97, 98, 99, 100, 101, 102, 107, 108, 111, 116, 131, 184, 185, 187, 207, 248, 254, 261
Javed Omar	274
Jayasuriya, ST	29, 35, 48, 50, 126, 133, 135, 188, 189, 190, 192, 207, 216, 262, 271
Jayawardene, DPMdS	25, 28, 30, 31, 33, 34, 122, 123, 125, 126, 130, 134, 135, 139, 158, 160, 161, 188, 189, 192, 207, 262, 271, 281
Jayawardene, HAPW	52, 126, 188, 191, 192, 193, 271
Johnson, IW	215, 231
Johnson, MG	38, 39, 40, 46, 213, 266, 276
Johnston, WA	47, 213, 231
Jones, AH	178, 181, 182, 209, 260
Jones, DM	100, 104, 105, 107, 124, 208, 250, 257
Jones, GO	51
Joseph, AS	285
Julien, BD	217, 245
Junaid Khan	215, 280
Kallicharran, AI	90, 91, 93, 97, 98, 208, 245
Kallis, JH	25, 27, 30, 33, 38, 43, 44, 48, 49, 93, 111, 120, 121, 122, 123, 125, 126, 127, 130, 133, 134,

135, 136, 137, 138, 140, 144, 148, 158, 159, 161, 193, 194, 195, 196, 197, 206, 214, 263, 272, 282
Kaluwitharana, RS 29, 52, 262
Kambli, VG 259
Kamran Akmal 29, 51, 134, 135, 153, 184, 185, 186, 187, 188, 211, 270
Kanhai, RB 25, 34, 73, 82, 86, 88, 94, 170, 171, 173, 207, 232, 238, 245
Kapil Dev 25, 38, 43, 45, 48, 49, 91, 100, 101, 103, 105, 106, 108, 110, 119, 133, 174, 175, 177, 210, 213, 219, 246, 252, 259
Karunaratne, FDM 33, 35, 150, 151, 154, 155, 188, 189, 190, 192, 208, 281, 287
Katich, SM 208, 266
Kelly, WL 70
Khaled Mashud 52, 202, 204, 205, 274
Khawaja, UT 33, 35, 150, 151, 154, 155, 208, 276, 285
Kippax, AF 70, 211
Kirmani, SMH 52, 174, 176, 177, 178, 246, 252
Kirsten, G 34, 193, 194, 196, 197, 207, 263, 272
Klusener, L 51, 116, 211, 216, 263
Knott, APE 49, 51, 91, 97, 98, 164, 165, 166, 210, 243
Kohli, V 31, 33, 34, 125, 131, 136, 137, 140, 141, 148, 174, 175, 177, 207, 278, 286
Kumar, B 214, 278
Kumble, A 37, 38, 41, 43, 45, 76, 110, 119, 121, 123, 125, 131, 132, 135, 158, 160, 161, 174, 175, 177, 212, 219, 259, 268

Labuschagne, M 33, 35, 150, 151, 154, 155, 208, 285
Laker, JC 37, 45, 72, 73, 76, 78, 79, 80, 162, 164, 166, 212, 230
Lakmal, RAS 188, 191, 192, 215, 281
Lamb, AJ 209, 249, 256
Langer, JL 32, 34, 124, 128, 166, 168, 169, 207, 257, 266
Langley, GRA 52, 75, 79, 80, 231
Lara, BC 27, 28, 29, 30, 31, 33, 74, 75, 109, 110, 112, 120, 121, 123, 124, 125, 130, 131, 134, 144, 145, 146, 158, 159, 161, 170, 171, 173, 181, 206, 258, 267
Larwood, H 62, 65, 66, 67, 68, 71, 214, 226
Latham, RT 178
Latham, TWM 178, 182, 183, 208, 279, 286
Lawry, WM 35, 81, 82, 83, 88, 208, 237
Lawson, GS 214, 250

Laxman, VVS 34, 124, 130, 174, 175, 177, 207, 268, 278
Leach, MJ 284
Lee, B 38, 47, 213, 266
Lehmann, DS 29, 208, 266
Leyland, M 67, 208, 226
Lillee, DK 38, 39, 40, 41, 44, 45, 85, 90, 91, 93, 94, 96, 97, 98, 100, 101, 102, 105, 108, 166, 167, 169, 212, 219, 244, 250
Lilley, AFA 52, 53, 56, 58, 59, 60, 223
Lindsay, DT 85, 91, 240
Lindwall, RR 46, 62, 73, 74, 213, 227, 231
Litton Das 51, 154, 155, 202, 204, 205, 210, 288
Lloyd, CH 25, 34, 86, 91, 93, 94, 95, 96, 97, 100, 101, 104, 107, 170, 171, 173, 207, 238, 245, 251
Lock, GAR 46, 72, 73, 76, 78, 79, 80, 213, 230
Logie, AL 211, 251
Lohmann, GA 36, 38, 47, 53, 54, 56, 59, 60, 94, 217, 223
Lords Cricket Ground 18, 21, 57, 63, 68, 74, 83, 84, 85, 95, 101, 105, 111, 112, 117, 127, 132, 133, 139, 143, 146, 153, 203, 219
Luckhurst, BW 212, 243
Lyon, NM 38, 41, 43, 45, 153, 155, 166, 168, 169, 212, 219, 276, 285

Macartney, CG 48, 50, 138, 209, 215, 224
MacGibbon, AR 215, 234
MacGill, SCG 38, 46, 213, 266
Mackay, KD 39, 51, 216, 231
MacLaren, AC 56, 57, 59, 211, 223
Madan Lal 217
Madugalle, RS 255
Mahanama, RS 212, 262
Maharaj, KA 214, 282, 287
Mahmood Hussain 217
Majid Khan 138, 209, 248
Malcolm, DE 215, 256
Malinga, SL 114, 188, 189, 191, 192, 215, 271
Mallett, AA 214, 244
Manjrekar, SV 210, 259
Manjrekar, VL 210, 233, 239
Mankad, MH 21, 50, 62, 73, 78, 79, 80, 211, 214, 233
Markram, AK 210, 282, 287
Marsh, GR 111, 211
Marsh, MR 217

Marsh, RW 49, 51, 90, 91, 93, 94, 97, 98, 101, 102, 107, 108, 114, 166, 168, 169, 170, 212, 244, 250
Marsh, SE 211
Marshall, MD 37, 38, 39, 40, 41, 45, 47, 99, 100, 101, 104, 106, 107, 108, 111, 115, 158, 160, 161, 170, 171, 173, 212, 219, 251
Martin, CS 30, 96, 178, 181, 183, 214, 269
Martyn, DR 208, 266
Masakadza, H 198, 201, 283
Mashrafe Mortaza 202, 203, 204, 205, 217, 274
Mathews, AD 33, 34, 152, 154, 188, 189, 192, 207, 281, 287
Matthews, CR 263
Matthews, GRJ 51, 210, 250
May, PBH 35, 73, 76, 77, 79, 208, 230
May, TBA 216
McCabe, SJ 51, 62, 70, 208, 227
McCosker, RB 210, 244
McCullum, BB 29, 35, 49, 51, 178, 179, 182, 183, 208, 269, 279
McDermott, CJ 38, 46, 110, 119, 121, 213, 250, 257
McDonald, CC 210, 231
McGlew, DJ 76, 77, 79, 209, 234
McGrath, GD 9, 30, 37, 38, 39, 40, 41, 43, 45, 110, 118, 121, 122, 123, 128, 129, 130, 134, 135, 143, 158, 160, 161, 166, 167, 169, 212, 219, 257, 266
McKenzie, GD 41, 46, 81, 82, 85, 88, 213, 237
McKenzie, ND 194, 210, 272
McLean, RA 234
McMillan, BM 50, 210, 216, 263
McMillan, CD 178, 181, 182, 210, 260, 269
Mehidy Hasan 202, 203, 204, 205, 214, 283, 288
Melbourne Cricket Ground (MCG) 9, 12, 53, 56, 79, 83, 87, 96, 112, 119, 125, 194, 219
Mendis, BKG 188, 190, 192, 209, 281, 287
Mendis, LRD 211, 255
Merchant, VM 64
Miller, CR 114
Miller, G 215
Miller, KR 37, 46, 48, 50, 62, 73, 74, 78, 80, 133, 210, 213, 227, 231
Misbah-ul-Haq 35, 184, 185, 187, 208, 280
Mitchell, B 35, 62, 193, 194, 196, 208, 228
Mitchell, DJ 178, 180, 182, 209, 286
Mitchell, JEP 180
Mitchell, TB 67
Mohammad Amir 215, 280
Mohammad Ashraful 198, 202, 203, 204, 274

Mohammad Hafeez 50, 209, 216, 280
Mohammad Mahmudullah 202, 203, 204, 205, 211, 283
Mohammad Rafique 29, 202, 204, 205, 216, 274
Mohammad Yousuf 27, 34, 122, 123, 127, 130, 134, 135, 184, 185, 187, 207, 270
Mohammed Shami 39, 40, 47, 174, 176, 177, 213, 278
Mohommad Rizwan 51, 184, 186, 187, 188, 210, 287
Mohsin Khan 210, 254
Moin Khan 52, 212, 261
Mominul Haque 202, 204, 205, 209, 283, 288
Mongia, NR 52, 259
More, KS 52, 259
Morkel, DPB 228
Morkel, M 38, 46, 124, 193, 195, 197, 213, 282
Morris, AR 62, 73, 208, 231
Morrison, DK 215, 260
Motz, RC 215, 241
Mudassar Nazar 50, 209, 217, 248, 254
Muralitharan, M 20, 29, 30, 37, 38, 41, 42, 43, 45, 47, 56, 110, 111, 115, 118, 119, 121, 122, 123, 124, 126, 128, 129, 132, 134, 135, 137, 142, 143, 158, 159, 161, 188, 189, 191, 192, 199, 212, 219, 262, 271
Murray, DL 52, 245
Murray, JR 52, 258
Mushfiqur Rahim 52, 203, 204, 205, 208, 283, 288
Mushtaq Ahmed 214, 261
Mushtaq Mohammad 48, 50, 73, 96, 97, 98, 185, 209, 215, 242, 248

Nadkarni, RG 39, 82, 87, 88, 214, 239
Nash, BP 212
Nash, DJ 178, 181, 183, 214, 260
Nash, MA 84
Nasim-ul-Ghani 216, 242
Nawab of Pataudi (Snr) 67, 239
Nel, A 215, 272
Nicholls, HM 210, 279, 286
Noble, MA 46, 50, 54, 58, 60, 213, 224
Nourse, AD 27, 34, 62, 67, 70, 193, 194, 196, 207, 228
Nourse, AW 67, 217, 225
Ntini, M 38, 43, 45, 116, 123, 124, 126, 131, 132, 135, 193, 195, 197, 213, 219, 272
Nurse, SM 208, 238

O'Neill, NC	209, 237
O'Reilly, WJ	37, 41, 45, 61, 62, 66, 67, 69, 70, 71, 166, 168, 169, 213, 227
O'Brien, IE	216, 269
Ojha, PP	214, 278
O'Keeffe, KJ	217, 244
Old, CM	106, 214, 243
Oldfield, WAS	52, 61, 62, 65, 66, 69, 70, 71, 75, 227
Oram, JDP	50, 211, 216, 269
Paine, TD	51
Panesar, M	214, 265
Pant, RR	28, 29, 51, 150, 151, 152, 154, 155, 174, 176, 177, 178, 209, 286
Parker, JM	247
Parks, JH	84
Parks, JM	52, 81, 82, 84, 87, 88, 89, 236
Parks, RJ	84
Parore, AC	51, 178, 182, 183, 260
Pataudi, MAK (Nawab of Pataudi, Jnr)	210, 239
Patel, AY	76
Patel, DN	217, 260
Patel, PA	52
Pathan, IK	214, 268
Patil, SM	210, 252
Patterson, BP	111, 215, 251
Paynter, E	27, 34, 62, 66, 67, 68, 70, 162, 164, 165, 207, 226
Peel, R	36, 45, 53, 57, 60, 162, 164, 166, 212, 223
Perera, MDK	188, 190, 192, 215, 281
Perera, MDKJ	28, 29, 212
Petersen, AN	211, 282
Phadkar, DG	51, 216, 233
Philander, VD	37, 39, 40, 45, 137, 145, 148, 193, 195, 197, 212, 282
Phillips, WB	250
Pietersen, KP	29, 34, 162, 163, 165, 207, 265, 275
Pollard, V	241
Pollock, PM	46, 81, 82, 84, 85, 88, 91, 118, 193, 195, 197, 213, 240
Pollock, RG	27, 34, 81, 82, 85, 88, 91, 118, 193, 194, 196, 197, 207, 240
Pollock, SM	38, 43, 45, 50, 110, 111, 116, 118, 121, 123, 131, 132, 133, 135, 143, 193, 194, 196, 197, 211, 212, 219, 263, 272
Ponsford, WH	62, 70, 112, 144, 146, 208, 227
Ponting, RT	25, 27, 30, 31, 33, 110, 113, 122, 123, 125, 126, 127, 130, 134, 135, 138, 158, 159, 161, 166, 167, 169, 206, 257, 266, 276
Pope, OJD	29, 210, 284
Powell, KOA	277
Prabhakar, MM	51, 216, 259
Pradeep, N	281
Prasad, BKV	215, 259
Prasad, KTGD	188, 191, 192, 216, 281
Prasanna, EAS	82, 87, 88, 214, 239, 246
Prince, AG	209, 272
Pringle, DR	216, 249
Prior, MJ	29, 49, 51, 162, 164, 165, 166, 209, 265, 275
Procter, MJ	85, 91, 240
Pujara, CA	35, 174, 175, 177, 207, 278
Pullar, G	209, 236
Pushpakumara, KR	217, 262
Qasim Omar	211, 254
Rabada, K	37, 38, 39, 40, 41, 45, 115, 137, 143, 145, 148, 150, 151, 152, 154, 155, 193, 194, 196, 197, 212, 282, 287
Rahane, AM	209, 278
Rajin Saleh	274
Ramadhin, S	213, 232
Ramchand, GS	233
Ramdin, D	51, 170, 172, 173, 174, 277
Ramiz Raja	211, 254, 261
Ramprakash, MR	256
Ranatunga, A	188, 190, 192, 209, 255, 262
Randall, DW	211, 243, 249
Ranjitsinhji, KS	59
Ransford, VS	56, 57, 59, 211, 224
Ratnayeke, JR	188, 191, 192, 216, 255
Raval, JA	279
Redpath, IR	91, 95, 97, 208, 244
Reid, BA	46, 213
Reid, JF	253
Reid, JR	48, 50, 87, 89, 210, 215, 234, 241
Reiffel, PR	214, 257
Rhodes, JN	211, 263
Rhodes, W	50, 53, 54, 55, 57, 58, 59, 60, 62, 94, 212, 214, 223, 226
Richards, BA	85, 91, 101, 240

Richards, IVA 27, 29, 34, 84, 90, 91, 92, 96, 97, 98, 99, 100, 101, 102, 104, 105, 107, 108, 170, 171, 173, 179, 207, 220, 245, 251
Richardson, DJ 51, 79, 193, 196, 197, 263
Richardson, MH 178, 180, 182, 209, 269
Richardson, PE 210, 230
Richardson, RB 35, 100, 104, 105, 107, 208, 251, 258
Richardson, VY 70
Roach, KAJ 38, 46, 170, 172, 173, 213, 277, 285
Roberts, AME 46, 90, 91, 94, 95, 97, 98, 100, 170, 172, 173, 213, 245, 251
Rogers, CJL 209, 276
Root, JE 27, 28, 30, 31, 33, 50, 137, 138, 142, 143, 144, 148, 150, 151, 154, 155, 158, 159, 161, 162, 163, 165, 166, 206, 275, 284
Rowan, EAB 209, 228
Rowe, LG 209, 245
Roy, P 79, 211, 233
Rubel Hossain 283
Rudolph, JA 210, 272
Rutherford, KR 260
Ryder, J 27, 62, 208, 227

Sadiq Mohammad 73, 185, 211, 248
Saeed Ahmed 51, 209, 242
Saeed Ajmal 41, 46, 137, 145, 146, 148, 184, 186, 188, 213, 280
Saeed Anwar 35, 110, 116, 120, 184, 185, 187, 208, 261
Saleem Altaf 217, 248
Saleem Malik 35, 107, 184, 185, 187, 208, 254, 261
Saleem Yousuf 52, 107, 108, 254
Samaraweera, TT 35, 126, 188, 189, 192, 207, 271, 281
Sammy, DJG 29, 216, 220, 277
Samuels, MN 210, 267, 277
Sangakkara, KC 27, 28, 30, 31, 33, 49, 51, 111, 123, 125, 126, 128, 130, 134, 135, 136, 137, 139, 141, 148, 158, 159, 160, 161, 162, 175, 188, 189, 191, 192, 193, 206, 271, 281
Santner, MJ 148, 279
Saqlain Mushtaq 20, 41, 47, 184, 186, 188, 200, 213, 261, 270
Sardesai, DN 210, 239
Sarfaraz Ahmed 28, 29, 51, 184, 186, 187, 188, 210, 280
Sarfraz Nawaz 102, 215, 248, 254

Sarwan, RR 208, 267
Schwarz, RO 214, 225
Sehwag, V 28, 29, 31, 32, 34, 122, 123, 124, 125, 127, 130, 134, 135, 137, 159, 171, 174, 177, 207, 268, 278
Shahadat Hossain 202, 203, 204, 205, 274
Shaheen Afridi 214, 287
Shahid Afridi 28, 29, 50, 124, 210, 217, 270
Shakib Al Hasan 29, 48, 49, 93, 147, 149, 202, 203, 204, 205, 209, 213, 283
Sharma, C 216, 252
Sharma, I 30, 38, 44, 174, 176, 177, 214, 268, 278
Sharma, RG 124, 142, 174, 176, 177, 208, 278, 286
Sharma, Y 252
Shastri, RJ 48, 50, 106, 210, 216, 252
Shoaib Akhta 188
Shoaib Akhtar 9, 39, 40, 44, 46, 122, 123, 129, 134, 135, 184, 186, 200, 213, 270
Shoaib Malik 211, 270
Shoaib Mohammad 73, 184, 185, 187, 209, 254, 261
Shrewsbury, A 211, 223
Shubman Gill 29, 211, 286
Siddle, PM 214, 276
Sidebottom, RJ 214, 265
Sidhu, NS 209, 259
Siedle, IJ 228
Sikander Bakht 216, 248
Simpson, RB 35, 50, 81, 82, 83, 87, 88, 89, 102, 207, 217, 237
Simpson, RT 212
Sinclair, BW 241
Sinclair, JH. 215, 225
Singh, H 29, 38, 41, 43, 46, 123, 125, 131, 132, 135, 174, 176, 177, 213, 219, 268
Singh, M 216, 252
Singh, Y 211, 268
Slater, MJ 110, 111, 117, 120, 208, 257
Smith, GC 31, 34, 133, 144, 193, 194, 195, 196, 197, 207, 272, 282
Smith, IDS 29, 52, 107, 108, 253
Smith, OG 51, 212, 216, 232
Smith, RA 208, 256
Smith, SPD 27, 30, 33, 136, 137, 138, 139, 140, 148, 152, 153, 154, 158, 159, 161, 166, 167, 169, 207, 276, 285
Snedden, MC 217, 253
Snooke, SJ 214, 225
Snow, JA 47, 213, 236, 243

Sobers, GStA 25, 27, 31, 33, 34, 43, 48, 49, 72, 73, 74, 75, 78, 79, 80, 81, 82, 84, 87, 88, 89, 93, 94, 112, 113, 125, 126, 127, 130, 131, 139, 140, 141, 142, 145, 153, 158, 160, 161, 168, 170, 171, 173, 207, 214, 232, 238, 245
Solkar, ED 246
Solomon, JS 238
Southee, TG 29, 38, 43, 46, 178, 180, 182, 183, 213, 279, 286
Spofforth FR 36, 47, 54, 57, 60, 217, 224
Srikkanth, K 252
Srinath, J 214, 259, 268
Stackpole, KR 210, 244
Starc, MA 29, 38, 39, 40, 44, 45, 114, 137, 142, 145, 146, 148, 166, 168, 169, 213, 219, 276, 285
Statham, JB 46, 73, 76, 82, 85, 213, 230, 236
Stewart, AJ 35, 49, 51, 110, 117, 120, 121, 162, 163, 164, 165, 166, 208, 256, 265
Stewart, MJ 117
Steyn, DW 37, 38, 39, 40, 41, 44, 45, 104, 115, 116, 123, 124, 126, 131, 132, 135, 136, 137, 142, 143, 148, 158, 160, 161, 193, 194, 195, 196, 197, 212, 219, 272, 282
Stokes, BA 48, 49, 114, 147, 149, 154, 155, 208, 214, 275, 284
Stollmeyer, JB 209, 232
Storer, W 59
Strang, BC 198, 199, 201, 216
Strang, PA 198, 199, 201, 216, 264
Strauss, AJ 35, 208, 265
Streak, HH 198, 199, 201, 214, 264, 273
Styris, SB 211, 269
Surti, RF 239
Sutcliffe, B 178, 181, 182, 209, 234
Sutcliffe, H 27, 34, 61, 62, 63, 64, 65, 67, 68, 70, 71, 74, 92, 159, 162, 163, 165, 207, 226
Swann, GP 29, 41, 46, 213, 275

Tahir, MI 217, 282
Taibu, T 198, 200, 201, 202, 273
Taijul Islam 202, 203, 204, 205, 214, 283, 288
Tamhane, NS 233
Tamim Iqbal 202, 204, 205, 208, 283
Tapash Baisya 274
Tate, MW 47, 61, 62, 65, 67, 70, 71, 213, 226
Taufeeq Umar 210, 270, 280
Tausif Ahmed 254

Tayfield, HJ 41, 46, 73, 77, 78, 80, 193, 195, 197, 213, 234
Taylor, BR 178, 181, 183, 214, 241
Taylor, BRM 198, 201, 210, 283
Taylor, HW 209, 228
Taylor, JE 215, 267
Taylor, JM 211
Taylor, LRPL 34, 178, 179, 182, 183, 207, 269, 279
Taylor, MA 34, 109, 110, 111, 112, 114, 117, 120, 121, 143, 166, 168, 169, 207, 257
Taylor, RW 52, 249
Tendulkar, SR 25, 27, 30, 31, 33, 101, 109, 110, 112, 113, 114, 117, 120, 121, 123, 124, 125, 126, 130, 131, 134, 138, 139, 142, 144, 158, 159, 161, 174, 175, 177, 206, 259, 268, 278
Thomson, JR 91, 94, 95, 96, 98, 213, 244
Thorpe, GP 35, 207, 256, 265
Tillakaratne, HP 188, 190, 192, 208, 262, 271
Titchmarsh, VA 59
Titmus, FJ 214, 236
Trescothick, ME 35, 208, 265
Trott, IJL 208, 275
Trueman, FS 37, 38, 39, 40, 41, 45, 73, 77, 78, 80, 81, 82, 85, 88, 162, 163, 164, 166, 212, 230, 236
Trumble, H 41, 45, 57, 58, 60, 166, 168, 169, 213, 224
Trumper, VT 53, 54, 55, 57, 59, 60, 138, 209, 224
Tuffey, DR 215, 269
Tufnell, PCR 215, 256
Turner, CTB 224
Turner, GM 91, 95, 97, 178, 179, 182, 183, 208, 247
Tyldesley, JT 59, 212

Umar Gul 215, 270, 280
Umrigar, PR 39, 50, 141, 208, 217, 233
Underwood, DL 38, 41, 43, 45, 90, 91, 94, 97, 98, 162, 164, 166, 212, 243

Vaas, WPUJC 38, 43, 46, 50, 126, 188, 189, 192, 199, 213, 219, 262, 271
Valentine, AL 214, 232
van Ryneveld, CB 234
Vandort, MG 211, 271
Vaughan, MP 208, 265
Vengsarkar, DB 35, 100, 104, 105, 107, 174, 175, 177, 208, 246, 252
Venkatapathy Raju, SL 259
Verity, H 46, 62, 66, 67, 68, 71, 213, 226

Vettori, DL	38, 43, 44, 46, 48, 50, 133, 135, 142, 178, 179, 180, 182, 183, 199, 210, 213, 219, 260, 269
Vijay, M	209, 278
Viljoen, KG	228
Vincent, CL	215, 228
Vincent, L	211, 269
Viswanath, GR	35, 91, 95, 97, 174, 175, 177, 208, 246
Voce, W	61, 62, 65, 66, 67, 68, 70, 71, 214, 226
Voges, AC	27, 34, 83, 137, 140, 142, 143, 144, 148, 166, 168, 169, 207, 276
Wadekar, AL	239
Wadsworth, KJ	52, 97, 98, 247
Wagner, N	38, 46, 178, 181, 183, 213, 279
Wahab Riaz	216, 280
Waite, JHB	52, 75, 79, 80, 87, 88, 89, 212, 234, 240
Walcott, CL	27, 34, 72, 73, 74, 75, 77, 79, 80, 170, 171, 173, 207, 232
Walker, CV	70
Walker, MHN	214, 244
Wall, TW	70
Walsh, CA	25, 30, 38, 43, 45, 100, 101, 105, 106, 108, 110, 111, 119, 121, 123, 129, 131, 132, 135, 170, 171, 172, 173, 212, 219, 251, 258, 267
Walters, KD	34, 48, 49, 81, 82, 83, 84, 88, 207, 215, 237, 244
Waqar Younis	38, 39, 40, 41, 45, 104, 109, 110, 111, 114, 115, 120, 121, 123, 184, 185, 187, 200, 212, 219, 261, 270
Wardle, JH	37, 46, 73, 77, 78, 80, 213, 230
Warne, SK	9, 20, 30, 37, 38, 41, 43, 45, 47, 84, 110, 118, 121, 122, 123, 128, 129, 132, 134, 135, 143, 158, 159, 161, 166, 167, 169, 212, 219, 257, 266
Warner, PF	28, 29, 31, 34, 55, 67, 136, 137, 138, 140, 148, 166, 167, 169, 207, 276, 285
Washbrook, C	209, 226
Wasim Akram	38, 41, 42, 43, 45, 50, 100, 101, 109, 110, 111, 114, 115, 116, 120, 121, 142, 184, 185, 187, 212, 219, 254, 261
Wasim Bari	49, 52, 248
Wasim Raja	51, 210, 217, 248, 254
Watling, BJ	49, 51, 141, 147, 148, 149, 178, 179, 182, 183, 210, 279
Watson, SR	48, 50, 125, 210, 216, 276
Waugh, ME	35, 50, 110, 111, 113, 116, 117, 120, 207, 257
Waugh, SR	25, 27, 28, 30, 34, 50, 101, 109, 110, 111, 113, 114, 116, 120, 121, 123, 125, 127, 166, 167, 169, 207, 216, 250, 257, 266
Wazir Mohammad	73, 235
Weekes, EDC	27, 34, 72, 73, 74, 75, 77, 79, 80, 170, 171, 173, 207, 232
Wessels, KC	206, 209, 250
Wettimuny, S	255
Whittall, GJ	198, 199, 200, 201, 217, 264
Wickramasinghe, GP	217, 262
Williamson, KS	27, 30, 31, 33, 34, 137, 143, 144, 148, 150, 151, 154, 155, 178, 179, 182, 183, 207, 279, 286
Willis, RGD	38, 46, 91, 95, 96, 98, 101, 107, 213, 243, 249
Woakes, CR	214, 275, 284
Wood, GM	211
Wood, MA	215, 284
Woodfull, WM	66, 70, 209, 227
Woolley, FE	48, 50, 54, 62, 69, 71, 76, 210, 215, 223, 226
Worrell, FMM	28, 35, 50, 73, 74, 75, 76, 77, 78, 79, 80, 146, 170, 171, 172, 173, 207, 216, 232
Wright, DVP	216
Wright, JG	178, 180, 182, 209, 253, 260
Wyatt, RES	67
Yadav, NS	216, 252
Yadav, UT	214, 278
Yallop, GN	209, 244, 250
Yardley, B	214, 250
Yasir Hameed	212, 270
Yasir Shah	41, 46, 66, 142, 146, 184, 186, 188, 213, 280
Young, BA	211, 260
Younis Khan	9, 27, 28, 30, 31, 34, 130, 131, 137, 143, 145, 148, 184, 185, 187, 207, 270, 280
Yousuf Youhana	9, 127
Zaheer Abbas	35, 91, 94, 101, 179, 184, 185, 187, 208, 248, 254
Zaheer Khan	38, 44, 174, 176, 177, 214, 268, 278
Zoysa, DNT	188, 191, 192, 216, 271